"OF WOOD AND STONE"

HARVARD SEMITIC MUSEUM PUBLICATIONS

Lawrence E. Stager, General Editor
Michael D. Coogan, Director of Publications

HARVARD SEMITIC MONOGRAPHS

edited by
Peter Machinist

Number 61
"OF WOOD AND STONE":
THE SIGNIFICANCE OF ISRAELITE CULTIC ITEMS
IN THE BIBLE AND ITS EARLY INTERPRETERS

by
Elizabeth C. LaRocca-Pitts

Elizabeth C. LaRocca-Pitts

"OF WOOD AND STONE"

THE SIGNIFICANCE OF ISRAELITE CULTIC ITEMS
IN THE BIBLE AND ITS EARLY INTERPRETERS

EISENBRAUNS
Winona Lake, Indiana
2001

"OF WOOD AND STONE":
THE SIGNIFICANCE OF ISRAELITE CULTIC ITEMS
IN THE BIBLE AND ITS EARLY INTERPRETERS

by
Elizabeth C. LaRocca-Pitts

Printed in the United States of America

Library of Congress Cataloging-in-Publication Data

LaRocca-Pitts, Elizabeth C., 1959–
    Of wood and stone : the significance of Israelite cultic items in the Bible and
    its early interpreters / Elizabeth C. LaRocca-Pitts.
        p.   cm. — (Harvard Semitic Museum publications) (Harvard Semitic
            Monographs ; no. 61)
    Includes bibliographical references and index.
    ISBN 1-57506-913-X (cloth : alk. paper)
    1. Worship in the Bible.   2. Bible. O.T.—Criticism, interpretation, etc.
3. High places (Shrines)   4. Asherahs (Jewish liturgical objects)   5. Stele
(Archaeology)   6. Altars in the Bible.   I. Title.   II. Series.   III. Series:
Harvard Semitic monographs ; no. 61

BS1199.W76 L37 2001
221.6'7—dc21
                                                                2001040870

The paper used in this publication meets the minimum requirements of the American
National Standard for Information Sciences—Permanence of Paper for Printed Library
Materials, ANSI Z39.48-1984.♾™

For my father of blessed memory,
Joseph Paul LaRocca
נעמת לי מאד נפלאתה אהבתך לי

And my mother,
Blair Camak LaRocca
עז־והדר לבושה ותשׂחק ליום אחרון

Table of Contents

Acknowledgments   ix
Abbreviations   xi
Introduction and Review of Scholarship   1

Part I: Source-critical Analysis of Texts Related to Cultic Items   17
    Chapter One: The Tetrateuchal Sources   19
    Chapter Two: Deuteronomy and the Deuteronomistic
       Historian   47
    Chapter Three: The Chronicler: Chronicles, Ezra, and Nehemiah   79
    Chapter Four: The Prophets and Remaining Writings   87

Part II: Synthesis of Biblical Data on Individual Items   125
    Chapter Five: Synthesis of the Data Regarding *bāmôt*   127
    Chapter Six: Synthesis of the Data Regarding *ǎšērîm*   161
    Chapter Seven: Synthesis of the Data Regarding *maṣṣēbôt*   205
    Chapter Eight: Synthesis of the Data Regarding *mizbǝḥôt*   229

Part III: Analysis of Material from the Ancient Translations   251
    Chapter Nine: The LXX and Other Greek Witnesses   253
    Chapter Ten: The Vulgate and Other Latin Witnesses   293
    Chapter Eleven: The Targumim and Other Early Jewish
       Interpretation   317

Conclusion   349
Bibliography   355
Index of Ancient Sources   377
Subject Index   379
Index of Scholars   383

Acknowledgments

The completion of this book has rested on the considerable collegial and financial support I have received since this project began as my doctoral dissertation. Those who have added the most insight, and for whose support and guidance I am most grateful, are the members my original committee, Jo Ann Hackett (who directed the dissertation), Theodore Hiebert, and Peter Machinist. My thanks also go to Frank Cross, who, prior to his retirement, helped me through the early stages of arriving at this thesis topic. Since my appointment to the faculty of the Divinity School at Duke University, I have also been blessed with generous insights from my Religion Department colleagues, Elizabeth Clark, Eric Meyers, and Melvin Peters. Their willingness to read portions of my work and to give me the benefit of their expertise is greatly appreciated. My thanks also extend to my two faculty mentors, Teresa Berger and James Crenshaw, for their consistent support and encouragement, and to Michael Coogan, who provided invaluable editorial advice for the preparation of this volume. For these and for all who have been my teachers and guides through the years, I am most grateful.

I am also grateful to those who supported this project financially: the Dempster Graduate Fellowship program of the General Board of Higher Education and Ministry of the United Methodist Church; the staff and congregation of the First United Methodist Church of Athens, Georgia; and my Deans, Dennis Campbell and L. Gregory Jones, who provided grants and other institutional support for the completion of the manuscript after my arrival at Duke. All else I owe to my husband Mark, my children Ellie and Joe, and the rest of our family members for their unwavering love and support.

Abbreviations

AB	Anchor Bible
ABD	*Anchor Bible Dictionary*
AHw	*Akkadisches Handwörterbuch*, Wolfram von Soden (3 vols.; Wiesbaden: 1965-81)
AOS	American Oriental Series
ARW	*Archiv für Religionswissenschaft*
ASORDS	American Schools of Oriental Research Dissertation Series
BA	*Biblical Archaeologist*
BAR	*Biblical Archaeology Review*
BASOR	*Bulletin of the American Schools of Oriental Research*
BDB	*Gesenius' Hebrew and English Lexicon of the Old Testament* (ed. Francis Brown, S. R. Driver, and Charles A. Briggs; Oxford: Clarendon, 1907)
BHS	Biblia Hebraica Stuttgartensia
BJRL	*Bulletin of the John Rylands Library*
BKAT	Biblischer Kommentar: Altes Testament
BZAW	Beihefte zur *Zeitschrift für die alttestamentliche Wissenschaft*
CAD	*The Assyrian Dictionary of the Oriental Institute of the University of Chicago*
CBQMS	*Catholic Biblical Quarterly* Monograph Series
CCL	*Corpus Christianorum Series Latina*
CHB	*The Hexateuch According to the Revised Version*, J. Estlin Carpenter and George Harford-Battersby (2 vols.; London: Longmans, Green, 1900)
CIS	*Corpus inscriptionum semiticarum*
CMHE	*Canaanite Myth and Hebrew Epic*, Frank Moore Cross (Cambridge: Harvard University Press, 1973)
CSEL	*Corpus Scriptorum Ecclesiasticorum Latinorum*
CTCA	*Corpus des tablettes en cunéiformes alphabétiques* (ed. Andree Herdner; 2 vols.; Mission de Ras Shamra 10; Paris: Imprimerie Nationale, 1963)
EncJud	*Encyclopaedia Judaica*
GKC	*Gesenius' Hebrew Grammar* (ed. Emil Kautzsch, tr. Arthur E. Cowley; Oxford: Oxford University Press, 1910)
HBD	*Harper's Bible Dictionary*
HSM	Harvard Semitic Monographs
HTR	*Harvard Theological Review*

HUCA	*Hebrew Union College Annual*
IDB	*Interpreter's Dictionary of the Bible*
IEJ	*Israel Exploration Journal*
JANESCU	*Journal of the Ancient Near Eastern Society of Columbia University*
JAOS	*Journal of the American Oriental Society*
JBL	*Journal of Biblical Literature*
JNES	*Journal of Near Eastern Studies*
JQR	*Jewish Quarterly Review*
JSOT	*Journal for the Study of the Old Testament*
JSOTSup	*Journal for the Study of the Old Testament*, Supplements
JSS	*Journal of Semitic Studies*
JTS	*Journal of Theological Studies*
KAI	*Kanaanäische und aramäische Inschriften*, Herbert Donner and Wolfgang Röllig (Wiesbaden: Otto Harrassowitz, 1962)
KJV	King James Version
KTU	*Keilalphabetischen Texte aus Ugarit* (ed. Manfried Dietrich, Oswald Loretz and Joaquín Sanmartín; Neukirchen-Vluyn: Neukirchener, 1976)
LSJM	*A Greek-English Lexicon*, Henry George Liddell and Robert Scott (revising ed., Henry S. Jones and Roderick McKenzie; Oxford: Clarendon, 1968)
NIDB	*New International Dictionary of the Bible*
NJBC	*The New Jerome Biblical Commentary*
NJPS	New Jewish Publication Society Version
NRSV	New Revised Standard Version
OBO	Orbis Biblicus et Orientalis
OCB	*Oxford Companion to the Bible*
OLD	*Oxford Latin Dictionary*
OLP	*Orientalia lovaniensia periodica*
OLZ	*Orientalistische Literaturzeitung*
OTL	Old Testament Library
PAAJR	*Proceedings of the American Academy of Jewish Research*
PL	*Patrologiae cursus completus . . . : Series Latina*
PRE	*Pirḳê de Rabbi Eliezer: (The Chapters of Rabbi Eliezer the Great) according to the Text of the Manuscript belonging to Abraham Epstein of Vienna* (tr. Gerald Friedlander; 4th ed.; New York: Sepher-Hermon, 1981).
PsG	Jerome's translation of the Psalms from the Old Latin

PsH	Jerome's translation of the Psalms from the Hebrew
RB	*Revue biblique*
RIMA	Royal Inscriptions of Mesopotamia, Assyrian Periods
SBLAS	Society of Biblical Literature Aramaic Studies
SBLMS	Society of Biblical Literature Monograph Series
SOTSMS	Society for Old Testament Study Monograph Series
TDOT	*Theological Dictionary of the Old Testament*
UF	*Ugarit-Forschungen*
UT	*Ugaritic Textbook*, Cyrus H. Gordon (4th ed.; Rome: Pontifical Biblical Institute, 1967)
VT	*Vetus Testamentum*
VTSup	*Vetus Testamentum*, Supplements
ZAW	*Zeitschrift für die alttestamentliche Wissenschaft*

Introduction and Review of Scholarship

Scholarly literature on ancient Israelite religion includes numerous discussions of what was considered either "normative" or "heterodox" in ancient Israel, from the worship of deities other than YHWH to the practice of child sacrifice or the employment of magic. There are also many works on various pieces of cultic paraphernalia used in ancient Israel, both those that are approved of and those that are disapproved of in the biblical text.

The designating of certain cultic apparatus as forbidden is a feature common to many of the ancient strata which make up the Hebrew Bible. *bāmôt* (so-called high places), *maṣṣēbôt* (standing stones), *ăšērîm* (so-called sacred poles or sacred trees), various types of cultic statuary (*gillûlîm, pəsîlîm, ʾĕlîlîm, massēkôt, tərāpîm,* etc.), and even altars (*mizbəḥôt*) are among those items that attract the negative attention of certain biblical authors. The source strata, however, are not unanimous, either in their assessment of the acceptability or unacceptability of individual cultic items, or in their grouping of these items into complexes upon which they then pass judgment. The subjects of the current study are *bāmôt, maṣṣēbôt, ăšērîm,* and *mizbəḥôt,* which share the common feature of appearing acceptable in certain biblical contexts and unacceptable in others. These four objects were chosen for this study over other possible groups of cultic items, in part because they are mentioned so frequently within the biblical text in varying combinations with each other (or with cultic statuary or other items such as incense burners); and in part because the clear divergence of opinion among the biblical authors concerning these objects, as well as their linkage with each other or with other cultic items, directly contradicts the depiction of these objects found in the secondary literature on the Hebrew Bible.

The secondary literature does not, as a rule, reflect the complexity of their treatment in the biblical text. What is lacking in the scholarly literature regarding these items in particular is a careful analysis of what each individual biblical source has to say about them, acknowledging that each writer's view of them may vary from the views of other writers because of how these items fit into a source's unique perspective on Israelite life and religion. These items are mentioned both in relatively minor references within major works of scholarship,[1] and in articles and monographs targeted at one specific item or artifact.[2] By and large, general scholarly works either

---

[1] Arthur B. Fowler, "High places," *NIDB* 439-40.
[2] Some examples concerning *bāmôt, ăšērîm,* and *maṣṣēbôt* are: W. F. Albright,

gloss over these items, rarely taking the time to focus on them or on how they were viewed by the sources, or generalize about them that they were universally disapproved of, because of some implied connection with the Canaanites or Canaanite religion.

Even works which focus on a specific source rarely deal with these cultic items in detail. Moshe Weinfeld's treatment of them in his work on the Deuteronomic School, for example, is largely confined to an appendix on the relation between Deuteronomy and Hosea.[3] Sara Japhet's work on Chronicles goes into more detail, though her discussion focuses mainly on *bāmôt*.[4] In his work on the Elohist, Alan Jenks discusses *maṣṣēbôt* only in terms of the relative merits of using the mention of them as a means of assigning a verse to E rather than J.[5] Martin Noth's *History of the Pentateuchal Traditions* deals specifically only with *maṣṣēbôt* and their role in the patriarchal stories of Jacob and Isaac.[6] Other source-critical studies rarely even mention cultic items by name;[7] and commentaries tend to discuss these items only under the verses in which the words appear.[8]

Unlike the studies mentioned above, Julius Wellhausen's *Prolegomena to the History of Ancient Israel* used the details of Israel's cult as the defining pieces of evidence in his larger discussion of the sources and

---

"The High Place in Ancient Palestine," in *Volume du Congrès: Strasbourg 1956* (VTSup 4; Leiden: E. J. Brill, 1957) 242-58; W. Boyd Barrick, "The Funerary Character of 'High-Places' in Ancient Palestine: A Reassessment," *VT* 25 (1975) 565-95; *idem*, "The Word BMH in the Old Testament" (Ph.D. diss., University of Chicago Divinity School, 1977); Patrick H. Vaughan, *The Meaning of 'Bāmâ' in the Old Testament: A Study of Etymological, Textual and Archaeological Evidence* (SOTSMS 3; Cambridge: Cambridge University Press, 1974); James Robert Engle, "Pillar Figurines of Iron Age Israel and Asherah/Asherim" (Ph.D. diss., University of Pittsburgh, 1979); William L. Reed, *The Asherah in the Old Testament* (Fort Worth: Texas Christian University Press, 1949); Carl Frank Graesser, Jr. "Studies in *maṣṣēbôt*" (Ph.D. diss., Harvard University, 1969).

[3]*Deuteronomy and the Deuteronomic School* (Oxford: Clarendon, 1972) 366-70.

[4]*The Ideology of the Book of Chronicles and Its Place in Biblical Thought* (Frankfurt am Main: Peter Lang, 1989) 217-21.

[5]*The Elohist and North Israelite Traditions* (SBLMS 22; Missoula: Scholars Press, 1977) 37.

[6]*History of the Pentateuchal Traditions* (tr. Bernhard Anderson; Chico: Scholars Press, 1981) 29, 80, 85, 107.

[7]Robert B. Coote and David Robert Ord, *In Defense of Revolution: The Elohist History* (Minneapolis: Fortress, 1991); idem, *In the Beginning: Creation and the Priestly History* (Minneapolis: Fortress, 1991); idem, *The Bible's First History* (Philadelphia: Fortress, 1989); Martin Noth, *The Chronicler's History* (tr. H. G. M. Williamson; JSOTSup 50; Sheffield: JSOT Press, 1987); idem, *The Deuteronomistic History* (tr. Jane Doull and John Barton; JSOTSup 15; Sheffield: JSOT Press, 1981).

[8]See, for example, Gerhard von Rad, *Deuteronomy: A Commentary* (OTL;

their relative dating. One of Wellhausen's primary tenets concerning Israelite religion was that it evolved from a completely decentralized cultic life (represented by J and E), to a stage in which cultic centralization was continuously mandated (D), to the final stage in which cultic centralization was assumed (P). It was this evolutionary model that fueled Wellhausen's argument concerning the late date of the Priestly source. Wellhausen noted the multiplicity of altars in J, and of *maṣṣēbôt* in E, as opposed to the complete denial in P of any religious activity outside the confines of the Tabernacle. In the middle of this spectrum he placed Deuteronomy, with its obviously anachronistic stress on God's demand for cultic centralization.[9] But in spite of the importance of cult for Wellhausen and those whose work depends on his, it is still the case that specific items of cultic paraphernalia have rarely occupied the sustained interest of the major scholars who, nonetheless, mention them in passing as part of larger synthetic treatments of Israelite religion, theology, or culture.

The studies which focus on one or more of these items are also often less than satisfying because they tend to be aimed at physically identifying the cultic objects mentioned in the text and relating them to archaeological remains found in Syria-Palestine.[10] Many of these studies make the facile assumption that all of the biblical authors (regardless of their presumed historical settings) had the same concrete object in mind when they used a common term in their writings (i.e. *bāmāh* or *ăšērāh*) and that this object can then be found in the ground or identified with known objects.

A similar type of study focuses on one of these items in isolation, conflating the various source descriptions of the item in order to produce a composite physical description of it, thereby homogenizing the distinctive views of the individual sources. The studies of Patrick H. Vaughan and W. Boyd Barrick on *bāmôt*, for example, demonstrate this tendency.[11] Focusing on the group of words *bāmāh, bāmôt, bāmôtê*, both Vaughan and Barrick seek to identify cultic *bāmôt* physically, using etymological (Vaughan)

London; SCM, 1966) 92, 115.

[9]Julius Wellhausen, *Prolegomena to the History of Ancient Israel* (tr. Black and Menzies; New York: Meridian, 1957; translated from the German edition, Berlin: Reimer, 1883). See especially his chapter on "The Place of Worship," pp. 17-51.

[10]See for instance, works which explore a connection between the Iron Age "pillar figurines" and the biblical *ašerim*: James Robert Engle, "Pillar Figurines;" and James B. Pritchard, *Palestinian Figurines in Relation to Certain Goddesses Known through Literature* (AOS 24; New Haven: AOS, 1943). S. Yeivin ("On the Use and Misuse of Archaeology in Interpreting the Bible," *PAAJR* 34 [1966] 141-54), rejects the notion that any of the numerous figurine types found throughout Israel are cultic.

[11]Vaughan, *The Meaning of 'Bāmâ'*; Barrick, "The Word BMH."

and/or syntactical arguments (Barrick). Vaughan's concern is to decide what, if anything, the original term had to do with the concept of "height," given the biblical mention of certain *bāmôt* erected in valleys. He comes to the conclusion that there were two types of *bāmôt*, some shaped like "truncated cones of some height," and some "low and oblong which may have had an altar standing on them."[12] Barrick is concerned with the assumption that all *bāmôt* were rural shrines. He uses syntactical evidence to argue that they were urban installations.

On the subject of *ăšērîm*, works by William L. Reed and Alice Lenore Perleman illustrate a tendency toward conflation of the biblical evidence.[13] Both seek to describe *ăšērîm* physically, and both come to the conclusion that they were wooden poles, with Reed eventually arguing that they were poles shaped like a goddess.

In many such studies, the views of the early translated traditions such as the LXX, the Vulgate, and the Targumim are used as early witnesses to one or another of the proposed reconstructions of these items without considering the fact that these works, in themselves, represent the earliest *interpretations* of the items, perhaps better reflecting not the historical items themselves, but analogies to these items from the translators' own era.

It tends to be assumed that temporal proximity lends to the early interpretation of these items a better understanding and rendering of them than is now possible. An equation between *ăšērîm* and trees, for instance, is often fueled by the traditional LXX analogy between *ăšērîm* and the sacred groves of Hellenic religion, or the Mishnah's explanation of *ăšērîm* as trees under which idols were buried. Patrick Vaughan's study of *bāmôt* is one example of this trend, which begins with the LXX meaning of "high place" for *bāmāh* and tries to work backward from this into other etymological evidence which would explain why the meaning "high" was applied to *bāmôt*.[14] There is no acknowledgment in Vaughan's work that the meaning "high" might have originated with the LXX in response to its own cultural setting.

By and large, studies aimed at linking the biblical and archaeological record with regard to these items have been unsuccessful, but this is not entirely because they have taken too literally the evidence of the translated traditions. There is also an inherent difficulty in trying to identify items con-

---

[12]Vaughan, *The Meaning of 'Bāmâ'*, 55.
[13]Reed, *Asherah in the OT*; Alice Lenore Perleman, "Asherah and Astarte in the Old Testament and Ugaritic Literatures," (Ph.D. diss., Graduate Theological Union, 1978).
[14]Vaughan, *The Meaning of 'Bāmâ'*.

cerning which there is no consensus as well as no actual physical description in the biblical text.[15]

Aside from the conflating tendency inherent in identifying one dominant shape for all biblical *bāmôt* or *ăšērîm* or *maṣṣēbôt* so that they can be identified with specific archaeological remains, in the rest of the scholarly literature there is also a tendency toward generalization concerning these items. The most common (represented by larger works for which cultic items basically serve as illustrative details) has been to join these items together to reconstruct some sort of monolithic Canaanizing syncretism. Another is to state that this Canaanizing syncretism was universally understood to involve these items so that they were naturally disapproved of by all the biblical sources.[16]

The idea that "normative" YHWHism stood opposed to some type of unified Canaanite religious tradition is a view common especially in older works whose aim was to demarcate the ideological or cultural boundaries between ancient Israel and its neighbors. To cite just one example, Walther Eichrodt's *Theology of the Old Testament* maintains that localization of deity in natural objects or locations was a feature of Canaanite religion which Israelite religion overcame by a process of abstraction of the deity beyond image or locality. For Eichrodt, cultic phenomena like *bāmôt*, *ăšērîm*, and *maṣṣēbôt* typified primitive religiosity common to the Canaanites, beyond which pure Israelite theology had progressed. He stated of *bāmôt*:

> [Along with] the taking over of the Canaanite *bāmôt* "on every high hill and under every green tree" . . . went a process of localizing and limiting the covenant God which bound him indissolubly to land and people and occasionally even disintegrated him into different local deities.[17]

Eichrodt's statement concerning *bāmôt* illustrates not only his assessment that their use derives from the Canaanites in particular and represents some sort of religious regression, but also his reduction of the biblical descriptions of *bāmôt* to an equation with the "high hill/green tree" or *ʿēṣ raʿănān* formula which is by no means synonymous with *bāmôt* in the biblical text.

---

[15]In chapters five through eight, which deal with each of these items individually, more studies which deal explicitly with them will be discussed.

[16]One recent study aimed at reversing this tendency in regard to one of the items under discussion is Saul Olyan's treatment of the *ăšērîm* in, *Asherah and the Cult of Yahweh in Israel* (Atlanta: Scholars Press, 1988). Olyan argues that the polemic against ʾAsherah was limited to Deuteronomistic circles.

[17]Walther Eichrodt, *Theology of the Old Testament* (tr. J. A. Baker; Philadelphia: Westminster, 1961); a translation of his *Theologie des Alten Testaments* (6th ed.;

Of *maṣṣēbôt* and *ăšērîm*, Eichrodt stated that they were "alien from primitive Yahwism and introduced into the Yahweh cultus predominantly as a result of Canaanite influence."[18] These two objects, however, were examples of two different types of "digression" from advanced religion back into primitive forms for Eichrodt. Of *ăšērîm* he wrote:

> The sacred poles, called Asherahs, were always thought of in Israelite religion as incompatible with the nature of Yahweh . . . The explanation of this attitude . . . is the sense . . . that the pole, which symbolized the goddess Asherah . . . meant opening the door to the unequivocally sensual and sexual character of the vegetation deities introducing the element of bisexuality into the concept of God.[19]

While Eichrodt stated here that *ăšērîm* represented fertility religion as well as a worship of the goddess, he also revealed his belief in a type of normative YHWHism that "always thought of" *ăšērîm* as "incompatible with Yahweh." No consideration is given to the notion that some segments of Israelite society might have endorsed *ăšērîm* and their use as thoroughly YHWHistic. With regard to *maṣṣēbôt*, however, Eichrodt argued for a modification of prevailing theories regarding animism, usually used to assess *maṣṣēbôt* negatively or at least as primitive. He described them, not as dwelling places of divinity, as did other scholars, but rather as "mediums of the divine power effective at a holy place."[20] In this way Eichrodt attempted to explain the acceptable use of *maṣṣēbôt* within normative YHWHism.

There can be no doubt that Israelite religion owed much of its own traditions to a common heritage with Canaanite religion; however, most early discussions of this relationship compared the religion of Canaan negatively to the religion of Israel, usually by loading Canaanite religion with more than its share of sexual impulses and obsession with fertility.[21] The

---

Stuttgart: Klotz, 1959) 1.105.

[18]*Theology*, 1.115.

[19]*Theology*, 1.116.

[20]*Theology*, 1.115.

[21]See for instance, Max Weber, "The Fight of Yahwism against Orgiasticism" (*Ancient Judaism* [tr. Hans H. Gerth and D. Martindale; London: George Allen and Unwin, 1952] 187-93). A somewhat less polemical reconstruction of Canaanite religion can be found in Albright, *Yahweh and the Gods of Canaan*, and a further softening of its portrayal in Cross, *CMHE*. Cross's work especially pays careful attention to the ways in which Israelite religion demonstrated continuity with, as well as distinction from, Canaanite religion. For a useful article on the pitfalls of viewing Canaanite religion through the lens of biblical studies see, Delbert Hillers "Analyzing the Abominable: Our Understanding of Canaanite Religion," *JQR* 75 (1985) 253-69.

discussion of objects such as *bāmôt*, *maṣṣēbôt*, and *ǎšērîm* then, which many wished to see as foreign elements within "pure YHWHism," is plagued with sexual interpretations and connections with the Canaanites, neither of which is an absolute mandate of the biblical text as will be seen.

In fact, there is a type of modern anti-Canaanite polemic focusing on the notion that the use of these objects or their antecedents, particularly when used in forms of outdoor worship, included participation in sexual activity aimed at producing fertility. Such sexual activity is assumed to have its origin in actual Canaanite religious practices, even though one can actually find little or no trace of such practices in the primary literature of Canaan. It would hardly be possible to list every scholarly work that has concluded that Canaanite "fertility rites" included sexual intercourse, and that these "rites" were widely practiced by apostate Israel.[22] This assessment greets one at practically every turn.

One basic text, John Bright's *A History of Israel*, describes Canaanite religion as a "fertility cult" which engaged in "orgies."[23] Bright also writes that during Amos's day, "Many of the local shrines were no doubt overtly pagan. The fertility cult with its debasing rites was practiced everywhere."[24] Another basic text with a similar statement is Samuel Sandmel's *The Hebrew Scriptures: An Introduction to Their Literature and Religious Ideas*. In this work, Sandmel states that "Baal orgies took place on hills; hence hills and high places signify Baalism."[25] Still another introduction, *The Old Testament*, by H. Keith Beebe, states that:

> Asherah was a goddess and she accompanied Baal in fertility rites. Worship of these deities was conducted at high places and a large upright stone often symbolized the Baal while a wooden pole signified the presence of Asherah. Fertility rites made available both male and female sacred prostitutes.[26]

---

[22]Two of the more recent works that criticize this type of assumption are, Christina Bucher, "The Origin and Meaning of ZNH Terminology in the Book of Hosea" (Ph.D. diss., Claremont Graduate School, 1988); and Joan Westenholz, "Tamar, *Qědēšā, Qadištu*, and Sacred Prostitution in Mesopotamia," *HTR* 82 (1989) 245-65. Further analysis of how such subjects as "magic," "fertility religion," and "cultic prostitution" attributed to the Canaanites have entered and been perpetuated in the secondary literature has been taken up by authors such as Gary Anderson (*Sacrifices and Offerings in Ancient Israel: Studies in their Social and Political Importance* [HSM 41; Atlanta: Scholars Press, 1987] 1-19, 91-116), and Robert Oden (*The Bible Without Theology: The Theological Tradition and Alternatives to It* [New York: Harper and Row, 1987] 131-53).

[23]John Bright, *A History of Israel* (3d ed.; Philadelphia: Westminster, 1981) 102.

[24]Bright, *History*, 260.

[25]Samuel Sandmel, *The Hebrew Scriptures: An Introduction to Their Literature and Religious Ideas* (New York: Knopf, 1963) 132 n. 2.

[26]H. Keith Beebe, *The Old Testament* (Belmont, CA: Dickenson, 1970) 161.

A similar description is Norman Gottwald's *A Light to the Nations: An Introduction to the Old Testament*. In this work Gottwald writes:

> The female counterpart of the baʻal was the ʼasherah. The divinities were worshipped not only in temples but also in open-air sanctuaries or "high places." The baʻal was generally represented by a large standing stone or massebah, the ʼasherah by a wooden pole known by the same name . . . Orgiastic revelries and ritual prostitution made Canaanite religion crude and vitalistic . . . Corps of male and female temple personnel were recruited. Even with the best of intentions it is easy to see how such a practice would pander to lust and immaturity.[27]

Note that the overriding picture given by these texts is that *bāmôt* were Baʻalistic shrines used for orgiastic fertility rituals, and that *maṣṣēbôt* and *ʼăšērîm* served in this complex to represent Baʻal and ʼAsherah. Nothing in these statements would lead the reader to inquire as to whether *all bāmôt*, *maṣṣēbôt*, or *ʼăšērîm* were so used. The implication is that this is the predominant biblical evidence concerning these items.[28]

In addition to basic texts and introductions, dictionary articles are also rife with this type of interpretation. For instance, Arthur B. Fowler's article, "High places," from *The New International Dictionary of the Bible* describes Canaanite religion as one which worshipped "the barely personified forces of nature" which were "empty of moral character." He goes further to say that:

> In Canaan the high places had become the scenes of orgies and human sacrifice connected with the idolatrous worship of these imaginary gods . . . figured stones were covered with crude carvings . . . or talismans . . . used to mystify or terrorize worshipers.[29]

An unsigned article in the same dictionary describes ʼAsherah as:

> 1. A goddess of the Phoenicians and Syrians taken over by the Israelites when they fell into idolatry. 2. Image representing this goddess whose worship was lewd and associated with Baal (Exod 34:13; 1 Kgs 16:29-33).[30]

---

[27]Norman Gottwald, *A Light to the Nations: An Introduction to the Old Testament* (New York: Harper, 1959) 148.

[28]Other introductions and basic texts which describe *bāmôt* as if they were universally Baʻalistic, or *ʼăšērîm* and *maṣṣēbôt* as if their primary function was to represent ʼAsherah and Baʻal respectively at *bāmôt* or as a part of Canaanite fertility religion, are Harry M. Buck, *People of the Lord: The History, Scriptures, and Faith of Ancient Israel* ([New York: Macmillan, 1966] 44, 199), and Walter Harrelson, *Interpreting the Old Testament* ([New York: Holt, Rinehart, and Winston, 1964] 155).

[29]Arthur B. Fowler, "High places," *NIDB* 439-40.

[30]"asherah," *NIDB* 99.

Although K. D. Schunck, in his article "בָּמָה bāmāh," notes, in keeping with some biblical evidence, that:

> for centuries the *bamoth*, which were spread out over the whole land, championed the Yahweh religion primarily in spite of their inclination to support a syncretistic cult,[31]

he also makes the rather unsupported identification of *bāmôt* as a particularly *Canaanite* type of cult place, not on the basis of any Canaanite evidence, but rather on the basis of Num 33:52.[32] John Day, in his article on "asherah" for *The Anchor Bible Dictionary*, states that "the Asherim together with the *maṣṣēbôt* 'pillars,' as well as altars, were a regular feature of the local shrines, the 'high places' (*bāmôt*), where Canaanite or syncretistic Canaanitizing worship was practiced in ancient Israel."[33]

A similar assessment occurs in G. Henton Davies' article "High Place, Sanctuary," in the *Interpreter's Dictionary of the Bible*. He writes:

> High places were essentially Canaanite . . . and then Israelite sanctuaries situated on high hills and associated with green trees and leafy oaks. Equipped with altars of sacrifice, incense, stone pillars, trees, and/or poles, and water, they were objects of Yahweh's wrath.[34]

In his article, "high place," for *Harper's Bible Dictionary*, Joshua R. Porter repeats many of the same themes seen above. He writes:

> In the Old Testament, it [the "high place"] is characteristic of the Canaanite fertility religion and the worship of Baal (Jer 19:5; 32:35), and so it is generally strongly condemned, especially in Deuteronomic passages of the Books of Kings, in Chronicles, and in the prophets . . . The rites practiced at the high places and the cultic objects found there are typically Canaanite: ritual prostitution (1 Kgs 14:23-24; Ezek 16:16); child sacrifice (Jer 7:31; 19:5; 32:35; Ezek 16:20);

---

[31]K. D. Schunck, "בָּמָה bāmāh," *TDOT* 2.144.

[32]Schunck, "בָּמָה bāmāh," 143. A similar projection of biblical evidence onto Canaanite religion occurs in Joshua R. Porter's article on the "High Place," *HBD* 392. Porter writes, on the basis of Josh 24:26 and Judg 9:6, that "the pillar and the tree in the sanctuary [at Shechem] are the regular features of a Canaanite high place."

[33]John Day, "asherah," *ABD* 1.486b.

[34]G. Henton Davies, "High Place, Sanctuary,"*IDB* 2.602. Schunck ("בָּמָה, bāmāh," 142-43), also provides a rather full, and therefore largely conflated description of *bāmôt* and their accoutrements. He writes, "each bamah was furnished with an altar...Besides the altar, the most important furnishings were a wooden pole = 'asherah, and one or more stone pillars . . . finally each bamah seems to have had a tent or a smaller or larger room covered with some sort of roof where sacrificial meals were eaten and where the cultic vessels were stored (Ezek 16:16; 1 Sam 9:22; 1 Kgs 3:5)."

sacrifices and the burning of incense (1 Kgs 22:43; 2 Kgs 12:3), the stone pillar symbolizing Baal and the wooden pole symbolizing the goddess Asherah (1 Kgs 14:23; 2 Kgs 17:10).[35]

Close examination of the passages listed by Porter raises some interesting questions, one being how the Jeremianic references to child sacrifice he mentions at the top of the paragraph fit into his understanding of Canaanite *fertility* religion. In addition, Porter's connection of ritual prostitution with *bāmôt* requires further scrutiny in that Ezek 16:16 is employing the familiar prophetic metaphor of faithless Israel which *likens* her to, rather than *identifies* her with, a cultic prostitute; and 1 Kgs 14:24 states that the *qādēš* (understood by Porter as a type of ritual prostitute), was "in the land," not specifically practicing on *bāmôt*.

Thus, by far the most common description found in the general literature concerning the items of interest to this study is the view that *bāmôt* were Canaanite shrines and that *maṣṣēbôt* and *ăšērîm* were a conceptual pair that represented, as part of Canaanite fertility religion, the male god (frequently identified as Baʿal) and the goddess ʾAsherah.[36] While this explanation of *ăšērîm* is a strong possibility, it is by no means the only possible interpretation, nor is it correct to say that the biblical record limits *ăšērîm* to this interpretation. Similarly, the biblical *maṣṣēbôt* are not limited to examples which were accoutrements of Baʿal.

One dictionary article which nonetheless presents these traditional views regarding *ăšērîm* and *maṣṣēbôt* is that of Roger S. Boraas from *Harper's Bible Dictionary*. Boraas writes:

> The stone pillar representing the male deity and the lush tree or wooden post representing the female deity were standard parts of Canaanite Baalistic shrine equipment. Their presence symbolized the sexual union of the gods necessary to allow agricultural fertility.[37]

Another scholar with similar views is J. C. de Moor. de Moor states that "as the *ʾasherah* is the symbol of the fertility goddess, the *matstsebhah* is the symbol of the fertility god Baal (2 Kgs 3:2; 10:26)."[38] K. D. Schunck also

---

[35]Joshua R. Porter, "High Place," *HBD* 391.

[36]One notable exception to the insistence that paired *ăšērîm* and *maṣṣēbôt* must represent Baʿal and ʾAsherah is found Saul Olyan's article "The Cultic Confessions of Jer 2,27a," *ZAW* 99 (1987) 254-59. Olyan argues that Jer 2:27, under the influence of Dtr, is a polemic against dedication of *ăšērîm* and *maṣṣēbôt* to YHWH, not to Baʿal.

[37]Roger S. Boraas, "Pillars," *HBD* 799.

[38]J. C. de Moor, "אֲשֵׁרָה ʾăsherāh," *TDOT* 1.443.

echoes this view, but with a more negative tone toward the use of *ăšērîm* than toward the use of *maṣṣēbôt*. He writes:

> Old Canaanite fertility rites with their immoral practices were kept alive in conjunction with the *'asherah* and it was not difficult for the people to conclude that the *matstsebhah* represented the deity himself (whether it be . . . Baal, in the earlier period or Yahweh in the later).[39]

Another who favors a similar interpretation of *maṣṣēbôt* and *ăšērîm* is G. A. Barrois,[40] while William L. Reed states simply that:

> The antipathy toward the Asherah on the part of the Hebrew leaders was due to the fact that the goddess and the cult object of the same name were associated with the fertility religion of a foreign people and as such involved a mythology and a cultus which were obnoxious to the champions of Yahweh.[41]

While Reed does correctly state that 'Asherah the goddess was a foreign deity and that this fact in connection with *ăšērîm* may have led to their negative depiction by certain Israelite leaders, he does not entertain the notion that the use of these objects could be part of a thoroughly Israelite cult of 'Asherah.

As this review of scholarship shows, it is difficult to escape the conclusion in general introductions and dictionary articles that *bāmôt*, *maṣṣēbôt*, and *ăšērîm* in particular, and the altars that accompany them were predominantly reflexes of Canaanite religion, and particularly a Canaanite religion focussed on fertility issues. Little in these articles suggests that these objects may have had any purely Israelite uses. They are generally described as Canaanite in origin and described as condemned by the biblical writers. While some more recent articles avoid most of these pitfalls,[42] they are still currently outnumbered by those studies that perpetuate a stereotypical and generalized picture of *bāmôt*, *ăšērîm*, and *maṣṣēbôt*.

It is the contention of this study that any attempt to merge the many viewpoints of the biblical sources concerning prohibited religious practices or paraphernalia into a synchronic reconstruction of a monolithic Canaaniz-

---

[39]"בָּמָה bāmāh," 144.

[40]"Pillar," *IDB* 3.815-817.

[41]William L. Reed, "Asherah," *IDB* 1.252.

[42]See, Susan Ackerman, "Asherah," *OCB* 62; W. Boyd Barrick, "High Place," *ABD* 3.196-200; Robert M. Good, "Asherah," *HBD* 74-75; Dale Manor, "massebah," *ABD* 4.602; P. Kyle McCarter, "High Place," *OCB* 284-85; Emmett Russell, "Pillars," *NIDB* 790-91. On the relationship between Israelite and Canaanite religion, see Patrick D. Miller, "Israelite Religion," in *The Hebrew Bible and Its Modern Interpreters* (ed. Douglas A. Knight and Gene M. Tucker; Philadelphia: Fortress, 1985) 201-37.

ing syncretism in ancient Israel is essentially in error. Only by seeing the separate sources or strata individually and the unique data from the various communities which engaged in the earliest interpretation of these items does one arrive at a clearer and more detailed understanding of how these strata and traditions understood Israelite religion in relation to the religions of Israel's neighbors, and in this light, how they understood their own depiction of Israelite religion as normative.

METHODOLOGICAL APPROACHES

Source Criticism

In order to fill the gaps in the existing literature on these items and their use one must avoid the generalizing tendencies discussed above, and engage instead in a careful source-critical study of these items and the way in which they are treated within each of the separate source strata of the biblical text. Part I of this analysis, therefore, will discuss each of the biblical passages which mention *bāmôt, maṣṣēbôt, ʾăšērîm, mizbəḥôt* (noting their connection to other cultic paraphernalia such as incense burners and cultic statuary), grouping these passages into chapters and subdivisions according to source attribution, and addressing any problems of attribution that may exist. Part II reorganizes the data by item, comparing the views of all the sources, discussing in more detail the secondary literature related to each item, and noting any significant differences in source opinions regarding them which may appear over time, or may be due to associations made between one item and other items, or between a certain item and any specific group of people.

A Note Concerning Source-critical Method

Reference to particular items of cultic paraphernalia has become one of the main indicators for the assignment of passages to one of the Pentateuchal source traditions. Because of this, there is a danger of circularity for studies such as this one which seek to distinguish the attitudes of the various sources from one another on the very subject of cultic paraphernalia. Regardless of this risk, it is by no means futile to attempt a source division in passages related to cultic matters. A writer's assumed attitude toward cultic issues is only one of the overall characteristics of a source, and one which the modern critic may hold in abeyance until other criteria, whether of vocabulary, style, or ideology, have been addressed. The surest way to avoid the error of circular or reductionistic reasoning is to sustain the most complete understanding possible of the nature of J, E, and P so that simple mention of a cultic item is never the only criterion by which a given passage is assigned to any source.

This study adopts as a working hypothesis the majority opinion concerning the existence of the following sources within the Tetrateuch: J,[43] E,[44] the preexisting legal corpora preserved by J and E (Exod 20:1-17; 34; and the Covenant Code, 20:22-23:33), P,[45] and H (the Holiness Code, Leviticus 17-26).[46] In addition to the sources within the Tetrateuch, this study recognizes an interrelationship among Deuteronomy, DH, and certain editorial activities within the prophetic corpus,[47] as well as acknowledging that Dtr may have had access to fragments from the earlier source materials of the Tetrateuch in addition to other early materials (such as the Elijah-Elisha Cycle). This study also accepts Chronicles, Ezra, and Nehemiah as a

---

[43]For a list of features considered to be peculiar to J, see J. Estlin Carpenter and George Harford-Battersby (*The Hexateuch According to the Revised Version* [2 s.; London: Longmans, Green, 1900], hereafter abbreviated CHB) 1.185-92. For extended studies on this source, see Coote and Ord, *First History*; Peter F. Ellis, *The Yahwist: The Bible's First Theologian* (Notre Dame, Ind: Fides, 1968). For a recent review of scholarship which includes the work of those such as Hans Heinrich Schmid (*Der sogenannte Jahwist: Beobachtungen und Fragen zur Pentateuchforschung* [Zürich: Theologischer Verlag, 1976]), who does not believe there is an independent J source, and John Van Seters (*In Search of History: Historiography in the Ancient World and The Origins of Biblical History* [New Haven: Yale University Press, 1983]), who argues that J is a late source, see Albert de Pury, "Yahwist ('J') Source," *ABD* 6.1012-20.

[44]For a list of features considered to be peculiar to E, see CHB, 1.190-92. For extended studies on this source, see Coote and Ord, *Defense of Reution*, and Jenks, *Elohist*; idem, "Elohist," *ABD* 2.478-82. Jenks provides an excellent history of scholarship of E, in addition to addressing the views of scholars such as Wilhelm Rudolph (*Der 'Elohist' von Exodus bis Josua* [BZAW 68; Berlin: Töpelmann, 1938]) who argue against the existence of an independent E source.

[45]For a list of features considered to be peculiar to P, see CHB 1.208-221; Baruch Levine, "Research in the Priestly Source: The Linguistic Factor," *Eretz-Israel* 16 (1982) 124-31 [Heb]; Jacob Milgrom, *Leviticus 1-16: A New Translation with Introduction and Commentary* (AB 3; New York: Doubleday, 1991) 1-63; and Avi Hurvitz, *Linguistic Study of the Relationship between the Priestly Source and the Book of Ezekiel: A New Approach to an Old Problem* (Cahiers de la Revue Biblique 20; Paris: Gabalda, 1982). See also Coote and Ord, *In the Beginning*.

[46]On H, see Israel Knohl, *The Sanctuary of Silence: The Priestly Torah and the Holiness School* (Minneapolis: Fortress, 1995); Milgrom, *Leviticus 1-16*, 1-60; idem *Leviticus 17-22: A New Translation with Introduction and Commentary* (AB 3A; New York: Doubleday, 2000); idem *Leviticus 23-27: A New Translation with Introduction and Commentary* (AB 3B; New York: Doubleday, 2001). An extended discussion of all the Tetrateuchal sources and their characteristics is also found in S. R. Driver, *Introduction to the Literature of the Old Testament* (7th ed.; New York: Charles Scribner's Sons, 1898) 10-159.

[47]On these issues see Moshe Weinfeld, *Deuteronomy and the Deuteronomic School*, and Jon D. Levenson, "Who Inserted the Book of Torah?" *HTR* 68 (1975) 203-33.

body of related sources with a common world view, and refers to this per-specitve as that of "The Chronicler" without making specific claims regarding actual common authorship of this material, and despite the use in Chronicles of material already present in Dtr. This study will take into account evidence of redactional strata within certain prophetic books.

Early Interpretation

Part III of this study will address the views of *bāmôt*, *ʾăšērîm*, *maṣṣēbôt*, and *mizbəḥôt* held by the early translated versions of the Hebrew Bible, specifically the LXX, the Vulgate, and the early Jewish interpreters. This section will discuss the conventions used by these early interpreters to describe these items. For each of these traditions, an effort will be made to establish whether the translator is attempting to be literalistic in rendering a view of a particular item, or whether an analogy to current religious practice is being drawn upon to provide the vocabulary needed to arrive at a translation. Of particular interest in this regard is the way in which the versions draw upon cultic settings from Classical Greek and Roman culture for the descriptive vocabulary used in translations concerning ancient Israelite cultic practice. Any established trajectories of interpretation which continue from the biblical sources into the early interpretative traditions will also be noted.

Summary

This study will show how *bāmôt*, *maṣṣēbôt*, *ʾăšērîm*, and *mizbəḥôt* have a rich descriptive history in the biblical text, approved by some, disapproved by others, but viewed distinctively by virtually all the sources which mention them. In the biblical text, as well as in the early interpretative traditions, these items represent a subset of religious practices which lent themselves to debate and reconsideration in each new age and new community. To view them as a vestigial remnants of some primitive religious practice belies the biblical evidence which depicts their use as persistent and in many cases central to Israelite religion at one time or another.

The significance of this evidence goes to the heart of how we may now come to understand Israelite religion: not as a monolithic phenomenon which promoted one "orthodox" concept of YHWHism and suppressed all other expressions as "heterodox," but rather as a multifaceted phenomenon in which many different expressions of YHWHism may have coexisted and thrived without any perceived need for one dominant form to supersede all others. It is an essentially flawed approach to view the many strata of the Hebrew Bible as if they were always in dialogue with each other and then to attempt to synthesize the many opinions found there into one systematic theological worldview or centrally organized faith system. The material related to cultic matters in particular resists such homogenization and simplification and calls into question any assumed reconstruction of what may or may not have been considered "normative" religious practice within ancient Israel. What the data actually reveal is a considerable amount of religious pluralism in ancient Israel as well as remarkable flexibility on the part of later traditions which transformed references to ancient cult life in specific ways designed to make them relevant to the new cultural contexts that greeted successive generations.

PART I
Source-critical Analysis of Texts
Related to Cultic Items

The primary emerging from the data on *bāmôt, maṣṣēbôt, ăšērîm,* and *mizbəḥôt* is that virtually every source has its own way of viewing these items and their other cultic associations. They are sometimes mentioned in combination with each other or with other items, although the combinations are by no means uniform, either within a source or among the sources.[1]

Some strata condemn certain of these items which others portray at least neutrally if not positively. Deuteronomy (16:22) and the Holiness Code (Lev 26:1), for example, prohibit *maṣṣēbôt* for Israelite use while E portrays Jacob (Gen 28:18, 22; 31:13, 45, 51, 52; 33:20, 35:14, 20) and Moses (Exod 24:4) erecting them. Other sources treat a single cultic item both positively *and* negatively according to some internal criterion. The Deuteronomic History, for example, describes *bāmôt* which existed prior to the construction of the Jerusalem Temple positively, and those erected or in existence after the Temple's construction negatively.[2] Both the Covenant Code and Deuteronomy share internal criteria related to construction methods which were used to judge an altar acceptable or unacceptable (Exod 20:24-25; Deut 27:5-6). The sources also acknowledge that altars, while

---

[1]The combination *ăšērîm, maṣṣēbôt,* and *mizbəḥôt* occurs in Exod 34:13; Deut 7:5; 12:3; *ăšērîm* and *maṣṣēbôt* are discussed sequentially in Deut 16:21-22; *ăšērîm* and *mizbəḥôt* are combined in Deut 16:21; Judg 6:24-32; Isa 17:8; 27:9; Jer 17:2; *bāmôt* and *mizbəḥôt* are discussed together in 1 Kgs 3:4; 12:32-13:32; 1 Chr 16:39; 21:29; 2 Chr 1:3, 13; Ezek 6:6, 13; Hos 10:8; *ăšērîm, bāmôt,* and *mizbəḥôt* are combined in 2 Kgs 21:3; 23:15; 2 Chr 33:3; Jer 17:2-3; *ăšērîm, bāmôt,* and *maṣṣēbôt* are combined in 1 Kgs 14:23; 2 Kgs 17:10-11; 18:4; and all four items, *ăšērîm, bāmôt, maṣṣēbôt,* and *mizbəḥôt,* are combined in 2 Chr 14:2 and 31:1. They are also variously linked with other items such as types of cultic statuary (*gillûlîm, pəsîlîm, ĕlîlîm, massēkôt,* etc.); incense burners (*ḥammānîm*), the formulaic pair "high hill" and "leafy tree" (*ĕṣ raănān*), and other vocabulary related to trees, stones, and hills.

[2]See 1 Samuel 9 and 1 Kgs 3:2. Moshe Weinfeld believes that the silence of Deuteronomy on the subject of *bāmôt,* like its omitting the mention of Jerusalem by name, is simply an attempt to avoid obvious anachronism in its Mosaic speeches (*Deuteronomy,* 6).

perfectly legitimate within Israelite religion, might also be part of unacceptable worship devoted to gods other than YHWH (Exod 34:13; Deut 7:5; 12:3).

Some sources are more concerned with certain cultic items than with others. The Deuteronomic History, for example, devotes a disproportionate number of verses to altars in comparison to its discussion of other cultic items,[3] while Jeremiah makes a unique connection between *bāmôt* and child sacrifice.[4] Other sources mention some of these items but ignore others completely, voicing no opinion, either positive or negative. P and the Holiness Code, for example, never mention *ăšērîm*. J and Deuteronomy never mention *bāmôt*. E never mentions *ăšērîm* or *bāmôt*.

No simple harmonization of the ancient sources can be effected on the subject of whether any one of these items was either generally approved or proscribed. The exact items and practices that are forbidden, the combination of items or practices that occur together, as well as the vocabulary used to describe them, vary from one ancient witness to another, and within certain witnesses. It is precisely this variation that is of interest.

This part of the study will discuss separately each of the biblical sources which mention *bāmôt*, *maṣṣēbôt*, *ăšērîm*, or *mizbəḥôt*. References to cultic statuary will be included as well since some sources connect the use of cultic statuary with the use of the items central to this study. Because the use of cultic statuary was of major concern to many biblical writers, the linking or distancing of this practice to the use of the items under discussion here cannot be considered irrelevant. Discussion of each source will begin with a list of items the source mentions along with an acknowledgment of the items which the source fails to mention. It will then be determined whether the items which are mentioned are assessed negatively or positively, if such a determination can be made. In chapters five through eight, the data will be rearranged by item so sources or traditions which share opinions concerning these items can be clearly seen.

---

[3]Several lengthy stories preserved in Dtr feature altars prominently: Joshua 22 (a large part of which was originally a P story); Judg 6:11-32, 1 Kgs 12:32-13:32 (and 2 Kgs 23:15-20), 1 Kgs 18:1-46, 2 Kgs 16:10-16, and 2 Kgs 18:1-25.

[4]Jer 7:31; 19:5; 32:35. See also, however, connections between *bāmôt* and Moab (Num 21:19 (P), 20 (P), 28 (J); 22:41 (E); Josh 13:17; Jer 48:35; Is 15:2; 16:12), in light of 2 Kings 3 which connects the king of Moab with child sacrifice. See also, Jo Ann Hackett, "Religious Traditions in Israelite Transjordan," in *Ancient Israelite Religion: Essays in Honor of Frank Moore Cross* (ed. Patrick D. Miller, Jr., Paul D. Hanson, S. Dean McBride; Philadelphia: Fortress, 1987) 125-36. See further chapter five (pp. 140-45).

Chapter One
The Tetrateuchal Sources

As noted above, this study assumes the existence of the three traditional Tetrateuchal sources and adopts source-critical theory as a working
hypothesis.[5] This chapter will also treat separately certain legal corpora
(Exod 20:1-17; 20:22-23:33; 34) and the Holiness Code (Leviticus 17-26)
which originated independently of J, E, and P though incorporated into
them in later stages of the editorial process. Passages whose source attributions are problematic (such as Exod 24:4-6; 34:13;[6] Joshua 4; Joshua 22)
will be discussed in some detail. These passages (as well as others discussed
in subsequent chapters), whose attribution has been questioned by scholars,
have been assigned their most likely attributions for the purpose of discussion, but with the questions concerning them noted. Those passages for
which attribution is the subject of significant debate are listed within brack-
ets under the source and heading to which they have been assigned.

THE J SOURCE

bāmôt [Num 21:28][7]

---

[5]The source divisions in this study have generally followed these major works:
CHB, Martin Noth, *Traditions*, Julius Wellhausen, *Prolegomena* and *Die Composition
des Hexateuchs und der Historischen Bücher des Alten Testaments* (2d ed.; Berlin:
Reimer, 1889). This study is also greatly indebted to the invaluable methodological
insight of Theodore Hiebert.

[6]CHB notes, "the assignment of Exod 24:4 and Exod 34:13 to either J, E, P or the
Covenant Code source is complicated by their situation in the heavily redacted Sinai
narratives." Noting the extreme difficulty presented by the JE version of the Sinai
revelation (Exod 19-24, 32-34:28), CHB discusses it at length and provides a diagram
outlining its redaction (CHB 2.135-6).

[7]Jenks takes issue with previous scholars (CHB 2.221-23; Noth *Traditions*, 36;
and George Buchanan Gray (*Numbers* [International Critical Commentary; Edinburgh: T.
& T. Clark, 1903] 264-65) who attributed Num 21:21-31 to E based on what he considers
"inconclusive" stylistic criteria (*Elohist*, 80 n. 222). He argues that "no clear evidence of
E passages can be found [in Num 13-21] before the Balaam pericope, Num 22-24"
(*Elohist*, 55). Wellhausen argued that Num 20:14-21 and 21:21-31 evidence the
characteristic J manner of referring to nations in the singular (Num 20:18, "But Edom
said to him . . ."; Num 21:21, "Israel sent messengers . . ."), similar to that found in the J

J does not use the word *bāmôt* apart from one Moabite place name, Bamot Arnon; this occurs in Num 21:28 within an old poetic passage, the "Song of Heshbon" (Num 21:27-30), which J incorporates into a narrative. While the NRSV chooses to translate *bāmôt* here as "heights," it is also possible to read a two-part place name similar to Bamoth Ba'al, which occurs in E (Num 22:41) and in Dtr (Josh 13:17). The significance of the fact that all the sites whose names include the term *bāmôt* (including the site of Bamoth mentioned in P, Num 21:19- 20) are located in Moab will be discussed in chapter five.

ăšērîm: not mentioned

maṣṣēbôt: not mentioned.

Although J makes no mention of *maṣṣēbôt* or *ăšērîm*, legal material from Exodus 34 (Exod 34:13), which J incorporates into its narrative, contains an instruction to destroy *ăšērîm* and *maṣṣēbôt* when found among the inhabitants of the land. Regardless of J's attitude toward the legal stipulations of Exodus 34, however, it could be argued that the way in which J depicts Abraham in relation to various famous trees is relevant to a discussion of *ăšērîm*. Abraham camps by the Oak of Moreh near Shechem where he witnesses a theophany (Gen 12:6-7). From there he moves to the Oaks of Mamre near Hebron where he erects an altar to YHWH (13:18). God appears to Abraham while he is sitting under the Oaks of Mamre (18:1), where Abraham prepares a meal for his divine visitors. Outside of J, there is another witness to Abraham living near the Oaks of Mamre in Genesis 14 (v 13). In addition to settling near trees, Abraham is also said to plant an *ēšel*, or tamarisk tree, when he covenants with Abimelek at Beer Sheba (21:33). Many commentators have discussed theories concerning "sacred," "cosmic," or "oracular" trees in relation to Gen 12:6 but without making the kind of direct connection between such trees and *ăšērîm* as did W. F. Albright.[8]

---

strata of Exod 14 (Exod 14:30 "Israel saw Egypt dead on the seashore . . . "), though he allowed that this may be due to a J revision (*Hexateuchs*, 110). Ultimately, there is more evidence of J than E in Num 21:21-31.

[8]E. A. Speiser, *Genesis: Introduction, Translation, and Notes* (AB 1; Garden City, N.Y.: Doubleday, 1962) 86; Gerhard von Rad, *Genesis: A Commentary* (Philadelphia: Westminster, 1973) 162; Nahum Sarna, *Genesis* (JPS Torah Commentary; Philadelphia: Jewish Publication Society, 1989) 91; Claus Westermann, *Genesis 12-36: A Commentary* (tr. John J. Scullion; Minneapolis: Augsburg, 1985) 153-4; W. F. Albright, *Yahweh and the Gods of Canaan*, 189-91. See chapter six for a discussion of this recurring arboreal motif within the Abraham stories (pp. 175-80).

mizbǝḥôt: Gen 8:20; 12:7, 8; 13:4, 18; 26:25; Exod 17:15[9]; Num 23:1, 2, 4, 14, 29, 30.[10]

Several J characters set up *mizbǝḥôt* to YHWH. Noah erects one at the landing place of the ark (Gen 8:20). Abraham erects three, one at Shechem near the Oak of Moreh (Gen 12:7), one at Bethel (Gen 12:8; 13:4) and one at the Oaks of Mamre near Hebron (13:18). Isaac erects one at Beer Sheba (26:25), and Moses erects one at Rephidim (Exod 17:15). Balaam and Balak erect altars on YHWH's instruction at Bamoth Ba'al (Num 23:1, 2, 4), Pisgah (Num 23:14), and Peor (Num 23:29-30); however, these altars are not specifically identified as YHWHistic. The legal corpus of Exodus 34, which J incorporates, specifically mandates the destruction of *mizbǝḥôt* which do not belong to the Israelites (Exod 34:13); however, the altars built by Balaam and Balak are not condemned by J itself.

---

[9]The story of Moses erecting an altar at Rephidim (Exod 17:8-16) is thought by some to be J and by others, E. Martin Noth assigned 17:8-16 to J, and hypothesized that the original form of the name of the altar may have been *YHWH kisî*, "YHWH is my throne," rather than *YHWH nissî*, "YHWH is my banner" (*Exodus: A Commentary* [tr. J. S. Bowden; OTL; Philadelphia: Westminster, 1962] 141-44). Brevard Childs, however, while not making a choice between J and E, notes that "older commentators tended to assign [Exod 17:8-16] to E, chiefly because of the staff" which Moses wields in the story. (This is the view of CHB [2.107].) Childs notes that J. H. Grønbaek ("Juda und Amalek. Überlieferungs-geschichtliche Erwägungen zu Exodus 17, 8-16," *Studia Theologica* 18 [1964] 26-45) chose J on the grounds that the staff references are secondary (*The Book of Exodus: A Critical, Theological Commentary* [OTL; Philadelphia: Westminster, 1974] 313). Jenks argues that despite the staff references and whether they are secondary, Exod 17:8-16 should be placed with E because of the role played by Joshua in the battle with Amalek (*Elohist*, 43). Richard Elliott Friedman also considers this story to be E, viewing the special role of Joshua as an E trait (*Who Wrote the Bible?* [New York: Summit, 1987] 66, 251). J altar stories do not usually include the feature of the altar being given a name, while this is a trend in many E stories of altar construction (Gen 22:14; 33:20; 35:7). Still, Amalek is a southern tribal enemy, and therefore more likely to be featured in a J story than an E story. Also, the name of the altar, whether it is YHWH as a banner, or a throne, belies a J emphasis on tribal unity.

[10]Scholarly opinion varies widely concerning the division of the Balaam cycle into J and E strands. Jenks provides an excellent summary of the various opinions (*Elohist*, 55-57). CHB considers all of Numbers 23 except for verses 27-29 to be E (27-29 is determined to be J or the JE redactor, CHB 2.224). Jenks also ends E's presence in Numbers 23 at verse 26 (*Elohist*, 57), while noting that Wilhelm Rudolf (*Der 'Elohist' von Exodus bis Josua* [BZAW 68; Berlin: A. Töpelmann, 1938] 127-28) considered Num 23:1-26 to be an independent premonarchic piece edited into the whole cycle by the J writer (*Elohist*, 55).

Cultic statuary: not mentioned

Although J does not mention cultic statuary, Exodus 34 (which J incorporates) prohibits the use of *massēkôt* in Israel (Exod 34:17).

Summary

J does not mention *ăšērîm, maṣṣēbôt*, or cultic statuary as cultic items in use by the Israelites and uses the term *bāmôt* only as a component part of a Moabite place name. The only cultic items of which J obviously approves are *mizbəhôt*, which J associates with unquestionably respected figures such as Abraham and Moses. The Balaam materials also make it clear that J has no objection to a non-Israelite erecting an altar to YHWH. Balaam, though a foreigner, converses with YHWH and builds altars upon his instruction. It should be said, however, that the Balaam materials are exceptional in more than one aspect and for this reason might not be the best representatives of J's overall world view.

J does not condemn any items of cultic paraphernalia outright; however, J does incorporate the legal material of Exodus 34 into its narrative and in so doing, preserves the prohibitions of cultic paraphernalia (*ăšērîm, maṣṣēbôt, mizbəhôt*, and *massēkôt*) present in Exodus 34. This may imply a tacit agreement with these prohibitions though it need not.

EXODUS 34

This legal corpus has long been held to have preexisted the J writer who later incorporated it into the J narrative.[11] Only two verses in this chapter, however, deal with items of interest to the present study, Exod 34:13 and 34:17. Exod 34:13, however, is suspected by many scholars as a Deuteronomistic addition. For this reason, Exod 34:13 will be discussed at length.

bāmôt: not mentioned

ăšērîm: Exod 34:13

maṣṣēbôt: Exod 34:13

---

[11]For the opposing view that legal codes were formulated in response to existing narratives, see Calum M. Carmichael, *The Origins of Biblical Law: The Decalogues and the Book of the Covenant* (Ithaca: Cornell University Press, 1992).

mizbǝḥôt: Exod 34:13

Exod 34:13 mentions *ăšērîm*, *maṣṣēbôt*, and *mizbǝḥôt* as cultic paraphernalia belonging to foreign nations, and demands that they be destroyed by the Israelites. While there is a consensus that the bulk of Exodus 34 is legal material incorporated into J, there is still extensive debate concerning the attribution of Exod 34:13. There are three major theories regarding this verse:

1. It belongs to the distinct corpus of Exodus 34.
2. It belongs to J.
3. It belongs to Dtr.

The first option is adopted by Frank Moore Cross who considers that Exod 34:10-17 in particular is an example of cultic material woven into the epic tradition, and therefore not original to either J or E. Cross goes on to state that "the ordering and selection of materials here [Exodus 19-24, 32, 33, 34] by the Priestly editor . . . obscures the covenant formulary in E and, indeed, suppresses even the main part of Yahwistic decalogue."[12] Wellhausen assigned Exodus 34 in its entirety to J, arguing that Exodus 20 constituted an Elohistic "ethical" decalogue while Exodus 34 was an YHWHistic "ritual" decalogue. Brevard Childs and others, however, see Exod 34:13 as a later expansion by Dtr.[13]

One piece of evidence for the theory that 34:13 is the work of Dtr is the presence of the term *ăšērîm*. Elsewhere this term occurs predominantly in Dtr and Chronicles, with only four occurrences outside these two sources in books for which Deuteronomistic editorial activity has long been suggested (Isa 17:8, 27:9; Jer 17:3; Mic 5:13).[14] One might argue, then, that

---

[12]*CMHE*, 84 n. 15. On the issue of cultic material embedded in epic material, Cross cites D. J. McCarthy, *Treaty and Covenant* (Rome: Pontifical Biblical Institute, 1963) 152-67.

[13]Wellhausen, *Hexateuchs*, 85; Childs, *Exodus*, 613; Friedman, *Who Wrote the Bible?*, 248; Noth, *Exodus*, 260-62. CHB also argues that Exod 34:13 should be attributed to a redactor working at a later time than J. The hypothesis behind this view is that many verses in Exodus 34 were added in order to facilitate the transplanting of the J account of the covenant (34:10-27) which was moved to chapter 34 from its original place in chapter 20 to make room for the E version (CHB 2.134-5). For a discussion of the history of scholarship on Exodus 34, see Childs, *Exodus*, 604-9.

[14]On the subject of Deuteronomistic editorial activity in Jeremiah, see Weinfeld, *Deuteronomy*, 27-32; for Micah see the suggestions of Hans Walter Wolff, (*Micah* [Biblischer Kommentar 14/12; Neukirchen-Vluyn: Neukirchener Verlag, 1980]) summarized by Delbert Hillers (*Micah: A Commentary on the Book of the Prophet Micah* [Hermeneia; Philadelphia: Fortress, 1984] 3). For a good discussion of the intricate

Exod 34:13 is also the result of Deuteronomistic expansion. It is possible, however, that all of these other sources, notable for their southern provenance, owe their interest in and opinion of *ăšērîm* as items of "non-YHWHistic" origin to Exod 34:13.[15]

Aside from this argument based essentially on a lexeme, there is another argument for Deuteronomistic authorship of 34:13, based on the similarities between it and Deuteronomy 7.[16] Exod 34:11-13 reads:

> Observe what I command you today. See, I am driving out before you the Amorites, the Canaanites, the Hittites, the Perizzites, the Hivites, and the Jebusites. Take care not to make a covenant with the inhabitants of the land to which you are going, or it will become a snare among you. You shall tear down their *mizbəhôt*, break their *maṣṣēbôt*, and cut down their *ăšērîm*.

Deut 7:1-5 reads:

> When YHWH your God brings you into the land that you are about to enter and occupy, he will clear away many nations before you, the Hittites, the Girgashites, the Amorites, the Canaanites, the Perizzites, the Hivites, and the Jebusites, seven nations mightier and more numerous than you, and when YHWH your God gives them over to you and you defeat them, then you must utterly destroy them. Make no covenant with them and show them no mercy. Do not intermarry with them . . . for that would turn away your children from following me, to serve other gods . . . But this is how you must deal with them: tear down their *mizbəhôt*, break their *maṣṣēbôt*, hew down their *ăšērîm* and burn their *pəsîlîm*.

Both passages have the same pattern: 1) the list of nations YHWH will expel before Israel, 2) the command not to make a covenant with these nations, 3) the warning that such contact will lead Israel away from proper YHWHistic religion, 4) instructions on how to avoid this threat by destroying foreign cultic installations. Except for the addition of *pəsîlîm* in Deuteronomy 7, even the order and contents of the list of items to be

---

connections between the Deuteronomistic School and that of First Isaiah, especially with regard to historical issues, see Joseph A. Blenkinsopp, *A History of Prophecy in Israel: From the Settlement in the Land to the Hellenistic Period* (Philadelphia: Westminster, 1983) 108-15.

[15]Peter Ellis states that while Noth was "probably correct" in considering 34:11-17 to be a Deuteronomistic interpolation, he believes that 34:11-17 is in keeping with the YHWHist's "anti-Canaanite animus." He goes on to state that "there is no good reason why in its earliest form such a text would not have come from the Yahwist. The theological content, if not the phraseology, is typically Yahwistic" (*Yahwist*, 202-3).

[16]CHB 2.135. This view is supported by Childs (*Exodus*, 613) and Noth (*Exodus*, 262).

destroyed are the same. On the basis of this evidence, one might argue either that Deuteronomy borrowed the general outline of this instruction from Exodus 34 and expanded it, or that Dtr inserted an abbreviated version of this instruction into Exodus 34 because it was deemed crucial to do so.

The argument, however, that Dtr would consider the absence of such an instruction in Exodus to be a major oversight and was therefore compelled to add one is weakened by the conclusion to the Covenant Code, in Exod 23:23-24. It reads:

> When my angel goes in front of you and brings you to the Amorites, the Hittites, the Perizzites, the Canaanites, the Hivites, and the Jebusites, and I blot them out, you shall not bow down to their gods, or worship them, or follow their practices, but you shall utterly demolish them and break their *maṣṣēbôt* in pieces.

Here again we see a similar content: 1) a list of nations to be eradicated (in this case by God's agent), 2) a warning against adopting their religion, 3) instructions to destroy their cultic installations. This list varies from the previous passages in only two details. The instruction not to make a covenant with the foreigners is missing, and the list of cultic items to be destroyed includes only *maṣṣēbôt*. Now, it is possible to argue, on the basis of the similarities found here, that Exod 23:20-33 is also a Deuteronomistic addition.[17] One would be hard pressed, however, to develop a logic behind Dtr adding both of these passages to previously existing legal corpora.[18]

---

[17]Jenks, who considers Exod 23:20-33 to be the closing oration of the Covenant Code (a source which he distinguishes from E, *Elohist*, 124), notes that many earlier scholars who attributed the Covenant Code to E have noticed the similarities to Deuteronomic phraseology in 23:20-33 and have thus argued for a closer relationship between Deuteronomic and Elohistic circles than Jenks is prepared to defend (*Elohist*, 77-78 n. 170). Another link between this passage and Dtr is the fact that it contains an explanation of why the inhabitants of the land will not be driven out at once but rather over time, little by little. This explanation, coupled with the presence of God's "angel," reminds one of Judges 2:1-5, though in Judges, the angel's announcement concerning the gradual defeat of the tribes of the land is seen as a judgment against Israel's unfaithfulness. In Exodus 23, it is supposed to be a protection from the overpopulation of wild animals.

[18]Tomoo Ishida has devised a schema for relatively dating them on the basis of changes in the definition of the term "Hittite" ("The Structure and Historical Implications of the Lists of Pre-Israelite Nations," *Biblica* 60 [1979] 461-90). He argues that the term progressed from describing "Palestinian Hittites," (those who migrated into Palestine and settled in the land during the Bronze age), to "Neo-Hittite" citizens of Syria, to finally conforming to the Neo-Assyrian use of the term to refer to all inhabitants of Syro-Palestine in general. Ishida argues that six name lists which rank the Hittites first date to the Neo-Assyrian era, those with Hittites second to the end of the Solomonic era, and

While these three passages do resemble each other, this resemblance could well be the result of three different sources each having knowledge of the same formulaic speech or cliché. Upon closer examination of the wording used in these passages, certain basic differences emerge. The phrases for the eradication of the nations vary from passage to passage. Exod 34:11 states, with God speaking in the first person, "Behold, I am *driving* [the nations] *out before you*" (גֹרֵשׁ מִפָּנֶיךָ). Deut 7:1 refers to YHWH's action in the third person: "he will *clear away* many nations *before you*" (וְנָשַׁל גּוֹיִם רַבִּים מִפָּנֶיךָ). Exod 23:23 uses only the simple first person statement, "I will blot them out" (וְהִכְחַדְתִּי). The injunctions against covenant making with the nations also vary. Exod 34:12 reads: "Be careful not to make a covenant with the inhabitants of the land" (הִשָּׁמֶר לְךָ פֶּן תִּכְרֹת בְּרִית לְיוֹשֵׁב הָאָרֶץ). Deut 7:2 states: "do not make a covenant with them" (לֹא תִכְרֹת לָהֶם בְּרִית). Finally, different verbs are used for the destruction of the *ăšērîm*. Exod 34:13 instructs that the *ăšērîm* be "cut down" (*krt*). Deut 7:5 states that they are to be "hewn down" (*gdʿ*).

In light of these and other differences among the three passages mentioned above, it seems unlikely that they are actually the products of the same hand. If the same hand were at work, one might expect more agreement in basic vocabulary. There are other similarities in stock phrases known to exist between sources, which do not necessitate the conclusion that they have common authorship.[19] There seems to be no compelling reason, then, to excise Exod 34:13 from the larger legal corpus of Exodus 34. As for the point that Exod 34:13, if not attributable to Dtr, would constitute the only pre-Deuteronomistic occurrence of the term *ăšērîm*, this does not rule out the possibility that the author of Exodus 34 knew the term.

---

those with Hittites third earlier still. If Ishida's schema is correct, then the earliest of our three passages is Exod 34:11-13, followed by Exod 23:23-24, and then Deut 7:1-5. Thus one could argue that Exod 34:11-44 is original to Exodus 34 or J, Exod 23:23-24 to E or the Covenant Code, and Deut 7:1-5 is a later expansion. Kevin G. O'Connell has critiqued Ishida ("The List of Seven Peoples in Canaan," in *The Answers Lie Below: Essays in Honor of Lawrence Edmund Toombs* [ed. Henry O. Thompson; Lanham, Md.: University Press of America, 1984] 221-41), arguing that the original form of the list had seven nations, not six. However, because the additional nation never alters the order in which the Hittites appear, O'Connell's work appears not to affect Ishida's dating schema.

[19]Two examples of this are the shared use by E and D of the place name Horeb, and the shared use by many sources of the phrase "land flowing with milk and honey." J (Exod 3:8, 17; Num 13:27), E (Exod 13:5; 33:3), H (Lev 20:24), P (Num 14:8; 16:14), D (Deut 6:3; 11:9; 26:9, 15), and Dtr (Deut 27:3; 31:20) all use this familiar phrase.

Cultic statuary

massēkôt: Exod 34:17

Exod 34:17, which prohibits the use of *massēkôt* in Israel, constitutes the only prohibition of any type of cultic paraphernalia *for Israel* in Exodus 34. It is also the only reference to cultic statuary in the larger literature of the J redaction.

Summary

The only items of cultic paraphernalia which are forbidden for Israelite use in this corpus are *massēkôt*. No other items of cultic paraphernalia are even mentioned here in relation to Israel. *ăšērîm*, *maṣṣēbôt*, and *mizbǝḥôt* are mentioned only in relation to the prior inhabitants of the land. The Israelites are given instructions to destroy these items when found among the nations they are to dispossess. There is no indication in Exodus 34 either that Israelites were using *ăšērîm*, *maṣṣēbôt*, and *mizbǝḥôt* or that such use would be prohibited were it taking place. Israelite use of these items is simply not discussed. On the subject of *bāmôt*, Exodus 34 is silent, with regard to both Israelite and non-Israelite use.

THE E SOURCE

It should be noted that any discussion of E's view of cultic items can only be based on the parts of E preserved within the JE redaction. There is no way to know whether other references, later edited out of JE, may have originally existed in E.

bāmôt: Num 22:41

As with J, the term *bāmôt* occurs within E only as part of a Moabite place name, in this case Bamoth Ba'al (Num 22:41). This place name also occurs in Dtr (Josh 13:17).[20]

ăšērîm: not mentioned

Although E makes no mention of *ăšērîm*, chapter six will discuss what may be derived concerning E's views of *ăšērîm* on the basis of E stories of famous trees. The two famous trees mentioned by E are the Shechem oak, under which Jacob buries the *ĕlōhê hannēkār* belonging to his followers (Gen 35:4), and the "Oak of Weeping," under which Jacob

---

[20]Chapter five (pp. 140-43) will discuss the significance of Moabite place names to the overall biblical understanding of *bāmôt*.

buries Deborah, Rebekah's nurse (Gen 35:8). Chapter eleven will also deal
with Gen 35:4 since the Mishnaic understanding of *ăšērîm* more closely
resembles the tree mentioned in this passage than any other object called an
ăšērāh in the biblical text. While this does not directly testify to E's
opinion regarding *ăšērîm*, it is an example of the complex relationship
between the biblical sources and the early interpretative traditions.

maṣṣēbôt: Gen 28:18, 22; 31:13, 45, 51, 52; 35:14, 20; Exod 24:4

E endorses the use of *maṣṣēbôt* devoted to YHWH, mentioning them
frequently in relation to Jacob (Gen 28:18, 22; 31:13, 45, 51, 52; 35:14, 20).
The Covenant Code, which is the legal corpus most closely associated with
E, enjoins the Israelites to destroy *maṣṣēbôt* belonging to other nations
(Exod 23:24). While similar instructions from other sources (Exod 34:13
[related to J], Num 33:52 [P]; Lev 26:1 [H]; Deut 7:5) include *bāmôt*,
ăšērîm, *mizbəḥôt*, or types of cultic statuary in their prohibitions, Exod
23:24 lists only *maṣṣēbôt*. There is no such destruction of other foreign
cultic paraphernalia enjoined by either E or the Covenant Code. This special
attention given to *maṣṣēbôt* illustrates the great importance placed upon
them in E and related traditions.

One additional passage which is pertinent to the discussion of
maṣṣēbôt in E is Exod 24:4:

> And Moses wrote down all the words of YHWH. He rose up early in the morning,
> and built an altar at the foot of the mountain, and twelve *maṣṣēbôt* corresponding
> to the twelve tribes of Israel.

Although the verse as a whole is usually assigned to E, the unique details
presented in this passage are numerous and do not easily lend themselves to
any one simple analysis.[21]

---

[21]CHB 2.119. The passage shows some affinities to the Covenant Code. CHB
notes, "This passage [24:4] has occasionally been combined with 34:27 as the sequel of
Yahweh's Covenant with Israel 34:10-27. The repetitions in the text are certainly
noteworthy: in [v.] 3 Moses recites the Words to the people and they unanimously
promise obedience to them: in [v.] 7 they are solemnly read out of the Covenant book,
and a similar promise follows. Are these parts of one narrative? The mention of the
sacred pillars in [v.] 4 has usually been regarded as decisive in favor of E. But it will be
noticed that they are introduced without a verb: the term 'built' is nowhere applied to
pillars, which are said to be 'set up,' Gen 28:18, 31:45, 35:14; nor are altars and pillars
ever said to be erected together. Is it possible that there are here traces of combination to
which we may also owe the doublets in [v.] 3 and [v.] 7?" (CHB 2.119). Noth argued that
24:3-8 is attributable to neither J nor E, but belongs instead to the same source as
Covenant Code (*Exodus*, 198-99). Childs states that regardless of whether one assigns

Another feature which complicates the tradition history of this passage is its use of the motif concerning twelve stones to represent the twelve tribes of Israel. This motif occurs elsewhere in several strata of the Pentateuch. Here, in Exod 24:4, the "twelve stones" are *maṣṣēbôt*. In P (Exod 28:21; 39:14), they are jewels mounted in Aaron's breastplate. P also describes another set of two stones, each with the names of six of the tribes carved on it and mounted on the ephod (Exod 28:10, 12; 39:7). In Dtr there are two uses of this motif. Joshua 4 mentions the twelve stones which represent the tribes and constitute the monument at Gilgal (although they are referred to simply as "stones" and not as *maṣṣēbôt*).[22] 1 Kgs 18:31 mentions "twelve stones" representing the tribes which are used by Elijah to build his altar on Mt. Carmel. In 1 Kgs 18:32, however, the stones are said to represent the "sons of *Jacob*," not the "sons of *Israel*." This singular reference to the "sons of Jacob" may signify that the Elijah sagas have preserved a slightly different tradition of the "twelve stones" motif from that known to the Pentateuchal, or even the Deuteronomistic traditions.

As will be demonstrated many times throughout this study, there seem to be certain, presumably old, traditions which recur in various of the biblical strata and which defy analysis concerning their origin. This "twelve stones" motif is one such tradition. Because the example from Exodus 24 actually uses the term *maṣṣēbôt*, however, this chapter apparently preserves the form of tradition peculiar to E, where it provides another example of a key figure erecting *maṣṣēbôt* at an important location. As will be seen below in the discussions of the other sources which use this motif, the "twelve stones" take on very different roles in each context where they appear.

mizbəḥôt: Gen 22:9; 33:20; 35:1, 3, 7; Exod 24:4, 6; 32:5

E mentions *mizbəḥôt* in relation to Abraham and his impending sacrifice of Isaac (Gen 22:9), Jacob's establishment of Shechem (33:20) and Bethel (35:1, 3, 7), Moses's sacrifice at the base of Mt. Sinai (Exod 24:4, 6), as well as Aaron's sacrifice at the base of Mt. Sinai (Exod 32:5). All of these altars are dedicated to Israel's god, called ʾEl or ʾElohim prior to Sinai and YHWH afterward.[23]

24:3-8 to E, a second stratum of E, or to independent J material, "these verses [3-8] remain a foreign body which the chapter has difficulty absorbing" (*Exodus*, 500-1).

[22]There are also debates concerning the source attribution of fragments within Joshua 4. According to CHB (2.325-7), Josh 4:3, 6, 8b belong to J, while Josh 4:5, 20 are E verses. See further the discussion of Joshua 4 in chapter two (pp. 54-55).

[23]In Gen 35:1 ʾElohim instructs Jacob to dedicate the altar at Bethel to "the God

Cultic statuary

ĕlōhê hannēkār: Gen 35:4

massēkôt: Exod 32:4, 8

tərāpîm: Gen 31:19, 34, 35

E appears at first glance to have mixed views on the subject of cultic statuary. E is neutral, if not positive, on the subject of Rachel's stealing her father's *tərāpîm* (Gen 31:19-35), while soon thereafter E depicts Jacob as enjoining his entourage to give up their other/foreign gods (*ĕlōhê hannēkār*), which he then buries beneath the oak which was at Shechem (Gen 35:1-4). The passage implies that these "gods" were portable objects which could be carried in one's hand (Gen 35:4), pointing possibly to some type of cultic statuary. E's "mixed view" of cultic statuary may not be mixed at all, however, if those scholars who believe that *tərāpîm* were something other than divine images are correct.[24]

Along with the "gods" Jacob's followers are to bury, however, they also bury the "rings" (*hannəzāmîm*) which were worn in their ears (35:4). Mention of these earrings calls to mind Exod 32:2, in which E indicates that the golden *massēkāh* made by Aaron at Sinai was manufactured out of the golden rings (*nizmê hazzāhāb*) which the Israelite women and children wore in their ears (Exod 32:4-8). Through this oblique connection between the *massēkāh* which Aaron makes and the *ĕlōhê hannēkār* which Jacob buries, E may be portraying the golden calf incident as a type of moral and religious regression, at the same time portraying Aaron as a type of "anti-Jacob."[25]

---

who appeared to you when you fled before your brother Esau." In response, he builds the altar and names its place El-Bethel (Gen 35:7). The altar at Shechem he calls "El Elohe Israel" (Gen 33:20). In Exod 24:4-6 and 32:5, both Moses and Aaron build their altars without naming them, but then proceed with a sacrifice to YHWH. For discussion of a textual variant on the name of the altar site in Genesis 22, see James R. Davila, "The Name of God at Moriah: An Unpublished Fragment from 4QGenExod^a," *JBL* 110 (1991) 577-82.

[24]See further, Karel van der Toorn ("The Nature of the Biblical Teraphim in Light of the Cuneiform Evidence," *CBQ* 52 [1990] 203-22), who argues that *tərāpîm* may have been "ancestor statuettes."

[25]The "golden calf" pericope does not use *pəsîlîm*, the term for cultic statuary found in the E related legal material of Exod 20:1-17, as might be expected, but rather *massēkôt*, the term found in the legal material more closely associated with J, Exodus 34.

Summary

E is silent concerning *ăšērîm* and mentions *bāmôt* only as part of a Moabite place name. E endorses *maṣṣēbôt* and *mizbəḥôt* as acceptable components of YHWHistic worship. Notably, in light of E's positive views of *maṣṣēbôt*, the Covenant Code singles out foreign *maṣṣēbôt* for destruction, but makes no such demand concerning other religious paraphernalia used by foreigners. This may signify that part of the shared perspective of E and the Covenant Code was that *maṣṣēbôt* were the most significant YHWHistic cultic items and thus had to have no competition from foreign *maṣṣēbôt*. Finally, although E's opinion regarding *tərāpîm* is ambiguous, E does openly disapprove of cultic statuary elsewhere.

EXODUS 20:1-17

This legal corpus is widely believed to have been composed separately from the JE and later P redactions responsible for its inclusion into the Tetrateuch. For this reason it will be treated separately from the rest of the E materials.[26] On the subject of cultic paraphernalia, however, this material contains only one verse of particular interest.

bāmôt: not mentioned

ăšērîm: not mentioned

maṣṣēbôt: not mentioned

mizbəḥôt: not mentioned

Cultic statuary

pəsîlîm: Exod 20:4

In Exod 20:4 cultic statuary referred to as *pəsîlîm* are prohibited for use by Israelites. The J-related passage in Exod 34:17 uses the term *mas-*

---

[26]Wellhausen assigned the "Decalogue" of Exod 20:1-17 to E (*Hexateuchs*, 97), while Noth held that the passage represents a special source unrelated to J or E (*Exodus*, 154-155). While Childs goes into great detail concerning the redactional and interpretive history of the Sinai revelation story (Exod 19:1-25, 20:18-21) and the Decalogue (*Exodus*, 337-439), he does not make any special effort to assign the Decalogue to any one source, stating only that Wellhausen's analysis for all but chapter 19 has been widely accepted by later scholars (*Exodus*, 345).

sēkôt.[27] The prohibition of the use of cultic statuary is particularly
emphasized, stretching over three verses, even though the injunction to worship only YHWH has already been given in verses 2-3. Although one frequently thinks of the prohibition against cultic statuary as a command that
Israel's worship of YHWH be aniconic, this passage does not refer to
images which might be made of YHWH. Exod 20:4-5a states:

> You shall not make for yourself a *pesel* in the form of anything that is in heaven
> above, or that is on earth beneath, or that is in the water under the earth. You shall
> not bow down to them or worship them; for I, YHWH your god, am a jealous god.

The implication of verses 4-6 is that the Israelites will be tempted to
make statuary depicting some entity other than YHWH and thus worship
that other deity. It is not the manufactured items themselves which cause
offense, but rather the distraction from YHWH that they constitute. The reason given for the prohibition is that YHWH is a "jealous" god (*ʾēl qannāʾ*).
The verses, then, are actually more a command to monolatry than to
aniconism.[28]

Summary
        Exod 20:1-17 mentions only cultic statuary and prohibits its use by
Israel. The lengthy prohibition implies that it is referring to statuary
modelled, not on YHWH, but on some created being or natural
phenomenon, thereby constituting a departure from the exclusive worship of
YHWH. Statuary of YHWH is not even suggested as a possibility.

THE COVENANT CODE
        Many scholars consider Exod 20:22-23:33 a separate source, called
the "Covenant Code," representing legal material which was a part of JE
and not P.[29] Childs noted that Wellhausen at first assigned these verses to J
but was later convinced by Kuenen that this was in error. Childs went on to
say that a majority of scholars viewed the Covenant Code as an independent
legal corpus which predated the other sources, though most believed it had
been incorporated to the E material.[30] In agreement with the essence of this

---

[27]The duplicate verse Deut 5:8 will be discussed in chapter 2 (p. 50).

[28]For a study on Israelite aniconism, see Ronald S. Hendel, "The Social Origins of
the Aniconic Tradition in Early Israel," *CBQ* 50 (1988) 365-82.

[29]See, for example, Noth, *Exodus*, 173.

[30]*Exodus*, 452. CHB ultimately assigned the Covenant Code to E (2.112).
Friedman however, agrees with those mentioned by Childs who feel that the originally
independent Covenant Code was only later incorporated into E material (*Who Wrote the*

assessment, the Covenant Code will be recognized as a legal code closely related to E, but will be treated as a separate source. It should be noted, however, that there is no longer a clear scholarly consensus that the Covenant Code predates the other sources.[31] This study, however, is less concerned with its dating than with its linguistic and ideological affinities to other sources, the closest of which appears to be E.

bāmôt: not mentioned

ăšērîm: not mentioned

maṣṣēbôt: Exod 23:24

As noted above, Exod 23:24 commands that *maṣṣēbôt* belonging to foreign nations be destroyed when Israel takes possession of the land. This instruction is unique among such commands enjoined in the other sources (Exod 34:13 [J], Num 33:52 [P]; Lev 26:1 [H]; Deut 7:5), in that *maṣṣēbôt* are the only items marked for destruction here. This special attention given to *maṣṣēbôt* may be the result of their prominent place in northern patriarchal stories.

mizbəḥôt: Exod 20:24, 25, 26; 21:14

As discussed above, Exod 20:24 dictates certain construction methods for *mizbəḥôt* and prohibits others, stating that YHWH's *mizbəḥôt* could be made simply of earth (*ădāmāh*), and might be erected in "any place" where God caused the divine name to be remembered.[32] If one wished to make *mizbəḥôt* of stone, however, this was allowed provided that the stones were natural field stones,[33] and that the *mizbəḥôt* were constructed without steps (vv 25-26). Exod 20:26 reads, "You shall not go up by steps to my altar, so that your nakedness may not be exposed on it." There has been

---

Bible?, 259).

[31]See for example, Cornelius Houtman (*Exodus* [3 vols.; Leuven: Peeters, 2000] 3.90), who argues that the Covenant Code is "no younger than Deuteronomy."

[32]The possibility that this one particular instruction may be the product of the J writer has been suggested to me by Theodore Hiebert. The fact that altars are to be constructed out of *ădāmāh* and natural stones coincides well with J's attitudes toward the sanctity of the natural order. This verse is treated here in the discussion of the Covenant Code, however, because the nuanced analysis which would be needed to justify assignment of Exod 20:24 to J is beyond the scope of the present study.

[33]See also later references to this instruction in Deut 27:5-6; Josh 8:31; 1 Macc 4:47.

much discussion of the intent behind this prohibition.[34] Some scholars believe that the prohibition against chiseled altars and altars with steps is a reference to the types of altars that people of other ancient cultures built.[35] That this type of altar was the particular preference of any specific group of people is nowhere stated, however. Other scholars imply that the reference to "nakedness" in this passage has a sexual connotation and refers to sexual activity, presumably engaged in by other cultures as part of religious ceremony.[36] This depiction of the religion of the cultures surrounding Israel, however, is not found in the primary literature of these cultures.

The remaining verse in the Covenant Code that deals with *mizbǝḥôt* is Exod 21:14. This law refers to the right of refuge and implies that one who has killed another person could flee for asylum to the altar of YHWH. The verse instructs the Israelites to take any person who is found guilty of willful murder away from YHWH's altar for execution.[37]

Cultic statuary

ĕlōhê kesep/zāhāb: Exod 20:23
Without using any technical terms for cultic statuary, Exod 20:23 instructs the Israelites to refrain from making "gods of silver" or "gods of gold." No particular method of manufacture is indicated.

Summary
The Covenant Code is concerned that Israel worship only YHWH and avoid the worship of other gods, either by making images of them out of metal or by offering sacrifices to them. In fact, Exod 22:19 [Eng 22:20], states that offering sacrifices to any god other than YHWH is a capital offense. As for other cultic specifications, only *mizbǝḥôt* seem to be of any interest, though this interest is rather detailed. The Covenant Code appears

---

[34]For a review, see Childs, *Exodus*, 466.

[35]Childs appears to suport D. Conrad's view ("Studien zum Altargesetz: Ex 20:24-26" [Ph.D. diss., Marburg; 1968]) that this verse represents a rejection of an altar construction technique used specifically by the Canaanites (*Exodus*, 466).

[36]Noth expressed such a suspicion in his Exodus commentary. He wrote: "The prohibition of altar steps (v. 26) which would form part of the altar rests on the idea that the sexual sphere is part of a dark, mysterious realm, a realm which played an elevated role in many cults in the ancient East. For this very reason, however, it was impossible for it to be associated with the sphere of the holy in Israel" (*Exodus*, 177).

[37] 1 Kgs 1:49-53 and 2:28-34 describe this process concerning Solomon's executions of Adonijah and Joab.

minimalist on the subject of cultic paraphernalia, in that altars are all it requires, and even they need not be elaborately constructed, but rather might be built out of plain soil and field stones in any place where God is perceived. With regard to cultic installations which Israel might find in the land upon their arrival, the Covenant Code mentions only *maṣṣēbôt* and instructs that these should be destroyed. *Bāmôt* and *ăšērîm* are not mentioned, either as Israelite or as non-Israelite cultic paraphernalia.

THE P SOURCE
bāmôt: Num 21:19, 20; 33:52

The word *bāmôt* is present in P in the Moabite place name Bamoth (Num 21:19-20), and in one verse listing religious items belonging to the inhabitants of the land which the Israelites are to destroy upon occupation (Num 33:52). In this verse, *bāmôt* are linked with "molten images" (*ṣalmê massēkōtām*), and some variety of sculpted stones referred to as "carved things" (*maśkîyōt*: see discussion below under *maṣṣēbôt*). P does not discuss Israelite use of *bāmôt*.

ăšērîm: not mentioned

P does not mention *ăšērîm* used either by Israel or by the prior inhabitants of the land. Certain arboreal motifs occur in P, such as the tradition concerning Aaron's staff breaking into bloom (Num 17:1-11), other references to magical "rods," and the tree-like structure of the Tabernacle menorah, but these subjects will be discussed in chapter six.[38]

maṣṣēbôt: not mentioned

maśkîyōt: Num 33:52

P does not use the term *maṣṣēbôt*. Num 33:52, however, uses the rare term *maśkîyōt*, which means "carved things," in a passage describing religious articles of the inhabitants of the land that are to be destroyed (Num 33:52). This term is usually thought, on the basis of passages from the Holiness Code (Lev 26:1) and Ezekiel (8:12), to refer to a type of carved stone or stone image of some type.[39] Num 33:52 links these "carved things" with

---

[38]For a detailed study of the menorah, see Carol L. Meyers, *The Tabernacle Menorah: A Synthetic Study of a Symbol From the Biblical Cult* (ASORDS 2; Missoula: Scholars Press, 1976).

[39]Susan Ackerman has argued that the Hebrew term *maśkît* "certainly means 'relief'" in Ezek 8:12, as she believes it does in Num 33:52 and Lev 26:1, although she notes that *KAI* 215.18 (Panammû II) contains the term *mśky* meaning "image" or "statue"

bāmôt and "cast images" (*ṣalmê massēkōtām*), leaving open the possibility that the term *maśkîyōt* represented either stone images or the same class of objects usually referred to as *maṣṣēbôt*. While H distinguished between *maṣṣēbôt* and *'eben maśkît*, mentioning them both in a list of prohibited items, it is not possible to argue such a distinction on the part of P who does not mention *maṣṣēbôt*.[40]

As noted above, P also uses the image of "twelve stones, one for each of the twelve tribes of Israel" (Exod 28:21; 39:14) which is found in Exod 24:4, Joshua 4, and 1 Kgs 18:31. Just as these "twelve stones" are appropriately *maṣṣēbôt* in E, a source in which *maṣṣēbôt* feature prominently as cultic items, the "twelve stones" in P are just as appropriately found among the ornamentation of the priesthood, P's central cultic concern. They are the "twelve" jewels mounted in Aaron's breastplate (Exod 28:21; 39:14) and accompanied by two other stones inscribed with the names of the tribes and mounted on the ephod (Exod 28:10, 12; 39:7). The fact that this motif of "twelve stones, one for each of the twelve tribes of Israel" occurs in P, with the stones themselves taking the form of jewels rather than the monuments or field stones found in the other surces, attests to the versatility of this motif.

(*Under Every Green Tree: Popular Religion in Sixth-Century Judah* [HSM 46; Atlanta: Scholars Press, 1992] 44 n. 30). Victor A. Hurowitz has recently found what he believes to be an Assyrian parallel to this type of stone in a recently restored inscription of Sennacherib. The Assyrian text describes an inscribed stone in the doorway of the temple on which the king would stand, bow down, kiss the ground, and make a petition or wish. In light of this text, as well as the Targum Onkelos which translates the *'eben maśkît* as an אבן סגידה , or "stone of prostration," Hurowitz argues that prohibitions related to these stones are not essentially aimed at the stones themselves as much as at a specific "foreign ritual practice." See Victor Avigdor Hurowitz, "אבן משכית—A New Interpretation," *JBL* 118 (1999) 201-8.

[40]An editorial addition to Gen 35:14a (an E verse that P displaced from the rest of Gen 35:1-8 in order to link the original P material in Gen 35:9-13 to the rest of the E narrative) explaining what a *maṣṣēbāh* is may shed some light on the absence of the term *maṣṣēbôt* in P. Gen 35:14a reads: "Jacob erected a *maṣṣēbāh* at the place where he had spoken to him, (that is,) an *erected stone*." וַיַּצֵּב יַעֲקֹב מַצֵּבָה בַּמָּקוֹם אֲשֶׁר-דִּבֶּר אִתּוֹ מַצֶּבֶת אָבֶן Nowhere else in the MT is such an explanation concerning *maṣṣēbôt* given, and while it is possible that this addition to Gen 35:14 was not added by P (the construct form מַצֶּבֶת occurs in a secondary addition to another E verse [Gen 35:20], Dtr [2 Sam 18:18] and in First Isaiah [6:13]; the construct form מַצֶּבֶת and suffixed form מַצַּבְתָּהּ occur in Dtr [2 Kgs 3:2; 10:27] and Isaiah 6:13 respectively), the fact that P editorial activity is clearly present in the chapter makes P at least a possible candidate. Were P responsible for this addition, one could argue the term *maṣṣēbôt* may not have been current at the time of P's activity, or that P felt, for whatever reason, that the term needed clarification, and so had a greater need to refer to other stone objects, such as *maśkîyōt*, when writing original material.

mizbəḥôt: Exodus 27-Leviticus 15; Numbers 3-18; Joshua 22[41]

P mentions only Israelite altars, and approves only those altars of the Tabernacle compound, which it discusses in great detail. The altars of the Tabernacle are mentioned 130 times in Exodus 27-Leviticus 15, 21 times in Numbers 3-18, and 3 times in Joshua 22 (vv. 19, 28, 29). The only other "altar" mentioned by P is preserved by the Deuteronomistic History in Joshua 22. In this passage there is an altar which the Transjordanian tribes erect on their border with Israel (vv. 10, 11, 16, 23, 26, 34). This "altar" is potentially unorthodox at the beginning of the story because it competes with the Tabernacle's altar, located at that time in Shiloh. Its builders, however, insist that it is only symbolic of a real altar and will never be used for sacrifice. The main point of the story seems to be the validation of the singular nature of the approved altar at the Tabernacle. Phineas ben Eleazar demonstrates this by his outrage at the mere existence of any other altar and his willingness to declare holy war over it. The situation is resolved by the subsequent explanation of this altar as simply a large-scale model to serve as a remembrance of YHWHistic tribal unity for future Tranjordanian YHWHists.[42]

Cultic statuary

ṣalmê massēkôt: Num 33:52

---

[41]Joshua 22 is included in the discussion of the P writer because there is ample evidence within this chapter of Priestly language, as well as emphases. For an excellent review of scholarship on this chapter, as well as a detailed analysis of it, see John S. Kloppenborg, "Joshua 22: The Priestly Editing of an Ancient Tradition," *Biblica* 62 (1981) 345-71. Kloppenborg notes that scholars have long accepted that 22:1-8 is the product of the Deuteronomist, while 22:9-34 is a Priestly composition ("Joshua 22," 351). For a fuller discussion of the use made of this older priestly material by Dtr, see further chapter two (p. 57).

[42]Another explanation of this pericope is offered by Frank Moore Cross in his article, "Reuben, First-Born of Jacob," *ZAW* 100 Supplement issue (1988) 46-65, now in his *From Epic to Canon: History and Literature in Ancient Israel* (Baltimore: Johns Hopkins University Press, 1999) 53-70. Cross believes that this passage, in demonstrating P's polemic against the Transjordanian "altar," secondarily testifies to traditions which trace the origins of Israel's primary cultic traditions in the southern Transjordanian desert where they were formed under Midianite influence in what later came to be known as Reubenite territory. According to Cross, there was a resultant polemic against Midianites, Reubenites, and Mushites in response to these traditions carried on by the P writer, who represents the rival Aaronids ("Reuben," 63).

maśkîyōt: Num 33:52

P commands Israel to destroy the "molten images" *(ṣalmê mas-sēkōtām)* of the people of the land, which he mentions in connection with *bāmôt* and the "carved things" *(maśkîyōt)* discussed above (Num 33:52). Everywhere else in P the word *ṣelem* is used in the absolute and carries a positive connotation, while here it is used to describe a type of idol (possibly in contrast to *maśkîyōt*, meaning "stone idols").

P never uses *ṣelem* in its absolute form to describe cultic statuary as do other biblical sources.[43] Rather, *ṣelem* describes the common "image" or "likeness" that is shared between God and humanity (Gen 1:26, 27), and between Adam and Seth (Gen 5:3). It is this shared "image of God" that P gives as the basis for the reprehensibility of murder (Gen 9:6).[44]

Summary

P does not mention *'ăšērîm*. P only uses the term *bāmôt* as part of the Moabite place name Bamoth, and in regard to cultic installations belonging to the inhabitants of the land which P enjoins the Israelites to destroy. P discusses *mizbǝḥôt* at length and views them as central pieces of equipment for Israelite worship. P does not mention *mizbǝḥôt*, however, in relation to people of other cultures. On the subject of *maṣṣēbôt*, P is silent. P does instruct the Israelites to destroy *maśkîyot*, however, which may have been either some type of monumental stone or some type of stone statuary. Cultic statuary, labelled by the more common term *ṣalmê massēkôt*, is also condemned by P (Num 33:52).

Also of interest in P is the combination of various items into complexes which are then linked to another cultural group. In Num 33:52, P links *bāmôt*, cultic statuary *(ṣalmê massēkōt)*, and carved (probably stone) objects *(maśkîyōt)* as features of the worship of the inhabitants of the land. While these "inhabitants of the land" are not given any specific ethnic

---

[43]2 Kgs 11:18 [= 2 Chr 23:17]; 2 Chr 33:15; Ezek 7:20; 16:17; 23:14; Amos 5:26; Ps 73:20; Dan 2:31, 32, 34, 35; 3:1-3, 5, 7, 10, 12, 14-15, 18.

[44]For an extensive study of *ṣelem* and its meaning in P, as well as a thorough review of scholarship on the theological concept of the "image of God," see Phyllis A. Bird, "'Male and Female He Created Them': Gen 1:27b in the Contest of the Priestly Account of Creation," *HTR* 74 (1981) 129-59, now in her collected essays, *Missing Persons and Mistaken Identities: Women and Gender in Ancient Israel* (Minneapolis: Fortress, 1997) 123-54. For further discussion, see James Barr, "Man and Nature: The Ecological Controversy and the Old Testament," *BJRL* 55 (1972) 9-32, and Claus Westerman, *Genesis 1-11: A Commentary* (tr. John J. Scullion; Minneapolis: Augsburg, 1984) 142-60, 461-69.

designation, P shares the feature of locating a place name containing the particle "*bāmôt*" in Moab with J, E, and Dtr. P shares with H the idea that those who used *bāmôt* also used cultic statuary.[45]

THE HOLINESS CODE

bāmôt: Lev 26:30

H describes Israelites using *bāmôt* (Lev 26:30) in a passage that details God's destruction of these *bāmôt* among the other types of destruction which God will visit upon the Israelites for covenant breaking. In this passage, *bāmôt* are linked with incense burners (*ḥammānîm*), and cultic statuary (*gillûlîm*).

It is not clear that H wishes to cite the mere existence of these *bāmôt* as an example of covenant-breaking, since some of the other expressions of YHWH's anger predicted in this same passage are targeted at otherwise acceptable forms of worship, such as sacrifices to YHWH and worship in YHWHistic sanctuaries (Lev 26:31). God will punish all who disobey covenant stipulations by completely wiping out Israelite society and all it involves.[46]

ăšērîm: not mentioned

Despite a long list of religious behaviors and cultic items mentioned in Leviticus 26, H does not mention *ăšērîm* as one of the features of Israelite religious life, nor does H mention them as a component of the religious practices of Israel's neighbors.

maṣṣēbôt: Lev 26:1

'eben maśkît: Lev 26:1

Lev 26:1 mentions the use of *maṣṣēbôt* within Israel, and like the P verse Num 33:52, also uses the rare term *'eben maśkît*, "carved stone." These "carved stones," which were probably some subset or variety of cultic stones, are prohibited for Israelite use in Lev 26:1 just as they are marked for destruction if found among the peoples of the land Num 33:52.[47] It is possible, on the basis of Num 33:52, to argue that the "carved stones" of

---

[45]See summary of H below (p. 41).

[46]A parallel between the vocabulary and content of this verse and Amos 7:9 has been noted by Shalom Paul, *Amos: A Commentary on the Book of Amos* (ed. Frank Moore Cross; Hermeneia; Minneapolis: Augsburg Fortress, 1991) 237.

[47]See studies cited above under Num 33:52 (p. 35, n. 39).

Lev 26:1 were stone idols, distinguished in P from molten idols (*ṣalmê mas-sēkôt*). It is not clear, however, whether H's distinction of them from *maṣṣēbôt* implies that they were an entirely separate category of object from *maṣṣēbôt*, or that they were a subset of that category.

Lev 26:1 could be used to argue that H interpreted *maṣṣēbôt* as a type of cultic statuary for the verse prohibits, along with *maṣṣēbôt,* two items that are clearly types of cultic statuary (*ĕlîlîm* and *pəsîlîm*), and one that may have been another type (the *'eben maśkît*). *maṣṣēbôt* would then be the only item in the list that is not usually so interpreted. As will be discussed in chapter eleven, the notion that *maṣṣēbôt* were idols appears in certain early Jewish sources. It is possible that this view of *maṣṣēbôt* began here in H and continued into early Jewish interpretation.

mizbəḥôt: Lev 17:6, 11; 21:23; 22:22

H discusses only the *mizbəḥôt* of the Tabernacle and regulations concerning them. As with P, no other altars, foreign or Israelite, are mentioned in H.

Cultic statuary

'eben maśkît: Lev 26:1

ĕlîlîm: Lev 19:4; 26:1

gillûlîm: Lev 26:30

massēkôt: Lev 19:4

pəsîlîm: Lev 26:1

H is much more expressive on the subject of cultic statuary than is P. As already noted, H specifically prohibits Israelite use of cultic statuary known by various names: *ĕlîlîm* (Lev 19:4, 26:1), *massēkôt* (Lev 19:4), *pəsîlîm* (Lev 26:1), and possibly *'eben maśkît* (Lev 26:1) and *maṣṣēbôt* (for the later two as statuary, see discussion above). In Lev 26:30, discussed above with regard to *bāmôt*, H also describes the destruction of incense burners (*ḥammānîm*) and the piling of corpses upon the idols (*gillûlîm*) of the Israelites as a feature of God's judgment against Israel.[48]

---

[48]The term *gillûlîm* appears to be a pejorative term originally derived from the word for dung. See further Horst Dietrich Preuss, "גִּלּוּלִים gillûlîm; גִּלֻּלִים gillulîm," *TDOT* 3.1-5. This term will be discussed below in the Postscript (pp. 41-43) with regard to its

Summary

H does not mention *ăšērîm*. H depicts God as destroying the *bāmôt* of the Israelites out of anger over covenant disloyalty. H discusses *mizbəhôt* as central pieces of equipment for Israelite worship, yet does not mention them in relation to people of other cultures. H condemns both *maṣṣēbôt* and "carved stones" (*'eben maśkît*), as well as cultic statuary called by various other names. The diversity of H's vocabulary concerning cultic statuary (when compared, for instance, to that of P) may demonstrate a special interest in these items on the part of H, or may simply be a feature of H's unique style, which, as will be discussed below, tends to include a wider variety of cultic terminology in lists of objects than does P.

Like P, H contains lists (Lev 26:1, 30) which group cultic objects into complexes. Lev 26:1 names two types of stone objects, *maṣṣēbôt* and the simple "carved stone" (*'eben maśkît*), and two words for cultic statuary, *pəsîlîm* and *'ĕlîlîm*, stating that all are prohibited for Israelite use but not describing these as associated with any other group of people. Although their identification remains inclear, if one views the *'eben maśkît* as a type of idol and not some other type of carved stone, one could argue that H viewed *maṣṣēbôt* as a form of cultic statuary as well. Three other terms are linked by H in Lev 26:30, a passage describing worship being practiced by Israelites when God's wrath descends to destroy them. These are *bāmôt*, *ḥammānîm*, and *gillûlîm*. As noted above in the summary on P, both P and H link *bāmôt* and cultic statuary. Unlike P, however, H also links *maṣṣēbôt* with cultic statuary.

POSTSCRIPT

One other detail worthy of note with regard to the material from P and H is that parts of it support the view of some scholars that H may be of a later date than P.[49] While traditionally, scholars have favored a later date

---

increased frequency in the later biblical sources.

[49]Some recent scholars who favor a pre-exilic date for P include Richard Friedman (*Who Wrote the Bible*, 210), Menahem Haran (*Temples and Temple Service in Ancient Israel: An Inquiry into Biblical Cult Phenomena and the Historical Setting of the Priestly School* [Winona Lake, Ind.: Eisenbrauns, 1985] 146-48), Israel Knohl ("The Conception of God and Cult in the Priestly Torah and in the Holiness School" [Ph.D. diss., Hebrew University of Jerusalem, 1988] [Heb]; idem *The Sanctuary of Silence*), Milgrom (*Leviticus 1-16*, 13-35; idem "Rejoinder to Israel Knohl," in *Leviticus 23-27*, 2440-6), Robert Polzin (*Late Biblical Hebrew: Toward an Historical Typology of Biblical Hebrew Prose* [Missoula: Scholars Press, 1976]), Gary Rendsburg ("Late Biblical Hebrew and the Date of 'P'," *JANESCU* 12 [1980] 65-80), and Ziony Zevit ("Converging Lines of Evidence Bearing on the Date of P," *ZAW* 94 [1982] 481-511).

for P than for H,[50] the data from P and H regarding cultic items of interest to this study tend to support those who contend that H may, in fact, be the later work.

H's use of certain terms which do not occur in P, but which do occur in Ezekiel, is a feature of the vocabulary in H which has been noted already by Avi Hurvitz and used to argue a late date for H relative to P.[51] Examples of this phenomenon from the current study are the terms ḥammānîm (Lev 26:30) and gillûlîm (Lev 26:30), both of which occur in Ezekiel, as well as in Chronicles, late sections of Jeremiah, and late redactional levels of Isaiah.[52] The term gillûlîm also occurs in Dtr (Deut 29:16; 1 Kgs 15:12; 21:26; 2 Kgs 17:11; 21:11, 21); however, it is the increased frequency of this term through time that is instructive with regard to the relative dating of P and H. P never uses gillûlîm at all, although H does and Ezekiel uses it more than any other source. While the above data of themselves are not entirely convincing, added to the other material gathered by Hurvitz they appear to have relevance.

Another recent scholar who has argued that H is later than P is Israel Knohl.[53] Unlike Hurvitz, whose approach to the dating of P is primarily linguistic, Knohl believes that beyond the linguistic distinctions, basic differences in attitude and expression exist between P and H. In his summary of Knohl's work, Jacob Milgrom distills the following features of H according to Knohl's scheme: 1) H is less linguistically precise in its terminology than is P; 2) H tends to add motive clauses and exhortations to the basic teachings of P, leading, at times, to the production of a type of "halakhic midrash" on P; 3) H portrays a more direct and anthropomorphic style of interaction between God and humanity.[54] At the end of his summary, Milgrom states, "Knohl's terminological study reveals a gaping ideological chasm that divides P from H far beyond what has been proposed by any prior critic."[55] Knohl himself uses the term "priestly-popular" to describe

---

[50]For recent reviews of scholarship on the relative dating of P and H, see Milgrom (*Leviticus 1-16*, 26-27), and Henry T. C. Sun, "Holiness Code," *ABD* 3.256.

[51]*Linguistic Study.*

[52]*ḥammānîm*: Ezek 6:4, 6; 2 Chr 14:4; 34:4, 7; Isa 17:8; 27:9 (a related verb occurs in Isa 57:5). *gillûlîm*: Ezek 6:4, 5, 6, 9, 13; 8:10; 14:3, 4, 5, 6; 16:36; 18:6, 12, 15; 20:7, 8, 16, 18; 20:31, 39; 22:3, 4; 23:7, 30, 37, 39, 49; 30:13; 33:25; 36:18, 25; 37:23; 44:10, 12; Jer 50:2.

[53]In addition to his dissertation, and his *Sanctuary of Silence,* see idem, "The Priestly Torah Versus the Holiness School: Sabbath and the Festivals," *Shnaton* 7-8 (1983-84) 109-46 [Heb], English translation in *HUCA* 58 (1987) 65-117.

[54]Milgrom, *Leviticus 1-16,* 13-42. See further, idem *Leviticus 23-27,* 2440-6.

[55]Milgrom *Leviticus 1-16,* 42.

what he believes to be H's tendency to add features of popular religious practice to the more formal ritual laws of P.[56]

Two examples in the data from the current study illustrate Knohl's point about H adding "popular" terminology alongside the more traditional terms used by P. As noted above with regard to Lev 26:1, it is not clear whether H means to imply that the "carved stone," the ʾeben maśkît, was an entirely separate category of object from the maṣṣēbôt or that it was a subset of that category. If Knohl is correct in characterizing H as a source which included popular notions and folk terms alongside technical understandings of cultic matters, one could argue that Lev 26:1 illustrates this phenomenon. If this is true, by mentioning the ʾeben maśkît alongside maṣṣēbôt, H might merely be providing more than one known term (possibly a folk term or popular term) for a more well-known form of the same type of object.

The second example relevant to Knohl's theory involves cultic statuary and the terms used to describe it in P and H. P uses two unusual, possibly technical terms for cultic statuary (ṣalmê massēkôt, and maśkîyōt, Num 33:52). H mentions two similar terms (massēkôt, Lev 19:4 and ʾeben maśkît, Lev 26:1), but also includes three more (pəsîlîm, Lev 26:1; ʾĕlîlîm, Lev 19:4, 26:1; gillûlîm, Lev 26:30) without implying any distinctions among them. That H uses many more terms in referring to cultic statuary than does P may again be an example of what Knohl identifies as H's blending of "popular and priestly" cultic elements,[57] or what Milgrom characterizes as H's "blurring" the distinctions made explicit in P.[58] Further study of the issue of the relative dating of H and P may shed even more light on this issue.

CONCLUSIONS

The sources which make up the Tetrateuch represent a wide variety of interests concerning cultic matters. Far from being unified in opinion regarding cultic items, the Tetrateuchal sources display a rich diversity of opinion. Some of these items are barely mentioned in the Tetrateuch. ʾăšērîm, for instance, are mentioned only in Exodus 34 where ʾăšērîm, maṣṣēbôt, and mizbəḥôt constitute the worship paraphernalia of the inhabitants of the land prior to Israelite occupation. As such they are to be destroyed. In the whole Tetrateuch, however, no mention is made of the use of ʾăšērîm by Israel.

---

[56]"Priestly Torah," 105-6.
[57]"Priestly Torah," 65-106.
[58]*Leviticus 1-16*, 38.

Similarly, only P and H mention *bāmôt* as cultic installations, although J and E, as well as P, mention the term as part of Moabite place names. Neither P nor H offers clear condemnation of *bāmôt*. P discusses only foreign *bāmôt* to be destroyed upon entrance into the land. H mentions *bāmôt* as part of a judgment oracle in which YHWH wipes out all worship in Israel (Leviticus 26). From this context it is clear that H knows of Israelite use of *bāmôt*, and that these installations might sometimes be connected to the use of cultic statuary (*gillûlîm*); however, even this statement does not prove that H viewed *bāmôt*, in and of themselves, to be illegitimate installations.

Some of the sources are primarily interested in one item to the exclusion of others. J, for instance, is primarily interested in YHWHistic *mizbəḥôt* which are approved in all cases regardless of location or other concerns. None of the other cultic items of interest to this study is mentioned by J. E is interested in *maṣṣēbôt* and *mizbəḥôt*, but features *maṣṣēbôt* more often in its narrative. The chart below summarizes the Tetrateuchal material. If a column is blank, this means that the item is not mentioned by the source. The entries in the chart describe the examples of each item found within the source. The term "forbidden" refers to items forbidden for use by Israelites.

Source:	*bāmôt*	*ʾăšērîm*	*maṣṣēbôt*	*mizbəḥôt*	statuary
Exod 34		foreign & condemned	foreign & condemned	condemned if foreign	*massēkôt* forbidden
Exod 20					*pəsîlîm* forbidden
J	Moabite GN's only			YHWHistic & approved	
E	Moabite GN's only		YHWHistic & approved	YHWHistic & approved	*massēkôt* forbidden
CovCode			foreign & condemned	must not be chiseled	statuary forbidden
P	Moabite GN's or foreign & condemned			must be at Tabernacle condemned if foreign	*massēkôt*, *maśkiyôt* foreign & condemned

Source:	*bāmôt*	*'ăšērîm*	*maṣṣēbôt*	*mizbăḥôt*	**statuary**
H	Israelite & neutral?		forbidden in Israel	must be at Tabernacle,	*massēkôt, pəsîlîm, 'ĕlîlîm, gillûlîm, 'eben maśkît,* & *maṣṣēbôt?* forbidden in Israel

In addition to the distinctions revealed by this chart, certain distinctions among the Tetrateuchal sources appear they discuss the same person or subject in the same type of account. One classic example appears in the patriarchal stories of Bethel. J has Abraham visit there, erect an altar, and call upon YHWH (Gen 12:7-8). Later J has Jacob name the site after an encounter with God (Gen 28:13-16). E, however, has Jacob erect a *maṣṣēbāh* on the site, name the site, and return later to put up an altar there (Gen 28:11-12, 17-18, 20-21a, 22; 35:1-8). P also credits Jacob with the founding of Bethel, retaining the E detail of the *maṣṣēbāh* in the course of editing new material into the chapter but omitting the altar (Gen 35:9-15). This one example illustrates several of the typical tendencies of these sources as noted by Wellhausen and others. J prefers altar stories while E prefers *maṣṣēbāh* stories;[59] P refuses to recognize as legitimate any altars except those of the Tabernacle, as Josh 22:9-34 clearly demonstrates.

Distinctions among the sources can also be seen when they each discuss the same type of object, but evaluate it according to different criteria. J and E, for example, approve of altars in various locations, as long as the altars are Israelite. P and H approve only those of the Tabernacle which are very carefully constructed. The Covenant Code approves only those altars which are simply constructed of earth or unchiseled field stones. Not for P, H, or the Covenant Code is YHWHistic dedication alone sufficient to insure that an altar will be approved. For the Covenant Code, only certain construction techniques are approved. For P and H, only one location is approved.

An additional type of distinction between the sources is illustrated by the "twelve stones for the twelve tribes" motif. In E, these stones are the favored *maṣṣēbôt*. In P they are ornamental additions to priestly vestments. This reveals much about the distinctive emphases of P and E. Both find this motif of value, and both feature it in a cultic context, but the particular manifestations of the motif for each writer are distinctive of their major emphases.

---

[59]J altar stories: Gen 8:20; 12:6-8; 13:4 and 18; 26:25; Exod 17:15. E *maṣṣēbāh* stories: Gen 28:18; 31:13; 31:45-52; 35:20; Exod 24:4. This former example features *maṣṣēbôt* as well as an altar.

The Tetrateuchal sources have as rich a variety of opinion concerning cultic items as they have about other more notable issues such as divine anthropomorphism, names of God, or the relative importance of northern and southern concerns. This diversity of opinion continues throughout the remainder of the biblical sources as well, making clear that no one reconstructed theory of "normative" YHWHistic religious practice can be sustained as representative of all biblical viewpoints.

Chapter Two
Deuteronomy and the Deuteronomistic Historian

THE D SOURCE

Before beginning any discussion of Deuteronomy one must acknowledge the existence of strata within the book. Though not completely homogeneous, chapters 4:44-28:28 are generally held to be the older core of the tradition, while chapters 1:6-4:40 and 29-30 are believed to have been added by later members of the Deuteronomic school. Still other later materials in chapters 31 and 34, relating to the career of Joshua and the death of Moses, flank a mixture of archaic poetic sections (32:1-43 and 33:9-28) and bits of both the Elohist (31:14-23) and the Priestly writer (32:48-52), incorporated in order to sum up the life of Moses and account for the elevation of Joshua as his successor.[1] All of the verses from Deuteronomy which deal with *ăšērîm*, *bāmôt*, *maṣṣēbôt*, and *mizbǝḥôt*, however, are confined to either the old core of the book (7:5; 12:3, 27; 16:21, 22; 26:4; 27:5-6) or to the archaic poetic chapters (32:13; 33:10, 29). The material from Dtr (Joshua through Kings) will be discussed later in this chapter, along with the references to cultic statuary which occur in the Dtr strata of Deuteronomy.

bāmôt: not mentioned

Although D does not mention *bāmôt*, either as features of the worship of other nations (as in P), or as components of Israelite worship (as in H), or even as a part of any place name (as in J, E, P, and Dtr), Deuteronomy does incorporate archaic poetic sections which use the term *bāmôtê*, meaning "heights" (32:13) or "backs" (33:29). How the two terms are related, however, is a matter of some debate, which will be outlined in chapter five.[2]

---

[1]For discussions of the strata within Deuteronomy, see Moshe Weinfeld, "Deuteronomy, Book of," *ABD* 2.168-83; and Jon D. Levenson, "Who Inserted the Book of Torah?," *HTR* 68 (1975) 203-33.

[2]For a detailed, yet somewhat circular linguistic analysis of the relationship between *bāmôt* and *bāmôtê*, see Vaughan, *The Meaning of 'Bāmâ'*.

ăšērîm: Deut 7:5; 12:3; 16:21

Deut 7:5 and 12:3 mention *ăšērîm* along with *pəsîlîm, maṣṣēbôt*, and *mizbəḥôt* as items used in the religions of the prior inhabitants of the land. Deut 12:2 states that these items were used on "mountain heights, high hills, and beneath every 'leafy tree'" (*ʿēṣ raʿănān*).[3] According to Deut 16:21, *ăšērîm* are made of wood, and are not to be placed next to any altar of YHWH. D, like Dtr (Judges 6), may have known that *ăšērîm* were sometimes located near altars of foreign gods, and therefore condemned any similar placement of them near altars of YHWH. More difficult to prove, yet equally possible, is the idea that D also understood these objects to represent the goddess ʾAsherah, and prohibited them for this reason as well. The fact that the prohibition exists, however, implies that placement of *ăšērîm* next to altars of YHWH was, in fact, being practiced by some YHWHists.[4]

It can also be argued on the basis of Deut 16:21 that D understood *ăšērîm* to be live trees. The passage is difficult. It reads:

לֹא-תִטַּע לְךָ אֲשֵׁרָה כָּל-עֵץ אֵצֶל מִזְבַּח יהוה אֱלֹהֶיךָ

Do not plant for yourself an *ăšērāh*, any tree/wooden thing, next to an altar of YHWH your God.

If one takes this passage to be a prohibition of the juxtaposition of YHWHistic altars and live trees which were considered to be *ăšērîm*, one might recall the J stories of trees at which Abraham and Isaac erected altars to YHWH.[5] Whether D is reacting against this type of piety specifically is unclear. Chapter six will discuss the significance of the numerous landmark trees mentioned in the Pentateuch for the study of *ăšērîm*.

---

[3]The combined images of the "high hill" and the "leafy tree" (*ʿēṣ raʿănān*), occur in several places in the Hebrew Bible: Deut 12:2; 1 Kgs 14:23; 2 Kgs 16:4; 17:10; Jer 2:20; 3:6, 13; 17:2; Ezek 6:13. Isa 57:5 mentions the *ʿēṣ raʿănān*, but without reference to the "high hill." For a more complete discussion, see chapter four on Hos 4:13 (pp. 92-93).

[4]Saul Olyan makes the case that *ăšērîm* were being used near altars of YHWH and that members of the Deuteronomistic school actively polemicized this practice ("The Cultic Confessions of Jer 2,27a," *ZAW* 99 [1987] 254-59).

[5]Abraham's trees and altars were in Shechem (Gen 12:6) and Hebron (13:18). Isaac's altar was erected in Beer Sheba, where YHWH spoke to Abraham (Gen 26:25) and where Abraham planted a tamarisk tree (Gen 21:33).

maṣṣēbôt: Deut 7:5; 12:3; 16:22

As noted above, D twice links *maṣṣēbôt* with *ăšērîm*, *mizbəḥôt*, and *pəsîlîm* in descriptions of the worship practices of the prior inhabitants of the land (7:5, 12:3). Directly following the prohibition against *ăšērîm* in 16:21, 16:22 specifically prohibits Israelite use of *maṣṣēbôt*, stating that they are things which YHWH hates.

It is possible, however, given descriptions of large stone monuments within D and Dtr (Deut 27:2-8; Josh 4, 8:30-35, 24), that the Deuteronomic school may have been conflicted on the issue of stone monuments and their acceptability. While D condemns Israelite use of *maṣṣēbôt*, it none-etheless includes traditions which described the erection of monumental stones. While Weinfeld sees both Deuteronomy 27 and Joshua 3-5 as pre-Deuteronomic Shechem and Gilgal foundation traditions linked here to Moses' instructions on the plains of Moab,[6] the fact that the Deuteronomic school incorporated, and therefore preserved these traditions implies a type of validation of them, or at least an attempt to coopt them for Deuteronomic purposes.

The issue of what these stone monuments represent for D and Dtr will continue to surface throughout this study. Either these monuments were significantly different from *maṣṣēbôt* in the eyes of D and Dtr, so that the term did not seem appropriate for them, or D and Dtr consciously chose a more common term for them so that they might include the traditional stories they inherited without mentioning *maṣṣēbôt* of which they themselves disapproved. It is also entirely possible that D and Dtr could have inherited an appreciation of stone monuments from some early tradition similar to E, but did not feel that *maṣṣēbôt* were included in the class of monuments of which they approved.

mizbəḥôt: Deut 7:5; 12:3, 27; 26:4; 27:5, 6; 33:10

Mizbəḥôt appear to be the only type of Israelite cultic paraphernalia of which D approves. D mandates the presentation of offerings on altars dedicated to YHWH (12:27; 26:4; 33:10) and gives instructions for the construction of an altar to YHWH which is to be built on Mt. Ebal (27:5, 6).[7] Following the instructions concerning YHWHistic altars found in the Covenant Code (Exod 20:25), the Mt. Ebal altar is to be built of field stones; however, the altar is not the only item which is to be constructed there.

---

[6]"Deuteronomy," 171-73.
[7]This destination is also mentioned earlier in Deut 11:29-30.

Deuteronomy 27 also commissions the erection of monumental stones which are to be plastered and then inscribed with the words of the covenant (27:2, 4, 8). As noted above, there is some dissonance between D's negative view of *maṣṣēbôt* and D's instructions for setting up these stones. Either there was some stylistic distinction which set the Mt. Ebal stones apart from *maṣṣēbôt*, or D is simply avoiding the term *maṣṣēbôt* in this account of the Shechem covenant ritual for theological reasons.

Cultic statuary

pəsîlîm: Deut 5:8; 7:5, 25; 12:3; 27:15

massēkôt: Deut 9:12, 16; 27:15

D is most expressive concerning types of cultic statuary, having no less than eight separate injunctions against them: five against *pəsîlîm* and three against *massēkôt*. These eight references represent the highest number of references to cultic statuary within any one strand of the Pentateuch.[8] Like the legal terminology found in E's Decalogue (Exod 20:4), D uses the term *pəsîlîm* in its Decalogue injunction against cultic statuary (5:8), but also employs the term *massēkôt*, which occurs in the legal material incorporated by J (Exod 34:17), as well as in P (Num 33:52). The terms *pəsîlîm* and *massēkôt* appear together in Deut 27:15 which is part of the Shechem covenant ceremony.

The Israelites are instructed not to construct cultic statuary in any form, human or non-human (5:8; 27:15). Along with *ăšērîm, maṣṣēbôt*, and *mizbəḥôt, pəsîlîm* are to be destroyed when discovered among the prior inhabitants of the land (7:5; 12:3), and the gold and silver used in their construction is to be discarded (7:25). D also identifies *massēkôt* with the covenant breaking calves of Sinai (9:12, 16).

Summary

D does not mention *bāmôt*, either in regard to Israel or the prior inhabitants of the land, though the archaic term *bāmôtê*, meaning "heights" or "back," does occur in Deuteronomy in certain old poetic passages

---

[8]Such items are mentioned only once in J (*massēkôt*, Exod 34:17), once in the Covenant Code (*ĕlohê kesep/zāhāv* Exod 20:23), twice in P (*pəsîlîm* Exod 20:4; *ṣalmê massēkôt* Num 33:52), five times in H (*massēkôt* Lev 19:4; *pəsîlîm* Lev 26:1; *gillûlîm* Lev 26:30; *ĕlîlîm* Lev 19:4, 26:1), and six times in E, of which the three references to *tərāpîm* can be taken as value neutral (*tərāpîm* Gen 31:19, 34, 35; *ĕlōhê hannēkār* Gen 35:4; *massēkôt* Exod 32:4, 8). There are five additional references to cultic statuary in

(32:13; 33:29). While D condemns the use of *ăšērîm*, *maṣṣēbôt*, and cultic statuary, this negative assessment cannot be completely derived from the fact that D does connect these items with the prior inhabitants of the land. *Mizbəḥôt* are also said to be used by the prior inhabitants of the land in conjunction with *ăšērîm*, *maṣṣēbôt*, and *pəsîlîm* (Deut 5:8; 12:3), but while these last three items are prohibited for the Israelites by D, *mizbəḥôt* are not. D thus reveals an opinion that while *mizbəḥôt* might be legitimately dedicated to YHWH, there was something inherent in *ăšērîm*, *maṣṣēbôt*, and *pəsîlîm* that made YHWHistic dedication impossible.

D expressly endorses only *mizbəḥôt* as legitimate items of cultic paraphernalia for Israel (12:27; 26:4; 27:5, 6; 33:10), although it also mandates the setting up of ceremonial "stones" which then figure prominently in the Shechem covenant ceremony (27:2, 4, 8). Even though these "stones" are not called *maṣṣēbôt*, which Deut 16:22 prohibits, they appear to be functionally equivalent to them. In forming complexes of cultic features, D confines itself to one description of the worship practiced by the prior inhabitants of the land involving *ăšērîm*, *maṣṣēbôt*, *mizbəḥôt*, and *pəsîlîm* (7:5, 12:3), and one prohibition of Israelites linking their altars of YHWH with *ăšērîm* (16:21) and possibly *maṣṣēbôt* as well (16:22).

THE DEUTERONOMISTIC HISTORY

Dtr is, perhaps, the most explicit of the biblical sources when it comes to cultic activity and the objects used in it. Not all the objects of interest in this study, however, are mentioned in each of the books which make up Dtr. For this reason, each book which comprises the Deuteronomistic corpus will be treated individually before combining the results into an overall picture of Dtr. Under the sections on Samuel and Kings, parallel passages which appear in Chronicles will be listed; however, passages in Chronicles which present a unique view will be discussed in chapter three.[9]

DEUTERONOMY 1-4; 28:29-30:20

bāmôt: not mentioned

Deuteronomy; however, these are from the later strata belonging to Dtr.

[9]For more on the relationship between these two sources, see Steven L. McKenzie, *The Chronicler's Use of the Deuteronomistic History* (HSM 33; Atlanta: Scholars Press, 1984).

ăšērîm: not mentioned

maṣṣēbôt: not mentioned

mizbəḥôt: not mentioned

Cultic statuary

gillûlîm: Deut 29:16 [Eng 29:17]

"gods of wood and stone": Deut 4:28; 28:36, 64; 29:16 [Eng 29:17]

pəsîlîm: Deut 4:16, 23, 25

The Dtr strata of Deuteronomy, while not mentioning any of the four items which are of primary interest to this study, do mention cultic statuary several times. Dtr uses a variety of terms to refer to cultic statuary in these chapters, of which only *pəsîlîm* is familiar from previous strata. Deuteronomy 4 mentions *pəsîlîm* three times, instructing that they not be made in the image of any creature, male or female, animal or human (4:15-18) and repeating this prohibition twice (4:23, 25). The same rationale is given here as in Exodus 20. YHWH is a jealous god who will not share humanity's devotion with any other being, and certainly not with a manufactured image. As in Exodus 20, there is nothing to suggest that images of YHWH are being discussed. The *pəsîlîm* are presumably images of other deities.

Another term for cultic statuary, found in Deut 29:16 [Eng 29:17] is the distinctively late term *gillûlîm* discussed in the "Postscript" to chapter one. In this verse, Dtr reminds the Israelites that they should be well acquainted with and repulsed by cultic statuary, having been exposed to the *gillûlîm* of the Egyptians and the peoples of the land.

In addition to these terms, however, Dtr also refers to cultic statuary simply as "gods" or "objects of wood and stone" (Deut 4:28; 28:36; 28:64; 29:16 [Eng 29:17]). This characteristic phrase is repeated once more in Dtr (1 Kgs 19:18), and three times in the prophetic literature (Jer 2:27; 3:9; Ezek 20:32). Furthermore, whenever this phrase is used, Dtr specifically identifies these "gods of wood and stone" as the gods Israel will be forced to serve if they break the covenant and are sent into exile. In Deut 4:25b, 27a, and 28, Dtr issues the warning:

> If you act corruptly by making an idol (*pesel*) in the form of anything, thus doing what is evil in the sight of YHWH your God, and provoking him to anger . . . the Lord will scatter you among the peoples . . . There you will serve other gods made by human hands, objects of wood and stone that neither see, nor hear, nor eat, nor smell.

Dtr apparently shared an ideology with the archaic poetic passage Deut 32:8-9 which dictated that each nation confine itself to the worship of one particular god to whom that nation had been assigned. This sentiment is echoed in the Shechem covenant-making scene in Deuteronomy 29. In this passage, after the people are assembled to engage in the covenant with YHWH, the penalty for breaking the covenant through the worship of other gods is spelled out (Deut 29:25, 27 [Eng 29:26, 28]):

> [Because] they turned and served other gods, worshiping them, gods whom they had not known and whom he had not allotted to them . . . YHWH uprooted them from their land in anger, fury and great wrath and cast them into another land as is now the case.

The temporal vantage point at the end of this passage reveals that Dtr is placing on the lips of Moses the eventual judgment visited upon Israel and Judah in the editor's own time. Moreover, this passage typifies Dtr's overall understanding of cultic statuary and the ramifications of its use upon Israel's covenant relationship with YHWH. For Dtr, the worship of manufactured cultic statuary was a hallmark both of those alien cultures in which Israel was once captive, and of those cultures in which Israel was now once again captive because YHWH's rights to exclusive worship had been violated. The use of cultic statuary for Dtr was both the primary mode of covenant breaking, as well as a punitive sentence upon the covenant breaker. Those who used these objects voluntarily were later sentenced to exile in countries where their use was compulsory.

JOSHUA

bāmôt: not mentioned

Joshua does not mention *bāmôt*, although it does mention the place name Bamoth-Ba'al as one of the Transjordanian cities allotted by Moses to the Reubenites (13:17). This Moabite place name is also mentioned by E (Num 22:41). The Moabite connection to *bāmôt* will be discussed in chapter five.

ăšērîm: not mentioned

Although Joshua does not mention *ăšērîm*, chapter six will discuss the possibility of a connection between *ăšērîm* and the "oak in the sanctuary of the Lord" at Shechem under which Joshua sets up the "large stone" upon which he has written the laws of the covenant (24:26-27). This oak may or may not be the same as those mentioned in Deut 11:30, and Gen 35:4. Further discussion of this oak can be found below under *maṣṣēbôt*.

maṣṣēbôt: not mentioned

While the word *maṣṣēbôt* does not occur in Joshua, three narratives speak of Joshua's setting up stone monuments himself, or ordering them to be set up. The first, in Joshua 4, describes two stone monuments erected by Joshua near Gilgal. The passage explains that after twelve men, one from each tribe, have been selected to retrieve twelve stones and set them down at the Gilgal camp, Joshua sets them up there as a monument (4:20). In a curious duplication, however, the chapter also states that Joshua erected twelve stones in the middle of the river itself, though no mention of tribal symbolism occurs in this case (4:9).

This narrative has many signs of layers of tradition and repetitions, which have raised for some the issue of whether it contains actual fragments of J, E, and P[10]; however, because extensive redaction in Joshua 4 has obscured the original nature of these sources, if they do exist, for the purposes of this study, the chapter will be considered properly part of Dtr. As noted in chapter one, the "twelve stones for the twelve tribes" motif is one which occurs in both E and P. The presence of the "twelve stone" motif in and of itself, however, is not necessarily indicative of the presence of either of these Tetrateuchal sources in Joshua 4.

Joshua 4 is the first of only two passages in Dtr to use this motif, the second being in the Elijah material (1 Kgs 18:31-32). In Joshua 4, however, the motif depicts the erection of a stone monument which, unlike E's

---

[10]CHB insists that "the existing text contains elements from all four hands, J E R^d and P." (CHB 2.322-27). CHB's division is as follows: J = 3:1a, 1c, 5, 9-10a, 11, 13, 17a; 4:3b, 6-7a, 8b, 10b-11, and 18. E = 3:1b, 2-3, 6, 12, 14; 4:1b-3a, 4-5, 20. D = 3:4b, 7, 10b, 17b; 4:1a, 9-10a, 12, 14, 21-24. P = 3:4a, 8, 15-16; 4:7b-8a, 13, 15-17, 19. A very thorough and complex analysis of eight possible source divisions in Joshua 3-4 is that of F. Langlamet, *Gilgal et les récits de la traversée du Jourdain (Jos., III-IV)* (Cahiers de la Revue Biblique 11; Paris: Gabalda, 1969). For further discussion of Joshua 3-4, see Robert G. Boling and G. Ernest Wright, *Joshua: A New Translation with Introduction and Commentary* (AB 6; Garden City, N.Y.: Doubleday, 1982) 151-81.

use of the motif, does not consist of twelve individual *maṣṣēbôt*. In Joshua 4, the stones are placed in a pile and are simply referred to as "stones" (*ăbānîm*), demonstrating Dtr's characteristic depiction of major stone monuments which are never likened or referred to as *maṣṣēbôt*.

A second narrative in Joshua which illustrates this treatment of stone monuments is Josh 8:30-35. Here, Joshua partially fulfills Moses's commandment concerning an altar and a stone monument with the covenant written upon it which were to be built on Mt. Ebal, above Shechem (Deut 11:29-30; 27:1-8). In Joshua 8, however, the "stones" (*ăbānîm*) which Moses instructed Joshua to build are not set up. The stones upon which Joshua writes are the field stones used to construct the altar. Neither is any plastering of the stones mentioned, despite this instruction in Deuteronomy 27.

Deut 27:1-8 states that this setting up of an altar and stone monument was to be done immediately upon entry into the land. In Dtr, however, the Gilgal monument is erected first. If Jon Levenson is correct in his theory that it was Dtr² and not Dtr¹ which inserted the old core of D into the history,[11] this passage may illustrate the fact that Dtr¹ knew nothing of the stone monument mandated in Deuteronomy 27, or the instruction to proceed to Mt. Ebal straight away. It is also possible that some textual difficulty, or intentional decision on the part of Dtr has resulted in the omission of the stone monument from Joshua 8.

A final narrative which portrays Joshua setting up a stone monument is Josh 24:1-28. Here, Joshua gathers the people at Shechem for a covenant ceremony. After recounting the great acts of YHWH and accepting the people's promise that they would put away their foreign gods (*ĕlōhê hannēkār*) and worship YHWH alone, Joshua writes the words of the covenant that the people have sworn to keep on a "large stone" (*ʾeben gədōlāh*) which he then sets up (*wayqîmehā*) under the oak (*hāʾallāh*) which was in the sanctuary of YHWH. The stone is then said to become a "witness" (*ʿēdāh*) to the covenant the people have made.

The location of this ceremony, held in Shechem under a prominent oak tree, is reminiscent of several passages in the Pentateuch. In Gen 12:6, J indicates that Abraham travelled to "that place at Shechem, to the oak of Moreh" (*ʿad məqôm šəkem ʿad ʾēlôn môreh*) and put up an altar there after receiving the promise of the land from YHWH. The term "sanctuary" (*miqdāš*), used in Josh 24:26, then, may be intended to refer to the precinct surrounding the tree and Abraham's altar. Even closer to the events in

---

[11]Levenson, "Torah," 212-21.

Joshua 24 is the E story concerning Jacob and his followers, who, prior to their settlement at Bethel (Gen 35:1-4), put away their foreign gods (*ĕlōhê hannēkār*) and bury them beneath the oak (*hā 'ēlāh*) which was near Shechem.[12] Given these connections, it appears that Dtr meant to connect the "oak" under which Joshua set up his stone as covenant witness to the people's putting away their foreign gods, with the oak under which Jacob buried the foreign gods carried by his followers, and the oak of Moreh under which Abraham built an altar after YHWH promised to give his descendants the land.[13]

It is noteworthy that in none of the Joshua stories concerning stone monuments does the term *maṣṣēbôt*, or even the verb *nṣb*, occur. This detail could mean one of two things. Dtr might be consciously eschewing the term *maṣṣēbôt* out of some theological disapproval of them (similar to D's opinion voiced in Deut 16:22), while at the same time preserving traditional pericopes that deal with them by substituting the common term for stone. The second possiblity is that Dtr is actually speaking of a different phenomenon from *maṣṣēbôt* altogether. Chapters six and seven will discuss the nature of Dtr's prominent stories of landmark trees and monumental stones and how they might relate to Dtr's views of *'ăšērîm* and *maṣṣēbôt*.

mizbəḥôt: Josh 8:30, 31; 9:27; [22:10-34]

Mizbəḥôt are the only items of cultic paraphernalia that Joshua mentions overtly, and as is the case in Deuteronomy, they are the only cultic items of which Joshua approves. In addition to the altar that Joshua erects on Mt. Ebal (8:30-35), two other stories in Joshua mention *mizbəḥôt* dedicated to YHWH. 9:27 remarks that the Gibeonites will be absorbed within Israel, but only as "hewers of wood and drawers of water for the congregation and for the altar of YHWH." Joshua 22 discusses the altar/monument which the Transjordanian tribes erect on their border with Israel.

---

[12]Michael D. Coogan has noted that the phrase "put away the foreign gods in your midst" (Josh 24:23) is "an almost verbatim quotation of Gen 35:2," such that this and other connections between the two passages are designed to connect Joshua "not just with Moses but also with ancestral tradition" ("Joshua," *NJBC* 131).

[13]In Deut 11:29-30, Moses gives the Israelites directions to Mt. Ebal and Mt. Gerizim, indicating that they are some distance west beyond the Jordan, opposite Gilgal, beside "the oaks of Moreh" (*'ēlônê mōreh*). This passage implies that for D the oaks were a better known landmark than the mountains themselves.

A note concerning Joshua 22

Joshua 22 has been discussed above in chapter one because it most probably belongs to P. Joshua 22 is, nonetheless, preserved in Dtr, and therefore must have served some agenda within this source. This Priestly pericope, with its emphasis on cultic centralization, was preserved by the Deuteronomist, most probably because it supports views central to Deuteronomistic theology later in the Dtr narrative. Dtr's centralization emphasis, however, does not truly enter the text until after the erection of the Temple in Jerusalem, and even then is not applied in all possible cases. For instance, the Deuteronomistic redactor of Joshua 22 does not bother to explain what status is to be afforded the altar on Mt. Ebal, constructed in Joshua 8, in comparison to the importance of the Tabernacle expressed by the P stratum of Joshua 22. Nor does Dtr shy away from depicting Samuel officiating at a *bāmāh* at Ramah with the *miškān* nowhere in sight (1 Samuel 9).[14] Obviously, although Josh 22:9-34 agreed with Dtr's overall emphasis on centralization, it was not a perfect fit. This fact has led many scholars to set aside the issue of Dtr's motivation for including it, in order to search for its original purpose within Priestly circles.[15]

Cultic statuary: not mentioned

The only possible reference to cultic statuary in Joshua occurs in 24:23 where Joshua instructs the Israelites to put away the foreign gods (*ĕlōhê hannēkār*) that were among them. It is not essential, however, to read the physical presence of cultic statuary into this mandate. The people are promising total devotion to YHWH which certainly extends beyond the mere absence of cultic statues into an expectation of complete ideological rejection of foreign gods as well.

JUDGES

bāmôt: not mentioned

---

[14]As part of his argument for the relatively late inclusion of D into the Dtr history, Levenson points out how the issue of cultic centralization is treated differently by D (his Dtn) and Dtr[1]. Levenson demonstrates that D mandates cultic centralization from the instant of the giving of the law, whereas Dtr leaves this issue until after the Temple is constructed ("Torah," 228-29).

[15]For a discussion of this issue, see Kloppenborg, "Joshua 22."

maṣṣēbôt: not mentioned

There is no use of the technical term *maṣṣēbôt* in Judges. Judg 9:6, however, contains a phrase which could be taken to describe a *maṣṣēbāh*. The object in question in this story stands next to an oak tree and is located, perhaps not surprisingly, in Shechem. In Judg 9:1-6, Abimelek, the son of Gideon by his concubine, receives the royal endorsement of the "lords of Shechem" (*baʿălê šəkem*), who then finance his slaughter of his half-brothers out of the treasury of the temple of Baʿal-Berith.[16] They then are said to declare him king "by the oak of the pillar which is at Shechem" (*ʾim-ʾēlôn muṣṣāb ʾăšer bišəkem*). While this translation, "oak of the pillar," is acceptable, it is also possible to translate this unusual phrase, "by the erected/standing oak which is at Shechem," thus removing the necessity of reading a *maṣṣēbāh* in the passage. Given the many Pentateuchal references to the landmark oak at Shechem, and the fact that Dtr described a stone monument erected under this oak by Joshua himself (Josh 24:26), it seems an obvious inference that this was the very same oak.

The use to which this monument is put, however, and the persons engaging in the action imply that Dtr viewed this incident in a negative light. That *mūṣṣāb* (a term derived from the same verbal root as the word *maṣṣēbāh*) is used in Judg 9:6, especially given that no terms derived from this same root, either verbal or nominative, appear in Josh 24:26 or in Joshua 3-4, suggests that the obliqueness of the reference to the oak and the even more oblique suggestion of a *maṣṣēbāh* in Judg 9:6 served to free the author to paint this episode negatively while at the same time reduced the possibility that any of its negative taint would be connected to the traditions of Joshua 24's stone of "witness."

The ordering of material in Judges 9 is also worthy of note. Here the author juxtaposes the story of Abimelek's coronation with Jotham's Parable. In this sequence, the first story portrays a famous and previously respectable tree, and the stone monument beneath it which once witnessed Israel's covenant with YHWH, being coopted for the purpose of witnessing the election of an illegitimate king. Following is the parable, in which various "trees" from the most valuable to the most worthless debate the merits of kingship and conclude that it is a goal that only the most worthless would seek. In an odd way, the parable serves as the verbal "witness" of the coopted Shechem oak and monument.[17]

---

[16]In 9:46, this temple is called the Temple of *ʾĒl*-Berith.

[17]Other notable trees featured by Judges include the palm tree under which Deborah holds court (Judg 4:5) and the tree implied in the place name *ʾĒlôn Məʿōnənîm* (Judg 9:37) usually translated, "Oak of the Diviners." These and other trees will be

ʾăšērîm: 6:25, 26, 28, 30[18]

mizbǝḥôt: 2:2; 6:24, 25, 26, 28, 30, 31, 32; 13:20; 21:4

ʾăšērîm are discussed in Judges only in chapter 6, which connects their use with the use of Baʿalistic altars. The stage for Judges 6 is set in Judg 2:1-5, in which the people of Israel are condemned by the malʾak-YHWH to a long period of struggle against the prior inhabitants of the land because they have ignored their promise to avoid making covenants with these people and to tear down their mizbǝḥôt. Judg 6:11-32 begins with another visit by the malʾak-YHWH, this time to the Oak (hāʾēlāh) which was at Ophrah where he commissions Gideon to become Israel's war leader against the Midianites (Judg 6:11-24). In a scene reminiscent of the J story of YHWH's visit to Abraham beneath the Oaks of Mamre (Gen 18:1-15), Gideon serves a meal to the malʾak-YHWH. Genesis states that Abraham had built an altar to YHWH at the Oaks of Mamre prior to his visitation (Gen 13:18). Similarly, Gideon builds and altar to YHWH under the Oak at Ophrah, but only *after* he has served YHWH's surrogate a meal, and has realized that he has been visited by the divine.

This story is then followed immediately by one in which Gideon is told by YHWH in the night to destroy his father's altar to Baʿal and to cut down (krt) the ʾăšērāh which stands beside it in order to build an altar to YHWH (Judg 6:25-32). In keeping with the understanding of ʾăšērîm in Deut 16:21, the ʾăšērāh in Judges 6 stands beside an altar and is made of wood, for the passage states that the wood of the ʾăšērāh is to be burned on the new YHWHistic altar. As in the case of Deut 16:21, it is not possible to prove whether the ʾăšērāh in question here is a wooden object or a live tree.

The juxtaposition of these two stories, however, the first of which parallels Gideon's altar beneath the Oak at Ophrah with Abraham's altar to YHWH which stood beneath the Oaks of Mamre, and the second of which

---

discussed in chapter six (pp. 175-80).

[18]In addition to the ʾăšērāh mentioned in Judges 6, there is one occurrence of ʾăšērāh in the less frequent feminine plural form (ʾăšērôt) in Judg 3:7. 2 Chr 19:3 and 33:3 are the only other occurrences of the feminine plural form. In Judg 3:7, however, the term occurs within the phrase, "And they served the Baʿals and the ʾAsherahs" (wayyaʿabdû ʾet-habǝʿālîm wǝʾet-hāʾăšērôt), implying that the proper name in plural form is intended. The two references from Chronicles refer to the cult object in the feminine plural. If Judg 3:7 presents a true reading, therefore, it would represent the only reference to the proper name ʾAsherah in the feminine plural. It is more likely, however, based on several references which elsewhere link the proper names Baʿal and ʿAstarte in the plural form, two of which are in Judges (Judg 3:13; 10:6; 1 Sam 7:4; 12:10), that

orders the destruction of an altar of Ba'al and the *ăšērāh* which stood beside it, strongly suggests a comparison between acceptable and unacceptable trees or tree surrogates, as well as acceptable and unacceptable altars. One could also argue, however, that Dtr merely juxtaposes here two parallel foundation stories for a YHWHistic precinct that once existed in Ophrah.

The final two passages from Judges which mention *mizbəḥôt* are Judg 13:20, in which an altar provides the site of a visitation by the *mal'ak-YHWH* to the parents of Samson, and Judg 21:4, in which an altar is built by Israel at Mizpeh in the aftermath of the clan war against Benjamin.

Cultic Statuary

pəsîlîm: 17:3, 4; 18:14, 17, 18, 20, 30, 31[19]

massēkôt: 17:3, 4; 18:14, 17, 18

tərāpîm: 17:5; 18:14, 17, 18, 20

Although there are three distinct items under discussion regarding Judges' views of cultic statuary, all three items are mentioned only in the narrative concerning Micah the Ephraimite and the Danite migration to Laish (Judg 17-18). In addition, this narrative also features an ephod.[20] This story, which shows signs of the merging of more than one stratum, similar to the signs of merging between J and E parallels in the Pentateuch,[21] credits Micah both with the possession of "a *pesel* and a

---

wə'et-hā'ăšērôt in Judg 3:7 is a textual corruption of *wə'et-hā'aštārôt* (cf. Judg 10:6).

[19]The term *pəsîlîm* also occurs in Judg 3:19 and 26. It is possible, however, that these two references form an oblique reference to the stone monuments at Gilgal. The NRSV translates the phrase in question here, *happəsîlîm 'ăšer 'et-haggilgāl*, as "the sculptured stones near Gilgal"; however, the KJV reading "quarries" is another possible translation for *happəsîlîm*, as is the more common "idols." The NJPS translation renders this word as a separate place name, Pesilim. Because of this ambiguity, these verses will not be considered to be a clear reference to cultic statuary, even though the connection of Gilgal, and by association, its monument, is intriguing.

[20]Judg 17:5; 18:14, 17, 18, 20.

[21]Verses which resemble a "southern" tradition similar to J include: 17:1-5 which call the main character Mica*iahu*, refer to his shrine simply as a "house," and call God YHWH; 17:7-13 which explain the origin of Micah's clergy as his adoption of a wandering Levite, an action blessed by YHWH; and 18:6 in which the Levite declares that the Danite's mission has the sanction of YHWH. Verses which resemble a "northern" tradition similar to E are: 17:5, which uses the short form of the name Micah, calls the shrine a *bêt 'ĕlōhîm*, and explains the presence of clergy in the shrine as

massēkāh,"[22] on the one hand, and an ephod and *tərāpîm* on the other. By 18:14-20, however, the two versions have merged to the extent that the "house" of Micah is said to contain all of the items, the ephod, *tərāpîm*, *pesel,* and *massēkāh.* When the Danites arrive and conquer Laish, they set up the *pesel* and the story ends by saying that the Danites "maintained Micah's *pesel* as their own as long as the house of God was at Shiloh" (18:31). No further mention is made of the ephod, *tərāpîm,* or *massēkāh.*

This passage provides an early etiology for the presence of a cult statue at Dan, tracing this cultic tradition not to Jeroboam ben Nebat, but to Micah, his YHWHistic and/or Elohistic shrine, and its descendent shrine at Dan, presided over by a Mosaic Levite (Judg 18:30). It appears that on the earliest level, this story is making an apology for the origin of the cult at Dan, explaining how there came to be a *pesel* there, seemingly validating this practice by placing it under the auspices of Mosaic Levites. Going one better than this, the seemingly "northern" stratum of this story appears to deny the presence of anything but an ephod and *tərāpîm* in Micah's shrine, which elsewhere are generally value neutral or even positively charged items. It is apparent by the end of the story, however, when all the items except the *pesel* have vanished and the Mosaic care of the *pesel* is said to terminate with the termination of the presence of the house of God at Shiloh, that this cultic activity at Dan is being linked with a tradition which was terminated because of corruption. While the condemnation of the practice is not overt, the statement that it ceased when Shiloh ceased implies that it too met the same fate as the doomed Mosaic Levitical house.

Micah's appointment of his biological sons as priests there; 18:5, which has the Danites ask Micah's Levite to inquire of 'Elohim for them; and 18:10, which has the Danites declaring that 'Elohim has blessed their efforts. Other variations occur in chapter 18, without showing signs of either J or E. One passage has the Danites return to Laish with only a war party of six hundred men (18:11-13). Another indicates that the whole tribe of Dan, women and children included, made the trip north (18:21). Verse 18:24, however, appears to be more like the "southern" stratum in that Micah charges the Danites with taking his "gods" and the "priest." No mention is made of the ephod; and if this were the "northern" version, one might have expected Micah to identify the "priest" as his son.

[22]The NRSV takes the phrase *pesel ûmassēkāh* as a hendiadys describing one object rather than two, reading "an idol of cast metal" rather than "an idol and a cast metal cultic statue."

1 AND 2 SAMUEL

bāmôt: 1 Sam 9:12, 13, 14, 19, 25; 10:5, 13

    1 Samuel 9-10 provides the first episodes involving *bāmôt* within the Deuteronomistic corpus. In 9:11-24, Samuel himself, here called a "seer" (*rō'eh*), blesses a sacrificial meal at the *bāmāh* in his home town of Ramah. After the meal to which he invites Saul, he takes Saul home with him. On the next morning, he anoints Saul king and sends him on a journey during which Saul is to meet and join a band of ecstatic prophets on their way down from another *bāmāh* located in a place called Gibeath-'Elohim, or "Hill of 'Elohim" (1 Sam 10:1-13). These two episodes make it clear that despite the condemnation of *bāmôt* which will pervade the books of 1 and 2 Kings, Dtr nonetheless associated *bāmôt* which existed prior to the construction of the Temple in Jerusalem with the early days of prophetic activity and acceptable YHWHistic worship.

    2 Samuel does not mention *bāmôt* though there are three occurrences in 2 Samuel of the archaic poetic term *bāmôtê*, meaning "heights." Two appear in David's lament over Saul and Jonathan (2 Sam 1:19, 25); and one appears in the poetic passage in 2 Samuel 22 (v. 34) which is a parallel of Psalm 18 (v. 33). The relation between this archaic poetic term and the cultic term *bāmôt* will be discussed in chapter five.

'ăšērîm: not mentioned

maṣṣēbôt: 2 Sam 18:18

    1 Samuel does not mention *maṣṣēbôt*, although a stone monument does appear in 1 Sam 7:12. This monument, which Samuel erects, is called *'eben-hā'āzer*, "stone of help," and commemorates YHWH's help in a recent battle. While this stone is not called a *maṣṣēbāh* it appears to be functionally equivalent to one.

    2 Sam 18:18 does mention *maṣṣēbôt*, however. It states that Absalom erected a *maṣṣēbāh* in the King's Valley, in order to "keep his name in remembrance," for he had no son.[23] It is said he named it after himself, and that it was called *yad 'abšālōm*, "Absalom's Monument." No indication is given by the author that this action was looked on with either

---

[23]This statement is in conflict with 2 Sam 14:27 which lists the names of Absalom's children. The Targum resolves this difficulty by reading "he had no *living* son" in 2 Sam 18:18; see Alexander Sperber, *The Bible in Aramaic* (5 vols.; Leiden: E. J. Brill, 1973) 4b.42.

favor or disfavor. P. Kyle McCarter, however, explains this passage, as have others before him, with a reference from the Ugaritic tale of Aqhat. McCarter states that in Aqhat "the ideal son was 'one who erects the stela of the god of his father,' that is, his father's shade or ghost . . . Since Abishalom has no son to do this, he must do it 'for himself.'"[24]

mizbəhôt: 1 Sam 2:28; 14:34; 2 Sam 24:18, 21, 25 (= 1 Chr 21:18, 22, 26)

1 Sam 2:28 mentions only the altar at Shiloh, and an altar on which Saul attempts to repair damage done when his soldiers butcher and consume animals taken in battle, without concern for the laws of ritual slaughter (1 Sam 14:33). Saul orders a large field stone rolled out to him on which he plans to kill and prepare the animals in a proper manner. 1 Sam 14:35 then states that Saul built an altar to YHWH, possibly out of the large field stone, and that this was the first altar Saul built for YHWH.

Similar to the story of the field stone which functioned like a *maṣṣēbāh* in 1 Sam 7:12, there is a story in 1 Samuel in which a field stone functions as an altar, though it is not designated as such. In 1 Samuel 6, the ark, which was placed in an ox cart and set free by the Philistines, runs aground at Beth Shemesh, hitting a large field stone upon which the oxen pulling the cart are later sacrificed (1 Sam 6:14-15).

Mizbəhôt feature in 2 Samuel only in the passage which describes David's purchase of the threshing floor from Araunah the Jebusite, and his building of an altar to YHWH on the site (24:18-25). Gad instructs David to build the altar in order to avert the plague brought on by his census.[25] It is here that Solomon later builds the Temple. Oddly, there are no *mizbəhôt* mentioned in relation to the "tent" in which David installed the ark of the covenant, though it is said that David offered burnt offerings (*ōlôt*) and offerings of well-being (*šlomîm*) to YHWH upon the ark's arrival (2 Sam 6:17-18).[26]

---

[24]*II Samuel: A New Translation with Introduction and Commentary* (AB 9; Garden City, N.Y.: Doubleday, 1984) 408. The Aqhat text cited is *CTCA* 17 [= *UT*⁴ 2 Aqht] 1.27,45; 2.16. For further discussion of a possible cult of dead ancestors in Israel, see Theodore Lewis, *Cults of the Dead in Ancient Israel and Ugarit* (HSM 39; Atlanta: Scholars Press, 1989). Lewis discusses 2 Sam 18:18 on pages 33, 96, 118, 126, and 173.

[25]The Chronicler alters this story slightly by stating that an "angel of YHWH" instructed Gad to give David instructions on building the altar (1 Chr 21:18-25). For more concerning the Chronicler's unique portrayal of David as the mastermind behind construction of the Temple, see chapter three (pp. 82-83).

[26]The Chronicler makes clear that David moved only the ark to Jerusalem, leaving the Tabernacle and its *mizbəhôt* in Gibeon under the supervision of Zadok the priest (1 Chr 16:39-40). The Chronicler will return to this once more (1 Chr 21:29)

Cultic Statuary

ṣelem[27]

tərāpîm: 1 Sam 15:23; 19:13-16

1 Sam 15:23 presents the first clearly negative assessment of *tərāpîm* in the narrative sequence of the biblical text. This poetic passage labels sorcery (*qesem*) a sin, and *tərāpîm*, iniquity (*āwen*). The only other mention of *tərāpîm* in 1 Samuel, however, portrays them neutrally, if not positively. In 1 Sam 19:13-16, Michal uses *tərāpîm* to assist David in an escape from the palace by putting one in a bed to make it look as if David were sleeping.[28]

ăṣabbîm: 1 Sam 31:9 (= 1 Chr 10:9); 2 Sam 5:21

1 Sam 31:9 states that the Philistines sent runners to inform the temples of their idols (*bêt ăṣabbêhem*) that Saul was dead. 2 Sam 5:21 also uses the term *ăṣabbêhem* to refer to the gods of the Philistines and indicates that these idols were portable. It states that after the Philistines abandoned them, David and his men carried them away.[29] This term for cultic statuary does not occur in the biblical narrative prior to 1 Sam 31:9.

1 AND 2 KINGS

bāmôt: 1 Kgs 3:2, 3, 4; 11:7; 12:31, 32; 13:2, 32, 33; 14:23; 15:14 (= 2 Chr 15:17); 22:43 (= 2 Chr 20:33); 2 Kgs 12:4; 14:4; 15:4; 15:35; 16:4 (=2 Chr 28:2); 17:9, 11, 29, 32; 18:4, 22 (= 2 Chr

---

before recounting the trip Solomon made to Gibeon prior to building the Temple (2 Chronicles 1), an account that varies from the Dtr account of that visit (1 Kings 3). See further chapter three (p. 79).

[27]The term *ṣelem* appears in 1 Sam 6:5 and 11, describing the gold offerings in the shape of mice and "tumors" that the Philistines sent out with the ark. It is not imperative, however, that these tokens be thought of as a type of cultic statuary.

[28]This passage raises the question of how large these objects were. If the *ĕlōhê hannēkār* which the followers of Jacob carried in their hands in Gen 35:8 are to be identified with the *tərāpîm* which Rachel stole from Laban, then these objects could hardly be expected to pass for a man lying in bed.

[29]For more on the ark narratives of 1 and 2 Samuel as a dramatic retelling of the conflict between YHWH and foreign gods, see Patrick D. Miller and J. J. M. Roberts, *The Hand of the Lord: A Reassessment of the Ark Narrative of 1 Samuel* (Baltimore: Johns Hopkins University Press, 1977).

32:12; Isa 36:7);[30] 21:3 (= 2 Chr 33:3); 23:5 (= 2 Chr 34:4), 8, 9, 13, 15, 19, 20

Kings clarifies Dtr's transition away from *bāmôt* and toward the legitimization of YHWHistic worship in the Temple only. Dtr's stance on this subject is encapsulated in 1 Kgs 3:1-4 which reads:

> Solomon made a marriage alliance with Pharaoh King of Egypt; he took Pharaoh's daughter and brought her into the city of David, until he had finished the building of his own house and the house of YHWH and the wall around Jerusalem. The people were sacrificing at the *bāmôt*, however, because no house had yet been built for the name of YHWH. Solomon loved YHWH, walking in the statutes of his father David; only he sacrificed and offered incense at the *bāmôt*. The king went to Gibeon to sacrifice there for that was the principal *bāmāh*; Solomon used to offer a thousand burnt offerings on that altar.

Although the sequencing of these verses is slightly odd, the perspective of Dtr on the subject of *bāmôt* is explicit here. *Bāmôt* were allowed as legitimate places for the worship of YHWH until the construction of the Temple, at which point they became illegitimate.[31] Solomon, who receives his dream commissioning the building of the Temple while worshipping YHWH at the *bāmāh* of Gibeon, is later denounced in 1 Kgs 11:7-8 [LXX 11:5-6] for building *bāmôt* for the gods of his foreign wives. All of the later kings of Judah are condemned for either building *bāmôt* or failing to destroy them.[32]

The people of Judah during the reign of Rehoboam are condemned for using *bāmôt* (among other items).[33] Beginning with Asa, the formulaic phrase "but the *bāmôt* were not taken away" (1 Kgs 15:14) is used by Dtr to render at least partially, if not completely, negative assessments of the

---

[30]As noted in chapter four (p. 101), although Isa 36:7 is preserved in the work of Isaiah, it most probably originated with Dtr.

[31]The Chronicler explains Solomon's use of the *bāmāh* at Gibeon by stating that David left the Tabernacle and its altars there when he moved the ark to Jerusalem (1 Chr 16:39-40; 21:29; 2 Chr 1:1-13). See further chapter three (p. 79).

[32]See the chapter, "The במות Theme in the Book of Kings," in Iain Provan, *Hezekiah and the Books of Kings: A Contribution to the Debate about the Compostion of the Deuteronomistic History* (BZAW 172; Berlin: de Gruyter, 1988) 57-170.

[33]Their offenses included the use of *ăšērîm* and *maṣṣēbôt*, worship on "every high hill and under every green tree (*ʿēṣ raʿănān*)," in addition to allowing *qādēšim* to remain in the land (1 Kgs 14:23-24). For other references to the *ʿēṣ raʿănān* formula, see Deut 12:2; 2 Kgs 16:4; 17:10; Jer 2:20; 3:6, 13; 17:2; Ezek 6:13; and Isa 57:5 which mentions the *ʿēṣ raʿănān* without the "high hill." For further references, see the discussion of Hos 4:13 in chapter four (pp. 92-93).

reigns of various Judahite kings.[34] This phrase, either in brief or expanded form, is used in the summary accounts of the reigns of Jehoshaphat (1 Kgs 22:43), Jehoash (2 Kgs 12:4), Amaziah (2 Kgs 14:4), Uzziah (2 Kgs 15:4), and Jotham (2 Kgs 15:35).[35] In all of these cases, the formulaic phrase is expanded from the short version dealing with Asa in 1 Kgs 15:14. The longer formula reads "But the *bāmôt* were not taken away, and the people still sacrificed (*zbḥ*) and offered incense (*qṭr*) on the *bāmôt*." This formula is only used of southern monarchs whose "sins" were somewhat limited in the eyes of Dtr. Those who had a more negative reputation were treated in more detail.[36]

This "*bāmôt*" formula is not used in relation to the northern kings. Instead, their indiscretions are described this way: "He did what was evil in the sight of YHWH, walking in the way of Jeroboam and in the sin that he caused Israel to commit." This is said of Nadab (though the phrase "his ancestor" is substituted for the name of Jeroboam, 1 Kgs 15:26), Baasha (1 Kgs 15:34), and Zimri (1 Kgs 16:19). Following Zimri's assessment, all of the judgment formulae on northern kings add "son of Nebat" to "Jeroboam," whether keeping the formula essentially the same, as in the case of Jehoahaz, (2 Kgs 13:2), Jehoash (2 Kgs 13:11), Jeroboam II (2 Kgs 14:24), Zechariah (2 Kgs 15:9), Menahem (2 Kgs 15:18), Pekahiah (2 Kgs 15:24), and Pekah (2 Kgs 15:28), or expanding it, as in the following cases.

Ahab's assessment is greatly expanded, including the familiar phrases "did evil in the sight of YHWH more than all who were before him," "walked in the sins of Jeroboam son of Nebat," and "provoked the

---

[34]The Chronicler has conflicting evaluations of Asa. 2 Chr 15:17 parallels 1 Kgs 15:14, stating that Asa left the *bāmôt* standing. 2 Chr 14:2-4, however, credits Asa with the removal, not only of the *bāmôt*, but of *ăšērîm*, *maṣṣēbôt*, *ḥammānîm*, and foreign *mizbǝḥôt* as well. The Chronicler also credits Asa with repairing the altar of YHWH. These variations will be discussed in chapter three (p. 80).

[35]The Chronicler also has varying accounts of the attitude of Jehoshaphat toward the *bāmôt*. While 2 Chr 20:33 parallels 1 Kgs 22:43, stating that Jehoshaphat left the *bāmôt* standing, 2 Chr 17:6 credits him with destroying *bāmôt* and *ăšērîm*, with 2 Chr 19:3 reiterating his destruction of *ăšērîm*. Dtr makes no mention of *ăšērîm* in relation to Jehoshaphat (see further chapter three, p. 80). 2 Chr 21:11 also faults Jehoram, son of Jehoshaphat, for building *bāmôt* in the hill country, a detail not found in Dtr's negative evaluation of Jehoram (2 Kgs 8:18).

[36]Construction and use of *bāmôt* was only one of the negative behaviors attributed to Ahaz (2 Kgs 16:2-4=2 Chr 28:2-3) and Manasseh (2 Kgs 21:3-9=2 Chr 33:3-9). The Chronicler recounts of the careers of Ahaz and Manasseh differently than does Dtr, though the assessments in the above passages remain largely unchanged. See further chapter three (p 80-81).

anger of YHWH, the God of Israel more than had all the kings of Israel who were before him" (1 Kgs 16:30-33). Ahaziah, the son of Ahab and Jezebel, has their memories invoked in his assessment phrase along with Jeroboam son of Nebat (1 Kgs 22:52-53). Jehoram is said to have done evil in YHWH's sight, though not like Ahab and Jezebel, only like Jeroboam son of Nebat (1 Kgs 3:2-3). Hoshea ben Elah's assessment goes on for a whole chapter, including a lengthy discussion of Jeroboam ben Nebat and his sins (2 Kings 17).

Only in the phrase related to Jehu is Jeroboam's sin identified and described as "the golden calves that were in Bethel and Dan" (2 Kgs 10:28). Similarly, it is said of Elah that he and his father Baasha erred through sins consisting of "provoking God to anger with their 'worthless things' (hablêhem)," usually interpreted as another reference to the calves of Dan and Bethel (1 Kgs 16:13). Omri's formula is similar: "Omri did what was evil in the sight of YHWH; he did more evil than all who were before him, for he walked in the way of Jeroboam son of Nebat, and in the sins that he caused Israel to commit, provoking YHWH, the God of Israel, to anger by their worthless things" (hablêhem, 1 Kgs 16:25-26).

Thus, the name of Jeroboam ben Nebat became synonymous with northern cultic violations. Unlike the south, however, where the use of bāmôt is focused upon by Dtr, in the north it is the institutionalization of cultic statuary which is considered by Dtr to be the most serious offense. Jeroboam is credited with the building of bāmôt (1 Kgs 12:31-32; 13:2, 32-33), and all of northern Israel is credited with their use (2 Kgs 17:9-32), but it is the use of cultic statuary that is mentioned most often as the primary offense of the northern kingdom.[37]

Outside the references to bāmôt listed above, Dtr also mentions bāmôt a number of times in relation to religious reforms which sought to end their use. These are the reforms of Hezekiah (2 Kgs 18:4) and Josiah (2 Kgs 23:4-24), respectively.[38] Because these passages combine so many

---

[37]Another unique feature of the northern bāmôt is the fact that they are described, five times, as "temple bāmôt" (bêt bāmôt, 1 Kgs 12:31; 13:32; 2 Kgs 17:29, 32; 23:19). This term, which implies a substantial structure, is not used for bāmôt in the south. See further chapter five (p. 145).

[38]While Dtr devotes only one verse to Hezekiah's reform, crediting him with the destruction of ăšērîm, bāmôt, maṣṣēbôt, and Moses' bronze serpent Nehushtan, which the Judahites had begun to worship, Chronicles discusses it for an entire chapter plus some additional verses (2 Chr 29:18-27, 30:14, 31:1). The Chronicler's account of Josiah's reform, however, is limited to five verses (2 Chr 34:3-7) in which the Chronicler adds pəsîlîm, massēkôt, and ḥammānîm to the list of items purged, and including only the ăšērîm, bāmôt and foreign mizbəḥôt mentioned in Kings. Another

items, they will be treated at length below, at the end of the discussion of 1
and 2 Kings.

ǎšērîm: 1 Kgs 14:15, 23; 16:33; 2 Kgs 13:6; 17:10, 16; 18:4; 21:3 (= 2
      Chr 33:3); 23:14, 15

Kings first mentions ǎšērîm in the passage in which Ahijah curses
the house of Jeroboam ben Nebat (1 Kgs 14:15). Although ǎšērîm are not
mentioned in 1 Kings 12-13 as items that Jeroboam installed in the north,
they are added to Ahijah's original indictment against the house of
Jeroboam. It appears that the original indictment ended with the destruction of Jeroboam and his children because he endorsed the use of massēkôt
(14:6-14), while the two verses adding ǎšērîm to the list of his crimes
(14:15-16) promise exile "beyond the Euphrates" as Israel's punishment.
In the chapter indicting the northern kingdom for its crimes, ǎšērîm are
mentioned again as a cause of its destruction (2 Kgs 17:10). Of the
southern kings, Rehoboam is credited with the use of ǎšērîm (1 Kgs
14:23), and Josiah with their destruction (2 Kgs 23:14).

In addition to these references to the plural cult objects, ǎšērîm,
Kings and its parallel verses in Chronicles are also responsible for the only
possible references to the goddess ʾAsherah in the Hebrew Bible. Although
the name of the goddess could, and possibly should, be read in the following verses, they are mentioned here and will be discussed in chapter six
because in all of these cases it is possible instead to read a singular noun
referring to the cult object. All of these verses attach either a definite article, or a prefix that may obscure a definite article, to the noun.[39]

The only instances in Kings of the noun ǎšērāh without a prefix are
2 Kgs 17:16 (where we read that in addition to the two calf massēkôt, the
north "made ʾAšērāh"), 2 Kgs 21:3 (where Manasseh is said to have "made
ʾAšērāh" just as Ahab did), and 2 Kgs 23:15 (where it is stated that those
who destroyed Bethel "burned ʾAšērāh"). The absence of a prefix, however, does not indicate that these verses refer to the goddess by name. On
the contrary, they undoubtedly refer to a cult object or statue of the goddess, and not to the goddess herself. In fact, even the famous "'Asherah of
Samaria," may in fact have been a cult object or shrine of some sort, and

---

notable omission in the Chronicles account is the elimination of Hilkiah as a major
participant in the reform of the cult (2 Kgs 23:4). In Chronicles, Hilkiah instead receives
money collected from Manasseh and Ephraim and hands it over to the workers who
made repairs on the Temple (2 Chr 34:9). See further chapter three (p. 81).

[39]l-ʾAsherah (1 Kgs 15:13 [= 2 Chr 15:16]; 2 Kgs 23:4, 7); h-ʾAsherah (1 Kgs
18:19; 2 Kgs 21:7 [=2 Chr 33:7]; 2 Kgs 23:6).

not a statue of the goddess. 1 Kgs 16:33 states that Ahab "made *the ăšērāh*" (*'et-hā ăšērāh*). 1 Kgs 18:19 describes half of Ahab and Jezebel's clergy as "prophets of *the ăšērāh*" (*nəbî'ê hā ăšērāh*), and 2 Kgs 13:6 states that long after Jehu's purge, "the *ăšērāh*" (*hā ăšērāh*) remained in Samaria. Now while it is possible to read the name of the goddess in all of these instances, or to infer that what is being discussed is a cult image, it is also possible to come to the conclusion that there was *an ăšērāh*, a singular cult object or shrine, in Samaria, to which reference is being made.[40] The same argument could be made for "the *'ăšērāh*" (*'et-hā ăšērāh*) that Hezekiah is credited with destroying in 2 Kgs 18:4.

maṣṣēbôt: 1 Kgs 14:23; 2 Kgs 3:2; 10:26, 27; 17:10; 18:4; 23:14

 Maṣṣēbôt dedicated to Ba'al are said to stand in Ba'al's temple in Samaria (2 Kgs 10:26-27), and Jehoram, though a northern king and otherwise disapproved of, is credited with destroying one of these (2 Kgs 3:2). *Maṣṣēbôt* are mentioned four times elsewhere without any direct connection to Ba'al. They are listed along with *ăšērîm* as items that Rehoboam used (1 Kgs 14:23), that the north is being punished for using (2 Kgs 17:10), and that both Hezekiah (2 Kgs 18:4) and Josiah (2 Kgs 23:14) destroyed.

mizbəḥôt: 1 Kgs 1:50, 51, 53; 2:28, 29; 3:4; 6:20, 22; 7:48 (= 2 Chr 4:19);
   8:22 (= 2 Chr 6:12), 31 (=2 Chr 6:22), 54 (= 2 Chr 7:7), 64
   (=2 Chr 8:12); 9:25; 12:32, 33; 13:1, 2, 3, 4, 5, 32; 16:32;
   18:26, 30, 32, 35; 19:10, 14; 2 Kgs 11:11 (= 2 Chr 23:10), 18
   (= 2 Chr 23:17); 12:10 [Eng 12:9]; 16:10, 11, 12, 13, 14, 15;
   18:22 (= 2 Chr 32:12); 21:3 (= 2 Chr 33:3), 4 (=2 Chr 33:4), 5
   (= 2 Chr 33:5); 23:9, 12, 15, 16, 17, 20.

 Throughout Kings, references are made to legitimate YHWHistic *mizbəḥôt* and illegitimate *mizbəḥôt*, either dedicated to YHWH or to other deities. Dtr's watershed of acceptability for multiple YHWHistic altars, in most cases, appears to be the construction of the Jerusalem Temple. Prior to its construction, there was an altar to YHWH at the *bāmāh* of Gibeon

---

[40]This type of reading would support those who feel that the divine name 'Asherah cannot be read in the pithos inscription from Kuntillet 'Ajrud because of the 3ms suffix on the word *šrth*. If one does not read the proper name, one must read "Blessed be PN by YHWH Šomron and his *ăšērāh*," referring to some cult object or shrine associated with YHWH at Samaria. Frank Cross (pers. comm.) is one who now derives the name 'Asherah from a word meaning "shrine."

upon which Solomon made sacrifices (1 Kgs 3:4),[41] as well as a
YHWHistic altar in Jerusalem which David built on the Jebusite threshing
floor (2 Samuel 24), which may or may not have been the location of the
sacrifices made upon arrival of the ark (2 Sam 6:17-18), or the altar to
which both Adonijah and Joab flee for refuge (1 Kgs 1:50-53; 2:28-29).[42]

Shortly after his ascension to the throne, Solomon is credited with
the construction and dedication of the *mizbəḥôt* of YHWH's Temple in
Jerusalem. Discussion of these altars occupies a large part of Dtr's interest
in the subject.[43] In addition to the altars of the Temple, however, Dtr
allows the altar Elijah builds on Mt. Carmel in his contest with the priests
of Baʿal to remain legitimate, even though it stands outside Jerusalem during an era in which the Temple of YHWH exists.

As noted above in the discussions of Exod 24:4 and Joshua 4,
the motif of the "twelve stones for the twelve tribes" occurs in the description of Elijah's altar on Carmel (1 Kgs 18:31-38); however, the Elijah story
calls the tribes the "sons of Jacob," not the "sons of Israel." This slight
alteration from the pattern of the motif is unique to this passage. Another
oddity about the Elijah material with regard to the Dtr's view of *mizbəḥôt*
is the fact that Elijah is depicted lamenting the destruction of YHWH's
many altars (19:10, 14), altars presumably in the north, and presumably

---

[41]See above (p. 65, n. 31).

[42]In addition to these presumed altars of sacrifice there is also mention of a
stone, *haz-zoḥelet*, upon which Adonijah makes the sacrifices announcing his claim to
the throne (1 Kgs 1:9).

[43]1 Kgs 6:20-22, and 7:48-50 (=2 Chr 4:19-22) describe the golden altar, while 2
Chr 4:1 has Solomon constructing a bronze altar as well in order to conform more
closely to the Priestly description of the *mizbəḥôt* of the Tabernacle. 2 Chr 4:20 notes
that Solomon manufactured the various items "as prescribed." For the inauguration of
the Temple and its altar see 1 Kgs 8:22 (= 2 Chr 6:12), 1 Kgs 8:31 (= 2 Chr 6:22) and 1
Kgs 8:54 (= 2 Chr 7:7). In its parallel to the last passage, Chronicles adds a slight
embellishment by stating that fire descended from heaven to consume the sacrifice. See
also 1 Kgs 8:64 (=2 Chr 8:12) and 1 Kgs 9:25. For other references in Kings to the altars
of the Temple in Jerusalem, see 2 Kgs 11:11 (=2 Chr 23:10); 12:10 [Eng 12:9]; 18:22 (=
2 Chr 32:12 = Isa 36:7); 23:9. See also 2 Kgs 16:10-15 for the account of the
Damascene altar that Ahaz commissions for the courtyard of the Jerusalem Temple.
While Dtr does not condemn its construction, the foreign origin of its design is stressed,
and it is noted that the original bronze altar of the courtyard was moved from its place
and replaced by the new altar and then relegated to use only by the king. Chronicles
lacks any mention of this episode. 2 Chr 28:22-25, however, states that Ahaz
worshipped the gods of Damascus because they had been powerful enough to defeat
him, and credits Ahaz with constructing numerous *mizbəḥôt* and *bāmôt* throughout
Judah and Jerusalem.

postdating the Temple in Jerusalem. This departure from the Dtr's program concerning centralization of worship in Jerusalem lends credence to the idea that the Elijah material preserves separate source material originally independent of Dtr.

With regard to illegitimate altars, Kings mentions many rulers who erected altars to Ba'al or other deities.[44] Kings also considers the altar that Jeroboam ben Nebat built in Bethel to be illegitimate. It is not referred to by Dtr as an altar of YHWH, but rather as if it were an altar dedicated to the calf *massēkāh* of Bethel only. Of course, no connection between YHWH and this calf, or the calf of Dan, is made by Dtr, though most modern scholars see no reason to insist that the calf iconography of the north should have been anything other than YHWHistic.[45] Dtr condemns the altar at Bethel from the moment of its construction (1 Kgs 12:32-33, 13:1-5, 32) until its thorough and predicted destruction at the hands of Josiah (1 Kgs 13:2; 2 Kgs 23:14-17). In fact, it is the construction and destruction of the altar at Bethel which forms the primary object lesson of Dtr, Josiah's court historian. The north erected the parallel shrine at Bethel and made *massēkôt* and the north was destroyed. Thus the south should have taken notice and cleansed itself from the sins of idolatry and noncentralization if it had wished to avoid a similar fate.

Cultic Statuary

gillûlîm: 1 Kgs 15:12; 21:26; 2 Kgs 17:12; 21:11, 21; 23:24

"gods of wood and stone": 2 Kgs 19:18

massēkôt: 1 Kgs 12:28, 32; 14:9; 2 Kgs 17:16

pəsîlîm: 2 Kgs 17:41; 21:7 (= 2 Chr 33:7)

ṣelem: 2 Kgs 11:18 (= 2 Chr 23:17)

---

[44]Monarchs said to have erected altars to Ba'al were Ahab (1 Kgs 16:32), Jezebel and her priests (1 Kgs 18:26), Athaliah (possibly) (2 Kgs 11:18 [=2 Chr 23:17]), and Manasseh (2 Kgs 21:3 [=2 Chr 33:3]). Manasseh is also said to have erected various illegitimate altars throughout Jerusalem, as well as altars to the Hosts of Heaven in the Temple court (2 Kgs 21:4-5). Josiah is said to have destroyed altars on rooftops and in the courtyard placed there by Ahaz and Manasseh (2 Kgs 23:12, cf 2 Chr 28:24-25).

[45]For a recent discussion of this issue, see John R. Spencer, "Golden Calf," *ABD* 2.1065-69.

tərāpîm: 2 Kgs 23:24

In addition to the verses which refer to ᵓAsherah in the singular, Kings can be read to testify to the existence of cult statuary either of her or for her (1 Kgs 16:33; 18:19; 2 Kgs 13:6; 17:16; 18:4; 21:3; 23:4, 6, 7, 15). Two passages specifically identify these objects as some type of image. 1 Kgs 15:13 calls the object that Maacah, mother of Asa, had made of/for ᵓAsherah a "monstrosity" (*mipleṣet*). 2 Kgs 21:7 (= 2 Chr 33:7) is less poetic, referring to Manasseh's statue of/for ᵓAsherah, which he installed in the Temple, as a *pesel*.[46] The term *pəsîlîm* occurs only once more in Kings, referring to those cultic statues revered in the northern kingdom by the Assyrian deportees (2 Kgs 17:41).

The term *gillûlîm* is used six times in connection with Asa (1 Kgs 15:12) and Josiah (2 Kgs 23:24) who purged them, and Ahab (1 Kgs 21:26), the northern Israelites (2 Kgs 17:12), Manasseh (2 Kgs 21:11), and Amon (2 Kgs 21:21), who used them. Two of these verses specifically connect the use of *gillûlîm* with the Amorites as representatives of the nations who inhabited the land before the Israelites (1 Kgs 21:26; 2 Kgs 21:11). *tərāpîm* are mentioned only once, along with *gillûlîm*, as objects of Josiah's reform (2 Kgs 23:24), and *ṣəlāmîm* are mentioned only once in connection with images of Baʿal that were destroyed along with Jerusalem's Baʿal temple following the deposing of Athaliah (2 Kgs 11:18 [=2 Chr 23:17]). Once Kings uses the formula "gods of wood and stone" found elsewhere in Dtr, to describe foreign deities (2 Kgs 19:18).

The term *massēkôt* occurs four times in Kings, and each time it is used to refer to the cult statuary of Dan and Bethel (1 Kgs 12:28, 32; 13:33; 2 Kgs 17:16). One might expect Dtr to refer to these primary offending objects of the north as *pəsîlîm*, given the fact that *pesel* is the term for cultic statuary used in the prohibitions of the Deuteronomic Decalogue (Deut 5:8). This is not the case, however.[47]

---

[46]2 Chr 33:7 does not use the name ᵓAsherah in this verse. It substitutes, instead, the term *semel*. The Septuagint, whose traditional translation of *ăšērîm* is "sacred grove/precinct" (ἄλσος), and which apparently had no knowledge of the proper name ᵓAsherah, had particular difficulty with 2 Kgs 21:7, slavishly translating, τὸ γλυπτὸν τοῦ ἄλσους ἐν τῷ οἴκῳ, "the statue of the grove which was in the house/Temple." See further the discussion of the Septuagint's treatment of *ăšērîm* in chapter nine (pp. 254-65).

[47]Again, this seeming discontinuity between Dtr and D might simply be additional evidence for Levenson's theory that D was added to the history by Dtr² after the composition of Dtr¹ (Levenson, "Torah," 222-23). For further discussion of the myriad ways in which Deuteronomy and Dtr discuss idolatry, see Weinfeld, *Deuteronomy*, 322-26.

Note on the grouping of cultic items in Kings

One of the most interesting features of Kings in relation to *ăšērîm*, *bāmôt*, *maṣṣēbôt*, and *mizbəḥôt* is the manner in which they are combined into sets of items at various places in the narrative. For instance, the description of worship involving these items "on every high hill and under every green tree" (*ẽṣ ra ănān*), is used three times in Kings.[48] *bāmôt*, *ăšērîm*, and *maṣṣēbôt* are connected to the *ẽṣ ra ănān* formula in 1 Kgs 14:23 and 2 Kgs 17:10-11, and in the latter reference incense burning is also mentioned. 2 Kgs 16:4 connects *bāmôt* and the *ẽṣ ra ănān* formula and mentions sacrifice (*zbḥ*) as well as incense burning (*qṭr*) taking place there.[49]

Other combinations of cultic items occur elsewhere in Kings. In terms of YHWHistic use of these items, *bāmôt* and *mizbəḥôt* are combined in the description of the *bāmāh* at Gibeon (1 Kgs 3:4) as well as in the Rab Shaqeh's charges that Hezekiah's centralization efforts were hostile to YHWH (2 Kgs 18:22 [=2 Chr 32:12 = Isa 36:7]). While it is not explicitly described as YHWHistic, Hezekiah also stops the Judahites from burning incense to Moses' bronze serpent Nehustan in his process of clearing the land of *bāmôt*, *ăšērîm*, and *maṣṣēbôt* (2 Kgs 18:4). According to Dtr's formula regarding *bāmôt*, the routine rituals held on *bāmôt* were incense burning and sacrifice which would have necessitated the presence of *mizbəḥôt* (1 Kgs 3:3, 4; 22:43; 2 Kgs 12:4; 14:4; 15:4; 15:35; 17:11).

In relation to the worship of other gods, both altars and images of Ba'al are purged from his temple in Jerusalem (2 Kgs 11:18 [=2 Chr 23:17]).[50] As for Samaria, ba'alistic *mizbəḥôt* as well as *maṣṣēbôt* are mentioned, as is an *ăšērāh* (1 Kgs 16:32-33; 2 Kgs 3:2; 10:26-27), though none of the references indicate that these objects stood together in one sacred precinct. In 2 Kgs 21:3-7, an *ăšērāh*, as well as *mizbəḥôt* for the "Hosts of Heaven" are erected in the Temple of YHWH; and *mizbəḥôt* for

---

[48]1 Kgs 14:23; 2 Kgs 16:4; 17:10. See also Deut 12:2; Jer 2:20; 3:6, 13; 17:2; Ezek 6:13; Isa 57:5; and the discussion of Hos 4:13 in chapter four (pp. 92-93).

[49]Several important issues raised by the *ẽṣ ra ănān* formula will be discussed in chapters five and six. For instance, the argument that *ăšērîm* were live trees is hampered by their location beneath trees in these passages (see pp. 180-83). Also, the location of *bāmôt* on high hills in these verses may account for the equation of *bāmôt* with "high places" that the Greek translators have introduced into the standard Western translations concerning *bāmôt* (see pp. 156-57).

[50]The only difference here between the Kings and Chronicles account is that Chronicles reduces the reference to the "people of the land" who destroy the temple in Kings, to a simple reference to "the people."

Ba'al are built along with an *ăšērāh*. Again, however, it is not clear that this *ăšērāh* was dedicated to Ba'al. Similarly, 2 Kgs 17:16 charges the north with erecting an *ăšērāh*, and worshipping the calf *massēkôt*, Ba'al, and all the Host of Heaven without indicating that these actions were performed together. Finally, Assyrian settlers install their gods and goddesses in the *bêt bāmôt* of the northern kingdom after the Israelites are deported (2 Kgs 17:29-34).

Descriptions of the Josianic reform also make lists of items which imply their use together either in the worship of YHWH or in the worship of other gods. 2 Kgs 23:4 and 6-7 describe "vessels" of Ba'al, 'Asherah (or *the ăšērāh*), and the Host of Heaven being purged from YHWH's Temple. 2 Kgs 23:5, and 8-9 describe the destruction of an apparently YHWHistic priesthood that made offerings on the *bāmôt* in the cities of Judah and Jerusalem, as well as those clergy who served the cults of other gods. During the reform, the lives of the YHWHistic *bāmôt* priests were apparently spared, though they were no longer allowed to serve on YHWH's purified altar (2 Kgs 23:9). The various *mizbəḥôt* that Ahaz and Manasseh had erected, as well as the *bāmôt* that Solomon had built for the gods of his foreign wives were destroyed, presumably along with the *maṣṣēbôt* and *ăšērîm* they were said to contain within their precincts. *gillûlîm* and *tərāpîm* used by mediums and wizards, perhaps for divination, were also destroyed (2 Kgs 23:13-14).[51]

At Bethel, the altar destroyed by Josiah is equated with a *bāmāh*, and both are said to be torn down along with the *ăšērāh* there, though there is no previous mention of an *ăšērāh* at Bethel (2 Kgs 23:15). The priests of the *bêt bāmôt* in the "towns of Samaria" are slaughtered with no explanation of what made them greater offenders than the *bāmôt* priests of the south. Perhaps we are to assume that these were the Assyrian settlers' priests who served foreign gods there, but this is not specified (2 Kgs 23:20).

Kings also connects *bāmôt*, *maṣṣēbôt*, and *ăšērîm* with the *'ēṣ ra'ănān* formula. In what might be a Deuteronomistic addition, Jeremiah locates *ăšērîm*, *bāmôt*, and *mizbəḥôt* next to the *'ēṣ ra'ănān* (Jer 17:2-3). This image is also found in Hosea and Third Isaiah, though they do not use the technical terms *bāmôt*, *ăšērîm*, or *maṣṣēbôt* in relation to this setting as does Kings. Ezekiel mentions only *bāmôt* in connection with the *'ēṣ ra'ănān*. Ezekiel, Jeremiah, and Hosea also connect the use of cultic statuary with the *'ēṣ ra'ănān*, though Kings does not.

---

[51]See further the discussion of *tərāpîm* as omens in Zech 10:2 (p. 120).

Summary

Concerning *ăšērîm*, Dtr limits its discussion to the Gideon story in Judges 6, until reaching the accounts of the monarchy in which *ăšērîm* are mentioned as objects to be purged. Similarly, *maṣṣēbôt* are not discussed outright in Dtr until the accounts of the monarchy, in which, with the exception of Absalom's monument, they are listed as items to be purged. Perhaps, because it was understood as a memorial substitute for children, Absalom's monument was not considered to be the same type of object as other *maṣṣēbôt* which were prohibited. Regardless of the reason for its escape from condemnation, however, the rather passing treatment it receives raises the question of whether all *maṣṣēbôt* were considered illegitimate by Dtr, or only those which were erected in certain contexts.

Many stone monuments and landmark trees which are approved of are described by Dtr, but without using the terms *maṣṣēbôt* or *ăšērîm*. Such references (to the stone monument of Gilgal, Joshua 4; the stone and the oak at Shechem, Joshua 24; the oak at Ophrah, Judges 6; the *'eben-hā'āzer*, 1 Sam 7:12) all give the impression that Dtr is attempting to preserve traditions which revered certain trees and stone monuments while at the same time purging them of any connection to *maṣṣēbôt* or *ăšērîm* which might have been considered to be of questionable religious character. The only alternative to this explanation is that Dtr did not consider the stone monuments or landmark trees of which it approved to be the equivalent of *ăšērîm* and *maṣṣēbôt*, but rather some other types of objects.

The juxtaposition that Judges 6 sets up between the J-type YHWHistic oak/altar combination at Ophrah and the *ăšērāh*/ba'alistic altar combination in the pericope that follows implies that Dtr is making a distinction between traditions which are acceptable and those which are forbidden. The same might be said of the covert contrast between Joshua 24 and Judges 9. Both involve the stone monument and oak at Shechem: the former being a legitimate use of tree and stone, and the latter being illegitimate (a point driven home by Jotham's parable).

Beginning in 1 Samuel, *bāmôt* are portrayed as acceptable to Dtr, an evaluation, however, which ends with the building of the Temple. The combination of *bāmôt* with *ăšērîm* and *maṣṣēbôt* which occurs in Kings makes it appear that Dtr considered the latter two to be accoutrements of the *bāmôt*. This grouping of cultic items in Kings is also the most likely source for the projection of this complex onto the whole of the biblical witness to *bāmôt* by modern scholars.[52] In fact, this grouping tendency is by

---

[52]See the Introduction (pp. 8-9) for examples of this view.

no means representative, even of Dtr's views taken as a whole, much less those of the entire text. Even within Kings, *bāmôt* could be dedicated to YHWH or to other gods, but after the erection of the Temple in Jerusalem, even *bāmôt* dedicated to YHWH were considered illegitimate. During Josiah's reform, however, a distinction seems to have been made between *bāmôt* dedicated to YHWH and those dedicated to other gods, with the clergy of the YHWHistic *bāmôt* being spared and rehabilitated somewhat, while the priests of *bāmôt* in the north, and those of non-YHWHistic *bāmôt* in the south were slaughtered.

Mizbəḥôt, which are portrayed by Dtr as accoutrements both of illegitimate and of legitimate worship, are condemned if located anywhere other than in Jerusalem inside YHWH's Temple, once that Temple has been constructed. The only exception to this rule is the altar Elijah builds on Mt. Carmel, and the YHWHistic altars about which he laments.

The use of cultic statuary is summarily disapproved of by Dtr in both the north and the south and in both YHWHistic and non-YHWHistic contexts, because this practice resembles the pagan worship of gods other than YHWH. Dtr describes the use of cultic statuary as a primary feature of the religion of the foreign cultures surrounding Israel (Deut 29:16 [Eng 29:17]), and introduces a formulaic expression describing foreign gods as "gods of wood and stone" whose worship leads to exile for the worshiper (Deut 4:28; 28:36, 64; 29:16 [Eng 29:17]). In fact, it is this prohibition of the use of cultic statuary with which Dtr frames Deuteronomy in an effort to drive home its belief that it was the gradual abandonment of YHWH for the worship of other gods that caused the exile of both Israel and Judah. The only items usually thought of types of cultic statuary on whose use Dtr preserves conflicting evaluations are *tərāpîm*. Michal's possession of them is not condemned (1 Sam 19:13-16), but Micah, in Judges 17–18, appears to use his in conjunction with condemned items, *pəsîlîm* and *massēkôt*. Dtr's view of Micah's collection of cultic items remains unclear, however, in that he also possesses an ephod which is normally an approved item. Given this, *tərāpîm* might also be approved by Dtr.

CONCLUSIONS

With regard to cultic items, certain distinctions do appear between the core of D and the later Deuteronomistic history. D does not mention *bāmôt*, which Dtr features and assesses positively prior to the Temple's construction but later condemns. D prohibits Israelite use of *massēbôt* (16:21-22), but Dtr mentions at least one such monument without negative comment (2 Sam 18:18). Similarly, D prohibits the planting of trees next to YHWHistic altars (Deut 16:21) while Dtr portrays such trees as acceptable (Judges 6) as does J. D stresses cultic centralization even prior to the construction of the Temple, while Dtr preserves traditions of multiple altars prior to the Temple and even some which existed after its construction (1 Kings 18). Both D and Dtr share an appreciation for *mizbəḥôt* but only D shows any concern for the construction techniques preferred by the Covenant Code (Exod 20:25; Deut 27:5-6). While Dtr depicts unworked field stones being used as altars (1 Sam 6:14-15; 14:33-35; 1 Kgs 1:9), Dtr also allows Ahaz's altar constructed on the model of a Syrian altar to be installed in the Temple without negative comment.

There are also some clear similarities between D and Dtr. Both include stories of revered stone monuments which are not referred to as *maṣṣēbôt*; and both share a central objection to cultic statuary, even though D uses only the traditional terms for them (*pəsîlîm* and *massēkôt*) while Dtr adds additional terms and phrases including *ăṣabbîm*, *gillûlîm*, and "gods of wood and stone."

The data from D and Dtr drive home the point that the theory of a particular type of monolithic normative YHWHism based on these sources does not withstand close scrutiny. It is generally accepted that one of Dtr's main concerns is cultic centralization. A close reading of the data, however, demonstrates that prior to the Temple's construction this was a non-issue for Dtr, and even after the Temple's construction the Elijah material is exempted from this concern. Dtr also preserves conflicting references to *maṣṣēbôt*, condemning most, but excusing Absalom's. Even Dtr's views on the installation of foreign cult objects in the Temple is not totally clear. Most who do this are clearly condemned, but Ahaz, who installs his own altar of Damascene design does so without comment from Dtr. Dtr even preserves views of *bāmôt*, *ăšērîm*, and *tərāpîm* which imply that they were seen as YHWHistic by some Israelites. Ultimately these data reveal Dtr's own witness to the fact that accepted YHWHistic worship in pre-exilic Israel took many forms, some of which run counter to modern reconstructions of what constituted "normative YHWHism."

Chapter Three
The Chronicler: Chronicles, Ezra, and Nehemiah

In chapter two, certain passages from the Chronicler were discussed along with those passages from the books of Samuel and Kings to which they are parallel. This chapter will devote its discussion to those passages in which the Chronicler presents material not found in Samuel and Kings. It is the assumption of this study that the works of Ezra and Nehemiah are integrally related to the books of Chronicles. Given the relatively small amount of data regarding cultic items in Ezra and Nehemiah, however, the current study will not attempt to contribute to the debate concerning whether these three books are actually the work of a single hand.

CHRONICLES

bāmôt: 1 Chr 16:39; 21:29; 2 Chr 1:3, 13; 11:15; 14:2, 4; 15:17 (= 1 Kgs 15: 13-14); 17:6; 20:33 (= 1 Kgs 22:43); 21:11; 28:4, 25; 31:1; 32:12 (= 2 Kgs 18:22); 33:3 (= 2 Kgs 21:3), 17, 19; 34:3 (= 2 Kgs 23:4)

The most interesting differences between the accounts of the Chronicler and those of Dtr, with regard to cultic items, occur in the passages concerning of the *bāmāh* at Gibeon. Apparently, it was unacceptable to the Chronicler for Solomon simply to go to Gibeon and sacrifice, unless there was an undeniably legitimate reason for him to have done so. In addressing this problem, Chronicles adopts a view that solves two questions at once, namely, "Why did Solomon go to Gibeon?" and "What happened to the Tabernacle?" Chronicles states that David left the Tabernacle at Gibeon under the cultically acceptable care of Zadok when he moved the Ark of the Covenant to Jerusalem (1 Chr 16:39-40; 21:29; 2 Chr 1:3, 13). These statements not only incorporate traditions concerning the Tabernacle into the flow of monarchic history, they also legitimate Solomon's use of the *bāmāh* at Gibeon.

Some variations in Chronicles on the Dtr accounts of *bāmôt* erected during the divided monarchy are relatively minor. 2 Chr 11:15 adds the detail of so-called "goat demons" being worshipped on the *bāmôt* of the northern kingdom in addition to the calves worshipped at Bethel. Other variations concerning *bāmôt*, however, can be seen in dual evaluations of particular kings which Chronicles appears to be trying to balance. For instance, in evaluating Asa, 2 Chr 14:2-4 states that he removed *ăšērîm*, *bāmôt*, *maṣṣēbôt*, *mizbəḥôt nēkār*, and *ḥammānîm*. This positive evaluation of Asa is lacking from Kings, and is, in fact, contradicted by Kings' assessment of Asa quoted by the Chronicler in 2 Chr 15:17 (= 1 Kgs 15:13). This assessment merely credits Asa with the destruction of his mother's statue of ʾAsherah, while stating that he left the *bāmôt* standing. 2 Chr 14:2-4, as well as 2 Chr 11:15, are also good examples of a trend that will recur throughout the work, namely, the Chronicler tends to expand lists that occur in Kings, either by adding items of cultic paraphernalia to the lists, or by adding adjectives in order to clarify items, such as the *mizbəḥôt* above which are specifically identified as "foreign." References to *ḥammānîm* are frequently added in Chronicles (perhaps as an expansion on the image of incense burning) whereas they appear not at all in Kings.

Similar to the account of Asa, the Chronicler's account of Jehoshaphat contains contradictions concerning *bāmôt*. 2 Chr 17:6 states that Jehoshaphat had the *ăšērîm* and the *bāmôt* torn down throughout Judah and 2 Chr 19:3 again credits him with the destruction of *ăšērîm*. 2 Chr 20:33, however, repeats the Kings assessment of Jehoshaphat (1 Kgs 22:43) which simply states that he left the *bāmôt* intact during his reign. Conversely, Chronicles credits Jehoram of Judah with the building of *bāmôt*, a detail that Kings does not mention (2 Chr 21:11). 2 Chr 28:24-25 also credits Ahaz with erecting *mizbəḥôt* all over Jerusalem and *bāmôt* in every city of Judah on which to burn incense to foreign gods. 2 Chr 28:2-4, however, repeats the only assessment of Ahaz that exists in Kings (2 Kgs 16:2-4), crediting Ahaz not with building *bāmôt*, but simply using *bāmôt* that already existed.[1]

Perhaps the most striking comment in the Chronicler concerning *bāmôt*, however, occurs in the description of the reign of Manasseh (2 Chr 33:1-20). Chronicles adds to the assessment of Manasseh which it quotes from Kings (2 Chr 33:3-9 = 2 Kgs 21:3-9) only the fact that the tophet where Manasseh sacrificed his children was in the valley of Ben Hinnom, and deletes only the passing reference which Kings makes to Ahab of Israel. However, Chronicles expands the Kings account concerning Manasseh by stating that the notorious king repented of his evil youth and reformed himself later in life (2 Chr 33:10-17). 2 Chr 33:15-17 states that Manasseh

---

[1] Other details that the Chronicler adds to this assessment of Ahaz are that the tophet at which he sacrificed his children was in the valley of Ben Hinnom, and the images he made were images of "the Baʿals."

did away with the altars he had made, repaired the altar of YHWH, and discarded the image (*semel*, presumably of ʾAsherah, though this is not stated) which he had put up in the Temple, and that although the people continued to worship at the *bāmôt*, they only went there to worship YHWH. Although its historicity cannot be ascertained, this is the only passage, either in Kings or in Chronicles, that specifically states that *bāmôt* continued to be used to worship YHWH even after the Temple was constructed. In the concluding statement concerning Manasseh, Chronicles recounts his early apostasy by crediting him with building *bāmôt*, and installing *ăšērîm* and *pəsîlîm*, but states that these things were done before he humbled himself.

The only other references to *bāmôt* in Chronicles are part of the accounts of Hezekiah and Josiah's reforms (2 Chr 31:1 = 2 Kgs 18:4, 2 Chr 34:3-7). The accounts of both of these reforms differ in Chronicles from the Kings counterparts. The Chronicler devotes an entire chapter (2 Chronicles 29) and several verses to the reform of Hezekiah, which Kings treats in a single verse (2 Kgs 18:4). Also, while the *ăšērāh* that Hezekiah purges in Kings is singular, the Chronicles version depicts plural *ăšērîm* being destroyed. This may be another of the Chronicler's attempts to clarify issues it considered inexact or incomplete.

In regard to Josiah's reform, the Chronicles version (2 Chr 34:3-7) gives a much shorter account than the Kings version (2 Kgs 23:4-24), but adds several items, *pəsîlîm*, *massēkôt*, *mizbəḥôt* dedicated to "the Baʿals," and *ḥammānîm*, perhaps as a type of shorthand for the details concerning foreign gods and their rituals that it omits. Another unique feature of the Chronicles account is its reduction of the role of Hilkiah in the actual religious reforms. In Kings he carries out the reforming orders of Josiah. In Chronicles he merely accepts collected funds for the renovation of the Temple.

ăšērîm: 2 Chr 14:2; 17:6; 19:3; 24:18; 31:1; 33:3 (= 2 Kgs 21:3), 19; 34:3, 4, 7 (= 2 Kgs 23:3-4)

Aside from the passage relating to Hezekiah's reform mentioned above, there is only one major change in the Chronicler's treatment of *ăšērîm* from that of Kings, dealing with the career of Josiah. Unlike Kings, which portrays Josiah in complimentary terms, 2 Chr 24:18 states that after the death of his priestly mentor Jehoiada, Josiah and the people lapsed and began to employ *ăšērîm* and *ăṣabbîm*. This slight tarnish on the career of Josiah goes hand in hand with the short shrift his reform receives in Chronicles.

Another distinction of the Chronicler, while not a major change from the assessment of *ăšērîm* found in Kings, appears in relation to the Chronicler's attitude toward 'Asherah the goddess. There are two passages related either to her cult object or to cultic statuary of her, in which the Chronicler differs from Kings by attempting to eschew the use of her proper name. 2 Chr 33:7 refers to a statue installed by Manasseh (which 2 Kgs 21:7 calls the *pesel hā ăšērāh*) as the *pesel-hassemel*. In a second reference to that same statue (2 Chr 33:15), for which there is no corresponding passage in Kings, Manasseh is said to remove the *semel* mentioned in 33:7. The only other source to use the term *semel* is Ezekiel. Ezek 8:3-5 uses the term in reference to the "image of jealousy" which he describes standing in the Temple. If this term is, in fact, borrowed from Ezekiel, the implication is that the author of Chronicles believed Ezek 8:3-5 to be references to a statue of 'Asherah.

maṣṣēbôt: 2 Chr 14:2; 31:1

Chronicles mentions *maṣṣēbôt* only as items destroyed by Asa (2 Chr 14:2) and Hezekiah (2 Chr 31:1) respectively. While both these purges are mentioned along with the destruction of *bāmôt*, *ăšērîm*, and *mizbəḥôt*, it is not clear that these items were viewed as parts a single complex.

mizbəḥôt: 1 Chr 6:34 [Eng 6:49]; 16:39, 40; 21:18, 22, 26, 29 (= 2 Sam
        24:18-25); 22:1; 28:18; 2 Chr 1:5, 6; 4:1, 4:19 (= 1 Kgs 7:48);
        5:12; 6:12 (= 1 Kgs 8:22), 22 (= 1 Kgs 8:31); 7:7 (= 1 Kgs
        8:54), 9; 8:12 (= 1 Kgs 8:64); 14:2; 15:8; 23:10 (= 2 Kgs
        11:11), 17 (= 2 Kgs 11:18); 26:16, 19; 28:24; 29:18, 19, 21, 22,
        24, 27; 30:14; 31:1; 32:12 (= 2 Kgs 18:22); 33:3 (= 2 Kgs
        21:3), 4, 5, 15, 16; 34:4 (= 2 Kgs 23:5), 5, 7; 35:16

The first mention of *mizbəḥôt* in Chronicles is the assertion that it was Aaron who was granted the right to sacrifice and present incense on the *mizbəḥôt* of YHWH (1 Chr 6:34 [Eng 6:49]). Following this statement, Chronicles goes on to make clear whom it considers responsible for the Temple, its *mizbəḥôt* and all its ritual, namely David and not Solomon. In Chronicles it is David who plans all the aspects of the Temple prior to his death and the passing of the specifications on to Solomon.[2] The Chronicler

---

[2]For Chronicles's view of David and Solomon concerning the *mizbəḥôt* of YHWH's Temple, see 1 Chr 21:18-26; 22:1; 28:18; 2 Chr 4:1; 5:12; 7:7, 9; 8:12. For an excellent treatment of the Chronicler's program concerning David and the Temple, see Carol L. Meyers, "David as Temple Builder," in *Ancient Israelite Religion: Essays in Honor of Frank Moore Cross* (ed. Patrick D. Miller, Paul D. Hanson, S. Dean McBride;

has strict notions concerning the purity of YHWH's altar, depicting Uzziah being struck with leprosy for daring to approach the altar with incense (2 Chr 26:16-19).

The Chronicler also devotes the entirety of 2 Chronicles 29 to Hezekiah's cleansing of the Temple and its altars. In the material unique to Chronicles, the only items of cultic paraphernalia besides the *mizbəḥôt* of YHWH that are mentioned with regard Hezekiah's reform, are foreign *mizbəḥôt* and *ḥammānîm*, which the people destroy in preparation for the Passover celebration instituted by Hezekiah (2 Chr 30:14).[3] In addition to the altars mentioned in the passages above, the only other *mizbəḥôt* mentioned by the Chronicler are those which Ahaz erected all over Jerusalem (2 Chr 28:24), and those purged from the countryside during Josiah's reform (2 Chr 34:4, 5, 7). Oddly, Kings includes a lengthy description of Ahaz's construction of a Damascene altar, but Chronicles does not. It merely states that Ahaz worshipped the gods of Damascus (2 Chr 28:22-23).

Cultic Statuary

ăṣabbîm: 1 Chr 10:9 (= 1 Sam 31:9); 2 Chr 24:18

ĕlîlîm: 1 Chr 16:26 (= Ps 96:5)

massēkôt: 2 Chr 28:2 (= 2 Kgs 16:4); 34:3, 4 (= 2 Kgs 23:5), 7

pəsîlîm: 2 Chr 33:22 (= 2 Kgs 21:21); 34:3, 4 (= 2 Kgs 23:5), 7

ṣelem: 2 Chr 23:17 (= 2 Kgs 11:18)

semel: 2 Chr 33:7 (= 2 Kgs 21:7), 15

Quoting 1 Sam 31:9, 1 Chr 10:9 refers to the gods of the Philistines as *ăṣabbîm*. The term *ăṣabbîm* also occurs in 2 Chr 24:18 in the negative verse added by the Chronicler to its assessment of the reign of Josiah.

Philadelphia: Fortress, 1987) 357-76.

[3]Kings reveals no knowledge of this Passover celebration of Hezekiah, crediting only Josiah with such an observance (2 Kgs 23:21-22). Chronicles also retains in its account of Josiah's Passover celebration the Deuteronomic sentence which states that "No Passover like [Josiah's] had been kept in Israel since the days of the prophet Samuel; none of the kings of Israel had kept such a Passover as was kept by Josiah . . . " (2 Chr 35:16-19).

Quoting Psalm 96:5, 1 Chr 16:26 refers to the gods of the nations as *ĕlîlîm*. Quoting 2 Kgs 11:18, 2 Chr 23:17 refers to the idols in Baʿal's temple in Jerusalem as *ṣəlāmîm*. In a slight variation of 2 Kgs 21:21, 2 Chr 33:22 refers to the idols worshipped by Amon as *pəsîlîm* instead of *gillûlîm*. In a slight variation of 2 Kgs 16:4, 2 Chr 28:2 identifies the *massēkôt* used by Ahaz as *massēkôt* of Baʿal. The only designation for cultic statuary in Chronicles not found in Kings is the term *semel* (2 Chr 33:7, 15), which may, in fact, be borrowed from Ezek 8:3-5. In addition to these references, the Chronicler adds the terms *massēkôt*, *pəsîlîm*, and *ḥammānîm* to his account of Josiah's reform while the use of these terms is lacking in the Kings account (2 Chr 34:3, 4, 7).

EZRA AND NEHEMIAH

bāmôt: not mentioned

ăšērîm: not mentioned

maṣṣēbôt: not mentioned

mizbəḥôt: Ezra 3:2, 3; Neh 10:35 [Eng 10:34]
    Neither Ezra nor Nehemiah mentions *ăšērîm*, *bāmôt*, or *maṣṣēbôt*, though both of them discuss the repair of YHWH's *mizbēᵃḥ*, and the reinstitution of the sacrificial cult (Ezra 3:2-3, Neh 10:35 [Eng 10:34]).

Cultic statuary

massēkôt: Neh 9:18
    In Ezra's speech found in Nehemiah 9, in which the great acts of God and the sins of the people are recounted, the only cultic object which is mentioned in relation to the people's sin is the calf *massēkāh* of Sinai (9:18). In terms of sinful actions engaged in by Israel, and whose punishment was the exile, only the killing of prophets and the committing of generalized blasphemy are mentioned (9:26). No other cultic violations or items appear.

CONCLUSIONS
    Aside from the addition of *ḥammānîm*, *pəsîlîm*, *massēkôt*, and clarifying comments concerning the deity to which certain *mizbəḥôt* were dedicated, the Chronicler's grouping of cultic items has remained virtually

the same as that of Kings. Even the Chronicler's only reference to the *ʿēṣ raʿănān* complex mentioned so frequently by other authors is a quote from Kings (2 Chr 28:4 = 2 Kgs 16:4). Although sharing with Kings its negative assessment of *bāmôt*, Chronicles twice elaborates on Kings passages on the use of the use of *bāmôt*, first with the explanation of the presence of the Tabernacle at Gibeon when Solomon went there (2 Chr 1:3), and second with the statement that the people in Manasseh's time used *bāmôt* only in the proper worship of YHWH (2 Chr 33:17). Chronicles also shares with Kings a negative assessment of *ʾăšērîm* but in this case goes even farther than Dtr in eschewing the proper name of the goddess ʾAsherah in passages where it is used in Kings.

Chronicles mentions *maṣṣēbôt* only twice, crediting Asa and Hezekiah with their destruction. Chronicles credits the design and ritual planning of YHWH's *mizbəḥôt* to David, while agreeing with Kings that it was actually Solomon who had them built. Foreign *mizbəḥôt* appear in much the same contexts in Chronicles as they do in Kings, with the exception of Ahaz's Damascene altar, which Chronicles fails to mention. Finally, Chronicles includes only a few added references to *pəsîlîm* and *massēkôt*, which are added, along with *ḥammānîm*, in the manner of a cultic laundry list, to the items purged in the reforms of Josiah.[4] By not dealing with the history of the northern kingdom, Chronicles forfeited many of the occasions afforded the books of Kings to express opinions concerning cultic statuary.

Ezra and Nehemiah make only the most cursory comments concerning cultic paraphernalia which simply echo the views already expressed in Chronicles. YHWH's altar in the Temple at Jerusalem is approved of and *massēkôt* are disapproved of. No other cultic items are mentioned. Because Ezra and Nehemiah deal with a different era in Israel's history than does the Chronicler, most of the cultic matters with which Chronicles deals are not mentioned in Ezra and Nehemiah. It is possible, however, that the mention of the calf at Sinai and the general blasphemy referred to in Nehemiah 9 are meant as a shorthand for all the cultic violations of Israel's past.

Similarities between Dtr and the Chronicler on the subject of cultic matters can be attributed, at least in part, to the fact that both share a concern for cultic centralization. Both seek to make a virtue out of what

---

[4]Chronicles is not the only source that provides lengthy lists of cultic terminology. See the "Postscript" at the end of chapter one (pp. 41-43), for a discussion of Israel Knohl's theory on H's tendency to expand cultic terminology in comparison with P.

was, most probably, a necessity for both communities. Judah was essentially confined to Jerusalem and its environs both in the last days of the southern kingdom and in the first days of the Restoration.

Those points at which the Chronicler differs greatly from Dtr are the result of the Chronicler's desire to portray the era of Judah's first monarchy as a type of golden age. This is best seen in the passages regarding *bāmôt*, in which the *bāmāh* at Gibeon is only used because the Tabernacle is there, and those *bāmôt* admittedly in use after the construction of the Temple are used *only* to worship YHWH. In spite of a tendency to justify certain characters and their actions which Dtr condemns (such as Manasseh), the Chronicler shares most of the views of Dtr regarding cultic items.

Chapter Four
The Prophets and Remaining Writings

Within this chapter, the books of the prophets are arranged roughly according to a presumed date of composition. Isaiah and Zechariah, books for which there is a widely recognized division into sections from different time periods, have been divided with the sections placed in the larger chronological ordering. Following the books of the prophets are discussions of the three remaining biblical books from the Writings (Psalms, Job, and Lamentations) which mention the items of interest to this study.

AMOS

bāmôt: 7:9[1]

In Amos, only 7:9 mentions cultic *bāmôt*. This verse predicts the destruction of the "high places of Isaac" (*bāmôt yiṣḥāq*), paralleling them with the "sanctuaries of Israel" (*miqdəšê yiśrā'ēl*).[2] The overall emphasis of verse 7:9, however, is a judgment oracle against the northern kingdom. 7:9 reads:

> The *bāmôt* of Isaac will be destroyed and the sanctuaries of Israel will be laid waste, and I will rise up against the House of Jeroboam with a sword.

As will be seen with regard to many judgment oracles throughout the prophetic material, it is not required that one read disapproval of a particular cultic item into the views of a prophet because destruction of that cultic item is mentioned as part of a judgment oracle. Shalom Paul argues that one should not assume, on the basis of Amos 7:9, that Amos views *bāmôt* as illegitimate cultic installations.[3] Following Sellin, Paul recounts that *bāmôt* were, in some cases, perfectly acceptable cultic installations. This is the view of Dtr regarding *bāmôt* which existed prior to the construction of the

---

[1]In addition to this one reference to *bāmôt*, Amos 4:13 uses the archaic cultic term *bāmôtê* meaning "heights." The relation between the term *bāmôt* and *bāmôtê* will be discussed in chapter five (pp. 127-29).

[2]The meaning of the parallelism between *bāmôt* and *miqdaš* in 7:9 will be discussed in chapter five (pp. 145-48).

[3]*Amos: A Commentary on the Book of Amos* (ed. Frank Moore Cross; Hermeneia; Minneapolis: Augsburg Fortress, 1991) 236.

Temple. Paul goes on to state, however, that in this passage "they represent
. . . the entire religious establishment that Amos time and again censures
and condemns."[4]

It could also be argued, however, that Amos may have held a completely different view of *bāmôt* than the one eventually expressed by Dtr,
considering *bāmôt* to be illegitimate regardless of their relationship to the
Temple in Jerusalem. If it were the case that Amos viewed all *bāmôt* negatively, then calling the cultic centers of Jeroboam's kingdom *bāmôt* might
have been Amos's way of expressing a derogatory sentiment toward these
cultic centers. Unfortunately, given the fact that Amos does not actually discuss *bāmôt*, but only uses the term as part of a judgment oracle against the
cult and royal house of the northern kingdom, it is not possible to say
whether Amos viewed *bāmôt*, in and of themselves, positively or negatively.

ăšērîm: not mentioned

Although *ăšērîm* are not mentioned by Amos, 8:14 makes an interesting statement which may refer to the "*ăšērāh* which stood in Samaria,"
possibly a statue or cult center for the goddess 'Asherah (2 Kgs 13:6). 8:14
mentions "those who swear by the 'Guilt of Samaria'" (*'ašmat šōmrôn*). The
word "guilt" here might represent a substitution for the name 'Asherah.[5] It
might also be a substitution for the construct form of the word *ăšērāh*,
referring to the "*ăšērāh* of Samaria" as a cultic installation. One Kuntillet
'Ajrud inscription seems to represent a similar practice to "swearing by the
'ašmat šōmrôn" because it invokes a blessing "by YHWH *šōmrôn* and his
ăšērāh" (*lyhwh šmrn wl'šrth*).[6] It is also possible, however, that there was
an actual goddess named 'Ašimah mentioned here in Amos 8:14 as well as

---

[4]Paul, *Amos*, 236. Hans Walter Wolff agrees that this passage is an oracle against
the "cult and court circles" of the north, but states that the *bāmôt* in this passage refer to
the many *bāmôt* scattered through the countryside in the northern kingdom, and that the
"sanctuaries" mentioned are the larger state shrines of the north, presumably Dan and
Bethel (Wolff, *Joel and Amos: A Commentary on the Books of Joel and Amos* [tr.
Waldemar Janzen, S. Dean McBride, and Charles A. Muenchow; ed. S. Dean McBride;
Hermeneia; Philadelphia: Fortress, 1977] 301).

[5]This interpretation is mentioned, though not supported, by Francis Andersen and
David Noel Freedman, *Amos: A New Translation with Introduction and Comentary* (AB
24A; Garden City, N.Y.: Doubleday, 1989) 828-29.

[6]Scholarly debate concerning whether this inscription and others like it are
actually speaking of the goddess 'Asherah, or the cultic object known as an *ăšērāh* will
be discussed chapter six (pp. 165-68).

in 2 Kgs 17:30. This is the view of many commentators,[7] who support their reading with references to a deity אשמביתאל found at Elephantine.[8] In short, it is not essential to read an allusion to an *ăšērāh* in Amos 8:14, even though there is some evidence to suggest that one may be present.

maṣṣēbôt: not mentioned

Amos does not mention *maṣṣēbôt*; however, there are references to pilgrimages to Gilgal (4:4; 5:5), the site of Joshua's stone monuments, which the prophet describes as sinful (4:4). The nature of this sin is not directly explained in the text, and has been variously interpreted by commentators. Andersen and Freedman argue that what these passages describe are national festivals celebrating military victories over Israel's enemies. As such, they argue that for Amos these festivals represented,

> the use of religion to legitimate militarism, to equate victory with divine blessing, to use such tokens of divine approval as evidence to contradict the argument that oppression of the poor has made them forfeit the favor of heaven.[9]

Paul voices a similar view, stating that what Amos objected to was the fact that the north saw worship and ritual as ends in and of themselves, instead of means for producing justice and righteousness.[10] There is little to suggest, however, that the prophet's dislike for these pilgrimages to Gilgal had anything to do with an aversion to the stone monuments located there. Because of this, nothing concerning Amos's possible views of *maṣṣēbôt* can be derived from these contexts.

mizbəḥôt: 2:6-8; 3:14; 9:1

Amos specifically mentions *mizbəḥôt* in three passages. 2:6-8 lists several transgressions of Israel, one of which is that "they lay themselves down beside every altar on garments taken in pledge" (2:8). This passage refers to those who engaged in the extraordinary religious practice of reclining beside altars (possibly all night), while simultaneously showing dis-

---

[7]Andersen and Freedman, *Amos*, 829; Paul, *Amos*, 269-70. See Paul's discussion for other scholars who have expressed this view.

[8]For this evidence, Paul cites the works of B. Porten, *Archives from Elephantine: The Life of an Ancient Jewish Military Colony* (Berkeley and Los Angeles: University of California Press, 1986) 160-73; and idem, "The Religion of the Jews of Elephantine in Light of the Hermopolis Papyri," *JNES* 28 (1969) 118-21 (Paul, *Amos*, 269 n. 13).

[9]*Amos*, 434.

[10]*Amos*, 139.

regard for the rights of the poor, in this case, the right to have garments taken as collateral returned before nightfall (Exod 22:26).[11] Amos 3:14 predicts the destruction of Bethel's altar by the cutting off of the altar's horns. Amos 9:1 describes a vision of YHWH standing beside an altar and delivering an oracle of doom upon Israel.[12]

In all of these passages, Amos's views of the altars themselves can be said to be neutral. It is the use to which they are put, or their association with larger cultic issues which attracts the attention of the prophet. The altar at Bethel, for instance, is not going to be destroyed because it is evil in and of itself, but because it is part of the Bethel cultus of which the prophet disapproves. Similarly, the fact that persons use altars to perform extraordinary rituals while they neglect their ordinary covenant obligations does not make the altars suspect. There is nothing to suggest that Amos objects to the mere existence of the altars of the northern kingdom. Amos's quarrel with the north appears to center on their neglect of social justice, not on a concern for cultic centralization.

Cultic statuary

ṣelem: 5:26

Aside from a reference to the "god" of Dan (8:14), very little mention of cultic statuary is made in Amos. There are a few general references to Bethel, but they lack specific mention of any cultic statuary found there (3:14; 4:4; 5:5, 6; 8:14). Only Amos 5:26, makes a specific reference, describing a procession of manufactured images (*ṣəlāmîm*) of two astral deities, Sakkuth and Kiyyun, who were venerated by the citizens of the northern kingdom.[13]

---

[11]Paul notes that because verse 7b reads "father and son go in to the same girl, so that my holy name is profaned," several scholars have sought to connect verses 7b and 8a in such a way that cultic prostitution is implied (see his discussion of this interpretation, *Amos*, 81). This reading is uncalled for, however. Amos may have considered a father and son having sex with the same woman, even outside of marriage, to be an example of "uncovering the nakedness" of one's son or father as prohibited by Lev 18:7-8, and 15-16. Thus, he would need no additional "cultic" overtones to view the behavior as unacceptable. Wolff describes this passage as an oracle against "the abuse of maidens," noting that the girl in the passage is *not* portrayed as a temple prostitute (Wolff, *Joel and Amos*, 166-67).

[12]Although the MT of Amos 9:1 can read "I saw YHWH standing *on* the altar," implying a conflict with Exod 20:26, reading "I saw YHWH standing *beside* the altar" is equally possible. See Paul, *Amos*, 274.

[13]For extra-biblical references to Sakkuth and Kiyyun (or Kaiwan) see Paul,

This reference comes at the end of one of the most famous passages in the book of Amos. 5:21-27 reads:

> I have hated and despised your pilgrimages; and I will not partake[14] of your sacred assemblies. If you offer me burnt offerings, or your grain offerings, I will not accept them. And the peace offerings of your fatlings I will disregard. Take the noise of your songs away from me! I will not listen to your harp songs. But rather let justice roll like water, and righteousness like an eternal stream! Did you offer me sacrifices and grain offerings during the forty years in the wilderness, O house of Israel? [Whereas now], you carry Sikkut your king, and Kiyyun, your image, the Star, your god, all of which you yourselves made; so I will exile you beyond Damascus, saith YHWH, whose name is the God of hosts.

In this passage, the prophet has made the use of cultic statuary to worship gods other than YHWH an afterthought in a list of cultic violations which centers on observance of ritual without a concern for social justice. For Amos this constitutes incomplete obedience to YHWH. Since YHWH is the real God of Hosts, worship of the manufactured hosts of heaven is futile; nor is YHWH a god who can be manipulated by offerings.

Summary

Amos, apparently, had nothing to say concerning *ʾăšērîm* or *maṣṣēbôt*. The prophet appears neutral with regard to *bāmôt* and *mizbəḥôt*. Amos does, however, reject the use of *mizbəḥôt* by people who emphasize the ritual laws over laws related to social justice (2:6-8; 4:4; 5:5; 8:14). This type of rejection also applies to the *bāmôt* of Isaac (7:9), the *massēkāh* implied in the phrase "god of Dan" (8:14), and the images of astral deities mentioned in 5:26. It might be said of Amos that he considered all cultic activity, YHWHistic or otherwise, and all types of cultic paraphernalia equally suspect if the use of them was divorced from the observance of laws related to economic and other forms of social justice within Israel.

HOSEA

bāmôt: 10:8

Hos 10:5-8 includes the prophet's only reference to *bāmôt*. This passage declares that the inhabitants of Samaria will fear on behalf of the "calves of Beth-Aven" (which shall be carried as tribute to the King of Assyria), and that *Bāmôt-ʾĀwen*, the "sin" (*ḥaṭṭaʾt*) of Israel, would be

---

Amos, 195-98.

[14]Literally, "smell," hiphil denominative from רוח.

destroyed and its *mizbəḥôt* overgrown with thorns. Beth-Aven, "House of Trouble" or "Wickedness," was apparently a nickname Hosea used for Bethel,[15] so one can infer that *Bāmôt-ʾĀwen* refers to Bethel as well.

As in the case of Amos, Hosea's views on the legitimacy of *bāmôt* are difficult to discern on the basis of this one reference, which is not actually talking about *bāmôt*, but rather about the center of northern cultic life, Bethel. One could argue that because Bethel is associated with *massēkôt* by Hosea, and the site itself is called the "sin of Israel," that Hosea uses the term *bāmôt* in a derogatory sense here. This is the view of Andersen and Freedman who relate *bāmôt* to the hill-side worship discussed in Hos 4:13. They go on to state:

> What ever the cult at such places, the use of the word [*bāmôt*] in the present chapter, especially in connection with Awen, shows that familiar and reprehensible practices are the target of the prophet's criticism.[16]

There is no real evidence, however, that Hosea connected *bāmôt* with any particularly "familiar and reprehensible practices." This is the only verse which mentions *bāmôt* in the whole of the prophet's work and the only connection made in this passage is to Bethel.

Hosea's main prophetic concern was the departure of the Israelites from the singular worship of YHWH, and there is really no evidence to suggest that *bāmôt*, in and of themselves, signified such a departure for Hosea. It is more likely that it is not *bāmôt*, but Bethel and its molten calf which are being referred to in 10:8 as the cardinal "sin of Israel," namely the abandonment of YHWH. It is not possible to decide from this particular verse what Hosea's actual opinion of *bāmôt* might have been.

ăšērîm: not mentioned

While Hosea does not mention *ăšērîm*, he does describe worship which took place beneath live trees. 4:13 reads, "They sacrifice on the tops of the mountains, and make offerings upon the hills, under oak, poplar, and terebinth, because their shade is good." Moshe Weinfeld believes Hos 4:13 to be the forerunner of the formulaic expression "on every high hill and under every green tree (*ʿēṣ raʿănān*)," which is used in Dtr and elsewhere to describe the location of heterodox rituals (Deut 12:2; 1 Kgs 14:23; 2 Kgs

---

[15]4:15; 5:8; 10:5.

[16]Frances Andersen and David Noel Freedman, *Hosea: A New Translation with Introduction and Commentary* (AB 24; Garden City, N.Y.: Doubleday, 1980) 559.

16:4; 17:10; Jer 2:20; 3:6, 13; 17:2; Ezek 6:13; Isa 57:5).[17] This description of outdoor worship will be discussed in chapter six; however, it is not possible to make a direct connection between this passage and any opinion Hosea might have had about *ăšērîm*.[18]

maṣṣēbôt: 3:4; 10:1, 2

Hosea discusses *maṣṣēbôt* in two contexts. 3:1-5 depicts the prophet purchasing the services of his wife who has become an adulteress. He pays her a fee and instructs her to go without the company of any man including himself for a certain period of time. Hos 3:3-4 reads:

> And I said to her, "For many days you will remain with me; you will not be unfaithful, you will not belong to any man, nor I to you." For the Israelites shall remain many days without king or prince, without sacrifice or *maṣṣēbāh*, and without ephod or *tərāpîm*.

A surface reading of this passage implies that *maṣṣēbôt* are items of a type with the acceptable items listed such as "kings" and "sacrifices" which the nation will be forced to do without as YHWH's punishment for the worship of other gods. Seen this way, it appears that *maṣṣēbôt* are approved by Hosea.

Carl Graesser and others, however, have argued that Hosea is listing pairs of both licit and illicit items which will be withheld from Israel just as both licit and illicit sexual relations will be withheld from the prophet's wife.[19] While it is easy to see how "ephod and *tərāpîm*" and "sacrifice and

---

[17]*Deuteronomy*, 322, 366-367. See also William L. Holladay, "'On Every High Hill and Under Every Green Tree'" (*VT* 11 [1961] 170-76). In all but three of the verses mentioned above (Jer 2:20; 3:6, 3:13), items under discussion in this study are specifically mentioned: *bāmôt* (1 Kgs 14:23; 2 Kgs 16:4; Ezek 6:13), *ăšērîm* (Deut 12:2; 1 Kgs 14:23; 2 Kgs 17:10; Jer 17:2), *maṣṣēbôt* (Deut 12:2; 1 Kgs 14:23; 2 Kgs 17:10), *mizbəhôt* (Deut 12:2; Jer 17:2; Ezek 6:13) and cultic statuary (*pəsîlîm*, Deut 12:2; *gillûlîm*, Ezek 6:13). Jeremiah may also be making oblique references to cultic statuary in 3:9-10 and 13, just as Second Isaiah may be making reference to *hammānîm* in 57:5.

[18]As noted above (p. 92), Andersen and Freedman do attempt to draw connections between this verse and *bāmôt* in their discussion of Hos 10:8 (*Hosea*, 559). They do not, however, mention *ăšērîm* or *bāmôt* in their discussion of 4:13 (*Hosea*, 368).

[19]"Studies in *maṣṣēbôt*," 251. Graesser lists R. Brinker (*The Influence of Sanctuaries in Early Israel* [Manchester: Manchester University Press, 1946] 32) and Peter Ackroyd ("Hosea," *Peake's Commentary on the Bible* [London: Thomas Nelson and Sons, 1962] 607) as those who preceded him in this interpretation. This interpretation also appears in Andersen and Freedman, *Hosea*, 303-6.

maṣṣēbāh" might be considered pairs in which the first item is acceptable and the second unacceptable, the pattern does not hold as well for "king and prince" (*śār*).[20]

There are two equally possible interpretations for Hos 3:1-5. Either the prophet accepted *maṣṣēbôt* as legitimate cultic emblems and thus described their destruction as a form of punishment for cultic transgression, or the prophet viewed *maṣṣēbôt* as examples of cultic transgression on the part of Israel, parallel to the illegitimate behavior of the prophet's wife. If this second statement is true, however, it should also be argued that the *maṣṣēbôt* to which Hosea refers are non-YHWHistic. For Hosea, the metaphor of marital unfaithfulness is typically applied to Israelite unfaithfulness to its exclusive covenant relationship with YHWH. It is a virtual certainty, given his major emphasis on faithfulness to YHWH, that Hosea would disapprove of *maṣṣēbôt* dedicated to other gods. This would not prove, however, that all *maṣṣēbôt* were objectionable to the prophet.

The second passage from Hosea which deals with *maṣṣēbôt* is Hos 10:1-2. This passage portrays Israel increasing its number of *mizbəḥôt* and *maṣṣēbôt* as their prosperity increases. The passage reads:

> Israel is like a rich vine that produces its fruit. Just as the quantity of his fruit increases, he increases the quantity of his *mizbəḥôt*. Just as his country improves, the *maṣṣēbôt* improve. Their heart is divided;[21] now they will be considered guilty. He will break down their *mizbəḥôt* and destroy their *maṣṣēbôt*.

There is a double entendre in verse one in that the term describing the vine usually translated as "rich or luxuriant" (בּוֹקֵק) is identical to a term formed off the root בקק meaning "to be depleted."[22] Thus, Israel is likened to a vine which, though productive, constantly uses up or depletes its resources and wastes its gains. In what amounts to a type of "futility curse," Israel may produce much fruit, but continually multiplies altars on which to offer it, and makes many societal improvements, all the while learning also how to make bigger and better *maṣṣēbôt*. Given this picture, YHWH decides that

---

[20]As will be noted in chapter eleven (p. 330), Targum Jonathan of Hosea expands and paraphrases this verse so that it contrasts Jerusalem and Samaria. It reads: "For the people of Israel shall dwell many days with no king *from the house of David and with no one to exercise authority over Israel, no one to offer an acceptable* sacrifice *in Jerusalem*, and without cult pillar *in Samaria*, and without ephod or *interpreters*." See Sperber, *Bible in Aramaic*, 3.390.

[21]Reading חָלַק rather than חָלָק.

[22]BDB 132. For examples of בקק meaning "empty" or "laid waste," see Isa 19:3; 24:1, 3; Nah 2:3; Jer 51:2.

Israel's heart is divided, between expansion and waste, blindly creating excess without thought to its use. The more they grow, the smaller they become in YHWH's eyes.

While this indictment against the northern kingdom implies that there is something futile and pointless in Israel's multiplication of *mizbəḥôt* and *maṣṣēbôt*, it does not state that the items themselves were illegitimate. The prophet may, however, mean to imply that these *mizbəḥôt* and *maṣṣēbôt* were not YHWHistic, so that for every national improvement made by Israel a counterbalancing cultic violation occurred so that as they became stronger, they also became more corrupt.[23] While objection to cultic relations with other gods is certainly a prime concern of Hosea, this passage does not prove that the prophet saw all *maṣṣēbôt*, and certainly not all *mizbəḥôt*, as illegitimate objects in and of themselves.

Finally, in a manner similar to Amos's condemnation of pilgrimage to Gilgal, Hos 9:15 states: "Every evil of theirs began at Gilgal; there I came to hate them." While this passage may imply a rejection of the stone monument at Gilgal, it might also simply refer to the pilgrimage festivals that are thought to have been established there.[24]

mizbəḥôt: 4:19; 8:11; 10:1, 2, 8; 12:12 [Eng 12:11]

As noted above, Hos 10:1-2 is a judgment oracle which mentions *mizbəḥôt* along with *maṣṣēbôt* as items which YHWH will destroy out of dissatisfaction with the north. In another judgment oracle, 10:8 decrees that the altar of *Bāmôt-ʿĀwen*, meaning Bethel, would be destroyed and subsequently overgrown. 4:19 states that Ephraim shall be put to shame because of his altars. 8:11 expresses a similar sentiment by indicating that "When Ephraim multiplied *mizbəḥôt* to expiate sin, they became to him *mizbəḥôt* for sinning with." Hos 12:12 [E 12:11] states that the *mizbəḥôt* at Gilgal, which are used to sacrifice bulls, will be reduced to piles of stones (*galîm*).

The fact that all of the references to altars in Hosea occur in perjorative contexts raises the question of what the prophet found objectionable about these altars. Hosea 4:17 states that "Ephraim has been joined to idols." This implies that the altars at which the Israelites have been "promis-

---

[23]This is the interpretation favored by Wolff, *Hosea*, 173-74.

[24]For other seeming condemnations of pilgrimage making, see Amos 4:4; 5:4-5; 8:14. The first two of these citations also mention Gilgal and Bethel by name. Hosea also communicates YHWH's general rejection of sacrificial worship directed to him by Israel (6:6; 8:13; 9:4), and "festivals, new moons, sabbaths and appointed festivals," as well as festivals of Baʿal which were attended by Israel (1:11-13).

cuous" (18b) were used to worship gods other than YHWH. Similarly, 8:11 is located in a judgment oracle against the north seeking to make treaty alliances with other nations. Hosea likens this to "hiring lovers" (8:10). Their "multiplication of altars for sin offerings," then, has no value, because of the sin of unfaithfulness inherent in entering into covenants with foreign nations and their gods.[25]

10:1-2 is unclear in its disapproval of Israel's many altars, but 10:8 is best interpreted as a polemic against Bethel and the "image" which was installed there (10:6). Finally, the sacrifice of bulls at Gilgal mentioned in 12:12 may be another reference to a covenant ceremony between Israel and its foreign allies,[26] or as Andersen and Freedman argue, a reference to a ceremony in which gods other than YHWH were worshipped.[27]

As all the verses, with the possible exception of 10:1-2, demonstrate, Hosea's main objection to the altars of the northern Israelites was their use in ceremonies for gods other than YHWH. There is nothing in these contexts to suggest, however, that all altars were illegitimate in the eyes of the prophet. Hosea objects to the use of altars to worship gods other than YHWH. There is no reason to suppose that he objects to the altars themselves.

Cultic statuary

ăṣabbîm: 4:17; 8:4; 13:2; 14:9 [Eng 14:8]

massēkôt: 13:2

pəsîlîm: 11:2

tərāpîm: 3:4

---

[25]Andersen and Freedman (*Hosea*, 509), state that "It is not likely that we have in v 11a a polemic against a multiplicity of altars, in the interest of a policy of one central shrine, although the disenchantment of the prophets with the local shrines had reached the point where centralization of the cult might appear the most logical next move" (*Hosea*, 508).

[26]See Cross (*CMHE*, 266), for references to the Sefirê treaty inscriptions (Sefirê I.A.40), which mandate the sacrifical slaughtering of a bull as part of a treaty ritual.

[27]Andersen and Freedman arrive at this interpretation by reading *āwen* and *šāwʿ* as synonyms for idols. They read, "They were in Gilead with idols (*āwen*), indeed false gods (*šāwʾ*) in Gilgal" (*Hosea*, 594, 618). The NRSV reads "In Gilead there is iniquity, they shall surely come to nothing."

Hosea's overwhelmingly negative opinions concerning the religious behavior of the northern kingdom can be understood best in light of a passage in which the prophet makes indirect reference to Bethel and its cultic statuary. Hos 8:1-6 reads:

> They made kings but not through me; they set up princes, but without my knowledge. With their silver and gold they made *ăṣabbîm* for their own destruction. Your calf is rejected, O Samaria . . . For it is from Israel, an artisan made it; it is not 'Elohim. The calf of Samaria shall be broken to pieces.

Notably, it is *ăṣabbîm*, rather than the more common *pəsîlîm* or *massēkôt*, which Hosea uses most frequently to refer to cultic statuary. Hosea may use *ăṣabbîm* more because, unlike *pəsîlîm* or *massēkôt*, which are sometimes said to be made and used by Israelites, *ăṣabbîm* are almost always connected to a foreign nation, usually the Philistines (1 Sam 31:9 = 1 Chr 10:9; 2 Sam 5:21). 4:17 describes Ephraim as "joined to idols" (*ḥăbûr ăṣabbîm*). 13:2, like 8:1-6, mentions Ephraim's *ăṣabbîm* (this time of silver only), along with calf *massēkôt* which the people kiss. 14:9 [Eng 14:8] asks: "What more has Ephraim to do with *ăṣabbîm*? It is I who answer and look after him. I am like an evergreen cypress; your fruit comes from me."[28] In light of the foreign connotation of *ăṣabbîm*, these passages highlight Hosea's objection to political alliances with other nations and the implicit idolatry that they entail.

The only other direct references to cultic statuary in Hosea are 11:2, which describes Israel "sacrificing (*zbḥ*) to the Ba'alim, and burning incense (*qṭr*) to *pəsîlîm*," and 3:4, which, as mentioned above under *maṣṣēbôt*, links kings and princes, *maṣṣēbôt* and sacrifice, *tərāpîm* and the ephod as items Israel will be deprived of for a time before returning to YHWH and the Davidic monarch.[29]

---

[28]The term translated here "evergreen," is *raʿănān*. God is, therefore, being compared to an *ēṣ raʿănān*. John Day believes that the imagery likening YHWH to a tree in this passage is an anti-*ăšērāh* polemic ("A Case of Inner Scriptural Interpretation: The Dependence of Isaiah XXVI.13-XXVII.11 on Hosea XIII.4-XIV.10 (Eng. 9) and its Relevance to Some Theories of the Redaction of the Isaiah Apocalypse," *JTS* 31 [1980] 314-15).

[29]For oblique references to cultic statuary within Hosea, see the "wood" (*ēṣ*) which is consulted in 4:12a (though this might refer to the divining rods mentioned in 4:12b), "their precious silver things" (*maḥmad ləkaspām*) referred to in 9:6, the "detestable things" (*šiqqûṣîm*) which the Israelites came to resemble through their worship at Ba'al Peor (9:10), and the "work of our hands" mentioned in 14:3.

Summary

Hosea mentions only *mizbǝḥ ôt* of which he disapproves,
predominantly because the northern Israelites use them to perform rituals
for gods other than YHWH. By the same token, Hosea condemns the
north's use of cultic statuary, and condemns Bethel for, among other things,
its installation which incorporated a calf *massēkāh*. Although Hosea refers
to Bethel as *Bāmôt/Bêt-ʾĀwen*, it is unclear if this indicates more of a dislike
for Bethel or for *bāmôt* in general on the part of the prophet. Similarly,
Hosea's views of *maṣṣēbôt* are not clear. They are mentioned twice in judgment oracles, but the prophet's own opinions of them are not stated. Finally,
while Hosea does not discuss *ăšērîm*, it is possible that he does have some
knowledge of them based on 4:13 and possibly 4:19.

MICAH

bāmôt: 1:5; 3:12

Micah uses the archaic poetic term *bāmôtê*, meaning "heights," in a
description of YHWH "treading on the heights of the earth" (Mic 1:3), but
also refers to *bāmôt* as cultic installations (Mic 1:5; 3:12). The MT of Mic
1:5 asks "What is the transgression of Jacob (*pešaʿ yaʿăqōb*)? Is it not
Samaria? And what is the "high-place" of Judah (*bāmôt yǝhûdāh*)? Is it not
Jerusalem?"[30]

This verse portrays the two capital cities of the divided monarchy as
"capital offenders," so to speak, leading their respective nations in religious
corruption, which, in the case of Judah, is represented by *bāmôt*. The primary offense of Samaria, according to this passage, is the use of cultic
statuary. Verses 6-7 predict that Samaria will be transformed "into a ruin in
the open country, a place for planting vineyards . . . " and that her *pǝsîlîm*
and *ăṣabbîm* will be destroyed. In this passage there is an echo of the Dtr's
shorthand for the main cultic offenses of the northern and southern kingdoms repectively, use of cultic statuary and use of *bāmôt*.[31]

Although the ruin of Jerusalem is not discussed in chapter one, Micah
does return to the fate of Jerusalem in chapter three, again predicting the

---

[30]The opaque nature of the parallelism in this verse seems to have created a
problem for the some translators of the LXX, who translate *bāmôt* in Mic 1:5 as "sin,"
ἁμαρτία. This may indicate that the LXX translators did not understand the meaning of
bāmôt in this context and therefore simply chose not to translate it, substituting instead a
word which was considered to be a better parallel for *pešaʿ*. It may also indicate, however,
that the LXX was translating a Hebrew text which read something other than *bāmôt* in
this verse. Other LXX variants for *bāmôt* are discussed in chapter nine (p. 271, n. 33).

[31]See chapter two for the discussion of *bāmôt* in 1 and 2 Kings (pp. 64-68).

transformation of the city into agricultural land, and again using the term *bāmôt* in the indictment against Jerusalem. Mic 3:12 reads "Zion shall be plowed as a field; Jerusalem shall become a heap of ruins, and the mountain of the Temple a 'wooded height' (*bāmôt yā'ar*)." Although the exact meaning intended by the phrase *bāmôt ya'ar* is not apparent,[32] the image is loaded with double entendre. Jerusalem, the center of Judean civilization with its magnificent Temple at its center will be reduced to a rural wasteland with only a "forest *bāmāh*" on its acropolis. Those who could not resist building *bāmôt* will have their crowning religious symbol reduced to one.

This indictment against the major cities of Judah and Israel fits well with the traditional understanding of Micah as a rural prophet who decried the corruption in large urban centers.[33] If it is true, however, that Micah viewed the used the term *bāmôt* as an allusion to the typical cultic violation of the southern kingdom, comparable to the use of cultic statuary in the north, then these passages might constitute a more direct condemnation of *bāmôt* than the mere mention of them in two anti-urban judgment oracles would dictate. It is not certain, however, that Micah is using references to *bāmôt* as a shorthand for Judah's religious corruption. He may be making a play on the idea of *bāmôt* as the primary symbol of cultic corruption in the south, indicating instead that it was the city of Jerusalem itself and the Temple itself which were the true "*bāmôt*," embodying more serious cultic offenses than the use of actual *bāmôt*.

ăšērîm: 5:13 [Eng 5:14]

maṣṣēbôt: 5:12 [Eng 5:13]

Maṣṣēbôt and *ăšērîm* are mentioned, along with *pəsîlîm*, in Mic 5:9-14 [Eng 5:10-15]. This passage announces that before YHWH executes vengeance against the nations, certain things will be purged, apparently from among the Israelites. The passage reads:

It will happen in that day, says YHWH,
I will cut off your horses from your midst,

---

[32]The phrase occurs only here and in the quotation of this verse in Jer 26:18. The LXX translation, ἄλσος δρυμοῦ "grove composed of thickets," will be discussed in chapter nine (pp. 274-75).

[33]For one expression of this view of Micah, see Philip J. King, "Micah," *Jerome Biblical Commentary* (ed. Raymond E. Brown, Joseph A. Fitzmyer, and Roland E. Murphy; Englewood Cliffs, NJ: Prentice-Hall, 1968) 283.

and I will destroy your chariots.
I will cut off the cities of your land,
 and raze all your strongholds.
I will cut off sorceries from your hand,
 and you will have no more diviners.
I will cut off your *pəsîlîm*,
 and your *maṣṣēbôt* from your midst;
You shall no longer bow down to the work of your hands.
I will uproot your *ăšērîm* from your midst.
I will destroy your cities.
I will take vengence in anger and in wrath
 against the nations which do not obey.[34]

In this judgment oracle Micah links *maṣṣēbôt* and *pəsîlîm* together as items made by Israelites which they then bow down and worship. It is not as clear in the reference to *ăšērîm* that Micah has the same view of them. *ăšērîm* may simply be objects caught up in the general destruction on YHWH's day of wrath. As for *maṣṣēbôt* and *pəsîlîm*, however, it appears that Micah views them as objects of idolatrous veneration on the part of the people.

mizbəḥôt: not mentioned
 Although Micah does not use the term *mizbəḥôt*, he, like Amos, issues an indictment against the practice of sacrificial rituals without an equal commitment to social justice (Mic 6:6-8).

Cultic statuary

ăṣabbîm: 1:7

pəsîlîm: 1:7; 5:12 [Eng 5:13]
 Micah uses only two terms for cultic statuary, *pəsîlîm* and *ăṣabbîm*. These two items are linked together in 1:7 as items which shall be purged from Samaria by the wrath of YHWH. The only other direct reference to

---

[34]There is some evidence to suggest that verses 13 and 14 may be later additions. For instance, while the verb *krt*, "to cut," is used at the beginning of each of the four bicola that begin the oracle (9b, 10, 11, 12a), the verb used in 13a to describe the destruction of the *ăšērîm* is *ntš*, "to uproot." While the shift away from the repetition of the verb *krt* may imply that verses 13 and 14 were not originally included in the oracle, it may also simply reveal a poet's practice of choosing expressive variant terminology. The implications of the use of the verb *ntš* with regard to *ăšērîm* will be discussed in chapter six under the discussion of the relationship between *ăšērîm* and live trees (pp. 173-85).

cultic statuary is in 5:12 [Eng 5:13] in which *pəsîlîm* are linked with *maṣṣēbôt* as items which the people worship and which will be purged from among them on the day of YHWH's wrath.

Summary

In 1:5, Micah appears to characterize the internal corruption of both the northern and southern kingdoms with much the same shorthand as does the Deuteronomist. Samaria is represented by the use of cultic statuary, and Jerusalem is said to be the "*bāmôt* of Judah." It is not clear, however, that this passage is truly directed at *bāmôt*. It may be directed obliquely at *bāmôt*, but primarily at urban centers and institutions of which the prophet disapproves. Micah does appear to disapprove of *maṣṣēbôt*, referring to them as manufactured objects which the people worship. *ăšērîm* are mentioned only in one judgment oracle context which does not make it clear that they themselves are the object of YHWH's disfavor. Finally, while *mizbəḥôt* escape condemnation in Micah, the use of even these, implied in descriptions of sacrificial rites, is not wholeheartedly endorsed unless accompanied by a sense of ethical responsibility.

FIRST ISAIAH

This study accepts the widely held opinion that the book of Isaiah exists in three basically discrete sections referred to as First Isaiah (chaps 1-39), Second Isaiah (chaps 40-55), and Third Isaiah (chaps 56-66), even though certain individual chapters within these divisions may derive from different sources (such as the postexilic chaps 24-27 and 34-35 most frequently known as the Isaianic Apocalypses, and the narrative sections of chaps 36-39 which are related to Dtr). For the purposes of the analysis in this chapter, however, each major section of the Isaianic corpus will be discussed separately and placed in historical order with other works from their own time period.

***bāmôt*: 15:2; 16:12; [36:7][35]**

First Isaiah mentions *bāmôt* as cultic installations (15:2; 16:12; 36:7), and also uses the archaic poetic term *bāmôtê*, designating the "tops" of clouds (14:14). Of the references to cultic *bāmôt*, 15:2 and 16:12 deal with *bāmôt* located in Moab.[36] Only Isa 36:7 refers to Israelite *bāmôt*, and links

---

[35]Although included in Isaiah, this verse is most probably the product of a Deuteronomistic editor.

[36]Isa 15:2 places the term *bāmôt* in parallelism with *bayit*, and 16:12 with *miqdāš*, implying that Moabite *bāmôt* might be a type of sanctuary structure. The implications of this parallelism will be discussed in chapter five (pp. 145-48).

these *bāmôt* with *mizbəḥôt*; however, as noted below, it is likely that this reference to the *bāmôt* surrounding Jerusalem is not original to the prophet Isaiah. The larger passage of which 36:7 is a part, the account of the siege of Sennacherib and the speeches of the Rab Shaqeh, most probably originated with Dtr (see 2 Kgs 18:22) and not with Isaiah. If, then, Isa 36:7 is ruled out as representative of the prophet's own views of *bāmôt*, First Isaiah would join the ranks of other biblical sources that speak of *bāmôt* only in connection to Moab.[37]

ăšērîm: 17:8; 27:9

First Isaiah mentions *ăšērîm* only twice (17:8; 27:9), and in both contexts they are linked with *mizbəḥôt* and *ḥammānîm*. In 17:8, these items are said to be the work of human hands from whose use the Israelites will turn to worship only YHWH once again. It is clear in this passage that the use of *ăšērîm* is considered a departure from the worship of YHWH. In 27:9 these items are slated for destruction as part of the process by which Jacob's sins will be forgiven (v. 9). Both of these verses, however, show signs of being late additions to First Isaiah. 17:8 is part of a small prose section placed between two poetic oracles, while 27:9 is part of an Isaianic Apocalypse.[38]

Another possible sign of late addition is the presence of the term *ḥammānîm*. As noted above in the "Postscript" to chapter one, *ḥammānîm*, or incense altars, are mentioned elsewhere only in Ezekiel (6:4, 6), 2 Chronicles (14:4; 29:27; 34:4, 7), and the Holiness Code (Lev 26:30), with a possible allusion to them in Third Isaiah (57:5), all of which are postexilic in date.[39] If these two verses were removed from consideration as secondary

---

[37]J (Num 21:28; 23:1) and E (Num 22:41) only use the term as a part of Moabite place names. In addition to one Moabite place name (21:19-20), P speaks only of *bāmôt* belonging to non-Israelites, but without specifying any one nationality which used them (Num 33:52). Jeremiah connects *bāmôt* both with Moab and with the kings of Judah and their practice of child sacrifice (19:5; 32:35 [LXX 39:35]; 48:35 [LXX 31:35]). For a discussion of this aspect of Jeremiah's views of *bāmôt*, see below (pp. 104-05). For a discussion of the possible presence of a *bāmāh* in Isa 6:13, see chapter five (p. 149).

[38]For further discussion of this passage and its possible relationship to polemics against *ăšērîm* in Hosea, see John Day, "A Case of Inner Scriptural Interpretation: The Dependence of Isaiah XXVI.13-XXVII.11 on Hosea XIII.4-XIV.10 (Eng. 9) and its Relevance to Some Theories of the Redaction of the Isaiah Apocalypse," *JTS* 31 (1980) 309-19.

[39]In chapter nine, the fact that most of the Greek textual traditions of Isaiah use the term "tree" (δένδρον), rather than the usual term "sacred grove" (ἄλσος), to translate *ăšērîm* in 17:8 and 27:9 will be discussed (pp.259-60). Also discussed in chapter six (p. 181, n. 53), is Isa 1:29 which states "You [who forsake YHWH] shall be ashamed of the oaks in which you delighted and you shall blush for the gardens you have chosen."

additions to the original work of First Isaiah, it could be argued that First Isaiah made no mention of *ăšērîm* whatsoever.[40]

maṣṣēbôt: 19:19

Isa 19:19 predicts that there will eventually be an altar to YHWH within Egypt, and a *maṣṣēbāh* to YHWH on Israel's border with Egypt. The installation of these two items is to be followed shortly thereafter by the conversion of both the Egyptians and the Assyrians to the worship of YHWH. While this passage may be a later addition to the book of Isaiah, it is noteworthy that this passage constitutes the first overt acknowledgment of a *maṣṣēbāh* dedicated to YHWH, outside of the early narratives of E.[41]

mizbəḥôt: 6:6; 17:8; 19:19; 27:9; [36:7]

In addition to the passages cited above in which *mizbəḥôt* are mentioned along with *bāmôt* (36:7), *ăšērîm* and *ḥammānîm* (17:8; 27:9), or *maṣṣēbôt* (19:19), the only other passage in First Isaiah which mentions an altar is 6:6, part of the famous scene of the call of the prophet.

Cultic statuary

ăṣabbîm: 10:11

ĕlîlîm: 2:8, 18, 20; 10:10, 11; 19:1, 3; 31:7

massēkôt: 30:22

pəsîlîm: 10:10; 21:9; 30:22

First Isaiah gives more attention to cultic statuary than to any other type of religious paraphernalia. Isaiah 2 describes Judah as full of *ĕlîlîm* made of silver and gold (2:8, 18, 20), a passage paralleled by a later addition in 31:7. 10:10-11 likens the *pəsîlîm* and *ĕlîlîm* of Assyria to those of

---

[40]*The New Oxford Annotated Bible with the Apocryphal/Deuterocanonical Books* ([ed. Bruce M. Metzger and Roland E. Murphy; New York: Oxford University Press, 1991] 875 OT), as well as BHS, mention in footnotes to Isa 6:13, a possible reading of the divine name 'Asherah. This passage fraught with textual difficulties. It may have originally likened the destruction of Israel to the destruction of *bāmôt*, including the uprooting of *maṣṣēbôt* and of trees sacred to 'Asherah. Given the current state of preservation of this verse, however, this reading requires extensive reconstruction.

[41]The only other possible reference to *maṣṣēbôt* in First Isaiah is 6:13 (see n. 40 above).

Samaria and Jerusalem, promising destruction to the *ĕlîlîm* of Samaria and the *ăṣabbîm* of Jerusalem.[42] 30:22 credits the Jerusalemites with the possession of *pəsîlîm* and *massēkôt* of silver and gold.[43] 19:1-3 refers to the gods of the Egyptians as *ĕlîlîm*, and 21:9 refers to Babylon's gods as *pəsîlîm*.

Summary

It is unclear whether the earliest strata of First Isaiah mention *ăšērîm*. There are two passages that do mention them negatively, but these verses occur in what appear to be late contexts (17:8; 27:9). Similarly, the views of Isaiah concerning *bāmôt* located within Israel cannot be determined based on 36:7, because this verse is probably the work of Dtr. Outside of this passage, First Isaiah speaks of *bāmôt* only in relation to Moab. *Maṣṣēbôt* are mentioned only once, but with a clear indication that the author understood them to be appropriate to the worship of YHWH (19:19). *Mizbəḥôt* are mentioned as appropriate to YHWH (6:6; 19:19), and as part of condemned complexes including *ăšērîm* and *ḥammānîm* (17:8; 27:9), or *bāmôt* (36:7). As noted above, however, these three verses are of questionable origin. All that can be said with absolute certainty about the views of First Isaiah is that he disapproved of cultic statuary, knew of *bāmôt* as Moabite cult sites, and approved of YHWHistic altars and *maṣṣēbôt*.

JEREMIAH

bāmôt: 7:31; 17:3; 19:5; 26:18; 32:35; 48:35

According to Jeremiah, the Judahites erected *bāmôt* in the Valley of Ben Hinnom on which to engage in child sacrifice. Jer 7:31 mentions the *bāmôt* related to the tophet (*bāmôt hattōphet*) which was built there, while Jer 19:5 and 32:35 [LXX 39:35] call them *bāmôt-habbaʿal*, a name which is reminiscent of the place name Bamoth-Baʿal in Num 22:41 and 23:1. Another Moabite connection to *bāmôt* appears in Jer 48:35 [LXX 31:35] which promises an end to Moabites who worship on *bāmôt*. These connections between *bāmôt*, Moab, and child sacrifice call to mind Mesha, king of Moab, who sacrificed his son during a battle with Israel (2 Kgs 3:27).[44]

---

[42]The choice of the term *ăṣabbîm* to describe Jerusalem's idols is suggestive. Dtr consistently uses this term only to name the gods of the Philistines (1 Sam 31:9; 2 Sam 5:21), and Micah (1:7) and Hosea use it only in relation to the north (Hos 4:17; 8:4; 13:2; 14:9 [Eng 14:8].

[43]The only other occurrence of the term *massēkāh* in First Isaiah is in 30:1, but most translators render the term "treaty" in this context of judgment against alliances with Egypt, based on the word's possible secondary meaning, "weaving."

[44]The Moabite Stone inscription credited to Mesha may refer to itself as a *bmt* for the Moabite god Chemosh. An alternate interpretation would be that it is the site on

The connection of *bāmôt* with Moab also occurs in Isaiah (15:2; 16:12), but the direct connection between *bāmôt* and child sacrifice seems to have begun and ended with Jeremiah. Dtr mentions kings who both sacrificed their children and continued to maintain and use *bāmôt* but there is no indication in Dtr that *bāmôt* were used for child sacrifice.[45] Dtr mentions the tophet in the valley of Ben Hinnom, but does not refer to it as a *bāmāh* (2 Kgs 23:10).[46] Jeremiah was apparently the only biblical writer who thought of these tophet installations as *bāmôt*.

The other references to *bāmôt* in Jeremiah are Jer 17:2 (which will be discussed below in connection with *ăšērîm*), and Jer 26:18 [LXX 33:18], the account of the prophet's trial, during which Mic 3:12, which prophesies the reduction of the Temple to a "forest shrine" (*bāmôt ya'ar*), is quoted.

ăšērîm: 17:2

Jeremiah uses the image of the "high hill" and the *'ēṣ ra'ănān* to describe unspecified cultic activity of which he disapproves (Jer 2:20; 3:6, 13);[47] but, he also preserves a positive image of the people likened to a beautiful "leafy olive tree" *zayît ra'ănān*. This imagery is found in the Psalms as well (37:35; 52:10 [Eng 52:8]). In 17:2, however, Jeremiah connects the "high hill" and the *'ēṣ ra'ănān* with specific cultic items, namely *mizbəḥôt*, *ăšērîm*, and *bāmôt*. The passage describes the "sin of Judah" for which the punishment is exile (17:4).[48] It is unclear, however, if the use of the items mentioned above constitutes this "sin." The relationship of the "high hill" and "green tree" to *bāmôt* and *ăšērîm* respectively will be discussed in chapters five and six.

In addition to the direct reference to *ăšērîm* in Jer 17:2, Jeremiah twice uses the common noun pair "tree" and "stone" to refer either to cultic statuary or possibly to *ăšērîm* and *maṣṣēbôt*. Jer 2:26-28 reads:

> As a thief is shamed when caught, so the house of Israel shall be shamed, they, their kings, their officials, their priests, and their prophets, who say to a tree, "You are my father," and to a stone, "You gave me birth . . ."But in the time of their

---

which the stone is erected that was a *bmt*.

[45]2 Kgs 16:2-4 [= 2 Chr 28:3-4]; 21:3-6 [= 2 Chr 33:3-6]; 23:8-10; see also Ezek 20:27-31, and the oblique references of Ezekiel 16.

[46]For another reference to child sacrifice carried on in valleys, see Isa 57:5.

[47]Other references to the *'ēṣ ra'ănān* complex of features are: Deut 12:2; 1 Kgs 14:23; 2 Kgs 16:4; 17:10; Ezek 6:13; Isa 57:5. For further references see discussion of Hos 4:13 (pp. 92-93). See also Jer 13:27, which makes reference to abominable activity carried out on hilltops.

[48]This entire passage is lacking in the LXX.

trouble they say, "Come and save us!" But where are your gods that you made for yourself? Let them come, if they can save you, in your time of trouble; for you have as many gods as you have towns, O Judah.

Saul Olyan has argued that Jer 2:27a, under Deuteronomistic influence, is a polemic against the use of *ăšērîm* and *maṣṣēbôt* to represent YHWH and his consort ʾAsherah within Israel's cult.[49] While Olyan's argument fits well within the context of Jer 2:27, it does not fit as well with Jer 3:9. In Jer 3:9, the prophet portrays Judah as a faithless woman who commits adultery with "tree" and "stone." The use of the verb *np*, "to commit adultery," suggests that in this context the prophet viewed the use of the tree and the stone as a complete departure from YHWH's worship, not as a wrongful way to worship YHWH.

maṣṣēbôt: 43:13
Aside from the oblique references to "stones" mentioned above which might be poetic descriptions of *maṣṣēbôt* worship, Jeremiah mentions *maṣṣēbôt* once in reference to the obelisks of Heliopolis in Egypt which YHWH will destroy (43:13).

mizbǝḥôt: 11:13; 17:1, 2
Aside from 17:1-2 which links *mizbǝḥôt* with *ăšērîm*, *bāmôt*, and the *ʿēṣ raʿănān* complex, Jeremiah's only other reference to *mizbǝḥôt* occurs in 11:13. This verse states, "your gods have become as many as your towns, O Judah," (as in Jer 2:28), going on to say, "and as many as the streets of Jerusalem are the *mizbǝḥôt* you have set up to shame, *mizbǝḥôt* to make offerings to Baʿal." Like Hosea, Jeremiah never mentions *mizbǝḥôt* in a positive light.

Cultic statuary

ăṣabbîm: 50:2

ĕlîlîm: 14:14

gillûlîm: 50:38

nesek: 10:14 (= 51:17)

---

[49]Olyan, "Cultic Confessions."

pəsîlîm: 8:19; 10:14 (= 51:17); 50:38; 51:47, 52

In addition to the references to "tree" and "stone" mentioned above which might refer to types of cultic statuary, Jeremiah uses numerous terms to refer to cultic statuary, the most frequent of which is *pəsîlîm*. In 8:19, Jeremiah parallels the term *pəsîlîm* with the phrase "foreign vanities" (*hablê nēkār*), in reference to idols which anger YHWH. Jeremiah frequently refers to the "idols" of Babylon, calling them *pəsîlîm* (50:38; 51:47, 52), *ăṣabbîm* (50:2), *gillûlîm* (50:2), and "terrors" (*ʾemîm*, 50:38).[50] 10:14, which is paralleled in 51:17, refers to the stupidity of those who make a *pesel* or a *nesek* out of gold, which is inert. Jeremiah also uses the terms "detestable thing" (*šiqqûṣ*, 7:30; 16:18; 32:34) and "abomination" (*tôʿēbāh*, 16:18; 44:4) to refer to cultic statuary.

Summary

Jeremiah is unique among the biblical sources in his explicit connection of *bāmôt* with the practice of child sacrifice. He also makes a connection between *bāmôt* and the Moabites. He mentions *ăšērîm* only once as part of the *ʿēṣ raʿănān* formula, and *maṣṣēbôt* only once in connection with Egyptian obelisks. The only *mizbəḥôt* that Jeremiah discusses are those which the Judahites are abusing by employing them in the worship of gods other than YHWH. Finally, Jeremiah, like Deuteronomy, seems to consider the worship of foreign deities to be the primary sin for which Israel is being punished with destruction. Although Jeremiah uses the technical term *pəsîlîm* most frequently of all the usual terms for cultic statuary, Jeremiah shares with Deuteronomy a wide variety of ways of referring to the worship of other gods, either through the manufacture of idols or through ideological devotion.[51] This worship of foreign gods and the use of cultic statuary is connected by Jeremiah with the practices of many other nations, including Babylon, Egypt, Canaan, Ammon, and Moab.

NAHUM

bāmôt: not mentioned

ăšērîm: not mentioned

---

[50]Jer 14:14 may refer to the use of cultic statuary (*ʾelîl*) in divination, though *ʾelîl* in this context may simply be an adjective meaning "worthless."

[51]For a list of the vocabulary concerning the worship of foreign gods which Jeremiah shares with Deuteronomy and Dtr, see Weinfeld, *Deuteronomy*, 322-24, 359-61.

maṣṣēbôt: not mentioned

mizbǝḥôt: not mentioned

Cultic statuary

massēkôt: 1:14

pǝsîlîm: 1:14
Nahum does not express an opinion concerning proper or improper Israelite religion since the entire book consists of an oracle directed at Assyria. He does, however, render an indictment against Assyrian cultic statuary (*pesel* and *massēkāh*) in 1:14, and against the practice of sorcery (*kešep*) by female practitioners in 3:4. Beyond this, Nahum gives us no information concerning his views of cultic matters.

HABAKKUK
bāmôt: not mentioned
Habakkuk does not mention *bāmôt*, although the archaic term *bāmôtê*, meaning "heights" does appear in 3:19.

ʾăšērîm: not mentioned

maṣṣēbôt: not mentioned

mizbǝḥôt: not mentioned

Cultic statuary

ʾĕlîlîm: 2:18

massēkôt: 2:18

pǝsîlîm: 2:18

"wood and stone": 2:19

Summary

Of the items of interest to this study, Habakkuk discusses only cultic statuary. In 2:18-19, Habakkuk uses three separate terms (*pesel, massēkāh, ĕlîlîm*), in addition to the generic terms "wood" and "stone," to refer to cultic statuary. 2:19 describes cultic statues as mere objects of wood and stone plated with silver and gold. Habakkuk does not mention any other cultic paraphernalia, either of a type of which he approves or of which he disapproves.

EZEKIEL

bāmôt: 6:3, 6, 13; 20:29; 36:2; 43:7

In chapter 6, Ezekiel locates *bāmôt* on the "mountains of Israel"[52] and connects their use with *mizbəḥôt, hammānîm, gillûlîm*, and shade trees including the *ēṣ raʿănān*. The only ritual action mentioned in this chapter is the presentation of "pleasing odors," presumably incense burning.[53] The judgment rendered concerning this activity is that YHWH will defile these cultic sites by killing those found there and scattering their corpses on the ritual ground. A similar punishment, again directed at those who use *bāmôt, hammānîm*, and *gillûlîm*, occurs in the Holiness Code (Lev 26:27-33). Unlike other judgment oracles in which it is difficult to discern the exact object of divine wrath, Ezekiel 6 makes it plain that the *bāmôt* themselves, as shrines used to worship idols, are the target of divine disfavor.

In chapter 20, Ezekiel focuses on *bāmôt* once again and goes so far as to suggest an etymology of the term *bāmāh/ôt* to his audience. Ezek 20:29 reads:

וָאֹמַר אֲלֵהֶם מָה הַבָּמָה אֲשֶׁר־אַתֶּם הַבָּאִים שָׁם וַיִּקָּרֵא שְׁמָהּ בָּמָה עַד הַיּוֹם הַזֶּה:

I said to them, "What is the high place to which you go? So it is called Bamah to this day."

This verse appears to derive the word *bāmāh* from the verb "to go," or "enter" (*bwʾ*). Exactly how we are to understand the connection between this verb and noun, however, is not altogether clear.[54] In addition to providing

---

[52] In what may be a related reference, see Ezek 7:7 for mention of *hēd hārîm*, "mountain revelry."

[53] Avi Hurvitz notes that anthropomorphisms such as the reference to pleasing odors reaching YHWH, become less and less frequent in the biblical text as one progresses toward Late Biblical Hebrew (*Linguistic Study*, 102-7).

[54] Other etymologies suggested for the term *bāmôt* are discussed in chapter five (pp. 127-29).

this etymology, Ezek 20:28 connects *bāmôt* with *gillûlîm*, the *ʿēṣ raʿănān*,[55] and ritual actions such as libation, incense burning, and sacrifice, indicating that these were activities that the exiles' ancestors did which displeased YHWH. 20:30-31 urges the exiles not to continue such abominable practices, this time including child sacrifice as one of them. The context of these verses, however, does not make it clear that Ezekiel wishes to connect *bāmôt* with child sacrifice. It is obvious, however, that the prophet considers both the use of *bāmôt* and the practice of child sacrifice to be abominations from Israel's past which should be excluded from her purified future.[56]

There are two remaining passages in which the term *bāmôt* appears in Ezekiel. The first is 36:2 which contains a taunt on the part of Israel's enemies "The ancient *bāmôt* (*bāmôt ʿôlām*) have become our possession." While this verse may imply that the enemies of Israel are rejoicing over capturing her ancient religious centers, it may also simply be a taunt celebrating that Israel has been extricated from her strongholds in the central hill country. In his study of *bāmôt*, Patrick Vaughan noted that the term *bmh*, meaning "foothills" or "territory," occurs in Mesopotamian sources in which monarchs celebrate their capture of enemy lands by stating that they have "trod" upon the territory of their enemies. Vaughan connects these passages with the term *bāmôtê* which frequently occurs in phrases in which YHWH is said to "tread" upon the cosmic heights, or on the backs of Israel's enemies.[57] Given this comparative material, it might be better to understand the "ancient *bāmôt*" of Ezek 36:2 as a reference to the long-held territory of Israel, rather than ancient cultic sites, though either interpretation is possible.

The final possible mention of *bāmôt* in Ezekiel is the problematic 43:7. This verse reads:

---

[55]Other references to the *ʿēṣ raʿănān* are: Deut 12:2; 1 Kgs 14:23; 2 Kgs 16:4; 17:10; Jer 2:20; 3:6, 13; 17:2; Isa 57:5. See additional references in the discussion of Hos 4:13 above (pp. 92-93, especially n. 17).

[56]Another oblique reference which might connect *bāmôt* with child sacrifice in Ezekiel occurs in chapter 16. In a lengthy metaphor of Jerusalem as an unfaithful woman, Ezekiel 16 mentions the "platform" (*gāb*) and "lofty place" (*rāmāh*) upon which faithless Jerusalem took her place to entice her lovers. This passage also portrays unfaithful Jerusalem sacrificing her children to abominable idols. These passages will be discussed further in chapter five. For a source that connects *bāmôt* and child sacrifice directly, see the discussion of Jeremiah, above (pp. 104-05).

[57]Vaughan, *The Meaning of 'Bāmâ'*, 9-12.

"He said to me, 'Mortal, this is the place of my throne and the place for the soles of my feet, where I will reside among the people of Israel forever. The house of Israel shall no more defile my holy name, neither they nor their kings, by their unfaithfulness, and by the corpses of their kings *at their death*.'"

The last phrase in this verse "and by the corpses of their kings *at their death*" represents the Hebrew phrase וּבְפִגְרֵי מַלְכֵיהֶם בָּמוֹתָם, which could also be translated "and by the corpses of their kings on their *bāmôt*." The meaning of this verse will be discussed in chapter five in light of W. F. Albright's interpretation of *bāmôt* as funeral mounds.[58]

ăšērîm: not mentioned

Although *ăšērîm* are not mentioned by Ezekiel, the many references to cultic activity in the vicinity of trees such as the *ēṣ raʿănān* might be seen as oblique references to *ăšērîm*.[59]

maṣṣēbôt: 26:11

The only *maṣṣēbôt* mentioned by Ezekiel are located in Tyre rather than in Israel, and appear to be architectural columns rather than cultic items (26:11). Chapter seven, however, will discuss whether the unusual references to "stones of fire" in Ezekiel 28 (a chapter which is also related to Tyre rather than Israel) could have any relation to *maṣṣēbôt*.

mizbəḥôt: 6:4, 5, 6, 13; 8:5, 16; 9:2; 40:46, 47; 41:22; 43:13, 18, 20, 22, 26, 27; 45:19; 47:1

Ezekiel discusses unsanctioned altars used in the worship of other gods, which he connects with *bāmôt*, *gillûlîm*, *ḥammānîm*, high hills, and green trees (6:1-14). He also discusses the proximity of unsanctioned objects to altars traditionally dedicated to YHWH. Ezek 8:5, for instance, decries the presence of an "Image of Jealousy" (*semel haqqinʾāh*) standing at the entrance to the gate of Jerusalem which is adjacent to the altar of YHWH. When viewed in light of 2 Kgs 21:7, which describes a cult statue of ʾĂšērāh, and 2 Chr 33:7, which calls the same statue a *semel*, it seems possible that Ezekiel also has in mind a statue of the goddess. Ezek 8:16 laments solar worship being practiced in YHWH's Temple, between the

---

[58]"High Place." Albright's thesis has been largely rejected by later scholars. See especially Barrick, "Funerary Character."

[59]This will be discussed below in chapter six along with the references to the trees of the Garden of Eden in Ezekiel 28 and 31 (pp. 180-83).

porch and the altar. Finally, in addition to these passages, Ezekiel deals in detail with the restoration of the Temple and its altar.[60]

Cultic statuary

ĕlîlîm: 30:13

gillûlîm: 6:4, 5, 6, 9, 13; 8:10; 14:3, 4, 5, 6, 7; 16:36; 18:6, 12, 15; 20:7, 8, 16, 18, 24, 31, 39; 22:3, 4; 23:7, 30, 37, 39, 49; 30:13; 33:25; 36:18, 25; 37:23; 44:10, 12

"gods of wood and stone": 20:32

ṣelem: 7:20; 16:17; 23:30

tərāpîm: 21:26 [Eng 21:21]

Ezekiel uses the term *gillûlîm* some 36 times, more than any other biblical writer. He depicts them being worshipped by Israel,[61] by Jerusalem, the "bloody city" (22:3-4),[62] by Levites in particular (44:10-12), and by the Egyptians (20:7-8; 30:13). Ezekiel 6 and 20 link their use with *bāmôt*. Ezekiel 6 and 18 locate this practice on hilltops, and Ezek 8:10 describes *gillûlîm* being portrayed in the Temple, possibly on wall reliefs.[63] Several passages in Ezekiel also link *gillûlîm* with child sacrifice (16:17-21; 20:31; 23:37-39).[64]

In addition to the term *gillûlîm*, Ezekiel also uses the term *ṣelem* in a negative sense three times: in relation to Israelite idols (7:20; 16:17) and Babylonian wall reliefs (23:14). Ezekiel uses the term *ĕlîlîm* once to describe the gods of Memphis (30:13) and *tərāpîm* once in a description of the

---

[60]Ezek 9:2; 40:42-47; 41:22; 43:13-27; 45:19; 47:1.

[61]6:4-13; 8:10; 14:3-7; 16:36; 18:6-15; 20:8, 16-24, 31-39; 23:7-49; 33:25; 36:18-25; 37:23.

[62]For a similar depiction of Nineveh, see Nah 3:1.

[63]The translation "wall reliefs," for the word "carved things" (*maśkîtô*) has been suggested most recently by Susan Ackerman (*Under Every Green Tree*, 44 n. 30). Victor Hurowitz suggests a type of carved symbol or other inscribed form on temple thresholds which marked a place where one would stand to make a petition ("אבן משכית," 206-7). This term occurs elsewhere only in P (Num 33:52) and H (Lev 26:1), in contexts which might, however, indicate references to *maṣṣēbôt*.

[64]See the "Postscript" to chapter one for a discussion of term *gillûlîm* as a possible indicator of Late Biblical Hebrew (pp. 41-3).

divinatory practices of the king of Babylon (21:26 [Eng 21:21]).[65] Ezekiel does not, however, use either of the most common terms for cultic statuary found in the Pentateuchal legal material and Dtr (*pəsîlîm* and *massēkôt*), though Ezekiel does use the typically Deuteronomistic description of cultic statuary as "gods of wood and stone" (20:32).

Along with more common terms, Ezekiel also uses generic terms such as "abomination" (*tôʿēbāh*) and "detestable thing" (*šiqqûṣ*) to refer to various unspecified religious violations. Both of these terms are used by other biblical traditions as well, but in more defined contexts. The term *tôʿēbāh* is used in J only to refer to Egyptian attitudes toward the Hebrews (Gen 43:32; 46:34; Exod 8:26 [Eng 8:22]). H uses this term only to refer to sexual misconduct (Lev 18:22, 26-30; 20:13). P does not use the term *tôʿēbāh* but does use the term *šiqqûṣ* frequently in the chapter which lists unclean animals.[66]

Ezekiel uses the term *tôʿēbāh* more than any other biblical source,[67] though with a semantic range most like that found in Deuteronomy. Both Deuteronomy and Ezekiel use the term to refer to sexual aberrations,[68] illegitimate ritual practices including child sacrifice,[69] as a general term for any aberrant practices of other nations,[70] and as an evaluation of the use of cultic statuary.[71] Both Deuteronomy and Ezekiel use the terms *tôʿēbāh* and *šiqqûṣ* together in verses that suggest a reference to the use of cultic statuary.[72]

With regard to purity laws, Deuteronomy uses the term *tôʿēbāh* to refer to unclean food (Deut 14:3), and the donation of illicitly acquired income in payment of vows (23:19 [Eng 23:18]). Ezekiel uses it to refer to

---

[65]For *tərāpîm* used in divination, see also Zech 10:2.

[66]Lev 11:10, 11, 12, 13, 20, 23, 41, 42, 43. The verbal form of this term is used regarding clean and unclean animals in H as well (Lev 20:25).

[67]Ezek 5:9, 11; 6:9, 11; 7:3, 4, 8, 9, 20; 8:6, 9, 13, 15, 17; 9:4; 11:18, 21; 12:16; 14:6; 16:2, 22, 36, 43, 47, 50, 51, 58; 18:12, 13, 24; 20:4; 22:2, 11; 23:36; 33:29, 26; 36:31; 43:8; 44:6, 7, 13.

[68]Deut 22:5; 24:4; Ezek 22:11; 33:26.

[69]Deut 18:9-12; Ezek 8:15-17; 16:22, 36. See also Dtr (2 Kgs 16:3 [=2 Chr 28:3]). See also Jer 32:35, where *bāmôt* are linked to the *tôʿēbāh* of child sacrifice.

[70]Deut 20:18; Ezek 5:9; 16:47. See also, Dtr (1 Kings 24; 2 Kgs 21:2 [=2 Chr 33:2], 11). See also Ezra 9:1, 11, 14.

[71]Deut 13:15 [Eng 13:14]; 17:4; 27:15; 32:16; Ezek 5:11; 7:20; 8:6, 9, 13; 14:6; 16:36; 22:2; 23:36. See also Dtr (1 Kgs 11:5, 7; 2 Kgs 23:13) where the deities ʿAstarte, Chemosh, and Milcom are referred to as either the *tôʿēbāh* or the *šiqqûṣ* of their respective countries. See also the abbreviated version of this passage, using only *tôʿēbāh*, in 2 Chr 34:33. Other prophets also use the term *tôʿēbāh* to refer to cultic statuary (Jer 16:18; 44:4; Isa 41:24; 44:19).

[72] Deut 7:25-26; Ezek 11:18, 21.

the admittance of foreigners into the Temple (44:6-13), and possibly to the practice of venerating dead kings buried within the city walls (43:7-8), though this passage may simply refer to the royal use of *bāmôt*.[73] The only meanings of the term that Ezekiel and Deuteronomy do not share are Deuteronomy's use of *tôʿēbāh* to refer to unfair weights and measures (25:13-16), and Ezekiel's use of the term in a generic sense to refer to any evil action perpetrated by Israel.[74] Ezekiel uses the term *šiqqûṣ* in many of the same ways in which he uses *tôʿēbāh*.[75]

Summary
In addition to his many general statements concerning "abominable" practices, and "detestable" objects, Ezekiel levels specific criticism at Israel, primarily for the use of *bāmôt* and cultic statuary (predominantly referred to as *gillûlîm*), which he variously combines with hilltop worship, shade trees, incense burning, libation, and possibly (though not directly) child sacrifice. Ezekiel does not discuss *ăšērîm* directly, though it could be argued that he assumes their presence in the complexes of features mentioned above. Neither does Ezekiel mention Israelite *maṣṣēbôt*, though he does locate them in Tyre, apparently as architectural features.

Ezekiel's concern for *mizbəḥôt*, their pure and impure use, is part of his concern for the restoration of proper cultic rites within Israel. Those rites which he wishes to see purged from the Temple include solar worship, veneration of images, and the particularly Mesopotamian ritual of "weeping for Tammuz."[76] Ezekiel's primary concern seems to be the reduction of

[73]2 Chr 36:14 echoes Ezekiel's opinion that "abominations" had been introduced into the Temple by the priestly hierarchy of the time just prior to the exile.

[74]Ezek 6:9, 11; 7:3, 4, 8, 9; 9:4; 11:18, 21; 12:16; 16:2, 43, 50-51, 58; 18:12-13, 24; 20:4; 33:29; 36:31. Other prophets use the term *tôʿēbāh* in this generic sense (Isa 1:13; Jer 2:7; 6:15; 7:9-10; 8:12; 44:22; Mal 2:11). Proverbs uses *tôʿēbāh* more than any other biblical source except Ezekiel, using the term to refer to various personality flaws such as perversity, arrogance, aggression, duplicity, dishonesty, foolishness, and generic "wickedness." See Prov 3:32; 6:16-19; 8:7; 11:20; 12:22; 13:19; 15:8-9, 26; 16:5, 12; 17:15; 21:27; 24:9; 26:25; 28:9; 29:27. Proverbs also shares Deuteronomy's use of the term to refer to unfair weights and measures (Prov 11:1; 20:10, 23).

[75]Describing divine images in wall reliefs (8:10), generic evil (5:11; 11:18, 21), and cultic statuary (7:20; 11:18, 21; 20:7, 8, 30; 37:23). For other references to *šiqqûṣ* referring to cultic statuary, or to deities of other cultures, see Deut 7:26; 29:16 [Eng 29:17]; 1 Kgs 11:5, 7; 2 Kgs 23:13; 2 Chr 15:8; Jer 7:30; 16:18; 32:34; Hos 9:10; Dan 9:27; 11:31; 12:11. For *šiqqûṣ* meaning generalized evil, see 2 Kgs 23:24; Isa 66:3; Jer 4:1; 13:27; Zech 9:7.

[76]For references to this observance, see Raphael Kutscher, "The Cult of Dumuzi/Tammuz," *Bar Ilan Studies in Assyriology* (ed. J. Klein and A. Skaist; Tel Aviv:

religious activity in Israel to only those activities properly carried out in the Temple, weeding out any rituals he considers to be imported from other cultures, and returning to a state of ritual purity and covenant faithfulness.[77]

SECOND ISAIAH

bāmôt: not mentioned

ăšērîm: not mentioned

maṣṣēbôt: not mentioned

mizbəḥôt: not mentioned

Cultic statuary

ăṣabbîm: 46:1; 48:5

massēkôt: 42:17

nesek: 41:29; 48:5

pəsîlîm: 40:19, 20; 42:8, 17; 44:9, 10, 15, 17; 45:20; 48:5

ṣîrîm: 45:16

Summary

Second Isaiah does not mention *ăšērîm*, *bāmôt*, *maṣṣēbôt*, or *mizbəḥôt*. The book, instead, focuses on cultic statuary and engages in numerous polemics against it. In these polemics, the author reveals a detailed knowledge of the artistic techniques used to craft cultic statuary out of wood which was then overlaid with metal and mounted on platforms so they could be carried in procession, either by human bearers or on animal carts. Several terms for cultic statuary are used by Second Isaiah; however, because the work refers to idols so frequently, many passages use none of these terms, relying on the reader to understand what is being discussed.[78] Second Isaiah's polemics against cultic statuary play upon the contrast

---

Bar Ilan University Press, 1990) 29-44.
[77]See especially Ezekiel 33.
[78]See, for instance, 41:7, 21-24; 46:6-7.

between the living God of Israel, and the inert gods of Babylon. No other type of polemic, against any other type of cultic paraphernalia, is engaged in by Second Isaiah.

THIRD ISAIAH

bāmôt: not mentioned

Although Third Isaiah, does not mention *bāmôt*, the archaic poetic term *bāmôtê*, meaning "heights" occurs in Isa 58:14, as it does in some preexilic prophets.[79]

ăšērîm: not mentioned

Oblique references to *bāmôt* and/or *ăšērîm* may appear in Isa 65:1-8, which mentions those who offer incense on mountains, sacrifice in gardens, and burn incense "on bricks" (*'al-hallǝbēnîm*). The consonantal text of the phrase *'al-hallǝbēnîm* allows for the reading "next to poplar trees."[80] Another reference to worshipping in gardens occurs in Isa 66:17. The implications of these passages for an understanding of *bāmôt* and *ăšērîm* will be discussed in chapter six.

maṣṣēbôt: not mentioned

In addition to the possible allusions to *ăšērîm* and *bāmôt* mentioned above, *maṣṣēbôt* and *ăšērîm* may be alluded to as well in 57:1-10, which addresses those who "warm themselves" (*hannēḥāmîm*) under oaks and beneath every *'ēṣ ra'ănān*,[81] and who sacrifice their children in the clefts of rocks (57:5). The passage also makes other more curious references. Isa 57:6-8 reads:

> Among the smooth [stones] of the river is your portion (*ḥallǝqê-naḥal ḥelqēk*), they, they are your lot (*gôrālēk*), to them you have poured out a drink offering (*nesek*) . . . upon a high and lofty mountain you have set your bed, and there you went up to offer sacrifice (*zbḥ*), behind the door and the door post you have set up your symbol (*zikrônēk*) . . . you have gazed on the monument (*yād*).

---

[79]Amos 4:13; Mic 1:3; Hab 3:19.

[80]For a reference to sacrificing on mountain sides and burning incense next to poplars, see Hos 4:13.

[81]This verbal form may be a veiled reference to the use of incense burners, *ḥammānîm*. For other references to *ḥammānîm*, see H, Lev 26:30; Isa 17:8; 27:9; Ezek 6:4, 6; and 2 Chr 14:4; 29:27; 34:4, 34:7. For other occurrences of *'ēṣ ra'ănān* see Deut 12:2; 1 Kgs 14:23; 2 Kgs 16:4; 17:10; Jer 2:20; 3:6, 13; 17:2; and Ezek 6:13. For further discussion, see above under Hos 4:13 (pp. 92-93).

This passage appears to be drawing on Deuteronomistic traditions concerning Joshua's monuments at Gilgal, and possibly the allotment of territory to the tribes as well. Joshua 4 identifies the stone monument of Gilgal as a group of Jordan river stones (4:2) which were made into a memorial (*zikārôn*) of their crossing the river (4:7). Josh 14:6 states that the division of the land into inheritances was done at Gilgal; while Josh 15:1 indicates that the process used to divide the land was lot (*gôrāl*). The connections with Shechem are less clear, though the "high mountain" referred to might signify Mt. Ebal, and the *yād* might signify the stone Joshua erected at Shechem (24:26-27).[82]

Whatever the cultic overtones to this passage may imply, however, the point of the passage seems to be to indicate that those whom Third Isaiah is implicating as the children of "adulterers" and "prostitutes" in 57:3 are the former citizens of the northern kingdom who were not exiled like those righteous now sleeping in their graves (57:2). Whether veiled references to the fact that these people continued to use *maṣṣēbôt* exist in this passage is unclear.

mizbəḥôt: 56:7; 60:7

Third Isaiah twice discusses the resumption of sacrifices on YHWH's altar, declaring that all the nations of the earth will bring sacrifices there which YHWH will accept (Isa 56:6-8; 60:7).

Cultic statuary: not mentioned

While none of the traditional language concerning cultic statuary occurs in Third Isaiah, there is a possible oblique reference to such items in 57:13. This verse refers to "collected ones" (*qibbûṣayik*) to whom the audience might cry for deliverance, which may be construed as small images or idols. Other such oblique references may also appear in 66:3 which uses the terms *ʾāwen* and *šiqqūṣ* to refer to entities to whom the misguided sacrifice.

---

[82] A *maṣṣēbāh* referred to as a *yād* appears in 2 Sam 18:18. This passage apparently contains a double meaning for the term *yād* (lit. "hand," fig. "phallus") in that the monument is to serve as a remembrance of Absalom, who had no children. This meaning is also supported by Isa 56:5 which promises eunuchs a "monument and a name (*yād wā-šēm*) better than sons and daughters . . . that shall not be cut off." In that this memorial is to be "heavenly" in nature, it can only be construed as a poetic reference based possibly on the memory of Absalom's *maṣṣēbāh*, and not a concrete reference to an actual one.

Summary
       Third Isaiah explicitly mentions the altar of YHWH, and mentions
other items only obliquely. Allusions to a knowledge of *maṣṣēbôt*, *ʾăšērîm*,
and *bāmôt* could be argued in many cases concerning Third Isaiah, but the
vocabulary employed in this source is not the overt traditional vocabulary of
other sources, making certain allusions so oblique that it is unclear whether
the practices referred to are truly those which were familiar from the
preexilic age or are innovations which greeted the returnees upon their
arrival back in Palestine.
       The vast difference between Second and Third Isaiah on the subject
of cult is striking. While Second Isaiah is concerned with the condemnation
of cultic statuary, Third Isaiah cannot be solidly proved to mention it at all.
Also, while Third Isaiah does at least mention altars dedicated to YHWH,
these central cultic items appear to be of little or no interest to Second
Isaiah. The differences between these two sections of the canonical book of
Isaiah appear to be attributable to their different settings and audiences,
Second Isaiah concerning itself with the experiences and needs of the exiles
in Babylon prior to their return, and Third Isaiah concerned with the
resumption of acceptable religious life within Palestine, with all its ancient
temptations.

JOEL

bāmôt: not mentioned

ʾăšērîm: not mentioned

maṣṣēbôt: not mentioned

mizbǝḥôt: 1:13; 2:17

Cultic statuary: not mentioned

Summary
       The only cultic item which is of any interest to Joel is the *mizbēᵃḥ*
YHWH. In 1:13, Joel laments that the sacrifices of YHWH's altar have been
cut off. Joel 2:17 depicts the ministers of YHWH weeping beside YHWH's
altar. Aside from these two references, there is no other mention of cultic
items in Joel.

MALACHI

bāmôt: not mentioned

ăšērîm: not mentioned

maṣṣēbôt: not mentioned

mizbǝḥôt: 1:7, 10; 2:13

Cultic statuary: not mentioned

Summary
        Like Joel, Malachi is not concerned with any item of cultic paraphernalia except the *mizbēᵃḥ* of the Jerusalem Temple. Malachi declares that the altar is polluted by imperfect sacrifices offered upon it (1:7, 10). The prophet also states that the altar's sacrifices are rejected (2:13-14) because the priests have not kept faith with the wives of their youth, but rather, have sought to divorce them. No other *mizbǝḥôt* are discussed by Malachi, nor are any other cultic items.

ZECHARIAH 1-8
        Although Zechariah 1-8 does not mention any of the items under discussion in this study specifically, the vision in Zechariah 4 concerning the olive trees and the lamp stand will be discussed in chapter six with regard to the relationship between *ăšērîm* and live trees.

ZECHARIAH 9-14

bāmôt: not mentioned

ăšērîm: not mentioned

maṣṣēbôt: not mentioned

mizbǝḥôt: 9:15; 14:20
        The *mizbēᵃḥ* of YHWH is favorably mentioned in Zech 9:15 and 14:20. No mention of any other types of altars occurs elsewhere in Zechariah 9-14.

Cultic statuary

ăṣabbîm: 13:2

tərāpîm: 10:2
Zech 10:1-2 is an interesting passage that gives insight into *tərāpîm* and their use. It reads:

> Ask rain from YHWH in the season of the spring rain, from YHWH who makes the storm clouds, who give showers of rain to you, the vegetation in the field to everyone. For the *tərāpîm* utter nonsense, and the diviners (*haqqôsəmîm*) see lies; the dreamers tell false dreams and give empty consolation.

This passage implies that the *tərāpîm* were used for obtaining oracular readings concerning agrarian concerns such as rainfall and crop potentials.[83] If this was the primary use of *tərāpîm*, then idolatry need not be seen as Rachel's motivation for taking those belonging to her father. Rather, she may have viewed them as tools essential for successful farming and as such, an appropriate asset to offer her husband.

The only other reference to cultic statuary in Zechariah 9-14 is 13:2, in which God vows to cut off the names of the *ăṣabbîm* from the land, and to remove the prophets (*hannəbîʾîm*), and the "unclean spirit" (*rûaḥ haṭṭumʾāh*) as well. In this extraordinary passage, the author predicts the dissolution of the institution of prophecy (because of its capacity to produce false prophets), as if the institution itself were tantamount to idolatry and divination of spirits.

Summary
Of the major items under discussion, Zechariah 9-14 mentions only the altar of YHWH. Zechariah 9-14 also makes reference to *tərāpîm* and *ăṣabbîm* in contexts which make it appear that they were used for obtaining oracles.

DANIEL

bāmôt: not mentioned

ăšērîm: not mentioned

maṣṣēbôt: not mentioned

---

[83]For another reference to *tərāpîm* used in divination, see Ezek 21:26 [Eng 21:21].

mizbᵊḥôt: not mentioned

Cultic statuary

ṣelem: 2:31, 32, 34, 35; 3:1, 2, 3, 5, 7, 10, 12, 14, 15, 18, 19

Summary
    The Book of Daniel makes no mention of any of the primary terms related to this study; however, it does make great use of cultic statuary as a literary image. *ṣelem* is the only term Daniel uses for cultic statuary. In chapter 2, King Nebuchadnezzar dreams of a statue made of various metals, yet having feet of clay. This the author uses to symbolize a succession of tyrannical regimes which will eventually be destroyed by a "stone" which God will cut out of a mountain, use to smash the statue's feet of clay, and then make to grow and fill the earth. In chapter 3, King Nebuchadnezzar sets up a golden statue and attempts to make his Hebrew subjects worship it, leading to their consignment to the "fiery furnace" when they refuse.
    One play on words which may imply that the author of Daniel intentionally picked the word *ṣelem* because of its double meaning, especially in the Priestly traditions, is the verse which describes the king's wrath as a distortion of his visage/face (*ṣelem*). The P writer uses the term *ṣelem*, not only to refer to cultic statuary, but also to describe the "image" of God in which humanity is made, and that Seth, as a child of Adam, was conceived and born in his "image." The statue in Daniel 3 is understood to be a statue of the king himself (a thinly veiled reference to the Antiochus IV Epiphanes). The image of the king's anger distorting his "*ṣelem*" calls to mind, then, the Priestly notion that there is an intrinsic connection between an individual and that which bears the individual's "image."[84] The statue carries the king's "image." When it is defied, the king's own physical self is affected.

---

[84]James Barr, "Man and Nature: The Ecological Controversy and the Old Testament," (*BJRL* 55 [1972] 9-32), makes the argument that the "image of god" which humanity shares places humanity in a type of "liturgical" role of leadership and stewardship over nature that mirrors God's role in the universe (p. 31). The scholarship on the nature of this "image of god," however, is vast. For a rather thorough review of this scholarship, see Phyllis A. Bird, "'Male and Female He Created Them': Gen 1:27b in the Contest of the Priestly Account of Creation," *HTR* 74 (1981) 129-59; now in her collected essays, *Missing Persons and Mistaken Identities: Women and Gender in Ancient Israel* (Minneapolis: Fortress, 1997) 123-54.

PSALMS

bāmôt: 78:58

Ps 78:58 [LXX 77:58] mentions *bāmôt* as well as *pəsîlîm*, describing *bāmôt* as items that anger ʾElohim and *pəsîlîm* as objects which provoke him to jealousy. Because Psalm 78 appears to be describing a time period prior to the construction of the Temple, and also appears to disapprove of *bāmôt* as installations which anger YHWH, Psalm 78 provides a unique contrast to Dtr. In Dtr, *bāmôt* are early cult sites which were fully acceptable to YHWH. Psalm 78, then, represents an alternate opinion concerning early *bāmôt*. The only other reference related to *bāmôt* in Psalms is Ps 18:34 which uses the archaic term *bāmôtê* meaning "heights."

ăšērîm: not mentioned

There is no mention of *ăšērîm* in the Psalms, although there are two positive uses of the term "leafy" (*raʿănān*, 37:35; 52:10 [Eng 52:8]) which occurs most frequently elsewhere in the *ʿēṣ raʿănān* formula describing illicit worship. The most suggestive of these positive references to an *ʿēṣ raʿănān* is Ps 52:10 [Eng 52:8], which likens the joyous worshiper to a "leafy olive tree in the Temple of ʾElohim." Jer 11:16 contains a parallel to this image. The possible relevance of these references will be discussed in chapter six.

maṣṣēbôt: not mentioned

mizbəḥôt: 26:6; 43:4; 51:21 [Eng 51:19]; 84:4 [Eng 84:3]; 118:27

Several Psalms make mention of the *mizbəḥôt* of YHWH (26:6; 84:4 [Eng 84:3]; 118:27) or of ʾElohim (43:4; 51:21 [Eng 51:19]). Altars dedicated to other gods, however, are not mentioned.

Cultic statuary

ăṣabbîm: 106: 36, 38; 115:4 (= 135:15)

ĕlîlîm: 96:5 (= 1 Chr 16:26); 97:7

massēkôt: 106:19

pəsîlîm: 78:58; 97:7

ṣelem: 73:20

In addition to Ps 78:58 which mentions *pəsîlîm* as objects which provoke the jealousy of ʾElohim, 97:7 portrays the worshipers of *pəsîlîm* and *ĕlîlîm* being put to shame. Ps 96:5, which is paralleled in 1 Chr 16:26, refers to the gods of the nations as *ĕlîlîm*. Ps 115:4, which is paralleled in 135:15, describes the gods of the nations as *ăṣabbêhem*, which are made of silver and gold, which neither speak, nor see, nor hear, etc. Psalm 106 also uses the term *ăṣabbêhem*, to refer to the gods of Canaan which the Israelites adopted and to whom they sacrificed their children (106:36-38). Psalm 106 also makes reference to the calf *massēkāh* made at Horeb (106:19). The only other possible reference to cultic statuary found in the Psalms is in Ps 73:20, in which the "phantoms" of the wicked (*ṣalmām*) are despised like a bad dream when one awakes. Whether this is a reference to cultic statuary, however, is unclear. The passage could be likening the wicked themselves to "phantoms" who will eventually disappear like nightmares when daylight comes.

Summary

The Psalms focus more on cultic statuary than on any of the other items under discussion, while they mention *ăšērîm* and *maṣṣēbôt* not at all. They do, however, mention *bāmôt*, as well as legitimate *mizbəḥôt*, and contain an intriguing reference to olive trees in the Temple precinct, using the familiar term *raʿănān*. Another unusual feature found in the Psalms is the pairing of cultic statuary (*ăṣabbîm*) with child sacrifice, and the tracing of this practice to the Canaanites (106:36-38). Ps 78:58, mentions *bāmôt* as items which anger God, and pairs them with *pəsîlîm* which provoke God's jealousy. This singular reference to early *bāmôt* of which YHWH disapproves provides a dissenting voice to that of Dtr which contains only positive views of early *bāmôt*.

JOB

bāmôt: not mentioned

While Job does not mention *bāmôt*, it does use the archaic term *bāmôtê*, to refer to the "backs/waves" of the sea (9:8).

ăšērîm: not mentioned

maṣṣēbôt: not mentioned

mizbǝḥôt: not mentioned

Cultic statuary

The only possible term related to the subject of cultic statuary used by Job is *ĕlil* (13:4), however, this term should probably be read simply as "worthlessness" in this context. No covert reference to cultic statuary is required here.

Summary

Job does not appear to be particularly concerned with cultic paraphernalia, making no overt references to any of the items of interest to this study. Job mentions only two peripherally related terms *bāmôtê* and *ĕlil*, both in contexts which do not require cultic interpretation.

LAMENTATIONS

bāmôt: not mentioned

ăšērîm: not mentioned

maṣṣēbôt: not mentioned[85]

mizbǝḥôt: 2:7; 4:1

Cultic statuary: not mentioned

Summary

Lamentations mentions only YHWH's *mizbē͏ᵃḥ*, which 2:7 describes as scorned and disowned along with YHWH's sanctuary (*miqdāšô*). Mothers killing their children is also mentioned (2:20; 4:10), but the reference here is not to child sacrifice, but to cannibalism practiced by those facing starvation.

---

[85]4:1 mentions the scattering of "sacred stones" (*ʾabnê-qōdeš*) at the top of every street, but this passage is an unlikely candidate for an allusion to *maṣṣēbôt*. Rather, it most probably refers to the "sacred" stones which once made up the walls and buildings of Jerusalem. For another use of this image, see Mic 1:6.

PART II
Synthesis of Biblical Data on Individual Items

This section of the study will devote a separate chapter to each of the four major items under discussion in order to organize all of the data regarding each object into a comprehensive assessment of the biblical evidence regarding them. In each of the four chapters in this section, a more comprehensive review of the scholarly literature on these items will precede the presentation of the biblical data regarding them. Most of the previous studies on these items, however, share the common obstacle of having as their task the identification of one of the objects based upon various types of comparative data (etymology, archaeology, comparative mythology, etc.). Because the identification of the object is their goal, most of these studies fail to prove their case because of the nature of the data. The current study will, nonetheless, present their findings before turning to the task at hand, namely the assessment of how these items were actually perceived within the biblical corpus.

Chapter Five
Synthesis of the Data Regarding *bāmôt*

A. SUMMARY OF PREVIOUS SCHOLARSHIP ON *bāmôt*

Previous studies focussed on *bāmôt* have largely been of three types: studies aimed at establishing a solid etymology of the term *bāmôt* from which some understanding of the object could then be derived; studies which seek to find *bāmôt* in the archaeological record of Syria-Palestine and connect these with the biblical text; and studies aimed at promoting a single understanding of what *bāmôt* were and how they functioned. Below is a brief discussion of the major studies of *bāmôt* according to these categories.[1]

A.1. Etymological study of the term *bāmôt*

One of the major difficulties in understanding *bāmôt* is the term *bāmāh* itself and its resistance to etymological analysis. The root of the term is obscure, and for this reason, the standard translation, "high place," suggested by the Greek and Latin translators, presents modern scholars with a mystery concerning the origin of this interpretation. Etymological studies often seek to discern whether the *bāmôt* were actually "high" as the Greek and Latin translations suggest and if so, in what way. Another issue with which etymological studies often deal is the question of relationship between the term *bāmôt* and the archaic poetic term *bāmôtê*. In short, etymological studies of *bāmôt* are usually undertaken in the hope that a correct etymology will offer a solution not only for what the name "*bāmāh*" means, but also for what *bāmôt* physically looked like, and how they were understood within the context of Israelite theology. Seldom is the question raised as to whether such issues can realistically be resolved through etymological analysis.

Patrick Vaughan made etymological analysis a major section of his work on *bāmôt*.[2] Vaughan summarizes the work of previous scholars and their search for the etymology of *bāmāh*, noting that its origin in the

---

[1] One exception to this categorization is the recent comprehensive study of *bāmôt* by Matthias Gleis (*Die Bamah* [BZAW 251; Berlin: de Gruyter, 1997]), which addresses many of the issues included by previous studies in addition to exploring certain of the textual connections between *bāmôt* and other cultic phenomena addressed in this study.

[2] *The Meaning of 'Bāmâ'*.

presumed root *bwm* was proposed as early the 1600s and was maintained by scholars such as Albright until as recently as 1956.[3] Vaughan notes, however, that this root does not occur in other Semitic languages and turns, therefore, to noting those possible cognates to *bāmôt* that are attested in other Semitic languages. He discusses Ugaritic *bmt*, which apparently referred to the "backs" of animals, Akkadian *bamtu*, which also carried an anatomical meaning of "flank" or "thorax," and Akkadian *bamâtu*, concerning which the *CAD* and von Soden have a difference of opinion, but which both agree is some technical topographical term for a category of land surrounding a city. *CAD* prefers a concept of level ground, while von Soden prefers a meaning closer to "slopes" or rolling hills.[4] Vaughan also notes that Albright changed his understanding of the derivation of *bāmāh* in 1956 by abandoning the search for a verbal root and positing instead an original pre-Semitic noun **bahmatu* as a source for the term.[5]

In addition to deriving a meaning for *bāmôt*, etymological studies such as Vaughan's attempt to decide how the cultic term *bāmôt* relates to the archaic poetic term *bāmôtê*. The assumption is that both terms must derive from the same root, which must, in turn, be related to the cognates mentioned above that deal with anatomical parts, either of humans or animals. Thus Vaughan provides a chart which traces the presumed derivation from a common root of all the potential Semitic language cognates listed above, including both *bāmôt* and *bāmôtê*.[6]

---

[3]Vaughan also notes, however, that J. D. Michaelis, in his *Supplementa ad Lexica Hebraica* (Göttingen, 1792), proposed that *bāmāh* might be a loanword from the Greek βωμός, a term for a type of altar. *The Meaning of 'Bāmâ'*, 57 n. 4.

[4]*The Meaning of 'Bāmâ'*, 4-9. Vaughan, following von Soden, notes that the *CAD*'s preferred meaning, "level ground" (2, pp. 76f.), does not facilitate understanding of phrases such as *ba-ma-at šadî* "level ground of the mountains?" (*AHw* 1.101b; Tiglath Pileser Prism; II 15; III 53; IV 92; published in A. K. Grayson, *Assyrian Rulers of the Early First Millennium BC: I (114-859 BC)* (RIMA 2; Toronto: University of Toronto Press, 1991) 15, 18, 21. Von Soden prefers the meaning "midsection of a mountain, slope (also in the steppe)" ("Hälfte eines Berges, Hang [auch in der Steppe]" *AHw* I; *bāmtu(m)* 101b). Both *CAD* and von Soden relate *bamâtu* to *bāmtu* as a frozen plural form. Albright also disliked the *CAD* translation and stated that the term "should be translated 'ridge(s)'" (*Yahweh and the Gods of Canaan*, 204 n. 114).

[5]*The Meaning of 'Bāmâ'*, 57 n. 6. See, also Albright, "High Place."

[6]Rather than pick one of the attested Semitic terms which he discusses as possible cognates to *bāmôt/bāmôtê*, Vaughan adopts Albright's theoretical Proto-Semitic noun **bahmatu*, meaning "rib cage," as the common ancestor of two families of words: those with anatomical meanings (Ugaritic *bmt*, Akkadian *bamtu*, and Hebrew *bāmôtê*, meaning "flank/chest/back" and eventually Hebrew *bəhēmāh*, meaning "animal") and those with topographical meanings (Akkadian *bamtu* and Hebrew *bāmôtê*, meaning "hill-sides")

Unfortunately, etymological discussions such as these have little light
to shed on *bāmôt* as cultic installations. Apart from suggesting possible cognate terms, even the most superficial reading of the biblical text can offer as
much certainty about what the Hebrew terms *bāmôt* and *bāmôtê* mean (as
well as their possible relation to each other) as the most in-depth etymological analyses. Both techniques lead to the same conclusion. Hebrew has two
terms, *bāmôt* and *bāmôtê*. The former refers to a type of cultic installation,
and the latter occurs only in poetic contexts and carries a variety of meanings ranging from the anatomical to the topographical.[7] Anything beyond
this has yet to be determined using etymological analysis.[8]

---

from which split a Hebrew term *bāmāh* meaning "grave mound" [as Albright argued] and
terms meaning "cultic platform" [Hebrew *bāmāh*, Moabite *bmt*, and Greek *βωμός*] and
finally "sanctuary" [Hebrew *bāmāh*]); *The Meaning of 'Bāmâ'*, p. 25. W. Boyd Barrick
also reproduces such a chart as part of his discussion of etymological studies of *bāmôt*
though his chart is not a theoretical proposal but rather a survey of traditional etymological interpretations of *bāmāh* ("The Word BMH," 8).

[7]Cognate studies shed much more light on the poetic term *bāmôtê* than on *bāmôt*.
Vaughan notes (*The Meaning of 'Bāmâ'*, 9-12) that of all the appearances of *bāmôtê* in
the biblical text, several have meanings reminiscent of the Akkadian topographical use of
bamâtu, especially in military contexts where the term describes regions conquered by the
victorious monarch. These include the "heights" on which Saul and Jonathan are killed (2
Sam 1:19, 25), as well as contexts in which YHWH either "treads," or "stands," on the
"heights" (*bāmôtê*) or on the "heights of the land," (*bāmôtê ʾareṣ*) or causes his chosen
favorite to do so (Deut 32:13; Amos 4:13; Mic 1:3; Isa 58:14; 2 Sam 22:34 [= Ps 18:34];
Hab 3:19). In other contexts, *bāmôtê* resembles the anatomical meanings of Akkadian
bamtu and Ugaritic *bmt* by representing the "backs" of objects (such as clouds; Isa 14:14)
or enemies (such as Yamm; Job 9:8) upon which YHWH or his victorious designate
stands (as in Deut 33:29). The only case in which one might prefer this more "military"
shading to apply to an occurrence of *bāmôt* is in Ezek 36:2 in which Israel's enemies
gloat over their conquest of the "ancient *bāmôt*." Perhaps the prophet is consciously
making a double entendre, implying in one image that Israel's enemies now "tread on
her" as YHWH once allowed Israel to "tread" on them, and also that Jerusalem has
become no more than a dilapidated *bāmāh* as a result of her unfaithfulness.

[8]The only biblical passage which even appears to attempt to derive a meaning for
bāmôt is the parenthetical statement in Ezek 20:29 which offers *bwʾ* as a verb related to
the meaning of *bāmôt* even though *bāmôt* is never spelled with *aleph* nor *bwʾ* with *mem*.
This apparent folk etymology, therefore, sheds no real light on the meaning of *bāmôt*. At
the end of his dissertation, Barrick was forced to state, after extensive analysis of
previous etymological studies as well as his own investigation ("The Word BMH," 1-20,
385-92), that "strictly speaking, the 'cultic' BMH is semantically 'opaque' and seems to
have been recognized as such at the close of the biblical period; it would be methodologi-
cally inappropriate, therefore, to supply a derivational transparency through etymological
guesswork. One must, at least for the moment, regard the 'cultic' word as an 'opaque'
termus technicus for a particular type of sanctuary installation in biblical Hebrew and

A.2. Archaeological studies of *bāmôt*

In addition to the etymological search for the meaning of *bāmôt*, many scholars have searched for physical examples of *bāmôt* in the archaeological record of Syria-Palestine, drawing their clues from the presence of other cultic remains and a presumed equation of *bāmôt* with small, often open-air, shrines. Those that Vaughan favors are the famous round stone platform with steps from Megiddo Stratum XVII (locus 4017); a series of cultic structures at Nahariya; a cultic enclosure from En Gedi; the altar complex from Tel Arad; certain *tumuli* located on the hills surrounding Jerusalem; the "cult places" identified at Hazor as area H, loci 8019 and 2554; the cultic complex at Tel Dan area T; and a low oblong structure found at Shechem identified as structure 968.[9]

Although Vaughan divides these structures into two types, those with "conical" surfaces and those which are flat on top, one is left at the end of the analysis with the same unsatisfied feeling expressed by Barrick: "a review of recent scholarly literature reveals a bewildering collection of dissimilar things currently being identified as *bāmôth* . . . surely not all [such reconstructions] can be correct!"[10] One additional structure described in published reports as a *bāmah* (discovered after the publication of both Vaughan and Barrick's studies), is the small stepped structure with an iconographic stela and related cultic vessels adjacent to the eastern city gate of Bethsaida (et-Tell).[11]

Aside from the disparate nature of these examples, some which are free-standing platforms (Megiddo), others of which are roofed structures with several rooms (Tel Dan), other problems exist for many of them if one

---

Moabitic." To his credit, therefore, Barrick voices early on the same scepticism regarding the search for root meanings which he found in the work of James Barr (*The Semantics of Biblical Language* [London: Oxford University Press, 1961], cited in Barrick, "The Word BMH," 9). This scepticism, at least in the case of *bāmôt/bāmôtê*, appears to be well justified.

[9] *The Meaning of 'Bāmâ'*, 37-48.

[10] "Funerary Character," 593-94. Barrick's note 147 lists many more discoveries which have been called *bāmôt*, as well as the "high places" at Petra which Albright identified as *bāmôt* ("High Place" 257). Vaughan spends some discussion arguing against this identification (*The Meaning of 'Bāmâ'*, 37-39), but regardless of their late provenance, K. D. Schunck, as late as 1974, upheld Albright's view of the Petra installations, stating: "There can be little doubt that they go back to Canaanite and Israelite prototypes or cultic practices" ("בָּמָה bāmāh," 142).

[11] The structure is referred to as a "high place" by the excavators, Rami Arav and Richard Freund in "The Bull from the Sea: Geshur's Chief Deity?," *BAR* 24/1 (1998) 42. For a more detailed study of the structure and its stela see, Monika Bernett and Othmar Keel, *Mond, Stier und Kult am Stadttor: Die Stele von Betsaida (et-Tell)* (OBO 161;

wishes to base some understanding of Israelite *bāmôt* on their structure and usage. Their dates of construction and use generally fall outside the Iron Age. Megiddo's stone structure 4017 dates to the Early Bronze Age with its latest use being in the Middle Bronze.[12] The Nahariya "*bāmāh*" dates to the MBI era with its latest use in LBI.[13] The Shechem structure 968 dates to the MBI.[14] Hazor's area H structures date to the LBI with latest use in the LBIIb,[15] and the En Gedi cult site is Chalcolithic.[16] Another site that is often referred to as a "high place" is the row of monoliths found by Macalister at Gezer. These also predate the Israelite period, dating as early as the MBIII with latest use in the LB.[17] Bethsaida, while in use during the Iron Age, is believed to be Geshurite not Israelite.[18]

Of those sites mentioned by Vaughan, only Arad, Tel Dan, and the Jerusalem tumuli date to the Iron Age, are located in Israelite territory, and might be Israelite constructions. Barrick notes, however, that the archaeological remains that are usually seen to be cultic at the Jerusalem sites (cooking pots and burned animal remains) were found *beneath* the stone tumuli which Vaughan and Albright found so suggestive of *bāmôt*. While this evidence might be reevaluated in future, it currently does not demand an interpretation connected to *bāmôt*.[19] Similarly, Yohanan Aharoni viewed Arad's sanctuary as a regional temple, not a *bāmāh*,[20] and Avraham

---

Göttingen: Vandenhoeck & Ruprecht, 1998).

[12]David Ussishkin, "Megiddo," *ABD* 4.668-69.

[13]See, William G. Dever, "Nahariyeh," *ABD* 4.995-96; Moshe Dothan, "Sanctuaries along the Coast of Canaan in the MB Period: Nahariyah," in *Temples and High Places in Biblical Times: Proceedings of the Colloquium in Honor of the Centennial of Hebrew Union College-Jewish Institute of Religion* (ed. Avraham Biran; Jerusalem: Keter, 1981) 74-81.

[14]Lawrence E. Toombs, "Shechem," *ABD* 5.1179. Even the larger "tower temple" structure found at Shechem dates from about 1650 to 1600, see Adam Zertal, "Shechem, Tower of," *ABD* 5.1186-87.

[15]William G. Dever, "Tell el-Qedah," *ABD* 5.579-80.

[16]David Ussishkin, "The 'Ghassulian' Temple in Ein Gedi and the Origin of the Hoard from Nahal Mishmar," *BA* 34 (1971) 23-39.

[17]William G. Dever, "Gezer," *ABD* 2.1000.

[18]Rami Arav and Richard Freund, "The Bull from the Sea: Geshur's Chief Deity?," *BAR* 24/1 (1998) 42.

[19]Barrick calls attention to the work of Z. Ron concerning these sites ("Agricultural Terraces in the Judean Mountains," *IEJ* 16 [1966] 48). Ron's explanation of these areas does not demand a cultic interpretation ("Funerary Character," 576-78, see especially n. 75).

[20]Yohanan Aharoni, *The Archaeology of the Land of Israel: From the Prehistoric Beginnings to the End of the First Temple Period* (tr. Anson Rainey; ed. Miriam Aharoni;

Biran has changed his views on the large shrine at Dan throughout the years.

As noted by Amihai Mazar, Biran first explained the cultic area of Area T as "an open-air platform, a *bamah* ("high place"), but later he changed his mind and concluded that the podium, recalling in function the palace's podium at Lachish, served as a foundation for a temple."[21] Recently, however, Biran has returned to his earlier nomenclature and refers to this large structure as a *bāmāh*.[22] Biran also refers to several smaller stela assemblages located at stages along the road leading into Dan through its southern gate, as *bāmôt*. Most of these lack any platform, steps, or major structures.[23]

It is unlikely that Biran means, by this wide use of the term *bāmāh,* that Dan's small stela shrines and the large platform structure of Area T would have been considered the same type of cultic installation by the ancients themselves. As he has stated in print many times, Biran believes the Area T structure to be the shrine described in the biblical text as one of two state-sanctioned temples of the northern kingdom, not just one of the various *bāmôt* of the Samarian countryside.[24] Biran's seemingly indiscriminate use of the term *bāmāh* is simply illustrates the complication of ancient Hebrew terms being borrowed into Modern Hebrew without a specific semantic range or specialized usage being borrowed along with them. Unfortunately, Israeli archaeologists often use the archaic biblical Hebrew term *bāmāh* to identify all types of open air cultic sites, without regard to formal or architectural criteria. This has led to a multiplicity of excavators reporting the presence of *bāmôt* without a general consensus of what the term actually means, either in modern or ancient usage.

So while there continue to be sites excavated which suggest to those who see them that they contain examples of *bāmôt*,[25] by and large, archaeology and biblical studies are in an impossible position when it comes to the

---

Philadelphia: Westminster, 1982) 229-34.

[21]Amihai Mazar, *Archaeology of the Land of the Bible: 10,000-586 B.C.E* (Anchor Bible Reference Library; New York: Doubleday, 1990) 493.

[22] Avraham Biran, "Dan (place)," *ABD* 2.14-15; idem, "Sacred Spaces: Of Standing Stones, High Places, and Cult Objects at Dan," *BAR* 24/5 (1998) 38-45, 70.

[23]Biran, "Sacred Spaces," 41-45.

[24]Biran, "Sacred Spaces," 40.

[25]See the following studies on the Mt. Ebal structure: Aharon Kempinski, "Joshua's Altar- An Iron Age I Watchtower," *BAR* 12/1 (Jan/Feb 1986) 42-49; Adam Zertal, "Has Joshua's Altar Been Found on Mt. Ebal?," *BAR* 11/1 (Jan/Feb 1985) 26-43; idem, "How Can Kempinski Be So Wrong!," *BAR* 12/1 (Jan/Feb 1986) 43-53; as well as studies on a small cult site found in the central hill country: Amihai Mazar, "Bronze Bull

identification of objects in the ground with objects mentioned in literature. Archaeologists can produce the physical evidence, but usually without the technical name attached, and biblical scholars can provide the ancient technical names of objects but often without any physical description along with them. Often the biblical text and the archaeological record both give multiple descriptions or examples of particular types of objects, frustrating the efforts of those who wish to arrive at a "standard image" or "definition" of them so that actual physical examples could be ruled in or out of the category. This embarrassment of riches with regard to both the literary and archaeological witnesses to *bāmôt* or possible *bāmôt* leaves biblical scholars and archaeologists looking to each other for evidence, connections, and or criteria for evaluation which neither can produce. Unfortunately, this situation is likely to persist until additional inscriptional evidence is recovered. At present, no studies have successfully identified any archaeological installations specifically as *bāmôt* as opposed to shrines or temples or other types of cultic structures.

A.3. Studies which reconstruct one particular understanding of *bāmôt*

Some longer works which deal with *bāmôt* are aimed at reconstructing one overarching understanding of what *bāmôt* were. Usually these works adopt a single understanding of *bāmôt* and attempt to prove it with relation to the biblical references at their disposal.

Perhaps one of the most narrowly focused views concerning *bāmôt* is that once held by W. F. Albright. Albright's theory of *bāmôt* was that they were funerary monuments which played a central role in an Israelite cult of the dead.[26] The best critique of Albright's unique, and highly theoretical thesis, is that of Boyd Barrick, who easily demonstrates the difficulties in

---

Found in Israelite 'High Place' From the Time of the Judges," *BAR* 9/5 (Sept/Oct 1983) 34-40; idem, "On Cult Places and Early Israelites: A Response to Michael Coogan," *BAR* 14/4 (July/August 1988) 45; Hershel Shanks, "Two Early Israelite Cult Sites Now Questioned," *BAR* 14/1 (Jan/Feb 1988) 48-52. For a recent discussion of the many archaeological features which have been identified as *bāmôt*, see Beth Alpert Nakhai, "What's a Bamah? How Sacred Space Functioned in Ancient Israel," *BAR* 20/3 (May/June 1994) 18-29, 77-78.

[26]"High Place." See also idem, *Yahweh and the Gods of Canaan*, 203-6; Elizabeth Bloch-Smith, *Judahite Burial Practices and Beliefs About the Dead* (JSOTSup 123; Sheffield: JSOT Press, 1992); Theodore J. Lewis, *Cults of the Dead in Ancient Israel and Ugarit* (HSM 39; Atlanta: Scholars Press, 1989); Brian B. Schmidt, *Israel's Beneficent Dead: Ancestor Cult and Necromancy in Ancient Israelite Religion and Tradition* (Winona Lake, Ind.: Eisenbrauns, 1996).

Albright's view.[27] Barrick himself, however, also undertook as his doctoral dissertation a study to define the essential nature of *bāmôt*.[28] Barrick rightly pointed out a chronic problem with works which deal with *bāmôt* when he wrote:

> A picture of these *bāmāh*-sanctuaries has been developed around . . . bits and pieces of information found scattered throughout the Old Testament, information routinely supplemented by archaeological discoveries and cross-cultural parallels. The well-known result needs only to be briefly outlined: A *bāmāh*-sanctuary is fundamentally an open-air sacred precinct situated atop a natural elevation or associated with a man-made elevation, whence its name. Roofed cult buildings may be present on occasion, but they are auxiliary and typologically secondary features. Its basic accoutrements are altars, *maṣṣēbôth*, and sacred trees or the surrogate *ăshērîm*. A *bāmāh*-sanctuary thus is a typically Canaanitish cult place of local importance and ubiquitous provenance expressive of a markedly fertility-oriented religiosity. This Canaanite heritage and concomitant orgiastic character necessitated their prohibition and ultimate eradication by the official religion of Israel.[29]

In his dissertation, Barrick provides a survey of previous scholarship on *bāmôt* and the nature of this scholarly analysis, as well as a thorough syntactical analysis of all the verses which mention *bāmôt*. His main objective, however, was to take issue with two of the features of the above description of *bāmôt* in secondary scholarship: first, that *bāmôt* were rural installations, and second, that they were part of what is frequently dubbed Israelite "popular religion." Barrick attempts to make the case that they were located within cities predominantly and that the active interest of the royal establishments of both Judah and northern Israel in them proves they were in some way "an organ of monarchical government and administration" rather than an example of "rustic" popular religion.[30] While many of Barrick's points are well taken (for example, the text does clearly imply that *bāmôt* were state-sanctioned cult sites [1 Kgs 12:31]), there is not sufficient evidence to prove all of his contentions (such that most *bāmôt* were urban as opposed to rural installations).

---

[27]"Funerary Character," 565-95.

[28]"The Word BMH."

[29]"Funerary Character," 566. The article which he cites as an example of this view is Schunck's article on *bāmôt* ("בָּמָה bāmāh," 139-45). An article which is free from this unfortunate generalizing tendency with regard to *bāmôt* is Barrick's own article for the *Anchor Bible Dictionary* ("High Place," *ABD* 3.196-200).

[30]See especially his conclusions, "The Word BMH," 279-384.

Another scholar with a single definition of *bāmôt* is Menahem Haran. He proposes that *bāmôt* are essentially a type of altar and nothing more. Haran argues for the dismissal of any evidence that suggests *bāmôt* were more substantial structures, believing that the type of cult activity which is described as taking place on *bāmôt* is not properly the province of a "temple" however small, but rather of a simple altar.[31]

As will be demonstrated by the analysis that follows, the weakness of any study that seeks to arrive at one definition for *bāmôt* and to force that definition on most or all of the examples is that, however carefully undertaken, this ultimately leads to a homogenization of the various biblical witnesses, leveling through any distinctions they might have preserved regarding their own particular opinion concerning *bāmôt*. While such studies seek to correct the work of previous scholars whose reconstructions of *bāmôt* did not fit all case examples, ultimately those who have a reconstruction of their own in mind simply end by displacing an older artificial unity among the witnesses with a newer one. In order to avoid this pitfall, the conclusions below are confined to specific statements concerning *bāmôt* made by the individual biblical witnesses. This sort of analysis of the data seeks to preserve the views of the witnesses, grouping them together only when they themselves have overtly voiced the same opinion concerning *bāmôt*.

B. SUMMARY OF THE BIBLICAL DATA ON *bāmôt*

The authors who mention *bāmôt* are P, H, Dtr, the Chronicler, Amos, Hosea, Micah, Isaiah, Jeremiah, Ezekiel, and Psalms.[32] The term *bāmôt* also occurs as a part of three different Moabite place names mentioned in the work of J, E, P, and Dtr.[33] The archaic poetic term *bāmôtê* occurs in D, Dtr, Amos, Micah, First Isaiah, Third Isaiah, Habakkuk, Psalms, and Job.[34]

---

[31]*Temples and Temple Service*, 18-25.

[32]P: Num 33:52; H: Lev 26:30; 1 Sam 9:12, 13, 14, 19, 25; 10:5, 13; 1 Kgs 3:2, 3, 4, 11:7; 12:31, 32; 13:2, 32, 33; 14:23; 15:14; 22:44 [Eng 22:43]; 2 Kgs 12:4 [Eng 12:3]; 14:4; 15:4, 35; 16:4; 17:9, 11, 29, 32; 18:4, 22; 21:3; 23:5, 8, 9, 13, 15, 19, 20; 1 Chr 16:39; 21:29; 2 Chr 1:3, 13; 11:15; 14:2 [Eng 14:3], 4 [Eng 14:5]; 15:17; 17:6; 20:33; 21:11; 28:4, 25; 31:1; 32:12; 33:3, 17, 19; 34:3; Amos 7:9; Hos 10:8, Mic 1:5; 3:12; Isa 15:2; 16:12; 36:7; Jer 7:31; 17:3; 19:5; 26:18; 32:35; 48:35; Ezek 6:3, 6; 16:16; 20:29; 36:2; 43:7; Ps 78:58.

[33]J: Bamoth-Arnon, Num 21:28; E: Bamoth-Ba'al, Num 22:41; P: Bamoth, Num 21:19, 20; Dtr: Bamoth-Ba'al, Josh 13:17.

[34]Deut 32:13; 33:29; 2 Sam 1:19, 25; 22:34; Amos 4:13; Mic 1:3; Isa 14:14; 58:14; Hab 3:19; Ps 18:34; and Job 9:8.

B.1. Biblical Opinions on the acceptability of *bāmôt*

Below is a chart listing those authors who evaluate *bāmôt* either positively or negatively, and categorizing them by whether they are speaking of "Israelite" *bāmôt*, "foreign" *bāmôt*, or both. The term "Israelite" refers to those *bāmôt* built or used by Israelite people from either the northern or the southern kingdoms. "Foreign" refers to those *bāmôt* built or used by non-Israelites. No distinction is made concerning whether the *bāmôt* in question are YHWHistic or non-YHWHistic because all of the *bāmôt* which are approved are YHWHistic. Of those Israelite *bāmôt* that are disapproved, some are YHWHistic, and some dedicated to foreign gods, though the majority are unspecified. Verses which contain the archaic poetic term *bāmôtê* are not included.

> Foreign *bāmôt* positive: -
> Foreign *bāmôt* negative: P & Jer
> Israelite *bāmôt* positive: Dtr & Chr (if built before the Temple)
> Israelite *bāmôt* negative: Dtr & Chr (if built after the Temple), Jer, Ps 78, Ezek

In addition to the authors above who indicate some positive or negative evaluation of *bāmôt*, several authors mention *bāmôt* only in judgment oracles against some other institution, thus obscuring their actual opinion regarding *bāmôt*. Authors who mention *bāmôt* only in judgment oracles are, H (Lev 26:30), Amos (7:9), Hosea (10:8), Micah (1:5; 3:12), and First Isaiah (15:2; 16:12). In the case of Isaiah, both the references to *bāmôt* refer to those located in Moab.[35] Finally, Jeremiah includes two judgment oracles which mention *bāmôt* (17:2-3; 26:18) along with other passages more indicative of Jeremiah's actual views of *bāmôt*, both Moabite and Israelite.

Of the biblical witnesses which mention *bāmôt*, P, H, Amos, Hosea, Micah, Jeremiah, Ezekiel, First Isaiah, and Psalms have primarily negative references to them, though as noted above, H, Amos, Hosea, First Isaiah, and Micah only mention *bāmôt* in judgment oracles that might well apply to some institution other than *bāmôt* and not to the *bāmôt* themselves. For H (Lev 26:30), *bāmôt* are items used by Israelites (mentioned alongside their use of idols) that YHWH will destroy as a punishment for unfaithfulness. In Amos and Hosea (Amos 7:9; Hos 10:8), *bāmôt* are mentioned in general indictments of the religious institutions of the northern kingdom. In Micah the term *bāmôt* is used twice as part of polemical speeches directed at the Solomonic Temple in Jerusalem (1:5; 3:12).

---

[35]Isa 36:7 is included with Dtr for the purposes of this chapter.

For P *bāmôt* are items used by the prior inhabitants of the land which Israel must destroy. The implication is that they were dedicated to gods other than YHWH (Num 33:52). P does not mention any Israelite use of *bāmôt*. Jeremiah, however, makes three references to a connection between child sacrifice and *bāmôt* built in the Valley of Ben Hinnom by Judah's royalty (7:31; 19:5; 32:35). Jeremiah also issues a judgment oracle against the "sins" of Judah which mentions *bāmôt* as items that will be destroyed. Jeremiah also mentions *bāmôt* in an oracle against Moab in which God declares an intention to destroy all the *bāmôt* of Moab that are used to worship idols. Finally, Jeremiah quotes Mic 3:12 in 26:18.

In a similar vein to Mic 3:12 and Jer 26:18, Ezekiel has the enemies of Israel gloat over the fact that the ancient *bāmôt*, presumably meaning Jerusalem and its environs, have now become their possession (36:2). Ezekiel makes only veiled connections between *bāmôt* and child sacrifice (16:16-22; 20:29-31), but clearly connects their use to the worship of idols (6:3, 6).[36] The single reference to *bāmôt* in Psalms (78:58) places them in parallelism with *pəsîlîm* and states that the use of *bāmôt* on the part of Israel's ancestors "angered" 'Elohim.

As noted above, of First Isaiah's three references to *bāmôt*, two are contained in judgment oracles against Moab (Isa 15:2; 16:12), and the third is in a duplicate of Dtr's speech of the Rab Shaqeh (Isa 36:7). If one accepts that Isa 36:7 is Dtr's material and not Isaiah, then there is no original Isaianic material that deals with Israelite *bāmôt*, and even those verses dealing with Moabite *bāmôt* cannot be demonstrated to condemn *bāmôt* separately from the condemnation of Moab.

The remaining witnesses which mention *bāmôt* are Dtr and the Chronicler. These are the only witnesses which clearly present the use of *bāmôt* in a positive light and as an acceptable way to worship YHWH prior to the construction of the Temple in Jerusalem. Psalm 78 appears to be describing the use of *bāmôt* prior to the construction of the Temple (contemporaneous with the existence of the shrine at Shiloh), but the Psalm does not view the use of *bāmôt* as acceptable in this context. Dtr, however, identifies three acceptable *bāmôt* at Ramah (1 Sam 9:12, 13, 14, 19, 25), Gibeah-Elohim (1 Sam 10:5, 13), and Gibeon (1 Kgs 3:4), as well as noting that the use of *bāmôt* to worship YHWH was widespread throughout Judah prior to the building of the Temple (1 Kgs 3:2, 3). The Chronicler deals only with the *bāmāh* at Gibeon, but expands on the explanation of its use found

---

[36]Ezek 43:7 is also a verse of condemnation, but it is uncertain whether a clear reference to *bāmôt* occurs in this passage.

in Dtr by stating that the Tabernacle and the Tent of Meeting were installed there and that Aaronide priests presided over the sacrifices there prior to the construction of the Temple (1 Chr 16:39; 21:29; 2 Chr 1:3, 13). The Chronicler also seeks to soften the negative impact of statements concerning the persistent use of *bāmôt* in Judah even after the construction of the Temple by insisting that these *bāmôt* were used only to worship YHWH (2 Chr 33:17).

The matter of clergy connected to *bāmôt* is also important to Dtr. The Deuteronomist seems to be as distressed by the fact that Jeroboam I chose non-Levitical priests to serve on his northern *bāmôt* as by the simple fact of their construction. It is as if this slighting of the Levitical priesthood added insult to injury as far as Dtr is concerned (1 Kgs 12:31, 32; 13:2, 32, 33; 2 Kgs 17:9, 11, 29, 32). 2 Chr 11:15 seconds this sentiment and goes further by insisting that not only were non-Levitical priests employed in the north, but genuine Levitical priests were consciously excluded from service there.

A final indication that Levitical priests who served at *bāmôt* were viewed differently from those priests who were not Levitical is found in Dtr in 2 Kings 23. In this passage, *bāmôt* priests (called *kəmārîm*) who served in the southern kingdom at idolatrous *bāmôt* (2 Kgs 23:5), and those priests (called *kōhănîm*) who served at other *bāmôt* whose dedication to foreign gods is not specifically mentioned (23:8-9) are deposed by Josiah and restricted from service on YHWH's altar in Jerusalem (23:9). This statement may imply that they *could* have "ascended" to YHWH's altar had they not served on *bāmôt* because they were Levitical priests. Support for the assumption that they were Levitical is that they were censured after their removal from the *bāmôt* by restriction from YHWH's altar, implying that they might once have been allowed access to it.[37] Those priests of *bāmôt* who remained in the north when Josiah arrived, however, whom Dtr has repeatedly stated were not Levitical priests (1 Kgs 12:31; 13:33; 2 Kgs 17:32), are executed and their bones burned on the altars of their *bāmôt* (23:20). This harsh justice meted out to the non-Levitical *bāmôt* priests from the north stands in sharp contrast to the relatively lenient treatment of the southern *bāmôt* priests who the text implies were Levitical.

The only author who appears to have a criterion for evaluating *bāmôt* either positively or negatively is Dtr, which bases this evaluation on whether or not they compete with worship in the Jerusalem Temple. It is not

---

[37]Menahem Haran argues the converse of this statement, namely that the fact that these priests were restricted from YHWH's altar makes it "very doubtful that these [*bāmôt*] priests really traced their descent to the tribe of Levi" (*Temples and Temple Service*, 100).

possible to discern if other authors also use this criterion to evaluate *bāmôt*. P does not acknowledge any use of *bāmôt* by Israelites, only by the prior inhabitants of the land who used them to worship their own gods. Ps 78:58 mentions the use of *bāmôt* as a type of unfaithfulness which causes God to abandon the shrine at Shiloh, thus demonstrating a negative view of *bāmôt* prior to the construction of the Temple, but possibly motivated by disapproval of competition with the shrine at Shiloh. Of the remaining authors besides Dtr, only H and the Chronicler deal with Israel's life prior to the construction of the Temple. H, however, does not mention *bāmôt* except in a passage concerning Israelite apostasy *after* the construction of the Temple (Lev 26:30). Dtr and the Chronicler appear to be alone, then, in the expressed opinion that *bāmôt* were acceptable parts of Israel's religious life prior to the Temple's construction.

Psalm 78 refers to the fall of the northern kingdom but not the fall of the southern kingdom, thus making it appear as if it belongs to a time period which is roughly contemporaneous with First Isaiah, prior to Dtr. It is the only reference which appears to be prior to Dtr that both discusses Israel's religious life prior to the construction of the Temple and mentions *bāmôt* as a part of that life. Because of the negative assessment of *bāmôt* in Psalm 78, then, it appears that Dtr's positive assessment of *bāmôt* prior to the Temple is either a development on Dtr's part, or evidence of a basic difference of opinion from the author responsible for Psalm 78. Whether Dtr's opinion concerning pre-Temple *bāmôt* was shared by anyone other than the Chronicler cannot be clearly demonstrated. Of those authors dated after Dtr, none can be clearly shown to be discussing *bāmôt* which existed prior to the Temple.[38]

It cannot be argued definitively, therefore, that any development in attitude concerning the acceptability of *bāmôt* occurred over time in Israelite thought in general. The authors which express negative views of *bāmôt* each have their own reasons for doing so, and their views may originally have been accompanied by views concerning circumstances in which *bāmôt* were acceptable. These later circumstances, however, if they existed, never surfaced in their writings. Dtr and the Chronicler are alone in affirming the use of *bāmôt* prior to the construction of the Temple. Psalm 78 condemns *bāmôt* use at this point in Israel's history, but without clearly stated reasons for this view. No other authors mention *bāmôt* used by Israelites in the pre-Temple years.

---

[38]Ezek 16:16 and 20:29 might be interpreted as referring to *bāmôt* which existed prior to the Temple but this interpretation is not clear.

B.2. Objects or peoples associated with *bāmôt*

Below is a series of discussions on the cultic objects or groups of people associated with *bāmôt* by the various biblical writers. As will be demonstrated, no one connection or association dominates, so that no one determination of the causes of negative views concerning *bāmôt* can be discerned. Certain connections, however, are shared by more than one author and will be discussed together.

B.2.a. *bāmôt* and Moab. The secondary literature on bāmôt often asserts that they are condemned by biblical authors because they were strongly associated with the Canaanites, or similarly, that *bāmôt* were nothing more than shrines previously used by Canaanites which Israelites took over.[39] In fact, the terms "Canaan" or "Canaanites" never occur in conjunction with *bāmôt*. To be sure, the P writer relates *bāmôt* to the "prior inhabitants of the land" (Num 33:52), and Dtr makes a few references to *bāmôt* along with practices also engaged in by the "nations whom YHWH dispossessed before" Israel (1 Kgs 14:23; 2 Kgs 16:4; 17:9-11; 21:3-9). P does not specify the names or nationalities of these "prior inhabitants of the land." Dtr has various lists of these "nations," however, which include the Canaanites along with the Hittites, Girgashites, Amorites, Perrizites, Hivites and Jebusites.[40] In as much as the "land" in question was viewed by biblical authors as the land of Canaan primarily (even though D extends the boundaries of the "promised land" east to the Euphrates, Deut 11:24), one might argue in a general way that these prior inhabitants were viewed collectively as Canaanites. However, the direct singling out and naming of the Canaanites specifically as those who worship on *bāmôt* never occurs in the biblical text.[41]

---

[39]For three examples of this opinion, see Walther Eichrodt (*Theology*, 105, 115), Helmer Ringgren (*Israelite Religion* [tr. David E. Green; Philadelphia: Fortress, 1966] 157), and Schunck ("בָּמָה bāmāh," 142-44).

[40]See further, Tomoo Ishida, "The Structure and Historical Implications of the Lists of Pre-Israelite Nations," *Biblica* 60 (1979) 461-90; Kevin G. O'Connell, "The List of Seven Peoples in Canaan," in *The Answers Lie Below: Essays in Honor of Lawrence Edmund Toombs* (ed. Henry O. Thompson; Lanham, Md.: University Press of America, 1984) 221-41.

[41]2 Kgs 23:13 states that 'Astarte was one of the deities for whom Solomon built *bāmôt* (though she is left out of the list provided in 1 Kgs 11:7) and Jeremiah states that *bāmôt* dedicated to Ba'al existed in the child sacrifice installations in the Valley of Ben Hinnom (Jer 19:5; 32:35); however, both of these authors indicate that those who built the *bāmôt* were Israelites. There is no indication that *bāmôt* per se were seen as shrines built according to some Canaanite model or tradition.

If one cites Gibeon as an example of a former Canaanite stronghold which is famous for its *bāmāh* (1 Kgs 3:4; 1 Chr 16:39; 21:29; 2 Chr 1:3, 13), one should note that the Gibeon *bāmāh* never receives even a hint of criticism from the authors who mention it (Dtr and the Chronicler), nor is it ever intimated that it was ever used to worship any other god but YHWH. In fact, one should not construe from the references listed in the previous paragraph, in which *bāmôt* are mentioned along with the "nations whom YHWH dispossessed," that it was the view of Dtr that all *bāmôt* were shrines of Canaanite origin and were therefore suspect. Dtr and Chronicles are the only two authors who openly maintain that *bāmôt* could be completely respectable YHWHistic shrines, providing they belonged to a time period when they were not in competition with the Jerusalem Temple. Given this evidence, the assertion that *bāmôt* were viewed by *all* biblical writers as thoroughly Canaanite installations, built by Canaanites and dedicated to Canaanite gods, which heterodox Israelites simply visited, is erroneous.

The text intimates, however, that *bāmôt* did have a traditional connection to another nation besides Israel. The national association recurring in the references to *bāmôt* is with Moab. All of the authors who mention place names of which the term *bāmôt* is a part locate these places in the land of Moab (J: Num 21:28; P: Num 21:19, 20; E: Num 22:41; Dtr: Josh 13:17). There is no biblical place name containing the term *bāmôt* which is not located in Moab.

The chart below indicates how often the authors who mention *bāmôt* connect them either with the land prior to Israelite settlement, the later kingdoms of Israel or Judah, or with Moab.

Source	Land Prior	Israel	Judah	Moab
J				1 place name
E				1 place name
Amos		1		
Hosea		1		
Micah			2	
Psalm 78		1		
First Isaiah				2
Dtr		12	22	1 place name
				2 Chemosh
Jeremiah			5	
P	1			
H			1	
Ezekiel		4	2	
Chronicles		1	18	

Out of thirteen authors who mention *bāmôt* either as cultic installations or as part of place names, six of these make a connection between *bāmôt* and Moab: J, E, First Isaiah, Dtr, Jeremiah, and P.

Of these authors, Isaiah and Jeremiah mention *bāmôt* as loci of Moabite worship. In Isa 15:2, the Moabite nation personified goes up to the *bāmôt* to lament its fate. In Isa 16:12, Moab is worn out with fruitless entreaty on a *bāmāh*. In this passage, the next colon states that when Moab enters his sanctuary (*miqdāšô*) to pray it will avail him nothing. This verse makes it apparent that Moabite *bāmôt* were viewed not simply as "heights" from which one looked out, but as the locus of religious activity such as prayer or ritual lament. Jeremiah 48:35 states that *bāmôt* are places at which Moabites offer sacrifice and burn incense to their gods.

Aside from simple mentions of *bāmôt* as worship sites, or as places located within Moab which contain the term *bāmôt* in their name, there is another type of connection made between *bāmôt* and Moab in Dtr. Twice Dtr states that one of the *bāmôt* constructed by Solomon was dedicated to Chemosh, god of the Moabites (1 Kgs 11:7; 2 Kgs 23:13).[42] Chemosh, however, is not the only god so honored by Solomon. He also built *bāmôt* for Sidonian ʿAstarte, Ammonite Milcom, and Molech[43] (1 Kgs 11:7; 2 Kgs 23:13). Jeremiah has two passages which link *bāmôt* to Baʿal (19:5; 32:35).

The significance of the Moabite connection to the overall understanding of *bāmôt* and of how this may have been perceived in ancient Israel is not easily determined. Since Dtr is the author for whom *bāmôt* were acceptable prior to the construction of the Temple in Jerusalem, it is noteworthy that there is a strong Moabite connection elsewhere in Dtr and in D. The entire narrative of Deuteronomy takes place in Moab. Moses, the Deuteronomic hero, is buried there (Deut 34:6). D and Dtr are also in agreement with P (Num 32) concerning the fact that the descendants of Reuben, Jacob's eldest son, are given Moab as their inheritance (Deut 3:12-18; Josh 13:15-23).

---

[42]One other possible point of connection between Dtr and Moab is the fact that the term *bêt bāmôt*, which occurs in the biblical text only in Dtr (with reference to cult sites in the north), also occurs in the Mesha Stone inscription (*KAI* #181, line 27; 1.31; 2.168-179). It is probable, however, that the בת במה of the Mesha Stone is a place name similar to others in the inscription formed by the combination of בת with some other particle: Bêt Bamot (בת במת) ln 27; Bêt Diblatin (בת דבלתן) ln 30; Bêt Baʿal Meon (בת בעלמען) ln 30. For a discussion of the occurrence of *bêt bāmôt* in Dtr, see the discussion below on the comparison of *bāmôt* to temples (pp. 145-48).

[43]For more on Molech, see the discussion of child sacrifice below (pp. 143-45).

Frank Moore Cross has skillfully pointed out the ambivalence and exchanges of polemic within the biblical text regarding traditions which linked Moses with Transjordanian cultures such as Midian and Moab.[44] The fact that the most favorable assessment of *bāmôt* in the biblical text comes from an author (Dtr) whose larger tradition (D) has strong positive associations with both Moses and Moab, may indicate that the connections between *bāmôt* and Moab, as well as the mixture of assessments regarding this connection, may be an additional part of this larger biblical dispute over the value of religious traditions which Israel may have inherited from Transjordan.[45] While this dispute cannot be responsible for every negative assessment of *bāmôt* in the biblical text (accounts of *bāmôt* dedicated to foreign gods would carry their own weight), it is possible that the positive connections between Moses and Moab in D derive from a commonly held tradition, reflected also in the positive assessment of pre-Temple *bāmôt* in Dtr, which existed independently of any negative connections drawn by other authors between *bāmôt* and Moab.

B.2.b. *bāmôt* and child sacrifice. In 2 Kgs 17:31, Dtr implies that child sacrifice went on at *bāmôt* abandoned by the citizens of the northern kingdom when they were deported to Assyria. Dtr states that the foreign people resettled by Assyria in northern Israel took over the abandoned *bêt bāmôt* shrines there and converted them to centers of worship for their own gods (17:29). Among these foreign people were those from Sepharvaim who sacrificed their children to their gods, Adrammelech and Anammelech. It is implied, though not stated explicitly, that this activity would have been conducted at one of the local *bāmôt* shrines currently in reuse by this new group. However, the passage is not speaking of Israelite use of *bāmôt* and so cannot be used as an indicator that Dtr viewed child sacrifice as the standard ritual practice of *bāmôt*. Given Dtr's singularly positive assessment of *bāmôt* built prior to the Jerusalem Temple, it seems unlikely that Dtr equated *bāmôt* rituals with child sacrifice.

Jeremiah, on the other hand, mentions *bāmôt* six times, three of which connect the use of *bāmôt* with the practice of child sacrifice on the part of Israelites (7:31; 19:5; 32:35). The larger contexts of 19:5 and 32:35

---

[44]See Cross, "Reuben," 46-64; now in his *Epic and Canon: History and Literature in Ancient Israel* (Baltimore: Johns Hopkins University Press, 1998) 53-70. A related discussion by Cross can be found in *CMHE*, 195-215.

[45]See further Jo Ann Hackett, "Religious Traditions in Israelite Transjordan," in *Ancient Israelite Religion: Essays in Honor of Frank Moore Cross* (ed. Patrick D. Miller, Jr., Paul D. Hanson, S. Dean McBride; Philadelphia: Fortress, 1987) 125-36.

indicate that the highest levels of Judean society, even including the Judean royal family, were actively involved in child sacrifice.[46] Another term for the place of child sacrifice is *tōpet*. Jeremiah includes the term *tōpet* along with *bāmôt* in 7:31 and 19:5-6.[47]

Jeremiah is the only biblical author who makes explicit the connection between *bāmôt* and child sacrifice on the part of Israelites, although there are additional veiled allusions possibly meant to connect the two in Ezekiel 16 and 20. In Ezekiel 16 there is a *bāmāh* which faithless Jerusalem constructs (16:16), and presumably on which she later sacrifices her children (16:20-22).[48] In Ezekiel 20:27-31, a condemnation of worship on "high hills" and under "green trees," includes an unusual derivation for the term *bāmāh* from the verb בוא, and closes with a condemnation of the practice of child sacrifice.

Another possible allusion to Israelite child sacrifice on *bāmôt* occurs in 1 Kgs 11:7 which states that Solomon built a *bāmāh* for "Molech, the abomination of the Ammonites." If this is not a mistake for Milcom, god of the Ammonites (who is mentioned instead of Molech in 11:5 and 2 Kgs 23:13),[49] it may be a reference to the cult of child sacrifice which the biblical text describes as "causing one's sons and daughters to pass through the fire to Molech."[50]

---

[46]2 Kgs 16:3 states that Ahaz sacrificed his son in a sacrificial practice once used by the former inhabitants of the land. The Chronicler repeats this assessment in 2 Chr 28:3. Dtr and the Chronicler also charge that Manasseh practiced child sacrifice (2 Kgs 21:6; 2 Chr 33:6). Others who sacrificed their children, according to Dtr, were Jephthah (Judg 11:30-39), Hiel of Jericho (1 Kgs 16:34), and (interesting in light of the connections between *bāmôt* and Moab), Mesha, king of Moab (2 Kgs 3:27).

[47]The term *tōpet* is used by only two biblical authors, Jeremiah (7:31, 32; 19:6, 11, 12, 13, 14) and Dtr (2 Kgs 23:10).

[48]Following this is a statement that she also built a "lofty place [*rāmāh*] in every square" of the city (16:23-25). Perhaps it is not a coincidence that the word chosen here is also the name of a place, Ramah, which was famous for having a *bāmāh* over which the prophet Samuel presided (1 Sam 9:12, 13, 14, 19, 25). It also implies that there was a connection in the mind of the prophet between *bāmôt* and physical height.

[49]The LXX translates "Molech" in 1 Kgs 11:5 as "the king (τῷ βασιλεῖ), the idol of the Ammonites."

[50]Jeremiah mentions Molech in one verse linking child sacrifice with *bāmôt* (32:35). Molech is mentioned elsewhere within the biblical text only in H (Lev 18:21; 20:2, 3, 4, 5), and Dtr (1 Kgs 11:7; 2 Kgs 23:10). The literature related to Molech is extensive and complicated. Much of the debate centers on whether the term "molech" (Heb מלך) refers to a god who was worshipped through child sacrifice or to a type of child sacrifice ritual. *mlk* is also part of the compound names of the gods of Sepharvaim who are said to receive child sacrifice in 2 Kgs 17:31 (Adrammelech and Anammelech). See

In short, only Jeremiah makes explicit the connection between Israelite *bāmôt* and child sacrifice. Dtr mentions the *tōpet*, *bāmôt*, Molech, and child sacrifice, but never clearly connects Israelite *bāmôt* with any of the other three though it does imply that Assyrian deportees may have sacrificed their children on the *bāmôt* left behind by the inhabitants of the northern kingdom (2 Kgs 17:31). Ezekiel implies a connection between *bāmôt* and child sacrifice, but fails to make such a connection indisputably explicit.

B.2.c. *bāmôt* and temples. When speaking of the religious sites of the northern kingdom, Dtr uses a term that is not found elsewhere. Five times Dtr refers to a type of northern cult site called a "house" or "temple of *bāmôt*." This construct occurs in various forms: "house/temple of *bāmôt*," *bêt bāmôt* (1 Kgs 12:31), "house/temple of *the bāmôt*," *bêt hābbāmôt* (2 Kgs 17:29, 32), and "houses/temples of the *bāmôt*," *bātê habbāmôt* (1 Kgs 13:32; 2 Kgs 23:19).[51] Dtr does not use this construct phrase when speaking of the *bāmôt* found in the southern kingdom. It is possible that Dtr is saying that the *bāmôt* of the north were larger structures than southern *bāmôt*, so large that they qualified as temples. It is more likely, however, that Dtr is making a disparaging comment about temples in the north. Perhaps it is not their *bāmôt* that were temples, but their temples that were essentially *bāmôt*.

In fact, the designation *bayit*, meaning "temple," is used very sparingly by Dtr with reference to anything other than the Jerusalem Temple, and Dtr never uses the term *bayit* or any other term meaning temple to refer to the cult sites at Dan and Bethel.[52] Dtr's usual way of referring to

---

further, George C. Heider, "Molech," *ABD* 4.895-898; idem "Molech," in *Dictionary of Deities and Demons in the Bible* (ed. Karel van der Toorn, Bob Becking, and Pieter W. van der Horst; Leiden: E. J. Brill, 1999) 581-85; Elizabeth C. LaRocca-Pitts, "Daughter (or Son or Child) Passed Through Fire, Burned, or Sacrificed," in *Women in Scripture: A Dictionary of Named and Unnamed Women in the Hebrew Bible, The Apocryphal/Deuterocanonical Books, and the New Testament* (ed. Carol Meyers, Toni Craven, and Ross S. Kraemer; Boston: Houghton Mifflin, 2000) 224-25.

[51]It was Albright's view that the phrase *bêt bāmôt* should be understood as "stela temple," designating a shrine in which memorial stelae stood, similar to the obelisk temple at Byblos (*Yahweh and the Gods of Canaan*, 205). This view also figures as part of Albright's theory that *bāmôt* were burial mounds or funerary stelae ("High Place," 242-58). For a discussion of this theory, see above page 133-34. Also, as noted above (p. 142, n. 42), the term *bēt bāmôt* occurs in the Mesha Stone inscription (*KAI* #181, line 27; 1.31; 2.168-179), but it is most probable that this phrase does not refer to a type of sanctuary, but rather to a city whose name happened to be Bêt Bamot.

[52]The term *hêkāl*, meaning "temple," is used in Dtr to refer to the temple at Shiloh (1 Sam 1:9; 3:3), YHWH's heavenly abode (2 Sam 22:7), the Jerusalem Temple (1 Kgs

the cult center in Bethel is to call it simply "the altar" of Jeroboam. Only in the passage which tells how Josiah returned to destroy Bethel (2 Kgs 23:15) does Dtr appear to designate this site as anything other than a simple altar, and here the term used is *bāmāh*.[53] However, the *bāmāh* mentioned in 2 Kgs 23:15, as well as an *'ăšērāh* that is said to exist at Bethel (attested only in this verse), were in another part of Bethel than the site of the calf shrine itself. It is also possible that the references to a *bāmāh* and an *'ăšērāh* at Bethel are embellishments on the part of a later Deuteronomistic editor.

In addition to Dan and Bethel (1 Kgs 12:31), the structures referred to as "temples of the *bāmôt*" are mentioned in the passages describing their establishment and were said to exist "in all the towns of Samaria" (1 Kgs 13:32; 2 Kgs 17:29; 23:19). Regardless of whether the designation of the calf shrine at Bethel as a *bāmāh* was an afterthought on the part of Dtr, the fact remains that the status of "temple" was withheld by Dtr from the shrines established by Jeroboam in Bethel and elsewhere. It is possible that Dtr wished to diminish the status of northern cult sites by referring to them as "temples of the *bāmôt*" and by referring most frequently to the major sites of Dan and Bethel without using any term denoting a significant structure.

6:3, 5, 17, 33; 7:21, 50; 2 Kgs 18:16; 23:4; 24:13), the palace of Ahab (1 Kgs 21:1), and the palace of the king of Babylon (2 Kgs 20:18). There are no northern cult sites which Dtr deigns to call a temple using this specific term. The term *bayit* is also restricted by Dtr with regard to the northern kingdom. Outside of the five references to *bêt bāmôt* (1 Kgs 12:31; 13:32; 2 Kgs 17:29, 32; 23:19) and beyond common references to domestic dwellings and place names, *bayit* is used most often by Dtr to refer to northern dynasties or family groups (1 Kgs 13:34; 14:10, 13, 14; 15:27, 29; 16:3, 7, 11, 12; 18:18; 20:31; 21:22, 29; 2 Kgs 9:7, 8, 9; 10:3, 10, 11, 30; 13:6; 21:13), and the northern palaces (1 Kgs 16:9, 18; 18:3; 20:6, 43; 21:2, 4; 22:39; 2 Kgs 7:9, 11; 10:5). Dtr uses *bayit* to refer to cult sites beside the Jerusalem Temple, but only three such cult sites: the temple of Ba'al in Jerusalem (2 Kgs 11:18), the temple of Ba'al in Samaria (1 Kgs 16:32; 2 Kgs 10:23, 25, 26, 27), and the temple of Rimmon (an additional manifestation of Ba'al Hadad, cf. Zech 12:11) in Aram (2 Kgs 5:18).

[53]As noted above (p. 135), Menahem Haran states that he believes the *bāmôt* were simple altars and not temples at all, however small (*Temples and Temple Service*, 23). Later on in this same work, however, he makes the following statement, "We must, however, think at least of the possibility that in the Deuteronomistic terminology the terms *bāmôt*, 'high-places' and especially *bêt bāmôt*, 'house of high-places' may include provincial temples, apart from the chosen place, just as the phrase *bêt bāmôt* is also used as a negative designation for heathen temples (2 Kgs 17:29, 32)" (*Temples and Temple Service*, 82). Elsewhere he also states that *bêt bāmôt* serves "as a derogatory designation for Jeroboam's temple in Bethel (1 Kgs 12:31)" (*Temples and Temple Service*, 25), although the verse cited in this last example by Haran contains no mention of Bethel specifically.

Amos, Hosea, Micah, and First Isaiah confine their mention of *bāmôt* to use in judgment oracles directed at major cult centers, whether the temples or sanctuaries of the northern Israel (Amos 7:9; Hos 10:8) or of Jerusalem and its Temple (Mic 1:5; 3:12 [= Jer 26:18]), or of the nation of Moab (Isa 15:2; 16:12). In all of these judgment oracles, *bāmôt* are identified with a sanctuary of some type.

Amos may be including the sanctuary at Bethel when he speaks of the "*bāmôt* of Isaac" (7:9); however, Hosea pointedly directs his only reference to *bāmôt* toward the sanctuary at Bethel which he calls the Bamoth-Aven (Hos 10:8). Micah twice refers to the Jerusalem Temple as a *bāmāh*, calling Jerusalem the "*bāmôt* of Judah" (*bāmôt yəhûdāh*) in parallelism to a description of Samaria as the "sin of Jacob" (*pešaʿ yaʿăqōb*; 1:5), and predicting that YHWH's judgment would reduce the Temple to "forest shrines" (*bāmôt yāʿar*; 3:12).[54] Jeremiah valued Mic 3:12 enough to quote it when the conquest of Jerusalem appeared imminent (Jer 26:18).

In both references to *bāmôt* in First Isaiah, the term is placed in parallelism with a term for shrine. In 15:2, *bāmôt* is parallel to *bayit*, "temple," and in 16:12 *bāmāh* is parallel to *miqdāš*, "sanctuary." This implies that for Isaiah, Moabite shrines and Moabite *bāmôt* were essentially synonymous. It is also possible, however, that Isaiah makes these statements to imply that Moab had no shrines which were equal in scale to Jerusalem's Temple. They had temples, yes, but they were the equivalent of *bāmôt* in the prophet's eyes.

All of these passages place *bāmôt* in a class with other types of sanctuaries, but some (such as those in Micah) imply that comparison between *bāmôt* and a temple or a major center of civilization constitutes a reduction in stature of the temple so compared. The implication is that *bāmôt* were seen as small-scale sites of worship which, when compared with greater state-level cult centers, are on a lesser scale of importance, or perhaps, of size. Usually *bāmôt* are spoken of in the plural. This may imply that *bāmôt* would have been seen as installations of relatively lesser importance than certain temples simply because there were many of them.

---

[54]Although the singular form *bāmāh* occurs (1 Sam 9:12-14, 19, 25; 10:5, 13; 1 Kgs 3:4; 11:7; 2 Kgs 23:15 (3x); 1 Chr 16:39; 21:29; 2 Chr 1:3, 13; Isa 16:12; Jer 48:35; Ezek 20:29), there are examples of the use of the plural form that appear to be part of singular constructions (Hos 10:8 *bāmôt ʾāwen*; Mic 1:5 *bāmôt yəhûdāh*; Mic 3:12 // Jer 26:18 *bāmôt yāʿar*; Jer 7:31 *bāmôt hat-tōpet*). This variation has no pattern with regard to approval by the author or location of the structure (Israelite or foreign). This is mixing of singular and plural forms also occurs in the construct pair *bêt bāmôt*. See above discussion, p. 145.

Temples, being less numerous, might have been seen as more important. Similarly, implications of unsanctioned religious practice connected to *bāmôt* (dedication to foreign gods or use for child sacrifice) could be understood to signify a brand of sanctuary that was somehow "lesser than" other sanctuaries. All of these images combine to form a depiction of *bāmôt* as somehow "lesser than:" lesser in scope, lesser in sophistication, and lesser in efficacy than right worship in YHWH's chosen Temple in Jerusalem.

    B.2.d. *bāmôt* and *ăšērîm*. Only Dtr (1 Kgs 14:23; 2 Kgs 18:4; 21:3; 23:13-14, 15), the Chronicler (2 Chr 14:2; 17:6; 31:1; 33:19; 34:3), and Jeremiah (17:2-3) mention *bāmôt* in the same context as *ăšērîm*. All of these authors, however, have other references to *bāmôt* which make no mention of *ăšērîm*, leading to the conclusion that though these two items might at times be associated, the presence of *ăšērîm* was by no means a required feature of *bāmôt* in their eyes. In fact, only 1 Kgs 14:23, 2 Kgs 23:13-15, 2 Chr 33:19, and Jer 17:2-3 give the impression that these two objects could, in fact, have been part of the same sacred complex. In the case of Jer 17:1-4, however, there is some evidence to suggest that the insertion of verse 2 into the oracle is secondary, making any theory about a strong connection in Jeremiah between *ăšērîm* which occur in verse 2, and *bāmôt* which occur in verse 3, questionable.[55] All the other verses which mention *bāmôt* and *ăšērîm* together simply list them as items either erected or purged without indication that they actually stood side by side on any given site.[56] This implies that the two items were free to coexist, but need

---

    [55]Holladay makes this argument in "Every High Hill," 174. He notes that while many scholars have questioned the authorship of the whole oracle (vs 1-4), in that its content is basically repeated in Jer 15:12-14, there is no reason to discount the oracle as non-Jeremianic. Holladay argues, however (following Volz and Rudolph), that verse 2 is intrusive into the larger oracle of verses 1-4. If this analysis is correct, it becomes difficult to affirm that Jeremiah linked *bāmôt* with *ăšērîm* at all.

    [56]In 2 Kgs 18:4 the *bāmôt* and *maṣṣēbôt* are plural while the *ăšērāh* is singular, making it appear as if only one of the *bāmôt*, at most, could have been located on the exact same site as the *ăšērāh*, even though all of these items may have been located in and around Jerusalem. In 2 Kgs 21:3, again there is a singular *ăšērāh* which is listed after the statement that *bāmôt* were built and altars to Ba'al established. There is no indication that any of the items stood together as part of one complex. In 2 Kgs 23:15, Josiah is said to destroy the altar at Bethel, and the *bāmāh* which Jeroboam had made, and the *ăšērāh*. This is the only mention of an *ăšērāh* at Bethel and the objects are listed in sequence so that it is unclear whether they stood all together or were simply all present in the environs of the town. Likewise 2 Chr 14:2 and 31:1 list *bāmôt* and *mizbǝḥôt* as a pair, followed by *ăšērîm* and *maṣṣēbôt*. 2 Chr 17:6 says Asa abolished *bāmôt* and *'ăšērîm* but does not indicate their proximity to each other. 2 Chr 34:3 mentions *bāmôt*, *ăšērîm*, *pǝsîlîm*, and

not do so. Nothing about one automatically implied the presence of the other.

B.2.e. *bāmôt* and *maṣṣēbôt*. Part of Albright's view that *bāmôt* were primarily funerary monuments was his argument that the term *bāmôt* could at times be applied to memorial stelae alone without the presence of any other structure. This view implies that, at times, *bāmôt* and *maṣṣēbôt* were identical objects. Support for this theory could be found in the LXX translation *bāmôt* = στήλη; however, Albright's views were derived from a rather complicated reading of a few biblical passages. For instance, with a rather cavalier approach to Hebrew syntax, Albright interprets the portion of Ezek 43:7 which reads:

וּבְפִגְרֵי מַלְכֵיהֶם בָּמוֹתָם   "and by the corpses of their kings at their death"

as "by the funerary stelae of their kings in their *bāmôt*."[57] This reading is only possible if you ignore the absence of the preposition "in" which would require a second ב. Albright also reads the Ugaritic *pgr* which means "stela."[58] Albright proceeds to argue that the 1QIsa[a] reading of "stela of the *bāmāh*" in Isa 6:13 is another testimony to an Israelite practice of erecting stelae on *bāmôt*, which for Albright could be a simple mound of stones.[59] He concludes, using the Mesha Stone as an example, either a mound of stones or a stela could be considered a *bāmāh*.[60]

In actuality, however, the biblical text says little about any connection between *bāmôt* and *maṣṣēbôt*. Only Dtr (1 Kgs 14:23; 2 Kgs 18:4; 23:13-14) and the Chronicler (2 Chr 14:2; 31:1) link *bāmôt* with *maṣṣēbôt*.[61] In all

---

massēkôt serially as items purged by Josiah.

[57]"High Place," 247.

[58]See David Nieman, "PGR: A Canaanite Cult-object in the Old Testament," *JBL* 67 (1948) 55-60. The Ugaritic inscription (*KTU* 6.13, 6.14) which Nieman cites as an example of this use of *pgr* was first published by Claude Schaeffer and René Dussaud in the report of the sixth season of excavation of Ras Shamra (*Syria* 16 [1935] 177). See also, Julian Obermann ("Votive Inscriptions from Ras Shamra," *JAOS* 61 [1941] 31-45); Theodore Lewis (*Cults of the Dead*, 72-79); and Manfried Dietrich, Oswald Loretz, and Joaquín Sanmartín, *The Cuneiform Alphabetic Texts from Ugarit, Ras Ibn Hani and Other Places* (Abhandlungen zur Literatur Alt-Syrien-Palestinas und Mesopotamiens 8; Munster: Ugarit-Verlag, 1995) 501-02.

[59]"High Place," 255.

[60]*Yahweh and the Gods of Canaan*, 205. See also Barrick's critique of Albright in "Funerary Character."

[61]In Num 33:52, P links *bāmôt* with stone objects called *maśkîyōt* which belonged to the prior inhabitants of the land. Whether these objects were equivalent to *maṣṣēbôt*,

of these passages *ăšērîm* are also mentioned. As with *bāmôt* and *ăšērîm*, however, *bāmôt* and *maṣṣēbôt* are not always listed in such a way as to imply that the two objects could regularly be found together. To be sure, in 1 Kgs 14:23, mentioned above, it is implied that *bāmôt*, *maṣṣēbôt*, and *ăšērîm* were regularly constructed together on the same sites by the inhabitants of Judah. Likewise, in 2 Kgs 23:13-14, *maṣṣēbôt* and *ăšērîm* are items removed from the *bāmôt* which Solomon had built for the gods of his foreign wives ('Astarte, Milcom, Chemosh).

On the other hand, in 2 Kgs 18:4, both *bāmôt* and *maṣṣēbôt* are listed in the plural as items destroyed while the *ăšērāh* that is destroyed is singular. This alone, however, does not necessarily mean that each *bāmāh* had a *maṣṣēbāh* as part of its fixtures. They could just as easily have stood on different sites. In 2 Chr 14:2 and 31:1, the four items listed as purged are mentioned in pairs, but in neither verse are *bāmôt* paired with *maṣṣēbôt*.[62] In neither verse is it explicit that these objects stood together on one site. For Dtr and the Chronicler, *maṣṣēbôt*, like *ăšērîm*, could have been part of *bāmôt* installations, but there was no tacit assumption that they were always present there.

B.2.f. *bāmôt* and *mizbǝḥôt*. Menahem Haran has argued that "*bāmāh* serves as a concept synonymous to altar, actually indicating a special kind of altar."[63] Haran further states that "the high-places fall within the general category of altars and have nothing to do with temples" and that "several unmistakable signs illustrate this point." The first of these "unmistakable signs" is that one verb used to describe the destruction of *bāmôt* is *swr* "to remove or take away" which he believes "cannot appropriately be applied to a building," and so indicates "that the *bāmôt* were simple, solid, and exposed constructions located in the open."[64]

The use of this verb to describe the destruction of *bāmôt* actually says nothing about how they were constructed, or how big they were, or whether they fall into the category of "building." It certainly says nothing about how "simple" they might have been or how relatively "exposed." Aside from the general meaning of "take away" or "remove," *swr* is also used in situations which depict removing smaller components of a larger object such as the

---

however, is unclear. For a new treatment of *maśkîyōt*, see Victor Horowitz, "אבן משכית."

[62] In 2 Chr 14:2 *mizbǝḥôt* and *bāmôt* are followed by *maṣṣēbôt* and *ăšērîm*. In 2 Chr 31:1, *maṣṣēbôt* and *ăšērîm* are followed by *bāmôt* and *mizbǝḥôt*.

[63] *Temples and Temple Service*, 20.

[64] *Temples and Temple Service*, 23.

covering over Noah's ark (Gen 8:13), or the wheels of a chariot (Exod 14:25), or a person's head through decapitation (1 Sam 17:46; 2 Sam 4:7; 16:9; 2 Kgs 6:32). While these are not architectural references, it is apparent that a general meaning of "dismantle" or "take apart" is also within the semantic range of *swr*. This might imply that *bāmôt* were not simply carried off, but that they might have had to be dismantled first in order to be "removed." Other verbs used for the destruction of *bāmôt* are *ntṣ* (2 Kgs 23:8, 15), *šmd* (Lev 26:30; Num 33:52; Hos 10:8), *ṭhr* (in the sense of "cleansing" Judah of their presence, 2 Chr 34:4), *ʾbd* (Ezek 6:3), and *yšm* (Ezek 6:6). Verbs used for the construction of *bāmôt* are *bnh* (1 Kgs 11:7; 14:23; 2 Kgs 17:9; 21:3; 23:13; 2 Chr 33:3, 19; Jer 7:31; 19:5; 32:35) and *ʿšh* (2 Chr 11:15; 21:11; 28:25; 1 Kgs 12:31; 2 Kgs 12:32; 17:29, 32; 23:19; Ezek 16:16), either of which can be applied to architectural features or to common objects, whether concrete or abstract.[65]

Haran's second sign that *bāmôt* are altars is the fact that the ritual activities which went on at *bāmôt* are those which require an altar; ergo *bāmôt* are altars. He rejects the possibility that *bāmôt* were structures or enclosures which might contain an altar. Even in the case of the *bāmāh* where Samuel treated Saul to a meal (1 Sam 9:11-25)--a story which certainly suggests a substantial structure--Haran dismisses the implied presence of an eating chamber or *liškāh* by stating that:

> the *liškāh* . . . is regarded as one of the auxiliary structures which in the course of time could be put up beside the high-place to provide comfortable quarters for gatherings and overnight visits, but nothing in the nature of the *liškāh*, or any other annex, need obscure the fact that, by its basic character, the high-place was only a large altar.[66]

Haran makes no effort to prove this contention with positive examples. Instead, he attempts to explain away those references which intimate that *bāmôt* might have been viewed by some as more than simple altars.

Many of the witnesses that discuss *bāmôt* make references which do not describe any sacrificial activity taking place there, and which do not

---

[65]*bnh* is used of various architectural items including the Temple at Jerusalem (2 Sam 7:5, 7; 1 Kgs 3:1; 5:32; 6:2 and so on), but it is also used of non-architectural items such as the woman YHWH fashions out of Adam's rib (Gen 2:22). Likewise *ʿšh* is used with regard to architectural items such as Noah's ark (Gen 8:6), or rooms within a building (Neh 13:7), but it is also used of abstract things as in phrases such as "to make a name" for oneself (2 Sam 7:9; 1 Chr 17:8).

[66]*Temples and Temple Service*, 24-25.

mention the presence of altars at *bāmôt*.[67] Other verses by some of the same authors, however, mention the presence of priests on *bāmôt*, whose job, presumably, would include offering sacrifices,[68] or mention sacrifices performed there which implies the presence of an altar on which they were offered.[69] Other references mention *bāmôt* and *mizbəḥôt* together without making a direct statement that the *bāmôt* contained *mizbəḥôt* within their confines,[70] while still others indicate specifically that *bāmôt* had *mizbəḥôt* as part of their furnishings.[71] These citations undercut Haran's contention that the terms *bāmôt* and *mizbəḥôt* were essentially synonymous.[72]

---

[67]Num 33:52; 1 Sam 10:5, 13; 1 Kgs 14:23; 15:14; 2 Kgs 23:13; 2 Chr 15:17; 17:6; 20:33; 21:11; 33:19; 34:3; Amos 7:9; Isa 15:2; 16:12; Ezek 36:2; 43:7; Ps 78:58.

[68]1 Kgs 12:31, 32; 13:2, 32-33; and 2 Chr 11:15 describe how Jeroboam ben Nebat appointed *bāmôt* priests to serve at the Bethel altar or at various *bāmôt*. 2 Kgs 17:29-32 describes the presence of priests on the *bāmôt* of the northern kingdom used by the Assyrian deportees, some of whom practiced child sacrifice. 2 Kgs 23:9 states that *bāmôt* priests were restricted from service on YHWH's altar at the Temple in Jerusalem after the *bāmôt* on which they served were destroyed by Josiah.

[69]The types of sacrifice vary. 1 Sam 9:12, 13, 14, 19, 25 (*zbḥ*); 1 Kgs 3:2 (*zbḥ*), 3 (*zbḥ* and *qṭr*); 11:7-8 (*qṭr* and *zbḥ*); 22:44 (*zbḥ* and *qṭr*); 2 Kgs 12:4; 14:4; 15:4, 35; 16:4 (*zbḥ* and *qṭr*); 17:9-11; 18:4; 23:5, 8 (*qṭr*); 2 Chr 28:4 (*zbḥ* and *qṭr*), 25 (*qṭr*); 33:17 (*zbḥ*); Jer 48:35 (*ʿlh* and *qṭr*); Ezek 20:28-29 (*zbḥ*). While not connecting *bāmôt* and sacrifice explicitly, the wider context of Ezek 16:16 makes reference to incense (*qṭr*) and child sacrifice. Similarly, in Jeremiah several verses describe making one's children "pass through the fire" (7:31; 19:5; 32:35). This suggestion of child sacrifice is made explicit in 19:5 which states that the children became *ʿōlôt lab-baʿal*, "burned offerings to Baʿal." Other references that locate *ḥammānîm* (which are evidently a type of incense altar [Albright, *Archaeology and the Land of Israel*, 215]) on *bāmôt* are: H (Lev 26:30); 2 Chr 14:4; and Ezek 6:4, 6. Apparently, *ḥammānîm* was a term more familiar to later biblical authors than to their predecessors. Other references to *ḥammānîm* occur in 2 Chr 34:4, 7; Isa 17:8; 27:9 without mention of *bāmôt* making it unlikely that *bāmôt* were the only places where these objects could be found.

[70]2 Kgs 18:22; 21:3; 23:15; 2 Chr 14:2; 31:1; 32:12; 33:3; Isa 36:7; Jer 17:3; Ezek 6:3, 6. Mic 1:5; 3:12 and Jer 26:18 may imply a connection between *bāmôt* and *mizbəḥôt* indirectly when they compare the Jerusalem Temple with its many altars to *bāmôt*.

[71]1 Kgs 3:4; 2 Kgs 23:19, 20; 1 Chr 16:39-40; 21:29; 2 Chr 1:3-5, 13; Hos 10:8. All of the Chronicles references as well as 1 Kgs 3:4 refer to the *bāmāh* of Gibeon. The additional references in Kings refer to the *bāmôt* of the hill country of Samaria built by Jeroboam ben Nebat. Hosea 10:8 refers to *bāmôt* in the environs of Bethel.

[72]Though Hos 10:8 reads, נִשְׁמְדוּ בָּמוֹת אָוֶן . . . קוֹץ וְדַרְדַּר יַעֲלֶה עַל-מִזְבְּחוֹתָם: . . . ., "Ruined will be the *bāmôt* of Aven . . . thorns and thistles shall come up on their altars." Haran states that *bāmôt* is here in parallelism with *mizbəḥôt* (*Temples and Temple Service*, 20 n. 12). It seems more likely that the altars in question are features of the *bāmôt* which are represented by the plural suffix on *mizbəḥôt*.

The chart below shows the types of references authors make regarding a connection between *bāmôt* and *mizbǝḥôt* or other sacrificial activity.

Sources	*mizbǝḥôt* located on *bāmôt*	*mizbǝḥôt* mentioned with *bāmôt*	priests appointed to *bāmôt*	sacrifices offered on *bāmôt*	No such ref.
Amos					1
Hosea	1				
Micah		2			
Psalm 78					1
First Isaiah		1			2
Dtr	3	3	7	18	5
Jeremiah		2		4	
P					1
H				1[73]	
Ezekiel		2		2	2
Chronicles	4	4	1	3	6

As this chart demonstrates, the number of biblical authors who make no connection between *bāmôt* and either *mizbǝḥôt* or sacrificial ritual (P, Amos, and Psalm 78), and those who make only tentative connections between them (Micah and Isaiah), are slightly greater than those which make this connection explicit (Hosea, Dtr, Jeremiah, H, Ezekiel, and the Chronicler). Thus, the evidence from Hosea, Dtr, and the Chronicler goes against Haran's views of *bāmôt* as simple altars and leads instead to the conclusion that at least for these authors, *bāmôt* might be larger structures or enclosures which themselves contained *mizbǝḥôt*.

B.2.g. *bāmôt* and cultic statuary. The chart below indicates the biblical authors who mention *bāmôt* as cultic installations and whether they directly connect the use of *bāmôt* with the use of cultic statuary, or with the worship of gods other than YHWH. A direct connection is a statement that expressly locates the use of cultic statuary or the worship of other gods at *bāmôt*. Other verses mention cultic statuary or other gods in contexts which also mention *bāmôt* but without making a direct connection between them.

---

[73]Lev 26:30 mentions *ḥammānîm* but not *mizbǝḥôt* or a specific type of sacrifice.

Source	statuary located at *bāmôt*	statuary mentioned with *bāmôt*	other gods worshipped at *bāmôt*	other gods mentioned with *bāmôt*	No ref.
Amos					1
Hosea		1			
Micah		1			1
Psalm 78		1			
First Isaiah			2[74]		[75]
Dtr		2	4	3	30
Jeremiah			3	1	2
P		1			
H		1			
Ezekiel	1				2
Chronicles	1		1	2	13

Of the witnesses which discuss *bāmôt*, only two directly link the use of *bāmôt* with the use of cultic statuary. The Chronicler states that Manasseh went to the *bāmôt* to worship *pəsîlîm* (2 Chr 33:19). Ezekiel describes faithless Israel as a woman who constructed *bāmôt* and then consorted upon them with "male images," *ṣalmê zākār* (Ezek 16:16-17). Dtr (1 Kgs 11:7; 2 Kgs 17:29, 32; 23:13), Isaiah (15:2; 16:12), Jeremiah (19:5; 32:35; 48:35), and the Chronicler (2 Chr 28:25), state that other gods were worshipped at *bāmôt* without using any of the technical terms for cultic statuary, leaving open the question of whether the worship of these gods necessitated the presence of cultic statuary at *bāmôt* dedicated to them.[76]

Aside from these verses which directly link the use of cultic statuary or the worship of other gods with *bāmôt*, still other passages mention cultic statuary in contexts which also mention *bāmôt*, but they do not make clear that they coexisted in one location. Such verses often list *bāmôt* and cultic statuary as items to be purged without indicating whether they were used together. References of this type are found in P (Num 33:52), H (Lev 26:30), Ps 78:58, Micah (1:5-7), Hosea (10:5-8), Dtr (2 Kgs 17:11-12), the Chronicler (2 Chr 11:15, 34:3), and Ezekiel (6:3, 6; 20:29).

Dtr gets closer to making an overt connection between the two, however, in 1 Kgs 12:32. Here Dtr states that the calf *massēkāh* set up by

---

[74]The *bāmôt* in question here are not Israelite but Moabite.

[75]Isa 36:7 is counted among the examples from Dtr.

[76]Dtr mentions certain gods worshipped on *bāmôt* by name: Chemosh and Molech, 1 Kgs 11:7; Succoth-benoth, Nergal, ʾAshima, Nibhaz and Tartak, Adrammelech and Anammelech, 2 Kgs 17:29-32; ʿAstarte, Chemosh, and Milcom; 2 Kgs 23:13. Jeremiah once neglects to state the deity to which the child sacrifice in the Valley of Ben Hinnom was directed (Jer 7:31); however, in other references the gods who were said to have benefitted were Baʿal (19:5) and Molech (32:35).

Jeroboam at Bethel was ministered to by the *bāmôt* priests he had appointed. It is not explicitly stated, however, that the *bāmôt* in question were actually in Bethel, or that the calf was positioned in one.

In addition to these verses which place in close proximity references to *bāmôt* and cultic statuary, there are others which mention the worship of other gods, if not specific types of cultic statuary, in contexts that also mention *bāmôt*. These are found in Dtr (2 Kgs 18:4; 21:3; 23:5), and the Chronicler (2 Chr 14:2; 33:3) These references, however, do not make the type of direct connections that can be used to argue that such practices were actually conducted on the *bāmôt*.

The great majority of references to *bāmôt* make no mention of cultic statuary by any name, or of gods other than YHWH.[77] Dtr and the Chronicler acknowledge the use of *bāmôt* in the worship of YHWH, and despite the Chronicler's inferences concerning *bāmôt* and cultic statuary, the Chronicler elsewhere defends *bāmôt*, even *bāmôt* constructed after the Temple in Jerusalem, as strictly YHWHistic (2 Chr 33:17).

As we have noted, only Ezekiel and Chronicles directly connect *bāmôt* with the use of cultic statuary. It should be noted, however, that Ezekiel makes numerous other references to cultic statuary without connecting their use with *bāmôt*. Likewise, Chronicles has nineteen total references to *bāmôt* with only six making any reference to other gods or to cultic statuary, and only two of these six making any direct connection. Amos and Isaiah make no connection between Israelite *bāmôt* and cultic statuary, either directly or indirectly. Jeremiah, however, does make direct connections to other deities in three of his six verses on *bāmôt*, and an indirect reference in one additional verse. P, H, Psalm 78, Hosea, Micah, and Dtr have only verses which mention *bāmôt* and cultic statuary together but without any clear connection between their use.

As one moves forward, however, in relative time of composition, the connections between *bāmôt* and cultic statuary, or with deities other than YHWH, become more common. The only author who has no such reference is Amos. The only authors who make such a connection explicit are Ezekiel and Chronicles. Beginning with Dtr, connections begin to be made between specific foreign deities and *bāmôt*, and inferences begin to be made concerning cultic statuary and *bāmôt*, though only Ezekiel and Chronicles have

---

[77]1 Sam 9:12, 13, 14, 19, 25; 10:5, 13; 1 Kgs 3:2, 3, 4; 12:31; 13:2, 32, 33; 14:23; 15:14; 22:44; 2 Kgs 12:4; 14:4; 15:4; 15:35; 16:4; 17:9; 18:22; 23:8, 9, 15, 19, 20; 1 Chr 16:39; 21:29; 2 Chr 1:3, 13; 14:4; 15:17; 17:6; 20:33; 21:11; 28:4; 31:1; 32:13; 33:17; Amos 7:9; Mic 3:12; Isa 36:7; Jer 17:3; 26:18; Ezek 36:2; 43:7.

explicit statements of connection. Still, Dtr and Chronicles make numerous references to *bāmôt* which do not mention cultic statuary, and Ezekiel makes many references to cultic statuary which do not mention *bāmôt*. Thus, even according to those who do make an overt connection between *bāmôt* and cultic statuary, it cannot be assumed that the two always coexisted.

B.2.h. *bāmôt* and the *ʿēṣ raʿănān* formula. The description of Israel's unsanctioned worship "on every high hill and under every green tree" (*ʿal kōl gibʿāh gəbōhāh wətaḥat kōl ʿēṣ raʿănān*) occurs several times in this exact formula and a few additional times in variations on it within the biblical text.[78] The image of Israelites performing rituals in the countryside, on hilltops and beneath shade trees, has given birth to many creative theories concerning ancient Israelite religion.[79] One interpretation of this biblical image which relates to the current study is that *bāmôt* might be synonymous with high hills and *ăšērîm* with green trees.[80]

While this interpretation is suggestive, some biblical passages make a simple equation of *bāmôt* with high hills and *ăšērîm* with green trees difficult. 1 Kgs 14:23 states that *bāmôt* and *ăšērîm* were constructed on every high hill and under every green tree during the reign of Rehoboam. If the hill itself could simply be considered a *bāmāh* and the green tree an *ăšērāh*, why would such items then be said to have been constructed there? This verse implies that more than simple natural phenomena constituted *bāmôt* and *ăšērîm* respectively. 2 Chr 28:4 lists *bāmôt* along with high hills and green trees as the loci of Ahaz's rituals, as if three distinct types of locations were meant.

Jeremiah and Ezekiel, however, come close to equating *bāmôt* with the "high hill/green tree" formula. Jer 17:2-3 juxtaposes high hills and green trees (beside which *mizbəḥôt* and *ăšērîm* are located) with *bāmôt* at which

---

[78]The exact formula occurs in 1 Kgs 14:23; 2 Kgs 17:10; Jer 2:20; Hos 4:13. Variations in wording but with the same intent occur in Deut 12:2; 2 Kgs 16:4; 2 Chr 28:4; Hos 4:13; Jer 3:6, 13; 17:2; Ezek 6:13; 20:28. Isa 57:5 mentions the "high hill," but not the "green tree." For an in-depth study of this formula, see Holladay, "Every High Hill."

[79]One such theory involves the use of these trees as the location of sexual rituals which were part of a fertility cult supposedly borrowed from the Canaanites. An example is Hans Walter Wolff's commentary on Hosea under the discussion of Hos 4:11b-14 (*Hosea: A Commentary on the Book of the Prophet Hosea* [tr. Gary Stansell; ed. Paul D. Hanson; Hermeneia; Philadelphia: Fortress, 1974] 86-88). For examples of other studies which argue for or against this theory, see the Introduction above, pp. 7-8.

[80]Chapter eleven will discuss rabbinic opinions regarding *bāmôt* and *ăšērîm*

the people sin. Ezek 6:3 portrays YHWH speaking to the mountains and hills (as well as the ravines and valleys), saying that their *bāmôt* will be destroyed. Ezek 6:13 describes a scene of idolatrous worship in which *mizbǝḥôt* (located on every high hill and mountaintop, under every green tree and leafy oak) are used to make sacrifices to *gillûlîm*. While the term *bāmôt* does not occur in 6:13, mention of *bāmôt* earlier in chapter 6, along with the similarity between 6:13 and Lev 26:30, in which H describes the destruction of *bāmôt* in which corpses are strewn among the *gillûlîm* (Lev 26:30), make it appear that Ezekiel intends to equate the *bāmôt* in the early portion of the chapter with the hilltop worship in the latter portion.[81] Finally, Ezek 20:28-29 begins with a description of Israel's worship on high hills and under green trees and then provides an etymology of *bāmôt* as if the two images were synonymous.

Both Ezekiel and Jeremiah, however, can be interpreted as merely locating *bāmôt* on high hills, rather than equating them with the actual hills. Both authors also have references to *bāmôt* located in low-lying sites (Jer 7:31; 19:5; 32:35; Ezek 6:3), making it impossible to argue that for either of them *bāmôt* were always equated with hilltops.

The idea that the presence of *bāmôt* in contexts containing the *ʿēṣ raʿănān* formula demonstrates that all references to hilltops on which worship took place are actually veiled references to *bāmôt* ignores the full picture of *bāmôt* in the biblical record. While many references to *bāmôt* located on hills do occur in the biblical text in Dtr, the Chronicler, Isaiah, Jeremiah, and Ezekiel,[82] Jeremiah and Ezekiel also locate certain *bāmôt* in valleys. Dtr, the Chronicler, Hosea, and Ezekiel give evidence that not all of the *bāmôt* with which they were acquainted were located in the open countryside. Many are said to have been built within cities throughout both Judah and northern Israel.[83] This evidence leads to the conclusion that while certain authors connected *bāmôt* with hilltop worship, the mention of *bāmôt* along with the *ʿēṣ raʿănān* formula does not prove that *bāmôt* were always located on hills.

---

which make this equation (pp. 321-29, 334-36).

[81] For a recent summary of scholarship on the connection between Ezekiel and the Holiness Code, see Henry T. C. Sun, "Holiness Code," *ABD* 3.256. See also Hurvitz, *Linguistic Study*.

[82] 1 Kgs 11:7; 14:23; 2 Kgs 16:4; 23:13; 16:4; 23:13; 2 Chr 21:11; 28:4; Isa 15:2; Jer 17:3; Ezek 6:3, 6; 20:28-29; 36:2. Certain specific cities or locations said to have *bāmôt* also have names which mean "high" (Ramah: 1 Sam 9:12, 13, 14, 19, 25) or "hill" (Gibeah Elohim: 1 Sam 10:5, 13; Gibeon: 1 Kgs 3:4; 1 Chr 16:39; 21:29; 2 Chr 1:3, 13).

[83] 1 Sam 9:12, 13, 14, 19, 25; 1 Kgs 3:4; 13:32; 2 Kgs 17:9, 11, 29, 32; 23:5, 8, 9, 15, 19, 20; 1 Chr 16:39; 21:29; 2 Chr 1:3, 13; 14:2, 4; 28:25; 31:1; Hos 10:8; Ezek 16:16;

CONCLUSIONS

In contrast to those who would try to merge all biblical references to *bāmôt* into one synthetic understanding of what they were and how they were understood, this chapter has demonstrated that the various biblical witnesses had distinct, and frequently divergent, views concerning *bāmôt*. No consistent concrete image of *bāmôt* emerges from the data. One does get a sense, however, of how each author viewed *bāmôt* and their proper, or improper, place within Israelite religion.

For Dtr and the Chronicler, *bāmôt* were acceptable worship sites prior to the construction of the Temple at Jerusalem. And while not endorsing the use of *bāmôt* after the Temple's construction, the Chronicler seems to apologize for their continued use by asserting that the people of Judah who continued to use *bāmôt* used them only to worship YHWH (2 Chr 33:17). In the passages concerning Sennacherib's siege of Jerusalem (2 Kgs 18:22; Isa 36:7; 2 Chr 32:12), the charge of the Rab Shaqeh, namely that the *bāmôt* which Hezekiah has destroyed were dedicated to YHWH, is not denied. For Dtr and those authors dependent on it, the fact that particular *bāmôt* were dedicated to YHWH was not at issue. The only issue for Dtr was its insistence that the only acceptable site of YHWHistic worship, once the Temple was constructed, was the Temple itself. *bāmôt* in and of themselves are neither legitimate nor illegitimate. Shrines which competed with the Temple were illegitimate, including all worship sites in the northern kingdom as well as the *bāmôt*. The only exceptions are the altars mentioned in the Elijah material.

For J and E, we only have evidence which shows that they knew the term *bāmôt* as part of the names of locations within Moab (places also known by Dtr and P). First Isaiah (excluding the passage relating the speech of the Rab Shaqeh) speaks only of *bāmôt* located in Moab. Jeremiah makes a link between *bāmôt* and Moab, but also between *bāmôt* and child sacrifice, a view which is found elsewhere only in vague references by Ezekiel.

For Amos, Hosea, Micah, First Isaiah, and Dtr (in references to the northern kingdom) *bāmôt* may have represented cult sites of diminished importance (if not of diminished sanctity) and as such, featured in judgment oracles directed at major cultic centers. For these authors, the use of the term *bāmôt*, or even *bêt bāmôt*, may have been to indicate a diminution or denigration of the value of worship practiced at *bāmôt* or at sites such as Bethel or even the Jerusalem Temple, all of which are compared to *bāmôt*.

43:7.

As time progressed through the biblical witnesses, inferences of a connection between *bāmôt* and the use of cultic statuary became more prevalent, with Ezekiel and Chronicles making direct statements of connection between these two phenomena. However, the use of either *bāmôt* or cultic statuary was not considered by any biblical author to automatically imply the use of the other. The later authors had a tendency to associate the two items while stopping short of portraying cultic statuary as a permanent feature of *bāmôt* worship.

Chapter Six
Synthesis of the Data Regarding *ăšērîm*

A. SUMMARY OF PREVIOUS SCHOLARSHIP ON *ăšērîm*

Since the discovery of the Ugaritic mythological corpus in 1928, much has been written concerning the goddess 'Athirat (Hebrew 'Asherah) and her relation to Israelite religion. Following William Reed's comprehensive 1949 study of *ăšērîm* and their connection to the goddess,[1] other longer works such as those of Walter Maier[2] and Saul Olyan,[3] have shed light on who 'Asherah was and of what her cult may have consisted in ancient Israel. In addition to works focusing on 'Asherah in particular,[4] there have also been studies which touch upon her while dealing with the subject of goddesses within Israel in general.[5] Finally, there have been numerous studies undertaken which seek to interpret archaeological evidence which may be related either to the goddess 'Asherah, or to the cult objects called *ăšērîm*, or to both.[6] The studies of most interest here are

---

[1]*The Asherah in the Old Testament* (Fort Worth: Texas Christian University Press, 1949).

[2]*'Ašerah: Extrabiblical Evidence* (HSM 37; Atlanta: Scholars Press, 1986).

[3]*Asherah and the Cult of Yahweh in Israel* (Atlanta: Scholars Press, 1988).

[4]Tilde Binger, *Asherah: Goddesses in Ugarit, Israel and the Old Testament* (JSOTSup 232; Sheffield: Sheffield Academic Press, 1997); Christian Frevel, *Ashera und der Ausschliesslichkeitsanspruch YHWHs: Beiträge zu literarischen, religions-geschichtlichen und ikonographischen Aspekten der Asheradiskussion* (Bonner Biblische Beiträge 94/1-2; Weinheim: Beltz Athenäum, 1995); Alice Lenore Perlman, "Asherah and Astarte in the Old Testament and Ugaritic Literature" (Ph.D. diss., Graduate Theological Union, 1978); Richard J. Pettey, "Asherah: Goddess of Israel?" (Ph.D. diss., Marquette University, 1985); Steve Wiggins, *A Reassessment of 'Asherah': A Study According to the Textual Sources of the First Two Millennia B.C.E.* (Neukirchen-Vluyn: Neukirchener, 1993); Tadanori Yamashita, "The Goddess Asherah" (Ph.D. diss., Yale University, 1964).

[5]Tikva Frymer-Kensky, *In the Wake of the Goddesses: Women, Culture, and The Biblical Transformation of Pagan Myth* (New York: Macmillan Free Press, 1992); Raphael Patai *The Hebrew Goddess* (3d ed.; Detroit: Wayne State University Press, 1990).

[6]Pirhiya Beck "The Drawings from Horvat Teiman (Kuntillet 'Ajrud)," *Tel Aviv* 9 (1982) 3-68; William G. Dever, "Asherah, Consort of Yahweh? New Evidence from Kuntillet 'Ajrud," *BASOR* 255 (1984) 21-37; idem, "Recent Archaeological Confirmation

those which deal primarily with the issue of the cult objects known as
ʾăšērîm and seek to posit what they were or how they were viewed in
ancient Israel. Most of these studies focus on seeking a definition or physical description of *ʾăšērîm*. Such theories concerning *ʾăšērîm* tend to be of
two types: literary studies or archaeological studies. Below is a discussion
of a selection of these approaches, followed by an analysis of the actual
biblical data regarding *ʾăšērîm*.

A.1. The literary approach to *ʾăšērîm*

The best example of a literary approach to the nature of the cult
objects known as *ʾăšērîm* is William Reed's *The Asherah in the Old Testament*.[7] In part, Reed's work was a reaction to previous scholarship which
either did not know of, or refused to recognize, the possibility that *ʾăšērîm*
might be directly related to a goddess named ʾAsherah.[8] Reed himself
defended the thesis that *ʾăšērîm* were gynomorphic wooden sculptures of
the goddess ʾAsherah, not simple wooden poles or sacred trees. To support
his argument, Reed analyzed the biblical vocabulary which describes either

---

of the Cult of Asherah in Ancient Israel," *Hebrew Studies* 23 (1982) 37-43; J. A.
Emerton, "New Light on Israelite Religion: The Implications of the Inscriptions from
Kuntillet ʿAjrud," *ZAW* 94 (1982) 2-20; James Robert Engle, "Pillar Figurines of Iron
Age Israel and Asherah/Asherim" (Ph.D. diss., University of Pittsburgh, 1979); Judith M.
Hadley, "Some Drawings and Inscriptions on Two Pithoi From Kuntillet ʿAjrud," *VT* 37
(1987) 180-213; Ruth Hestrin, "The Lachish Ewer and the Asherah," *IEJ* 37 (1987) 212-
23; idem, "Understanding Asherah: Exploring Semitic Iconography," *BAR* 17/5 (Sept/Oct
1991) 50-59; André Lemaire, "Who or What was Yahweh's Asherah? Startling New
Inscriptions from Two Different Sites Reopen the Debate about the Meaning of
ʾAsherah," *BAR* 10/6 (Nov/Dec 1984) 42-51; Zeʾev Meshel, *Kuntillet ʿAjrud: A Religious
Centre From the Time of the Judaean Monarchy on the Border of Sinai* (Jerusalem: Israel
Museum, 1978); James B. Pritchard, *Palestinian Figurines in Relation to Certain
Goddesses Known Through Literature* (AOS 24; New Haven: AOS, 1943); Moshe
Weinfeld, "Kuntillet ʿAjrud Inscriptions and their Significance," *Studi Epigrafici e
Linguistici* 1 (1984) 121-30.

[7]Although this work is primarily literary, Reed did address previous
archaeological theories in a chapter on "extra-biblical evidence" (*Asherah in the OT*, 69-
72). For the best recent work on the role of the goddess ʾAsherah in Israelite religion, see
Olyan, *Asherah*.

[8]*Asherah in the OT*, 11-28. In his chapter III, Reed provided an excellent summary
of the scholarship on *ʾăšērîm* and ʾAsherah up to the time of his work, sorting the studies
into categories based upon the solution they offered for the problem, either of who
ʾAsherah was ("ʾAsherah identified with Ashtaroth" pp. 11-16), or what the cult objects
were (pp. 16-22), or how they related to each other (pp. 22-28).

the construction or destruction of *ăšērîm*, as well as references to the other cultic objects with which *ăšērîm* are associated.[9]

Reed argued, against scholars who viewed *ăšērîm* as live sacred trees,[10] that the majority of verbs used in relation to establishing an *ăšērāh*, *śh*, *bnh*, *ʿmd*, and *nṣb*, imply an object of human manufacture, not a natural phenomenon. He correctly notes that even *nṭʿ*, which is used only once, and usually means "to plant" as one might plant a live tree (Deut 16:21), can also be used to refer to inanimate objects such as tents. Reed then used the terms to describe the destruction of *ăšērîm* to support part of his reconstruction, namely that *ăšērîm* were made of wood. He notes that verbs such as *krt*, *gdʿ*, *bʿr*, and *śrp* imply a combustible object that might also be "hewn" or "chopped down," suggesting wood as the material of manufacture.[11]

In the case of 2 Chr 34:3-7, however, where the verbs *šbr*, *ntṣ*, and *dqq* occur, verbs that do not bring to mind a wooden object, Reed suggests that:

> The Chronicler's choice of verbs may have been determined by his eagerness to show how zealous Josiah was in the abolition of the objects of the pagan cult.[12]

Similarly, he explains inflections of *yṣʾ*, *swr*, and even *ntš* (which usually means "to uproot," but is also used with reference to objects without actual roots such as "people" or "nations") as simple expressions of "removal" with no relevance to the material of the object.[13]

Thus Reed arrived at the theory of *ăšērîm* as manufactured wooden objects. He wished, however, to argue that they were not simple poles, but rather physical likenesses of the goddess ʾAsherah carved out of wood. To do so he had to explain references to them which occur alongside references to items such as *pəsîlîm* or *ʿăṣabbîm* which are believed to be sculpted images of deities also. If *ăšērîm* were sculpted images of a deity, why the separate reference to them and to *pəsîlîm*? To this Reed argued:

---

[9]*Asherah in the OT*, 29-58.

[10]*Asherah in the OT*, 22. He cites among those, W. F. Badé, *The Old Testament in the Light of Today* (New York: Houghton Mifflin, 1915) 33; R. A. S. Macalister, *Bible Side-Lights from the Mound of Gezer* (London: Hodder and Stoughton, 1906) 64; Stanley A. Cook, *The Religion of Ancient Palestine* (Schweich Lecture, 1925; London: Oxford University Press, 1930) 64; Sidney Smith, *Early History of Assyria* (New York: E. P. Dutton, 1928) 123; W. M. Flinders Petrie, *Palestine and Israel* (London: SPCK, 1934) 51.

[11]*Asherah in the OT*, 29-35.

[12]*Asherah in the OT*, 36.

[13]*Asherah in the OT*, 36.

> The fact that the graven images are mentioned in conjunction with the Asherahs need not be understood as an indication that they were totally unlike. The Asherah, made of wood and in the shape of a female figure, would come under the general classification of *pǝsîlîm* but would be sufficiently different to have a name of its own.[14]

In the final analysis, however, Reed was unable to offer concrete evidence to support his theory that these wooden objects were actually carved to resemble the goddess, although he does make a good case that both the object and the goddess are referred to by the same name in the biblical text.[15] While Reed's treatment of the nature of *ăšērîm* has much to commend it, it assumes that all *ăšērîm* were alike, that a uniform type of construction existed, and that all the biblical sources which mention *ăšērîm* had exactly the same type of object in mind when they did so. Since this may not have been the case, any attempt to discern such a standard definition of *ăšērîm* may be in error.

A.2. The archaeological approach to *ăšērîm*

One archaeological study which supported Reed's work on *ăšērîm* was that of James Engle.[16] Following on the work of James B. Pritchard, as well that of Raphael Patai,[17] Engle set about to identify a particular type of Palestinian cultic figurine (usually referred to as a "pillar figurine" because of its wide pillar-type base) as a representation of the goddess ʾAsherah. After demonstrating his belief that the pillar figurines are evidence of a cult of ʾAsherah in Iron Age Palestine (supporting the previous statements of Reed and Patai on this subject), Engle went on to suggest that the pillar figurines themselves should qualify as a type of the *ăšērîm* cult objects in addition to the wooden images posited by Reed.[18]

Engle's theory correctly supposes that not all *ăšērîm* look alike. There are two basic weaknesses, however, in his suggestion that the pillar

---

[14]*Asherah in the OT*, 49.

[15]*Asherah in the OT*, 55-58. One convincing parallel which Reed mentions in connection to this last issue is that Judg 16:23 and 1 Sam 5:2, 3, and 4 make it clear that for Dtr, the term Dagon refers both to the name of a Philistine deity and to his cult statue (*Asherah in the OT*, 57).

[16]"Pillar Figurines of Iron Age Israel and Asherah/Asherim" (Ph.D. diss., University of Pittsburgh, 1979).

[17]James B. Pritchard, *Palestinian Figurines in Relation to Certain Goddesses Known Through Literature* (AOS 24; New Haven: AOS, 1943); Raphael Patai, *The Hebrew Goddess* (3d ed.; Detroit: Wayne State University Press, 1990).

[18]Engle, "Pillar Figurines," 60.

figurines might be examples of the biblical cult objects called ăšērîm. First, there cannot be any direct connection made between the two objects without inscribed examples or other types of physical or literary evidence which could prove this connection. Second, the predominant contexts of discovery for the pillar figurines do not resemble the contexts in which the biblical text locates the ăšērîm. Engle states concerning the provenance of the pillar figurines:

> A distressingly large number, about half . . . of our figurines . . . have no solid archaeological context, being a surface find, coming from a dump area of the excavation, or having no recorded information of their provenience. A significant number, about one quarter, approximately 40, come from a designated context which can be interpreted as primarily domestic, with an occasional hint of a public (as along a road) or an industrial (as near a dye vat) setting. Thus the pillar figurines did apparently have some common household use.[19]

Engle goes on to state that some of the figurines come from contexts which "point to a religious use;" however, his examples of this type of context are tombs or burial sites (12 examples out of roughly 150) and favissae, or dumps which also contained other "cultic" objects (3 examples out of 150).[20] None of these find sites correspond to biblical descriptions of where ăšērîm could be found, unless the three examples found in favissae were removed to there from a nearby sanctuary. Engle's evidence actually suggests that if the pillar figurines did, in fact, function as cultic ăšērîm from time to time, this use was secondary to their use in "secular" or "domestic" contexts.

Additional theories concerning ʾAsherah and ăšērîm based upon archaeological evidence have been posited since the discovery of inscriptional evidence at Kuntillet ʿAjrud which seems to invoke the name of ʾAsherah alongside the name of YHWH.[21] There are two inscriptions from Kuntillet ʿAjrud of particular interest in this regard. The first reads:

---

[19]Engle, "Pillar Figurines," 30.

[20]"Pillar Figurines," 30.

[21]See Pirhiya Beck, "The Drawings from Horvat Teiman (Kuntillet ʿAjrud)" *Tel Aviv* 9 (1982) 3-68; Dever, "Asherah, Consort of Yahweh?"; idem, "Recent Archaeological Confirmation;" Emerton, "New Light;" Hadley, "Some Drawings;" Lemaire, "Who or What;" P. Kyle McCarter, Jr., "Aspects of the Religion of the Israelite Monarchy: Biblical and Epigraphic Data," in *Ancient Israelite Religion: Essays in Honor of Frank Moore Cross* (ed. Patrick D. Miller, Jr., Paul D. Hanson, S. Dean McBride; Philadelphia: Fortress, 1987) 137-55; Zeʾev Meshel, *Kuntillet ʿAjrud*; Weinfeld, "Kuntillet ʿAjrud."

ברכת אתכם ליהוה שמרן ולאשרתה

May you be blessed by YHWH of Samaria (*šmrn*) and by his 'asherah.

The excavator of Kuntillet ʿAjrud, Zeʾev Meshel, first read this inscription "May you be blessed by God, who guards us and by his asherah (cella or symbol)."[22] Meshel and others, however, now believe that שמרן should be translated "of Samaria."[23]

A second Kuntillet ʿAjrud inscription is similar to the first, with the exception of the location named in the invocation. It reads:

את ברכתך ליהוה תמן ולאשרתה. יברך וישמרך שיהי אם אד[נ]י

I bless you by YHWH of Teman and by his 'asherah. May he bless you and keep you and be with my lord.[24]

The difference of opinion concerning these inscriptions is not whether they, or the similar inscription from Khirbet el-Qom,[25] have some relation to the biblical text and the subject of *ăšērîm*, but whether they refer to a cult object or to the goddess herself.

William G. Dever holds the opinion that it must be the goddess who is being invoked,[26] while others argue, on grammatical and other grounds, that it must be the cult object which is mentioned.[27] Moshe Weinfeld avoids the conflict by stating that the "'Asherah' embodies the female element of the divinity, whether the term is taken as a reference to a goddess, or to a tree, or wooden pole."[28] Perhaps the most involved explanation, however, is that of Kyle McCarter who argues:

---

[22]Meshel, *Kuntillet ʿAjrud*, 9 [Eng].

[23]For a discussion of the history of this translation, see Hadley, "Some Drawings," 183.

[24]Hadley, "Some Drawings," 185.

[25]See André Lemaire, "Les inscriptions de Khirbet El-Qôm et l'ashérah de YHWH," *RB* 84 (1977) 595-608, pl. 31; Ziony Zevit, "The Khirbet el-Qom Inscription mentioning a Goddess," *BASOR* 255 (1984) 39-48.

[26]See his articles, "Asherah, Consort of Yahweh?"; and "Recent Archaeological Confirmation."

[27]Emerton, "New Light," 19; Hestrin, "Understanding Asherah," 57; André Lemaire, "Who or What," 46; Meshel, *Kuntillet ʿAjrud* 9 [Eng].

[28]Weinfeld, "Kuntillet Ajrud," 121-30.

In the cult of Yahweh's *ăšērâ*, his trace, sign, or effective presence, was marked with an upright wooden pole, called an asherah . . . At the same time, the *ăšērâ* - the "trace" of Yahweh in the cult - was attributed substance, personified, and worshiped as a hypostatic personality . . . the asherah was thought of as feminine and thus as the consort of the deity . . . Yahweh's *ăšērâ* is not, however, the Canaanite Asherah. She is the Israelite Asherah, the personification of a hypostatic form of Yahweh.[29]

While this explanation is compelling, there is neither textual nor artifactual data to support the idea that 'Asherah was viewed as an hypostasis of YHWH himself. It seems unlikely that the Israelites could have maintained such a belief alongside the knowledge of Canaanite 'Asherah without eventually connecting the two.

Another view concerning *ăšērîm* based on archaeological evidence is the iconographic work of Ruth Hestrin. Hestrin argues that a particular type of symbolism typified by symetrical animals flanking a tree is actually a representation in art of the Israelite goddess 'Elat, also known as 'Asherah. Hestrin supports her theory with a series of artifacts, most important of which is the Lachish Ewer which actually has the word אלת inscribed above the motif in question.[30] Hestrin also relates her theory concerning this iconography to the materials from Kuntillet ʿAjrud,[31] taking issue with those who would identify 'Asherah as the seated woman who appears on one of the pithoi that bears an inscription.[32] Hestrin states instead:

That Asherah is not pictured in this drawing is confirmed by another drawing on the same pithos . . . a grouping by now familiar to us: ibexes flanking a sacred tree. Here is the Asherah beside Yahweh - in the form of a sacred tree representing the Goddess. This grouping - from Egypt, to Lachish, to Ugarit - stands for Asherah. In short, the Asherah mentioned in the inscription is not a divine name but an object or a cult symbol.[33]

---

[29]McCarter, "Aspects," 149. McCarter notes that his theory, at some points, "agrees closely with that of Lemaire," (McCarter, "Aspects," 155 n. 68), who states that at Kuntillet ʿAjrud and Khirbet el-Qom "we are witnessing a kind of birth of a hypostasis," (Lemaire, "Who or What," 51).

[30]Hestrin, "The Lachish Ewer," 212-23.

[31]Hestrin, "Understanding Asherah," 50-59. For the original technical drawings of the artwork from Kuntillet ʿAjrud, see the work of Pirhiya Beck, "The Drawings from Horvat Teiman (Kuntillet ʿAjrud)" *Tel Aviv* 9 (1982) 3-68.

[32]See, Dever, "Asherah, Consort of Yahweh?" and "Recent Archaeological Confirmation."

[33]"Understanding Asherah," 57, illus., 58.

For Hestrin, then, 'Asherah the goddess is represented at Kuntillet ʿAjrud, and other sites such as Lachish and Taanach,[34] by the "sacred tree" motif featuring symetrical animals flanking a tree. Hestrin does not state, however, whether she believes all *ăšērîm* needed to be live trees. She does appear to argue, in the case of the Kuntillet ʿAjrud material, that a simple drawing of the motif she describes qualifies as an *ăšērāh* cult symbol. While this may be true in this one case, the biblical *ăšērîm* appear to have been produced in three dimensions. Still, Hestrin's argument must be taken into account when considering the relationship between *ăšērîm* and trees, whether live, or stylized.

B. SUMMARY OF THE BIBLICAL DATA ON *ăšērîm*

ăšērîm pose a challenge to modern interpreters because of the inexact nature of the biblical references to them. The biblical authors who mention *ăšērîm* assume that their audience knows what these items were. No description of their physical appearance occurs in the biblical text, nor are the details of their manufacture explained. There is some ambiguity concerning whether some passages which mention an *ăšērāh* are speaking of a cult object or of a divine personage. The consonantal text can be read either way in all cases.

The only biblical witnesses which mention *ăšērîm* are Exodus 34, D, Dtr, the Chronicler, Micah, First Isaiah, and Jeremiah.[35] All of these imply that the use of *ăšērîm* was to be discouraged; yet, as Saul Olyan has demonstrated, Dtr witnesses, in spite of its polemic against *ăšērîm*, that their use persisted in ancient Israel and even withstood Jehu's violent purge of foreign cult elements in the northern kingdom (1 Kgs 13:6).[36] Below is a summary of biblical opinions on whether *ăšērîm*, as either Israelite or non-Israelite cultic paraphernalia, were positive or negative items.

---

[34]Two incense stands recovered at Taanach depict the "sacred tree" motif. See Hestrin, "Understanding Asherah," 58.

[35]Exod 34:13; Deut 7:5; 12:3; 16:21; Judg 6:25, 26, 28, 30; 1 Kgs 14:15, 23; 15:13; 16:33; 18:19; 2 Kgs 13:6; 17:10, 16; 18:4; 21:3, 7; 23:4, 6, 7, 14, 15; 2 Chr 14:2; 15:16; 17:6; 19:3; 24:18; 31:1; 33:19; 34:3, 4, 7; Isa 17:8; 27:9; Jer 17:2; Mic 5:13. The feminine plural form *ăšērôt* (אשרות) which occurs in Judg 3:7 is most probably a textual corruption of *ʿaštārôt* (עשתרות).

[36]See Olyan, *Asherah*.

Israelite *ăšērîm* negative: D (1 v.[37]), Dtr (20 vs.[38]), Chr (11 vs.)
Non-Israelite *ăšērîm* negative: Exod 34 (1 v.), D (2 vs.), Dtr (1 v.[39])
Israelite or non-Israelite *ăšērîm* positive: -

As the summary shows, there are no references to any *'ăšērîm*, Israelite or non-Israelite, which are clearly viewed positively by the sources. In addition to the above references, there are additional references to *ăšērîm* which are part of judgment oracles directed at some other institution. These are Mic 5:13; Jer 17:2; and Isa 27:9. It could be argued, then, that Jeremiah and Micah viewed *ăšērîm* without direct disapproval. Isa 17:9, however, implies that use of *ăšērîm* constitutes a rejection of YHWH.

It is instructive that the majority of the references to *ăšērîm* listed above apply to Israelite *ăšērîm*, with only Exodus 34, D, and possibly Dtr making any reference to non-Israelite use of *ăšērîm*. What is implied by certain authors, however, is that their use was related, if not directly connected, to the worship of gods other than YHWH. Other references in the same works (outlined below), may indicate, without connecting *ăšērîm* to other gods, that their use was inappropriate in the worship of YHWH.

Source	Dedication to other gods indicated	Other gods implied or mentioned	Dedication to YHWH prohibited	No dedication
Exodus 34	1			
D	2		1	
Dtr	5	5	7	4
Chronicles	2	3	2	3
First Isaiah		1		1
Jeremiah				1
Micah		1		

[37]In addition to the prohibition of *'ăšērîm* in Deut 16:21, 12:4, while not mentioning Israelite *'ăšērîm*, implies that *'ăšērîm, maṣṣēbôt,* and *pəsîlîm* may not be dedicated to YHWH. it refers to the use of these items by the nations YHWH dispossessed mentioned in 12:3, and goes on to state that the Israelites are not to worship YHWH in the same way as the nations who use these items worship their gods.

[38]One of the verses referred to in this set is Judg 3:7 which states that the Israelites sinned by worshipping the Baʿals and the *'ăšērôt.* If this is not a mistake for *'ăštārôt,* then one must assume that Israelite worship or veneration of 'Asherah or her cult symbol is being prohibited. 1 Kgs 14:23 indicates that although it was the citizenry of Judah who constructed *'ăšērîm* and *bāmôt* and *maṣṣēbôt,* they were imitating the practices of the prior nations in doing so.

[39]2 Kgs 23:14 states that *'ăšērîm* were destroyed that were once located in the shrines which Solomon built for his foreign wives. If these shrines were the particular province of foreign royal women, then they might best be classified as non-Israelite despite the fact that Solomon had the shrines built.

For Exodus 34, the only *ăšērîm* mentioned are those belonging to other nations and dedicated to their gods (34:13). For D the issue is more complicated. While it is acknowledged that *ăšērîm* are items used by the prior inhabitants of the land, D also enjoins Israel not to make such objects for themselves, or use them in the worship of YHWH (Deut 12:4; 16:21). The material from Dtr is even more complex. On the issue of *ăšērîm* dedicated to other gods, the material in Judges 6 (which depicts an *ăšērāh* dedicated to Ba'al), along with 2 Kgs 23:14 (which states that *ăšērîm* were removed from the *bāmôt* which Solomon built for the gods of his foreign wives), demonstrate that Dtr recognized examples of *ăšērîm* dedicated to specific foreign deities. Verses in Dtr which simply mention *ăšērîm* in contexts which also mention or imply the presence of other gods are Judg 3:7 (which is most likely a textual corruption for a reference to 'Astarte in the plural form), 1 Kgs 16:33 (which mentions that Ahab built an *ăšērāh* in addition to his temple of Ba'al), 1 Kgs 18:19 (which mentions the priests of 'Asherah [or the *ăšērāh*] along with Ba'al clergy), 2 Kgs 17:9-12 (which mentions the worship of *gillûlîm* along with the cultic practices of the prior inhabitants of the land), and 2 Kgs 17:16 (which mentions an *ăšērāh* which the northern Israelites built along with Ba'al and the Host of Heaven which they worshipped).

On the subject of prohibiting the dedication of *ăšērîm* to YHWH, Dtr states, in 1 Kgs 14:15, that the Israelites "vexed" (*kʿs*) YHWH by making *ăšērîm*, implying that he would not welcome them even if they were associated with his own cult. Similarly, 1 Kgs 14:23 implies that the attempt to worship YHWH in the same manner that the prior nations worshiped their gods was an error on the part of the Judahites who constructed for themselves *ăšērîm*, *bāmôt*, and *maṣṣēbôt*. While references to an *ăšērāh* placed in YHWH's Temple (2 Kgs 21:3, 7; 23:4, 6, 7) imply that their presence was considered by some to be appropriate to the larger cult of YHWH, this is a view with which Dtr obviously disagrees. It may also be the case, however, that these singular *ăšērāh*s were not the same as the plural *ăšērîm*.[40] Finally, Dtr has several references to *ăšērîm* lack any statement about their dedication (1 Kgs 15:13; 2 Kgs 13:6; 18:4; 23:15).

The material from Chronicles outlined on the chart above is equally complex. On the subject of *ăšērîm* indicating worship dedicated to a god other than YHWH, 2 Chr 24:18 states that Israel forsook the House of YHWH in order to participate in a cult that included *ăšērîm* and *ăṣabbîm*. 2

---

[40]This issue will be discussed below under the relationship between *ăšērîm* and the goddess 'Asherah (pp. 187-91).

Chr 33:19 implies that Manasseh built *bāmôt* in which he installed both *ăšērîm* and *pəsîlîm*, presumably of other gods, which he then worshipped. Other more distant connections between *ăšērîm* and other gods in Chronicles include 2 Chr 33:3 (which states that Manasseh built altars for Baʿal and *ăšērîm* but does not directly connect the two) and 2 Chr 34:3, 4, and 7 (which mention *ăšērîm* along with the use of *pəsîlîm* and *massēkôt* but do not state that they were all part of one complex of worship). Chronicles appears to prohibit the use of *ăšērîm* to worship YHWH in 2 Chr 14:2, and 2 Chr 19:3. Finally, like Dtr, Chronicles has other references to *ăšērîm* which do not mention their relation to any specific deity (2 Chr 15:16; 17:6; 31:1).

In the prophetic material, a range of similar views is expressed. Isa 17:8 implies that to trust in objects, such as *ăšērîm*, which Israel has manufactured themselves, constitutes a turning away from YHWH, presumably to the objects themselves as gods. Isa 27:9 and Jer 17:2 indicate that the use of *ăšērîm* is a sin, but no dedication of them to any particular god is mentioned. Similarly, Mic 5:12 refers to *pəsîlîm* but no direct connection is made between them and the *ăšērîm* mentioned in 5:13.

As the above chart and discussion demonstrate, the reason why *ăšērîm* might be disapproved of by any one source is a complicated matter. What appears consistent in all the references is the suggestion that the use of *ăšērîm* (related to the cult of YHWH, the cults of other gods,[41] or unrelated to either), is a breach of religious protocol. The nature of this breach is not explained at all in some sources (such as Jeremiah); it is defined as a form of worship of other gods in other sources (such as Exodus 34 and D); as a form of worship inappropriate to YHWH in others (also D); while in still others (such as Dtr and the Chronicler), several possible reasons for this opinion present themselves. Below further discussion will explore the various nuances of the biblical record concerning *ăšērîm*.

B.1. *ăšērîm* and live trees

One of the most enduring scholarly suspicions concerning *ăšērîm* is that there is some relationship between them and live trees, frequently referred to as "sacred trees." This is the view of early interpreters who translate *ăšērîm* as sacred groves (LXX and Vulgate) or as individual live trees (Mishnah). In modern times this idea is fueled, in part, by the evidence which Reed used to argue that *ăšērîm* are wooden objects, and by

---

[41]See below the discussion of possible connections between *ăšērîm* and cultic statuary (pp. 197-200).

references related to trees, especially in J and E, which make it appear that certain trees were venerated in ancient Israel. If *ăšērîm* were equated with live trees in the minds of some authors, this would soften the predominantly negative view of them which comes through in the sources which refer to them by name.

The issue of whether *ăšērîm* were equated with live trees by sources such as J and E, or even Dtr, is a one for which there is no easy answer.[42] Albright believed there was no doubt on this issue: *ăšērîm* were once live trees: as demonstrated, in part, by the connection between the Canaanite biform of the name of the goddess 'Asherah, 'Elat, and the Hebrew term for the oak or terebinth, *ēlāh/ ēlôn*.[43] Some authors, such as Reed, resist this suggestion and prefer to seek one unified definition of *ăšērîm* which would fit every example. As noted above, Reed argues that *ăšērîm* must be con-structed objects on the basis of verbs used in relation to them, such as *bnh* and *śh*. This assumes that those biblical authors (such as Dtr) who state that *ăšērîm* were constructed speak for all biblical authors concerning *ăšērîm*.

If any author believed that live trees were the equivalent of *ăšērîm*, that author might refer to them as trees without ever using the technical term *ăšērîm*, and also would never need to use verbs of construction to refer to them. It is possible that what began as a veneration of live trees, or simply the location of cult sites beneath landmark trees, could have developed into the production of stylized trees (*ăšērîm*) which could be installed at any

---

[42]Many commentators infer the presence of "sacred trees" from the contexts discussed above, without directly arguing that *ăšērîm* were a type of "sacred tree;" Speiser, *Genesis*, 86; von Rad, *Genesis*, 162; Sarna, *Genesis*, 91; Westermann, *Genesis 12-36*, 153-4. Carol Meyers prefers to see the "sacred tree" as an arboreal image equated with YHWH and represented in cultic apparatus by the menorah, as is suggested, for example, by the vision of Zechariah 4, *The Tabernacle Menorah: A Synthetic Study of a Symbol from the Biblical Cult* (ASORDS 2; Missoula: Scholars Press, 1976). Meyers does, however, acknowledge that the *ăšērîm* may have been representations of the sacred tree motif as well (*Tabernacle Menorah*, 200 n. 87). Another type of sacred or magical wooden object mentioned in the biblical text are miraculous staffs belonging to Moses according to JE (Exod 4:1-4, 17-20; 9:23; 10:13; 14:16; 17:5, 9) and Aaron according to P (Exod 7:9-20; 8:1 [Eng 5], 12-13 [Eng 16-17]; 17:5, 9; Num 17:16-26 [Eng 17:1-11]). It is unlikely, however, that these magical staffs are to be connected with *ăšērîm*. In Numbers 17, there is double entendre between the staff (*maṭṭeh*) of Aaron and the tribe (*maṭṭeh*) of Levi in the contest which establishes Aaron's right to the high priesthood. The point of the other references is that God uses an ordinary walking stick to work miracles. This would be negated if the object itself were cultic, or magical, in its own right.

[43] *Yahweh and the Gods of Canaan*, 189-91. Lemaire also favors the interpretation of *ăšērîm* as live trees, "Who or What," 50.

new cult site.[44] That live trees may actually have been planted at certain cultic sites as *ăšērîm* has been suggested, in light of certain archaeological evidence, by Lawrence Stager.[45] It is also possible that there were groups within Israel who may have continued to equate *ăšērîm* with live trees, even if there were an eventual development of a stylized version. If this is the case, the opinions of certain biblical authors regarding live trees could indirectly reveal their otherwise unstated views of *ăšērîm*.

Because the issue of the relation between *ăšērîm* and live trees is complicated, there follows an analysis which treats the evidence for and against the proposition that live trees were viewed by some biblical authors as either equivalent objects to or early prototypes of later *ăšērîm*. As will be seen, there are certain authors who disapprove of *ăšērîm*, yet at the same time, preserve stories in which landmark trees figure prominently and positively. The nature of the relationship between *ăšērîm* and live trees, then, is relevant to an understanding of how such a source viewed *ăšērîm*.

B.1.a The evidence for *ăšērîm* as live trees. Deut 16:21 is the only verse which provides anything even vaguely approaching a definition of *ăšērîm* in the biblical text. As such, it can be used to support the theory that *ăšērîm* were once live trees, at least for D. The verse reads:

לֹא תִטַּע לְךָ אֲשֵׁרָה כָּל־עֵץ אֵצֶל מִזְבַּח יהוה אֱלֹהֶיךָ אֲשֶׁר תַּעֲשֶׂה לָךְ׃

Do not plant for yourself an *ăšērāh*, any tree, beside the altar of YHWH your god which you will make for yourself.

---

[44]Edward Lipiński believed that *ăšērîm* were originally sacred trees but that during the monarchy they developed into a type of small sanctuary or shrine ("The Goddess Atirat in Ancient Arabia, in Babylon, and in Ugarit: Her Relation to the Moongod and the Sun-goddess," *OLP* 3 [1972] 112). See further the discussion of *ăšērîm* as shrines or sanctuaries below (pp. 185-87).

[45]Stager believes that there are examples of this phenomenon at the Phoenician and Late Bronze temples at Kition, and suspects that many so-called *favissae* uncovered in Israel (such as the one from the Fosse Temple at Lachish) may actually be the remains of pits in which sacred trees were planted (see the chapter "Religious Institutions," in Lawrence E. Stager and Philip J. King, *Life in Biblical Israel* [Louisville: Westminster/John Knox, 2001]). For classical examples of this phenomenon, see the work of Darice Birge, "Sacred Groves in the Ancient Greek World," (Ph.D. diss., University of California at Berkeley, 1982), especially pp. 295-96 for plans of the sanctuary of Apollo Hylates at Kourion showing a circular construction with pits for the planting of sacred trees.

This rendering clearly makes it sound as if D understood *ăšērîm* to be live trees which one installs by means of planting them in a sacred area. It is also possible, however, to translate the same verse in such a way as to leave open the possibility that *ăšērîm* were merely made of wood, but need not be understood as living, or even as "tree-shaped." Such a rendering might read:

> Do not put up for yourself an *ăšērāh*, any wooden thing, beside the altar of YHWH your god which you make for yourself.

As Reed pointed out, the verb *nṭ*ʿ is used idiomatically for "fixing" or "establishing" things in place, such as tents (Dan 11:45), the heavens (Isa 51:16), or the people within their land (2 Sam 7:10). It need not refer to an actual plant which one plants in the ground. Similarly *ʿṣ* can mean "tree" or simply "wood" or "wooden object." There is no indication of the shape of any such wooden object, any wooden object, a pole, a wooden statue (as Reed suggests), or even a small wooden shrine could be the intended meaning.

Deut 12:2-3, which mentions both the "leafy tree" under which the prior inhabitants of the land worshipped their gods as well as the *ăšērîm* which Israel is to destroy, may also provide proof that for D, *ăšērîm* could not be live trees like the *ʿēṣ raʿănān*.[46] It is equally possible, however, to read verse 3 in apposition to verse 2, as if the *ăšērîm* which the Israelites were to destroy were the live trees under which the prior nations worshipped.

The most straightforward argument against reading objects other than actual trees into Deut 16:21 is that the plain reading of the text, which combines the verb meaning "to plant" with a noun whose basic meaning is "tree," suggests that a live tree is the most obvious choice for the meaning of *ăšērāh* in this context. Similarly, Reed's argument that the use of *ntš* ("to uproot") as a verb of destruction for *ăšērîm* (Mic 5:13a) is not to be taken literally (because it is elsewhere used metaphorically), destroys the beauty of the possible metaphor, especially in passages such as 1 Kgs 14:15, where the people's manufacture of *ăšērîm* inspires YHWH to "uproot" the people from the ground given to them, ground in which YHWH had previously "planted" them (*nṭ*ʿ, 2 Sam 7:10). Even if one were positive that Deut 16:21 refers to live trees, however, all that one could safely state is that for D, *ăšērîm* were live trees. This says nothing about what any of the other witnesses believed concerning *ăšērîm*.

---

[46]Other verses using the term *ʿēṣ raʿănān* will be discussed below, pp. 180-83.

B.1.a.i. Famous trees in biblical narrative. As noted in the previous chapters, although Exodus 34 is the only Tetrateuchal source to mention *ăšērîm*, the patriarchal stories are filled with examples of significant trees which serve as the sites of settlements and even theophanies. In fact, three separate sources related to the patriarchal period have references of this type: J, E, and Genesis 14.

Genesis 14 (v 13) mentions that Abraham lived near the Oaks (*ēlōnîm*) of Mamre. In J, Abraham initially camps by the Oak (*ēlôn*) of Moreh near Shechem (Gen 12:6), and moves from there to the Oaks (*ēlōnîm*) of Mamre near Hebron, where he erects an altar to YHWH (13:18), and where God later appears to him and shares a meal with him (18:1). J also mentions Abraham planting an *ēšel*, or tamarisk tree, when he moves to Beer Sheba and makes a covenant with Abimelek there (21:33). The Vulgate apparently views this as a ceremonial action, in that the name of the tree is translated with the term *nemus*, which can mean either "forest" or "sacred grove."[47]

J is obviously not bothered by the presence on one site of both an altar of YHWH and the oaks of Mamre. This could imply several things. Either J would not have agreed with the injunction prohibiting trees near YHWH's altar which is later articulated in Deut 16:21; or J would have agreed with such a view, but did not consider the injunction to refer to live trees, but rather only to *ăšērîm* which were significantly distinct from live trees for J; or J *did* consider live trees and *ăšērîm* to be essentially the same, but still would not have agreed with D that they should be prohibited. Unfortunately, all of these options are equally plausible. All that can be said is that for J, trees near YHWH's altar or even the ceremonial planting of trees in a religious context posed no difficulty. Trees, for J, were prominent objects which were perceived completely positively, and served as the scene of significant religious experiences in the life of Abraham.

E also contains references to important trees within the stories of its preferred patriarch, Jacob. The first is the Shechem oak (*ēlāh*), under which

---

[47]The term *ēšel* is also translated with *nemus* in the Vulgate of Dtr's 1 Sam 22:6 (where Saul sits beneath a tamarisk at Gibeah and hears a report concerning David), and 31:13 (where Saul and Jonathan's remains are interred beneath a tamarisk at Jabesh). It is possible that Gibeah reminded Jerome of Gibeath ʾElohim, or Gibeon, where Dtr states there were *bāmôt*, and thus inspired the reading of *nemus* in 1 Sam 22:6, just as the burying of Saul and Jonathan's remains may imply a sacred context in 31:13. But the Vulgate may use *nemus* simply because Jerome did not know exactly what type of tree an *ēšel* was. These are the only verses in which the noun appears. For further discussion of this type of tree and its possible relation to *ăšērîm*, see James Barr, "Seeing the Wood for the Trees? An Enigmatic Ancient Translation," *JSS* 13 (1968) 11-20.

Jacob buries the *ĕlōhê hannēkār* belonging to his followers (Gen 35:4), and the second is the *'allôn bākût*, "Oak of Weeping," under which Jacob buries Deborah, Rebekah's nurse (Gen 35:8). The narrative does not identify E's oak at Shechem as the Oak of Moreh mentioned by J. It is, however, the scene of an important covenant making for E where the people promise to serve only 'Elohim and put away all other gods before proceeding to establish the shrine at Bethel. In D, the oaks (*ēlônîm*) of Moreh are mentioned as landmarks so prominent that Mt. Ebal and Mt. Gerizim, where the first recitation of the law in the promised land is to take place, are to be located in relation to them (Deut 11:29-30).

The most prominent tree in Dtr, however, is the oak (*'allāh*), again near Shechem where Joshua erects a stone monument and convenes a covenant ceremony (Josh 24:26). This oak near Shechem (which is not identified as the Oak of Moreh, or equated with E's unnamed oak of Gen 35:4, where Jacob and his followers covenant themselves to YHWH) is said to stand in the *miqdaš YHWH* (Josh 24:26). One possible explanation of how Dtr, in light of Deut 16:21, lets stand this reference to a tree in a sacred precinct of YHWH, is that this tree was not considered, by Dtr, to be an *'ăšērāh*. Another possible explanation is that like *bāmôt*, which were allowed prior to the construction of the Temple, this tree was considered appropriate to the shrine at Shechem because the Temple and its more proper cultic procedures had not yet been instituted. Still another possiblity is one suggested by the work of Jon Levenson, namely that Dtr[1] did not include the core of D into its own work, but rather, Dtr[2] included it. Thus Dtr[1] may have been oblivious to the injunction in Deut 16:21.[48]

Another possible explanation, however, is that this story derives from material which preexisted Dtr, and intends as its referent the same unnamed tree which E mentions in Gen 35:4, and which J and D call the Oak of Moreh, and that for the originator of Joshua 24, if not for the rest of Dtr as well, the presence of this tree in the sacred precinct was a completely acceptable form of Israelite piety. So acceptable was it that Joshua, like Jacob, is depicted commemorating a covenant renewal at this tree. The stone placed beneath the tree is said to be a "witness" (*ēdāh*) to the covenant made there, just as the *maṣṣēbāh* and stone heap which E says were erected by Jacob and Laban in Gen 31:44-52 serve as witnesses to their truce.

In Gen 31:44, Jacob invites Laban to make a covenant which will "witness" (*lə 'ēd*) between the two of them. E then notes twice that Jacob named the monument erected on that occasion, *gal 'ēd*, "Heap of Witness"

---

[48]See Levenson, "Torah."

(31:47, 48), while Laban calls the heap by the Aramaic equivalent of *gal ʿēd*, *yəgar śāhădûtāʾ* (31:47). Laban then states repeatedly that the stone heap is to be a "witness" (*ʿēd*) between himself and Jacob (31:48), just as God is a "witness" (*ʿēd*) between them (31:50), and again that the stone heap and the *maṣṣēbāh* both will be "witnesses" (*ʿēd* and *ʿēdāh*, 31:52), that they will do each other no harm. All told, the term *ʿēd* occurs, in one form or another, eight times in nine verses. The prominence of inanimate objects serving as witnesses in this E story gives support to the notion that some shared tradition exists between E and the material in Josh 24:26.

Another similarity exists between Joshua 24 and E, again in the very story in Genesis 35 in which Jacob and his followers removed from themselves their pagan gods and buried them under the oak (*ʾēlāh*) at Shechem. In both Joshua 24 and Genesis 35, the people separate themselves from the *ʾĕlōhê hannēkār* and promise to follow YHWH only. In both stories, the oak at Shechem features prominently.

The only other reference to an oak at Shechem is negative. Judg 9:6 states that the lords of Shechem stood beside the *ʾēlôn muṣṣab*, "standing oak," which was at Shechem, when they made Abimelek king. This scene calls to mind a covenant ceremony, but of a different type of covenant, one between a potential king and his supporters. Again, an oak at Shechem is the scene of a covenant ritual.

One final prominent oak in Dtr bears a striking resemblance, not to an oak from a prior E story, but to one from a prior J story. This is the oak (*ʾēlāh*) at Ophrah beneath which Gideon provides a meal for the angel of YHWH (Judg 6:11-24) in a manner very similar to the meal prepared by Abraham for YHWH's emissaries beneath the Oaks (*ʾēlōnîm*) of Mamre (Gen 18:1-15). This theophanic scene in Dtr concludes with the statement that Gideon built an altar under the oak and named it YHWH Shalom. This is followed directly by the story of how Gideon tore down Baʿal's altar at Ophrah and the *ăšērāh* which stood beside it and burned it on the new altar he then built for YHWH. The juxtaposition of these two stories, as has been noted in chapter two, implies a contrast between approved and disapproved trees for Dtr.

There are other prominent trees in Dtr's narrative. One is the palm tree (*tōmer*) beneath which Deborah holds court during her tenure as a judge in Israel (Judg 4:5). Like the scene in 1 Sam 22:6, where Saul sits under an *ʾēšel* while others come to report to him, Deborah sits *tahat tōmer dəbôrāh*, "beneath Deborah's palm tree" and the citizens come to her for judgment. There is also an unusual place mentioned in Dtr that seems to imply that

some sort of cultic activity was once associated with it. This is the place
known as *ʾĒlôn Məʿōnənîm* (Judg 9:37), usually translated "Oak of the
Diviners." The origin of this unusual name is not certain and may merely
have been the place where one came to meet a diviner, and not an integral
part of the diviner's work. Other landmarks or place names related to trees
in Dtr are *ʾēlôn bəṣaʿănannîm*, understood as "the oak which is in
Ṣaʿanannîm," (Josh 19:33; Judg 4:11), and *ʾalammelek*, understood as
"king's oak" (Josh 19:26).

What then can be decided concerning Dtr's view of live trees and
their possible relation to *ăšērîm*? There is no doubt that for J and E, trees
were significant features of the patriarchal traditions and served as sites for
theophany as well as symbols of covenant. Similarly, D locates Mt. Gerazim
and Mt. Ebal in relation to their location near the Oak of Moreh at Shechem,
and Dtr depicts Joshua and Abimelek performing covenant rituals at a
Shechem oak.

It is highly improbable that Shechem had four famous oak trees: one
at which Abraham camped, which J and D call the Oak of Moreh; another at
which Jacob buries his followers' foreign gods; another at which Joshua
sets up his stone of witness; and still another beside which Abimelek is
declared king. It is most likely that the same tree, in some form of sacred
precinct (as indicated by Dtr in Josh 24:26), is the site of all these incidents
related by J, E, D, and Dtr.

Unlike J and E, D and Dtr mention both landmark trees and *ăšērîm*.
D has landmark trees in the Oaks (*ʾēlônîm*) of Moreh mentioned in Deut
11:30, but does not locate any cultic activity there, which would be consistent with the prohibition of *ăšērîm* in YHWH's sanctuaries (Deut 16:21)
if D truly understood *ăšērîm* to be live trees.[49] Dtr also has Gideon receive
a theophany beneath an oak (*ʾēlāh*), and while Dtr may know of the prohibition in Deut 16:21, it still depicts the oak (*ʾallāh*) at Shechem standing
within a sacred precinct of YHWH (Josh 24:26). How is this to be
understood? There are several possible explanations:

1. Dtr did not consider the Shechem oak to be an *ăšērāh* and therefore did not see
   it as a violation of Deut 16:21.
2. Dtr did understand the Shechem oak to be a type of *ăšērāh* but since this story
   takes place prior to the construction of the Temple, did not consider Deut
   16:21 to be in force.

---

[49]Both J and E place covenant-making rituals, and in the case of J, theophanies, at
prominent trees, but neither of these writers mentions *ăšērîm*.

3. Dtr believed the Shechem oak to be an *ăšērāh* and simply did not agree with the prohibition in Deut 16:21 or did not know it.

4. Dtr knew that some within Israel believed the Shechem oak to be an *ăšērāh* and so intentionally avoids the term, referring to the tree simply as a tree, in an attempt to reconcile the story of Joshua's covenant at the tree with Deut 16:21.

While option 1 is the most straightforward, option 4 is equally plausible. However, both explanations are problematic. There is no evidence with which to determine whether the author of Dtr thought the Shechem oak was an *ăšērāh*. The connection is never made. Options 2 and 3 require additional analysis of the remaining material in Dtr before it can be decided whether they offer the best solution to this question.

Option 2 raises the question of whether Dtr saw Deut 16:21 to be in force prior to the construction of the Temple. Judg 6:25-32 depicts Gideon destroying the *ăšērāh* which stood by Baʿal's altar and burning it on the new altar he constructs for YHWH. This story, however, has no bearing on Dtr's understanding of Deut 16:21, because the *ăšērāh* in question, although destroyed, is not YHWHistic. It stands beside the altar of Baʿal and might have been destroyed for that reason alone.

As for option 3, there is, again, no evidence upon which to base the argument that Dtr approved of YHWHistic *ăšērîm* even though Deut 16:21 does not, or to definitively state that Dtr did not know of any injunction like the one in Deut 16:21. Even if Dtr[1] did not incorporate D into its work, it is still possible that some knowledge of an injunction against *ăšērîm* was known to Dtr. After the construction of the Temple Dtr disapproves of all *ăšērîm* regardless of the deity to which they might have been dedicated. Prior to the construction of the Temple there is no reference to YHWHistic *ăšērîm* in the way that there are references to YHWHistic *bāmôt*. Because it is not possible to prove that Dtr saw live trees as equivalent to *ăšērîm*, it is not possible to state that Dtr approved of *ăšērîm* on this basis. It can be proven, however, that Dtr approved of the prominence given to certain landmark trees.

The tree under which Gideon has his theophany and erects his first altar to YHWH (Judg 6:11-24) is viewed in a completely positive light by Dtr, just as the Oaks of Mamre are viewed by J, and the oak at Shechem is viewed by both E and Dtr. These oaks are live trees beneath which ceremonies dedicated to YHWH occur and there is no condemnation of the practice. The juxtaposition of Judg 6:11-24 with 6:25-32 also raises a contrast. While altars to Baʿal had *ăšērîm* (6:25-32), altars to YHWH were constructed beneath live trees (6:11-24). This juxtaposition might have been meant to convey the meaning that live trees were distinct from *ăšērîm* and to be preferred as sites for YHWHistic worship, or that some development from the use of live trees to the use of *ăšērîm* in worship was taking place and was considered to be a negative development. Still, Dtr does not address the subject of YHWHistic *ăšērîm* and therefore any attempt to supply an opinion for Dtr on this issue is suspect.

B.1.a.ii. *ăšērîm* and the *ʿēṣ raʿănān* formula. As noted in previous chapters, among the biblical witnesses which mention *ăšērîm* and those which do not, there is the recurring description of worship that takes place on high hills, or under every leafy tree (*ʿēṣ raʿănān*), or both. One argument against seeing *ăšērîm* as live trees is that certain sources locate *ăšērîm* "on high hills and under leafy trees." The combination of this "*ʿēṣ raʿănān*" formula with *ăšērîm* occurs in Dtr (1 Kgs 14:23; 2 Kgs 17:10) and Jeremiah (17:2).[50] In the case of Jer 17:2, the verse describes *ăšērîm* that were "next to" (עַל) an *ʿēṣ raʿănān* as opposed to "under" (תַּחַת) one; however, one could argue on the basis of all of these verses that *ăšērîm* are unlikely to have *been* live trees if they were situated *under* or *next to* live trees.[51] But while this may say something about the view of *ăšērîm* held by those witnesses which make this connection, it says nothing about the view of trees as *ăšērîm* in those which do not use the term *ăšērîm*, or this *ʿēṣ raʿănān* formula.

Below is a chart showing which authors use the *ʿēṣ raʿănān* formula and how it relates or does not relate to their use of the term *ăšērîm*. Because some authors alter the formula, it will be indicated whether they mention both the hill and the tree, or just one.

Source	high hill	green tree	ʾăšērîm
D	Deut 12:2	Deut 12:2	Deut 12:3
Dtr	1 Kgs 14:23	1 Kgs 14:23	1 Kgs 14:23
	2 Kgs 16:4	2 Kgs 16:4	
	2 Kgs 17:10	2 Kgs 17:10	2 Kgs 17:10
First Isaiah	Isa 30:25		

---

[50]The most thorough discussion to date on this formula is Holladay, "Every High Hill."

[51]D (Deut 12:2-3) also mentions *ăšērîm* in a passage that mentions the *ʿēṣ raʿănān*; however, the passage instructs the Israelites to destroy the sites on which other nations once worshiped their gods, "on high hills, mountains, and under every *ʿēṣ raʿănān*," then goes on to list *ăšērîm* among the items to be purged. There is no direct indication that the *ăšērîm* were located under the *ʿēṣ raʿănān*.

Source	high hill	green tree	*ʾăšērîm*
Second Isaiah		Isa 57:5	
Third Isaiah	Isa 65:7		
Jeremiah	Jer 2:20	Jer 2:20	
	Jer 3:6	Jer 3:6	
		Jer 3:13	
		Jer 11:16	
	Jer 17:2	Jer 17:2	Jer 17:2
Ezekiel	Ezek 6:13	Ezek 6:13	
	Ezek 20:28	Ezek 20;28	
	Ezek 34:6		
Hosea	Hos 4:13	Hos 4:13	
Chronicles	2 Chr 28:4	2 Chr 28:4	
Psalms		Ps 52:10	

Of the above witnesses, D, Dtr, First Isaiah, and Chronicles have other references to *ăšērîm* which do not mention the high hill/green tree formula.

The above chart demonstrates that the relationship between *ăšērîm* and the *ʿēṣ raʿănān* formula is by no means constant in the authors who use it. Only Dtr and Jeremiah mention the *ʿēṣ raʿănān* along with *ăšērîm*, but Jeremiah does this in only one of his four uses of the formula. D mentions *ăšērîm* and the *ʿēṣ raʿănān* in adjacent verses but without direct connection. Second Isaiah, Ezekiel, Hosea, and Chronicles mention the formula but not *ăšērîm*,[52] and First and Third Isaiah reduce the formula to a mention of the high hill without the green tree and make no mention of *ăšērîm* in this context.[53] Ps 52:10, however, does not mention worship on high hills or under leafy trees, nor does it mention *ăšērîm*, but it does liken the joyous wor-

---

[52]John Day argues that there is a polemic against *ăšērîm* which plays on images of live trees in Hos 14:9 and Isa 27:9 ("A Case of Inner Scriptural Interpretation: The Dependence of Isaiah XXVI.13-XXVII.11 on Hosea XIII.4-XIV.10 [Eng. 9] and its Relevance to Some Theories of the Redaction of the Isaiah Apocalypse," *JTS* 31 [1980] 309-19).

[53]Similar, but most probably unrelated, both to the discussion of the *ʿēṣ raʿănān* formula and to the discussion of *ăšērîm*, is the reference to worship in gardens that occurs in First and Third Isaiah (1:29-30; 65:3; 66:17). First Isaiah states that Israel will "be ashamed of the oaks (*ʾēlîm*)" in which it delighted and the gardens that it has chosen (1:29-30); however, this could be a reference to military alliances. The "Oaks of Bashan" and the "Cedars of Lebanon" are used as symbols for the real or supposed strength of Syria and Phoenicia throughout the prophetic material. Ezekiel expands the image of the garden of Eden to depict the king of Tyre as a former resident of the garden (Ezekiel 28), and later depicts Pharaoh as a mighty tree that dwarfs the trees of Eden (Ezekiel 31). Such imagery, though suggestive of sacred groves or trees, is more akin to the symbolism of royal largesse than to the issue of *ăšērîm* or trees as cultic loci.

shiper to a "leafy (*ra'ănān*) olive tree in the Temple of Elohim," calling to mind the tree in the sanctuary of YHWH at Shechem mentioned in Joshua 24.[54] Jer 11:16 uses the same image of the worshipper as a *zayît ra'ănān* which is found in Ps 52:10, however, Jeremiah uses this image as a contrast to the temple corruption and false hope in ritual which leads to the destruction of the people. In this oracle the verdant olive is torn down and destroyed.

Only in the case of Dtr and Jeremiah can it be argued that the presence of the *'ēṣ ra'ănān* formula indicates that *'ăšērîm* and live trees were not identical objects. That Dtr had at least one definition of *'ăšērîm* which included constructed objects, however, is demonstrated by Dtr's use of verbs such as *bnh* and *'śh* for their manufacture. In the case of Jeremiah, however, 17:2 is the only reference to *'ăšērîm* in the prophet's work. This makes the presence of the *'ēṣ ra'ănān* formula in 17:2 the only evidence to suggest that for Jeremiah, *'ăšērîm* could not be live trees. In the case of the other sources which do not mention *'ăšērîm* but do describe worship under trees and on high hills it is as difficult to argue that they saw these trees as *'ăšērîm* as it was to argue that J saw the landmark trees this way or that E, or even Dtr did.

One additional point in relation to the use of the *'ēṣ ra'ănān* formula is that with the description of the construction of the Temple, references to landmark trees related to YHWH disappear from Dtr. From this point on, only references to the *'ēṣ ra'ănān* mention the use of trees in worship, and only in Ps 52:10 and Jer 11:16 is the reference to an olive tree which is *ra'ănān* a positive one related to YHWHistic worship (even though the olive in Jeremiah's oracle is eventually destroyed). When Dtr uses the *'ēṣ ra'ănān* formula, all of its references and one parallel reference in Chronicles, while never claiming that this worship is non-YHWHistic, still point out that by worshipping under the *'ēṣ ra'ănān*, the Israelites were worshipping in the forbidden style of the prior inhabitants of the land (1 Kgs 14:23; 2 Kgs 16:4, 17:10; 2 Chr 28:4).

It was the opinion of D that the former inhabitants of the land worshipped their gods beneath the *'ēṣ ra'ănān* (Deut 12:2), and along with Dtr, all the remaining authors who mention the *'ēṣ ra'ănān* also mention the worship of other gods in that context. Ezekiel and Hosea state directly that the worship of other gods was practiced at such sites (Ezek 6:13; 20:28; 34:6; Hos 4:13), while Second Isaiah, Third Isaiah, and Jeremiah make this

---

[54]Another occurrence of *ra'ănān* appears in Ps 37:35, though the meaning of the term is not clear in this passage.

inference (Isa 57:5-7; 65:7; Jer 2:20; 3:6, 13). It appears, then, that there is a chronological progression from *ʿēṣ raʿănān* as a description of a tree in a YHWH precinct (Ps 52:10 and the allusion in Jer 11:16), to inferences that its use was prohibited for Israel because it resembled foreign worship (Dtr, Chronicles), to a belief that Israelites, like the prior inhabitants of the land mentioned by D (Deut 12:2), worshipped foreign gods under the *ʿēṣ raʿănān*.

B.1.b. *ăšērîm* **as live trees in the early translated traditions.** Part III of this study will demonstrate how of early Greek, Latin, and Jewish translations provide meanings for *ăšērîm* that suggest that they believed *ăšērîm* to be live trees, whether referred to in the plural as a "grove," as in the Greek and Latin, or as a singular "tree," as in the Mishnah. By the time of the Mishnah the accepted Jewish interpretation of *ăšērîm* included the belief, not only that these items were actual live trees, but that they were likely to have idols hidden beneath them, as did the landmark oak in Gen 35:4. This interpretation of *ăšērîm* is the most explicit and complete of any found in the early translated traditions.

It would be a mistake, however, to assume that these sources, by virtue of their proximity in time to the biblical text, have some pride of place and increased trustworthiness when it comes to providing an explanation of *ăšērîm* as cult phenomena. In fact, as will be demonstrated in Part III, the early translated traditions exhibit the same homogenizing tendency in interpretation that is now common in the secondary scholarship concerning *ăšērîm*. All of these traditions level through their particular understanding of *ăšērîm* (understandings which no doubt had meaning during the translators' own times), and apply that understanding to the entire biblical corpus.

Conclusions regarding *ăšērîm* and live trees

As the above material indicates, ancient Israel had a long history of worship beneath live trees, beginning with J and E's patriarchal traditions and extending through Dtr's descriptions of covenantal events, and on into the image in the elohistic Psalm 52 of a "leafy" olive tree which stands in the Temple, ending with later references to the *ʿēṣ raʿănān*, where Israel either worshipped YHWH or gods other than YHWH. All of these references make it clear that trees served various cultic functions in Israel for almost the entire span of biblical history. Beyond this simple statement concerning the importance of trees in Israelite religion, however, little else can be said about how this practice developed or what it signified in relation to other aspects of Israelite religion.

However, only over the course of some time are we told that Israel's use of trees in worship was eventually associated with the worship of other gods. Sources such as D, which describe Israelite religion prior to the entrance into the land, state that foreign nations used trees for this purpose, but only the prophetic sources, beginning with Hosea and extending to Third Isaiah, which describe the later periods of the Israelite monarchy, state that Israel used high hills or trees for this purpose. Dtr does not make the statement that Israel used trees to worship other gods during any of the historical periods which it describes.

Thus the evidence reveals that worship beneath trees could evoke either the image of the *ʿēṣ raʿănān* and its possible negative connotations, or it could evoke the image of the revered patriarchs worshipping at some of the most important cultic sites in Israel. If *ăšērîm* are to be equated with live trees, either of these images might equally be applied to them. J might be said to approve of *ăšērîm* on the basis of J's approval of cultic activity beneath trees. Dtr might be said to disapprove of the same style of worship, identifying the *ăšērîm* as a type of *ʿēṣ raʿănān*.

It remains unclear, however, whether the use of trees for worship, either of YHWH or of other gods, was equated in the minds of the biblical writers with the use of *ăšērîm*. Only D provides a definition of *ăšērîm* which appears to refer to a living tree (Deut 16:21). Only Dtr and Jeremiah make statements that imply that the *ăšērîm* were erected under or immediately next to live trees and therefore were unlikely to be live trees themselves. Dtr also describes the manufacture of *ăšērîm* in such a way as to imply that they were not living things. Other writers who use verbs of construction which might imply the planting of a living tree also use verbs that imply manufacture of inanimate objects.[55]

Where *ăšērîm* are mentioned but cannot be shown to be equated with live trees, other sources, namely J, E, Genesis 14, Dtr, and Psalm 52, contain references to significant trees which cannot be proven to be equated with *ăšērîm* or to give a tacit approval of them. The scene in Gen 35:4 appears to provide the basis for the Mishnah's predominant image of *ăšērîm*, namely live trees under which idols are buried, which indicates that the tree of Gen 35:4 would have qualified as an *ăšērāh* according to Mishnaic law although it is not called one in the biblical text.

---

[55]Dtr: *ʿmd* (2 Kgs 13:6); *nṣb* (2 Kgs 17:10); *ʿśh* (1 Kgs 14:15; 15:13; 16:33; 2 Kgs 17:16; 21:3, 7); *bnh* (1 Kgs 14:23); Isaiah: *qwm* (Isa 27:9); *ʿśh* (Isa 17:8); The Chronicler: *ʿmd* (2 Chr 33:19); *ʿśh* (2 Chr 15:16; 33:3).

Although it cannot be proven beyond question, if *ăšērîm* are to be equated with live trees, it could be argued that J, E, Psalm 52, and even some of the sources used in the early books of the Deuteronomistic History might have viewed the use of *ăšērîm* positively and connected them, not with any foreign deity, but with proper YHWHistic religion. Whether they would have been emblems of YHWH personally, as creator and sustainer of life, or of a companion deity such as 'Asherah, cannot be assertained. It is not impossible, however, that just as Dtr polemicized *bāmôt* after the construction of the Temple, Dtr also polemicized at that stage trees which others viewed as completely YHWHistic. The *ēṣ raʿănān* and possibly the *ăšērîm* as well might have seemed to sources unconnected with Dtr to be completely acceptable and even venerable cultic institutions.

B.2. *ăšērîm* as a type of shrine.

As noted above, some scholars believe that wooden poles and live trees are not the only possible objects to which the biblical writers might have been referring when they used the term *ăšērîm*. Edward Lipiński has argued that although *ăšērîm* may have started out as live trees, "in the monarchic period, the *ăšērā* could also be a chapel or shrine." Lipiński bases this view on the existence of Semitic cognate terms to *ăšērāh* which carry the meaning "sanctuary," "shrine," "chapel," "holy place," or the like.[56] Examples of such terms listed by Lipiński are: Akkadian *aširtu*, *ešertu*, *iširtu*, *išertum*, *ašrū*, and *ašratu*,[57] Phoenician or Punic *šrt*[58] or *šr*,[59] Old Aramaic *šrt*,[60] Aramaic *ʾtrt*,[61] and late Aramaic *ʾtr*.[62]

Positing that *ăšērîm* were shrines solves certain problems presented by the inscriptions at Kuntillet ʿAjrud and Khirbet el-Qom. It eliminates the need to read the name of the goddess 'Asherah in the inscriptions, which raises theological problems for some scholars (in that she is said to belong to YHWH) and grammatical problems for others (in that her name would have an anomalous pronominal suffix attached). Both these problems could

---

[56]"The Goddess Aṯirat," 112, 114-16. This view is also reflected, in part, in Zeʾev Meshel's initial translation of אשרתה in the Kuntillet ʿAjrud inscription as "cella or symbol" (*Kuntillet ʿAjrud*, 9 [Eng]).

[57]*CAD* 2.436-39; *AHw* 1.82b-83b.

[58]Maʿṣub inscription, *KAI* 19, 4; Punic inscription *CIS* 1.3779, 5-6.

[59]Pyrgi inscription, *KAI* 277, 1-5. See also the translation by J. A. Fitzmyer, "The Phoenician Inscription from Pyrgi," *JAOS* 86 (1966) 285-97.

[60]Sefirê I, *KAI* 222 B 11.

[61]Sardis inscription; *KAI* 260, 3.

[62]Palmyra inscription; *CIS* 2.3917, 3.

be solved by reading the biblical cult object in these inscriptions rather than
the goddess, but this solution raises other problems. For one, it associates
YHWH directly with the cult objects, thus making the inscriptions evidence
of some a syncretistic form of YHWHism of which the biblical text would
disapprove.[63] For another, there is insufficient parallel evidence to suggest
that blessings were routinely invoked by cultic objects related to a god,
whereas there are parallels to the practice of personifying or "deifying"
shrines or cult sites.

Albright identified what he saw as deified shrines at Elephantine,
where divine names occur such as *Eshem-bêth'el*, which he translates as
"Name of the House of God," and *Ḥerem-bêth'el*, which he renders "Sacred-
ness of the House of God."[64] This deification of the house of god was discussed at length, prior to Albright, by Otto Eissfeldt.[65] The Elephantine
evidence is not always used to argue in favor of the theory that *ăšērîm* were
shrines, however. P. Kyle McCarter uses the material from Elephantine to
argue that the *ăšērāh* of YHWH at Kuntillet 'Ajrud was an hypostasis of
YHWH similar to that suggested by the titles *'Anath-bêth'el*, "Sign of the
House of God," and *'Anath-Yahu*, "Sign of YHWH," which occur at
Elephantine.[66]

In short, the theory interpreting biblical *ăšērîm* as shrines is supported by material contemporaneous to the biblical text in which the noun
'šr/'šrt/'šrh and its cognates most often mean "shrine" or "cult place," rather
than some other object, or even the name of the Canaanite goddess
'Asherah.[67] It is also possible to read the biblical passages, as does the LXX,

---

[63]In certain biblical texts, however, *ăšērîm* seem, to some, to be appropriate
accoutrements for YHWH's worship. The instruction not to erect *ăšērîm* near an altar of
YHWH (Deut 16:21) suggests that the idea had at least occurred to some individuals.
There were also eras in which *ăšērîm* were installed in YHWH's Temple in Jerusalem (2
Kgs 21:3-7; 23:4-7), and as Saul Olyan has pointed out (*Asherah and the Cult of Yahweh
in Israel* [SBLMS 34; Atlanta: Scholars Press, 1988] 74), the *ăšērāh* of Samaria survived
Jehu's purge implies that it was seen as YHWHistic in some way, or at least not in
conflict with YHWHism (2 Kgs 13:6).

[64]*From the Stone Age to Christianity* (2d ed.; Garden City, N.Y.: Doubleday
Anchor, 1957) 373.

[65]"Der Gott Bethel," *ARW* 28 (1930) 1-30.

[66]"Aspects," 147.

[67]Lipiński and Lemaire, for instance, argue that the name 'Asherah does not occur
in any Phoenician inscriptional material from the Iron Age. Lipiński makes the statement
that "the goddess Atirat is never mentioned in Phoenician or Punic texts," and then
emends one such reading of *CIS* 1.13, 3 to eradicate a reading of the goddess's name
("The Goddess Atirat," 114 n. 82). Likewise, Lemaire states "Phoenician texts of the first
millennium . . . make no mention of a goddess asherah," but adds a note to the effect that

with a cult site or small shrine in mind rather than a tree or pole. This explanation, however, while possibly solving certain problems with the inscriptional material from Kuntillet ʿAjrud and Khirbet el-Qom, offers little interpretative benefit for students of the Hebrew Bible.

The reading of *ăšērîm* as shrines is no better than the reading of them as poles from the perspective of the biblical text. In fact, one must posit a development away from *ăšērîm* as poles or trees to *ăšērîm* as shrines (as does Lipiński), if one wants to read the plain meaning of Deut 16:21. Similarly, the idea of *ăšērîm* as shrines or places of worship conforms to the LXX understanding in one way, but it loses the sense that these sites were comprised of trees.

It is possible that, for certain biblical writers, *ăšērîm* were small shrines. This argument can be made with regard to Dtr as well as other sources which indicate that *ăšērîm* were manufactured. It is even possible to argue that they were small wooden shrines in order to agree more closely with verbs of destruction such as *gdʿ*, *śrp*, and *krt*. Still, this theory, however suggestive, really has no more evidence to support it than prior theories that *ăšērîm* were live trees or poles. It has the benefit of the comparative data, but is also has the drawback of constituting a major change in form from images such as those invoked by Deut 16:21 and Judges 6.

Most scholars who argue that *ăšērîm* were pagan do so by arguing that *ăšērîm* were essentially related to the goddess ʾAsherah. If, in fact, YHWH's ʾAsherah were not a consort at all, but a type of shrine that YHWH might have occupied quite alone, the argument that sources disapproved of *ăšērîm* because they were Canaanite or dedicated to ʾAsherah as a separate deity would dissolve. The opinion of the sources which condemn *ăšērîm*, then, would not be based on any issue of polytheism, but on the issue of cultic centralization or on some other issue concerning the proper form of otherwise YHWHistic worship. If Dtr, for instance, viewed *ăšērîm* as shrines, then it is safe to say that the usual explanation of this source's objection to *ʾăšērîm* has been largely misunderstood. Unfortunately, it is not possible to prove whether the identification of *ăšērîm* with shrines is valid.

B.3. *ăšērîm* as depictions or symbols of ʾAsherah
An enduring scholarly assumption made with regard to *ăšērîm* is that they were inseparably related to the goddess ʾAsherah and as such

---

the examples mentioned by Engle in his work on pillar figurines are uncertain ("Who or What," 46, 51 n. 12).

represented Canaanite fertility religion which met with the wrath of
monotheistic YHWHistic purists. Beyond the issue of whether the name
applied to *ăšērîm* indicates that they were dedicated to the goddess
'Asherah, is the question of whether use of *ăšērîm*, then would have constituted a departure from YHWHism into a pagan worship of 'Asherah, or
rather symbolized 'Asherah's persistent incorporation into the cult of
YHWH. The discussion which follows will attempt to assess whether a connection between *ăšērîm* and 'Asherah is an imperative in the biblical text,
thus giving some indication of whether the use of *ăšērîm* may have been
viewed by those that opposed them as a form of idolatry at worst, or a
heresy within YHWHism at best.

The cognate evidence concerning the term *šr/t/h* as "sanctuary or
shrine" collected in the previous section of this chapter makes it at least
possible that another meaning for *ăšērîm* exists which is not connected to
the name of the goddess. What of those passages, however, where the
singular form of the term *ăšērîm*, namely *ăšērāh* occurs in the text? Do
they, in fact, make reference to the goddess, or to some object or location
(such as the "grove" suggested by the LXX)?

The singular noun *ăšērāh* occurs only in D, Dtr, and one Chronicles
parallel to Dtr:

Examples with the definite article:

Judges 6:25, 26, 28, 30 refer to the *ăšērāh* at Ophrah, next to Ba'al's altar, which
Gideon cuts down (*krt*) and burns.

1 Kgs 16:33 refers to the *ăšērāh* made (*'šh*) by Ahab in Samaria.

1 Kgs 18:19 refers to Jezebel's prophets of the *ăšērāh* or of 'Asherah.

2 Kgs 13:6 refers to the *ăšērāh* that remained (*'md*) in Samaria after Jehu's purge.

2 Kgs 18:4 refers to an *ăšērāh* cut down (*krt*) by Hezekiah.

2 Kgs 21:7 refers to a *pesel* of or for 'Asherah or the *ăšērāh* that Manasseh made
(*'šh*) and installed in the Temple in Jerusalem.

2 Kgs 23:6 refers to an *ăšērāh* or 'Asherah which is brought out of the Temple
during Josiah's reform, burned (*śrp*), and beaten to dust (*dqq*).

Examples with preposition:

1 Kgs 15:13 and 2 Chr 15:16,[68] refer to the "monstrosity" (*miplēṣet*) made (*'šh*) by
Asa's mother Maacah, of or for 'Asherah or the *ăšērāh*.[69]

---

[68]In all but one of the cases of *ăšērāh* with *lamed* prefixed, (the exception being 2
Chr 15:16), the Masoretes provided pointing that indicated the presence of the definite
article (לַ). In the case of 2 Chr 15:16, the pointing indicates that the Masoretes were not
reading the article (לַ). The consonantal text, however, is the same in all cases.

[69]As noted above (n. 68), the Masoretes did not indicate the presence of a definite
article in 2 Chr 15:16 although the consonantal text could be read to include one.

2 Kgs 23:4 refers to vessels made for ʾAsherah or the *ăšērāh* which was installed in the Temple which Hezekiah removes and destroys.

2 Kgs 23:7 refers to the women who weave *bāttîm* of or for ʾAsherah or the *ăšērāh*.

Examples without prefix:
Deut 16:21 prohibits the planting (*nṭʿ*) of any tree or wooden object as an *ăšērāh* next to an altar of YHWH.

2 Kgs 17:16 refers to an *ăšērāh* made (*ʿśh*) by the northern Israelites.

2 Kgs 21:3 refers to an *ăšērāh* made (*ʿśh*) by Manasseh which is compared to the one made by Ahab.

2 Kgs 23:15 refers to an *ăšērāh* which was burned (*śrp*) by Josiah at Bethel.

Lemaire has argued that the definite article, when prefixed to the noun *ăšērāh*, poses an "insuperable grammatical obstacle to interpreting these passages as references to the name of a goddess."[70] If so, then only those examples without prefix of any kind can be examples of the goddess's name.[71] All of the examples without prefix, however, refer to objects which were constructed by human beings. Given this evidence, it would appear that ʾAsherah the goddess does not appear in the text. There is a problem with Lemaire's logic, however. Divine names other than that of ʾAsherah appear in the text with the definite article attached. The names Baʿal and ʾElohim or ʾEl (applied to YHWH) often appear with the article.[72] If one dismisses Lemaire's objection, then, do any of the other verses above suggest a reading of the goddess ʾAsherah's name?

The best candidates for passages containing the name of the goddess are 1 Kgs 18:19 (which speaks of prophets related to something or someone called *ăšērāh*); 1 Kgs 15:13; 2 Kgs 21:7; and 2 Chr 15:16 (which discuss cultic statuary made for someone or something called *ăšērāh*); and 2 Kgs 23:4 and 7 (which state that there were cultic items such as vessels and

---

[70]"Who or What," 47.

[71]The presence of the preposition masks the presence of the definite article in the consonantal text. If one wishes to focus on the views of the Massoretes on this subject, however, one must consider whether the preposition is pointed to include the article.

[72]Baʿal: Judg 2:13; 6:25, 28, 30, 31, 32; 1 Kgs 16:31, 32; 18:19, 21, 22, 25, 26, 40 (and 25 more times in Dtr); 2 Chr 23:17; Jer 2:8; 7:9; 11:13, 17; 12:16; 19:5; 28:13, 27; 32:29, 35; Hos 2:10; 13:1; Zeph 1:4. ʾEl: Gen 31:13; 35:1, 3; 46:3; 2 Sam 22:31, 33, 48; (and elsewhere, see BDB 42; see also הָאֵל יהוה; Isa 42:5; Ps 85:9). ʾElohim: Deut 4:35, 39; 7:9; 1 Kgs 8:60; 18:39; 2 Chr 33:13 (and elsewhere, see BDB 43). GKC explains these examples by seeing them instances where "terms applying to whole classes" of terms "are restricted (simply by usage) to particular individuals . . . or things" (405, paragraph 126 d).

bāttîm in the Temple dedicated to something or someone called *ăšērāh*). Although these verses could be read to mean that a shrine or a cult emblem called an *ăšērāh* was equipped with prophets, statues, and vessels, it is less awkward to view these items as the possessions of someone, namely the goddess.

An additional reference which is suggestive is 2 Kgs 17:16. In 2 Kgs 17:10, the people of the northern kingdom are said to make *ăšērîm* and *maṣṣēbôt* for themselves on "every high hill and under every green tree." In 17:16, however, an *ăšērāh* is said to have been made (*śh*), and reference to it is listed, not with other cultic items, but with other objects or deities believed by Dtr to have been worshipped by the Israelites. The verse reads:

> They rejected all the commandments of YHWH their God and made for them-selves *massēkôt* of two calves; they made an *ăšērāh*, worshipped all the host of heaven, and served Ba'al.

In this context, the *ăšērāh* is manufactured and apparently represents a deity other than YHWH which the Israelites worshipped. The mention of *ăšērîm* in 17:10 might suggest that this *ăšērāh* was a substantially different object meriting its own mention among the gods whose worship competed with YHWH's in Israel. It could also be read simply as an indication that any *ăšērāh* or *ăšērîm* which were made, whether plural, or singular, con-stituted the worship of a god, or in this case, a goddess, other than YHWH.

If one accepts the above data as evidence that the goddess 'Asherah was worshipped in ancient Israel, the original question of her relationship to the *ăšērîm* becomes an important one for a fuller understanding of how *ăšērîm* were viewed and evaluated by the biblical authors. It is not suffi-cient to assert that the *ăšērîm* represented the goddess and her worship simply because their name is the plural form of her name. As demonstrated above, the common noun *ăšērîm* may derive from some other term meaning "shrine" rather than from the name of the goddess. The *ăšērāh* in 2 Kgs 17:16, might be a type of sculpture of the goddess similar to those implied by 1 Kgs 15:13; 2 Kgs 21:7; and 2 Chr 15:16, and thus constitute an entirely separate type of object from the plural *ăšērîm*.

Still another interpretation of this evidence, which appears to be con-tradicted by 2 Kgs 17:16, but supported by 2 Kgs 13:6, is that *ăšērîm* were connected, not to 'Asherah's, but to YHWH's worship. This appears to be the sense of the Kuntillet 'Ajrud inscriptions, but even the statement that *ăšērîm* were connected to YHWH can be understood several ways:

1. The *ăšērîm* are representations of YHWH's consort, 'Asherah.
2. The *ăšērîm* are shrines of YHWH.
3. The *ăšērîm* are symbolic representations of something about YHWH's own personality (fertility, a feminine hypostasis, etc.).

It is also the case that the cult objects referred to in the plural as *ăšērîm* and in the singular as *ăšērāh* are not treated, in the text, as if they actually represent a specific god or goddess. The text implies or states outright that they might appear in shrines of Baʿal (Judges 6), or a shrine of YHWH (Deut 16:21), or even in shrines of ʿAstarte, Chemosh, or Milcom (2 Kgs 23:14). Regardless of whether certain passages seem to describe the worship of 'Asherah in Israel, other passages make it appear as if these objects called *ăšērîm* were interchangeable cult images which could be installed in the shrine of any god. If one is tempted to argue that *ăšērîm* represented a type of interchangeable consort for any god, how then does one understand an *ăšērāh* dedicated to ʿAstarte (2 Kgs 23:13-15)?[73]

In the final analysis, all that can be stated is that there is evidence that the goddess 'Asherah was known to Dtr, and possibly to the Chronicler as well through the Dtr materials. There is no irrefutable evidence, however, that *ăšērîm*, in the various biblical contexts in which we find them, always represented the worship of 'Asherah. In fact, the view that they *ever* represented her worship could be called into question in light of the fact that other types of objects (such as statuary and vessels), dedicated to 'Asherah are described in the text. It is equally possible, however, that these sculptures and vessels represented a state version of her cult which, in the smaller shrines, contented itself with the simple *ăšērîm* symbols. Unfortunately, whether *ăšērîm* represent the goddess 'Asherah in Israelite religion, either as a fully YHWHistic expression of some aspect of the god or of his consort, or as a completely separate divine personage worshiped alongside YHWH, remains unclear. The data do not support one theory to the exclusion of all others.

---

[73]It is not out of the realm of possibility that an *ăšērāh* in a shrine of ʿAstarte might represent a smaller shrine for the goddess's mother, or sister, on the analogy of Mary chapels found in many Christian cathedrals. Less far removed in time, however, is the Pyrgi inscription which gives a direct parallel to an *šr* of ʿAstarte presumed to be a type of shrine, not dedicated to another goddess, but to ʿAstarte personally (*KAI* 277, 1-5). The biblical text, however, implies that ʿAstarte had a shrine in which the *ăšērāh* was installed, making Pyrgi an inexact comparison.

B.4. Objects or peoples associated with *ăšērîm*

    B.4.a. The connection between *ăšērîm* **and** *bāmôt.* As noted in chapter five, Dtr (1 Kgs 14:23; 2 Kgs 18:4; 21:3; 23:13-14, 15), the Chronicler (2 Chr 14:2; 17:6; 31:1; 33:19; 34:3), and Jeremiah (17:2-3) mention *ăšērîm* in the same context as *bāmôt*, although there is some question about this connection in Jeremiah.[74] 17:2 is the only reference to *'ăšērîm* in Jeremiah, however, while verses referring to *bāmôt* occur elsewhere in the prophet's work. This makes it unlikely that *ăšērîm* were considered to be an integral part of *bāmôt* complexes for Jeremiah.

    As for Dtr and the Chronicler, of their ten references which mention *bāmôt* and *ăšērîm*, only 1 Kgs 14:23, 2 Kgs 23:13-14, and 15, and 2 Chr 33:19 give the impression that these two objects could have been part of the same sacred complex. All the other verses simply list *bāmôt* and *ăšērîm* together as items either erected or purged without indication that they actually stood side by side on any given site.[75] Contrary to the views of some scholars, there is very little evidence to suggest that *ăšērîm* were considered to be standard features of *bāmôt*.[76] Dtr, Chronicles, and possibly Jeremiah connect the two, but even in these corpora not all references to *bāmôt* and *ăšērîm* coincide. This implies that these two items were viewed as essentially independent phenomena which might, from time to time, coexist. References to their coexistence, in fact, are outnumbered by independent references to them.

---

[74]See p. 148, n. 55.

[75]In 2 Kgs 18:4 the *bāmôt* and *maṣṣēbôt* are plural while the *ăšērāh* is singular, making it sound as if only one, if any, of the *bāmôt* could have been located on the same site as the *ăšērāh*. In 2 Kgs 21:3, again there is a singular *ăšērāh* which is listed after the statement that *bāmôt* were built and altars to Ba'al established. There is no indication that any of the items stood together as part of one complex. In 2 Kgs 23:15, Josiah is said to destroy the altar at Bethel, and the *bāmāh* which Jeroboam had made, and the *ăšērāh*. This is the only mention of an *ăšērāh* at Bethel and the objects are listed in sequence so that it is unclear if they stood all together or were simply all present in the environs of the town. Likewise 2 Chr 14:2, and 31:1 list *bāmôt* and *mizbəḥôt* as a pair, followed by *ăšērîm* and *maṣṣēbôt*. 2 Chr 17:6 says Asa abolished *bāmôt* and *ăšērîm* but does not indicate their proximity to each other. 2 Chr 34:3 mentions *bāmôt*, *ăšērîm*, *pəsîlîm*, and *massēkôt* serially as items purged by Josiah.

[76]See the Introduction of this study (pp. 7-9), for quotes to this effect from the following scholars (as well as others): Beebe, *Old Testatment*, 161; Gottwald, *Light to the Nations*, 133; Schunck, "בָּמָה bāmāh," 139-45.

B.4.b. *ăšērîm* **and** *maṣṣēbôt.* Eleven passages, found in Exodus 34, D, Dtr, the Chronicler, and Micah connect *ăšērîm* with *maṣṣēbôt.*[77] In most of these verses, *ăšērîm* are listed with *maṣṣēbôt* as items to be destroyed without direct indication that they ever stood together on one site. The only verses which make it appear that they were erected at least near one another are Deut 12:2-3 and 2 Kgs 23:14. 1 Kgs 14:23 and 17:10 state that *ăšērîm*, *maṣṣēbôt*, and *bāmôt* were constructed on every high hill and under every green tree, but this does not explicitly indicate that each hill or tree had one of each object. This stock phrase should be taken to mean that both items were to be found in various places around the countryside.

There, however, a pattern here. In Exodus 34 and D, *ăšērîm* and *maṣṣēbôt* are accompanied by *mizbəḥôt* whenever they are mentioned together. They are also connected to the worship of other gods in these verses, with the exception of Deut 16:21-22 which does not mention other gods, but rather states that YHWH hates *ăšērîm* and *maṣṣēbôt* near his altars. In Dtr, *ăšērîm* and *maṣṣēbôt* are accompanied by *bāmôt* whenever they are mentioned together, and in Chronicles, *ăšērîm* and *maṣṣēbôt* together are always accompanied by both *mizbəḥôt* and *bāmôt*. Apparently, the Chronicler is making the complex an accumulation of previous lists, with Micah standing outside this development. The chart below illustrates this point:

Verse	*ăšērîm*	*maṣṣēbôt*	*mizbəḥôt*	*bāmôt*	*pəsîlîm*	other gods
Exod 34:13	✓	✓	✓			✓
Deut 7:5	✓	✓	✓		✓	implied
Deut 12:2-3	✓	✓	✓		✓	✓
Deut 16:21-22	✓	✓	✓			
1 Kgs 14:23	✓	✓		✓		implied
2 Kgs 17:10-12	✓	✓		✓		*gillûlîm*
2 Kgs 18:4	✓	✓	✓			
2 Kgs 23:13-14	✓	✓		✓		✓
2 Chr 14:2	✓	✓	✓	✓		implied
2 Chr 31:1	✓	✓	✓	✓		
Mic 5:12-13	✓	✓			✓	implied

It appears that the Chronicler has combined all the elements into one complete list of Israel's offenses. Chronicles takes the *ăšērîm*, *maṣṣēbôt*, and *mizbəḥôt* of Exodus 34 and D, and combines them with the *ăšērîm*, *maṣṣēbôt*, and *bāmôt* preferred by Dtr. Micah, while mentioning the *pəsîlîm*

---

[77]Exod 34:13; Deut 7:5; 12:3; 16:21-22; 1 Kgs 14:23; 2 Kgs 17:10; 18:4; 23:14; 2 Chr 14:2; 31:1; Mic 5:12-13.

which D mentions on two occasions, omits mention of either *bāmôt* or *mizbǝḥôt*.

In conclusion, while *ăšērîm* and *maṣṣēbôt* are linked in Exodus 34, D, Dtr, the Chronicler, and Micah, this pairing takes place only within stock descriptions of either the religion of the former inhabitants of the land (Exodus 34, D), whose style of worship is not to be emulated by Israel (Deut 16:21-22, 1 Kgs 14:23-24; 2 Kgs 17:10-12), or of errant Israel itself (Dtr, Chronicler, Micah). In the case of Exodus 34 and D, no other references to either *ăšērîm* or *maṣṣēbôt* occur apart from these passages where they (along with *mizbǝḥôt*) become a shorthand for worship in the style of the prior inhabitants of the land. This implies that for Exodus 34 and D *ăšērîm* and *maṣṣēbôt* may or may not have been seen always to coincide on one site, though they were seen as like objects, sharing in common an association with gods other than YHWH and the nations who worshiped those other gods. For Micah, *maṣṣēbôt* and *pǝsîlîm* are objects, manufactured by Israel, to which they bow down, leading God to uproot Israel from its land just as its *ăšērîm* are uprooted.

Dtr mentions *ăšērîm* and *maṣṣēbôt* along with *bāmôt* every time the first two appear together, although Dtr also has other references to these three items separately or in other combinations with additional objects.[78] Chronicles adds mention of *bāmôt* and *mizbǝḥôt* to its references to *ăšērîm* and *maṣṣēbôt*, when they occur together; however, it also has references to *ăšērîm* without *maṣṣēbôt*, whether alone or paired with other objects.[79] So while *ăšērîm* suggested *maṣṣēbôt* and the religion of other cultures to Exodus 34, D, and possibly Micah, Dtr and the Chronicler give more information concerning *ăšērîm* to the reader, including their use by Israel and their connection to other items.

---

[78]Dtr mentions *ăšērîm* without *maṣṣēbôt* or *bāmôt* in Judges 6 (where they appear with *mizbǝḥôt*) and 1 Kgs 14:15 (where they appear alone). *ăšērîm* appear with *bāmôt* and *mizbǝḥôt* but not with *maṣṣēbôt* in 2 Kgs 21:3 and 23:15.

[79] *ăšērîm* appear with *bāmôt* only in 2 Chr 17:6, with *ăṣabbîm* only in 2 Chr 24:18; with *bāmôt* and *pǝsîlîm* in 2 Chr 33:19; with *bāmôt*, *pǝsîlîm*, and *massēkôt* in 2 Chr 34:3; with *mizbǝḥôt*, *hammānîm*, *pǝsîlîm*, and *massēkôt* in 2 Chr 34:4; with *mizbǝḥôt*, *pǝsîlîm*, and *hammānîm* in 2 Chr 34:7; and alone in 2 Chr 19:3. The Chronicler, however, only mentions *maṣṣēbôt* in the two verses under discussion here. This means that independent references to *maṣṣēbôt* separate from other objects do not occur in Chronicles.

B.4.c. *ăšērîm* and *mizbəḥôt*. *ăšērîm* and *mizbəḥôt* are connected in Exodus 34, D, Dtr, the Chronicler, First Isaiah, and Jeremiah.[80] As noted above, Exodus 34 and D connect *ăšērîm* with *maṣṣēbôt* and *mizbəḥôt* in a description of the religion of the prior inhabitants of the land which the Israelites are to avoid (Exod 34:13; Deut 7:5; 12:3; 16:21-22). As is the case with *ăšērîm* and *maṣṣēbôt* in the above section, the fact that both of these sources mention *ăšērîm* only in these few passages means that they never mention *ăšērîm* apart from *mizbəḥôt* and *maṣṣēbôt*, and the context that suggests this collection of features constitutes the basic cultic equipment of the prior inhabitants of the land.

As in the case of *ăšērîm* and *maṣṣēbôt*, however, Dtr does mention *ăšērîm* and *mizbəḥôt* together without *maṣṣēbôt*. Dtr's most prominent passage linking *ăšērîm* and *mizbəḥôt* is Judges 6 where an *ăšērāh* stands beside an altar of Baʿal in just such a way as it is prohibited from standing by an altar of YHWH in Deut 16:21. 2 Kgs 21:3 states that Manasseh made an altar for Baʿal and an *ăšērāh* just as Ahab had done, although neither this context, nor the one related to Ahab (1 Kgs 16:33) indicates that the two stood side by side as did the pair at Ophrah. Similarly, 2 Kgs 23:15 locates an *ăšērāh* at Bethel, which is famous for its altar, but does not indicate that they stood together. The altar in 2 Kgs 23:15 is the only altar near which Dtr situates an *ăšērāh* which is not specifically stated to be an altar of Baʿal.

The Chronicler has two verses, mentioned above, in which it mentions *ăšērîm* and *maṣṣēbôt* together with *bāmôt* and *mizbəḥôt* in a sort of cultic "laundry list" based upon similar collections in D, Exodus 34, and Dtr (2 Chr 14:2; 31:1). There are two additional verses in Chronicles which link *ăšērîm* and *mizbəḥôt*, without *maṣṣēbôt*, to cultic statuary and *ḥammānîm* (2 Chr 34:4, 7). 2 Chr 33:3 is a parallel to 2 Kgs 21:3 which lists the building of *bāmôt*, an *ăšērāh*, and *mizbəḥôt* of Baʿal among the offenses of Manasseh.

In 2 Chr 34:3 it is stated that Josiah began to purge Judah and Jerusalem of *bāmôt*, *ăšērîm*, *pəsîlîm*, and *massēkôt*, but in verse 4, certain details concerning them and their arrangement are provided. The *mizbəḥôt* which Josiah purges are altars of Baʿal above which were hung *ḥammānîm*, or incense altars. *ăšērîm* and the cultic statuary are destroyed next. In 34:7, this procedure is repeated with *ăšērîm* and *mizbəḥôt* being purged from the northern tribal areas along with *pəsîlîm* and *ḥammānîm*.

---

[80]Exod 34:13; Deut 7:5; 12:3; 16:21-22; Judg 6:25, 26, 28, 30; 2 Kgs 21:3; 23:15; 2 Chr 14:2; 31:1; 33:3; 34:4, 7; Isa 17:8; 27:9; Jer 17:2.

What is interesting about these passages is that, omitting 2 Chr 33:3 which is a parallel to a Dtr passage, the rest seem to be of two types: one which links *ăšērîm* and *mizbəḥôt* to *maṣṣēbôt* (2 Chr 14:2; 31:1), and a second which links *ăšērîm* and *mizbəḥôt* to cultic statuary and to *ḥammānîm* (2 Chr 34:3-7). Because these passages are not directly paralleled in Kings, however, it cannot be argued that the Chronicler used one set of features in inherited material and a different set in newly composed material. 2 Chr 33:3 does not fit either pattern. Apparently, the Chronicler viewed *ăšērîm* and *mizbəḥôt* as a combination which might occur with a variety of other items, but because both *ăšērîm* and *mizbəḥôt* occur separately elsewhere in the Chronicler, it does not appear that the presence of one demanded the presence of the other for the Chronicler.

First Isaiah and Jeremiah, however, both mention *ʾăšērîm* and *mizbəḥôt* together in the only verses in their books which discuss *ăšērîm* and First Isaiah adds *ḥammānîm* to these verses as well (Isa 17:8; 27:9; Jer 17:2). This implies that for First Isaiah and Jeremiah, the presence of *ăšērîm* suggested the presence of altars, whether for sacrifice or for incense burning. It is important to note, however, that there is some evidence which suggests that all three of these verses are secondary to their respective books. All three verses constitute prose connections between poetic oracles, and all three show some anomaly in their LXX translations. In the case of the Isaiah passages, the presence of the term *ḥammānîm*, which occurs elsewhere only in H, Ezekiel, and Chronicles suggests that the editorial process of Isaiah which connected the oracles together with these prose sections may have occurred much later than the composition of the poetic sections. These two verses are also the only ones in the LXX in which *ăšērîm* is translated with the term δένδρον rather than the term ἄλσος. In the case of the Jeremiah passage, this reference to *ăšērîm* occurs as part of the *ʿēṣ raʿănān* formula, which might also be a sign that this verse is part of a late editorial addition of a Deuteronomistic sort. Moreover, Jer 17:1-4 is missing from the LXX.

Given this information, it is possible to argue that other parties added what they considered to be stock descriptions of the use of *ăšērîm*: in the case of Isaiah, combining *ăšērîm* with *mizbəḥôt* and *ḥammānîm*, and in the case of Jeremiah, adding a recounting of the *ʿēṣ raʿănān* formula along with reference to *ăšērîm* and *mizbəḥôt*.

In the final analysis, the only source which mentions *ăšērîm* which does not also mention *mizbəḥôt* with them from time to time is Micah who has only one reference to *ăšērîm* and mentions them along with *pəsîlîm* and *maṣṣēbôt*. All of the other sources which mention *ăšērîm* depict them at least once in conjunction with *mizbəḥôt*. Some sources never mention *ăšērîm* without mentioning *mizbəḥôt* as well (Exodus 34, D, First Isaiah, and Jeremiah). This list of sources which always mention *ăšērîm* and *mizbəḥôt* together constitute four of the seven sources which mention *ăšērîm*, and an additional two of the seven (Dtr and the Chronicler) mention them together more than once.

For Exodus 34 and D, *ăšērîm*, *mizbəḥôt*, and *maṣṣēbôt* form a complex describing the religion of the prior inhabitants of the land which Israel was not to emulate. For Dtr, *ăšērîm*, when paired with *mizbəḥôt*, are pictured with either an altar of Ba'al (Judg 6:25, 28, 30, 2 Kgs 21:3) or the unacceptable altar of Bethel (2 Kgs 23:15). For the Chronicler, *ăšērîm* and *mizbəḥôt* are two items among many that are either purged or reinstituted by various Judean kings. For Isaiah and Jeremiah, *ăšērîm* and *mizbəḥôt* appear in secondary material which uses stock expressions to describe religious abnormalities within Israel.

All but one of the sources which mention *ăšērîm* mention *mizbəḥôt* along with them. Only Micah fails to mention *mizbəḥôt* along with *ăšērîm*, but this should not be surprising in that Micah is listing items to be eliminated from Israel. *mizbəḥôt*, then, regardless of whether Micah saw them as standard complements to *ăšērîm*, could hardly be listed along with *ăšērîm* in this context.

B.4.d. *ăšērîm* and cultic statuary. Three sources of the seven which mention *ăšērîm* (D, the Chronicler, and Micah) connect their use with the use of cultic statuary of one type or another. In all of these cases, the noun referring to the cult object appears in the masculine plural form, *ăšērîm*.[81] D connects them with *pəsîlîm*, as well as with *maṣṣēbôt* and *mizbəḥôt*, and attributes this type of worship to the prior inhabitants of the land. In Dtr, individual examples of this cult object are also mentioned along with cultic statuary, but all cases, the object is mentioned in the singular form, *ăšērāh*.[82] This produces a situation in which all of these verses in question could be interpreted as referring to the goddess 'Asherah instead of the cult emblem. In 1 Kgs 15:13 (which is paralleled in 2 Chr 15:16), Maacah, the

---

[81]Deut 7:5; 12:3; 2 Chr 15:16; 24:18; 33:19; 34:3, 4, 7; Mic 5:12-13.

[82]1 Kgs 15:13; 2 Kgs 17:16; 21:7. 2 Kgs 18:4 mentions the bronze serpent which the people were worshipping and which Hezekiah destroyed as he destroyed the *bāmôt*, *ăšērîm*, and *maṣṣēbôt* from Judah. There is no indication in the text, however, that the bronze serpent was closely associated with the *ăšērîm* or with any of the other items.

mother of King Asa is said to make a *mipleṣet*, a monstrosity of some sort, either of, or for 'Asherah. This object is cut down (*krt*) by Asa, burned (*śrp*), and thrown in the Wadi Kidron. This description makes it possible that the object in question was either a wooden sculpture of 'Asherah or a wooden cult object which was dedicated to 'Asherah. It is also possible that it was an object made to be installed in a shrine called an *ăšērāh*. In a similar passage, 2 Kgs 21:7, Manasseh is said to have made a *pesel* of (or perhaps for) 'Asherah which he then installed in the Temple. In the case of this verse, all the possible options for interpretation exist as for 1 Kgs 15:13.

In 2 Kgs 17:16, an *ăšērāh* is listed among the items worshiped in the northern kingdom, along with the calf *massēkôt*, Baʿal, and all the host of Heaven. This context, as discussed above, suggests that the *ăšērāh* in question is a representation of the goddess, just as all the other items listed represent gods, goddesses, or statues which Dtr takes to be representative of gods other than YHWH.

Thus, while the cult objects referred to in the plural as *ăšērîm* are associated with *maṣṣēbôt*, *mizbəhôt*, *bāmôt*, and a host of other objects by Dtr, they are not connected with cultic statuary by Dtr. What appears to be connected with cultic statuary in Dtr is the term *ăšērāh* in the singular, most likely referring to the goddess 'Asherah or possibly to a type of shrine called an *ăšērāh*.[83] One might argue, as does Reed, that all *ăšērāh*s, whether mentioned in the plural or in the singular, were a type of cultic statuary made to resemble the goddess 'Asherah, and thus the mention of cultic statuary along with them would have been redundant in most cases. This is, however, an argument from silence. Just because Dtr never lists *ăšērîm* in the plural together with cultic statuary does not prove the two were identical in the mind of Dtr.

The Chronicler does list the plural term *ăšērîm* along with cultic statuary. In 2 Chr 24:18, *ăšērîm* and *ăṣabbîm* are listed as the entities which Judah began to worship after the death of Jehoiada, abandoning the Temple of YHWH. Nothing else is mentioned in the passage; and there no parallel passage in Kings.[84] All of the other references to *ăšērîm* and cultic statuary in the Chronicler linked these items with other items.

---

[83]The interpretation of the singular *ăšērāh* as a shrine does not seem to be the sense of 2 Kgs 17:16; and would also require that we read the installation of a small shrine within the larger Temple in 2 Kgs 21:7. While awkward, however, this interpretation is still possible.

[84]As noted in chapter two (p. 64), *ăṣabbîm* appears in Dtr only twice, referring to the gods of the Philistines (1 Sam 31:9; 2 Sam 5:21). 1 Chr 10:12 parallels 1 Sam 31:9 and also uses *ăṣabbîm* in this manner.

2 Chr 33:19 states that the "Record of the Seers" recorded all the sites at which Manasseh built *bāmôt* and at which he set up *ăšērîm* and *pəsîlîm*. This verse implies that *ăšērîm* and *pəsîlîm* were part of the complex associated with *bāmôt*. 2 Chr 34:3-7 also mentions *bāmôt* along with *ăšērîm*, *pəsîlîm*, *massēkôt*, *mizbəḥôt* for Baʿal, and *ḥammānîm*. The sheer number of items in this passage makes it appear possible, however, that in condensing the account of Josiah's reform, on which Dtr spends twenty verses (2 Kgs 23:1-20), into five verses, the Chronicler lumped together many items which might not otherwise have been mentioned together.

Unlike D, who always mentions *ăšērîm* with *pəsîlîm*, and Dtr which does not mention the plural *ăšērîm* with any items of cultic statuary, Chronicles lists *ăšērîm* both with and without the presence of cultic statuary. In fact, 2 Chr 19:3 is the only verse in the biblical text in which the plural cult objects (here called by the feminine plural, *ăšērôt*) are mentioned without any other cultic items alongside them. The Chronicler does not describe a fixed cultic assemblage featuring *ăšērîm* which could not be changed, combined with other features, or discontinued altogether.

The final source to connect *ăšērîm* with cultic statuary is Micah (5:12-13), who lists *ăšērîm*, *maṣṣēbôt*, and *pəsîlîm* among the items YHWH will eradicate from Israel. Some of the other items which Micah lists as targeted for destruction are not cultic items. He lists horses, chariots, cities, and strongholds before he turns to sorcery, divination, *pəsîlîm*, and *ăšērîm*. The nature of this judgment oracle, then, obscures the actual target of YHWH's wrath. Micah may not actually intend to connect *ăšērîm* with cultic statuary, or to indicate that YHWH's general wrath is directly related to Israel's use of *ăšērîm*.

All of the biblical witnesses which connect *ăšērîm* to cultic statuary appear to have their own distinct reasons for doing so. For D, *ăšērîm* and *pəsîlîm* were connected in the religious life of the prior inhabitants of the land who used them in the worship of their own gods. For Dtr, plural *ăšērîm* are not connected to cultic statuary, although *ăšērāh* in the singular sometimes is. Dtr has several passages which imply that cultic images either of or for 'Asherah were constructed at various points in Israel's history. Beyond this connection, *ăšērîm* and terms for cultic statuary do not occur together in Dtr. In the Chronicler, *ăšērîm* and cultic statuary appear as items of worship used by Judah in times of apostasy and which constituted the unorthodox cult which Manasseh installed and which Josiah later purged. The Chronicler displays a variety of groupings of different objects with *ăšērîm*, neither limiting the mention of other objects to cultic statuary,

nor excluding them. Micah mentions *ăšērîm* and *pəsîlîm* as objects which
will be destroyed on the day when YHWH judges Israel.

B.4.e. *ăšērîm* and other gods or cultures. As noted above, Exodus
34 and D associate the use of *ăšērîm* with the prior inhabitants of the land
and their gods. So strong was the association for D that Israel is instructed
not to worship YHWH in the same way. In Dtr and the Chronicler, however,
specific gods are mentioned in connection with *ăšērîm*.

As noted previously in this study, Judg 3:7 contains a reference to
Israel's worship of the Ba'alim and the *ăšērôt*. This is most probably not a
reference to Ba'al and 'Asherah, but the corruption of a reference to Ba'al
and 'Astarte as in formulas combining their names in just this way
elsewhere in Dtr (Judg 2:13; 10:6; 1 Sam 7:4; 12:10). There are other
references, however, in which *ăšērîm* are connected with Ba'al. An *ăšērāh*
appears in concert with an altar of Ba'al in Judges 6. Manasseh erects altars
for Ba'al and an *ăšērāh*, and worshipped the whole Host of Heaven,
although it is not certain that all of this activity took place on the same site
(2 Kgs 21:3). 2 Kgs 23:14, however, states that Josiah destroyed the *bāmôt*
made by Solomon for the gods and goddesses of his wives and removed the
maṣṣēbôt and *ăšērîm* from them and destroyed them. This implies that any
or all of the *bāmôt* dedicated to 'Astarte, Chemosh, and Milcom might have
had *ăšērîm* in them.

The last type of citation linking *ăšērîm* to other gods in Dtr might be
better considered references which mention 'Asherah along with Ba'al and
other gods. These are 1 Kgs 18:19, in which the priests of Ba'al dine with
the prophets of 'Asherah (or the *ăšērāh*) at Jezebel's table in Samaria; 2
Kgs 17:16, in which 'Asherah (or an *ăšērāh*) is listed along with Ba'al, the
Hosts of Heaven, and the calf *massēkôt* as objects of worship in the northern
kingdom, and 2 Kgs 23:4, in which vessels made for Ba'al, for 'Asherah (or
the *ăšērāh*), and for all the Host of Heaven are removed from the Temple
and destroyed by Josiah. The only verse in which the Chronicler connects
ăšērîm to other gods is the account of Josiah's reform in (2 Chr 34:4) in
which *ăšērîm*, altars of Ba'al, and other cultic items are destroyed.

What the evidence demonstrates is that only in Exodus 34 and D are
ăšērîm connected specifically to other nations, namely the nations that
inhabited the land prior to Israel's settlement there. In Dtr and Chronicles,
ăšērîm are at times linked to Ba'al, but those who are using them for worship in conjunction with the worship of Ba'al are Israelites for the most part.
Only in 2 Kgs 23:14, where it is stated that Solomon's *bāmôt* for his wives'

gods had *ăšērîm* in them, does one get the sense that people of other cultures outside Israel used *ăšērîm*. The worship of ʾAsherah appears to have been a court institution under Ahab and Jezebel, but the use of *ăšērîm* is not directly attributed to Jezebel even though she is Tyrian.

When one adds to this data the fact that Micah, First Isaiah, and Jeremiah also indicate that it was Israel who used *ăšērîm*, it appears that the majority of the biblical writers viewed the use of *ăšērîm* as a particularly Israelite practice. Even if there were some general biblical view, derived from D, that *ăšērîm* were invented by the prior inhabitants of the land, no foreigners are ever directly depicted using them. D and Exodus 34 are disturbed by Israel's use of *ăšērîm* because of this connection to other nations and their gods, but Dtr and Chronicles, as well as First Isaiah and Jeremiah focus their disapproval of ʾ*ăšērîm* on their use by Israelites without mentioning other nations. Dtr indicates that *ăšērîm* were apparently used in connection with the worship of YHWH as well and that this alone was enough to earn the disapproval of Dtr without any connection to foreign persons or deities.

CONCLUSIONS

Any study of the biblical material related to *ăšērîm* is complicated by the fact that despite their continuous use throughout the years of the monarchy, they are the only objects of interest to this study concerning which there are no clear affirmative statements made in the text. There is no source that champions their use. There are only the oblique witnesses in Dtr, such as 2 Kgs 13:6, to their continuous popularity in Israel.

Thus in an ironic development of Israel's literary history, Dtr has become the only clear witness to the popularity and persistence of *ăšērîm* in Israelite religion through the very polemic which it directs toward them. This has led recent scholars to the inevitable conclusion that *ăšērîm* were, quite possibly, approved by a large segment of Israelite society whose opinions on them have been overshadowed by the views of the Deuteronomistic Historian.[85] A search for the roots of this hidden approval leads to the type of examination of inferences in the text found in the current study and in others. Searching for the causes of disapproval of *ăšērîm* and for any hidden approval through connection to approved phenomena such as landmark trees requires that the connections between *ăšērîm* and other cultic institutions in Israel be explored.

---

[85]See especially Olyan, *Asherah*.

If one could prove that *ăšērîm* were roughly equivalent to live trees, either of the venerated or denigrated variety, one could add the approval or disapproval of the cultic role of live trees to an understanding of a particular author's view of *ăšērîm*. If one could prove that *ăšērîm* were small shrines one might argue that they violated a certain source's opinions concerning cultic centralization. If one could prove that *ăšērîm* were emblems of ʾAsherah then one could explain their denigration by certain authors as a disapproval, either of a non-YHWHistic or a YHWHistic veneration of ʾAsherah the goddess. If one could prove that the use of *ăšērîm* was a departure from Israelite religion into the full-scale religion of Canaan one could add this understanding to the disapproval of *ăšērîm* by a given author. If one could prove they were manufactured objects one might argue that a particular author disapproved of them on these grounds.

Despite efforts to prove any of the above hypotheses concerning *ăšērîm*, however, the biblical evidence remains resistant to any one global definition of them. The conclusions concerning *ăšērîm* which can be gleaned from the text are as follows:

1. Verbal descriptions of the installation of *ăšērîm* suggest that they could either be live trees or manufactured objects.

2. While early sources such as J and E, and passages with affinity to either E or some other early northern source (such as Joshua 24 and the elohistic Psalm 52), have references to trees which served a cultic role, either for the patriarchs or their descendants in the land, *ăšērîm* are not directly connected to them, nor do they appear in any source until Exodus 34, D, and later works (Dtr, Micah, First Isaiah, Jeremiah, Chronicles).

3. In later references, worship beneath live trees, as described with the *ʿēṣ raʿănān* formula, gradually becomes synonymous with the worship of other gods, beginning in Hosea and continuing in the later prophets, though the authors who connect this formula with *ăšērîm* (D, Dtr, and Jeremiah) do not state that Israel worshipped other gods by using their *ăšērîm* beneath the *ʿēṣ raʿănān*. Only D makes the connection between this worship and other gods, but the people engaging in this worship are not Israelites. They are the prior inhabitants of the land.

4. *ăšērîm* are linked with foreign cultures only rarely. Exodus 34, D, and Dtr state that the prior inhabitants of the land used *ăšērîm*, but do not refer by name to any one foreign culture which may have used them. Dtr states that the *bāmôt* built for Solomon's foreign wives contained *ăšērîm*, *bāmôt* built for Sidonian, Ammonite, and Moabite gods.

5. *ăšērîm* are linked with cultic statuary in only three of the seven sources which mention them (D, the Chronicler, and Micah), while Dtr mentions only *ăšērāh* in the singular with cultic statuary.

6. Of all the objects related to *ăšērîm*, *mizbəḥôt* are connected to them in all the sources which mention them except Micah. They are linked with *maṣṣēbôt* and *mizbəḥôt* wherever they appear in Exodus 34 and D. They are linked with cultic statuary in four of the seven sources which mention them, though Dtr is noticeably absent from this list.

7. Mention of the goddess 'Asherah appears to occur in Dtr, but the connection between *ăšērîm* and 'Asherah remains uncertain.

While the biblical material summarized above offers many details that may form the grounds of informed speculation concerning *ăšērîm* and how they were viewed by the biblical sources, it contradicts many of the understandings of *ăšērîm* that pervade the secondary scholarship. As demonstrated in the Introduction to this study, secondary scholarship tends to generalize concerning *ăšērîm* that they not only represented specifically Canaanite worship dedicated to 'Asherah and some ill-defined fertility cult dedicated to her, but that they might also represent some type of animistic sacred tree worship, and involve such questionable practices as ritualized sexual intercourse and cultic prostitution.

What the biblical material actually suggests is that *ăšērîm* were of no significant interest to any but seven of the biblical authors, some of whom mention *ăšērîm* only in passing. None specifically name the Canaanites as the inventors of *ăšērîm* though they are listed as one of the many nations who once used them (Exod 34:11; Deut 7:1). Dtr and the Chronicler, the only sources which could even remotely be said to mention 'Asherah, do not specifically connect her with *ăšērîm*; and worship on high hills and green trees, often held up as the culprit responsible for cultic offenses involving sex, is rarely linked with *ăšērîm*. What can be said about *ăšērîm* is that they were cultic objects used by the Israelites and that some biblical sources (Exodus 34, D, Dtr) considered this practice wrong because it resembled a style of worship with which the prior inhabitants of the land once worshipped their gods. They were used by Israelites during the monarchic period primarily and may or may not have had some connection to 'Asherah or the reverence for live trees demonstrated during the patriarchal period.

The connections between *ăšērîm* and 'Asherah, as well as between *ăšērîm* and live trees once venerated in Israel, remain, however, the most likely speculations regarding *ăšērîm* which are implied by the text. It can certainly be argued that D viewed *ăšērîm* as live trees, just as it can be argued that J (and probably E) viewed trees as important features of Israelite worship. While there is no direct evidence for a chronological development from the cultic use of live trees to the cultic use of *ăšērîm* as stylized trees, it is possible, on the basis of the data, to speculate that such a transformation did take place.

If trees were an important symbolic presence in early shrines, as J, E and Joshua 24 suggest, then it is possible that a portable representative of the tree might be invented to place in newer or smaller shrines. If this were the case, Dtr's condemnation of both *ăšērîm* and the *ʿēṣ raʿănān* might be seen as a development away from the affirmation cultic trees (such as the one in Joshua 24) which is similar to Dtr's development away from the affirmation of *bāmôt*. Dtr would then be subsuming the importance of this earlier tradition to the central importance of the Temple.

On the subject of ʾAsherah, the speculation that the name of the goddess and the name of the cultic *ăšērîm* are identical, while by no means the only possible theory, is still perfectly plausible. This theory, however, leaves open the question of whether any given source considers the worship of ʾAsherah as a total departure from Israelite religion, or merely a reflex of it, and possibly a perfectly normal one.

The sources which mention *ăšērîm* do not make clear the reasons behind their generally negative assessment of them. When foreigners use them, as Exodus 34 and D point out, they might be condemned for that reason and in that instance only, as are altars. If they are used in the shrine of a god or goddess other than YHWH, as Dtr points out, they might be condemned purely for their context in this case as well. It could be argued that any negative statement regarding them made in a prophetic judgment oracle might be a feature of the larger judgment of Israel and not an essential judgment about *ăšērîm*.

What remains to be said of *ăšērîm* is that their use was a consistent tradition in monarchic Israel as demonstrated by the text as well as by epigraphic data, regardless of the generally negative view of them presented by Dtr and related sources. They do not appear to be any more foreign to Israel than any other cultic item, nor are they clearly demonstrated to be associated any less with YHWH than with any other deity; however, they remain the most resistant to clear interpretation of any of the items of interest to this study.

Chapter Seven
Synthesis of the Data Regarding *maṣṣēbôt*

A. SUMMARY OF PREVIOUS SCHOLARSHIP ON *maṣṣēbôt*

Unlike *bāmôt* and *ăšērîm*, regarding which there is a large amount of ambiguity in the biblical text, and which have, therefore, generated considerable interest among scholars seeking to identify them more fully, *maṣṣēbôt* are fairly well defined in the text (by passages such as Genesis 28), and have been discussed less in the secondary literature because of this. One of the few major studies in recent years devoted entirely to *maṣṣēbôt* is that of Carl Graesser, Jr.[1]

Graesser's study was aimed at defining how *maṣṣēbôt* were used and why they were approved in the early stages of Israel's history and proscribed in later time periods. According to Graesser, the early scholarship on *maṣṣēbôt* was mostly generated by those in the History of Religions School because two aspects of *maṣṣēbôt* interested them, namely "primitive stages of religion where the veneration of sacred stones was thought to play a major role," and the "development in religious beliefs and practices" which the change in biblical attitudes toward *maṣṣēbôt* seemed to represent.[2] Graesser summarizes the work of Georg Beer and W. Robertson Smith on *maṣṣēbôt*, noting how, for Beer, *maṣṣēbôt* were simply a carryover from prehistoric stone worship practiced by Israelites, whereas Robertson Smith regarded *maṣṣēbôt* as a special type of stone erected by worshipers to provide a dwelling place for the god in areas designated as cultic, constituting the "visible symbol or embodiment of the deity." According to Graesser, both Beer and Robertson Smith saw stone altars, as well as *maṣṣēbôt*, as objects which could be traced back to primitive stone worship.[3]

---

[1]"Studies in *maṣṣēbôt*," (Ph.D. diss., Harvard University, 1969); "Standing Stones in Ancient Palestine," *BA* 35 (1974) 34-63.

[2]"Studies in *maṣṣēbôt*," 1-2.

[3]The works summarized by Graesser are: Georg Beer, *Steinverehrung bei den Israeliten* (Berlin: de Gruyter, 1921); and W. Robertson Smith, *Lectures on the Religion of the Semites* (Edinburgh: Adam and Charles Black, 1894). Graesser notes that Robertson Smith's views on *maṣṣēbôt* are carried over into the work of George F. Moore ("Massebah," *Encyclopaedia Biblica* [New York: Macmillan, 1902] 3.2982) and Immanuel Benzinger (*Hebräische Archäologie* [Tübingen: J. C. B. Mohr, 1907] 315). See Graesser, "Studies in *maṣṣēbôt*," 3-8.

Graesser noted that in addition to attempting to trace the use of stones in worship back into primitive times, other members of the History of Religions School also sought to determine the original significance of sacred stones. This led to theories such as Benzinger's in which *maṣṣēbôt* originally functioned as phallic symbols or representations of sacred mountains, paired with the female divine presence in the sacred tree.[4] Graesser himself dismisses the phallic symbolism theory of *maṣṣēbôt* by stating "there were probably certain Freudian individuals in every age who read such a significance into the *maṣṣēbôt*. It is difficult, however, to treat seriously the suggestion that a phallic symbolism played a major role in Israel."[5]

Graesser's study aimed at collecting the archaeological and comparative data related to *maṣṣēbôt* which had accumulated in the nearly fifty years between his work and that of Georg Beer.[6] Graesser organized this material into discussions of four distinct types of standing stones: commemorative stones "which commemorate an event for the purpose of honoring the divine and/or human participants in that event"; memorial stones which are "used to memorialize the dead"; legal stones which "witness to a legal relationship between two or more individuals, such as a boundary or contract"; and cultic stones which "indicate the place at which the deity is

---

[4]Benzinger, *Archäeologie*, 322. For Graesser's discussion see, "Studies in *maṣṣēbôt*," 8-11. In note 2 on page 10, Graesser lists those scholars who either supported or opposed the phallic interpretation of *maṣṣēbôt*. Those in favor were H. H. Spoer ("Versuch einer Erklärung des Zusammenhanges zwischen Dolmen, Mal- und Schalensteinen in Palälstina," *ZAW* 28 [1908] 271-90), B. D. Eerdmans ("The Sepulchral Monument 'Maṣṣēbāh'," *JBL* 30 [1911] 109-13), Ernst Sellin ("Zu der ursprünglichen Bedeutung der Mazzeben," *OLZ* 15 [1912] 119-26), and Benzinger. Those against this interpretation were Robertson Smith (*Lectures*, 457-58), Hugo Gressmann ("Dolmen, Masseben, und Napflöcher," *ZAW* 29 [1909] 113-28), and Karl Budde ("Zur Bedeutung des Mazzeben," *OLZ* 15 [1912] 248-50, 469-71).

[5]"Studies in *maṣṣēbôt*," 11-12.

[6]Another recent study which attempts to draw connections between archaeological remains and textual issues, much of which centers on *maṣṣēbôt* is Tryggve N. D. Mettinger's, *No Graven Image? Israelite Aniconism in Its Ancient Near Eastern Context* (Coniectanea Biblica OT Series 42; Stockholm: Almqvist & Wiksell, 1995). Mettinger is mostly interested, however, not in *maṣṣēbôt* themselves, but in the connection between them and the practice of aniconic religion. Mettinger, unfortunately, errs by including as much archaeological data as possible without attempting to discern if the examples he includes are valid or if any connection between them and textual descriptions can actually be verified. For a recent review of this work, see Theodore J. Lewis, "Divine Images and Aniconism in Ancient Israel," *JAOS* 118 (1998) 36-53.

immanent in the cult so that cultic intercourse with the deity can occur." Graesser notes that the various functions outlined above may overlap in some cases.[7]

Graesser's study provides an extensive analysis of the various types of standing stones, recovered not only within Israel, but throughout the ancient Near East. He discusses, among other examples of standing stones, Assyrian victory stelae, Ugaritic votive stelae, Egyptian funerary stelae, Aramaic *napšā*, Sumerian boundary stones, Kassite *kudurru*s, the Sefirê treaty stelae, Hittite *huwaši*, and Nabatean betyls. He then provides a section in which he discusses archaeological examples of standing stones from throughout the ancient Near East[8] before addressing the biblical evidence and Albright's theory that *bāmôt* were funerary standing stones.

Graesser himself acknowledges the inherent difficulty in his categorization of *maṣṣēbôt* by conceding that there is something vaguely cultic about all of these functions, and the precise nature of what made a particular *maṣṣēbāh* important to the ancients is as open to interpretation now as it was in ancient times. He notes that:

> modern interpreters are not the only ones who have experienced difficulty in understanding the function of *maṣṣēbôt*. Different ancient individuals probably interpreted a single stone in a number of ways even though they had the benefit of oral tradition concerning the stone . . . This probably reflects not only the fact that stones can perform several functions at once, but also the varying interpretations of different individuals or different generations.[9]

If, then, one cannot with any certainty draw a line between a cultic stone and a boundary stone or a funerary monument or a victory stela, then a system dividing *maṣṣēbôt* into precise categories may be less useful than one would wish.

As might be expected, Graesser's final analysis of why the stones were eventually prohibited is also less than compelling. He admits that "the possible cause of the prohibition of the *maṣṣēbôt* in Israel is notable primarily for its sketchiness and its large silent gaps."[10] In other words, no specific reason for their proscription is given in the text, leaving Graesser, in the final page of his work, to speculate along some of the same lines as the former members of the History of Religions School which he critiques at

---

[7]"Studies in *maṣṣēbôt*," 31–32.
[8]"Studies in *maṣṣēbôt*," 34–218.
[9]"Studies in *maṣṣēbôt*," 301.
[10]"Studies in *maṣṣēbôt*," 306.

the beginning of his work. He theorizes, as did scholars such as Robertson Smith who tended toward developmental theories concerning religious phenomena, that:

> these holy cultic stones came to be used more and more as magical instruments of cultic manipulation and thus fell under the prohibition of the second command-ment. The recognition of the impropriety of the *maṣṣēbôt* was undoubtedly due in part to a heightened and more sophisticated religious conscience.[11]

This appears to be a theory that posits Israel's early acceptance of *maṣṣēbôt* as an unsophisticated practice out of which they later evolved. Graesser's work is valuable, however, for its review of scholarship and the wealth of material it collects concerning sacred stones, even if the final conclusions regarding the various types of stones and the underlying reason for their lack of sanction in later Israel are not completely convincing.

B. SUMMARY OF THE BIBLICAL DATA ON *maṣṣēbôt*.

Before presenting the biblical data, one major difference between the current study and that of Graesser should be explained. Graesser considered any stone set up by an individual (or group), specifically those without ornamentation of any kind, to typify Syro-Palestinian *maṣṣēbôt*.[12] Graesser counted as *maṣṣēbôt*, then, any of the biblical stones which fit into one of his categories, regardless of whether that stone is called a *maṣṣēbāh* in the text (Deut 27:2-8; Josh 4:8; 5:22; 24:27; 1 Sam 7:12; 15:12).[13]

The current study has avoided this practice in the case of verses such as the above examples from Dtr precisely because Dtr does know the term *maṣṣēbāh* and yet does not use it for these monuments. It is unknown whether Dtr had some functional definition for *maṣṣēbôt* in mind which these stones did not fit, or rather refused to call them *maṣṣēbôt*, even though they did fit the definition, because they were seen as acceptable in spite of earlier law prohibiting *maṣṣēbôt* (Deut 16:22). The fact remains that these monuments are consciously referred to by Dtr with another term, and this makes blurring the distinctions between these stones and those which Dtr does call *maṣṣēbôt* undesirable if one's goal is to avoid homogenizing the

---

[11]"Studies in *maṣṣēbôt*," 307. Throughout his introductory chapter (especially pp. 8-16), Graesser takes issue with the overly evolutionary nature of the work of the History of Religions school. He also tacitly criticizes the theory of earlier scholars, including de Vaux, that *maṣṣēbôt* eventually became idols (p. 14, n.3; p. 19).

[12]"Studies in *maṣṣēbôt*," 298.

[13]"Studies in *maṣṣēbôt*," 302-4.

biblical data. For this reason, the current study will first deal with those passages which actually use the term *maṣṣēbāh* and introduce evidence regarding additional monumental stones only secondarily.

B.1. The biblical data regarding *maṣṣēbôt* and their function

The sources which mention *maṣṣēbôt* are: E, the Covenant Code, Exodus 34, H, D, Dtr, the Chronicler, Hosea, Micah, First Isaiah, Jeremiah and Ezekiel.[14] Not all of these sources, however, acknowledge the existence of *maṣṣēbôt* within Israel. Jeremiah and Ezekiel mention only foreign *maṣṣēbôt* dedicated by their builders to foreign gods.[15] Both of these prophets predict the destruction of such *maṣṣēbôt* at the hands of the Babylonian king Nebuchadnezzar. In the case of Jer 43:1, the *maṣṣēbôt* in question are Egyptian. In Ezek 26:11, they are Tyrian and may even be simple architectural features rather than cultic items. First Isaiah acknowledges Israelite use of *maṣṣēbôt*, but mentions the term only once, and only in a description of the establishment of a YHWHistic *maṣṣēbāh* and a YHWHistic altar in Egypt as a signal of Egypt's eventual conversion to YHWH (Isa 19:19). The *maṣṣēbāh* is erected on the border with Egypt also, making it unclear whether it served any religious function beyond marking the border of YHWH's land.[16]

Isa 19:19 and the remainder of the references (excluding Jeremiah and Ezekiel) all deal with *maṣṣēbôt* which are either located within the land of Israel (existing prior to Israel's occupation of the land or erected within the land at some later time by Israelites), or which were erected by Israelites in some other land. Of these references, several have positive views toward *maṣṣēbôt*. E and First Isaiah make only positive references to *maṣṣēbôt*.[17] E also has positive references to *maṣṣēbôt*, but only to those *maṣṣēbôt* erected by Israelites.[18] The E-related Covenant Code (Exod 23:24), instructs Israel

---

[14]Gen 28:18, 22; 31:13, 45, 51, 52; 35:14, 20; Exod 23:24; 24:4; 34:13; Lev 26:1; Deut 7:5; 12:3; 16:22; 2 Sam 18:18; 1 Kgs 14:23; 2 Kgs 3:2, 10:26, 27; 17:10; 18:4; 23:14; 2 Chr 14:2; 31:1; Hos 3:4; 10:1, 2; Mic 5:12; Isa 19:19; Jer 43:13; Ezek 26:11. Judg 9:6 and Isa 6:13 constitute possible, though not definite references to *maṣṣēbôt* and will be mentioned only tangentially to the main discussion.

[15]For a discussion of a possible reference to an Israelite *maṣṣēbāh* dedicated to YHWH in Jer 2:27, see Olyan, "Cultic Confessions."

[16]The use of *maṣṣēbôt* as boundary stones discussed below, pp. 212-13.

[17]In addition to Isa 19:19, Isa 6:13 uses the term *maṣṣēbāh* in reference to a tree stump that remains standing even when the tree has been felled. This stump is then likened to the remnant of Israel which God will preserve.

[18]Gen 28:18, 22; 31:13, 45, 51, 52; 35:14, 20.

to destroy the *maṣṣēbôt* which the prior inhabitants of the land erected and dedicated to their gods.

The remainder of the sources deal with "Israelite" *maṣṣēbôt* and assess them negatively (H, D, Dtr, Chr), or mention them only in the negative contexts of judgment oracles (Hos 3:4; 10:1-2; Mic 5:12). Some of these sources share as one reason for disapproval the fact that the *maṣṣēbôt* in question were dedicated to gods other than YHWH. This view is shared by H, D, Dtr, the Chronicler, and possibly Hos 3:4 and Mic 5:12. D, Dtr, and the Chronicler, however, express disapproval of *maṣṣēbôt*, regardless of whether they might be dedicated to YHWH. Deut 16:22 states that YHWH hates *maṣṣēbôt*. Dtr continually mandates the destruction of *maṣṣēbôt* in the Judahite and Israelite countryside without suggesting that they are dedicated to any foreign deity (1 Kgs 14:23; 2 Kgs 17:10; 18:4), although others are specified as dedicated to other gods (2 Kgs 3:2; 10:26, 27; 23:14). Likewise the Chronicler mandates the destruction of *maṣṣēbôt* whose dedication is not specified (2 Chr 14:2; 31:1).

Despite the predominantly disapproving assessment of *maṣṣēbôt* by Dtr, however, even this source has one reference to a *maṣṣēbāh* which it apparently finds acceptable. This is the reference to the monument erected by Absalom to memorialize himself (2 Sam 18:18). Perhaps it is approved because it, like the grave marker for Rachel mentioned by E (Gen 35:20), is not dedicated to any god, but rather serves as a memorial monument to a person. The chart below illustrates biblical opinions concerning *maṣṣēbôt* in order to clarify the distinctions which exist in the evidence.

> **E:** *maṣṣēbôt* approved, all erected by Jacob, serving the following functions:
> Gen 28:18-22: anointed theophany marker at Bethel, witness to vow
> Gen 31:13-52: border marker with Gilead, witness to treaty
> Gen 35:14:anointed theophany marker at Bethel, witness to fulfilled vow
> Gen 35:20: grave marker
> **Covenant Code:** *maṣṣēbôt* condemned, erected by prior inhabitants of the land
> Exod 23:24: dedicated to foreign gods
> **Exodus 24:** *maṣṣēbôt* approved, erected by Moses
> Exod 24:4: theophany marker at Sinai commemorating the twelve tribes
> **Exodus 34:** *maṣṣēbôt* condemned, erected by prior inhabitants of the land
> Exod 34:14: dedicated to foreign gods
> **Holiness Code:** *maṣṣēbôt* condemned and prohibited for Israelite use
> Lev 26:1: possibly viewed as dedicated to idols
> **D:** *maṣṣēbôt* condemned, erected by prior inhabitants, prohibited for Israelites
> Deut 7:5: dedicated to foreign gods
> Deut 12:3:dedicated to foreign gods
> Deut 16:22: dedicated to gods but not to be erected for YHWH

Dtr: One *maṣṣēbāh* approved
    2 Sam 18:18:approved memorial for himself erected by Absalom
All other *maṣṣēbôt* condemned
    1 Kgs 14:23: unspecified cultic use resembling prior nations, erected in Judah
    2 Kgs 3:2: dedicated to Baʿal, erected by Ahab in Samaria, destroyed by
        Jehoram
    2 Kgs 10:26-7: dedicated to Baʿal, erected in Samaria, desroyed by Jehu
    2 Kgs 17:10: unspecified cultic use resembling prior nations, erected by Israel
    2 Kgs 18:4: unspecified cultic use with *bāmôt* and *ʾăšērîm*, erected Judah
    2 Kgs 23:14: dedicated to Astarte, Milcom, and Chemosh, erected in
        Jerusalem by Solomon, purged by Josiah
Chronicler: *maṣṣēbôt* condemned
    2 Chr 14:2: dedicated to foreign gods, located in Judah, destroyed by Asa
    2 Chr 31:1: unspecified use, destroyed by Hezekiah
Hosea: View of *maṣṣēbôt* unclear
    Hos 3:4: unspecified cultic use, YHWH removes so Israel will repent?
    Hos 10:1-2 unspecified cultic use, proliferated in northern kingdom
Micah: View of *maṣṣēbôt* unclear
    Mic 5:12: unspecified cultic use, removed by YHWH along with *pəsîlîm*
First Isaiah: *maṣṣēbôt* approved, erected by, or symbolizing, Israel
    Isa 6:13: term used for the image of a stump symbolizing a remnant of Israel
    Isa 19:19: border marker with Egypt, a sign of YHWH's worship in Egypt
Jeremiah: *maṣṣēbôt* condemned, erected by Egyptians
    Jer 43:1: dedicated to Egyptian gods, to be destroyed by Nebuchadnezzar
Ezekiel: *maṣṣēbôt* condemned, erected by Tyrians
    Ezek 26:11:pillars of unspecified use to be destroyed by Nebuchadnezzar

The above chart demonstrates the many uses of *maṣṣēbôt* and the evaluations of them by various authors as either approved or disapproved. Below is a discussion of the various uses and associations linked with *maṣṣēbôt* in the biblical material.

B.1.a. *maṣṣēbôt* as markers of covenant. E depicts important personages erecting *maṣṣēbôt* on the sites of theophanic experiences which lead to covenant making (Gen 28:18-22; 35:14; Exod 24:4). In all three of these cases, the *maṣṣēbôt* become the witnesses, as it were, to the covenant or vow made by either the person who erected the *maṣṣēbāh* (Jacob in Gen 28:18-22 and 35:14), or to the parties present who are entering into covenant with YHWH (Moses and the twelve tribes in Exod 24:4). In E, Jacob's *maṣṣēbāh* at Bethel has the effect of commemorating a theophany, witnessing his vow to build Bethel, as well as witnessing his fulfillment of that vow. In Gen 31:13-52, the *maṣṣēbāh* erected by Jacob does not commemorate a covenant made between YHWH and a worshipper, but it does witness the covenant and vow of truce made between Jacob and Laban.

Although E is the only source which uses the term *maṣṣēbôt* to describe standing stones used as markers or witnesses to covenant, in D, this
same function is fulfilled by the stones (*ăbānîm*) at Mt. Ebal (Deuteronomy
27), and in Dtr, by the monuments of Gilgal (Joshua 4), and the stone
beneath the oak at Shechem (Joshua 24). It is also possible that Samuel's
monument to a military victory, called the *ʾeben hā-ʿāzer*, "Stone of Help" is
a witness to the divine intervention believed to aid in the battle (1 Sam
7:12). Although these stones are not said to be *maṣṣēbôt*, it is possible that
they are also reflexes of a shared tradition, perhaps a particularly northern
tradition, of stones as witnesses to theophany or covenant.

B.1.b. *maṣṣēbôt* as grave markers or memorial stelae. E, Dtr, and
perhaps First Isaiah, record two types of *maṣṣēbôt* which are representative
of individual people or groups of people. The first type, found in E, is a
maṣṣēbāh that commemorates a dead person, namely Rachel (Gen 35:20).
The second type, found in Dtr, and perhaps First Isaiah, is a *maṣṣēbāh* used
to honor, represent, or commemorate live persons. As well as marking the
site of a theophany, E's reference in Exod 24:4 to twelve *maṣṣēbôt* which
represent the twelve tribes' presence at the site of the Sinai covenant may fit
this pattern also. In 2 Sam 18:18, Dtr records that Absalom erected a
monumental *maṣṣēbāh* for himself because he had no sons. In Isa 6:13, the
prophet states that a tree stump left behind after the felling of a mighty oak
is like the remnant of Israel that shall be left behind after YHWH's judgment against Israel is fulfilled. The use of the term *maṣṣēbāh* for a tree
stump is curious here unless one understands the word play that evokes the
image of the commemorative *maṣṣēbāh*, in this case, a stump which witnesses to both the fallen glory of Israel as well as the survival of the remnant. As stones which represented individuals, either on the site of their
burial (Gen 35:20) or as a record of their life which would stand after they
had died (Exod 24:4; 2 Sam 18:18), *maṣṣēbôt* appear to have been accepted,
even by Dtr, who elsewhere rejects them. As will be discussed below, common stones were also said to serve this commemorative purpose,
particularly in the "twelve stones for the twelve tribes," motif found in Dtr,
P, and the Elijah cycle.

B.1.c. *maṣṣēbôt* as boundary stones. E and Isa 19:19 record the use
of *maṣṣēbôt* as boundary markers. In the E example mentioned above, Gen
31:13-52 records the boundary stone erected between the lands of Jacob and
Laban. It witnessed their truce and their vow of nonencroachment. This pas-

sage states that the boundary stone is there to watch that neither passes over the border to harm the other, in keeping with the vow made in the presence of the stone. In Isa 19:19, a *maṣṣēbāh* is erected on the border between Israel and Egypt, not as a witness to nonaggression per se, but to the presence of YHWH (or YHWH's worshipers) in the land of Egypt, and the future conversion of the Egyptians to YHWH.

This function of *maṣṣēbôt* as markers of national boundaries also appears to be approved by those who use it. As with the above cases, however, Dtr also mentions plain stone monuments (*ăbānîm*) which served the same function. In Joshua 4 they stand on the Jordan river border and mark the presence of YHWH's people in the land. Again, it is possible that some shared tradition concerning stone boundary markers is behind this image but it was not one that suggested use of the term *maṣṣēbôt* to Dtr.

B.1.d. Disapproval of certain cultic functions of *maṣṣēbôt*. The Covenant Code, H, D, Dtr, and the Chronicler, appear to disapprove of certain *maṣṣēbôt* for cultic reasons. The Covenant Code and D disapprove of *maṣṣēbôt* which were erected by the prior inhabitants of the land because they were dedicated to the gods of those nations and not to YHWH (Exod 23:24; Deut 7:5; 12:3). D goes farther by prohibiting Israel from constructing them and dedicating them to YHWH, stating that they are objects which YHWH "hates" (Deut 16:22). H also prohibits the Israelites from manufacturing *maṣṣēbôt* (as well as *pəsîlîm*, *ĕlîlîm*, and the *ʾeben maśkît*), for the purpose of worship (Lev 26:1).

Given that the Covenant Code is so closely associated with E, which heavily endorses Israelite *maṣṣēbôt*, it is not unexpected that this legal corpus is negative toward the *maṣṣēbôt* of other cultures which are used in the worship of their gods probably in the same way as they were used by Israel in the worship of YHWH. Similarly, H does not specifically state that *maṣṣēbôt* were used to worship the idols also mentioned in Lev 26:1; however, it is likely that this was the intent of the passage.

Dtr contains several verses which evaluate the use of *maṣṣēbôt* negatively without specifically stating what it is about them that is undesirable. In 1 Kgs 14:23 and 2 Kgs 17:10 the use of *maṣṣēbôt* is said to resemble the worship conducted by the prior inhabitants of the land. 2 Kgs 18:4 lists *maṣṣēbôt* among the items removed by Hezekiah when he became king. Other items listed are *bāmôt* and *ăšērîm* and the bronze serpent Nehushtan which the people had begun to worship. Other Dtr verses, discussed below, mention *maṣṣēbôt* that are disapproved, presumably because they are part of the cult of specific foreign gods (2 Kgs 3:2; 10:26-27; 23:14). The Chronicler, as mentioned in chapter six, mentions *maṣṣēbôt* only twice in lists of items including *ăšērîm*, *bāmôt*, and *mizbəḥôt*, which are purged by the kings Asa and Hezekiah respectively (2 Chr 14:2; 31:1). This relative lack of interest in *maṣṣēbôt* on the part of the Chronicler is interesting in that both of these passages are from material original to the Chronicler. Why more references to *maṣṣēbôt* did not enter the Chronicler's work from Dtr remains a mystery.

Passages which convey disapproval of *maṣṣēbôt* without giving specific motivation for that disapproval, along with passages in the section below dealing with foreign gods, are often cited in generalizations concerning *maṣṣēbôt* in secondary literature. The above evidence, however, shows that many uses of *maṣṣēbôt* existed about which various sources, including Dtr, are quite positive. While it is true that D, H, and the Chronicler have only negative views of *maṣṣēbôt*, E has only positive ones regarding Israelite *maṣṣēbôt*, and Dtr's views vary according to their usage.

B.2. Objects or peoples associated with *maṣṣēbôt*

B.2.a. *maṣṣēbôt* and specific foreign gods. Dtr makes direct connections between *maṣṣēbôt* and the worship of specific foreign deities. Ba‘al is mentioned most often in relation to *maṣṣēbôt* which Dtr states were part of the furnishings of his temple in Samaria built by Ahab (2 Kgs 3:2; 10:26-27).[19] *maṣṣēbôt* are also said to have been removed by Josiah when he destroyed the *bāmôt* which Solomon erected for ‘Astarte, Milcom, and Chemosh, the gods of his foreign wives (2 Kgs 23:14). Dtr, however, is the only source which makes a direct connection between *maṣṣēbôt* and other gods referred to by name. As expected, Dtr applauds the destruction of *maṣṣēbôt* dedicated to foreign deities, just as the destruction of *maṣṣēbôt* found within Israel's cult life is applauded.

B.2.b. *maṣṣēbôt* and foreign cultures. In addition to Dtr's references concerning *maṣṣēbôt* as part of the cult of Ba‘al, and possibly those of ‘Astarte, Milcom, and Chemosh as well, Jeremiah and Ezekiel witness to the presence of *maṣṣēbôt* in foreign cultures. Jer 43:13 predicts the destruction of the *maṣṣēbôt* found in Heliopolis of Egypt, as well as the rest of the temples of Egypt's gods at the hands of Nebuchadnezzar. Ezek 26:11 also

---

[19]For *mizbəḥôt* in construct with Ba‘al, see Judg 6:25, 28, 30; 1 Kgs 16:32; 18:26; 2 Kgs 11:18; 21:3; 2 Chr 23:17; 33:3; 34:4; Jer 11:13. *bāmôt* are mentioned in construct with Ba‘al in Jer 19:5; 32:35.

predicts Nebuchadnezzar destroying *maṣṣēbôt* found in Tyre. The *maṣṣēbôt* mentioned here, however, may simply be architectural pillars toppled along with the walls and houses of the city.

Jeremiah and Ezekiel, however, are the only two sources which mention *maṣṣēbôt* belonging to other specific cultures.[20] Isaiah 19 also mentions a *maṣṣēbāh* on Israel's border with Egypt, but this monument is YHWHistic and most probably seen as erected by Israelites at some future time. In Jeremiah and Ezekiel, the *maṣṣēbôt* in question are representative symbols of the glory of Egypt and Tyre respectively, Egypt with her great temples and Tyre with her rich architecture. In both passages, these *maṣṣēbôt* and their destruction by Nebuchadnezzar represent the thoroughness of the defeat of these once powerful nations at the hand of the king YHWH has allowed to triumph over them. Cultic *maṣṣēbôt* are associated with Egypt in Jer 43:13 in a way similar to the association between *bāmôt* and Moab in Jer 48:35. It appears that for Jeremiah these two cultic items are the stereotypical cultic features of these cultures, and as such, their destruction reveals the weakness of the deities to whom they were dedicated.

B.2.c. *maṣṣēbôt* and *bāmôt*. As noted above, Albright proposed that *bāmôt* frequently had *maṣṣēbôt* as part of their fixtures, and that because these objects were so frequently present on the same site, these two terms were in fact used interchangeably for this type of installation, namely a burial cairn.[21] *maṣṣēbôt* and *bāmôt* are not actually mentioned together frequently, however.

As noted in chapter five, *maṣṣēbôt* and *bāmôt* are mentioned together only five times, in Dtr (1 Kgs 14:23; 2 Kgs 18:4; 23:13-14) and the Chronicler (2 Chr 14:2; 31:1). Contrary to the conclusion of Albright that *maṣṣēbôt* and *bāmôt* occur together so frequently they became synonymous terms, it should be noted that only two sources actually mention them together (Dtr and the Chronicler) and of the five total passages in which these two sources mention them together, only two passages make the overt statement that *maṣṣēbôt* and *bāmôt* were constructed together on the same sites (1 Kgs 14:23; 2 Kgs 23:13-14). The other references which combine the mention of *maṣṣēbôt* and *bāmôt* simply list them as items which were purged at the same time. This implies that even for Dtr and the Chronicler, *maṣṣēbôt*, like *ăšērîm*, could have been part of *bāmôt* installations, but there was no tacit assumption that they always were.

---

[20]Exodus 34, D, and Dtr connect *maṣṣēbôt* with the prior inhabitants of the land as a group without specifically naming any one particular group that was partial to them.

[21]"High Place," 242-58.

B.2.d. *maṣṣēbôt* and *ăšērîm*. As noted in chapter six, Exodus 34, D, Dtr, and the Chronicler mention *maṣṣēbôt* together with *ăšērîm*. In Exod 34:13 and D (Deut 7:5; 12:3), *maṣṣēbôt*, *ăšērîm*, and *mizbəḥôt* represent a complex of objects used by the prior inhabitants of the land to worship their gods. D goes farther to instruct that Israelites not use *maṣṣēbôt* and *ăšērîm* in the worship of YHWH or erect them near YHWH's altars (Deut 16:21-22). The implication is that YHWH does not wish to be worshipped in the same style as the gods of other nations.

Dtr picks up on this theme in 1 Kgs 14:23 and 2 Kgs 17:10 when the use of *maṣṣēbôt* and *ăšērîm* on every high hill and under every *ʿēṣ raʿănān* is pointed out as a mistake because it resembles the worship practices of other nations. No mention is made that these installations were used to worship any god other than YHWH, only that their use was a practice borrowed from another culture. In Dtr's other two passages linking *maṣṣēbôt* with *ăšērîm*, they are items removed during religious reforms (2 Kgs 18:4; 23:14). In 2 Kgs 23:14, however, they are connected with the worship of gods other than YHWH in that they are removed from *bāmôt* dedicated to ʿAstarte, Milcom, and Chemosh.

Dtr also has other verses which mention these objects separately, however, and one verse apparently approves of Absalom's use of a *maṣṣēbāh* as a memorial to himself. This implies that for Dtr, the issue of *ăšērîm* and *maṣṣēbôt* was more nuanced than it was for Exodus 34 and D. *maṣṣēbôt* and *ăšērîm* were connected with the prior inhabitants of the land and their style of worship, but they were also used by Israelites separately as well as together with varying levels of acceptability.

In Chronicles (2 Chr 14:2; 31:1) *maṣṣēbôt* and *ăšērîm* are merely objects purged (along with *bāmôt* and foreign *mizbəḥôt*) during reforms with no mention of their dedication to specific gods or any statement of their location together on one site. Mention of *ăšērîm*, *bāmôt*, and *mizbəḥôt* occurs elsewhere in the Chronicler without the mention of *maṣṣēbôt*, however, which leads to the conclusion that rather than seeing *maṣṣēbôt* as constant companions to *ăšērîm*, the Chronicler viewed *maṣṣēbôt* as rather minor items listed with other more prominent ones for the sake of completeness.

B.2.e. *maṣṣēbôt* and *mizbəḥôt*. E, Exodus 34, D, Dtr, the Chronicler, Hosea, and Isaiah all mention *maṣṣēbôt* together with *mizbəḥôt*. For E, the coexistence of an altar and a *maṣṣēbāh* at Bethel must be presumed on the basis of passages which state that both types of objects were constructed there by Jacob. E mentions the *maṣṣēbāh* which Jacob erects in Bethel in Gen 28:18, 22; 31:13; and 35:14. E mentions the altar in 35:7. There is no statement that the two objects stood side by side, but they are both said to be present. No references to Bethel in the other sources, however, mention the *maṣṣēbāh* of Jacob. Only an altar of Bethel, presumably the altar built by Jeroboam ben Nebat, is mentioned in Dtr and the prophets.

In Exod 24:4, E depicts Moses erecting twelve *maṣṣēbôt* representing the twelve tribes of Israel beside the altar he constructs at the foot of Sinai. Exod 34:13 and D (Deut 7:5; 12:3) list *maṣṣēbôt* and *mizbǝḥôt* as fixtures in the cultic life of the prior inhabitants of the land. In Deut 16:22, D also mentions *maṣṣēbôt* after a prohibition against constructing *ăšērîm* near *mizbǝḥôt* of YHWH, implying that *maṣṣēbôt* as well are prohibited from proximity to YHWH's *mizbǝḥôt*. Dtr states that the Temple of Ba'al in Samaria had both *maṣṣēbôt* and *mizbǝḥôt* (2 Kgs 10:26-27). Chronicles merely lists *maṣṣēbôt* along with *mizbǝḥôt* as items to be purged in religious reforms, again, as noted above, without any suggestion of how closely connected they might actually have been.

Hos 10:1-2 mentions *maṣṣēbôt* and *mizbǝḥôt* together in a passage which states: "Israel is like a rich vine that produces its fruit. Just as the quantity of his fruit increases, he increases the quantity of his *mizbǝḥôt*. Just as his country improves, the *maṣṣēbôt* improve." The passage ends with the indictment that YHWH will now break down their altars and destroy their *maṣṣēbôt*. It has been argued above in chapter four that this passage is a type of "futility curse," which implies that Israel's multiplication of *mizbǝḥôt* and *maṣṣēbôt* is a futile process which ultimately angers YHWH. While the passage seems judgmental toward *maṣṣēbôt*, it is not clear that Hosea means to depict all *maṣṣēbôt* as illegitimate. If one were to assume this, one would have to make the same case concerning *mizbǝḥôt*.

Regardless of how Hosea meant his audience to understand 10:1-2, *maṣṣēbôt* and *mizbǝḥôt* formed some sort of conceptual pair. In fact, in Hos 3:4, the only other verse in Hosea to mention them, *maṣṣēbôt* are mentioned in a pair with a term related to *mizbǝḥôt*, namely *zebaḥ*. This passage states that YHWH will sentence Israel to go without "king, prince, sacrifice (*zebaḥ*), *maṣṣēbāh*, ephod, and *tǝrāpîm*," before they eventually learn to abandon their other gods and return to YHWH.

As noted in chapter four, the surface meaning of this passage implies that *maṣṣēbôt* are items of a type with acceptable items such as "kings" and "sacrifices" which the nation will be forced to do without as YHWH's punishment for the worship of other gods. Graesser and Andersen and

Freedman, however, are among those who demonstrate that here is a reflec-
tion, in societal and cultic terms, of the legitimate and illegitimate
relationships in which Israel has engaged. Just as the prophet's wife is to be
denied legitimate sexual union with her husband, Israel is to be denied her
kings, her sacrifices, and her ephod. Just as the prophet's wife will be
denied illegitimate sexual union with another man who is not her husband,
Israel will be denied her princes (presumably lesser leaders than kings), her
maṣṣēbôt, and her *tərāpîm*.[22]

The analogy which is said to exist here, however, is not perfect.
Without mentioning *maṣṣēbôt* it can be stated that not all sources see
tərāpîm or princes negatively. If this interpretation is the right one, however, it would reinforce the interpretation of Hosea 10 as a passage which
saw the proliferation of *maṣṣēbôt* and *mizbəḥôt* as a sign of corruption
within northern Israel's national expansionism. It does not, however, say
anything definitive concerning Hosea's opinion of *maṣṣēbôt* or *mizbəḥôt* in
and of themselves.

The final source which mentions *maṣṣēbôt* and *mizbəḥôt* in the same
context is First Isaiah. As part of his vision for the conversion of Egypt to
YHWHism, Isa 19:19-22, the prophet states that two objects will be erected
there. In the center of Egypt there will be an altar to YHWH and on its border with Israel a *maṣṣēbāh*. These two objects represent the YHWHistic
presence in Egypt. Thus for Isaiah (who only mentions *maṣṣēbôt* in this one
context), the use of *maṣṣēbôt* as boundary markers was approved and considered a YHWHistic practice, and that along with *maṣṣēbôt* on one's bor-
ders, *mizbəḥôt* in one's midst provided a stable presence of YHWH in a foreign land such as Egypt. While these two objects do not stand together in
Isaiah, they do constitute a pair of objects which represent YHWH.

In short, along with Exodus 34, D, Dtr, the Chronicler, and Hosea
who saw *maṣṣēbôt* and *mizbəḥôt* as parts of illegitimate or ineffectual worship, whether on the part of the prior inhabitants of the land (Exodus 34, D),
or of Israel (D, Dtr, the Chronicler, Hosea), E and Isaiah see *maṣṣēbôt* as
legitimate companions to YHWHistic *mizbəḥôt*, either as parallel
YHWHistic symbols (Isaiah 19) or as witnesses to covenant with YHWH
(E). A final note concerning these references is that with the exception of E
and Dtr, the verses in which the rest connect *maṣṣēbôt* with *mizbəḥôt* (or
with sacrifices) are also the only verses in these sources which mention
maṣṣēbôt at all. This means that for them, the presence of *maṣṣēbôt* called to

---

[22]Graesser, "Studies in *maṣṣēbôt*," 251; Andersen and Freedman, *Hosea*, 303-6.

mind the presence of *mizbǝḥôt*. It is not evident, however, that any specific sacrificial ritual involving both items was also in the minds of these authors.

B.2.f. *maṣṣēbôt* and cultic statuary. Chapters ten and eleven of this study will demonstrate how the Vulgate and the early Jewish interpreters apparently viewed *maṣṣēbôt* as a type of cultic statuary based on the interpretation of *maṣṣēbôt* as "things which are made to stand up." Because idols must be made to stand up, these interpreters formed the opinion that *maṣṣēbôt* were a type of cultic image or statue. This interpretation, however, even though it has been championed in modern times,[23] appears to be another leveling through of one possible interpretation onto the whole of the biblical data.

Of the sources which mention *maṣṣēbôt* (E, The Covenant Code, Exodus 24, Exodus 34, H, D, Dtr, the Chronicler, Hosea, Micah, First Isaiah, Jeremiah, and Ezekiel), several have views which are inconsistent with the theory that *maṣṣēbôt* were a type of idol. E views Israelite *maṣṣēbôt* as respected tools of testimony, to covenant with YHWH (Gen 28:18, 22), to covenant between persons (Gen 31:45-52), or to persons themselves (Gen 35:20). First Isaiah (19:19) likewise sees *maṣṣēbôt* as monuments wholly appropriate to YHWHism in a way that idols would not be. Ezekiel mentions *maṣṣēbôt* in a context that implies that they were primarily understood as Tyrian architectural features and does not comment at all on their religious significance (26:11). The Covenant Code (Exod 23:24), Exod 34:13, D (Deut 7:5; 12:3; 16:22), and Jeremiah (43:13) mention a connection between *maṣṣēbôt* and the gods of other nations, but in such a way as to imply that *maṣṣēbôt* were items used in the worship of these gods, not that they themselves were worshipped as gods by these nations.

Other biblical passages mention *maṣṣēbôt* along with terms for cultic statuary in passages which seem to be differentiating between them. D (Deut 7:5; 12:3) mentions how the prior nations used *maṣṣēbôt* to worship *pǝsîlîm*, which in 12:3 are referred to as *pǝsîlê ʾĕlōhêhem*, "the carved images of their gods." While the text does not state exactly how these objects were used, leaving open the possibility that D meant to state that the *maṣṣēbôt* were a type of idol, it is not imperative that one read the text this way. Similarly, in the case of the Chronicler, in which *maṣṣēbôt* appear only twice in lists of items to be purged (2 Chr 14:2; 31:1), the possibility of reading these objects as idols exists, but is not likely.

---

[23]See above, "A: Summary of Previous Scholarship on *maṣṣēbôt*," pp. 205-08.

Dtr has mixed references to *maṣṣēbôt*, some which definitely should not be interpreted as idols (such as Absalom's monument, 2 Sam 18:18), others which definitely could be interpreted as idols (such as the *maṣṣēbôt* which Ahab erected either of, or for, Baʿal, 2 Kgs 3:2; 10:26-27), and others which might or might not be so interpreted (1 Kgs 14:23; 2 Kgs 17:10; 23:14). Similarly, the passages in Hosea which mention *maṣṣēbôt* (3:4; 10:1-2) would read as well if a term meaning "idol" was substituted for the term *maṣṣēbāh*, but there is no compelling reason to suppose that Hosea viewed *maṣṣēbôt* as a type of idol.

Two sources which could be seen to imply that *maṣṣēbôt* are a type of idol are H and Micah. In Lev 26:1, H lists *maṣṣēbôt* along with two other items used by the prior inhabitants of the land which are types of cultic statuary: *pəsîlîm* and *ʾĕlîlîm*. Also mentioned is the *ʾeben maśkît*, which, while not clearly identified as a type of idol, is most closely related to either pictorial reliefs or ritual carvings like those found in Mesopotamian temples, both of which would have some connection to gods of other nations.[24] If the *maṣṣēbôt* themselves are not a type of idol or artifact intimately connected to the worship of gods other than YHWH, they appear to be the only item in the list that clearly is not.

Similarly, Mic 5:10-13 lists pairs of related items which YHWH will destroy: horses and chariots, cities and strongholds, sorcery and divination, *pəsîlîm* and *maṣṣēbôt*. It is possible to understand this passage as placing *pəsîlîm* and *maṣṣēbôt* in the same class. While this class might simply be "cultic items upon which Israel relies" just as "horses and chariots" are items in the war machine upon which Israel relies, Micah nonetheless refers to *maṣṣēbôt* and *pəsîlîm* as "works of" Israel's hands to which they "bow down." This may imply that *maṣṣēbôt* as well as *pəsîlîm* were understood by Micah to have been worshiped in Israel.

Though the interpretation of *maṣṣēbôt* as statues or idols is prominent in the Vulgate and in certain midrashim, of all the biblical sources which mention *maṣṣēbôt*, only H and possibly Micah provide examples of sources which may have seen *maṣṣēbôt* as a type of cultic statuary. Dtr has a few verses which make this interpretation appear possible and others which make it appear impossible. The verses from Hosea and Chronicles could be interpreted as references to statuary, but they need not be so interpreted. Exodus 34, D, the Covenant Code, and Jeremiah have references which

---

[24]For the theory that these objects were reliefs, see Ackerman, *Under Every Green Tree*, 44, n. 30. For the view that they are temple carvings indicating where one should stand to petition the god, see Hurowitz, "אבן משכית."

connect *maṣṣēbôt* to other gods, but in such a way as to make it seem they were not synonymous with idols of these gods. In contrast, Ezekiel apparently mentions *maṣṣēbôt* only as Tyrian architectural features, while First Isaiah and all of E's references to Israelite *maṣṣēbôt* represent *maṣṣēbôt* as legitimate YHWHistic emblems.

Apparently it is the H passage (and possibly that of Micah) which has been leveled through in certain of the midrashim, and from there the interpretation of *maṣṣēbôt* as idols made its way into Jerome's translation. See further, chapters ten and eleven.

B.2.g. **_maṣṣēbôt_ and the 'ēṣ ra'ănān formula.** Only three occurrences of the 'ēṣ ra'ănān formula mention *maṣṣēbôt* as part of this image. These occur in D (Deut 12:2-3) and Dtr (1 Kgs 14:23; 2 Kgs 17:10). There are a greater number of examples of this formula which do not mention *maṣṣēbôt*. These can be found in Dtr (2 Kgs 16:4), First and Third Isaiah (30:25; 57:5-7), Jeremiah (2:20; 3:6, 13; 17:2), Ezekiel (6:3-13; 20:28; 34:6), Hosea (4:13), and Chronicles (2 Chr 28:4).

Of the witnesses which omit *maṣṣēbôt* from the 'ēṣ ra'ănān formula, Ezekiel, Jeremiah, and Third Isaiah also lack any reference to Israelite *maṣṣēbôt* and First Isaiah has only positive references to *maṣṣēbôt*. Hosea and the Chronicler have both the 'ēṣ ra'ănān formula and negative views of *maṣṣēbôt*, but they fail to connect *maṣṣēbôt* with the formula where it occurs.

Apparently, *maṣṣēbôt* were not an essential feature of the 'ēṣ ra'ănān formula for any source except D. Dtr does not include them in one of its three uses of the formula, and the other sources which use the formula do not mention *maṣṣēbôt* at all as a part of it, even if they have references to *maṣṣēbôt* elsewhere in their writings (as do First Isaiah, Jeremiah, Ezekiel, Hosea, and the Chronicler). This material demonstrates that any who see *maṣṣēbôt* as a permanent feature of worship on high hills and under green trees are leveling through the views of D only.[25]

B.2.h. The relationship of _maṣṣēbôt_ to other stones not so named.

B.2.h.i. maṣṣēbôt and 'eben maśkît. As noted above the term *'eben maśkît*, which means "carved stone," appears in Lev 26:1, in addition to *maṣṣēbôt*, *pəsîlîm*, and *'ĕlîlîm*, as a type of object that the Israelites are not to have in their land. Similarly, P states that the Canaanites had *maśkîyôt*, "carved things," as well as *bāmôt* and cast images which Israel was to

---

[25]See, for example, Davies, "high place," 602-4.

destroy upon entrance into the land (Num 33:52). Ezekiel 8:12 uses this term apparently to refer to wall reliefs, while Prov 18:11; 25:11; and Ps 73:7 use the term to mean something akin to "imagination." Because the term is so obscure in its Hebrew usage, scholars have for many years assumed these items to be a type of *maṣṣēbāh* whose distinction from the ordinary type had been lost through time.

It appears now, however, that the only connection between these stones and *maṣṣēbôt* is their material and the fact that both are carved. If Victor Hurowitz is correct, and these carvings were traditionally found in Mesopotamian temples marking the spot on the threshold where petitioners were to stand, or if Susan Ackerman is correct and these stones are wall reliefs,[26] then there would have been ample reason for H, P, and Ezekiel to single them out as syncretistic and therefore unacceptable. The reason for their rejection would, in both these cases, have nothing to do with any connection to *maṣṣēbôt*.

B.2.h.ii *maṣṣēbôt and peger.* W. F. Albright and other scholars, particularly David Nieman, have long seen the possibility of interpreting the term *peger* in Hebrew not only as "corpse" but also as "grave marker" or "stela."[27] Nieman argued that *pgr* could mean "stela" on the basis of inscriptional evidence from Ugarit.[28] This evidence was also invaluable to Albright who used it in his translation of Ezek 43:7. Albright argued that *pgr* in this context was a reference to funeral stelae erected on *bāmôt*. This allowed him to connect *bāmôt* with his theories concerning the cult of the dead, and to interpret *maṣṣēbôt* at times as simple grave markers.[29]

That *peger* may have come into Hebrew with the meaning of "grave marker," however, has no wider bearing on the interpretation of *maṣṣēbôt* than to witness to the existence of a synonym for *maṣṣēbôt* in their function as grave markers. It certainly cannot be used to connect *maṣṣēbôt* in other contexts to some funerary ritual as Albright attempted.

B.2.h.iii. *maṣṣēbôt and ăbānîm with similar functions.* As noted above, D and Dtr depict stone monuments which serve the same purpose as

---

[26]See above, p. 220, n. 24.

[27]"PGR: A Canaanite Cult-object in the Old Testament," *JBL* 67 (1948) 55-60.

[28]As noted above in chapter five (p. 149, n. 58), Nieman cites as evidence for this theory, KTU 6:13 and KTU 6:14, first published by Claude Schaeffer and René Dussaud (*Syria* 16 [1935] 177), now in Dietrich, Loretz, and Sanmartín, *Cuneiform Alphabetic Texts*, 501-02.

[29]"High Place," 242-58.

maṣṣēbôt in other contexts without referring to them by any other term but *ʾeben*. Examples of this are the monuments at Gilgal (Joshua 4), the stones on Mt. Ebal (Joshua 8), the stone beneath the oak at Shechem (Joshua 24), and Samuel's "Stone of Help" (1 Samuel 7). The reason D and Dtr do not call these stones *maṣṣēbôt* remains obscure. It is possible that D and Dtr are making a distinction between these stone monuments and *maṣṣēbôt* based purely on physical criteria of appearance or construction technique. It is also possible, however, that D and Dtr are attempting to sanitize these respected monuments from any possible connection with *maṣṣēbôt* which had later fallen out of favor. Refusing to call them *maṣṣēbôt* would not only insulate these monuments from any hint of illegitimacy, it would also prevent any attempts to legitimize later prohibited *maṣṣēbôt* by noting the reverence given these monuments.

One bit of evidence that seems to support the theory that Dtr is intentionally avoiding the term *maṣṣēbāh* for monuments which are approved of is the reference in Judg 9:6 to the "oak of the pillar" *ʾēlōn mūṣṣab* which stood at Shechem and beside which Abimelek was declared king. If this is a reference to the same oak tree under which Joshua erects the stone monument in Joshua 24, then the use of a term related to *maṣṣēbāh* in Judg 9:6 may be an intentional means of casting aspersions on Abimelek, without directly calling Joshua's stone a *maṣṣēbāh*. If the oak is the same, it is possible that the stone has become a *maṣṣēbāh* in this Judg 9:6 reference specifically to underscore the unsanctioned nature of Abimelek's kingship ceremony. If this is seen as a conscious word choice of Dtr, then one could theorize that the term *maṣṣēbôt* is being intentionally avoided elsewhere for reasons related to Dtr's cultic agenda.

Other stones which appear in contexts where some sources use the term *maṣṣēbôt* are the "twelve stones which represent the twelve tribes." In E these are *maṣṣēbôt* (Exod 24:4). There are twelve stones representing the twelve tribes of "Jacob" in 1 Kgs 18:31 in Dtr's story of Elijah's altar on Mt. Carmel, and stones which represent the twelve tribes of "Israel" in the ornamentation of the ephod and the high priest's breastplate in P (Exod 28:10-12, 21; 39:7, 14). This image occurs in three different sources, E, P, and Dtr, and in one occurrence, the stones are actually called *maṣṣēbôt*. Dtr and P do not use the term *maṣṣēbôt* most probably because their contexts call for other types of stone, field stones or gem stones. However, all the sources retain the detail that the stones represent the tribes, just as the *maṣṣēbôt* at the foot of Mt. Sinai testify to the covenant between the tribes and YHWH.

For whatever reason, D and Dtr do not use the term *maṣṣēbôt* in every context in which one might expect to find it. Stone monuments were erected in several D and Dtr stories in which the term *maṣṣēbôt* does not occur. Whether this was an attempt to sanitize these monuments from any future interpretation as *maṣṣēbôt*, to avoid lending support to later cultic use of *maṣṣēbôt* by Israelites (a practice which they actively discouraged), or whether it demonstrates that they were making a distinction between *maṣṣēbôt* and these other monuments on purely aesthetic or technological grounds remains unknown. That Dtr and P also know of the "twelve stones for the twelve tribes" motif, but do not use the term *maṣṣēbôt* for these stones as E does, sheds more light on the endurance and flexibility of this image than on the views of these sources regarding *maṣṣēbôt*.

B.2.h.iv. *maṣṣēbôt* and Ezekiel's "stones of fire." In Ezekiel 28 there is a unique reference to "stones of fire," *ʾabnê ʾēš*, located in Eden, among which the king of Tyre once walked. Verse 13 portrays the king in Eden, called "the garden of ʾElohim," where he is clothed with a covering of precious jewels and woven gold. Verses 14-16 add the detail of the "stones of fire," to the scene. They read:

> With an anointed cherub as protector I placed you (there),
> On the holy mountain of ʾElohim you were.
> Amid the stones of fire you came and went.
> Innocent in your ways you were.
> From the day you were created,
> until there was iniquity found in you,
> Through your abundance of trading,
> full of violence within you, you sinned.
> So I judged you too profane for the mountain of ʾElohim,
> and the cherub protector banished you
> from among the stones of fire.

There are many similarities between this scene and the scene of Eden in the J source. The cherub is present in both scenes (Gen 3:24), as are the riches described in terms of gold and precious stones (2:11-12). The king walks about in the garden (*hithallēk*) just as YHWH ʾElohim does (Gen 3:8). In that there are no references to "stones of fire" in J, the antecedent for this particular aspect of the scene appears obscure.

Some commentators connect these stones with the "precious jewels" mentioned in verse 13.[30] In his commentary on Ezekiel, Walther Zimmerli

---

[30]See, for example, Andrew W. Blackwood, *Ezekiel: Prophecy of Hope* (Grand

notes many other possible explanations for this reference offered by scholars. Marvin Pope, for instance, offered the parallel to Canaanite myth in which Ba'al's palace is constructed by a process of smelting precious stones and metals. The "stones of fire," then, are smelted precious stones which formed the king's palace.[31] Another explanation discussed by Zimmerli was that of F. Charles Fensham in his article "Thunder-Stones in Ugaritic."[32] Zimmerli, however, misstates Fensham's interpretation:

> F. C. Fensham, on the basis of Akkadian *aban išāti*, with which he compares the Ugaritic *abn brq* of text V AB.C 23, thinks of "lightning stones, thunderbolts" hurled in a thunderstorm by the weather-god Ba'al who lives on *ṣpn*.

This is not, however, Fensham's argument. It is an argument of M. D. Cassuto, which Fensham quotes,[33] that seeks to connect the *'abnê 'ēš* of Ezekiel with the *'bn brq* of the Ugaritic text. Fensham notes that Cassuto found what he thought was a parallel in the attested Akkadian phrase *zunnu u abnê*[mes] *birqu išātu*, "rain and hail, lightning and fire"; Fensham, however, does not believe the phrase is a good parallel to Ezekiel 28. Fensham himself states that the phrase *'abnê 'ēš* of Ezekiel 28 refers to flint, which he then argues was believed by the ancients to be the remnant of thunderbolts because it produces fire.[34] As Fensham noted, he was preceeded in the identification of these stones with flint, based on Akkadian *aban išāti*, by Herbert May.[35]

Zimmerli himself prefers to interpret the "stones of fire" as "fellow inhabitants" in the garden with the king. He writes:

> After the magnificent creature himself has been compared with a signet [v. 12], it is more likely, in the case of the "stones of fire" in whose midst he dwells, that the reference is to his fellow inhabitants--who are thus thought of as creatures of light, either the stars or the originators of the powerful flashes of lightning that fall from heaven . . . In any case the polytheistic environment on the "mountain of assembly" is clear. It is only lightly concealed by the image.[36]

Rapids, Mich.: Baker, 1965) 186; J. W. Wevers, *Ezekiel* (Century Bible; London: Nelson, 1969) 217.

[31]Walther Zimmerli, *Ezekiel 2* (Hermeneia; Philadelpha: Fortress, 1983) 93. Pope's work, to which Zimmerli refers, is *El in the Ugaritic Texts* (VTSup 2; Leiden: E. J. Brill, 1955).

[32]*JNES* 18 (1959) 273-74.

[33]Fensham cites Cassuto, *From Adam to Noah* (2d ed.; Jerusalem: Magnes, 1953) 50-51.

[34]"Thunder-stones," 273-74.

[35]"Ezekiel," *The Interpreter's Bible* (New York: Abingdon, 1956) 6.221.

[36]Zimmerli, *Ezekiel 2*, 93.

It appears that the only thing upon which all of the commentators agree is that some sort of Canaanite mythological imagery is involved in this passage.

An additional reference may contribute to this discussion. In a tradition concerning Tyre, preserved in the writings of Philo of Byblos (as quoted by Eusebius) two stelae are mentioned, dedicated to Fire and Wind. Below is a translation of the reference from Eusebius's *Praeparatio evangelica* (I.10.10):

> Then he [Philo] says that Hypsouranios settled Tyre and that he invented huts made of reeds, rushes, and papyrus. He quarreled with his brother Ousoos who first discovered how to gather a covering for the body from the hides of animals which he captured . . . He [Ousoos] dedicated two steles for Fire and Wind. He worshipped them and poured out to them libations of blood from the animals which he had hunted . . . They worshipped the steles and conducted annual festivals for them.[37]

While this reference is not situated in Eden, it does constitute a tradition, connected with Tyre, and placed at the beginnings of human history which speaks of "stelae of fire and wind." This does not prove that Ezekiel knew the exact tradition that Philo preserves, but the comparison is suggestive. Perhaps Ezekiel knew something of Tyrian legend and so uses an image similar to the Tyrian image of primordial "stelas of fire" in his description of the king of Tyre's fall from power. While Ezekiel does not use the term *maṣṣēbāh* here in chapter 28, he does use the term in 26:11 to speak of architectural features in Tyre. Even if one were to conclude, however, that these "stones" were the poetic equivalent of stela or *maṣṣēbôt*, this would say nothing of Ezekiel's views of *maṣṣēbôt* as Israelite items. It merely implies that Ezekiel knew certain traditions concerning standing stones beyond those *maṣṣēbôt* mentioned in 26:11.

CONCLUSIONS

This chapter has demonstrated that various scholarly generalizations concerning *maṣṣēbôt* cannot be supported by the biblical evidence. Contrary to the views of Albright, *maṣṣēbôt* cannot be seen as synonymous with *bāmôt*. Nor can *maṣṣēbôt* be demonstrated in any sources except H and

---

[37]Harold W. Attridge and Robert A. Oden, Jr. *Philo of Byblos: The Phoenician History- Introduction, Critical Text, Translation, Notes* (CBQMS 9; Washington D.C.: CBA, 1981) 43. For additional treatments of Philo of Byblos, see James Barr, "Philo of Byblos and his 'Phoenician History'" *BJRL* 57 (1974) 17-68; and Albert I. Baumgarten, *The Phoenician History of Philo of Byblus: A Commentary* (Leiden: E. J. Brill, 1981).

Micah, to be the equivalent of idols, although this is the view of the Vulgate and certain of the midrashim. *maṣṣēbôt* are not always present in the scene depicting worship on high hills and under green trees except in D.

What the text shows is that *maṣṣēbôt* had a variety of functions in ancient Israel. They could be grave markers (E, Dtr), border markers (E, First Isaiah), personal monuments (Dtr), monuments to covenant (E), or objects used in the worship of a god, be that god YHWH (E, First Isaiah), Baʿal (Dtr), ʿAstarte, Milcom, Chemosh (Dtr), the gods of Egypt (Jeremiah), or some other indeterminate deity (E, Exodus 34, H, D, Dtr, the Chronicler). They could be approved as YHWHistic (E, First Isaiah), or condemned when seen as remnants of the cult used by the prior inhabitants of the land (E, Exodus 34, H, D, and Dtr). They could simply be referred to as architectural features from foreign lands (Ezekiel).

They could be associated always with *ăšērîm* and *mizbəḥôt* (Exodus 34 and D) or with *ăšērîm, mizbəḥôt,* and *bāmôt* (the Chronicler). They might be considered a type of idol (H), or in a class of objects with idols (Micah), or they could be mentioned along with idols as if they were distinct from them (D). Their use was not restricted to any one nation in that they were viewed as appropriate to Israel by E and First Isaiah, to Egypt by Jeremiah, to Tyre by Ezekiel, and to the nations who used to inhabit the land by Exodus 34, D, and Dtr.

Essentially, *maṣṣēbôt,* more so than any of the other items in this study, have the potential to be seen in a variety of different settings, performing a multitude of functions, and representing traditions which could be sanctioned or condemned depending on the point of view of the author who mentions them. Dtr appears to single out one function of *maṣṣēbôt* as accepted (that of personal memorial or grave marker) and condemn the rest due to the fact that many stone monuments which serve the same functions in Dtr as *maṣṣēbôt* do in other sources (such as E) are not always called *maṣṣēbôt* by Dtr. The only object for which Dtr allows this term is Absalom's monument (2 Sam 18:18). E and the Covenant Code, when considered together, makes the distinction that *maṣṣēbôt* of all types are allowed, provided that they are YHWHistic, while *maṣṣēbôt* of other nations are to be destroyed.

Because the biblical material regarding *maṣṣēbôt* is so varied, the tendency to level one conception of *maṣṣēbôt* throughout the entire text cannot be supported; whether it be H's (and possibly Micah's) view that *maṣṣēbôt* were idols, or D and Exodus 34's view that *maṣṣēbôt* were representative of the worship practiced by the prior inhabitants of the land, or even E's view that all *maṣṣēbôt* used by Israelites were YHWHistic. *maṣṣēbôt* appear to have been used for a variety of purposes throughout most of the biblical time periods, both within and without Israel, and each source which discusses them gives its own view of whether they should be accepted or destroyed.

Chapter Eight
Synthesis of the Data Regarding *mizbəḥôt*

A. SUMMARY OF PREVIOUS SCHOLARSHIP ON *mizbəḥôt*

Of all the items of interest in this study, *mizbəḥôt* are the most positively evaluated in the biblical text. Regardless of their periodic use in unsanctioned contexts, *mizbəḥôt* remained the primary cultic fixture in Israelite religion. Because of this, there are not as many studies aimed at identifying *mizbəḥôt* or defining the term as there are in the case of the other objects under discussion.[1] Most recent studies which mention *mizbəḥôt* or sacrificial offerings are aimed at understanding Israelite cult and ritual, rather than *mizbəḥôt* themselves.[2]

Perhaps one reason for the relative lack of studies related to *mizbəḥôt* in Israel is the wealth of archaeological evidence regarding them. Unlike the other items of interest in this study, Israelite *mizbəḥôt* are represented in the archaeological material by many clear examples which leave little doubt as to how *mizbəḥôt* looked in biblical times. Large horned altars of ashlar construction have been recovered from Tel Dan and Beer Sheba, while smaller monolithic stone altars and field stone altars have been recovered from Arad.[3] Similar monolithic altars to those at Arad have been recovered from

---

[1]Kurt Galling, *Der Altar in den Kulturen des alten Orients: eine archaologische Studie von Kurt Galling mit zwei Abschnitten von Hugo Gressman* (Berlin: K. Curius, 1925); Harold Marcus Wiener, *Altars of the Old Testament* (Leipzig: Hinrich, 1927).

[2]See, for example, Gary A. Anderson, *Sacrifices and Offerings in Ancient Israel: Studies in their Social and Political Importance* (HSM 41; Atlanta: Scholars Press, 1987); Haran, *Temples and Temple Service*; Jacob Milgrom, *Studies in Cultic Theology and Terminology* (Studies in Judaism in Late Antiquity 36; Leiden: E. J. Brill, 1983); Anson Rainey, "The Order of Sacrifices in Old Testament Ritual Texts," *Biblica* 51 (1970) 485-98; Among older studies on this subject are: George Buchanan Gray, *Sacrifice in the Old Testament: Its Theory and Practice* (Oxford: Clarendon, 1925); Rolf Rendtorff, *Studien zur Geschichte des Opfers im Alten Israel* (Neukirchen-Vluyn: Neukirchener, 1967); Norman Henry Snaith, "Sacrifices in the Old Testament," *VT* 7 (1957) 308-17; Roland de Vaux, *Studies in Old Testament Sacrifice* (Cardiff: University of Wales Press, 1964).

[3]Avraham Biran, "Dan (place)," *ABD* 2.15; Yohanan Aharoni, "The Horned Altar of Beer-sheba," *BA* 37 (1974) 2-6. For photographs, see also Aharoni *Archaeology*, photo 44; and Mazar, *Archaeology*, 496; Yohanan Aharoni, "The Israelite Sanctuary at Arad," in *New Directions in Biblical Archaeology* (ed. David Noel Freedman and Jonas Green-

Megiddo, Dan, Lachish, Tel Qedesh, and most recently at Tel Miqne-Ekron, where many of these small altars have been recovered in what appears to be an oil producing installation.[4] Also excavated recently are what may be a large ramp-style altar on Mt. Ebal,[5] and a smaller rural altar discovered in the hill country. This second site is being referred to as the "Bull Site," because a small statuette of a bull was found there.[6] Given the numerous examples of altars of varying manufacture found in Iron Age strata in Israel, there is no need to engage in lengthy discussion aimed at identifying *mizbəḥôt* as artifacts, or expounding on biblical terminology such as "horns" in relation to *mizbəḥôt*.

B. SUMMARY OF THE BIBLICAL DATA ON *mizbəḥôt*

The sources which mention *mizbəḥôt* are: J, E, the Covenant Code, Exodus 34, P, H, D, Dtr, the Chronicler (Chronicles, Ezra, and Nehemiah), Amos, Hosea, First Isaiah, Third Isaiah, Jeremiah, Ezekiel, Joel, Zechariah, Malachi, Psalms, and Lamentations.[7] The great majority of these references are to altars used in the worship of YHWH, and certain of the biblical wit-

---

field; Garden City, N.Y.: Doubleday, 1971) 28-44.

[4]See a discussion of these and other cultic finds in Mazar, *Archaeology*, 499-501.

[5]See Zertal, "Joshua's Altar." There is some debate concerning whether this structure is, in fact, an altar. For this debate, see Kempinski, ("Joshua's Altar," 42-49) and Zertal's response ("How Can Kempinski," 43-53).

[6]Mazar, "Bronze Bull," 34-40.

[7]J: Gen 8:20; 12:7, 8; 13:4, 18; 26:25; Exod 17:15; E: Gen 22:9; 33:20; 35:1, 3, 7; Exod 24:4, 6; Covenant Code: Exod 20:24, 25, 26; 21:14; P: Exod 27:1, 5, 6, 7; 28:43; 29:12, 13, 16, 18, 21, 25, 36, 37, 38, 44; 30:1, 18, 20, 27, 28; 31:8; 32:5; 34:13; 38:1, 3, 4, 7, 30, 38; 40:5, 6, 10, 26, 29, 32, 33; Lev 1:5, 7, 8, 9, 11, 12, 13, 15, 16, 17; 2:2, 8, 9, 12; 3:2, 5, 8, 11, 13, 16; 4:7, 10, 18, 19, 25, 26, 30, 31, 34, 35; 5:9, 12; 6:2, 3, 5, 6, 7, 8; 7:2, 5, 31; 8:11, 15, 16, 19, 21, 24, 28, 30; 9:7, 8, 9, 10, 12, 13, 14, 17, 18, 20, 24; 10:12; 14:20; 16:18, 20, 25, 33; Num 3:31; 4:11, 13, 14; 5:25, 26; 7:1, 10, 11, 84, 88; 17:3, 4, 11; 18:3, 5, 7, 17; 23:1, 2, 4, 14, 29, 30; Josh 22:10, 11, 16, 19, 23, 26, 28, 29, 34; H: Lev 17:6, 11; 21:23; 22:22; Deut 7:5; 12:3, 27; 16:21; 26:4; 27:5, 6; 33:10; Josh 8:30, 31; 9:27; Judg 2:2; 6:24, 25, 28, 30, 31, 32; 13:20; 21:4; 1 Sam 2:28, 33; 7:17; 14:35; 24:18, 21, 25; 1 Kgs 1:50, 51, 53; 2:28, 29; 3:4; 6:20, 22; 7:48; 8:22, 31, 54, 64; 9:25; 12:32, 33; 13:1, 2, 3, 4, 5, 32; 16:32; 18:26, 30, 32, 35; 19:10, 14; 2 Kgs 11:11, 18; 12:10; 16:10, 11, 12, 13, 14, 15; 18:22; 21:3, 4, 5; 23:9, 12, 15, 16, 17, 20; 1 Chr 6:34; 16:40; 21:18, 22, 26, 29; 22:1; 28:18; 2 Chr 1:5, 6; 4:1, 19; 5:12; 6:12, 22; 7:7, 9; 8:12; 14:2; 15:8; 23:10, 17; 26:16, 19; 28:24; 29:18, 19, 21, 22, 24, 27; 30:14; 31:1; 32:12; 33:3, 4, 5, 15, 16; 34:4, 5, 7; 35:16; Ezra 3:2, 3; Neh 10:3; Amos 2:8; 3:14; 9:1; Hos 4:19; 8:11; 10:1, 2, 8; 12:12; Isa 6:6; 17:8; 19:19; 27:9; 36:7; 56:7; 60:7; Jer 11:13; 17:1, 2; Ezek 6:4, 5, 6, 13; 8:5, 16; 9:2; 40:46, 47; 41:22; 43:13, 18, 22, 26, 26, 27; 45:19; 47:1; Joel 1:13; 2:17; Zech 9:15; 14:20; Mal 1:7, 10; 2:13; Ps 26:6; 43:4; 51:21; 84:4; 118:27; Lam 2:7.

nesses make reference only to YHWHistic *mizbəḥôt*. Those which mention no other altars except those dedicated to YHWH/ʾElohim are J, E, P, H, Third Isaiah, Joel, Zechariah, Malachi, Ezra, Nehemiah, Lamentations, and Psalms.

Of the remaining authors who mention *mizbəḥôt*, some speak only of *mizbəḥôt* which are condemned, and do not speak of approved *mizbəḥôt* of any kind. These are Exodus 34, Amos, Hosea, and Jeremiah. Those which remain mention both YHWHistic altars and non-YHWHistic ones. These are the Covenant Code, D, Dtr, Chronicles, First Isaiah, and Ezekiel. Below each of the groups outlined above will be discussed separately.

B.1. Biblical witnesses which mention only YHWHistic *mizbəḥôt*

J mentions altars which are built for YHWH by Israelite patriarchs such as Noah (Gen 8:20), Abraham (Gen 12:7, 8; 13:4, 18), Isaac (Gen 26:25), and Moses (Exod 17:15). J also mentions one notable non-Israelite who is depicted building *mizbəḥôt* presumably dedicated to YHWH, namely Balaam (Num 23:1-2, 4, 14, 29, 30). J is apparently untroubled by the fact that Balaam is non-Israelite or by the fact that these *mizbəḥôt* are situated in Moab.

E depicts Abraham (Gen 22:9), Jacob (Gen 33:20; 35:1, 3, 7), Moses (Exod 24:4-6), and Aaron (Exod 32:5) building *mizbəḥôt* for ʾElohim/ YHWH. In Exod 24:4-6, Moses builds an altar for YHWH following the revelation at Sinai, but also erects twelve *maṣṣēbôt* which are seen positively as representing the twelve tribes of Israel. Although Aaron's altar in 32:5 is used in a festival involving the golden calf, the altar itself is said to be built for a festival for YHWH.

P, in all its numerous references to *mizbəḥôt*, approves only those *mizbəḥôt* which are situated in front of the Tabernacle.[8] Even the P tradition preserved in Joshua 22 serves to underscore the fact that only the Tabernacle's *mizbəḥôt* are sanctioned for Israelite use. If the Transjordanian tribes wish to make sacrifices to YHWH, in P's view, they must come over the Jordan and use the altars of the Tabernacle. H also approves only altars related to the Tabernacle.

---

[8]Exod 27:1, 5, 6, 7; 28:43; 29:12, 13, 16, 18, 21, 25, 36, 37, 38, 44; 30:1, 18, 20, 27, 28; 31:8; 32:5; 34:13; 38:1, 3, 4, 7, 30, 38; 40:5, 6, 10, 26, 29, 32, 33; Lev 1:5, 7, 8, 9, 11, 12, 13, 15, 16, 17; 2:2, 8, 9, 12; 3:2, 5, 8, 11, 13, 16; 4:7, 10, 18, 19, 25, 26, 30, 31, 34, 35; 5:9, 12; 6:2, 3, 5, 6, 7, 8; 7:2, 5, 31; 8:11, 15, 16, 19, 21, 24, 28, 30; 9:7, 8, 9, 10, 12, 13, 14, 17, 18, 20, 24; 10:12; 14:20; 16:18, 20, 25, 33; Num 3:31; 4:11, 13, 14; 5:25, 26; 7:1, 10, 11, 84, 88; 17:3, 4, 11; 18:3, 5, 7, 17; 23:1, 2, 4, 14, 29, 30; Josh 22:10, 11, 16, 19, 23, 26, 28, 29, 34.

Lamentations and Joel mention YHWH's altar in the course of lament over the destruction of the nation. Lam 2:7 states that YHWH has scorned his own altar and his sanctuary, while Joel's two passages tell of how the priests lament the downfall of the people and the withholding of sacrifices from YHWH's altar (1:13; 2:17). Five different Psalms mention the altar of YHWH. One is a song of thanksgiving (Psalm 26), while the rest are hymns to Zion, both Elohistic (Psalms 43 and 51) and YHWHistic (Psalms 84 and 118). Psalm 118 features a procession up to YHWH's altar.

Sources which deal with the Second Temple era, Ezra, Nehemiah, Third Isaiah, Malachi, and Zechariah, discuss only the altars of the Jerusalem Temple which need to be restored. Ezra deals with the rebuilding of the altar (3:2-3) and Nehemiah deals with the resumption of sacrifices (10:35). Malachi warns the priesthood and those who would renew sacrifice at Jerusalem's altar that sacrifices must be done in a proper manner (1:7) for God would prefer the Temple closed rather than defiled (1:10; 2:13). Zechariah compares Israel's revenge upon her enemies as like the horns of the altar that drink blood (9:15), and later states that restored Israel will ultimately be so pure that even horse tack and cooking pots will be as holy as the altar vessels from the Temple (14:20). The most optimistic by far of all these Restoration sources is Third Isaiah who twice depicts the conversion of the whole world to YHWH and the offerings of all the new converts flowing to YHWH's (56:7; 60:7).

There can be no doubt that the authors listed above, even though they speak only of YHWHistic *mizbəhôt*, knew that *mizbəhôt* were part of the religious paraphernalia of other cultures. These sources simply do not choose to discuss other *mizbəhôt*. All of the *mizbəhôt* they discuss are sanctioned (if in need of repair and purification in some sources) primarily because they are dedicated to YHWH, and secondarily, in some cases, because they are located at the central shrine. As Wellhausen observed,[9] J affirms all altars of YHWH regardless of who builds them or where. E approves of all altars to 'Elohim/YHWH, no matter where they exist, and even if they are accompanied by *maṣṣēbôt*. For both J and E, construction of *mizbəhôt* was a simple process without any elaborate instuctions as to their manufacture. P and H, however, mention no altars but the carefully crafted altars of the Tabernacle, and P appears to condemn even Israelites who try to build altars to YHWH at any other place (Joshua 22).

That these authors only mention *mizbəhôt* of YHWH and in so doing have only references to altars which are approved, does not mean that for

---

[9]See his chapter on "The Place of Worship," *Prolegomena*, 17-51.

these authors all altars were acceptable. Each portrays the use of *mizbəḥôt* in the manner they found acceptable. The failure to condemn other types does not indicate tacit approval of them.

B.2. Biblical witnesses which mention only disapproved *mizbəḥôt*

Exod 34:13 mentions only those altars which were built by the prior inhabitants of the land, and with which, along with *ăšērîm* and *maṣṣēbôt*, they worshipped their gods. This passage demands that the Israelites tear down these objects as they find them, and make no treaties or covenants with their owners (34:12, 15). The rest of the biblical authors who have only negative references to *mizbəḥôt* are all in the prophetic material.

Amos depicts the hypocritical citizens of the northern kingdom performing supposedly pious acts such as sleeping all night before the altar of YHWH while at the same time sleeping on garments taken in pledge from the poor (2:8). While the altar itself is not criticized, the use to which it is put is obviously unacceptable to Amos. Elsewhere the prophet condemns the state shrine at Bethel (3:14) and depicts YHWH standing beside the offending altar to proclaim judgment on the people (9:1). For Amos, the show of piety in the north was completely annulled by their lack of concern for the poor. Their ceremonies, their shrines, and their *mizbəḥôt* were all worthless, even if dedicated to YHWH, because they did not know how to keep their covenant responsibilities.

Hosea condemns the altars of Ephraim (4:19) which are said to be dedicated to *ăṣabbîm*. In 8:11 and 10:1-2 Hosea states that the nation multiplies its *mizbəḥôt* and also *maṣṣēbôt* (in the case of 10:1-2) but that this expansion of cult sites will not bring an expansion of God's appreciation for them. The prophet seems to state that Israel has come to rely on her ability to hold territory, build cities and expand but that sheer number and distribution of *mizbəḥôt*, even if they are dedicated to YHWH, presumably, will not satisfy YHWH who has marked the north for destruction. In Hos 10:8 the nation's central shrine at Bethel is likened to a *bāmāh* and its altar destined for decay and abandonment. In 12:12, the popular pilgrimage festival at Gilgal is condemned. The heart of the message of Hosea, however, in addition to its disapproval of Israel's overconfidence in itself, is the belief that the north had essentially abandoned the worship of YHWH by worshipping other gods as well. This transgression renders all other efforts to please YHWH null and void in the eyes of Hosea.

Jeremiah also rejects cultic overconfidence, in his case, on the part of the southern kingdom (Jeremiah 7). Jeremiah, however, reserves his comments on *mizbəḥôt* for those *mizbəḥôt* which are dedicated to gods other than YHWH. In 11:13, Jeremiah notes how the Judahites have erected altars to Baʿal in Jerusalem and in all the cities of Judah. 17:1-4 tells how the sin of Judah is to be inscribed on the horns of their altars because of how their children use *ăšērîm* along with *mizbəḥôt* on every high hill and under every *ʿēṣ raʿănān*.

The reasons for disapproving of certain altars vary among the biblical authors. Exodus 34 and Hosea acknowledge that certain *mizbəḥôt* were dedicated to gods other than YHWH and therefore were illegitimate. Amos rejects *mizbəḥôt* and the sacrifices carried out on them if the rest of the nation's religious life is not in keeping with covenant loyalty. Hosea, likewise, rejects the north's confidence in its ability to expand and improve as a nation, but also underscores the eventual destruction awaiting the north for its worship of gods other than YHWH. Although the *mizbəḥôt* of Hosea are not always directly related to the worship of other gods, the fact that this goes on at all in Israel, makes even any YHWHistic cult worthless for Hosea. Likewise, Jeremiah condemns the use of *mizbəḥôt* specifically because they are dedicated to gods other than YHWH, and in the face of this, not even the Temple in Jerusalem is protected.

Throughout the work of these writers, with the possible exception of Amos, is the realization that *mizbəḥôt* are central, not only to the worship of YHWH but to the worship of other gods as well. For Exodus 34, Hosea, and Jeremiah, the use of *mizbəḥôt* to worship other gods deserved attention and special censure. Only Amos and Hosea seem to comment on the use of *mizbəḥôt* in YHWH's worship, and even in these passages, it avails Israel nothing because of how they offend in other ways.

B.3. Biblical witnesses which mention both approved and disapproved *mizbəḥôt*

The Covenant Code, D, Dtr, the Chronicler, First Isaiah, and Ezekiel all mention both approved *mizbəḥôt* and disapproved *mizbəḥôt*. This material, therefore, provides a good opportunity for comparing each type and coming to conclusions concerning the criteria by which each source determines whether an altar is approved or not.

In the case of the Covenant Code the difference between approved and disapproved *mizbəḥôt* appears to be in the method of manufacture. Exod 20:24-26 states that altars are to be built of earth wherever God appears to the people, or they may be built out of field stones, but never out of chiseled stone, and never with steps included. Altars not made in the simple style of earth and natural stone were not proper, but no restriction is placed upon where they may be built. In this regard the Covenant Code is closely related to J and E, both of which depict very simple altar construction at places in which God had been revealed.[10] Unlike P and H, the Covenant Code did not care about the location of the altar, only about its manufacture, and mandated that its manufacture be much more simple than that described in P and H.[11] The only other reference to *mizbǝhôt* in the Covenant Code is Exod 21:14 which indicates that the altar of God was a place to which accused murderers could flee for refuge.

D acknowledges three types of altars. The only one which is condemned is the type of *mizbǝhôt* built by the prior inhabitants of the land and used, along with *ăšērîm* and *maṣṣēbôt*, to worship their gods (Deut 7:5; 12:3; 16:21-22). Israel is to destroy these. The second type of altar that D acknowledges is one which the tribes are to build on Mt. Ebal and at which they are to perform a covenant ritual upon entering the land (Deut 27:5-6; 33:10).[12] This altar is approved; however, in the future, D notes, God will make his name to dwell in one specific spot and at that time, all acceptable ritual is to be located there and nowhere else (Deut 12:27; 26:4). This altar in the "place God chooses" is understandably approved. For D, the prohibition of worship outside this one spot can only take place in the distant future from the time of Moses which is the presumed setting of the book. However, D actually has two classes of approved altars and two of disapproved ones. Those that are approved are those which are YHWHistic and predate God's choosing of a central shrine and that central shrine which will one

---

[10]As noted in chapter one (p. 33, n. 32), Theodore Hiebert has suggested to the current author that this instruction may be the result of some influence by the J writer. That altars are to be constructed out of the natural material of simple earth (*ădāmāh*) and stone coincides well with J's attitudes toward the sanctity of the natural order.

[11]It will be noted below in chapter eleven (p. 345, n.76), that the Vatican manuscript tradition of *The Fragment Targums* may have attempted to reconcile these two conflicting opinions. The MT of Exod 20:24 states, "you shall make me an *altar made of soil*" (מִזְבַּח אֲדָמָה). *The Fragment Targum* reads, "you shall make me an *altar fixed in the earth*" (קביע בארעא). For this text, see the Michael L. Klein, *The Fragment Targums of the Pentateuch According to their extant sources* (2 vols.; Analecta Biblica 76; Rome: Biblical Institute, 1980) 2.134. This interpretation is also recounted in *Mekilta d'Rabbi Ishmael*. For this text, see the critical edition, (*Mechilta d'Rabbi Ismael*, H. S. Horovitz and I. A. Rabin, eds. [Jerusalem: Wahrmann: 1970] 242-45) or the English translation (Jacob Neusner, *Mekhilta According to Rabbi Ishmael: An Analytical Translation* [2 vols.; Brown Judaic Studies 154; Atlanta: Scholars Press, 1988] 2.99-103).

[12]It should be noted that Deut 27:5-6 mandates that the altar on Mt. Ebal be built of unhewn stones in keeping with Exod 23:24-6.

day exist. Those that are disapproved are non-YHWHistic altars and those, YHWHistic or not, which might one day exist contemporaneously with the central shrine and in addition to it.

Similarly, in Dtr, *mizbəḥôt* which are YHWHistic and which exist prior to the construction of the Temple in Jerusalem are approved,[13] as are those dedicated to YHWH which will one day exist or that do exist in the "place god chooses," namely in the Jerusalem Temple.[14] *mizbəḥôt* which are dedicated to gods other than YHWH are disapproved,[15] and *mizbəḥôt* which exist outside the Jerusalem Temple after its construction are disapproved,[16] with the notable exception of the YHWHistic *mizbəḥôt* either used or mentioned by Elijah (1 Kgs 18:30, 32, 35; 19:10, 14). Dtr is non-committal on the issue of whether the altar Ahaz saw in Damascus was good or bad in that it belongs to a foreign king, was located in a foreign land, and so might have been expected to be dedicated to foreign gods (2 Kgs 16:10). Even when Ahaz has it copied and installed in the Temple (2 Kgs 16:11-15) Dtr makes no comment, perhaps because it still fulfills Dtr's criteria for a good altar. It is dedicated to YHWH and it is in the Temple in Jerusalem.

It is worth noting that Dtr makes an exception from the cult centralization rule in the case of Elijah. Elijah obviously lived and worked after the construction of the Temple, and yet Dtr makes no disparaging comment about his use of *mizbəḥôt* outside the Temple and as far away as Mt. Carmel. Two explanations for this situation present themselves. Either the Elijah material was a separate unit which Dtr incorporated into the larger history without editorial revision, or the personage and stories of Elijah were so central to Dtr's image of the righteous prophet that he, and he alone is given special dispensation to erect altars to YHWH in places which YHWH did not choose.

The Chronicler has a similar division of approved and disapproved *mizbəḥôt* as does Dtr but with some interesting nuances that remind one of H and P. The first mention of an altar in Chronicles is in 1 Chr 6:34, which reports that the sons of Aaron had been given the responsibility for YHWH's altars connected with the Tabernacle. The Tabernacle is then mentioned again in relation to the *bāmāh* at Gibeon. Apparently it was not suffi-

---

[13]Josh 8:30-31; Judg 6:24, 26, 28; 13:20; 21:4; 1 Sam 2:28, 33; 7:17; 14:35; 1 Kgs 3:4.

[14]Josh 9:27; 2 Sam 24:18, 21, 25; 1 Kgs 1:50-51, 53; 2:28-29; 6:20, 22; 7:48; 8:22, 31, 54, 64; 9:25; 2 Kgs 11:11; 12:10; 16:11-15.

[15]Judg 2:2; Judg 6:25-26, 28, 30-32; 1 Kgs 16:32; 18:26; 2 Kgs 11:18; 21:3-5; 23:12.

[16]1 Kgs 12:32-33; 13:1-5, 32; 2 Kgs 18:22; 23:9, 15-17, 20.

cient for the Chronicler that the shrine at Gibeon predated the Jerusalem Temple. In order to underscore why it was acceptable for Solomon and other Israelites to worship there, the Chronicler notes that the Tabernacle or Tent of Meeting was there with Aaronide priests presiding (1 Chr 16:40; 21:29), and all of the Tabernacle fixtures, including its altars were in use (2 Chr 1:5-6). The rest of the acceptable altars in Chronicles are located either on the site of the future Temple (1 Chr 21:18, 22, 26) or in the Temple once it is constructed.[17] Altars dedicated to other gods are condemned,[18] as are those in locations outside the Temple.[19]

First Isaiah is another source which mentions both acceptable and unacceptable *mizbəḥôt*, but for this source, there are only two examples of approved *mizbəḥôt*. The first is in the prophet's vision of the Temple and the throne of YHWH in which he receives his commission (Isa 6:6). The second is an altar which will one day stand in the center of Egypt to mark the presence of YHWH and the fact that the Egyptian people will convert to his worship (Isa 19:19). Unlike D, Dtr, and the Chronicler, the prophet apparently has no problem with an acceptable altar of YHWH beyond the confines of the Temple, and even beyond the confines of the land. In this Isaiah is somewhat similar to J in outlook. One of the other references to *mizbəḥôt* in First Isaiah is, however, a quotation from the speech of the Rab Shaqeh, in which the altars outside the Temple are destroyed by Hezekiah (36:7). Because this material is shared between Isaiah, Dtr, and the Chronicler, it may not be considered representative of Isaiah's views concerning *mizbəḥôt*. The remaining two references to altars of which Isaiah disapproves are 17:8 and 27:9, both of which appear to be part of later editorial layers of the book, but in these two verses, turning away from the *mizbəḥôt* they had made and the *ăšērîm* they had worshipped or destroying them constitutes a return to YHWH on the part of Israel, making it appear as if the altars were dedicated to some other deity than YHWH.

Ezekiel is the last remaining source which contains both positive and negative views of *mizbəḥôt*. In Ezekiel 6:4-6 and 6:13, *mizbəḥôt* are disapproved as part of an entire complex of worship features condemned for its connections to idols representing gods other than YHWH. The rest of the references to *mizbəḥôt* in Ezekiel either lament the corruption of YHWH's Temple and its altar with improper and idolatrous practices (8:5, 16; 9:2), or

---

[17]1 Chr 22:1; 28:18; 2 Chr 4:1, 19; 5:12; 6:12, 22; 7:7, 9; 8:12; 15:8; 23:10; 26:16, 19; 29:18-19, 21-22, 24, 27; 33:16; 35:16.

[18]2 Chr 14:2; 23:17; 33:3-5, 15; 34:4, 7.

[19]2 Chr 28:24; 30:14; 31:1; 32:12; 34:5, 7.

predict the glorious renovation of the Temple and its altars when YHWH restores Israel.[20]

In short, of the writers who both approve and disapprove of *mizbəḥôt*, the Covenant Code appears to base its approval of YHWHistic altars on one issue, their manner of construction. The location of the altars appears irrelevant. D bases its approval or disapproval of *mizbəḥôt* on two issues, the dedication of the altar to YHWH, and the relation of the altar, either in time or in location, to the place God will choose, namely Jerusalem. Dtr shares a concern for these issues with D, but exempts the YHWHistic altars of Elijah from the requirement of location at Jerusalem.

The Chronicler, likewise approves only those altars which are YHWHistic and located in Jerusalem, but goes on to sanction the altars at the *bāmāh* of Gibeon. This means that for the Chronicler, no altar which is not either in the Temple or in front of the Tabernacle is approved. First Isaiah also disapproves of altars dedicated to other deities, and quotes Dtr's account of Hezekiah's restriction of YHWH's altars to the Temple, but allows for YHWHism outside of Israel, an idea not seen in other sources since J. Finally, Ezekiel condemns altars dedicated to gods other than YHWH and depicts the future restoration YHWH's Temple in Jerusalem and its altars which are temporarily corrupted. Ezekiel does not mention YHWHistic altars outside the Temple.

The evidence suggests that, for these writers, either manufacture, dedication, location, or attachment to a famous personage such as Elijah might constitute a reason for an altar to be approved when others were dis-approved. Dtr reserves the right to relax the rules of centralization in the case of Elijah, and First Isaiah reserves the right to predict the future con-version of Egyptians to YHWH's worship. All, except the Covenant Code, share the condemnation of the use of *mizbəḥôt* to worship gods other than YHWH. The fact that D, the Chronicler, and possibly Ezekiel strictly enforce the rule that not even any YHWHistic altar may exist outside the Temple in Jerusalem, only underscores the apparent need some biblical writers felt to control the use of *mizbəḥôt* and confine that use to the proper worship of YHWH.

B.4. Analysis of the biblical criteria for evaluation of *mizbəḥôt*

After review of the biblical data regarding *mizbəḥôt*, several nuances appear among the sources which defy generalization. For instance:

---

[20]40:46-47; 41:22; 43:13, 18, 22, 26-27; 45:19; 47:1.

1. One need not be Israelite, or a lifelong YHWHist to build an approved altar to YHWH, at least according to J (Num 23).
2. One need not be in Israel to build an approved altar to YHWH (J, E, First Isaiah).
3. One might build legitimate altars to YHWH outside Jerusalem, even after the Temple is constructed, if one were a revered figure such as Elijah (Dtr).
4. One could err in building even a YHWHistic altar if it was not constructed in the proper way (Covenant Code).
5. One could use a foreign culture's style of altar and escape criticism (as does Ahaz) if the altar is located in the Temple and used to worship YHWH (Dtr).

For some authors, only the dedication to YHWH/ʾElohim was vital (J, E, Exodus 34, D). For still others, centralization was vital (Dtr, P, H, Ezekiel, the Chronicler), but even among these Dtr waives the requirement for centralization in Jerusalem for important episodes such as Elijah's struggle against Ahab, Jezebel, and the priests of Baʿal.

Prophets such as Amos and Hosea place the use of altars and whether or not the cult in which they were central was approved in the context of larger religious life. For Hosea, the widespread practice of the worship of other gods rendered even the legitimate use of YHWHistic *mizbəḥôt* a hypocritical and futile pastime. For Amos the primary offense which might render even proper cultic worship futile was the failure to observe the whole law which mandated covenant loyalty toward the poor.

While it is true that the worship of other gods was a major restriction on the use of *mizbəḥôt* in Israel, the above evidence shows that it was not the only criterion by which the different writers evaluated *mizbəḥôt*. Altars must be YHWHistic, yes, but they must be made a certain way for some, located in Jerusalem or before the tabernacle for others, and for still others, they must be a part of a total religious life that is pure in all of its other aspects as well. For some, without social justice, sacrificial worship was a waste of time. For others without total devotion to YHWH, any devotion given to YHWH in addition to devotion to other gods was useless. Each writer may have shared some views concerning *mizbəḥôt* with the others, but ultimately, the particular theological concerns of each formed the ground rules under which *mizbəḥôt* were to be used.

B.5. Objects or peoples associated with *mizbəḥôt*

B.5.a. *mizbəḥôt* and *ḥammānîm*. In addition to the sacrificial rituals which involved *mizbəḥôt*, there were also altars which Israel used which the Bible refers to as *ḥammānîm*. *ḥammānîm* are believed to be incense altars,

similar perhaps to archaeological examples such as those found at
Taanach.[21] Whether the biblical *ḥammānîm* resembled these or other stands
from Israel is not certain, but the fact that the burning of incense in special
stands took place in Israel is certain both from archaeology and from the
biblical text.

With regard to *ḥammānîm*, it is noteworthy that the only biblical
references to them occur in H (Lev 26:30), the Chronicler (2 Chr 14:4; 34:4,
7), Ezekiel (6:4-6), and Isaiah 17:8 and 27:9. With the exception of Isaiah
17:8 and 27:9, all of these references occur in exilic or postexilic sources,
and the two references from Isaiah come not from the poetic prophetic
oracles in the book but from the prose connections between oracles, both of
which could be exilic in origin. In all of these sources, the use of *ḥammānîm*
are condemned as part of unacceptable worship.[22]

Of the four authors who mention *ḥammānîm*, only H does not also
mention *mizbəḥôt* in the same context. For Ezekiel (chapter 6) *mizbəḥôt* and
ḥammānîm are both present as part of the worship engaged in by Israel on
bāmôt. For Isa 17:8 and 27:9 *ăšērîm* are also present along with *mizbəḥôt*
and *ḥammānîm* as examples of the improper worship of Israel. For the
Chronicler, *ḥammānîm* are items which, along with *mizbəḥôt*, *pəsîlîm*, *massēkôt*, and *ăšērîm*, are purged from Judah and Israel by Josiah. Chronicles
also gives a description of how these items were arranged in relation to each
other. 2 Chr 34:4, states that the *ḥammānîm* hung above the *mizbəḥôt* dedicated to Ba'al. While this does not call to mind an object like the cult stand
from Taanach, which was built to stand on a level surface, this description
implies that incense could be burned in *ḥammānîm*, which might be hanging
censers situated above *mizbəḥôt*.

In essence, *ḥammānîm* appears to be a term which exilic or postexilic
authors used for small incense burners which might have hung above larger
altars. For all of the authors who mention *ḥammānîm*, the worship in which
they are used is not sanctioned. Apparently they were needed, in the minds
of certain writers (Ezekiel, Isaiah, and the Chronicler) for heterodox rituals

---

[21]A picture of the bigger of the two Taanach stands appears on the cover of *BAR*
17/5 (Sept/Oct 1991). See also Ruth Hestrin, "The Cult Stand from Ta'anach and its
Religious Background," *Studia Phoenicia V: Phoenicia and the East Mediterranean in
the First Millennium B.C.* (ed. E. Lipinski; Orientalia Lovaniensia Analecta 22; Leuven:
Uitgeverij Peeters, 1987) 61-77; and idem "Understanding Asherah," 50-59. For a further
discussion of incense burning and incense stands see Kjeld Nielsen *Incense in Ancient
Israel* (VTSupp 38; Leiden: E. J. Brill, 1986).

[22]The *piel* form for the verb *qṭr*, "to burn incense" is also believed to refer, almost
exclusively, to unacceptible religious ritual. BDB, 882.

that could not be performed on *mizbəḥôt*, or needed to be performed simultaneously with the use of *mizbəḥôt*. While the use of incense was appropriate to Israel, these *ḥammānîm* appear to constitute illicit incense burners which, when paired with *mizbəḥôt* or other objects, were used in the cult of gods other than YHWH.

B.5.b. *mizbəḥôt* **and** *bāmôt*. As noted in chapter five, Menahem Haran has argued that *bāmôt* are a subclass of *mizbəḥôt*, not a subgroup of building which might be called a temple or sanctuary.[23] Haran seeks to show that the *bāmôt* were *mizbəḥôt* by analysing the type of cultic ritual that is appropriate for temples and contrasting this with those which could be performed on a simple altar, thus placing *bāmôt* in a subgroup with altars and not with temples. This discussion, however, is more about what *bāmôt* are not than what *mizbəḥôt* are, and does not treat how *bāmôt* and *mizbəḥôt* are paired in the text.

The direct connections between *mizbəḥôt* and *bāmôt* are limited to Hosea, Dtr, and the Chronicler. For Hosea, Bethel is like a *bāmāh* whose altar will eventually be abandoned and overgrown with weeds (Hos 10:8). Dtr and the Chronicler mention the prominent example of Gibeon as a *bāmāh* which had altars for sacrifice, though for Dtr, these were simply altars of YHWH where sacrifices were made prior to the construction of the Temple (1 Kgs 3:4). For the Chronicler, the *mizbəḥôt* present at Gibeon were those of the Tabernacle.[24] In addition to these approved altars at Gibeon, Dtr has an additional reference to *bāmôt* whose priests were killed and altars defiled by Josiah (2 Kgs 23:19, 20).

Indirect connections between *mizbəḥôt* and *bāmôt* also exist in Dtr, the Chronicler, First Isaiah, Jeremiah, and Ezekiel. Dtr and the Chronicler have a variety of this type of indirect reference. At times they mention priests on *bāmôt* which implies sacrifice and altars upon which to make such sacrifice,[25] and at other times they mention the sacrifices themselves.[26] In still other contexts, Dtr and the Chronicler mention *bāmôt* and *mizbəḥôt* together in lists of items purged without directly connecting them.[27] Ezekiel also makes two of these types of indirect connection between *mizbəḥôt* and *bāmôt* by mentioning sacrifices on *bāmôt* which imply *mizbəḥôt* (20:28-29),

---

[23]See Haran, *Temples and Temple Service*.

[24]1 Chr 16:39-40; 21:29; 2 Chr 1:3-5, 13.

[25]1 Kgs 12:31, 32; 13:2, 32, 33; 2 Kgs 17:29-32; 23:9; 2 Chr 11:15.

[26]1 Sam 9:12, 13, 14, 19, 25; 1 Kgs 3:2, 3; 11:7-8; 22:44; 2 Kgs 12:4; 14:4; 15:4, 35; 16:4; 2 Chr 28:4; 33:17.

[27]2 Kgs 18:22; 21:3; 23:15; 2 Chr 14:2; 31:1; 32:12; 33:3.

and by listing them together but without direct connection (Ezek 6:3-6). First Isaiah and Jeremiah only mention *mizbəḥôt* and *bāmôt* together but without direct connection (Isa 36:7; Jer 17:3). Finally, just as there are many references to *mizbəḥôt*, licit and illicit, which make no mention of *bāmôt*, similarly, there are many references throughout the sources to *bāmôt* which do not mention or imply the presence of *mizbəḥôt*.[28]

Apparently *mizbəḥôt* were directly connected with *bāmôt* in the minds of Dtr, the Chronicler, and Hosea, while other sources such as First Isaiah, Jeremiah, and Ezekiel make this inference indirectly. In 2 Kgs 23:9, Dtr states that those priests who were spared after the purge of Judean *bāmôt* by Josiah (perhaps because their *bāmôt* were YHWHistic, or because they were Levitical priests), are allowed to eat the sacrificial meals with their kinsfolk but were forever after prohibited from serving on YHWH's altar in the Temple. This implies either that their service on other altars is what makes them ineligible (a sin against centralization), or their presumed service of other gods on these *bāmôt* disqualifies them (a sin against monolatry).

As is demonstrated in the material above, mere placement on *bāmôt* did not disqualify *mizbəḥôt* from the approval of the sources. Both Dtr and Chronicles approve the *mizbəḥôt* at Gibeon, apparently because they did not violate other principles for acceptance which these authors had (predating the Temple, dedicated to YHWH, or, in the case of the Chronicler, located in front of the Tabernacle).

B.5.c. *mizbəḥôt* and *ăšērîm*. As noted above in chapter six, Exodus 34, D, Dtr, the Chronicler, First Isaiah, and Jeremiah all mention *ăšērîm* and *mizbəḥôt* together in some fashion.[29] Exodus 34 and D connect *mizbəḥôt* with *ăšērîm* and *maṣṣēbôt* in a depiction of the worship style of the prior inhabitants of the land (Exod 34:13; Deut 7:5; 12:3; 16:21-22). In fact, Exodus 34 and D have no references to either *ăšērîm* or *maṣṣēbôt* which do not also mention *mizbəḥôt* and call to mind that this complex was used by others to worship gods other than YHWH. Exodus 34 mentions *mizbəḥôt* only in this passage.

Dtr mentions *ăšērîm* and *mizbəḥôt* together, three times in contexts which state that the *mizbəḥôt* in question were not dedicated to YHWH (Judges 6; 1 Kgs 16:32-33; 2 Kgs 21:3). In all of these passages, the altars

---

[28]Num 33:52; 1 Sam 10:5, 13; 1 Kgs 14:23; 15:14; 2 Kgs 23:13; 2 Chr 15:17; 17:6; 20:33; 21:11; 33:19; 34:3; Amos 7:9; Isa 15:2; 16:12; Ezek 36:2; 43:7; Ps 78:58.

[29]Exod 34:13; Deut 7:5; 12:3; 16:21-22; Judg 6:25, 26, 28, 30; 2 Kgs 21:3; 23:15; 2 Chr 14:2; 31:1; 33:3; 34:4, 7; Isa 17:8; 27:9; Jer 17:2.

are altars of Baʻal. In one other connection between *mizbəḥôt* and *ăšērîm*, Dtr locates an *ăšērāh* at Bethel in the passage which discusses its destruction as well the destruction of the altar which stood there (2 Kgs 23:15). While Dtr never directly charges that this altar was not YHWHistic, or that it was dedicated to some other god specifically, this altar was nonetheless one which violated Dtr's criteria for legitimacy.

The Chronicler mentions *mizbəḥôt* and *ăšērîm* along with *bāmôt* and *maṣṣēbôt* in two separate lists of items purged during cultic reforms (2 Chr 14:2; 31:1). Chronicles also has two verses from another account of religious reform which mention *mizbəḥôt* and *ăšērîm* along with cultic statuary and *ḥammānîm* as items purged (2 Chr 34:4, 7). The Chronicler also has a parallel to 2 Kgs 21:3 (2 Chr 33:3) which lists the building of *mizbəḥôt* for Baʻal, as well as *ăšērîm* and *bāmôt* among the offenses of Manasseh. As noted in chapter six, the Chronicler's original material has an equal number of verses which connect *mizbəḥôt* and *ăšērîm* to *maṣṣēbôt* and *bāmôt* as those which connect the two with *ḥammānîm* and cultic statuary, implying, perhaps, that for the Chronicler, *ăšērîm* and *mizbəḥôt* were a likely combination of objects which might then also be combined with other objects. It is also true, however, that both *ăšērîm* and *mizbəḥôt* occur separately elsewhere in the Chronicler so that one cannot argue that the presence of one demanded the presence of the other.

First Isaiah and Jeremiah, however, both mention *mizbəḥôt* along with *ăšērîm* and *mizbəḥôt* in the only verses in their books which discuss *ăšērîm*. First Isaiah also adds *ḥammānîm* to these verses as well (Isa 17:8; 27:9; Jer 17:2). This implies that for First Isaiah and Jeremiah, *mizbəḥôt* were likely to be found alongside *ăšērîm*.[30] Micah is the only source which mentions *ăšērîm* which does not also connect them with *mizbəḥôt* at some point. This implies that for most of the biblical writers who deal with *ăšērîm*, *mizbəḥôt* were their natural companion item.

Some biblical witnesses never mention *ăšērîm* without mentioning *mizbəḥôt* as well (Exodus 34, D, First Isaiah, and Jeremiah). Dtr and the Chronicler mention them together often, but not always. While it can be said that for a majority of the sources which mention *ăšērîm*, *mizbəḥôt* were also expected to be present, it cannot, of course, be stated that all *mizbəḥôt* stood near *ăšērîm*. It cannot even be stated that all *mizbəḥôt* which are disapproved of stood near *ăšērîm*. Use along with *ăšērîm* is only one among many prohibited uses of *mizbəḥôt*.

---

[30]See the chapter six (p. 196), for a discussion of whether these verses are original to First Isaiah and Jeremiah.

B.5.d. *mizbəḥôt* **and** *maṣṣēbôt.* As noted above in chapter seven, E, Exodus 34, D, Dtr, the Chronicler, Hosea, and Isaiah all mention *mizbəḥôt* along with *maṣṣēbôt*. E expressly mentions them side by side only in Exod 24:4-6, but E does mention the *maṣṣēbāh* which Jacob erects in Bethel (Gen 28:18, 22; 31:13; 35:14) as well as an altar he erects there (35:7). What is unusual about this juxtaposition of the altar of Bethel with a *maṣṣēbāh* is that after E, Jacob's *maṣṣēbāh* is never mentioned again. The altar, or its successor built by Jeroboam ben Nebat recurs, but the *maṣṣēbāh* disappears from Dtr, the Chronicler, and the prophetic sources which mention Bethel. In Exod 24:4, the altar which Moses erects at the base of Sinai after receiving the law is surrounded by twelve *maṣṣēbôt* which represent the twelve tribes of Israel.[31] It is possible that the acceptable view of *mizbəḥôt* erected in conjunction with *maṣṣēbôt* represented by E constitutes part of the northern tradition which viewed *maṣṣēbôt* as acceptable YHWHistic emblems. One additional example of the conjunction of *mizbəḥôt* and *maṣṣēbôt* seen positively is found in Isa 19:19.

The majority of linkages between *mizbəḥôt* and *maṣṣēbôt* in the text, however, are found in negative contexts. As noted elsewhere, *mizbəḥôt* and *maṣṣēbôt* as well as *ăšērîm* constituted the religious practices of the prior inhabitants of the land in the eyes of Exodus 34 and D (Exod 34:13; Deut 7:5; 12:3; 16:21-22). Deut 16:22 also explicitly rejects the use of *maṣṣēbôt* in YHWH's cult and presumably from proximity to YHWH's altars as stated concerning *ăšērîm* in Deut 16:21. In light of this prohibition, it is interesting that Dtr mentions only one combination of *mizbəḥôt* and *maṣṣēbôt*, namely that present in the temple of Baʿal in Samaria at the time of Jehu's purge (2 Kgs 10:26-27). In Chronicles, *mizbəḥôt* and *maṣṣēbôt* appear together only as items to be purged during religious reforms.

For Hosea, *mizbəḥôt* were connected with *maṣṣēbôt* in all the passages in which *maṣṣēbôt* are mentioned (3:4; 10:1-2), even though the connection in 3:4 is in the form of a reference to sacrifice and not to an altar specifically. Hos 10:1-2 issues a critique of the way northern Israel multiplies cult sites consisting of *maṣṣēbôt* and *mizbəḥôt*. It states that this practice does not increase the value of northern Israel's worship in YHWH's eyes. For First Isaiah, both *mizbəḥôt* and *maṣṣēbôt* are acceptable YHWHistic emblems which in 19:19 stand within Egypt and on its border with Israel as a testament to YHWH's worship there. The last source to affirm *maṣṣēbôt* as emblems of YHWHistic presence on par with *mizbəḥôt* is E.

---

[31]This motif of the "twelve stones for the twelve tribes" recurs in Dtr and P (Exodus 28, 39; Joshua 4; 1 Kings 18).

In short, several biblical witnesses (Exodus 34, D, Dtr, the Chronicler, and Hosea) depict the use of *mizbəḥôt* along with *maṣṣēbôt* as parts of either illegitimate worship on the part of the prior inhabitants of the land (Exodus 34, D), or illegitimate or other-wise futile worship on the part of Israel (D, Dtr, the Chronicler, Hosea). E, and First Isaiah, however, see *maṣṣēbôt* as legitimate features which might be located near YHWHistic *mizbəḥôt*. One additional note of interest is that E, Exodus 34, D, the Chronicler, and Hosea never mention *maṣṣēbôt* without also mentioning either *mizbəḥôt* or sacrifices which would have been performed on *mizbəḥôt*. This implies that for these authors, the presence of one implied the presence of the other. The reverse of this statement, however, is not true, except in the case of E and Exodus 34. With the exception of these, all the others have references to *mizbəḥôt*, both approved and disapproved, which do not include references to *maṣṣēbôt*.

B.5.e. *mizbəḥôt* and cultic statuary. Several terms for cultic statuary are linked with *mizbəḥôt* in the sources. D, the Chronicler and Ezekiel all mention *pəsîlîm* which were used along with *mizbəḥôt* in either of the worship of other gods (Deut 7:5; 12:3; 2 Chr 34:4, 7), or in the corrupted worship of YHWH (Ezek 8:5). Dtr uses the term *ṣelem* to describe the cultic statuary of Ba'al whose worship also included the use of *mizbəḥôt* (2 Kgs 11:18). Although the altar which Aaron builds at Sinai is dedicated to YHWH according to E, the golden calf which also appears in this story is a *massēkāh* (Exod 32:5-8). Dtr also uses the term *massēkôt* to refer to the cult statues of Dan and Bethel which were set up by *mizbəḥôt* there (1 Kgs 12:32).

The Chronicler also refers to both *massēkôt* (2 Chr 34:4) and *ṣəlāmim* (2 Chr 23:17; 33:15) in connection with *mizbəḥôt*. Hosea uses the term *'ăṣabbîm* when stating that "Ephraim is joined to idols," and that he will one day be ashamed of the altars used to worship them (Hos 4:17-19). The final term for cultic statuary connected to *mizbəḥôt* is *gillûlîm* which is found connected to *mizbəḥôt* only in Ezekiel (Ezek 6:4, 5, 6, 9, 13). This is by far Ezekiel's favorite term for cultic statuary and it occurs in Ezekiel some thirty-one times.[32] All of the above passages mention the use of *mizbəḥôt* with objects which are understood to be cultic statuary; however, Dtr,

---

[32]Ezek 8:10; 14:3-7; 16:36; 18:6, 12, 15; 20:7, 8, 16, 18, 24, 31, 39; 22:3, 4; 23:7, 30, 37, 39, 49; 30:13; 33:25; 36:18, 25; 37:23; 44:10, 12. The only other sources which use this term are, H: Lev 26:30; Dtr: Deut 29:16; 1 Kgs 15:12; 21:26; 2 Kgs 17:12; 21:11, 21; 23:24; and Jer 50:2.

Amos, and Hosea periodically mention Bethel and its *mizbəḥôt* in condemnation without directly mentioning the calf *massēkāh* which stood there, though one could assume that its presence is implied.[33]

Because *mizbəḥôt* are appropriate to the worship of other gods, it should not be surprising that they are mentioned as part of cults which used statuary, whether this was the state cult of the north with its presumably YHWHistic calf sculptures, or the state cult of Baʿal begun by Ahab, or the smaller sites which may have combined images of various gods with *mizbəḥôt* on which to make them offerings. Many, though not all, of the *mizbəḥôt* which are condemned in the sources appear to have been so used. This does not, of course, mean that all altars which were outside a given source's concept of acceptability had to have cultic statuary present. They were simply items that some unsanctioned installations are said to have had.

B.5.f. *mizbəḥôt* and other gods. Dtr, the Chronicler, and Jeremiah acknowledge that *mizbəḥôt* of Baʿal existed in both the north and the south at various times.[34] Dtr and the Chronicler mention that the Hosts of Heaven were worshipped using *mizbəḥôt*,[35] while Exod 34:13 and D (Deut 7:5; 12:3; 16:21-22) state that the prior inhabitants of the land used *mizbəḥôt* in the worship of their gods.

Among other references which imply the worship of other gods with *mizbəḥôt* but without mentioning specific gods are the Chronicler's reference to *mizbəḥôt hannēkār*, "alien altars" (2 Chr 14:2), and the various references in Jeremiah, Isaiah, and Hosea which imply that departure from the use of certain altars constitutes a return to right worship of YHWH.[36] In still other passages are altars which are condemned, though they are not said to have been dedicated to other gods, but for which one might make the presumption that some foreign dedication was implied. For instance, the Chronicler credits both Manasseh (2 Chr 33:4) and Ahaz (2 Chr 28:24; 30:14) with the building of altars outside the Temple and in various locations throughout Judah and Jerusalem. Whether these were non-YHWHistic or simply competitive with the Temple, however, is not stated as reason for their destruction (2 Chr 31:1). Similarly, Dtr mentions the *mizbəḥôt* which existed on the *bāmôt* in the north (1 Kgs 13:2; 2 Kgs 23:20). No statuary or

---

[33] 1 Kgs 12:33; 13:1, 3-5, 32; 2 Kgs 23:15-17; Amos 3:14; 9:1; Hos 10:8.

[34] Judg 6:25, 26, 28, 30-32; 1 Kgs 16:32; 18:26; 2 Kgs 11:18; 21:3; 23:12, 17; 2 Chr 33:3; 34:4; Jer 11:13.

[35] 2 Kgs 21:3-5; 23:12; 2 Chr 33:3, 5.

[36] Jer 17:1-2; Isa 17:8; 27:9; Hos 8:11; 10:1-2; 12:12.

foreign gods are mentioned, however, so that one might assume it is their mere location which makes them unacceptable.

Finally, in this unspecified category, are those altars and *bāmôt* which Hezekiah is said to have destroyed from the environs of Jerusalem in the course of his religious reform (2 Kgs 18:22; 2 Chr 32:12; Isa 36:7). The Rab Shaqeh makes the charge that these are *mizbǝḥôt* of YHWH, though whether they were, or whether this purge also included *mizbǝḥôt* to other deities as well cannot be determined.

In the final analysis, surprisingly few biblical references refer to the dedication of *mizbǝḥôt* to specific gods other than YHWH within Israel. Dtr, the Chronicler, and Jeremiah mention the cults of Baʿal that used *mizbǝḥôt*, while Dtr and the Chronicler also mention the dedication of *mizbǝḥôt* to the Hosts of Heaven by certain kings. This relative dearth of specific named deities, however, should not be taken as evidence that other gods were not regularly worshipped with *mizbǝḥôt* in Israel. The inference is made by many sources, listed here and in the above section on cultic statuary, that *mizbǝḥôt* were regular features in the worship of other gods. It remains true, however, that dedication to a god other than YHWH, while certainly a serious offense, was not the only possible reason for judging *mizbǝḥôt* negatively.

B.5.g. *mizbǝḥôt* and the *ʿēṣ raʿănān formula.* D (Deut 12:2), Jeremiah (17:1-2), and Ezekiel (6:13) mention *mizbǝḥôt* in verses which contain some form of the *ʿēṣ raʿănān* formula. In other instances of the formula, the verb *zbḥ* is present, though *mizbǝḥôt* are not. This occurs in Dtr (2 Kgs 16:4), Chronicles (2 Chr 28:4), Hosea (4:13), Second Isaiah (57:5), and Ezekiel (20:28). Not all the references to the *ʿēṣ raʿănān* include such references to *mizbǝḥôt* or sacrifice. In Dtr, 1 Kgs 14:23 simply states that Israel built *ăšērîm*, *bāmôt*, and *maṣṣēbôt* beneath the *ʿēṣ raʿănān*. In two additional verses, one from Dtr and one from Third Isaiah, those worshipping beneath the *ʿēṣ raʿănān* are said to burn incense (*qṭr*, 2 Kgs 17:9-12; Isa 65:7); while Jeremiah (2:20; 3:6, 13) uses a sexual metaphor with the verb *znh* in his description of how Israel's worship under the *ʿēṣ raʿănān* constituted unfaithfulness to YHWH.[37]

---

[37]For recent work which discourages taking this imagery literally to mean that Israel engaged in sexual intercourse beneath trees as some sort or fertility ritual, see Phyllis Bird, "'To Play the Harlot': An Inquiry into an Old Testament Metaphor," in *Gender and Difference in Ancient Israel* (ed. Peggy L. Day; Minneapolis: Augsburg Fortress, 1989) 75-94; Christina Bucher, "The Origin and Meaning of 'znh' Terminology in the Book of Hosea" (Ph.D. diss., Claremont Graduate School, 1988); and T. Drorah Setel,

While J has three examples of *mizbəḥôt* of YHWH which stand beneath live trees (Gen 12:7; 13:18; 26:25) and Dtr has one (Judg 6:11-24), what sets these trees apart from the *ʿeṣ raʿănān* is that they feature prominently in the lives of major figures and are seen as entirely acceptable YHWHistic sites. The *ʿeṣ raʿănān*, however, carries the hint of worship outside the confines of acceptable cultic behavior. Some form of sacrificial ritual, whether the type performed on *mizbəḥôt* or the burning of incense appears in the *ʿeṣ raʿănān* formula frequently.

The fact that *mizbəḥôt* are not always mentioned, however, need not mean that their use was not understood by the sources who used this image. Perhaps the type of unfaithfulness which Jeremiah describes using *znh* is best understood as offering sacrificial gifts to other gods as an unfaithful woman might offer sexual gifts to men not her husband. Whatever the meaning of this metaphor, the sense behind the *ʿeṣ raʿănān* formula is that Israel is performing rituals in unsanctioned places and perhaps directing this worship to gods other than YHWH. Both of these factors are primary in the approval or disapproval of *mizbəḥôt* in the sources, so that the *ʿeṣ raʿănān* formula represents the same type of cultic action disapproved of when *mizbəḥôt* are condemned. They are either in the wrong place, or dedicated to the wrong god.

CONCLUSIONS

While *maṣṣēbôt* appear to have more recognizably different, and still acceptable uses than any other of the objects of interest in this study, *mizbəḥôt* appear to have one specific use, but more reasons for being either approved or disapproved than any of the other items. Far from being a simple matter, each source apparently had its own reasons for allowing some altars and disallowing others.

Certain writers insist on a particular type of manufacture (Covenant Code). Others warn against the use of *mizbəḥôt* to worship other gods (Exodus 34, D, Dtr, the Chronicler, Hosea, Isaiah, Jeremiah, and Ezekiel). Others warn against seeming faithfulness with regard to sacrificial worship when other aspects of faithfulness to YHWH are not followed (Amos, Hosea, Jeremiah). Some sources insist that *mizbəḥôt* must exist only in Jerusalem once the Temple is built (D, the Chronicler) and some recognize

---

"Prophets and Pornography: Female Sexual Imagery in Hosea," in *Feminist Interpretation of the Bible* (ed. Letty M. Russell; Philadelphia: Westminster, 1985) 86-95. For only two of the many who take this imagery literally, see Samuel Terrien, "The Omphalos Myth and Hebrew Religion," *VT* 20 (1970) 326; and Wolff, *Hosea*, 86-88.

only those altars of the Tabernacle in times prior to the Temple's construction (H, P, the Chronicler). Others allow *mizbəḥôt* in any place where YHWH is worshipped (J, E, First Isaiah), and allow non-Israelites to construct YHWH's altars (J). Others make allowances for famous personages only to erect altars outside the Temple (Dtr). Still others speak only of the Temple's altars (Joel, Lamentations, Psalms), or those to be restored in the Second Temple (Ezra, Nehemiah, Malachi, Zechariah).

Perhaps it is precisely because *mizbəḥôt* were used by other people to worship their own gods, that some sources are so particular in the manner in which they will allow the use of *mizbəḥôt* by Israel. Some found the visual aspect of the altars important to convey meaning. Others wished to control all *mizbəḥôt* within the confines of state level centralized religious behavior. Others allowed the use of other items, such as *maṣṣēbôt* (E) and *bāmôt* (Dtr, the Chronicler) along with *mizbəḥôt* as long as the installations were YHWHistic. The fact that *mizbəḥôt* could be combined with so many items, and used in so many different types of religious behavior, makes the material concerning them particularly resistant to one generalized understanding of them and their function within ancient Israel.

PART III
Analysis of Material from the Ancient Translations

This section will discuss the vocabulary and conventions which the versions use to describe *bāmôt*, *ăšērîm*, *maṣṣēbôt*, and *mizbəḥôt*. Separate chapters within this section will be devoted to the LXX (chapter nine), the Vulgate (chapter ten), and the early Jewish interpretation found in the Targumim, the Mishnah, and certain Tannaitic midrashim (chapter eleven). In addition to a basic overview of the data from each of these traditions, special attention will be given to the ways in which each decides on a translation for these fixtures of ancient Israelite religion that speaks to its own era.

As will be seen, wherever a particular translation of a given item seemed a particularly apt analogy to a known cultic institution of the translator's own time it was leveled through in a formulaic manner at the expense of any ambiguities or contextual nuances in the Hebrew text (as in the LXX's use of ἄλσος for *ăšērāh*). Stereotypic translations also developed which seem to have no clear connection to any known object or institution (as in the LXX's use of ὑψηλός for *bāmāh*), perhaps because the nature of the object and any possible contemporary relevance of it remained obscure to the translator.

Nuances are also introduced into the translations at times where they are lacking in the Hebrew, especially in the case of items which were still fixtures, either of the accepted cult of the translator's time (as in all three of the translated traditions' treatments of *mizbəḥôt*), or of a pagan culture with which the translator is concerned (as in the Vulgate's treatment of *maṣṣēbôt*). Nuances were also introduced when current religious practice was believed to be informed by the biblical proscriptions regarding a particular item (as illustrated by the numerous Targumic renderings of *bāmāh*, and its interpretation of *ăšērîm* as live trees).

It will become evident after examination of the data from these traditions that they are less interested in providing a detailed picture of ancient Israelite religion than in communicating the essence of biblical teaching for their own time. In this way, the early translated versions are less valuable as a source of description or explanation of these objects, and more valuable as

251

witnesses to the way biblical interpretation functioned in each of their respective time periods. In many ways these translators appear to be the earliest employers of the trend toward generalization in translation that is still current in the treatment of these items by present-day scholars. They are also, however, the inheritors of biblical traditions with which their interpretations are at times in continuity and in other times in discontinuity. As the discussions in these chapters progress, the ways in which these traditions adapted the biblical message to their own time will become apparent.

Chapter Nine
The LXX and Other Greek Witnesses

INTRODUCTION

The Greek versions are relatively consistent in their translations of the items in question, even though many translators' hands were doubtless at work in the task of rendering the Hebrew Bible into Greek.[1] According to the classic work of H. B. Swete, there is ample internal as well as external evidence that the LXX translation of the Pentateuch predated the translation of the Prophets and Writings, even though Swete dated the completion of even this second stage of work prior to the date of Ben Sirach which gives the first witness to the tripartite division of Hebrew scripture (circa 132 BCE).[2] On the issue of internal evidence for multiple translators of the LXX, Swete had this to say:

> Strictly speaking the Alexandrian Bible is not a single version, but a series of versions produced at various times and by translators whose ideals were not altogether alike. Internal evidence of this fact may be found in the varying standards of excellence which appear in different books or groups of books. The Pentateuch is on the whole a close and serviceable translation; the Psalms and more especially the Book of Isaiah shew obvious signs of incompetence . . . If further proof is needed it may be found in the diverse renderings of the same Hebrew words in different parts of the Canon. This argument must be used with caution, for . . . such diversities are to be found not only in the same book but in the same

---

[1]A brief discussion of the theory of multiple LXX translators appears in the introductory chapter by Alfred Rahlfs, "History of the Septuagint Text," in *Septuaginta: Id est Vetus Testamentum graece iuxta LXX interpretes* (2 vols. in 1; Stuttgart: Deutsche Bibelgesellschaft, 1979) lvi. For a much more detailed discussion, including a review of modern scholarship on the issue, see Emanuel Tov, *The Text-Critical Use of the Septuagint in Biblical Research* (Jerusalem: Simor, 1981) 29-72; and Melvin K. H. Peters, "Septuagint," *ABD* 5.1093-104. Extensive bibliographies on Septuagint scholarship are also currently available; see for example, Sebastian P. Brock, C. T. Fritsch, Samuel Jellico, ed. *A Classified Bibliography of the Septuagint* (Arbeiten zur Literature und Geschichte des Hellenistischen Judentums VI; Leiden: E. J. Brill, 1973); Cecile Dogniez, *Bibliography of the LXX 1970-1993* (Leiden: E. J. Brill, 1995); and M. Harl, G. Dorival, and E. L. Munnich, *La Bible Grecque des Septante: Du Judaisme Hellenistique au Christianisme Ancien* (Paris: Cerf, 1988).

[2]*An Introduction to the Old Testament in Greek* (2d ed.; Cambridge: Cambridge University Press, 1914; repr. Peabody, Mass.: Hendrickson, 1989) 23-24.

context. But after making allowance for variations of this kind, there remain abundant instances in which the diversity can only be attributed to a change of hand.[3]

Swete also believed that the instances of variation increase as the relative level of canonicity decreases for a particular work. He believed that though the Prophetic books, like the Pentateuch, were translated for use in the synagogue, they were treated with a "diminished sense of responsibility" because they were "not regarded as sharing the peculiar sanctity of the Law." Even greater latitude appeared to Swete to have been taken with the Writings because they were viewed as "national literature which . . . might be treated with the freedom allowed by custom in such cases to the interpreter and the scribe."[4]

As the data on each individual item of interest to this study are presented, attention will be given to how this data fits into the prevailing theory of multiple translators within the LXX and their relative care for their task.[5] Each item will be treated separately followed by a general discussion and conclusions. Special attention will also be given to the Hellenistic culture of the period and how it prompted adaptation of biblical material to suit the needs of the translators' communities.

A: GREEK TRANSLATIONS OF THE TERM *ăšērāh/îm/ôt*

ἄλσος: 35 out of 40 occurrences

δένδρον: 2 out of 40 occurrences

Ἀστάρτη: 2 out of 40 occurrences

One verse lacks any LXX translation: Jer 17:2

---

[3]Swete, *Introduction*, 315-17.

[4]Swete, *Introduction*, 318.

[5]For the Septuagint text, this study relies upon the Göttingen Septuagint primarily (*Septuaginta, Vetus Testamentum graecum auctoritate societatis litterarum gottingensis editum* [2d ed.; Göttingen:1931-]) and the Cambridge Septuagint secondarily (A. E. Brooke, N. McLean, and H. St. J. Thackeray, *The Old Testament in Greek addording to the Text of Codex Vaticanus* [Cambridge: Cambridge University Press, 1906-1940]). All textual variants derive from the apparatus of these critical editions.

A.1. ἄλσος

With relatively few exceptions, the Greek translations of the Hebrew Bible regularly render the terms *ăšērāh*, *ăšērₑm*, and *ăšērₜt* with the Greek term *ἄλσος*.[6] According to Liddell and Scott,[7] *ἄλσος* is defined as follows:

> I. *grove*, II. esp. *sacred grove*, hence, *any hallowed precinct,* even without trees. [Special usages include] *Μαραθώνιον ἄ.*, of the field of battle, viewed as a holy place; and metaph., *ποντιον ἄ.* the ocean-*plain*[8].

This term for "grove" or "sacred precinct" is used to translate the Hebrew *ăšērāh* and related lexemes even when the term does not provide an easy match. Most prominent among these circumstances are those in which the divine name ʾAsherah presents itself to modern translators on the basis of context. These contexts in particular make it appear that the Greek translators were unaware of the existence of a goddess whose proper name was ʾAsherah. In many cases, the term "grove" or "sacred precinct" is smoothly interchangeable with the proper name of a goddess. Even in contexts in which the personal name of the goddess would seem to provide a superior reading, however, the Greek nonetheless slavishly persists in its chosen translation. One of the most obvious examples of this is 2 Kgs 21:7.

MT:

וַיָּשֶׂם אֶת פֶּסֶל הָאֲשֵׁרָה אֲשֶׁר עָשָׂה בַּבַּיִת אֲשֶׁר אָמַר יְהוָה אֶל דָּוִד וְאֶל שְׁלֹמֹה בְנוֹ בַּבַּיִת
הַזֶּה וּבִירוּשָׁלִַם אֲשֶׁר בָּחַרְתִּי מִכֹּל שִׁבְטֵי יִשְׂרָאֵל אָשִׂים אֶת שְׁמִי לְעוֹלָם:

---

[6]אֲשֵׁירָה, singular or masculine plural, spelled with medial *yōd*: Deut 7:5; 2 Kgs 17:16; Mic 5:13; אֲשֵׁרָה, singular or masculine plural, spelled without the *yōd*: Exod 34:13; Deut 12:3; 16:21; Judg 6:25, 26, 28, 30; 1 Kgs 14:15, 23; 15:13; 16:33; 18:19; 2 Kgs 13:6; 17:10; 18:4; 21:3, 7; 23:4, 6, 7, 14, 15; 2 Chr 14:2; 17:6; 31:1; 33:19; 34:3, 4, 7; and אֲשֵׁרָה, feminine plural, spelled without the *yōd*: Judg 3:7; 2 Chr 19:3; 33:3. Although the majority of manuscripts read *δένδρον* for *ăšērîm* in Isa 17:8 and 27:9, some witnesses to these verses also read *ἄλσος* (Isa 17:8, A and S only; 27:9, α′, σ′, and θ′ only). The LXX also adds *ἄλσος* to 1 Kgs 18:22 as part of an expansion which corrects the omission in the Hebrew of the prophets of ʾAsherah alongside the priests of Baʿal. The LXX supplies the missing reference to these prophets based on 18:19.

[7]*A Greek-English Lexicon* (revising ed., H. S. Jones and R. McKenzie; Oxford: Clarendon, 1968). For additional reference works on the LXX see Johan Lust, E. Eynikel, K. Hauspie, and G. Chamberlain, *A Greek-English Lexicon of the Septuagint* (Stuttgart: Deutsche Bibelgesellschaft: 1992); T. Muraoka, *A Greek-English Lexicon of the Sep-tuagint (12 prophets)* (Louvain: Peeters, 1993); and Friedrich Rehkopf, *Septuaginta-Vokabular* (Göttingen: Vandenhoeck & Ruprecht, 1989).

[8]LSJM 73b.

He placed the sculptured image of [the] 'Ašerah *which he made in the Temple concerning which the Lord had said to David and to Solomon his son, "In this House and in Jerusalem, which I chose out of all the tribes of Israel, I will establish my name forever."*

LXX (B):

καὶ ἔθηκεν τὸ γλυπτὸν τοῦ ἄλσους ἐν τῷ οἴκῳ ᾧ εἶπεν Κύριος πρὸς Δαυεὶδ καὶ πρὸς Σαλωμὼν τὸν υἱὸν αὐτοῦ Ἐν τῷ οἴκῳ τούτῳ ἐν Ἰερουσαλὴμ ἐξελεξάμην ἐκ πασῶν φυλῶν Ἰσραὴλ καὶ θήσω τὸ ὄνομά μου εἰς τὸν αἰῶνα,

And he put up the carved image of the grove *in the house of which the Lord said to David and to Solomon his son, "In this house in Jerusalem, which I chose for myself out of all the tribes of Israel, (and) I will set my name in perpetuity."*

Major variants:

καὶ ἔθηκεν τὸ γλυπτὸν τοῦ ἄλσους ἐν τῷ οἴκῳ] καὶ εθηκεν γλυπτον εν τω το περιβωμιον ο εποιησεν εν τω οικω (σ′)

"And he put up a carved image inside the area surrounding the altar which he had made in the Temple."[9]

τὸ γλυπτὸν τοῦ ἄλσους] το κρυπτον του οικου εν τω ασσει ως εποιησες (A)

"[He put up] the hidden/secret thing of the Temple in a nearby place which he had made [in the Temple]."

τὸ γλυπτὸν τοῦ ἄλσους] το χωνευτηριον και το γλυπτον του αλσους την εικονα ην εποιησεν (Did-gr)

"[He put up] a smelting furnace and the carved image of the grove, the idol which he had made."

Another example of a LXX passage that seems strained with the use of ἄλσος for *ăšērāh* is 2 Kgs 23:6.

MT:

וַיֹּצֵא אֶת הָאֲשֵׁרָה מִבֵּית יְהוָה מִחוּץ לִירוּשָׁלַ͏ִם אֶל נַחַל קִדְרוֹן וַיִּשְׂרֹף אֹתָהּ בְּנַחַל קִדְרוֹן וַיָּדֶק לְעָפָר וַיַּשְׁלֵךְ אֶת עֲפָרָהּ עַל קֶבֶר בְּנֵי הָעָם:

---

[9]See jmp-c₂, b of 2 Chr 34:3.

He took [the] ʾAšerah *out of the House of the Lord and outside Jerusalem, to the Wadi Kidron, then he burned it in the Wadi Kidron, beat it to dust, and scattered its dust over the burial ground of the common people.*

LXX B:

καὶ ἐξήνεγκεν τὸ ἄλσος ἐξ οἴκου Κυρίου ἔξωθεν Ἰερουσαλὴμ εἰς τὸν χειμάρρουν Κεδρών καὶ κατέκαυσεν αὐτὸν ἐν τῷ χειμάρρῳ Κεδρὼν καὶ ἐλέπτυνεν εἰς χοῦν καὶ ἔριψεν τὸν χοῦν αὐτοῦ εἰς τὸν τάφον τῶν υἱῶν τοῦ λαοῦ.

And he carried the grove *out of the house of the Lord, outside of Jerusalem into the Valley of Kedron and burned it in the Valley of Kedron and he reduced it to dust and scattered its dust on the burial ground of the "sons of the people".*[10]

Major variants:

τὸ ἄλσος] *της ασηρωθ* (bc₂), *τη ασηρωθ* (e₂), *της ασηρεθ* (o), *τη ασιρωθ* (g).

Although the Lucianic variations appear relatively minor, they raise the important issue of whether the Lucianic recension of the Greek witnesses did, in fact, know the proper name ʾAsherah. They, unlike the majority of the Greek witnesses, appear to be attempting to spell the term *ăšērāh* phonetically here, as if in this context they were aware that the term ἄλσος did not reflect the intended meaning of the Hebrew.

One might think that Judg 3:7, which mentions two divine names in conjunction with one another, might present a case in which the LXX would be forced to acknowlege that the lexeme *ăšērāh* represented the name of a diety. Because of the flexibility of the dative case in Greek, however, Judg 3:7 can be read to recognize Baʿalim as deities while simultaneously describing *ăšērôt* as "groves" in which one worships.[11]

MT:

וַיַּעֲשׂוּ בְנֵי יִשְׂרָאֵל אֶת־הָרַע בְּעֵינֵי יְהוָה וַיִּשְׁכְּחוּ אֶת יְהוָה אֱלֹהֵיהֶם וַיַּעַבְדוּ אֶת הַבְּעָלִים
וְאֵת הָאֲשֵׁרוֹת:

---

[10]The English renderings of the LXX in this chapter reflect the LXX's literal renderings of hebraisms such as the phrase "sons of the people." Quotation marks in the English translations indicate the presence of such hebraisms within the Greek.

[11]Although it can be argued that the best Hebrew reading in this verse is *ăštārôt* and not *ăšērôt* in light of other pairings of "Baʿalim and Ashtaroth" in Dtr (Judg 2:11-13; 10:6; 1 Sam 7:3-4; 12:10), the Greek witnesses to Judg 3:7 are clearly reading *ăšērôt* as a form of *ăšērāh* by virtue of their use of the traditional translation, ἄλσος. There is at least one ancient witness, Ethiopicᶜ, however, which has "'Astaroth" for *ăšērôt* in Judg 3:7.

The Israelites did that which was offensive to the Lord; they ignored the Lord their God and worshipped the Baʿalim and the ʾAšeroth.

LXX B:
Καὶ ἐποίησαν οἱ υἱοὶ Ἰσραὴλ τὸ πονηρὸν ἐναντίον Κυρίου καὶ ἐπελάθοντο Κυρίου τοῦ θεοῦ αὐτῶν, καὶ ἐλάτρευσαν τοῖς Βααλεὶμ καὶ τοῖς ἄλσεσιν.

And the "Sons of Israel" did that which was offensive in opposition to the Lord and they abandoned the Lord their God and they worshipped Baaleims and [in] the groves.

Major variants:
τοῖς Βααλεὶμ] τῃ Βααλ (MNahoyb2 Armenian, Syro-Hexapla)
"[they worshipped] Baʿal"
τοῖς ἄλσεσιν] ʿAstaroth (Ethiopicᶜ)

The dative case in Greek can be used several ways. It is used to indicate the indirect object in the case of verbs such as the verb "to worship" in which "worship" is thought of as rendered "to" someone or something. For example, one renders worship *to Baʿal*, as indicated with the dative. One also can be said to worship *in an ἄλσος*, a construction which is also rendered in the dative. Granted, the Greek witnesses had trouble with the plural form of the name Baʿal, but to read the dative case the same way for both objects of the verb would provide a curious reading in any case. One possible reading would be "They worshipped *in* the *Baaleims* and in the groves" as if Baʿalim were multiple place names or locations of some type. Another possible reading would be "They worshipped the *Baaleims* (Baʿals) and the groves," making the groves themselves objects of worship. This slavishly literal understanding is the most likely reading; however, the conundrum presented by the dative makes the option of reading the two objects of the verb as under two distinct functions of the dative, first as a dative of indirect object and the second a dative of location, at least one other possible solution.

At times the LXX alters the meaning of the Hebrew in order to give what it must have considered a more sensible meaning for a difficult passage. One good example of this is 1 Kgs 15:13.

MT:

וְגַם אֶת מַעֲכָה אִמּוֹ וַיְסִרֶהָ מִגְּבִירָה אֲשֶׁר עָשְׂתָה מִפְלֶצֶת לָאֲשֵׁרָה וַיִּכְרֹת אָסָא אֶת מִפְלַצְתָּהּ וַיִּשְׂרֹף בְּנַחַל קִדְרוֹן׃

He also removed his mother Maacah from the office of queen mother because she had made an abominable thing of/for [the] 'asherah and so Asa cut down her abominable thing and burned [it] in the Wadi Kidron.

LXX B:
καὶ τὴν Ἀνὰ τὴν μητέρα αὐτοῦ μετέστησεν τοῦ μὴ εἶναι ἡγουμένην, καθὼς ἐποίησεν σύνοδον ἐν τῷ ἄλσει αὐτῆς· καὶ ἐξέκοψεν Ἀσὰ τὰς καταδύσεις αὐτῆς καὶ ἐνέπρησεν πυρὶ ἐν τῷ χειμάρρῳ Κεδρών.

And Anna, his mother, he removed from being in a position of leadership, because she had held a new moon gathering[12] in her grove, and Asa cut down her hiding places and he consigned [them] to flames in the valley of Kedron.

The translator has rendered the troublesome Hebrew term *mipleṣet* with a term which does not imply a cult statue, as is the assumption of most English translators, but rather "gatherings" of some type. It also describes "hiding places" that the queen frequents which Asa cuts down and burns. The Greek implies that the groves used by the queen were places in which she presided over secret and objectionable rituals which her son abolished by destroying the groves. This is a fascinating interpretation which is quite a departure from the more simple, if obscure, meaning of the Hebrew.

A.2. δένδρον

One exception to the LXX translation of ἄλσος for *ʾăšērāh* is the use, on the part of some major Greek witnesses, of the term δένδρον, "tree" in Isa 17:8 and 27:9. In the case of Isa 17:8, ἄλσος is found in Alexandrinus and Sinaiticus while the Vaticanus has δένδρον. The variation between ἄλσος and δένδρον also occurs in Isa 27:9, but in the case of Isa 27:9, the evidence is more heavily weighted toward δένδρον as the favored choice of the Greek witnesses. In this case, only Aquila, Symmachus, and Theodotion read ἄλσος.

In light of Swete's negative evaluation of the competence of the translator of Isaiah, it is perhaps not surprising that the only two references to *ʾăšērîm* in this translator's work presented a variant translation which many textual traditions appear to have seen the need to correct back to the stereotypic translation ἄλσος. It is possible, however, that the translator of

---

[12]According to LSJM, the meaning "new moon festival" for σύνοδος is known from astronomical contexts such as the *Stoica* of Zeno Citieus (I.34), and is used elsewhere to connote other types of astral conjunctions (LSJM 1720b). The term σύνοδος might simply mean "gathering" of whatever type, but the LXX uses the term to denote lunar divisions of time in Deut 33:14, where it is used to translate יְרָחִים "months."

Isaiah was attempting to represent a view of *ăšērîm* which was in keeping with the current Jewish understanding of the objects as live trees.[13] Regardless of whether this is the source of the use of δένδρον in this passage, it is noteworthy that Aquila, who is believed to have extremely strong ties to the rabbinic community, nevertheless retains the stereotypic ἄλσος in Isa 27:9.[14]

A.3. Ἀστάρτη

The only other term used to translate *ăšērᵊm* in the LXX is the term Ἀστάρτη (2 Chr 15:16; 24:18). This substitution of the name of one goddess for another is perfectly understandable in 2 Chr 15:16 in which a statue of a goddess is the referent. If it is true that the LXX translators did not know 'Asherah as a proper divine name, it is logical that the translator of Chronicles would substitute the name of a known goddess in this verse. This explanation does not apply, however, to 2 Chr 24:18, in which the word being translated is *ăšērîm*, the plural form of the term which here suggests cult objects, and which is elsewhere rendered in the LXX of Chronicles with the traditional translation ἄλσος (2 Chr 14:2; 17:6; 31:1; 33:19; 34:3, 4, 7).

One might ask if the use of Ἀστάρτη was influenced by whether these verses are original Chronicles material, or are parallels to the material in Dtr. Unfortunately, no explanation is forthcoming from this avenue of inquiry. 2 Chr 15:16 is paralleled in Dtr (1 Kgs 15:13), while 2 Chr 24:18 is not. One might also ask if this translation reflects the translation of the feminine plural *ăšērôt* which exists along with the masculine plural *ăšērîm* in Chronicles. Unfortunately, this too is a dead end. *ăšērôt* occurs in 2 Chr 19:3 and 33:3 but in both cases it is translated by ἄλσος.

One might fall back on Swete's view of the less than careful nature of the translations of the Writings, to explain this apparently free variation on the part of LXX Chronicles. 2 Chr 24:18, however, also has an anomaly which might provide an explanation of why it, along with 2 Chr 15:16 (which apparently refers to a statue of a goddess), has the unusual translation of Ἀστάρτη for *ăšērāh/ăšērîm*. 2 Chr 24:18 states that the rulers of Judah "served" or "worshipped" the *ăšērîm* (*bd*). This use of the verb *bd* in conjunction with *ăšērîm*, which does not occur elsewhere in the Hebrew

---

[13]For a discussion see chapter eleven (pp. 321-27).

[14]On the tradition of Aquila's ties to rabbinic circles and the particular features of his translation, see Swete, *Introduction*, 31-42; and Dominique Barthélemy, *Les Devanciers d'Aquila: Première publication intégrale du texte des fragments du Dodécaprophéton* (VTSup 10; Leiden: E. J. Brill, 1963).

Bible, most probably suggested to the Greek translator of Chronicles that the goddess ʿAstarte was the intended referent. Further support for this may be seen in the fact that the verb *ʿbd* occurs with the term *ăšērôt* in Judg 3:7, a passage which clearly calls for correction to the reading *ăštārôt*. The fact that ἄλσος is used to translate *ăštārôt* by the Greek translator of First Samuel (see below), may also have given the translator of Chronicles the idea that the terms ἄλσος and Ἀστάρτη were essentially synonymous.

A.4. Other uses for the primary translation ἄλσος in the LXX

In addition to its use of ἄλσος to translate the term *ăšērāh* in its various forms, the LXX also uses ἄλσος for *bāmôt* in a rather unusual occurrence of that term (Mic 3:12; Jer 26:18).[15] ἄλσος is also used by the translator of First Samuel to render the divine name ʿAstarte in plural form, עַשְׁתָּרֹות (1 Sam 7:3, 4;[16] 12:10). The remaining two LXX uses of ἄλσος relate to terms for trees or vegetation. The first is עֵבִים, "thicket" (Jer 4:29), and the second is בְּכָאִים, a term whose exact meaning is obscure (2 Sam 5:23-24).[17]

A.5. Synopsis of the LXX's understanding of *ăšērāh*

The level of consistency with which the Greek witnesses chose ἄλσος to translate the term *ăšērāh* and its related forms, even in passages in which the name of the goddess ʾAsherah would be seen by modern translators as a

---

[15]The full term being translated here is *bāmôt yāʿar*, "forest *bāmôt*." It is plausible, however, that the term *yaʿar* rather than *bāmôt* governed the choice of ἄλσος δρυμου "thicketed sacred precinct" as the preferred translation.

[16]In this case, the LXX transforms the divine name ʿAstarte into a place name to which it appends the term ἄλσος. The altered verse reads: καὶ περιεῖλον ὁι υἱοὶ Ισραηλ τὰς Βααλιμ καὶ τὰ ἄλση Ασταρωθ καὶ ἐδούλευσαν κυρίῳ μόνῳ, "And the ʿSons of Israel' put aside the Baʿalim and the groves of ʿAstaroth and served the Lord only."

[17]The Hebrew term בְּכָאִים has been rendered many different ways by English translators. P. Kyle McCarter (*II Samuel: A New Translation with Introduction and Commentary* [AB 9; Garden City, N.Y.: Doubleday, 1984] 155-56) gives an excellent summary of the history of translation for this verse, much of which arrives at a meaning related to sounds heard in the top branches of a certain type of tree near David's encampment. The LXX renders the word as του κλαυθμωνος, "weeping," apparently reading the root בכה instead of בכא. McCarter notes that the reading του κλαυθμωνος is the standard LXX rendering of the placename, Bokim, which is derived from the root בכה (Judges 2:1-5, McCarter, *II Samuel*, 156). The term αλσος, however, enters the LXX in 2 Sam 5:24 in which it refers to το αλσους του κλαυθμωνος, "The grove of Weeping," or perhaps "The grove of Bochim." In a unique translation, McCarter choses to emend the MT consonantal text *brꜱšy hbkym* to agree with a retroverted Hebrew original based on the LXX. He reads *b šry hbk ym* "in the *ăšērîm* of Bakaim," with Bakaim being a place name which the

better option than *ἄλσος*, raises a question concerning these witnesses' view of the nature of the cult object and its relation, or lack of direct relation, to the goddess of the same name. To the modern interpreter, in possession of the Ugaritic mythic corpus and other epigraphic evidence from Canaan and Phoenicia, the reading of the goddess's name and the proposal of a connection between *ăšērîm* and the goddess 'Asherah are very compelling options.

Apparently these options were not so compelling for the translators of the LXX. This presents interpreters of the LXX with several possible explanations for the difference between current perceptions of *ăšērîm* and those of the LXX translators. Either the LXX knew of the goddess 'Asherah and simply saw no connection between her and the biblical *ăšērîm*, or the LXX knew of such a connection but considered it irrelevant to current interests, or the LXX did not know of 'Asherah the goddess at all. In any case, the LXX translators have leveled through an understanding of *ăšērîm* as sacred groves in all contexts without making any inference that such groves were dedicated to any specific deity. In this way, the LXX treatment of *ăšērîm* is very similar to the biblical treatment, where connection with 'Asherah is vague at best and where most *ăšērîm* are not connected specifically to any one deity.

Mention should be made of the invaluable work of Darice Birge on the subject of the *ἄλσος* among the ancient Greeks.[18] In her study, Birge undertakes the first ever systematic analysis of groves and their role in Greek religious life.[19] Birge makes clear in her study that the groves of the ancient Greeks were dedicated to a wide number of deities, semi-deities, and heros.[20] They were not restricted, as some might think, to deities who had some special jurisdiction over trees, fertility, or plant life. Birge writes:

> This survey of gods and their sacred groves has shown that the deities one associates with fertility of plants, animals, and humans do not possess the large number of groves that one expects them to have. Demeter and Kore, Zeus, Poseidon, and Aphrodite have fewer groves than Apollo does. At their wooded sanctuaries these gods are worshipped having jurisdiction over their usual

---

LXX rendered as equivalent to Bokim (*II Samuel*, 152-57).

[18]"Sacred Groves in the Ancient Greek World," (Ph.D. diss., University of California at Berkeley, 1982).

[19]One of the most exceptionally valuable features of this work is its Appendix entitled "Testimonia to Sacred Groves," which reproduces all literary references to *ἄλσος* in Greek literature, both in Greek and with accompanying English translation (Birge, "Sacred Groves," 298-636).

[20]See her chapter II, "Groves and their Gods," (Birge, "Sacred Groves," 16-43).

domains . . . A mythical grove in Atlantis is dedicated to Poseidon, and at
Onchestos he is concerned with horse-training; at these shrines Poseidon oversees
the ocean, earthquakes, and horses, all of which are usually in his care . . . Greeks
did not restrict groves in their sanctuaries to deities with a concern for forces of
nature . . . They were not inappropriate to the shrine of any god; Hephaistos had
sacred groves although he was not much concerned with the sorts of things that
Apollo or Demeter governed. One god did not possess sacred groves to such an
extent that they were excluded from the shrines of other deities. Jurisdiction over
one particular aspect of the universe was not the only prerequisite for a god's possession of a sacred grove.[21]

One way in which Birge's evidence on this point is important for the discussion of ἄλσος in the LXX may be that for the LXX translators, ’ăšērîm were
less the province of any one god (or goddess) other than YHWH, and more
a feature of unspecified worship of many gods other than YHWH, any of
whom might have had an ἄλσος. Perhaps it was this very feature of
universality among the gods that made ἄλσος the favored translation of
’ăšērîm for the LXX translators. In all of the cases in which the LXX uses
ἄλσος instead of the proper name ’Asherah where it might be expected, one
could argue that they are reading the existence, not of an additional deity
whose worship was in competition with the worship of YHWH, but rather
of a system of competing shrines, which may or may not have contained
emblems or images of any deity, or which might have been dedicated to any
number of deities.[22]

To close this section, one additional observation from the work of
Darice Birge should be mentioned. After investigating whether the origin of
the ἄλσος may be found in ancient Near Eastern veneration of sacred trees
(including ’ăšērîm in the discussion), Birge decides that it cannot. She bases
this view partly on the fact that Near Eastern sacred trees appear to occur in
the singular and Greek groves consist of a number of trees. She goes on to
state, however, that:

> Trees were not sacred [in Near Eastern cultures] because they belonged to a god,
> as Greek groves were, but because a divine spirit lived in them. Consequently, we
> do not find whole stands of trees dedicated to divinities, nor do we expect to. One

---

[21]Birge, "Sacred Groves," 42-43.

[22]As noted above in chapter six (pp. 185-87), there is epigraphic evidence for gods
possessing "’ăšērāhs," such as the Pyrgi inscription which refers to one individual who
built an "’šr for ‘Astarte," (*KAI* 277, 1-5), as well as the inscriptions from Kuntillet ‘Ajrud
and Khirbet el-Qom which mention YHWH and his "’ăšērāh." For the first report of the
excavator of Kuntillet ‘Ajrud, see Meshel, *Kuntillet ‘Ajrud*.

tree is sufficient. In the Septuagint's use of ἄλσος for a word denoting a pole or trunk [*ăšērāh*] . . . we may see attempts to make dissimilar elements of two cultures coincide.[23]

While this animistic interpretation of Near Eastern views of sacred trees is open to question, Birge's first observation concerning the singularity of Near Eastern sacred trees as opposed to plural trees in Greek groves is well taken. The two phenomena, on the outside, do not actually resemble one another that closely. Birge may be wrong, however, concerning her second point. It is impossible to know whether *ăšērîm* were believed, either by the LXX translators, or the authors of the Hebrew Bible, to be objects in which deities or their spirits resided. They may simply have been seen as emblems or accoutrements of deity, and as such, not quite so different from the ἄλσος as Birge states.

The *ăšērîm* of the Hebrew Bible were uniformly depicted as sacred precincts by the translators of the LXX. A question remains, however, concerning which aspect of ἄλσος was most responsible for its choice by the LXX translators as the stereotypic translation of *ăšērāh*. It has long been suspected that it was the arboreal nature of the ἄλσος alone which suggested its use to translate *ăšērāh*. Given the widespread occurrence of these groves for all the various gods of ancient Greece, however, it is also likely that the term suggested devotion to any number of gods, a sort of universal term for Hellenistic religious precincts. This sets up a contrast within the LXX between YHWH's one Temple and the numerous and therefore seemingly minor groves of the Greek gods.

The fact that the LXX chooses a term for *ăšērîm* which does not denote individually constructed cultic objects such as certain biblical *ăšērîm* seem to be, but rather a term which denoted a widely common type of Hellenistic shrine consisting of live trees, may indicate that the translators were not interested in representing exactly what they may or may not

---

[23]Birge, "Sacred Groves," 54. Birge's sources for this understanding of Near Eastern religion were Thorkild Jacobsen, (from his chapter "Mesopotamia," in Henri Frankfort's, *The Intellectual Adventure of Ancient Man* [Chicago: University of Chicago Press, 1946] 149), W. Robertson Smith (*Lectures on the Religion of the Semites*, [Edinburgh: Adam and Charles Black, 1894]), Geo Widengren ("Israelite-Jewish Religion," in *Religions of the Past* [ed. C. J. Bleeker and Geo Widengren; Historia Religionum: Handbook for the History of Religions; Leiden: E. J. Brill, 1969]), and Helmer Ringgren ("The Religion of Ancient Syria," in *Religions of the Past* [ed. C. J. Bleeker and Geo Widengren; Historia Religionum: Handbook for the History of Religions; Leiden: E. J. Brill, 1969]). These are cited in Birge, "Sacred Groves," 45, 249-50, notes 98, 99, and 113.

have thought biblical *ăšērîm* were. They may, rather, have been using peripheral aspects (such as construction out of wood or trees) shared by *ăšērîm* and groves to form a translation that mirrored and therefore challenged a common institution within Hellenistic religion, a religion which LXX era Judaism considered to be predominantly given over to idolatry. Just as the *ăšērîm* represented departure from pure worship of YHWH in ancient Israel, the ἄλσος may have represented for the readers of the LXX a departure from Judaism into idolatrous Hellenistic culture. The ἄλσος in the LXX, then, would represent the worship of any god other than YHWH just as any Greek god might be worshipped in an ἄλσος.

It may well be that the exact nature of ancient Israelite *ăšērîm* was either unknown or unimportant to the LXX translators. The importance of *ăšērîm* for the LXX appears to have been, not as a particular emblem of a specific goddess, but as a representation of worship located outside YHWH's precincts which was a direct analogy to the sacred groves of Hellenistic culture whose worship of foreign gods greeted Jews in virtually every corner of the Hellenistic world.

B. GREEK TRANSLATIONS OF THE TERM *maṣṣēbāh/ôt*

στήλη: 31 out of 35 occurrences

λίθος: 1 out of 35 occurrences

Two verses have contextually specific translations: Isa 6:13; Ezek 26:11

One verse contains a variation on the basis of parallelism: Hos 3:4

B.1. στήλη

The Hebrew term meaning "standing stone" exists in two feminine singular forms, *maṣṣebet* and *maṣṣəbāh*, apparently in free variation. In addition to these are the singular construct form (*maṣṣəbat*) and plural form (*maṣṣēbôt*). Aside from the verses which vary their translation according to context (Isa 6:13; Ezek 26:11),[24] or for purposes of parallelism (Hos 3:4),[25]

---

[24]In Isa 6:13, the term *maṣṣebet* apparently refers to a "tree stump." Likening the people to a tree that has been cut down, the verse reads: כָּאֵלָה וְכָאַלּוֹן אֲשֶׁר בְּשַׁלֶּכֶת מַצֶּבֶת בָּם זֶרַע קֹדֶשׁ מַצַּבְתָּהּ "Like a terebinth and like an oak which, when felled, still possess a stump, the holy seed is its stump." The Greek greatly paraphrases this verse as follows: καὶ πάλιν ἔσται εἰς προνομὴν ὡς τερέβινθος καὶ ὡς βάλανος ὅταν ἐκπέσῃ ἀπὸ τῆς θήκης αὐτῆς. "Until it shall once again be source of plunder, like a terebinth and like an oak when sent

and Exod 24:4 which uses the plural of λίθος for *maṣṣēbôt* (see below), the Greek witnesses translate the remaining examples of these forms related to *maṣṣēbāh* with comparable forms of the word στήλη.[26] Apparently, there was no question in the minds of the Greek translators as to what the term *maṣṣēbôt* meant, a meaning for which the Greek term στήλη appears to have been considered the most appropriate.

According to Liddell and Scott, στήλη is defined as follows:

> I. *block of stone*, II. *block* or *slab* used as a *memorial monument*, 1. *gravestone*, 2. *monument* inscribed with record of victories, dedications, votes of thanks, treaties, laws, decrees, etc., whether for honor or for infamy, also the *record* itself, *contract*, or *agreement*, 3. *post places on mortgaged ground*, as a record of the

---

to its grave." α΄, θ΄, σ΄ corrected this verse to the MT, and read the alternate forms στηλωσις or στηλωμα for *maṣṣebet*. In Ezek 26:11, a technical term for architectural column (ὑπόστασις; LSJM 1895a) replaces *maṣṣēbôt* in the prophet's description of the destruction of Tyre by Nebuchadnezzar.

[25]In Hos 3:4, the MT has *maṣṣēbāh* for which the major Greek witnesses substitute Θυσιαστήριον. The only text which reads στήλη is the Syro-Hexapla. Though it could be argued that the parallelism of זֶבַח וְאֵין מַצֵּבָה וְאֵין which the Greek reflects represents a better reading than the MT, the context of the passage suggests otherwise. As has been noted by several scholars, Hos 3:1-5 lists pairs of acceptable and unacceptable institutions within Israel, the destruction of which is analogous to the prophet's wife's deprivation of both licit and illicit sexual partners; see Graesser ("Studies in *maṣṣēbôt*," 251), who cites two scholars who stated this view prior to him: R. Brinker, *The Influence of Sanctuaries in Early Israel* (Manchester: Manchester University Press, 1946), 32; and Peter Ackroyd, "Hosea," *Peake's Commentary on the Bible* (London: Thomas Nelson, 1962) 607; see also Andersen and Freedman, *Hosea*, 306. On the basis of this insight alone *lectio difficilior* should be used to argue that the MT has the better reading. It cannot be argued that the translator of Hosea was unfamiliar with the traditional translation of στήλη for *maṣṣēbāh*. The translator of Hosea renders *maṣṣēbôt* and *mizbǝhôt* in Hos 10:1-2 with the traditional choices of στήλη and Θυσιαστήριον. These two points make it apparent that a conscious choice to deviate from the standard translation in the case of Hos 3:4 has taken place for the sake of parallelism.

[26]מַצֵּבָה: Gen 28:18, 22; 31:13, 45, 51, 52; 35:14, 20; Lev 26:1; Deut 16:22; Isa 19:19; מַצֵּבוֹת: Exod 23:24; 34:13; Deut 7:5; 12:3; 1 Kgs 14:23; 2 Kgs 10:26; 17:10; 18:4; 23:14; 2 Chr 14:2 [Eng 14:3]; 31:1; Jer 43:13 [LXX 50:13]; Hos 10:1, 2; Mic 5:13 [Eng 5:12]; מַצֶּבֶת: Gen 35:14, 20; 2 Sam 18:18; מַצֵּבָה: 2 Kgs 3:2; 10:27. In 2 Sam 18:18, A substitutes the related term στηλωσις for מַצֶּבֶת. Similarly, many Greek witnesses to Jer 43:13 [LXX 50:13] use the related term στυλος, which also means "pillar," instead of στήλη. Although it is not listed among the number of the references to *maṣṣēbôt* in the Hebrew, Judg 9:6 refers to אֵלוֹן מֻצָּב אֲשֶׁר בִּשְׁכֶם "the standing oak which is at Shechem," or "the oak of the pillar which is at Shechem." For this verses the Greek reads, τῇ βαλάνῳ τῇ εὑρετῇ τῆς στάσεως τῆς ἐν Σικίμοις, "the oak at which the uprising was devised, which is in Shechem."

fact, 4. *boundary-post, turning post* at the end of a racecourse, 5. for *Στῆλαι Ἡρακλήϊαι* (Strabo 3.5.5) so *σ. Διονύσου* mountains in India marking the limits of the progress of Dionysus.[27]

This definition demonstrates how well the semantic range of the Greek *στήλη* overlaps the biblical descriptions of the setting and function of *maṣṣēbôt*.

B.2. *λίθος*

The only verse with the translation *λίθος* for *maṣṣēbāh* is Exod 24:4 in which Moses erects twelve *maṣṣēbôt* representing the twelve tribes of Israel. Because the other references to *maṣṣēbôt* in Exodus use the more standard translation *στήλη* (Exod 23·24; 34·13), one cannot make the case that this is a translation typical of Exodus. Another possible explanation of the presence of *λίθος* here is that the Greek reflects dependence on a Hebrew text which reads *ʾăbānîm* rather than *maṣṣēbôt*. This is the view of John Wevers, who believes that this translation is "almost certainly not based on MT's מצבה . . . but on [the Samaritan Pentateuch's] אבנים."[28]

One additional way to account for this variation to note that Exod 24:4 constitutes the only positive reference to *maṣṣēbôt* within the Pentateuch, following the giving of the law. All other references to *maṣṣēbôt* in the Pentateuch after the giving of the law describe their use by the former inhabitants of the land (Exod 23:24; Deut 7:5; 12:7; 16:22) and or instruct that they are not to be used by Israelites (Deut 16:22; Lev 26:1). It is possible that the LXX translator of Exodus believed, as did the Samaritan Pentateuch apparently, that Moses should be insulated from connection with *maṣṣēbôt* because they were no longer seen as legitimate after the giving of the law. It is also possible that in addition to the Samaritan Pentateuch's reading, which Wevers attributes to the "influence" of Josh 4:20,[29] the translator of Exod 24:4 may also have known of other passages in Hebrew Scripture, in Deuteronomy in particular, which used the term *ʾăbānîm* in contexts in which one might expect the term *maṣṣēbôt*. These traditions may have influenced the translator to render Exod 24:4 in a way that portrayed the monuments Moses erected at Sinai as simple stones and not stelae.

---

[27]LSJM 1643b.

[28]John W. Wevers, *Notes on the Greek Text of Exodus* (Septuagint and Cognate Studies 30; Atlanta: Scholars Press, 1990) 381.

[29]Wevers, *Exodus*, 381.

B.3. Verses with variant Greek readings which suggest *maṣṣēbôt*

Other possible references to *maṣṣēbôt* in the Greek occur in two verses in which a number of Greek witnesses appear to be reading *maṣṣēbāh* in place of *mizbēᵃḥ*. These are 2 Kgs 12:10 [LXX 12:9] and 2 Chr 33:3. In the case of 2 Kgs 12:10, there seems to be confusion as to whether the collection box installed in the Temple was mounted next to an altar, or next to a pillar. The MT reads הַמִּזְבֵּחַ, and the Greek witnesses boc²e² read Θυσιαστήριον in agreement. However, LXX B has the odd phonetically rendered term ιαμειβεὶν, possibly reflecting a garbled version of the next word in the MT, בְּיָמִין. Various other Greek witnesses, however, have phonetic spellings of the word *maṣṣēbāh*.[30] Because these readings produce a seemingly acceptable *maṣṣēbāh* within the Temple, a feature which translators would be unlikely to consciously introduce, these variant Greek witnesses, though in the minority, may represent translations of a variant Hebrew text which was either unknown to the other Greek witnesses, or corrected back to *mizbəḥôt* by them.

In 2 Chr 33:3, the MT reads *mizbəḥôt* and the Greek witnesses read στήλη. In this case θ′ is alone in reading Θυσιαστήριον with the MT. The reason for this alternative reading may lie in an attempt to harmonize several biblical passages. In Dtr the construction of *maṣṣēbôt* for Baʿal is credited to Ahab (2 Kgs 3:2; 10:26-7), but in 2 Kgs 21:3, Manasseh is said to erect *mizbəḥôt* for Baʿal "just as Ahab had done." It is likely that the translator of 2 Chr 33:3 is attempting to harmonize these texts by stating that Manasseh built *maṣṣēbôt* for Baʿal.

B.4. Other uses for the primary translation στήλη in the LXX

In Gen 19:26, the verse in which Lot's wife becomes a "pillar of salt," στήλη is used to translate the Hebrew *nəṣîb*. In Ezek 8:3, στήλη is used to translate the difficult term מוֹשַׁב סֶמֶל. In Exod 29:29, LXX A reads στήλη, in an apparent mistake for στολη, a word meaning "garment." All of the remaining occurrences of the term στήλη in the Greek (Lev 26:30; Num 21:28; 22:41; 33:52) serve to translate the Hebrew term *bāmôt* or *bāmāh*. Of these four, Num 21:28 and 22:41 are references to place names, while Lev 26:30 and Num 33:52 constitute the only mention of cultic *bāmôt* in H and P respectively. It will be argued below, in the discussion of LXX translations of *bāmôt*, that what is demonstrated here is a uniform understanding of *bāmôt* as στήλη on the part of the LXX translators of Leviticus and Num-

---

[30]A, αμμασβη; Nnvy, αμμαζειβη; zₐ, αμμαζεειβι; j, αμμαζεειβη; f, αμμαζεηβι; e, αμαζειβι; hu, αμμαζιβην; x, αμμαζιβιν; g, αμαξικην; z, αμμαζειβι.

bers, or possibly the translators of the Pentateuch as a whole because Lev 26:30 and Num 33:52 are the only Pentateuchal references to *bāmôt* as cultic installations.

B.5. Synopsis of the LXX's understanding of *maṣṣēbôt*

Given the semantic range of στήλη, which included monuments in general as well as counterparts to the functions of biblical *maṣṣēbôt* as funeral monuments (Gen 35:20), boundary markers (Gen 31:45-52), and memorials (2 Sam 18:18), the LXX choice of στήλη to translate *maṣṣēbāh* seems the obvious one. There is one way, however, in which the Hebrew term *maṣṣēbāh* is not a direct parallel to the Greek term στήλη. Unlike biblical *maṣṣēbôt* which might be erected for cultic uses which did not include the marking of a boundary or a grave, and which might not have had inscriptions on them, στήλη is a technical term in Greek for stones which did have one of these particular functions or features. The term στήλη is not used for standing stones of indeterminant cultic function.

According to Walter Burkert, however, simple field stones, similar to the one erected by Jacob to mark the future site of the sanctuary at Bethel (Gen 28:28, 22), were often erected by the Greeks to mark sacred sites.[31] While the technical term στήλη is not used of these stones, their function matches the only function of biblical *maṣṣēbôt* which does not fall within the semantic range of στήλη. What the LXX translators did, apparently, was to extend the term στήλη to cover unmarked cultic stones rather than to introduce a distinction based on Greek usage into their treatment of biblical *maṣṣēbôt*. As will be noted below, some LXX translators do introduce a distinction in the translation of *mizbəhôt* which is not present in the Hebrew, but for the most part, this distinction is driven by the biblical context (based upon whether an altar was approved or disapproved) and not upon whether the biblical altars fit the description of either Greek Θυσιαστήριον or βωμός. Chapter ten will discuss how Jerome introduced a distinction in vocabulary related to *maṣṣēbôt* to separate approved and disapproved examples. The LXX translators apparently felt no need to do this. With the exception of the four passages discussed above, the term στήλη is chosen for *maṣṣēbāh* and leveled throughout the text. This leveling has nonetheless resulted in a translation which appears to be in complete continuity with biblical views of *maṣṣēbôt*.

---

[31]*Greek Religion: Archaic and Classical* (tr. John Raffan; Oxford: Basil Blackwell, 1985) 85.

C. GREEK TRANSLATIONS OF THE TERMS *bāmôtê* AND *bāmāh/āt/ôt*

C.1. Greek translations of *bāmôtê*

LXX treatment of the term *bāmôtê* is a separate issue from LXX translations of the terms *bāmāh*, *bāmāt*, and *bāmôt*. The many references to *bāmôtê* occur in archaic or archaizing poetic passages which are governed by a poetic image of the victorious God, or God's champion, "treading on the *heights*," or "on the *backs* of Israel's enemies." These passages do not appear to be making reference to the cultic installations referred to elsewhere as *bāmôt*. In each of the verses in which *bāmôtê* appears, a derived meaning appropriate to the context has been supplied by the Greek translator. These meanings in some cases are similar to lexemes used to translate terms related to *bāmôt*, but in most cases the translation is contextually specific.[32]

C.2. Greek renderings of *bāmāh*, *bāmāt*, *bāmôt*

βαμά/Αβαμα/βαμωθ: 13 out of 84 occurrences.

ὑψηλός: 49 out of 84 occurrences.

βουνος: 2 out of 84 occurrences.

Alternate translations based on cultic associations:

ἄλσος: 2 out of 84 occurrences.

στήλη: 4 out of 84 occurrences.

βωμός: 7 out of 84 occurrences.

Θυσιαστήριον: 1 out of 84 occurrences.

---

[32]Deut 32:13, *bāmôtê 'āreṣ* = τὴν ἰσχὺν τῆς γῆς "the might of the land;" Deut 33:29, *bāmôtê* = τὸν τράχηλον, "the necks" of Israel's enemies on which they shall tread; 2 Sam 1:19, 25; 22:34 *bāmôtê* = τὰ ὕψη, "the heights;" Amos 4:13 and Mic 1:3 *bāmôtê 'āreṣ* = τά ὕψη τῆς γῆς, "heights of the earth;" Hab 3:19 and Ps 18:34 [LXX 17:34; Eng 18:33], *bāmôtê* = ὑψηλός, "heights;" Isa 14:14, *bāmôtê 'āb* = ἐπάνω τῶν νεφελῶν "on the top of the clouds;" Isa 58:14, *bāmôtê 'āreṣ* = τά ἀγαθά τῆς γῆς "the good things of the earth" (α', σ', θ' τα ὑψηλα); Job 9:8, *bāmôtê yām* = ἐδάφους ἐπὶ θαλάσσης, "on the waves of the sea."

Five verses have variant readings: 2 Kgs 23:13; Mic 1:5; Ezek 16:16; 36:2; 43:7

One verse lacks any LXX translation: Jer 17:3

Aside from the five references to *bāmôt* in the Hebrew which are greatly altered in the Greek because of textual variation or corruption,[33] there are three main categories of translations within LXX renderings of terms related to *bāmôt* as cultic installations: simple transliterations from Hebrew to Greek, the predominant translated rendering with ὑψηλος or related terms, and alternate translations based on cultic associations.

C.2.a. Transliterations: βαμά/Aβαμα/βαμωθ. Aside from the transliteration of the place names which contain the element βαμωθ (Num 21:19-20; Josh 13:17), the remainder of the references in which the LXX transliterates *bāmôt* are found in 1 Samuel, Chronicles, and Ezekiel. The translator of 1 Samuel transliterates *bāmāh* as βαμά in every instance in which it occurs (9:12, 13, 14, 19, 25; 10:5) with the exception of 10:13. In 10:13, the translator choses τὸν βουνόν "the hill," perhaps under the influence of the nearby reference to the "hill of God" (10:5) at which Saul was to meet the ecstatic prophets, or the similar place name Gibeah, mentioned in 10:10.

The translator of Chronicles also transliterates the term *bāmāh* as βαμά but only in the references to the *bāmāh* of Gibeon that are unique to

---

[33]Two of these suggested "mistranslations" read τον οικον and so appear to be triggered by a reading of בית for במות (2 Kgs 23:13; Mic 1:5). The remaining three are examples of the translator of Ezekiel trying to make sense of an obscure Hebrew text. The LXX of Ezek 16:16 renders the obscure phrase במות טלאות, "colorful *bāmôt*," with the phrase εἴδωλα ῥαπτὰ "colorfully embroidered idols," based on the Hebrew which stated that these things were made from "garments," (Heb מבגדיך, Gk ἱματίων). Another possibility is that the reference to woven בתים, mentioned in 2 Kgs 23:8 suggested to the translator that בתים should be read here instead of במות. The LXX of Ezek 36:2 translates במות עולם, "ancient *bāmôt*," as ἔρημα αἰώνια, "ancient wastes/deserts/solitary places." BHS suggests that the Greek is reading שממת. The MT of Ezek 43:7 includes the obscure Hebrew phrase, וּבְפִגְרֵי מַלְכֵיהֶם בָּמוֹתָם, "and with the 'pegers' of their kings, their *bāmôt*." Ancient and modern commentators have suggested many different options for understanding this verse. The LXX translates this phrase, καὶ ἐν τοῖς φόνοις τῶν ἡγουμένων ἐν μέσῳ αὐτῶν, "and in the murder of those that come into their midst," apparently reading a form of הלך for מלכיהם, and either בביתם or בתוכם for במותם. The Targum understood במותם to mean "in their death." (Sperber, *Bible in Aramaic*, 4b.341). For a discussion of these and other suggested readings such as *peger* = stela, see Graesser, "Studies in *maṣṣēbôt*," 257-58; and Nieman, "PGR," 55-60. There is one additional verse in which *bāmôt* occurs in the MT but for which there is no LXX counterpart, Jer 17:3.

the Hebrew text of Chronicles (1 Chr 16:39; 21:29; 2 Chr 1:13)[34]. In trans-lating the one reference to the *bāmāh* of Gibeon which is loosely based on a Dtr passage (2 Chr 1:3 which parallels 1 Kgs 3:4) the LXX translator of Chronicles uses a term related to the term used to refer to this site by the LXX translator of Dtr (2 Chr 1:3, τὴν ὑψηλὴν; 1 Kgs 3:4 ὑψηλοτάτη). For the rest of the book of Chronicles, the LXX translator uses the more com-mon translation of ὑψηλος for *bāmôt/bāmāh*. Apparently out of pious regard either for Solomon or for the ark of the covenant, the LXX translator of Chronicles chose to "sanitize" references to the *bāmāh* of Gibeon whenever possible by substituting a transliteration of the term for the more common translation.[35]

The only other remaining example of transliteration of *bāmāh* is in Ezek 20:29. In this curious passage, the prophet is apparently punning on the terms *bāmāh* and *bā ʾîm* by asking:

> *māh habbāmāh ʾǎšer ʾattem habbā ʾîm šām? wayyîqqārēʾ šəmāh bāmāh ʿad hayyôm hazzeh.*

> 'What is this *bāmāh* to which you go?' And so it is called a bamah *(or Bamah)* to this day.

The LXX either does not understand the pun, or realizes that it cannot preserve the pun in the Greek, so it transliterates the Hebrew word *hab-bāmāh*, and renders the verse:

> Τί ἐστιν Αβαμα, ὅτι ὑμεῖς εἰσπορεύεσθε ἐκεῖ; καὶ ἐπεκάλεσαν τὸ ὄνομα αὐτοῦ Αβαμα ἕως τῆς σήμερον ἡμέρας.

> "What is Abama, that you should go in there? So its name is called Abama to this day."

The fact that the LXX translator of Ezekiel uses the standard translation of ὑψηλός for *bāmôt* elsewhere (6:3, 6) rules out that this rendering was unknown to this particular translator. The majority of occurrences of the term *bāmôt* in the Hebrew of Ezekiel, however, are not translated with ὑψηλός. In addition to these two occurrences of transliteration in Ezek

---

[34]2 Chr 1:13 is a partial parallel of 1 Kgs 3:15, but the Dtr passage only mentions Solomon returning to Jerusalem, but not the *bāmāh* of Gibeon. Therefore the occurrence of *bāmāh* in 2 Chr 1:13 constitutes original Chronicles material.

[35]A similar sanitizing of the Gibeon traditions in Chronicles can also be seen in the Targumim, although there the term *bāmāh* is not transliterated. It is replaced with entirely different terms, one of which is *miqdaš*. See further, see chapter eleven (p. 335).

20:29, three additional verses (Ezek 16:13; 36:2; 43:7) appear to be reading an entirely different text from the MT.[36] Unless one wishes to argue that multiple translators were at work on the Greek of Ezekiel, however, it is simpler, in the case of Ezek 20:29, to argue that the unusual nature of the word play produced this unique transliterated rendering.

C.2.b. $\dot{v}\psi\eta\lambda\acute{o}\varsigma$. The adjective $\dot{v}\psi\eta\lambda\acute{o}\varsigma$ understood substantively is used by the LXX to translate the terms *bāmāh* and *bāmôt* in the majority the MT's references to these terms.[37] According to Liddell and Scott, $\dot{v}\psi\eta\lambda\acute{o}\varsigma$ is defined as follows:

> I: *high, lofty*, of a highland country or alone; II: metaphorically, *high, lofty, stately, proud*; 1. to talk *high* and boastfully; 2. of persons 3. *upraised*, i.e. *mighty* 4. of poets, *sublime*, the *loftier*, or *sublimer* thoughts or language.[38]

It is most likely that the Greek choice of $\dot{v}\psi\eta\lambda\acute{o}\varsigma$ for *bāmāh* is responsible for the later Latin translations such as *excelsum* and *sublimis*, from which English versions eventually arrived at their standard translation for *bāmôt*, "high places."[39]

In his work on the etymology of *bāmāh*, however, which drew upon the work of de Vaux and Albright, Patrick Vaughan correctly noted that there is no known Hebrew root for *bāmôt* which contains the simple meaning of "highness" in its semantic range. Vaughan pointed out, however, that there is a cognate Akkadian term, *bamātu*, for which von Soden allows a topographical meaning of "hill slopes" or "foot hills," (literally "ribs of the mountains") connected to the original anatomical meaning of the singular term *bamtu*, "rib cage." Vaughan also noted the existence of a Ugaritic cognate *bmt* which means "back."[40] It was Vaughan's view that the Greek understanding of *bāmôt* as specifically "high" places evidenced a

---

[36]These apparently corrupted verses are discussed above (p. 271, n. 3).

[37] בָּמוֹת: 1 Kgs 3:2, 3; 12:31, 32; 13:2, 32, 33; 14:23; 15:14; 22:44 [Eng 22:43]; 2 Kgs 12:4; 14:4; 15:4, 35; 16:4; 17:9, 11, 29, 32; 18:4, 22; 21:3; 23:5, 8, 9, 19, 20; 2 Chr 11:15; 14:2; 15:17; 17:6; 20:33; 21:11; 28:4, 25; 31:1; 32:12; 33:3, 17, 19; 34:3; Isa 36:7; Jer 19:5; Ezek 6:3, 6; בָּמָה: 1 Kgs 11:7 [LXX 11:5]; 2 Kgs 23:15; 2 Chr 1:3. The superlative form $\dot{v}\psi\eta\lambda\text{o}\tau\alpha\tau\eta$ "highest" or "highest place," is used in 1 Kgs 3:4 to translate the Hebrew phrase הַבָּמָה הַגְּדוֹלָה, "the largest *bāmāh*."

[38]LSJM 1909b.

[39]For a brief outline of how the translation "high places" for *bāmôt* found its way from the Latin, into the German, and eventually into the English translations of the Hebrew Bible, see Barrick, "The Word BMH," 1-2.

[40]Vaughan, *The Meaning of 'Bāmâ'*, 3-28. See also, *AHw* 1.101b.

knowledge of the wider Proto-Semitic semantic range of the term *bāmāh* which these other cognates reveal. Vaughan's theory, however, requires that one accept that the topographical connotation of the root, more readily seen in *bāmôtê* than in *bāmôt*, somehow remained part of the Hebrew semantic range of the term *bāmôt*, even though the term *bāmôt* is never used by the Hebrew Bible in a purely topographical context.

Although the Akkadian evidence Vaughan presents is instructive, it is not likely that the LXX translators knew of a wider semantic range for *bāmôt* than the Hebrew Bible itself made use of. It is just as likely (or unlikely) that the anatomical meaning "back" as evidenced in the Ugaritic *bmt*, somehow suggested a meaning of "roundness" or "height" for *bāmôt* to the Greek translators. For the solution to the question of where the LXX got the meaning of "heights" for *bāmôt*, one might simply note that both the anatomical and topographical meanings are part of the semantic range of biblical *bāmôtê*. Regardless of whether the terms *bāmôt* and *bāmôtê* are actually semantically related, the *bāmôtê* passages, as well as those which combined mention of *bāmôt* with descriptions of hillside worship, are most probably the biblical contexts which suggested to the Greek translators that *bāmôt* were cultic sites located on topographical elevations.

C.2.c. βουνός. There are two verses in which the term *bāmôt* is translated with the Greek word for "hill," βουνός (1 Sam 10:13 and Ps 78:58 [LXX 77:58]). As noted above, this substitution in 1 Sam 10:13 might be attributable to the influence of nearby references to the place names Gibeath ʾElohim and Gibeah (1 Sam 10:5, 10). The reference in Psalm 78, however (while it could represent a simple poetic variation), illustrates that to at least one LXX translator, the term *bāmôt* was synonymous with the simpler term, "hill."

C.2.d. Alternate translations based on cultic associations.

C.2.d.i. ἄλσος. In Mic 3:12, the prophet predicts that the Temple in Jerusalem will be reduced to a "forest shrine," a *bāmôt yāʿar*. This phrase is rendered in Greek as ἄλσος δρυμοῦ, "grove of thickets." The same verse and translation are reproduced in Jer 26:18 [LXX 33:18].[41] While the term ἄλσος is most frequently used to translate *ʾăšērîm*, it is probable that the translator of Micah and Jeremiah picked this term because of its combina-

---

[41]As noted below in chapter eleven (p. 334, n. 52), *Targum Jonathan* to the Minor Prophets contains a similar rendering (חרשא חורשת חיש׳ת) in both these contexts.

tion of cultic connotations and connection with trees. The term *bāmôt* alone, without any reference to a forest, does not elsewhere suggest a translation involving the term ἄλσος.[42]

C.2.d.ii. στήλη. As noted in the section on *maṣṣēbôt*, there are two place names in which the LXX translator chose to use the term στήλη to translate *bāmôt*. These occur in Num 21:28 and 22:41. In Num 21:28, instead of understanding a two-part place name, Bamoth Arnon,[43] the Greek speaks of the στηλας Αρνων, "stelas of Arnon." In Num 22:41, instead of the place name Bamoth Ba'al, which, in Josh 13:17 is directly transliterated, βαμωθβααλ, the Greek refers to την στηλη του Βααλ, "the stelas of Ba'al." For Num 22:41 there are minuscules that read ὑψηλός, which is the most frequent LXX rendering of *bāmôt*.[44]

One cannot argue that the use of the translation στήλη for *bāmôt* in Numbers was simply a stereotypic rendering reserved for place names. The option of transliteration existed, and was used for βαμωθ in Num 21:19-20. One possible reason for the use of στήλη in these place names might be that the connection with Ba'al in Num 22:41 suggested to the translator the references to Ba'alistic stela mentioned elsewhere in the Hebrew Bible (2 Kgs 3:2; 10:26). In the case of Num 21:28, perhaps the situation of Arnon on the border with Israel suggested a στήλη in light of the border *maṣṣēbôt* in Genesis 31, and Isaiah 19. There is also the suggestion, however, based on the Mesha stone, that some objects which a modern eye might perceive as στήλη were actually called *bāmôt* in antiquity.[45] Another possibility is that this meaning for *bāmôt* was the only one with which the translator of Numbers was familiar.

The only two additional places in which the LXX uses στήλη to translate *bāmôt* are Lev 26:30 and Num 33:52. These two passages are the only references to cultic *bāmôt* in their respective sources, H and P, but they are also the only two references to *bāmôt* which are not part of place names in the entire Pentateuch. In both passages there are lists of items whose destruction is described, *bāmôt* being one. Lev 26:30 reads:

---

[42]There is a verse in Isaiah (10:34), in which the term *yā'ar* is translated with the term ὑψηλός. It is unlikely, however, that this verse is making a conscious allusion to *bāmôt yā'ar*. More likely, this highly paraphrased verse is attempting to emphasize the image of the tall forest soon to be felled.

[43]The NRSV reads "heights of Arnon."

[44]130-321'; F^b, 106 read τὸ ὕψος τοῦ εἰδώλου.

[45]See *KAI* 181:3.

MT:

וְהִשְׁמַדְתִּי אֶת בָּמֹתֵיכֶם וְהִכְרַתִּי אֶת חַמָּנֵיכֶם וְנָתַתִּי אֶת פִּגְרֵיכֶם עַל פִּגְרֵי גִּלּוּלֵיכֶם וְגָעֲלָה
נַפְשִׁי אֶתְכֶם:

I will destroy your *bāmôt*, cut down your *ḥammānîm*, and put your corpses on the corpses of your *gillûlîm*, and I will abhor you.

LXX:

καὶ ἐρημώσω τὰς στήλας ὑμῶν, καὶ ἐξολεθρεύσω τὰ ξύλινα χειροποίητα ὑμῶν, καὶ θήσω τὰ κῶλα ὑμῶν ἐπὶ τὰ κῶλα τῶν εἰδώλων ὑμῶν, καὶ προσοχθιεῖ ἡ ψυχή μου ὑμῖν·

I will desolate your stelas, and utterly destroy your artificial (handmade) wooden objects, and pile your limbs on the limbs of your idols and I will weary of you.

The translation of this passage suggests four possibilities that might explain its variation from the MT. Either the LXX translator considered these terms to be interchangeable; or worked from a Hebrew text that, unlike the MT, read *maṣṣēbôt* in place of *bāmôt*; or substituted, under the influence of 26:1, *maṣṣēbôt* for *bāmôt* in order to harmonize 26:30 with 26:1; or perhaps the LXX translator simply understood the term *bāmôt* to mean στήλη.[46]

A similar situation exists in the case of Num 33:52. The text reads:

MT:

וְהוֹרַשְׁתֶּם אֶת כָּל יֹשְׁבֵי הָאָרֶץ מִפְּנֵיכֶם וְאִבַּדְתֶּם אֵת כָּל מַשְׂכִּיֹּתָם וְאֵת כָּל צַלְמֵי מַסֵּכֹתָם
תְּאַבֵּדוּ וְאֵת כָּל בָּמֹתָם תַּשְׁמִידוּ:

You shall disposess all the inhabitants of the land before you, and then you shall destroy all their carved things and destroy all their molten images and tear down all their *bāmôt*.

LXX:

καὶ ἀπολεῖτε πάντας τους κατοικοῦντας ἐν τῇ γῇ πρὸ προσώπου ὑμῶν, καὶ ἐξαρεῖτε τὰς σκοπιὰς αὐτῶν καὶ πάντα τὰ εἴδωλα τὰ χωνευτὰ αὐτῶν ἀπολεῖτε αὐτά, καὶ πάσας τὰς στήλας αὐτῶν ἐξαρεῖτε·

And you shall destroy all the inhabitants/habitations in the land which is "before your face" and remove their watch towers and as for all their molten idols, you shall destroy them, and you shall remove all their stelas.

---

[46]Another complication to this passage is the possibility that the Hebrew *peger* was understood as a type of funerary stela. See Graesser, "Studies in *maṣṣēbôt*," 257-58; Nieman, "PGR," 55-60.

The LXX translator of Num 33:52 has taken a Hebrew verse which mentions *bāmôt*, carved items of some sort, and idols, and rendered the verse as if *maṣṣēbôt* and idols were the objects mentioned. At this point, given the passages discussed above, the possibility presents itself that in Leviticus and Numbers we are dealing with a translator who either did not understand what *bāmôt* were, or simply differed in understanding of what they were from the rest of the LXX translators.

The term *bāmôt* occurs six times in the books of Leviticus and Numbers (Num 21:19, 20, 28; 22:41; 33:52; Lev 26:30). In two cases the term is transliterated (Num 21:19, 20). In four cases it is rendered with στήλη (Num 21:28; 22:41; 33:52; Lev 26:30). In fact, the use of στήλη to translate *bāmôt* is limited to Leviticus and Numbers. This being the case, one must consider the possibility that these two books were translated by an individual whose understanding of *bāmôt* and what they constituted differed from the majority of LXX translators.

The examples provided by the various "*bāmôt*" place names in Numbers are particularly instructive in this regard. Rather than transliterate the place name Bamoth Ba'al as βαμωθβααλ (as the translator of Josh 13:17 does), or Bamoth Arnon as βαμωθΑρνων, as obviously could have been done given the transliteration of Bamoth as βαμωθ in Num 21:19-20, the translator, instead, chooses to translate the two former examples as στήλη, in keeping with renderings of *bāmôt* elsewhere in Leviticus and Numbers.

Perhaps the significant variable here is that Bamoth Ba'al and Bamoth Arnon suggested themselves to the translator, not as mere place names, but references to Moabite cult sites, thus the "cultic" translation, στήλη. Bamoth, being judged a place name, perhaps because it is not in construct with another term, was transliterated. It is entirely possible that the translator responsible for the renderings of Leviticus and Numbers into Greek simply understood *bāmôt* to be shrines composed of στήλη; thus, whenever what appeared to be shrines referred to as *bāmtt* are mentioned in the text, the translator uses the term στήλη to refer to them.

Finally, since these references to *bāmôt* in Leviticus and Numbers are also the only references to cultic *bāmôt* in the Pentateuch, it is also possible that the understanding of *bāmôt* as στήλη was a view held only by those translators responsible for the LXX of the Pentateuch and not by the translators of the remaining books. There is little in the Greek cultural millieu that would suggest that *bāmôt* were obvious cultic parallels of στήλη.[47]

---

[47]W. F. Albright suggested (see his article, "High Place"), that *bāmôt*, like the Greek στήλη which marks the burial sites of dead heros, were associated with the "cult of the dead" in ancient Israel. Albright's view on this issue, however, has been largely

What this suggests, then, is that for unknown reasons, the translator or translators of Leviticus and Numbers had a unique understanding of *bāmôt* as similar to Greek στήλη which was not adhered to by other translators.

C.2.d.iii. βωμός. Another term used to translate *bāmôt* that could be thought of as cultically derived is the term βωμός.[48] Liddell and Scott define βωμός as follows:

> 1. *raised platform, stand,* for chariots, *base* of a statue, but mostly, 2. *altar with a base,* 3. later *tomb, cairn,* 4. *title of poems* by Dosiades and Besantinus, 5. *altar-shaped cake,* 6. Ζεύς Βωμός, probably a Syrian god, 7. *central fire* in the system of Philolaus.[49]

In the case of Isa 15:2, the context is an oracle against Moab in which *bāmôt* appears to be in parallelism with *bayit*, though the text is obscure.[50] In Isa 16:12, the context is also Moab, though in this instance, *bāmāh* is in parallelism with *miqdāšô*.

Aside from these two verses, the term *bāmôt* recurs in Isaiah only in the speech of the Rab Shaqeh (Isa 36:7), which is a parallel passage to Dtr and which only certain witnesses include in their text of Isaiah.[51] All the witnesses which include this verse, however, use the translation of *bāmôt* which is in the parallel passage in Dtr, ὑψηλός (2 Kgs 18:22). The consistency in this choice of words among so many disparate witnesses, in addition to the fact that elsewhere in Isaiah the translation of *bāmôt* is βωμός, may suggest that the witnesses which include the missing end of Isa 36:7 have followed the text of 2 Kgs 18:22 in order to complete the verse. Even if the completion of this verse had existed in the major witnesses and had included the translation ὑψηλός instead of βωμός, one could still argue that harmonization with the translation of 2 Kgs 18:22 had taken place.

---

rejected, due in part to the extensively criticism it has received by more recent scholars such as Boyd Barrick (see his article, "Funerary Character"). See further discussion in chapter five, pp. 133-34.

[48] בָּמוֹת: Isa 15:2; Jer 7:31; 32:35 [LXX 39:35]; Hos 10:8; Amos 7:9; בָּמָה: Isa 16:12; Jer 48:35 [LXX 31:35].

[49] LSJM 334b.

[50] Eng: "He has gone up [to?] the temple, and Dibon, [to?] the *bāmôt* to weep. On Nebo and on Medeba, Moab wails. Baldness is on every head and every beard is shaved."

MT: עָלָה הַבַּיִת וְדִיבֹן הַבָּמוֹת לְבֶכִי עַל נְבוֹ וְעַל מֵידְבָא מוֹאָב יְיֵלִיל בְּכָל רֹאשָׁיו קָרְחָה כָּל זָקָן גְּרוּעָה:

[51] Greek witnesses that include the end of the verse are the Lucianic texts, α', σ', θ', and Theodoret. Other witnesses in languages other than Greek which attest to the second half of the verse include the Syrohexapla, Boharic, and Fayumic texts.

The preference for the translation βωμός = bāmôt in each case in which bāmôt occurs within original Isaianic material suggests that it, and not ὑψηλός, was the term which the original LXX translator of Isaiah felt best suited the meaning of bāmôt. Another possiblity, however, is that the Moabite context of Isa 15:2 and 16:12 suggested to the translator that some term other than ὑψηλός should be used to describe these foreign installations. In any case, the evidence suggests that the translator of Isaiah preferred the term βωμός as a translation for bāmôt, perhaps because it was a more overtly cultic term than ὑψηλός.[52]

It is also possible that the translator of Isaiah could be aware of early Jewish traditions regarding bāmôt, as could also be the case with the choice of δένδρον for ʾăšērîm in Isa 17:8 and 27:9. As will be seen in chapter eleven, early Jewish interpretation concerning bāmôt runs along the same lines as interpretation regarding mizbəḥôt. The later rabbinic sources discuss bāmôt most often in light of when and why their use for sacrifice was either approved or dissapproved. Perhaps some awareness of the early stages of this type of discussion prompted the translator of Isaiah to translate bāmôt with the term βωμός which means altar, and specifically in some LXX contexts, an unsanctioned altar.

Additional uses of the translation βωμός = bāmôt occur in Jeremiah (7:31; 32:35 [LXX 39:35]; 48:35 [LXX 31:35]), Hosea (10:8), and Amos (7:9). In both Hos 10:8 and Amos 7:9, this constitutes each book's sole mention of bāmôt. That both select βωμός instead of ὑψηλός to translate bāmôt simply raises the possibility that they, like the translator of Isaiah, felt βωμός better represented the meaning of bāmôt.

In the case of Jeremiah, there are only two additional verses to those listed above in which the MT mentions bāmôt. One is 17:3 for which there is no corresponding LXX passage.[53] The second is 19:5, in which the phrase bāmôt hab-baʿal is rendered ὑψηλὰ τῇ Βααλ. Unlike Jer 7:31, to which many commentators of the book of Jeremiah believe 19:5 is related,[54] 19:5 uses ὑψηλός for bāmôt rather than βωμός, the only time in which this particular choice for translation is made in Jeremiah.

---

[52]The term bāmôtê occurs twice in Isaiah (14:14; 58:14), but in both cases, the LXX translator paraphrases the Hebrew rather heavily in order to arrive at a reading. This need not be taken as evidence for a view that the translator did not understand this archaic term. Only in 58:14 does the paraphrase depart widely from the original.

[53]The texts which supply this verse, Syrohexapla, Theodoret, Origen, and the Lucianic texts, chose ὑψηλός to translate bāmôt.

[54]See W. L. Holladay Jeremiah I: A Commentary on the Book of the Prophet Jeremiah, Chapters 1-25 (Hermeneia; Philadelphia: Fortress, 1986) 536-37.

There are two additional verses in Jeremiah in which the LXX provides a reading of *βωμός* when the MT lacks mention of *bāmôt*. The first is 7:32, which provides the construct *bāmτt hat-tōpet*, in the form *Βωμὸς τοῦ Ταφεθ*, in order to harmonize with 7:31. The second is Jer 49:2 [LXX 30:18] in which the LXX apparently reads בָּמוֹתֶיהָ rendered as *βωμοὶ αὐτῆς* instead of the MT reading, בְּנֹתֶיהָ.

Thus, if correction to the favored vocabulary of the Dtr translator has occurred in 19:5, why only in this one verse? Why not also in 7:31, or in the addition to 7:32, or in 32:35 [LXX 39:35] where the same exact phrase found in 19:5 is rendered *τοὺς Βωμοὺς τῆς Βααλ*? If a pun is being made on the Moabite place name Bamoth Baʿal, why not render the name as it is rendered elsewhere in the LXX, as either *βαμωθβααλ* (Josh 13:17), or *τὴν στήλην τοῦ Βααλ* (Num 22:41), or even *τοὺς Βωμοὺς τῆς Βααλ*, which one might expect the LXX translator of Jeremiah to compose on the basis of 32:35 [LXX 39:35]? Perhaps the translator of Jeremiah knew two options for translating *bāmôt* and happened to pick the same translation as that favored by the translator of Dtr only once in Jer 19:5.

C.2.d.iv. Θυσιαστήριον. Only 2 Chr 14:4 appears to use the term *Θυσιαστήριον* to translate *bāmāh*. In this verse *bāmôt* and *hammānîm* are translated with the terms *θυσιαστήρια* and *εἴδωλα*. As will be noted below, *ὑψηλός* is used to translate *hammānîm* in 2 Chr 34:4 and 7. Since *bāmôt* is also translated with *ὑψηλός* in Chronicles, it seems likely that the appearance of both *bāmôt* and *hammānîm* in one verse presented the translator of Chronicles with a problem best solved by introducing novel renderings of both terms in this one instance only.

C.3. Other uses for terms used to translate *bāmôt* in the LXX.

The wider LXX use of the common noun *βουνος*, meaning "hill," does not require additional discussion in order to clarify its meaning to the LXX translators. The wider LXX uses of *ἄλσος* and *στήλη* have already been discussed in the sections above pertaining to *ăšērîm* and *maṣṣēbôt*, and wider uses of *Θυσιαστήριον* will be discussed below in the section pertaining to *mizbəḥôt*. What follows, then, is an examination of the remaining two terms used to translate *bāmôt* in the LXX, *ὑψηλός* and *βωμός*.

C.3.a. Additional uses for *ὑψηλός* in the LXX.

Outside its use as a translation for *bāmôt*, *ὑψηλός* is used elsewhere in the LXX to translate Hebrew terms for which the basic and most overt meaning is "high," "height," or "hill," or for which a metaphorical meaning such as "uplifted," in the sense of "exalted" is appropriate.[55] In one instance (Lam 3:41), the term ὑψηλός is used, either as a translation for אל, meaning "God," or as a translation of another textual tradition such as עליון.

It is also used to translate the formulaic phrase "outstretched arm," as in God's "mighty hand and outstretched arm," so the LXX translates, "mighty hand and uplifted arm."[56] This reading may derive from the fact that Hebrew root נטה, whose basic meaning is to "stretch out" can also be used to describe the process by which one puts up a tent,[57] or, as in Isa 3:16, the action by which arrogant women stretch their necks up to full height. These two examples give insight into the Greek choice of ὑψηλός to translate Hebrew terms formed on the root נטה.

In what might be considered derived translations from the one just mentioned, ὑψηλός is also used to translate roots whose basic meaning implies strength. In three cases, the root is חזק (Exod 6:1; Jer 21:5; Dan 9:15), and in two cases, עזז (Judg 9:51; Prov 18:19). In one other related

---

[55]גָּבֹהַּ/גְּבָה/גֹּבַהּ/גַּבְהוּת Gen 7:19; Deut 3:5; 28:52; 1 Sam 2:3; 9:2; 1 Kgs 14:23; 2 Kgs 17:10; Est 5:14; 7:9; Job 5:7; 11:8; 22:12; 35:5 [LXX 35:4]; 41:26 [LXX 41:25]; Ps 104:18 [LXX 103:18]; 113:5 [LXX 112:5]; 138:6 [LXX 137:6]; Eccl 5:7; 7:8 [LXX 7:9]; Zeph 1:16; Isa 2:11, 15; 10:33; 30:25; 40:9; 57:7; Jer 2:20; 3:6; 51:58 [LXX 28:58]; Ezek 17:22, 24; 21:31 [LXX 21:26]; 31:3; 40:2; Dan 8:3. רוּם/מָרוֹם Exod 14:8; Num 33:3; Deut 12:2; 32:27; 2 Sam 22:49; Ps 93:4 [LXX 92:4]; 99:2 [LXX 98:2]; 113:4 [LXX 112:4]; 138:6 [LXX 137:6]; Prov 8:2; 9:3; 25:3; Hos 5:8; Isa 2:13, 14; 6:1; 10:33; 22:16; 24:4; 26:5, 11; 32:15; 33:5, 16; Jer 49:16 [LXX 29:16]; 25:30 [LXX 32:30]; 31:15 [LXX 38:15]; Ezek 6:13; 20:28, 40; 34:6, 14; Dan 4:7; עָלְיוֹ 1 Kgs 9:8; 2 Chr 7:12; Ps 89:11 [LXX 88:11]; Ezek 9:2; נָשָׂא Isa 2:14; 57:15; גֵּאֶה/גֵּאוּת Isa 2:12; 12:15; גָּדֹל Isa 9:8 [LXX 9:9]; מִדָּה Isa 45:14. Gen 7:20 adds the word ὑψηλός to describe the height of the mountains over which flood waters rise. There is no corresponding word in the MT. In Jer 16:16, LXX A has ὑψηλός for βουνος. ὑψηλός is also used in other cases of derived meanings related to height, or greatness. These are: Isa 14:13 (Heb ירכתי); 28:4 (Heb גאון for גיא?); Prov 10:21 (Heb רבים). The LXX of Isa 10:34 also uses the term ὑψηλός twice, but the Hebrew is so paraphrased that it is unclear whether any attempt at direct translation was intended.

[56]Exod 6:6; Deut 4:34; 5:15; 7:19; 9:29; 11:2; 26:8; 2 Kgs 17:36; 2 Chr 6:32; Ps 136:12 [LXX 135:12]; Jer 32:17 [LXX 39:17], 21; Ezek 20:33, 34. Deut 6:21; 7:8; 9:26; 29:1 [Eng, LXX 29:2], in which the Hebrew text only mentions God's "mighty hand," are expanded in the Greek to include mention of God's "outstretched arm." These are Deut 6:21; 7:8; 9:26; 29:1 [Eng, LXX 29:2]. ὑψηλός is also used in Isaianic passages that echo this image by describing God's hand outstretched in anger over Israel's enemies: 5:25; 9:11 [Eng, LXX 9:12], 16 [Eng, LXX 17], 20 [Eng, LXX 21]; 10:4; 14:26, 27.

[57]Gen 12:8; 26:25; 33:19; 35:21; Exod 33:7; Judg 4:11; 2 Sam 6:17; 1 Chr 15:1; 16:1; 2 Chr 1:4; Jer 43:10; see BDB, 640.

case, the term ὑψηλός is used to translate a Hebrew term meaning "fortified." For the Hebrew of Neh 9:25, "fortress cities" ערים בצרות, the Greek of Esdras B 19:25 reads, πόλεις ὑψηλάς. ὑψηλός is also used, for reasons that are less clear, to translate two place names, "the Land of Moriah" (LXX: τήν γῆν τὴν ὑψηλήν, Gen 22:2), and the oak (Gen 12:6) or oaks (Deut 11:30) of Moreh (LXX Gen 12:6; τὴν δρῦν τὴν ὑψηλήν; LXX Deut 11:30; τῆς δρυὸς τῆς ὑψηλῆς). These translations are apparently based on the assumption that *hammōrîyāh* (Gen 22:2), *môreh* (Gen 12:6), and *mōreh* (Deut 11:30) are all terms derived from the root רום, "to be high or exalted." In the case of the oak/oaks of Moreh, however, it could well be a metaphorical translation which understands *mōreh* to mean "teacher," but with the additional nuance of understanding this title to derive from the status of a teacher as an exalted personage.

Finally, two verses from Chronicles contain the term ὑψηλός as a translation for the Hebrew term *hammānîm* (2 Chr 34:4, 7). One solution to this puzzle is to posit that the LXX was reading a Hebrew original which had the term *bāmôt* in the position which *hammānîm* now occupies in the MT. It is also possible, however, that the LXX is harmonizing the Hebrew of Chronicles with the Hebrew of Kings, which doesn't mention *hammānîm* in this episode. It is also possible that the LXX translator of Chronicles did not know what *hammānîm* were. As noted above, 2 Chr 14:4 translates *hammānîm* with εἴδωλα.

C.3.b. Additional uses for βωμός in the LXX. The only additional use for βωμός in the LXX is as a translation of the most basic word for "altar," *mizbēᵃh*.[58] It is intriguing that Exod 34:13, held by many to be a Deuteronomistic addition, shares the translation of βωμός = *mizbēᵃh* with the very Dtr verses on which it is thought to have been based, Deut 7:5, and 12:3. Elsewhere in both Exodus and Deuteronomy *mizbēᵃh* is translated with Θυσιαστήριον; however, Exod 34:13, Deut 7:5, and Deut 12:3 share the distinction of referring to foreign altars rather than Israelite ones. With no vocabulary distinction in the Hebrew, one is left with the conclusion that the LXX translator has specifically chosen to make a distinction in the Greek for foreign as opposed to Israelite altars.

---

[58]Exod 34:13; Num 23:1, 2, 4, 14, 29, 30; Deut 7:5; 12:3; Josh 22:10, 11, 16, 19, 23, 26, 34; 2 Chr 31:1; Isa 17:7; 27:9; Jer 11:13. There is an addition of βωμός in the Greek of Num 3:10, in which the sacred area of the tabernacle is referred to as a βωμός, but the Hebrew provides no antecedent for this passage. In Judg 7:1, the Lucianic witnesses refer to the βουνοῦ, or "hill" of Moreh as the βωμοῦ or "sacred precinct" of Moreh, but this may be only accoustic confusion and not an attempt to portray the site as sacred.

Further investigation reveals that throughout the books of Exodus, Leviticus, Numbers, Deuteronomy, and Joshua those altars which are built by non-Israelites, or which were considered to be non-YHWHistic for some other reason, such as those built by Balaam in Numbers 23 and the "symbolic" altar built by the Transjordanian tribes in Joshua 22, are translated in the LXX not with Θυσιαστήριον, but with βωμός. All altars referred to as Θυσιαστήριον are accepted. After Joshua, however, this distinction breaks down. Despite the many references to altars which are unacceptable throughout Dtr, the translation βωμός = mizbē^aḥ does not occur again in the historical books until 2 Chr 31:1, and although the altars being referred to here are those condemned to destruction, 2 Chr 30:14 also mentions altars which are being destroyed, yet refers to them using Θυσιαστήριον.

In the prophetic material there are two examples of βωμός = mizbē^aḥ. In two of these cases (Isa 17:7; 27:9), the reading mizbē^aḥ = βωμός conflicts with the translation bāmôt = βωμός found elsewhere in Isaiah (Isa 15:2; 16:12). Isa 17:7 and 27:9, however, demonstrate the same distinction from the other Isaianic references to altars (6:6; 19:19) as is found in the examples from Exodus through Joshua in that they refer to condemned altars while 6:6 and 19:19 refer to accepted YHWHistic altars. The last case, Jer 11:13, also conflicts with other Jeremianic translations of βωμός = bāmôt (7:31; 32:35 [LXX 39:35]; 48:35 [LXX 31:35]); however, it too refers to an altar condemned by the prophet. Unfortunately, the only additional references to mizbəhôt in Jeremiah are absent from the LXX text (17:1, 2), so that no comparison between LXX choices of terms is possible.

It appears, then, that βωμός was frequently used by LXX translators to indicate a type of altar that was not sanctioned by Israelite religious custom. Not all translators availed themselves of this distinctive device, but those who did appear to have used it consistently. As will be seen in chapters ten and eleven, the Vulgate and Targumim also use an alternate and negatively charged term for altar in their translations of mizbəhôt. However, the three translated traditions do not use their alternate term always in the same verses or according to the same criteria. A chart displaying the verses in which each of these traditions uses its alternate term for altar can be found in chapter eleven in the section on mizbəhôt.

C.4. Synopsis of the LXX's understanding of bāmôt

Although the primary understanding of bāmôt on the part of the Greek translators seems to be some type of cultic installation located on elevated terrain, evidenced by the choice of ὑψηλός as the primary translation, there appear to be several LXX translators who did not share this understanding. The translator of 1 Samuel transliterated the term βαμα in six of its seven occurrences in the Hebrew. Likewise, in all of its original references to the *bāmāh* at Gibeon (as opposed to those taken from Dtr), the translator of Chronicles too transliterates *bāmôt*. The only mention of *bāmôt* in the Psalms is translated with βουνος, which means "hill." Leviticus and Numbers seem to understand *bāmôt* as στήλη, even to the extent of using the term as part of certain place names formed with *bāmôt*. And finally, several of the prophetic books, Isaiah, Amos, Hosea, and Jeremiah, seem to prefer the translation βωμός for *bāmôt*, while Chronicles once substitutes another word for altar, Θυσιαστήριον, for *bāmôt*.

What this evidence implies is that various options for the translation of *bāmôt* suggested themselves to the translators of the LXX, with certain translators chosing the more conservative approach of transliteration, others the widely accepted translated meaning of "high place," or "hill," while others opted for more specifically cultic or perhaps more easily recognizable cultic items as equivalents such as στήλη, βωμός, Θυσιαστήριον, or even ἄλσος. That *bāmôt* were cultic installations must have been apparent to the Greek translators on the basis of context. The exact nature of what these installations included or consisted of, however, appears to have been a matter of opinion among the Greek translators.

Apparently the translators of Leviticus and Numbers understood *bāmôt* to consist of στήλη, a view which constitutes a substantial discontinuity with the majority of biblical depictions of *bāmôt*. When other books of the Hebrew Bible were translated into Greek, no other translators chose στήλη to render *bāmôt*. Instead, the rather "non-technical" term ὑψηλός became virtually a stereotypic translation. Unlike the LXX's use of στήλη to translate *maṣṣēbôt*, or ἄλσος to translate *ǎšērāh*, the use of ὑψηλός to translate *bāmāh* does not imply a direct analogy to any specific type of Hellenistic cultic installation on the part of the translators.

While there are so-called "peak sanctuaries" in the Mediterranean world,[59] ὑψηλός is not a technical term used to describe them in the same way that ἄλσος is a technical term for the sacred groves of Greek culture. ὑψηλός is simply an adjective meaning "high" or "lofty." The predominant

---

[59]See, Burkert, *Greek Religion*, 26-28; see also Doro Levi, "Features and Continuity of Cretan Peak Cults," and Spyridon Iakovidis, "A Peak Sanctuary in Bronze Age Thera," both in *Temples and High Places in Biblical Times: Proceedings of the Colloquium in Honor of the Centennial of Hebrew Union College-Jewish Institute of Religion* (ed. Avraham Biran; Jerusalem: Keter, 1981) 38-46, 54-60.

use of this term to translate *bāmāh/bāmôt*, then, implies that the LXX translators who used it were not interested in trying to draw a connection between the *bāmôt* and any specific Greek cultic institution. The later LXX translators appear to have leveled this interpretation through much of their work for lack of a more appropriate technical term.

The LXX's predominant use of the term *ὑψηλός* to translate *bāmôt* constitutes a type of continuity with the biblical text if one posits that the LXX translators believed that the cultic term *bāmôt* was directly related to the archaic poetic term *bāmôtê*. The contexts in which *bāmôtê* occurs often imply that "height" was part of the semantic range of this term. If the LXX translators were convinced that the two terms (*bāmôt* and *bāmôtê*) were cognate, their translation *ὑψηλός* for *bāmôt* would seem to be an attempt to maintain continuity with what they perceived to be the meaning of *bāmôt*. That this translation is not particularly apt in all cases, and cannot be proved to have any direct parallels in any known etymology of *bāmôt*, and in no way illuminates the cultic function of *bāmôt*, does not alter the fact that for the majority of LXX translators, this translation presented itself as the most appropriate term, and may therefore have seemed to them to be completely in line with the biblical text.

D. GREEK TRANSLATIONS OF THE TERMS *mizbēaḥ/ôt*

Θυσιαστήριον: 304 out of 330 occurrences.

βωμός: 20 out of 330 occurrences.

Two verses have variant readings: 2 Kgs 12:10; 2 Chr 33:3

Four verses lack any LXX translation: Exod 27:2; Jer 17:1, 2; Isa 36:7b

D.1. *βωμός*

As noted above in section dealing with LXX renderings of the term *bāmôt*, there are two Greek terms which are used to render the terms *mizbēaḥ* or *mizbəḥôt* in the LXX, *θυσιαστήριον*, and *βωμός*, with *βωμός* appearing in certain books as a distinctive term, over and against *Θυσιαστήριον*, to indicate altars that were viewed as inappropriate.[60] Both the Vulgate and the

---

[60]Exod 34:13; Num 23:1, 2, 4, 14, 29, 30; Deut 7:5; 12:3; Josh 22:10, 11, 16, 19, 23, 26, 34. Other verses which use the equation *βωμός* = *mizbēaḥ* even though the distinction between appropriate and inappropriate altars using *Θυσιαστήριον* and *βωμός* is not maintained throughout the books of which they are a part are: 2 Chr 31:1; Isa 17:8;

Targumim also introduce a distinction between accepted and unaccepted altars and choose an alternate and negatively charged word for the latter. These three sources, however, do not choose their alternate term in the same verses or apparently according to the same criteria. An analysis of this phenomenon appears in chapter eleven.

D.2. Θυσιαστήριον

Aside from verses in which the LXX translators use βωμός for *mizbəḥôt*, and verses for which the LXX either omits mention of an altar which the MT mentions,[61] or is apparently reading another term in place of *mizbē°ḥ* or *mizbəḥôt*,[62] the LXX consistently uses the term Θυσιαστήριον for *mizbē°ḥ* and *mizbəḥôt*.[63] According to Liddell and Scott, the common noun

---

27:9; Jer 11:13. For a more detailed discussion, including the definition of βωμός and a listing of other LXX uses for βωμός, see the section above dealing with the use of βωμός for *bāmôt* (pp. 278-80).

[61]The LXX of Exod 27:2 omits mention of the bronze plating of the altar, but it also expands Exod 38:2 [LXX 38:22] to include a reference to the Korah rebels and the use of their firepans for the altar plating. Num 17:3, 4, and 11 [Eng 16:38, 39, 46] also describe the overlaying of the bronze altar with copper from the firepans of the Korah rebels. It is Jacob Milgrom's view that the elimination of the first plating in Exod 27:2 and the expansion of Exod 38:2 represents the LXX's attempt to harmonize the Exodus accounts of altar plating with the episode in Numbers (*Numbers* [JPS Torah Commentary; Philadelphia: Jewish Publication Society, 1989] 140). Similarly, in 1 Kgs 6:20, the Greek rearranges a difficult Hebrew phrase which states that Solomon's altar was overlayed with cedar so that in some Greek witnesses to 6:20 it is the *dəbîr* which is overlaid and the altar is simply manufactured. Jer 17:1-2 and its references to *mizbəḥôt* are missing from the LXX as is the last half of Isa 36:7 which, in the MT, mentions YHWH's altars being destroyed by Hezekiah. The Lucianic recensions, Hexaplaric columns α′, σ′, θ′, and the SyroHexapla restore the MT reading of the latter half of Isa 36:7.

[62]As noted above in the section on *maṣṣēbôt* (pp. 265-69), the Hebrew of 2 Kgs 12:10 [Eng 12:9] has a wide variety of renderings among the Greek versions. Where the MT has *mizbēaḥ*, LXX B reads a strange transliteration, ιαμειβείν. LXX R which reads ἀμμαζειβί, and LXX A, which reads ἀμμασβή, are apparently attempting phonetic spellings of the Hebrew, *maṣṣēbāh*. Only boc²e² read Θυσιαστήριον in this verse. Also noted above is 2 Chr 33:3 for which θ′ among the Greek witnesses is alone in reading Θυσιαστήριον with the MT's *mizbēaḥ*. All other witnesses read στήλη, apparently having *maṣṣēbāh* their antecedent.

[63]Gen 8:20; 12:7, 8; 13:4, 18; 22:9; 26:25; 33:20; 35:1, 3, 7; Exod 17:15; 20:24, 25, 26; 21:14; 24:4, 6; 27:1, 5, 6, 7; 28:43 [LXX 28:39]; 29:12, 13, 16, 18, 21, 25, 36, 37, 38, 44; 30:1, 18, 20, 27, 28; 31:8; 32:5; 38:1 [LXX 38:22], 3 [LXX 38:23], 4 [LXX 38:24], 7 [LXX 38:24]; 38:30 [LXX 39:10], 38 [LXX 39:15]; 40:5, 6, 10, 26; 40:29, 32 [LXX 38:27], 33; Lev 1:5, 7, 8, 9, 11, 12, 13, 15, 16, 17; 2:2, 8 [LXX 2:9], 9, 12; 3:2, 5, 8, 11, 13, 16; 4:7, 10, 18, 19, 25, 26, 30, 31, 34, 35; 5:9, 12; 6:2 [LXX 6:9], 3 [LXX 6:10], 5 [LXX 6:12], 6 [LXX 6:13], 7 [LXX 6:14], 8 [LXX 6:15], 7:2 [LXX 6:32], 5

"altar" is the only attested meaning of the term Θυσιαστήριον.[64]

However, the term Θυσιαστήριον does not occur in Greek sources which predate the LXX. It is found only in the LXX and later Jewish and Christian works. This makes it appear as if the LXX translators have specifically coined a term for biblical altars, or perhaps for all Jewish altars, so that they would be immediately recognizable as different from Greek altars. This coining of a new term may have also served to insulate biblical legislation concerning altars from any confusion with the altars of Greek cult. In this new choice of terms, the LXX translators are accomplishing the opposite from their task in translating items such as *ăšērîm* and *maṣṣēbôt*. For these last two, an attempt was made to liken them to known Greek cultic institutions. In the case of *mizbǝḥôt*, however, the conscious blocking of any connection between them and their Greek counterparts appears to have been the goal.

[LXX 6:35], 31 [LXX 6:21]; 8:11, 15, 16, 19 [LXX 8:18], 21 [LXX 8:20], 24 [LXX 8:23], 28 [LXX 8:27], 30 [LXX 8:29]; 9:7, 8, 9, 10, 12, 13, 14, 17, 18, 20, 24; 10:12; 14:20; 16:12, 18, 20, 25, 33; 17:6, 11; 21:23; 22:22; Num 3:31; 4:11, 13, 14; 5:25, 26; 7:1, 10, 11, 84, 88; 17:3 [Eng 16:38], 4 [Eng 16:39], 11 [Eng 16:46]; 18:3, 5, 7, 17; Deut 12:27; 16:21; 26:4; 27:5, 6; 33:10; Josh 8:30 [LXX 9:2], 31 [LXX 9:2]; 9:27 [LXX 9:33]; 22:19, 28, 29; Judg 2:2; 6:24, 25, 26, 28, 30, 31, 32; 13:20; 21:4; 1 Sam 2:28, 33; 7:17; 14:35; 2 Sam 24:18, 21, 25; 1 Kgs 1:50, 51, 53; 2:28, 29; 3:4; 6:20; 7:48; 8:22, 31, 54, 64; 9:25 [LXX 3:1]; 12:32, 33; 13:1, 2, 3, 4, 5, 32; 16:32; 18:26, 30, 32, 35; 19:10, 14; 2 Kgs 11:11, 18; 16:10, 11, 12, 13, 14, 15; 18:22; 21:3, 4, 5; 23:9, 12, 15, 16, 17, 20; 1 Chr 6:34 [LXX 6:49]; 16:40; 21:18, 22, 26, 29; 22:1; 28:18; 2 Chr 1:5, 6; 4:1, 19; 5:12; 6:12, 22; 7:7, 9; 8:12; 14:2 [LXX 14:3]; 15:8; 23:10, 17; 26:16, 19; 28:24; 29:18, 19, 21, 22, 24, 27; 30:14; 32:12; 33:4, 5, 15, 16; 34:4, 5, 7; 35:16; Ezra [LXX 2 Esdras] 3:2, 3; 7:17 [Θυσιαστήριον = Aramaic מדבח]; Neh 10:35 [LXX 2 Esdras 20:35]; Amos 2:8; 3:14; 9:1; Hos 8:11; 10:1, 2, 8; 12:12 [LXX 11]; Isa 6:6; 19:19; 56:7; 60:7; Ezek 6:4, 5, 6, 13; 8:5, 16; 9:2; 40:46, 47; 41:22; 43:13, 18, 22, 26, 27; 45:19; 47:1; Joel 1:13; 2:17; Zech 9:15; 14:20; Mal 1:7, 10; 2:13; Lam 2:7; Ps 26:6 [LXX 25:6]; 43:4 [LXX 42:4]; 51:19 [LXX 50:19]; 84:4 [LXX 83:3]; 118:27 [LXX 117:27]. Several LXX verses supply the term Θυσιαστήριον, or repeat it a second time when an altar is implied but not mentioned explicitly in the Hebrew (Exod 27:3; 29:21, 38; 38:7 [LXX 38:24]; Lev 3:5; 2 Sam 24:25; 1 Kgs 3:15; 18:33; 2 Kgs 23:16; 2 Chr 4:11; Ezek 43:20; Joel 1:9). Three LXX verses contain the term Θυσιαστήριον in portions for which there is no MT counterpart, possibly due to haplography (Josh 9:27 [LXX 9:33]; 1 Kgs 2:29; Hos 8:12). Hos 4:19 reads Θυσιαστήριον in one instance in which the MT vocalizes the consonants מזבחותם as "sacrifices" rather than "altars."

[64]LXX *Exodus* 27:1; *Gospel according to Matthew* 23:18; Josephus *Antiquities of the Jews* 8.4.1; *Codex Justinianus* I.12.3.2; LSJM 812.

D.3. Other uses for the primary translation Θυσιαστήριον in the LXX

As noted above in the section on *maṣṣēbôt*, the MT of Hos 3:4 contains the term *maṣṣēbāh* while the major Greek witnesses read Θυσιαστήριον. It is most likely that this change occurred under the pressure of the potential parallelism of וְאֵין זֶבַח וְאֵין מִזְבֵּחַ which would result if Θυσιαστήριον were used instead of στήλη. One final term for which the LXX offers Θυσιαστήριον as a translation is נאה, which occurs in Ps 83:13. The MT of Ps 83:13b reads:

נִירְשָׁה לָּנוּ אֵת נְאוֹת אֱלֹהִים:

"Let us take possession of the pastures/habitations of God for ourselves." [Eng 83:12b]

The Sinaticus and Alexandrinus of this same verse read:

Κληρονομήσωμεν ἑαυτοῖς τὸ ἁγιαστήριον τοῦ θεοῦ.

"Let us take possession of the holy places of God for ourselves."
[LXX 82:13b]

The Vaticanus, however, reads Θυσιαστήριον for נאות.

Although Mitchell Dahood suggests that the the constructionנאות אלהים be interpreted as a superlative meaning "the very finest pastures,"[65] it is clear that the Greek translator of Psalms did not understand the construction this way. It is more likely that the translator understood נאות to derive its meaning in this context from the related noun נוה, which refers to the "habitation" or "dwelling places" of sheep or shepherds.[66] It is also possible, however, that the Hebrew נאות suggested to the LXX translators the Greek term ναός, meaning "sanctuary, or holy site."[67] Regardless of how the Greek witnesses inferred a holy site rather than a field in this verse, the Vaticanus has gone one step farther in providing the "altar," presumably within the "habitation" of God as the specific target of the aggressors.

---

[65]Mitchell Dahood, *Psalms II, 51-100: Introduction, Translation, and Notes* (AB 17; Garden City, N.Y.: Doubleday, 1968) 276.

[66]2 Sam 7:8; 1 Chr 17:17; Isa 65:10; Ezek 25:5. See BDB 627 for definitions of נוה I, II, and III.

[67]LSJM 1160a.

D.4. Synopsis of the LXX's understanding of *mizbəḥôt*

Of all the items under discussion in this study, *mizbəḥôt* appear to be the most clearly recognizable to the LXX translators. With the exception of three verses in which some idiosyncratic translation or alteration has been made (Hos 3:4; Ps 83:13 [LXX 82:13]; 2 Chr 14:4), two standard Greek terms for altars Θυσιαστήριον and βωμός are the routine terms used for the Hebrew *mizbəḥôt*. There are two aspects of the Greek treatment of *mizbəḥôt*, however, that shed light on the LXX's particular views of them.

First, the Greek translators chose a term for biblical altars of which they approved which is not used elsewhere in Greek literature to refer to Greek altars. Second, certain of the Greek translators introduce an alternate term for altar, βωμός, which is confined to altars of which the biblical text disapproves. These conventions, though the latter distinction is not adhered to in all the biblical books, shed light on an interesting feature of LXX hermeneutical method. Altars of the biblical text (and presumably those of the Jewish community by virtue of association) were distanced from pagan altars two different ways. A term other than the term for altars used in the Greek world at the time of the translators is used, and at times, the pagan altars of the ancient world were translated with a different term than the acceptable altars of the ancient world. This extremely careful treatment of altars is unlike the treatment given any other of the items of interest to this study, regardless of whether they were once favored by important figures, as in the case of *bāmôt* or *maṣṣēbôt*.

By introducing these two distinctions, the LXX translators add their own ideology to their translation. For some of them it was important to indicate that not all altars were approved, a view shared by the Vulgate and the Targumim, although the use of an alternative and negatively charged term for altar does not occur in the same verses among these three translations. It was also important to them to distinguish appropriate Jewish altars from Greek altars by the invention of a new Greek term with which to refer to them. These two indicators of value judgments related to biblical altars constitute a departure from the wording of the biblical text, although in most cases the distinctions made are in continuity with the sense of biblical contexts surrounding *mizbəḥôt*. In all cases where the negative term for altar is used, it is the original biblical context which dictated its use.

CONCLUSIONS

When rendering a translation for the Hebrew *mizbēᵃḥ/mizbəḥôt*, the LXX translators used a new term, otherwise unknown in Greek literature,

Θυσιαστήριον. This choice most probably functioned to distinguish the altars of ancient Israelite religion and later Judaism from confusion with the altars of ancient Greece and later Greek religion. Some translators introduced a second translation, βωμός, which was a more common Greek term for altar, but which was used only for those ancient altars which were disapproved of in the text. Although this distinction was not maintained by all translators, it appears to have been used throughout the Pentateuch and Joshua and to have been reintroduced in some, but not all, of the later books. This highly nuanced treatment of altars may be a testimony to the continued importance of altars in the Second Temple period and the need on the part of the translators to provide renderings of the scripture which would make the biblical statements concerning altars as clear as possible.[68]

The LXX translations of ʾăšērîm and maṣṣēbôt are less nuanced than the LXX translations of mizbəḥôt. For ʾăšērîm and maṣṣēbôt, the LXX translators tend to adopt one standard translation and level it through the text. Unlike biblical mizbəḥôt, ʾăšērîm and maṣṣēbôt had no currently acceptable counterparts in the Judaism of the LXX era. Because of this, these items may have represented to the LXX translators items of cultic paraphernalia which ultimately belonged to the category of "forbidden," or "idolatrous" religious practice. In the case of these two items, the translations chosen are the names of two well-known Greek cultic institutions, the ἄλσος and the στήλη. Thus the prohibitions against ʾăšērîm and maṣṣēbôt in the Hebrew text became prohibitions against the use of Greek religious institutions which persisted in the translators' own times. The fixtures of ancient heresy were permanently likened to features of the contemporary "heresy" inherent in Hellenistic religion.

The nature of the potential "heresy" of becoming involved in Hellenistic religion is not evidenced in the literature of the period in numerous prohibitions against the use of the ἄλσος or the στήλη. There is, however, an enormous amount of literature of the period decrying the worship of idols, a practice which confronted Jews throughout the Hellenistic era and into Roman times. One need only look at the books of Esther, Daniel, and Maccabees to see the importance placed on the resistance of pagan worship and custom by the Hellenistic and Roman era Jewish communities.[69] The

---

[68]Perhaps the best testimony to the heated conflict between pagan altars and Jewish altars during this time period is the episode from Maccabees (1 Macc 1:54-64) in which the Greek's desecration of the altar in the Temple of Jerusalem precipitates the Maccabean War.

[69]See also Wisdom 14:8-30; 15:15; Sirach 30:19.

entirety of the Letter of Jeremiah is a polemic against idol worship, and despite the pseudepigraphic attribution, it can hardly be argued that idolatry in Egypt and Babylon of 597 BCE is the subject of the work. The object is exhortation of Hellenisitic Jews to resist idolatry in their own time.

Even without explicit references, then, the fact that the *ἄλσος* was a standard type of cult center for the worship of Greek gods gives ample reason to suspect that their use would fall into the general category of idolatry for Hellenistic Jews. The connection between *maṣṣēbôt* and idolatry is less clear in the literature of this era because *maṣṣēbôt* are seldom discussed. There are, however, examples of early Jewish interpretation which link the *maṣṣēbôt* to the practice of idolatry.[70]

It can be seen then, that a desire for literal translation was by no means the only goal of the LXX translators. In the case of *maṣṣēbôt*, the translation *στήλη* fits very well. In the case of *ăšērîm* the translation *ἄλσος* ignores some major nuances within the Hebrew. In the case of both these objects, however, the LXX translators appear to make deliberate analogies to current Greek religion. Later the Rabbis appeared to do the same thing with *ăšērîm*, although they associated *ăšērîm* with a different type of item than did the LXX translators. As will be seen in chapter eleven, the Rabbis equated *ăšērîm* with single trees under which an idol might be hidden. This interpretation apparently reflects a phenomenon that was contemporaneous with the Rabbis themselves. Thus both the Rabbis and the LXX translators picked an interpretation for *ăšērîm* which made the biblical prohibitions against *ăšērîm* applicable to some cultic phenomenon which persisted into their own time and prevaded the culture to which they addressed their interpretative work.

Finally, in the case of *bāmôt*, the LXX translators appear to have no programatic agenda behind their translation, nor do they appear to have a very clear or consistent opinion concerning what *bāmôt* were. It is most likely that under the influence of the use of the term *bāmôtê*, and the biblical descriptions concerning hillside worship, the LXX translators came up with *ὑψηλός* as a rendering for *bāmôt* in the absence of any clear analogy to a cultic institution from their own time.

Throughout this chapter it has been demonstrated (especially in the discussion of *bāmôt*) that the LXX is a diverse collection of translations and interpretations. At times these translations are in direct continuity with the biblical text (as in the case of *maṣṣēbôt* and *mizbǝḥôt*), at times they are in relative discontinuity (as in the case of *ăšērîm*), and at times they seem to

---

[70]These are discussed in chapter eleven, pp. 329-33.

attempt continuity with less than complete success (as in the case of *bāmôt*).
What typifies the LXX's treatment of these objects as a group, however, is a
desire to make biblical teaching on matters of cult applicable to the present
time of the translation and to its particular audience, the Jewish citizens of
the Hellenistic world.

Chapter Ten
The Vulgate and Other Latin Witnesses

INTRODUCTION

There are two primary Latin witnesses to the Hebrew Bible, the body of manuscripts referred to as the Old Latin, or *Vetus Latina*, and the Vulgate translation of St. Jerome. Although it is the earlier of the two translations, the Old Latin is essentially a daughter translation of the LXX, having been translated from the Greek and not from a Hebrew text.[1] However, the Old Latin, along with the LXX, may at times witness to a Hebrew text tradition which is different from that of the Hebrew text which lies behind the Vulgate. The Hebrew text used by the Vulgate is closely related to the MT, whereas the Greek witnesses as well as the Old Latin preserve readings from other Hebrew text traditions. The witnesses to the Old Latin, however, are not conveniently accessible to modern scholars, existing primarily in various textual fragments and quotations from the Latin Church Fathers.[2]

Dennis Brown notes that it was the proliferation of variant readings in the Latin Bible during the fourth century which prompted Pope Damasus to commission Jerome to produce the Vulgate.[3] Brown quotes Jerome's own lament from the *Preface to the Four Gospels* concerning the state of the Old Latin, namely that there were "almost as many forms of the text as there are manuscripts."[4] Jerome did not, however, discard the readings of the Old

---

[1]For further discussion and works on the Old Latin, see Emanuel Tov, *Textual Criticism of the Hebrew Bible* (Minneapolis: Fortress, 1992) 139.

[2]For a list of the editions and fragments which contain the Old Latin, as well as a list of biblical verses contained in each fragment, see Swete, *Introduction*, 93-97. See also the work in progress of B. Fischer, et. al. *Vetus Latina: Die Reste der altlateinischen Bible* (Freiburg: Herder, 1949-). For further bibliography, see Pierre-Maurice Bogaert, "Versions, Ancient [Latin]," *ABD* 6.799-803.

[3]Dennis Brown, *VIR TRILINGUIS: A Study in the Biblical Exegesis of Saint Jerome* (Kampen: Kok Pharos, 1992) 97.

[4]*PL* 29, 115f, cited in *Vir Trilinguis*, 97-8. Brown also cites the following quotation from Augustine on this subject: "Those who translated the scriptures from Hebrew into Greek can be counted, but the Latin translators are out of all number. For in the early days of the faith, every man who happened to gain possession of a Greek manuscript (of the N.T.) and who imagined he had any facility in both languages, however slight that might have been, dared to make a translation," Augustine, *On Christian Doctrine* 2.16 (Brown, *Vir Trilinguis*, 98).

Latin. Along with his use of the LXX, the Hexaplaric recensions, and his study of Hebrew, Jerome also sought to harmonize and preserve the existing traditions in the Old Latin manuscripts. According to Brown, Jerome was "conscious of his commission to revise the existing Old Latin version, and changed this text only when it was necessary."[5] For the purposes of this study, then, the Vulgate will be treated as the primary witness to Latin interpretation of the Old Testament.[6]

One final distinctive feature of Jerome's work which is of particular interest is his use of rabbinic sources and opinions as part of his translations. According to Adam Kamesar, Jerome believed that a knowledge of Jewish scholarship "was an essential element in the study of the Bible."[7] Kamesar goes on to note that Jerome often used the witnesses of Jewish sources to justify translations which upheld the Hebrew text against the LXX.[8] Although there is some question as to how well Jerome knew Aramaic, such that it has been argued that his knowledge of certain Jewish opinions comes from his reading of Origen rather than the rabbis,[9] Jerome himself recounts visits to synagogue services, and remarks on the opinions of Akiba and others which he learned from the Jewish men with whom he read Hebrew.[10] Because Jerome is known to have had exposure to Jewish exegesis and to have used this knowledge for his own purposes in translation, special attention will be paid to evidence of Jewish influence upon Jerome's interpretation.[11]

---

[5]*Vir Trilinguis*, 100. For a further note on Jerome and his textual sources, see Tov, *Textual Criticism*, 153.

[6]One major witness to the Old Latin which will be discussed in this study is the translation of the book of Psalms from the Old Latin, adapted by Jerome (largely by correcting it to Origen's Hexapla). This psalter, hereafter abbreviated as PsG, is preserved in most critical editions of the Vulgate alongside Jerome's independent translation. Jerome's second translation of the Psalter, translated from the Hebrew, will hereafter be abbreviated PsH.

[7]*Jerome, Greek Scholarship, and the Hebrew Bible: A Study of the Quaestiones Hebraicae in Genesim* (Oxford: Clarendon, 1993) 177.

[8]*Jerome*, 190.

[9]Brown, *Vir Trilinguis*, 173, 196. For more on the subject of Jerome's interaction with the works of Origen, see Brown (*Vir Trilinguis*, 121-65), and Kamesar (*Jerome*, 4-28, 98-126).

[10]For example, see Jerome's *Commentary on Ezekiel* 34, 31 (*CCL* 75, 488), as well as the many other references cited by Brown in *Vir Trilinguis*, 179-81.

[11]For a full discussion of Jerome's use of Jewish scholarship, much of which is polemical in nature regardless of his stated appreciation of its usefulness, see Brown (*Vir Trilinguis*, 167-93) and Kamesar (*Jerome*, 176-91).

A. LATIN TRANSLATIONS OF THE TERM *ăšērāh/îm/ôt*

lucus: 36 out of 40 occurrences.

nemus: 3 out of 40 occurrences.

Ashtaroth: 1 out of 40 occurrences.

A.1. *lucus* and *nemus*

There are two Latin terms related to groves or trees used to translate all but one of the occurrences of the Hebrew terms *ăšērāh, ăšērîm,* and *ăšērôt*. These are *lucus* and *nemus*. The *Oxford Latin Dictionary* defines *lucus* as:

> **1** A sacred grove. **2.** (in general) A wood, copse, grove.[12]

The definition of *nemus* is:

> **1** A wood, forest. **2** A wood consecrated to a deity, sacred grove; (spec.) the grove of Diana at Aricia. **3** bushy foliage.[13]

Of these two terms, *lucus* is more frequently chosen to render *ăšērîm* and related words.[14] The term *nemus* for *ăšērîm* occurs only three times, all in Judges 6.[15] The only instance in which another term beside these two is chosen occurs in Judg 3:7. Here the term *ăšērôt* appears in conjunction with the plural of the name Baʿal. Unlike the LXX, which translates *ăšērôt* here with a form of the word ἄλσος meaning "grove," the Vulgate reads *Ashtaroth*, in harmony with Judg 2:13; 10:6; 1 Sam 7:4; and 12:10.

---

[12]*OLD* 1047c.

[13]*OLD* 1170b.

[14]Exod 34:13; Deut 7:5; 12:3; 16:21; Judg 6:28; 1 Kgs 14:15, 23; 15:13; 16:33; 18:19; 2 Kgs 13:6; 17:10, 16; 18:4; 21:3; 21:7; 23:4, 6, 7, 14, 15; 2 Chr 14:2 [Lat 14:2-3]; 15:16; 17:6; 19:3; 24:18; 31:1; 33:3, 19; 34:3, 4, 7; Isa 17:8; 27:9; Jer 17:2; Mic 5:13. One additional use of the term *lucus* occurs in 1 Kgs 18:22 in the Amiatinus codex of the Latin. This witness adds a reference, the "prophets of the *ăšērāh*," in harmony with 18:19, as do most of the Greek witnesses.

[15]Judg 6:25, 26, 30. The use of *lucus* in Judg 6:28 makes it appear that the two terms occur in free variation. In some cases, *ʿēṣ raʿănān* is translated *lignum nemorosum*; 2 Kgs 17:10; Ezek 6:13; 20:28. Other translations for *ʿēṣ raʿănān* are *arborem frondosam*; 1 Kgs 14:23; and *lignum frondosum* Isa 57:5; Jer 17:2.

Elsewhere, however, the Vulgate is like the LXX: it does not understand the term *ăšērāh* to represent the proper name of a goddess, but rather interprets it as some type of sacred wood.

A.2. Other uses for the primary translation *lucus* in the Vulgate

Unlike ἄλσος, the Greek translation for *ăšērîm*, which is also used to translate other terms in the LXX, the Latin *lucus* is used only to translate *ăšērîm* and its derivative terms.

A.3. Other uses for *nemus* in the Vulgate

The Vulgate uses *nemus* to translate several terms other than *ăšērāh/îm/ôt*. In Gen 21:33, 1 Sam 22:6, and 1 Sam 31:13, the term being translated is *ʾēšel*. In 2 Chr 9:16 the term being translated is *yaʿar*. In Est 1:5 and 7:8, *ginnat bîtan* is translated with a combination of *hortus*, which means "garden" and *nemus*. In Ps 104:12 [PsH 103:12], *nemus* translates the rare term *ăpāʾîm*, which is rendered with *petrarum* in the PsG version in keeping with the LXX reading τῶν πετρῶν. In Ezek 15:2 *lignis nemorum* is the translation for *ʿēṣ hazzəmôrāh* "wooden branch." For most of these readings, *nemus* carries the simple meaning of "tree," "branch," or "forest." Gen 21:33, Est 1:5, and Est 7:8, however, might be examples in which the idea of a unique or otherwise "sacred" tree or grove could also be understood in the use of *nemus*.

A.4. Synopsis of the Vulgate's understanding of *ăšērîm*

Like the LXX before it, the Vulgate evidences no knowledge of ʾAsherah as a proper name of a goddess. It might be argued, given Jerome's well documented appreciation for a literal, yet graceful, translation,[16] that Jerome could not have known of the existence of ʾAsherah or else he would have made reference to her. Brown notes, however, that Jerome at times "equates the literal sense of scripture with the Jewish understanding" of it.[17] This leads one to suspect that Jerome would have been inclined to see the Jewish view of *ăšērîm* as the literal one, regardless of whether he knew of ʾAsherah or not. By the time of Jerome, both the LXX and the Mishnah had solidified the understanding of *ăšērîm* as trees, so perhaps this understanding on the part of the Vulgate is not surprising.

Neither is it suprizing that Jerome uses two separate terms for *ăšērîm*, *lucus* and *nemus*, both of which carry a semantic range which includes the two meanings, "wood" and "sacred precinct." Brown notes that

---

[16]See Brown, *Vir Trilinguis*, 121-39.
[17]*Vir Trilinguis*, 127.

Jerome once fended off his critics by insisting that although he translated the Greek Fathers "sense for sense" because this made for a superior translation, he nonetheless translated scripture "word for word."[18] Brown demonstrates, however, that this is not actually the case in the Vulgate. Jerome often used more than one Latin translation for the same Hebrew or Greek antecedent, ultimately deciding that it was the meaning of the passage, and not a slavishly literal rendering that was most important.[19] This tendency to render the same antecedent in numerous ways will be seen again with regard to the other items under discussion, in particular *maṣṣēbôt*.

Finally, unlike the LXX, it is not certain that Jerome was engaging in a polemic against the use of sacred groves in his own time through his use of the terms *lucus* and *nemus* to translate *ăšērîm*. Although the existence of sacred groves within the Latin world has been much discussed, particularly in James G. Fraser's magnum opus, *The Golden Bough*,[20] the Christian community of the fourth century for which Jerome produced his translation likely had little cause to be overly concerned about being eclipsed by institutions such as the groves, which flourished in the early days of the Roman Empire, but which had, by the fourth century, long since ceased to hold much religious importance even for pagans. The philosophical teaching of ancient Greece and Rome were certainly popular at this time, but it is unclear that this popularity translated into a revival of actual worship in groves.[21]

While it is must be true that Jerome was aware of the suppression of Christianity and promotion of a return to paganism that was instituted by the Roman Emperor Julian (called "the Apostate," 361-63 CE), Henri Marrou argues that the church's progress toward becoming the dominant religion in the fourth century was "stopped and reversed for a few months only" during

---

[18]*Epistulae* 57, 5 (*CSEL* 54, 508), cited in *Vir Trilinguis*, 105-9.

[19]*Vir Trilinguis*, 108-9, 112-15.

[20](1st ed.; 2 vols.; London: Macmillan, 1890). Fraser expanded this work over a series of years, publishing a three-volume edition in 1900, a twelve volume edition beginning in 1911 and ending in 1915, and ultimately published an abridged edition in one volume in 1922. For a brilliant critique of Fraser's work, see Jonathan Z. Smith, "When the Bough Breaks," *History of Religions* 12 (1972) 324-71.

[21]Darice Birge notes that the later Roman affinity for groves was more philosophically than pietistically based. She writes, "Both Plutarch and Iamblichus looked to the Greek past for inspiration," but "instead of unconsciously expressing their piety at a rural grove . . . they consciously seek philosophical inspiration in the wooded sanctuaries of gods whose worship is in decline;" "Sacred Groves," 232.

Julian's time. He also argues that Julian's paganism was "very original and very different from that of ancient Rome . . . marked by the philosophic influence of Neo-Platonism."[22] So, while Jerome may well have been influenced by his teacher Appollinarius, who was a strong opponent of Julian's policies,[23] to connect the use of groves with the prohibitions against *'ăšērîm* when translating the Vulgate, there does not seem to be evidence that there actually was an increase in worship at groves due to Julian's influence. Jerome's treatment of groves as the equivalent of *'ăšērîm* appears to be a simple continuation of earlier Greek and Jewish interpretation. As will be discussed below, however, Jerome's references to the worship of idols, a topic much discussed in Christian scripture with regard to Roman custom, do appear to demonstrate a serious concern on Jerome's part concerning this practice.

B. LATIN TRANSLATIONS OF THE TERM *maṣṣēbāh/ôt*

statua: 15 out of 35 occurrences.

titulus: 10 out of 35 occurrences.

lapis: 3 out of 35 occurrences.

simulacrum: 3 out of 35 occurrences.

Three verses have alternate readings: 2 Kgs 10:27; Isa 6:13; Hos 3:4

One occurrence is omitted from the Latin: Gen 35:14

Unlike terms related to *'ăšērîm*, for which there are only two predominant Latin translations, terms for *maṣṣēbôt* have as many as four distinct Latin renderings, not including verses which have variant readings.[24] This diversity in the translation of *maṣṣēbôt* is absent in the

---

[22] *The Christian Centuries: A New History of the Catholic Church, Volume One: The First Six Hundred Years* (Jean Daniélou and Henri Marrou, ed.; 5 vols.; New York: Paulist, 1964) 1.237.

[23] Daniélou and Marrou, *Christian Centuries*, 336.

[24] In 2 Kgs 10:27 the noun *maṣṣēbāh* is replaced with a pronoun. In Isa 6:13 the term is translated according to context with a term meaning "tree stump." The Latin of Isa 6:13 reads: *Et adhuc in ea decimatio et convertetur et erit in ostensionem sicut terebinthus et sicuti quercus quae expandit ramos suos semen sanctum erit id quod steterit in ea.* In Hos 3:4, the Latin reads *altare*, reflecting *mizbəḥôt* as the Hebrew antece-

Greek which (barring the existence of a variant reading), chose στήλη in all but one instance. Jerome apparently felt that more nuances in the translation of *maṣṣēbôt* were called for than did the Greek translators.

Jerome's choice of terms divides roughly into two groups of two terms each, dividing the occurrences of *maṣṣēbāh/maṣṣēbôt* into groups according to whether they were viewed positively or negatively in context. The first group, using *statua* and *simulacrum*, represent verses which view *maṣṣēbôt* negatively. The second group, those using *titulus* and *lapis*, with only one exception, represent verses which view *maṣṣēbôt* positively. Thus Jerome provided a nuance of positive and negative *maṣṣēbôt*, similar to that provided for *mizbǝḥôt* by certain LXX translators, the Targumim, and Jerome himself.

B.1. *statua* and *simulacrum*

The most frequent of the four Latin terms used to translate *maṣṣēbôt* and related terms is *statua*, which occurs fifteen times.[25] There is only one basic Latin meaning for *statua*, namely, "a statue."[26] This choice of reading has a distinctly different connotation from the Greek understanding of *maṣṣēbôt* as stelas, in that *statua* can carry the connotation of a sculpted anthropo- or zoomorphic form.

All of the verses which use *statua* for *maṣṣēbāh* are passages in which *maṣṣēbôt* are viewed negatively. Some are linked with foreign nations and condemned for that reason (Exod 23:24; 34:13; Deut 7:5; 12:3; 16:22), and some are linked with Israelites whose use of them is condemned (1 Kgs 14:23; 2 Kgs 3:2; 10:26; 17:10; 18:4; 23:14; 2 Chr 14:2 [Lat 14:2-3]; Mic 5:12). In two verses these *maṣṣēbôt* are located in foreign lands and are being destroyed by the invading armies of Nebuchadnezzar (Jer 43:13; Ezek 26:11).

Whether Jerome meant to imply that all *maṣṣēbôt* which he describes as "statues" were sculpted images is open to question. The noun *statua* relates to the verb *statum*, "to stand" in the same way that *maṣṣēbāh* relates to the verb *nṣb*. Jerome may simply have chosen *statua* on the basis of

---

dent against *maṣṣēbôt* as in the MT. This is also the reading of the major Greek witnesses to Hos 3:4. It may well be that the Greek, and not a second Hebrew tradition, is the source of the Latin reading. Not counted above is the phrase אֵלוֹן מֻצָּב אֲשֶׁר בִּשְׁכֶם, which occurs in Judg 9:6. The Latin understands this phrase to mean "the oak *which stands* in Shechem" (*quercum quae stabat in Sychem*).

[25]Exod 23:24; 34:13; Deut 7:5; 12:3; 16:22; 1 Kgs 14:23; 2 Kgs 3:2; 10:26; 17:10; 18:4; 23:14; 2 Chr 14:2 [Lat 14:2-3]; Jer 43:13; Ezek 26:11; Mic 5:12.

[26]*OLD* 1815a.

etymological analogy, intending a simple meaning of "that which stands," rather than the specific semantic implication of anthropomorphic sculpture that *statua* implies elsewhere. As will be seen below, however, Jerome uses *statua* elsewhere in the Vulgate primarily to translate terms which represent either anthropomorphic objects or types of cultic statuary. Coupled with the fact that Jerome uses *statua* only in passages with negative opinions regarding *maṣṣēbôt*, this makes it seem as if Jerome implies that some *maṣṣēbôt*, a certain prohibited type, were sculpted images.

Jerome's knowledge of rabbinic opinions may provide further evidence that his use of *statua* for *maṣṣēbôt* is an intentional equation of certain *maṣṣēbôt* with cultic statuary. As will be discussed in chapter eleven, an early rabbinic opinion recorded in *Sifra* held that the use of *maṣṣēbôt* should be considered idolatrous because *maṣṣēbôt* must be made "to stand" as idols are made to stand.[27] While it is not possible to prove that first-hand knowledge of *Sifra* inspired Jerome to consider some *maṣṣēbôt* as a type of idol, this or another similar rabbinic viewpoint may be the source behind this equation in Jerome's translations.

The second negative translation for *maṣṣēbāh* is *simulacrum*, which occurs only three times.[28] *simulacrum*, like *statua*, carries a connotation of intentional structure in order to render a likeness. The *OLD* defines *simulacrum* as follows:

> **1** That which resembles something in appearance, sound, etc., a likeness. **2** A visual representation, image . . . **3** (spec.) **a** An image, statue (usu. of a god). **b** a pictorial representation, esp. as carried in triumphs.[29]

Additional meanings of *simulacrum* connote "images" which are not tangible (such as ghosts or dreams), or which, though real, are judged to be flawed or false.[30] The verses which use *simulacrum* are similar to those which use *statua* in that they describe Israelite use of *maṣṣēbôt* which is condemned by the source describing that use (2 Chr 31:1; Hos 10:1, 2).

B.2. *titulus* and *lapis*

The second most common translation of *maṣṣēbāh* in the Vulgate is more closely related to the meaning of the favored Greek translation, στήλη.

---

[27]*Sifra Qədōšîm* section ten, chapter 195.
[28]2 Chr 31:1; Hos 10:1, 2.
[29]*OLD* 1766b-c.
[30]*OLD* 1766c.

It is *titulus*, which occurs ten times.[31] Unlike *statua*, for which there is one basic meaning, *titulus* has several meanings, the first two of which appear to be most closely related to the Hebrew *maṣṣēbôt* and the Greek στήλη.

> 1 A flat piece of wood, stone or other material inscribed with a notice, identification, or other information, a placard, tablet, label, etc. **b** a commemorative tablet on which details of a person's career, etc., are inscribed **2** An inscription (dist. fr. the material on which it is inscribed). **b** a commemorative inscription giving details of a person's ancestry, career, etc.[32]

Additional meanings of the term *titulus* are similar to current uses of the English word "title."[33]

In direct contrast to the verses which use *statua* or *simulacrum* for *maṣṣēbāh*, the majority of the verses in which the Vulgate selected *titulus* for *maṣṣēbāh* are positive toward the use of *maṣṣēbôt*. Jacob's *maṣṣēbôt* from Gilead and Bethel are among them (Gen 28:18, 22; 31:45; 35:14, 20), as are Moses twelve *maṣṣēbôt* from Sinai (Exod 24:4), Isaiah's YHWHistic *maṣṣēbāh* on the border with Egypt (19:19), and Absalom's commemorative monument (2 Sam 18:18). Lev 26:1 is the only exception.

It is possible that the context of Lev 26:1 led Jerome to translate *maṣṣēbāh* with *titulus* in this passage. Lev 26:1 presented Jerome with a verse which had already mentioned two types of idols and where two terms occur which Jerome elsewhere translates with his negative terms for *maṣṣēbôt*. *pesel* occurs in Lev 26:1, and both *statua* (2 Chr 33:19) and *simulacrum* (2 Chr 34:3; Isa 10:10; 40:20; Hos 11:2) are used elsewhere by Jerome to translate *pesel*.[34] It is possible that the coincidence of the two terms *pesel* and *maṣṣēbāh*, both of which Jerome elsewhere translates with *statua* and *simulacrum*, suggested to Jerome that he use alternate translations for both of them in Lev 26:1 rather than risk confusion by using *statua* for either. Thus, it is likely that he inserted *titulus* in this negative reference more out of contextual necessity than out of any specific preference.[35]

---

[31]Gen 28:18, 22; 31:45; 35:14, 20 (2x); Exod 24:4; Lev 26:1; 2 Sam 18:18; Isa 19:19. The Hebrew of Gen 35:14 also contains a second reference to the *maṣebet ʾāben* which Jacob erects in Bethel. This second reference, however, is omitted in the Vulgate, and appears to be a late addition to the MT.

[32]*OLD* 1945a.

[33]*OLD* 1945a-b.

[34]*ʾĕlîlîm* also occurs in Lev 26:1 and *simulacrum* was used in the PsG version of Ps 97:7 [PsG 96:7] to translate *ʾĕlîlîm*. In his PsH translation of this passage, Jerome uses *idolis* to translate *ʾĕlîlîm* as he does in Lev 26:1.

[35]The use of either *lapis* or *titulos* for *maṣṣēbāh* may have been complicated in Lev 26:1 further by the occurrence of *ʾeben maskît* in this verse. Jerome uses *lapis* in his

The second positive translation for *maṣṣēbāh* is *lapis* which occurs three times in Genesis only.[36] In addition to meanings commonly related to stone objects and their mundane uses, *lapis*, the common Latin term for "stone," also has the following meanings:

> **1 b** a stone, usu. meteoric, supposed to have divine or magical properties . . . **2c** (used in religious ritual; *Iouem lapidem iurare*, a solemn form of oath) . . . **4d** a tombstone, funeral stele; also, a stone sepulchre. **e** a milestone (usu. w. numerals to indicate distance); (also) a boundary stone; a stone set up for these or other purposes, and treated as sacred.[37]

The verses in which the term *lapis* is used for *maṣṣēbāh* are all in the Jacob stories of Genesis. The first refers to the *maṣṣēbāh* erected at Bethel, but in this passage God is reminding Jacob of the "pillar" he erected and the promise he made to return to Bethel (Gen 31:13). Perhaps it is because Jacob had used a simple stone upon which he rested his head to make his *maṣṣēbāh* that Jerome was inspired to use the simple term *lapis* in this context. He does not use *lapis* in his account of the initial incident, however (Gen 22:18, 28). The remaining two verses in which *lapis* is used for *maṣṣēbāh* are part of the story of Jacob and Laban's border monuments (Gen 31:51, 52). In this story, Jerome has used the term *lapis* in Laban's dialogue concerning Jacob's *maṣṣēbāh*, but has used *titulus* in the verse which describes Jacob building the monument (Gen 31:45). Perhaps this variation also derived from the context which preserves Laban's name for the monument in Aramaic while Jacob's name for it is in Hebrew.

B.3. Other uses for *statua* in the Vulgate

The Latin term *statua* is used elsewhere to render five additional Hebrew terms. In Gen 19:26 it provides quite an apt anthropomorphic translation for *nəṣîb* in the description of the transformation of Lot's wife into a "pillar" of salt (*nəṣîb melaḥ*). Likewise, in 1 Sam 19:13, it provides an interpretive translation of *tərāpîm* in the passage in which Michal helps David escape by disguising her *tərāpîm* to look like him.[38] In both of these verses, the choice of *statua* appears to be governed by a context which calls for a

---

translation of this phrase, *insignem lapidem*, but in Num 33:52, the related term *maskîyōtām* is translated with *titulus*.

[36] Gen 31:13, 51, 52.

[37] *OLD* 1001c–1002a.

[38] As noted below (p. 304, n.49), in 1 Sam 19:16 *tərāpîm* is translated with *simulacrum*.

manufactured life-size replica of a human being. In the other verses which use *statua*, however, the Hebrew term being translated also overtly suggests such an object.

In 2 Chr 33:19, *statua* is used to translate *pəsîlîm* and in 28:2 it translates *massēkôt*. In Num 33:52, *statua* is used to render the phrase *ṣaləmê massēkotām*, "their cast images." In this instance, however, it is unclear whether the use of *statua* is dictated by the presence of *massēkôt* in the Hebrew. It could just as well be chosen to translate *ṣelem*, as it frequently does in Daniel (2:31, 32, 34, 35; 3:1, 2, 3, 5, 7, 10, 12, 14, 15, 18). Based on these uses of *statua* to translate Hebrew terms connected to "statuary," whether cultic or secular, it appears likely that for Jerome, illegitimate *maṣṣēbôt* were understood to be statues in human or divine likeness.

B.4. Other uses for *titulus* in the Vulgate

Aside from its use to translate *maṣṣēbôt* and related terms, *titulus* is also used to translate three additional Hebrew terms. The most frequent is the word *miḵətām* which appears as a part of the titles to several Psalms (16:1 [PsG 15:1]; 56:1 [PsG 55:1]; 57:1 [PsG 56:1]; 58:1 [PsG 57:1]; 59:1 [PsG 58:1]; 60:1 [PsG 59:1]). This translation, however, occurs only in the PsG translation of the Psalms and not in the PsH.[39]

The next most frequent use of *titulus* in the Latin is as a translation of rare word *ṣiyyûn* meaning "sign-post" (2 Kgs 23:17; Ezek 39:15). This term is only found three times in the Hebrew Bible and in two of the three cases, *titulus* is the chosen Latin translation.[40] The only additional use of *titulus* in the Vulgate is as a translation for *maśəkîyotām* "their carved things" in Num 33:52. This use of *titulus* may imply that the Latin translator understood these objects to be inscribed stele.

B.5. Other uses for *lapis* in the Vulgate

The predominant use of the term *lapis* in the Latin versions is to translate the common Hebrew term for stone, *ʾeben*.[41] The Latin also uses *lapis* to supply the noun "stone" in some verses which contain either of the

---

[39]In the PsH translation *miḵətām* is translated with the phrase *humilem et simplicem* rather than with *tituli inscriptione* as in the PsG. The only exception is Ps 60:1 [PsH 59:1] where *humilis et perfecti* is chosen.

[40]In Jer 31:21, the Latin translator chose *speculam*, "mirrors" as a translation for *ṣiyyûnîm*, and read *tamrûrîm*, another rare term in the parallel cola, as *amaritudines* "bitterness."

[41]Gen 2:12; 28:11, 18, 22; 29:2, 3, 8, 10; 31:45, 46; 49:24; Exod 15:5, 16; 17:12; 20:25; 21:18; 25:7; 28:9, 10, 17, 21; 35:9, 27, 33; 39:6, 14; Lev 14:40, 42, 43, 45; 20:27; 24:23; 26:1; Num 14:10; 15:35, 36; 35:17; Deut 4:28; 8:9; 13:10; 17:5; 21:21; 22:21, 24;

Hebrew verbs סקל or רגם, meaning "to stone to death."[42] Likewise, *lapis* is added to three verses to specify that the verb חצב should be understood to mean "to quarry stone," and not simply "to dig."[43] *lapis* is also supplied in other verses that have to do with construction terminology. The term *gāzît* which means "ashlar" is specified as a "block of stone" in five verses.[44] Three times the Latin specifies that a *rispāh*, which means "pavement," is made of stone.[45] In certain verses, *lapis* is used to make obscure terms clearer, such as *ṣûr*[46] and *ʿîy*.[47] The Latin renders the latter, usually translated "ruins," as *acervis lapidum*, "piles of stones." Similarly, the Latin of Jer 50:26 adds "stones" to the image of "heaps and destruction" (*ʿărēmîm wəhaḥărîmûhā*).

The remaining uses of *lapis* occur in contexts where minerals or precious stones are mentioned. The phrase *libənat has-sapîr* in Exod 24:10 is translated as "brickwork of sapphire *stone*." Similarly, the Latin phrase for the precious stone *šoham* in Job 28:16 is *lapidi sardonico*, "sardonyx stone." Finally, the Latin sometimes translates *paz*, a term for a type of gold, with the phrase *lapidem pretiosum*, "precious stones."[48]

B.6. Other uses for *similacrum* in the Vulgate

Most of the other uses for *similacrum* relate to cultic statuary, called by both technical and metaphorical names.[49] The only other Hebrew term

---

27:2, 4, 5, 8; 28:36, 64; 29:17; Josh 4:3, 5, 6, 7, 8, 9, 20, 21; 7:26; 8:29, 31, 32; 10:11; 15:6; 18:17 [Lat 18:18] 24:26, 27; Judg 9:5, 18; 20:16; 1 Sam 4:1; 5:1; 6:14, 15; 7:12; 17:40, 49, 50; 20:19; 25:37; 2 Sam 5:11, 16:6, 13; 18:17; 20:8; 1 Kgs 1:9; 5:17, 18; 6:7, 18; 7:9, 10, 11; 10:27; 15:22; 18:31, 32, 38; 21:13; 2 Kgs 3:19, 25; 12:12; 16:17; 19:18; 22:6; 1 Chr 22:2, 14; 29:2, 8; 2 Chr 1:15; 9:27; 16:6; 24:21; 26:14; 32:27; 34:11; Ezra [Lat 1 Esr] 5:8; 6:4; Neh [Lat 2 Esr] 4:2; 9:11; Job 5:23; 6:12; 8:17; 14:19; 28:2, 3, 6; 38:6, 30; 41:24 [Lat 41:15], 28 [Lat 19]; Ps 91:12 [PsG & PsH 90:12]; 102:14 [PsG & PsH 101:15]; 118:22 [PsG & PsH 117:22]; Prov 16:11; 24:31; 26:8, 27; Eccl 3:5; 10:9; Isa 8:14; 27:9; 28:16; 30:30; 37:19; 54:11, 12, 60:17; 62:10; Jer 2:27; 3:9; 43:9, 10; 51:26, 63; Lam 3:53; 4:1; Ezek 1:26; 10:1, 9; 13:11, 13; 16:40; 20:32; 23:47; 26:12; 27:22; 28:13; 38:22; 40:42; Dan 2:34, 35, 45; 6:17; 11:38; Mic 1:6; Hab 2:11, 19; Hag 2:15 [Lat 2:16]; Zech 3:9; 4:7, 10; 5:4; 9:15, 16; 12:3.

[42] סקל: Exod 8:22 [Lat 8:26]; 19:13; 21:28, 29, 32; Isa 5:2; רגם: Lev 24:16.

[43] 2 Chr 2:1 [Lat 2:2], 17 [Lat 18]; 24:12.

[44] 1 Kgs 6:36; 7:12; Isa 9:9 [Lat 9:10]; Lam 3:9; Amos 5:11.

[45] 2 Chr 7:3, Est 1:6; Ezek 40:17; 42:3.

[46] Job 24:8; Ps 31:3 [PsH 30:3].

[47] Ps 79:1 [PsH 78:1]; Isa 17:1; Jer 26:18; Mic 3:12.

[48] Ps 19:11 [PsG & PsH 18:11]; 21:4 [PsG & PsH 20:4]; Prov 8:19.

[49] *ʾĕlohêhem*, Exod 34:15; *ʿāmāl*, Num 23:21; *tərāpîm*, 1 Sam 19:16 (see above p. 302 on 1 Sam 19:13); Zech 10:2; *mipəleṣet*, 1 Kgs 15:13; 2 Chr 15:16; *ṣelem*, 2 Chr

translated with *similacrum* is *ḥammānîm*,[50] perhaps indicating that Jerome believed *ḥammānîm* to be a type of cultic statuary. This is an opinion which might also be derived from the Midrash *Sifra*, which states that *ḥammānîm* are part of idolatrous worship because they "stand in the sun."[51] As noted above, however, it is unclear if Jerome knew of this Rabbinic reference.

B.7. Synopsis of the Vulgate's understanding of *maṣṣēbôt*

Unlike the LXX translators, Jerome addressed the issue of acceptable and unacceptable *maṣṣēbôt* by providing two types of translations for them. Unacceptable *maṣṣēbôt* were rendered with terms which carried the connotation of cultic statuary, *statua* and *simulacrum*. Acceptable *maṣṣēbôt* were rendered with more generic terms for monuments, *titulus* and *lapis*. With the exception of Lev 26:1, all of Jerome's references to *maṣṣēbôt* are divided according to their positive or negative evaluation in the Hebrew text. This treatment of *maṣṣēbôt* does not occur in either the LXX or the Targumim. Both of these translations choose one predominant translation and, except for the LXX of Exod 24:4, level the predominant reading through every biblical occurrence of *maṣṣēbāh/maṣṣēbôt*.

It is unknown whether the interpretation of prohibited *maṣṣēbôt* as varieties of cultic statuary is dependent upon Jewish interpretation, or was Jerome's own attempt to make the prohibitions against *maṣṣēbôt* relevant to Christianity's rise to prominence over Greek and Roman culture.[52] According to Brown, Jerome did, upon rare occasion, indulge in the practice of "christianizing" certain passages from the Hebrew Bible which he believed to be important to the Church; and he also translated certain other passages under the direct influence of the New Testament.[53] Given this, as well as Jerome's practice of using Jewish opinion to support translations in which he went against the reading of the LXX,[54] it is possible that Jerome's equa-

---

23:17; *hassemel*, 2 Chr 33:15; *pəsîlîm*, 2 Chr 34:3; Isa 10:10; 40:20; Hos 11:2; *ĕlîlîm*, Ps 97:7 [PsG 96:7] (PsH *idolis*); Isa 2:20; 19:1, 3; Hab 2:18; *ăṣabîm*, Ps 115:14 [PsG 113:12] (PsH *idola*); Isa 10:11; 46:1; *nisəkêhem*, Isa 41:29; *gillûlîm*, Ezek 6:5; 30:13; *šiqqûṣêhem*, Ezek 7:20.

[50]Lev 26:30; 2 Chr 34:4; Ezek 6:4.

[51]*Sifra Qədōšîm* section ten, chapter 195.

[52]For New Testament references to the early Christian struggle against idols and idol worship, see Acts 7:41; 15:20, 29; 17:16; 21:25; Rom 2:22; 1 Cor 5:10, 11; 6:9; 8:1, 4, 7, 10; 10:7, 14, 19, 28; 12:2; 2 Cor 6:16; Eph 5:5; Gal 5:20; Col 3:5; 1 Thes 1:9; 1 John 5:21; 1 Pet 4:3; Rev 2:14, 20; 9:20; 21:8; 22:15.

[53]See Brown, *Vir Trilinguis*, 118-20.

[54]Kamesar, *Jerome*, 190.

tion of certain *maṣṣēbôt* with cultic statues or idols was an intentional interpretation, supported by the Jewish sources, and aimed at reinforcing the
later books of the Christian scriptures which describe Christian opposition
to Roman idol worship. As will be seen in chapter eleven, Jerome may have
found in certain negative rabbinic views of *maṣṣēbôt* an apt interpretation of
them which blended well with his own views concerning pagan religion.

C. LATIN TRANSLATIONS OF THE TERMS *bāmôtê* AND *bāmāh/āt/ôt*

excelsus: 73 out of 84 occurrences of *bāmāh/āt/ôt*

Bamoth: 3 out of 84 occurrences of *bāmāh/āt/ôt*

ara: 5 out of 84 occurrences of *bāmāh/āt/ôt*

altitudo: 1 out of 84 occurrences of *bāmāh/āt/ôt*

fanum: 1 out of 84 occurrences of *bāmāh/āt/ôt*

sublimis: 1 out of 84 occurrences of *bāmāh/bāmāt/bāmôt*

collis: once in the PsG version of Ps 78:58 [PsG 77:58]

C.1. *excelsus*

The most common Latin term used to translate *bāmôt* and related
lexemes is *excelsus*. The *OLD* defines *excelsus* as:

> **1** High ground, an eminence, height. **b** a high altitude; **2** Loftiness (of rank, sta-
> tion, etc.), high position.[55]

The Latin uses *excelsus* for both *bāmôt* meaning the cultic installations[56]

---

[55]*OLD* 633c.

[56]Lev 26:30; Num 21:28; 22:41; 33:52; 1 Sam 9:12, 13, 14, 19, 25; 10:5, 13; 1
Kgs 3:2, 3, 4; 12:31, 32; 13:2; 13:32, 33; 15:14; 22:44; 2 Kgs 12:4 [Lat & Eng 12:3];
14:4; 15:4; 15:35; 16:4; 17:9, 29; 18:4, 22; 21:3; 23:5, 9, 13, 15, 19, 20; 1 Chr 16:39;
21:29; 2 Chr 1:3, 13; 11:15; 14:2 [Lat 14:2-3]; 15:17; 17:6; 20:33; 21:11; 28:4; 31:1;
32:12; 33:3, 17, 19; 34:3; Amos 7:9; Hos 10:8; Mic 1:5; 3:12; Isa 15:2; 16:12; 36:7; Jer
7:31; 17:3; 19:5; 26:18; 32:35; 48:35; Ezek 6:3, 6; 16:16; 20:29; 43:7; Ps 78:58 [PsH
77:58]. The Vulgate of Isa 2:22 interprets the term במה as *excelsus* even through the MT
vocalizes it בַּמֶּה, clearly not taking this as a reference to a cultic *bāmāh*.

and the archaic poetic term *bāmôtê*.[57] Twice the term is used in place names (Num 21:28; 22:43) while other place names transliterate the term *Bamoth* (Num 21:19, 20; Josh 13:17). The term *excelsus* also features in the way in which *bāmôt* is translated in constructions with *bêt*. In four of the five incidences of this word-pair the term which translates *bāmôt* is *excelsus*.[58] In one instance *bāmôt* as part of this pair is translated with *sublimis*.[59] As with the LXX use of ὑψηλός for *bāmāh*, the Vulgate's choice of adjectives such as *excelsus* and *sublimis* to translate *bāmāh* does not reflect a conscious allusion to any specific cultic installation in Roman culture. Rather, it is likely that the Vulgate adopted this conventional rendering of *bāmôt* from the LXX translation.

C.2. *ara*

The second most frequent translation for *bāmôt* in the Latin is *ara*.[60] The *OLD* defines *ara* as:

> **1** An altar, usu. one built or 'raised' to a particular god. **2** (in geog. names). **3** The constellation Ara **4** (fig) **a** (applied to institutions, etc.) A source of protection, refuge. **b** a protector or champion. **5** A raised base or bed for supporting machinery, etc.[61]

This term is also used by Jerome to translate Hebrew *mizbē*ᵃ*ḥ/mizbəḥôt*. As will be noted below, *ara* is the term which Jerome uses to represent illegitimate altars in certain contexts while other contexts, most of which pertain to legitimate altars, use *altaria*. The fact that Jerome also uses this term to translate *bāmāh/bāmôt* in certain contexts which condemn their use suggests that Jerome viewed *bāmôt* as the equivalent of illegitimate altars in some cases. While, again, it cannot be definitely proven, this view may influenced by rabbinic opinion which discussed *bāmôt* primarily with regard to their role as installations of sacrifice.[62]

---

[57]Num 21:28; Deut 32:13; 2 Sam 1:25; 22:34; Amos 4:13; Mic 1:3; Hab 3:19; Ps 18:33 [PsG & PsH 17:34]. The Latin renderings of *bāmôtê* which do not use the term *excelsus* vary widely depending on context. The transliteration of *bāmôt/bāmôtê* in place names occurs three times (Num 21:19, 20; Josh 13:17). The term *altitudo* occurs twice (Isa 14:14; 58:14). The term *collum*, "neck," occurs once (Deut 33:29), as do the terms *mons*, "mountain" (2 Sam 1:19), and *fluctus*, "wave" (Job 9:8).

[58]*bêt bāmôt = fana in excelsis*: 1 Kgs 12:31; *bātê habbāmôt = fana excelsorum*: 1 Kgs 13:32; 2 Kgs 23:19; *bəbêt habbāmôt = fanis excelsis*: 2 Kgs 17:29.

[59]*bəbêt habbāmôt = fanis sublimibus*: 2 Kgs 17:32.

[60]1 Kgs 14:23; 2 Kgs 17:11; 23:8; 2 Chr 14:4 [Lat 14:5]; 28:25.

[61]Also funeral altars, pyres, and commemorative altars for the living, *OLD* 158c.

[62]See below chapter eleven, pp. 333-39.

These readings of *ara* for *bāmôt* in the Vulgate are also not, apparently, the result of LXX influence. Although the LXX also uses a term which means "altar" (Θυσιαστήριον) to render *bāmāh* in 2 Chr 14:4 [Lat 14:5], none of the other verses which use *ara* for *bāmôt* in the Vulgate also read Θυσιαστήριον or βωμός in the LXX. The majority of Vulgate verses which use this translation, then, are not dependent for this reading upon the LXX.

C.3. *fanum, altitudo, sublimis,* and *collis*

All of the remaining Latin translations for *bāmôt* listed above occur only once. The term *fanum,* which the *OLD* defines as "a piece of consecrated ground; (sus.) a shrine, temple,"[63] appears for *bāmôt* in 1 Kgs 11:7. The term *altitudo* occurs for *bāmôt* in Ezek 36:2. This term has eleven possible meanings, among which are both "height" and "depth," in the sense of "extension upwards" or "downward extension," as well as "a high structure or mass."[64] As noted above, the term *sublimis,* which the *OLD* defines as "high up, elevated aloft . . . tall . . . having lofty ambitions . . . exalted in rank,"[65] is used to translate *bāmôt* in 2 Kgs 17:32. The term *collis,* which the *OLD* defines as "a hill, eminence . . . a mountain . . . a mound or hummock,"[66] also appears in Ps 78:58 [PsG 77:58]. The PsH translation of this verse uses *excelsus,* making it clear that *collis* is specifically rendering the Greek βουνοῖς found in the LXX rather than *bāmôt* which occurs in the Hebrew.

C.4. Other uses for the primary translation *excelsus* in the Vulgate

The most frequent use of *excelsus* is to translate terms which were believed to derive from either of the verbal roots רום or רמם, meaning "to be high or exalted."[67] The second most frequent use of *excelsus* is to translate

---

[63]*OLD* 676b.

[64]*OLD* 109b-c.

[65]*OLD* 1843a-b.

[66]*OLD* 352c.

[67]Exod 14:8; Num 33:3; Deut 2:10; 12:2; 27:14; 32:27; 2 Sam 22:17, 28; 2 Kgs 19:22, 23; Neh 9:5 [Lat 2 Esr 9:5] Job 16:19 [Lat 16:20]; 21:22; 31:2; 38:15; Ps 18:28 [PsH 17:28]; 68:19 [PsH 67:19]; 71:19 [PsH 70:19]; 73:8 [PsG & PsH 72:8]; 75:6 [PsH 74:6]; 92:9 [PsH 91:9]; 93:4 [PsH 92:4]; 99:2 [PsG & PsH 98:2]; 102:20 [PsG & PsH 101:20]; 113:4 [PsG & PsH 112:4]; 118:16 [PsH 117:16]; 138:6 [PsG & PsH 137:6]; 144:7 [PsH 143:7]; 148:1 [PsG & PsH 148:1]; Prov 8:2; 9:14; 24:7; 30:13; Isa 2:12, 14; 6:1; 10:33; 22:16; 24:18, 21; 26:5; 32:15; 33:5, 16; 37:24; 38:14; 40:26; 57:15; 58:4; Jer 25:30; 51:53; Lam 1:13; Ezek 16:31; 20:28, 40; 34:6, 14; Mic 6:6; Hab 2:9. Job 28:18 understands *rāʾmôt* to be related to רמם/רום. In Jer 31:15, the word *rāmāh* is interpreted as

the term *'elyôn* or its Aramaic cognate *'illāyā'*, either as a common adjective or the divine name.[68] Two additional verses use *excelsus* to translate the related term *ləmā'əlāh* (2 Chr 1:1; 20:19). The third most frequent use of *excelsus* is to translate terms related to the root גבה.[69] The fourth most frequent use of *excelsus* is to translate *śāgab*.[70]

In addition to these terms whose basic meaning connotes "height," *excelsus* is used twice in translations of place names,[71] and twice to translate the term *nəṭûyāh* in the description of YHWH's "outstretched (or as both the Latin and the Greek understand it, 'upstretched') arm."[72] All of the other uses of *excelsus* occur only once, though many of them share a meaning related to topographic "heights."[73] Two final uses of *excelsus* occur in verses in which there is some textual variance.[74]

These uses of *excelsus* outside its use as a translation for *bāmāh* underscore what was stated above regarding Jerome's choice of this translation. There is no evidence to suggest that the choice was governed by a desire to draw an analogy to any existing cultic institution. Just like the LXX use of ὑψηλός, *excelsus* communicates only physical or metaphorical "height," or "loftiness," for *bāmôt*, most probably for lack of a more technical term or parallel to any specific Latin cultic institution. It is most likely that Jerome is simply following the LXX in this translation.

───────────

"height" (*vox in excelso audita*) rather than as the place name Ramah.

[68]Gen 14:19, 20, 22; 40:17; Deut 26:19; 28:1; 2 Sam 22:14; 2 Chr 27:3; Neh 3:25 [Lat 2 Esr 3:25]; Ps 21:8 [PsH 20:8]; 47:3 [PsG 46:3]; 73:11 [PsG & PsH 72:11]; 77:11 [PsG & PsH 76:11]; 78:17, 35, 36 [PsG & PsH 77:17, 35, 56]; 82:6 [PsG & PsH 81:6]; 83:19 [PsH 82:19]; 87:5 [PsH 86:5]; 89:28 [PsG & PsH 88:28]; 91:1, 9 [PsH 90:1, 9]; 97:9 [PsH 96:9]; 107:11 [PsH 106:11]; Dan 7:22. Aramaic *'illāyā'* Dan 3:26 [Lat 3:93], 32 [Lat 3:99, Eng 4:2]; 4:14 [Eng 4:17], 22 [Eng 24], 29 [Eng 34]; 7:25.

[69]Gen 7:19; Est 5:14; Ps 103:11 [PsH 102:11]; 104:18 [PsG & PsH 103:18]; 113:5 [PsH 112:5]; 138:6 [PsH 137:6]; Job 11:8; 22:12; Eccl 5:7; 12:5; Isa 2:15; 7:11; 30:25; 40:9; 57:7; Jer 3:6; 17:2; 51:58; Ezek 17:22; 31:3; 40:2; Dan 8:3; Zeph 1:16.

[70]Ps 139:6 [PsH 138:6]; Job 36:22; Isa 12:4; 30:13.

[71]*Gib'at hammôreh* = *collis excelsi*, Judg 7:1; *migdal 'ōz* = *turris excelsa*, Judg 9:51.

[72]Exod 6:6; Ps 136:12 [PsG 135:12].

[73]*gabnûnîm*, Ps 68:16, 17 [PsH 67:16, 17]; *'adîr*, Isa 10:34; *ṭillāh*, Jer 30:18; *hārim*, 1 Chr 15:16; *tô'āpôt*, Ps 95:4 [PsH 94:4]; *mišbāreyk*, Ps 42:8 [PsG 41:8] (PsH 41:8 has *gurgites* and the LXX has μετεωρισμοί).

[74]The Vulgate of Deut 26:15 reads *excelso caelorum* whereas the MT has only *haššāmayim*. The LXX also lacks any adjective on τοῦ οὐρανοῦ. The Vulgate of 2 Sam 21:20 reads *vir excelsus* "a tall man" where the Qirê reads *'îš mādôn*, "a contentious man." The Kᵉtiv of the MT reads *yš mdyn*. The the Lucianic Greek witnesses, in agreement with the Syriac, also read the quality of "height" in their translation προμετρος.

C.5. Other uses for *ara* in the Vulgate

As noted above, the Vulgate uses *ara* as a translation for *mizbəḥôt* as well as for *bāmôt*. This is the only other term for which the Vulgate uses *ara*. The use of *ara* for *mizbēªḥ/ mizbəḥôt* will be discussed at length below.

C.6. Other uses for *fanum* in the Vulgate

The only additional use of *fanum* in the Vulgate is to translate *bêt*. It is not used in every occurrence of this term in the Hebrew, but when it is used, the shrine in question is understood to be connected to a god or gods other than YHWH.[75] The *bāmôt* which are described with *fanum* are also dedicated to gods other than YHWH, specifically the gods of Solomon's wives (1 Kgs 11:7). Although this translation for *bāmôt* fits in well with the other uses of *fanum* in the Vulgate, it is unclear why Jerome did not also use this term in other passages in which *bāmôt* are linked with other gods. Even 2 Kgs 23:13, which describes the destruction of the same installations mentioned in 1 Kgs 11:7, uses *excelsus*.

C.7. Other uses for *sublimis* in the Vulgate

The great majority of uses for *sublimis* in the Vulgate are translations of terms derived from Hebrew verbal roots related to physical or metaphorical "height" or "highness," the most common of these being גבה.[76] It is also used to render the common preposition "above," *mē ʿal* (Gen 7:17; Deut 28:43; 2 Chr 17:12), as well as the more poetic term "heavenward," *šāmaymāh* (Judg 20:40). It is used for two basic terms meaning "height" as a measurement, *qômah* (2 Kgs 19:23) and *midāh* (Isa 45:14), as well as more metaphorical uses of the concept of "loftiness" or "veneration," *gāʾôn* (Isa 4:2), and *ʾadîr* (1 Sam 4:8). Like *excelsus* it is used to translate the term for God's outstretched (or "upstretched") arm from נטה (Josh 8:26) as well as terms forming divine titles, namely *ʿelyôn* (2 Kgs 15:35) and *šaday* (Ezek 1:24). The five remaining uses of *sublimis* occur in passages where there is either some textual variance or paraphrasing.[77]

---

[75]Deut 3:29; 4:46; Judg 9:4, 27, 46; 2 Kgs 10:26; 1 Chr 10:10. The Latin of 2 Chr 24:7 includes a reference to the *fanum Baalim* for which Athalia had cultic vessels made. The MT mentions the Baʿalim without reference to any shrine or temple.

[76] גבה: Deut 28:52; 1 Sam 2:3; 2 Kgs 17:10; Isa 2:11; 5:15; 52:13; Jer 2:20; Ezek 17:24; 21:31 [Lat 21:26]; Job 40:10 [Lat 40:5]; 41:26 [Lat 41:25]; רום/רמם: Deut 9:2; Isa 2:13; 10:33; Ezek 17:22, 23; Job 5:11; 25:2; Prov 6:17; Eccl 10:6; 2 Chr 5:13; נשא: Isa 57:7, 15; Mic 4:1; Prov 30:32; שגב: Isa 25:12; 26:5; Ps 148:13 [PsH 148:13]; גדל: 1 Kgs 1:37; Ezek 31:18; Aramaic רבה: Dan 2:48; 4:17.

[77]Isa 10:13 supplies *sublimis*, reading *sublime residentes*, where the Hebrew has only *yôšəbîm*. Isa 5:14 paraphrases *šə ʾônāh wə ʿālēz bāh* into *sublimes gloriosique eius ad*

C.8. Other uses for *altitudo* in the Vulgate

The most frequent use for *altitudo* in the Vulgate is as a translation for *qômāh*, meaning "height."[78] The second and third most frequent uses are also translations for terms meaning "height," specifically, those derived from the roots רום / רמם,[79] and those related to גבה.[80] The Vulgate also uses *altitudo* once for *ma'amōq*, "deep" (Ps 69:3 [PsG 68:3]), since "negative altitude" or "depth" is a perfectly acceptable meaning for the Latin *altitudo*. Also occuring once is the use of *altitudo* to translate *tô'apôt*, meaning "tops" (Ps 95:4 [PsG 94:4]). Finally, there are two verses for which some textual issue has resulted in the use of *altitudo* in a verse for which the MT has no parallel.[81]

C.9. Synopsis of the Vulgate's understanding of *bāmôt*

The majority of translated references to *bāmôt* which occur in the Vulgate select terms which somehow denote "height" or "elevation," whether physical or metaphorical. Only *fanum* and *ara* carry specifically cultic meanings and they occur in only six instances altogether. The preponderance of terms which denote "height" indicates that the interpretation of *bāmôt* which dominates the LXX also presented itself as the preferable translation for *bāmôt* to Jerome. Only infrequently did Jerome feel it necessary to use a term for *bāmôt* whose meaning had a specifically

---

eum. Num 23:14 renders the phrase *śᵊdēh ṣōpîm*, not as a placed name "Field of Ṣopim" as does the NRSV, but as "elevated place" (*locum sublimem*), based on the literal meaning of the phrase "field of those who keep watch." Dan 2:31 translates the Aramaic *zîwēh yatîr* "surpassing splendor" as *statura sublimis* "enormous height." The LXX has ἡ πρόσοψις αὐτῆς ὑπερφεής "its appearance was monstrous/extraordinary." Perhaps the dual meaning of the Greek adjective (abnormally large or surpassingly strange) influenced the Latin translation. Finally, 2 Chr 6:30 turns *min-haššāmayim mᵊkôn šibtekā* "from heaven, the place of your habitation," into *de caelo de sublimi scilicet habitaculo tuo*, "from heaven, from your truly sublime habitation." It is possible that graphic confusion has led the Latin to read *nākôn* rather than *mᵊkôn*.

[78]Gen 6:15; Exod 25:10, 23; 27:1, 18; 30:2; 37:1, 10, 25; 38:1, 18; 1 Kgs 6:2, 10, 20, 23, 26; 7:2, 15, 16, 23, 27, 32; 2 Kgs 25:17; Jer 52:21, 22; Ezek 31:3, 5, 10, 14; 2 Chr 4:1, 2; 6:13.

[79]Ps 12:9 [PsG 11:9]; Ps 56:3 [PsG 55:4]; Isa 2:11, 17; 10:12; 24:4; 37:23, 24; Jer 17:12; 48:29; 49:16; Hab 3:10; Aramaic *rûmēh*: Ezra 6:3 [Lat 1 Esr 6:3]; Dan 3:1; 4:7, 17.

[80]1 Sam 16:7; 17:4; Ezek 1:18; 19:11; 40:42; 41:8, 22; Amos 2:9; Ps 10:4 [PsH 9:25]; 103:11 [PsG 102:11]; Est 5:14; 7:9; 2 Chr 3:4.

[81]2 Chr 3:15 has *altitudo* for *'ōrek* which appears in the MT where one might expect *qômāh*. The LXX also has a term for "height" (τὸ ὕψος) rather than one for length in agreement with the Latin. Num 11:31 inserts *altitudo* as a minor explication.

cultic connotation. This implies that like the LXX translators, Jerome made no significant interpretative use of *bāmôt* to speak to or allude to any contemporaneous cultic institution with which his audience might be familiar.

D. LATIN TRANSLATIONS OF THE TERM *mizbēaḥ/mizbǝḥôt*

altaria: 290 out of 330 occurrences.

ara: 29 out of 330 occurrences.

Ten verses replace *mizbǝḥôt* with a pronoun or omit completely.

One verse has a variant reading: Hos 4:19

D.1. *altaria* and *ara*

The two primary terms which are used to translate *mizbēᵃḥ* and *mizbǝḥôt* in the Vulgate are *altaria* and *ara*, both of which have the basic meaning "altar." The predominant translation, however, is *altaria* which is found in all but 40 of the 330 uses of the terms *mizbēᵃḥ* and *mizbǝḥôt* found in the Hebrew Bible.[82] *ara* is found in 29 of the 330 uses of *mizbǝḥôt*.[83]

Although there are two terms used for "altar" in the Latin, as there are in the LXX and in the Targumim (as will be demonstrated in chapter eleven), the choice of *altaria* over *ara* does not always indicate that the former was used for legitimate altars and the latter for illegitimate ones. While the distinction made in the Targumim between *mizbēᵃḥ* and *'ēgôrā'* is clear, similar to the exchange between Θυσιαστήριον and βωμός in certain LXX books, the Vulgate does not sustain the distinction with the same frequency. The equation βωμός = *ara*, Θυσιαστήριον = *altaria* holds true in certain verses (Exod 34:13; Num 23:1-30; Deut 7:5; 12:3; Jer 11:13; Hos 10:8) but

---

[82]Verses which choose *ara* are: Exod 34:13; Num 23:1-2, 4, 14, 29, 30; Deut 7:5; 12:3; Judg 2:2; 6:25, 28, 30, 31; 1 Kgs 16:32; 2 Kgs 11:18; 21:3, 4; 2 Chr 23:17; 33:3, 15; 34:4; Jer 11:13; 17:1, 2; Ezek 6:4, 5, 6, 13; Verses which omit any translation, or replace the common noun with a pronoun are: Exod 30:28; 38:3; Lev 1:8, 12; 4:26; Deut 27:6; 2 Chr 33:5; Hos 8:11; 10:2, 8. The Latin of Hos 4:19 reads "sacrifices" (*sacrificiis*) as does the MT even though the LXX understood the consonants in this case to represent the word "altars" (Θυσιαστήριον).

[83]Exod 34:13, Num 23:1, 2, 4, 14, 29, 30; Deut 7:5, 12:3; Judg 2:2; 6:25, 28, 30, 31; 1 Kgs 16:32; 2 Kgs 11:18; 21:3, 4; Jer 11:13; 17:1, 2; Ezek 6:4, 5, 6, 13; 2 Chr 23:17; 33:3, 15; 34:4.

not in others (Josh 22:10-34;[84] Judg 2:2; 2 Chr 33:1). The Vulgate occasionally, however, maintains a distinction between legitimate and illegitimate altars contrasting *ara* and *altaria* in books where the LXX neglects any such distinction (Judg 6:25-31; 1 Kgs 16:32; 2 Kgs 11:18; 21:3, 4; 2 Chr 33:3, 15; 34:4; Ezek 6:4, 5, 6, 13; Hos 8:11; 10:2), while at times abandoning the distinction where one might expect it (1 Kgs 18:26; 2 Kgs 21:5; 2 Chr 14:2 [Lat 14:2-3]; 23:17; Hos 10:1).

Similarly, the Targumim's use of an alternate and negatively charged term for altar does not coincide with the Vulgate's use of its alternate term. In chapter eleven, this phenomenon among all three translated versions will be discussed at length. It appears, however, that although Jerome made use of this distinction at times, he did not apply this distinction systematically throughout his translation.

D.2. Other uses for *ara* and *altaria* in the Vulgate

The only term beside *mizbǝḥôt* for which *ara* is used as a translation in the Vulgate is *bāmôt*.[85] There are no other Hebrew terms besides *mizbǝḥôt* for which the Vulgate uses *altaria* as a translation. There are several verses, however, in which the Latin supplies the term *altaria* in a context in which the Hebrew either makes indirect reference to *mizbǝḥôt* or represents the noun with a pronominal suffix.[86] Jerome apparently did not understand the term *ḥammānîm*, for which one might expect the use of *altaria* or *ara*, as a type of altar.[87]

D.3. Synopsis of the Vulgate's understanding of *mizbǝḥôt*

The treatment of *mizbǝḥôt* in the Vulgate is similar to that in the LXX and the Targumim in that all three use two terms, one predominantly positive, and one negative, to translate the one Hebrew antecedent. Jerome is not entirely consistent in this division, however, just as not all LXX trans-

---

[84]Josh 22:16 choses to use the phrase *altare sacrilegum* rather than *ara* as a distinctive term for illegitimate altars.

[85]1 Kgs 14:23; 2 Kgs 17:11; 23:8; 2 Chr 14:4 [Lat 14:5]; 28:25. For further discussion, see the section above on Latin translations for *bāmôt* (pp. 306-12).

[86]Exod 29:43; 30:4, 6; Lev 6:15 [Lat 6:22]; 10:15; 1 Chr 21:30.

[87]Of the three terms used to translate *ḥammānîm*, one gives the impression that the translator was picturing a type of statue or image (*simulacrum*: Lev 26:30; 2 Chr 34:4; Ezek 6:4) while the remaining two give the impression of a shrine or sanctuary of some type (*fanum*: 2 Chr 14:4 [Lat 14:5]; *delubrum*: 2 Chr 34:7; Isa 17:8; 27:9; Ezek 6:6). There does not appear to be any consistency in these translations, even within the same chapter (see Ezek 6:4 and 6:6).

lators made use of this device. There are some verses in which a negative assessment of an altar is implied in the Hebrew, but for which Jerome does not use *ara* (as in Joshua 22). It is true, however, that every time *ara* is used, there is a contextual reason why the altar might be viewed in a negative manner.[88] Therefore, it can be stated that Jerome did use *ara* as a negative term for altar, but that he did not use this term in every context in which the LXX and Targumim felt the distinction was called for.

CONCLUSIONS

The Vulgate's witness to the objects of interest to this study shares many interpretive features with the LXX, and also with some early Jewish interpretation. The Vulgate shares with both the LXX and the Jewish sources the lack of recognition of the goddess ʾAsherah as well as the interpretative device of distinguishing altars from one another with regard to their relative sanctity. The Vulgate shares with the LXX the idea that the primary meaning of *bāmôt* needed to include the concept of "height," and that the use of terms for "sacred grove" should be used to translate *ăšērîm*. The Vulgate shares with certain Jewish sources the suggestion that the use of some *maṣṣēbôt* constituted idolatry.

On the subject of *maṣṣēbôt*, however, Jerome introduces a dual translation not found in the other versions. For *maṣṣēbôt*, Jerome uses two positive terms and two negative terms, the latter of which conveyed the idea that certain biblical standing stones were "likenesses" (*simulacra*) or "statues" (*statua*). The implied anthropo- or zoomorphism here is not strictly required by the Hebrew, nor is it reflected in the LXX understanding of *maṣṣēbôt* as στήλη. It is possible that Jerome was influenced by early Jewish opinion that the class of objects called *maṣṣēbôt* could properly include idols; however, this view did not influence the Targum translators to use a term for "statue" as their translation for *maṣṣēbāh*.[89] It appears that the dual evaluation of *maṣṣēbôt* in the Hebrew presented Jerome with an opportunity to nuance his translation of these items with both positive and negative terms; however, the decision to choose terms which imply that certain *maṣṣēbôt* were sculpted images constitutes more than a mere evaluation of some *maṣṣēbôt* negatively and some positively.

---

[88]Most of the references are to foreign, Baʿalistic, or illegitimate Israelite altars (Exod 34:13; Deut 7:5, 12:3; Judg 2:2; 6:25, 28, 30, 31; 1 Kgs 16:32; 2 Kgs 11:18; 21:3, 4; Jer 11:13; 17:1, 2; Ezek 6:4, 5, 6, 13; 2 Chr 23:17; 33:3, 15; 34:4). The remaining verses refer to the altars of Balaam, which, though apparently YHWHistic, were built in Moab by a non-Israelite (Num 23:1, 2, 4, 14, 29, 30).

[89]The predominant Targum rendering of *maṣṣēbāh* is *qāmāh/qāmtāʾ* which is a

In introducing the connection between condemned *maṣṣēbôt* and idols, Jerome is at once acknowledging the change of status visited upon these objects while at the same time explaining why they were condemned. The fact that *maṣṣēbôt* are connected with idols in this way may demonstrate a desire on Jerome's part to add additional condemnation of idol worship to his translation. Such condemnation would be in keeping with Christianity's historical animosity to Roman cults in which the veneration of statues played a crucial role, and so would constitute an example of "christianizing" in Jerome's translation similar to those identified by Brown and other scholars of Jerome.

Jerome stood farther outside the biblical time period than did the LXX or Targum translators. Consequently, Jerome's translation of the cultic items under discussion did not often seek to draw new parallels between their use in the idolatry of ancient Israel and cultic corruption in his own time. Jerome's audience was the Christian Church, by his day the dominant religious force in the formerly pagan Roman Empire. And although the supression of pagan practice and the destruction of pagan worship sites was still a very active enterprise in the fourth and early fifth centuries,[90] the production of biblical support for this effort through his translation work does not appear to have been an essential part of Jerome's mission. Jerome's primary task was to provide a translation for the Christian community which would be accurate, yet in continuity with the established interpretative traditions they had inherited from the LXX and the Old Latin.[91]

While it is possible that the interpretation of *ăšērîm* as groves underscored a pressing religious issue at the time of the translation of the LXX, it is not clear that this was a burning issue for Jerome's era. Jerome most likely adopted it because it had become the standard interpretation of *ăšērîm*, and also could be seen to be in agreement with Jewish interpretation. Similarly, Jerome adopted the standard LXX interpretations of *bāmôt* and *mizbəḥôt* in large part, apparently finding no need to modify them. Only in his treatment of *maṣṣēbôt* is Jerome's interpretation significantly differ-

---

near synonym to the Hebrew.

[90]See Johannes Geffcken, *The Last Days of Greco-Roman Paganism* (tr. Sabine MacCormack; Europe in the Middle Ages 8; Amsterdam: North-Holland Publishing; 1978) 155-222. See also section 16.10 of the *Codex Theodosianus* which discusses the suppression of paganism, "On Pagans, Sacrifices, and Temples;" *The Theodosian Code and Novels and the Sirmondian Constitutions* (tr. Clyde Pharr; Princeton: Princeton University Press, 1952) 472-76.

[91]Brown, *Vir Trilinguis*, 87-8.

ent from the LXX, and even for this departure, he has the support of certain Jewish sources. For whatever reason, Jerome acted on the opportunity directly to link *maṣṣēbôt* with idols in a way the LXX and even the Targumim did not. It may be, then, that for Jerome, the use of cultic statuary was of more interest than any of the other practices represented by the items of interest to this study, likely due to Christianity's historic conflict with Rome.

Chapter Eleven
The Targumim and Other Early Jewish Interpretation

INTRODUCTION

This chapter will explore the views of certain early Jewish interpreters concerning the cultic objects under discussion. Unlike the previous two chapters, however, which were based on materials found in the major translations of scripture from the Greek and Latin speaking communities respectively, this chapter will not confine itself to the views expressed in the Targumim. The reason will become clear as the discussion progresses. The linguistic similarity between the Hebrew of the Bible and the Aramaic of the Targumim presents a much different body of information than that which appears in the LXX or the Vulgate. With the exception of a few interpretative expansions, direct transcription or translation by cognate terms without comment is the most common type of Targumic reference to the objects of interest to this study.

Because of this characteristic of the Targumim, additional descriptions and opinions expressed concerning these objects in the early Midrashim and the Mishnah are vital to a fuller understanding of the early Jewish interpretation of them. Due to the vast scope of the early Jewish commentary on the Hebrew Bible, however, the following discussion will be limited to the views of only a selected group of witnesses from among the early rabbinic materials.

In choosing the materials for this chapter, the discussion is confined to the best preserved examples of early Jewish interpretation. Of the Targumim, the Pentateuch Targums of *Onqelos*,[1] *Codex Neofiti I*,[2] and *The*

---

[1] See Sperber, *Bible in Aramaic*, volume 1.

[2] A. Díez Macho, *Neophyti I: Targum Palestinense. MS de la Biblioteca Vaticana* (5 vols.; Madrid-Barcelona: Consejo Superior de Investigaciones Científicas, 1968-78). See also, Stephen A. Kaufman and Michael Sokoloff *A Key-word In-context Concordance to Targum Neofiti: A Guide to the Complete Palestinian Aramaic Text of the Torah* (Baltimore: Johns Hopkins University Press, 1993); Shirley Lund and Julia Foster, *Variant Versions of Targumic Traditions Within Codex Neofiti 1* (SBL Aramaic Studies 2: Missoula: Scholars Press, 1977); Martin McNamara, *Targum Neofiti 1: Genesis Translated, with Apparatus and Notes* (The Aramaic Bible 1a; Collegeville, Minn.: Michael Glazier/Liturgical, 1992).

Fragment Targums,[3] as well as *Targum Jonathan* to the prophets,[4] were chosen. An arbitrary cut-off date for inclusion was set at the end of the Late Roman period (fourth-fifth century C.E.).[5] When no early Targum of a particular book is extant, however, as in the case of Chronicles, later materials were consulted.[6] Certain early texts, however, such as the *Cairo Genizah Fragments* and the *Toseftot* were excluded from the discussion primarily in the interests of time and space, but also because of the relatively superior state of preservation of the witnesses which were chosen.[7]

In addition to the Targumim mentioned above, views from the Mishnah[8] and certain of the Tannaitic Midrashim were also included such as the two commentaries on Exodus, *Mekhilta de-Rabbi Ishmael*[9] and *Mekhilta de-Rabbi Shimon bar Yohai,*[10] *Sifre Deuteronomy,*[11] *Sifre Numbers,*[12] and *Sifra*

---

[3]Michael L. Klein, *The Fragment Targums of the Pentateuch According to their extant sources* (2 vols.; Analecta Biblica 76; Rome: Biblical Institute, 1980).

[4]Sperber, *Bible in Aramaic*, vols. 2 and 3. See also Kevin L. Cathcart and R. P. Gordon, *The Targum of the Minor Prophets* (The Aramaic Bible 14; Wilmington, Del.: Michael Glazier, 1989); Bruce Chilton, *The Isaiah Targum: Introduction, Translation, Apparatus and Notes* (The Aramaic Bible 11; Wilmington, Del.: Michael Glazier, 1987).

[5]*Pseudo-Jonathan* was excluded from the general discussion because of the ongoing debate concerning its date of composition. For more on *Pseudo-Jonathan*, see Philip S. Alexander "Targum, Targumim," *ABD* 6.322-23; and Michael Maher, *Targum Pseudo-Jonathan: Genesis Translated, with Introduction and Notes* (The Aramaic Bible 1b; Collegeville, Minn.: Michael Glazier/ Liturgical, 1992).

[6]Sperber, *Bible in Aramaic*, volume 4.

[7]For further discussion of the extant Targumim, their dating and relative states of preservation, see Alexander, "Targum," 320-31; Bernard Grossfeld, "Bible: Translations, Ancient Versions," *EncJud* 4.841-51; and Martin McNamara, *Targum and Testament: Aramaic Paraphrases of the Hebrew Bible: A Light on the New Testament* (Shannon: Irish University Press, 1972).

[8]Philip Blackman, *Mishnayoth* (7 vols.; Gateshead: Judaica Press, 1983).

[9]H. S. Horovitz and I. A. Rabin, ed. *Mechilta d'Rabbi Ismael* (Jerusalem: Wahrmann, 1970). See also, Jacob Neusner, *Mekhilta According to Rabbi Ishmael: An Analytical Translation* (2 vols.; Brown Judaic Studies 154; Atlanta: Scholars Press, 1988); Elaine A. Philips, "On Mekhilta d'Rabbi Ishmael: A study in Composition and Context," (Ph.D. diss., Annenberg Research Institute, 1991); Jakob Winter and August Wünsche, ed. *Mechiltha: Ein tannaitischer Midrasch zu Exodus* (Zürich: Georg Olms Verlag, 1990).

[10]J. N. Epstein and E. Z. Melamed, ed. *Mekhilta d'Rabbi Šim'on b. Jochai: Fragmenta in Geniza Cairensi reperta digessit apparatu critico, notis, praefatione instruxit* (Jerusalem: American Academy for Jewish Research, 1955).

[11]Louis Finkelstein, ed. *Sifre on Deuteronomy* (New York: Jewish Publication Society, 1969). See also Reuven Hammer, *Sifre: A Tannaitic Commentary on the Book of Deuteronomy* (Yale Judaica Series 24; New Haven: Yale University Press, 1986); Hans Bietenhard, *Sifre Deuteronomium* (Judaica et Christiana 8; Frankfurt am Main: Peter

on Leviticus.[13] While this is by no means the full extent of early Jewish interpretation it is a place to begin.[14]

As with both the LXX and Vulgate, the early Jewish interpreters were not always concerned with presenting an historically based assessment of what the objects under discussion in this study were in biblical times. Their work was seldom, if ever, motivated by such antiquarian interest. Rather, the Jewish interpreters shaped their treatment of these objects to issues relevant to their own time. At times this interpretation is in continuity with certain trajectories within biblical tradition; at other times it is discontinuous. The discussion below will endeavor to demonstrate the nature of this continuity and discontinuity so that the distinct views of the Jewish interpreters can be seen.

A. EARLY JEWISH INTERPRETATION CONCERNING *ăšērîm*

A.1. Targumic renderings

ăšērāh/ăšêrāh/ăšērtā/ăšêrtā: 39 out of 40 occurrences

One verse has a variant reading: Mic 5:13

The Targumim do not generally translate *ăšērāh* but rather transliterate the term wherever it occurs. William Reed has implied that this tendency signifies either that the Targumim felt the term needed no explanation or that they had no clear idea concerning *ăšērîm* and therefore did not

---

Lang, 1984).

[12]H. S. Horovitz, ed. *Siphre d'Be Rab. Fasciculus primus: Siphre ad Numeros adjecto Siphre zutta cum variis lectionibus et adnotationibus* (Leipzig: 1917, reprinted Jerusalem: Wahrmann, 1966). See also Dagmar Börner-Klein, *Midrasch Sifre Numeri: Voruntersucheungen zur Redaktionsgeschichte* (Judentum und Umwelt 39; Frankfurt am Main: Peter Lang, 1993).

[13]A. H. Weiss, ed. *Sifra de-Ve Rav* (Vienna: 1862). See also Jacob Neusner, *Sifra: An Analytical Translation* (3 vols.; Brown Judaic Studies 140; Atlanta: Scholar's Press, 1988); and *Sifra: Halachischer Midrasch zu Leviticus* (tr. Jacob Winter; Schriften der Gesellschaft zur Forderung der Wissenschaft des Judentums 42; Breslau: Stefan Munz, 1938).

[14]The relative dating of the Tannaitic Midrashim and the Mishnah, and the possible literary relationships between them is a topic of some debate, the essence of which is outside the subject of the present study. A good discussion can be found in Reuven Hammer's introduction to *Sifre Deuteronomy* (*Sifre*, 3-4).

venture a guess.[15] Regardless of this practice of transliteration, however, the Aramaic translators did, apparently, have a clear opinion concerning the nature of ăšērîm.

The Aramaic rendering of ăšērāh is אֲשֵׁירָה/אֲשֵׁרְה, for which Marcus Jastrow offers the following definition: "asherah, tree (grove) devoted to idolatry."[16] Although the references Jastrow cites in support of this interpretation are found in the Mishnah, Talmud, and late Midrashic commentary,[17] the interpretation of ăšērîm as trees also comes, at least in part, from the Targumim. The Targumim of Deut 16:21 read:

> *Targum Onqelos*:
>
> לא תיצב לך אשירת כל אילן בסטר מדבחא דיוי אלהך
>
> *Targum Neofiti*:
>
> לא תצבון לכון אשרה כל אילן סמיך למדבחה דייי אלהכון
>
> Do not plant for yourself an *ăšērāh* consisting of any tree next to the altar of YHWH your god.

In these translations, the Targumim remove the ambiguity between live trees and objects made of wood which is inherent in the Hebrew term עֵץ by translating it with the common Aramaic noun for "tree," indicating that they understood ăšērîm to be not simple wooden objects, but rather live trees.

Another passage which sheds some light on the Targumic understanding of ăšērîm is Targum Jonathan to Micah. Mic 5:13 is the only biblical verse mentioning ăšērîm for which the Targum has a distinctive reading. The MT of Mic 5:13 reads:

> וְנָתַשְׁתִּי אֲשֵׁירֶיךָ מִקִּרְבֶּךָ וְהִשְׁמַדְתִּי עָרֶיךָ׃

---

[15]*Asherah in the OT*, 6.

[16]Marcus Jastrow, *A Dictionary of the Targumim, the Talmud Babli and Yerushalmi, and the Midrashic Literature* (2 vols.; London: Luzac, 1903; reprinted, 2 vols. in one; Brooklyn: Traditional, 1975) 127. All citations from this work in the current study are from the reprinted edition.

[17]*'Ăbôdāh Zārāh* 3.5, 7; Talmud *Sûkkāh* 31b; Talmud *Pəsāḥîm* 27a; *Pirke de Rabbi Eliezer* 26 (Jastrow, *Dictionary*, 127). Jastrow's chapter reference to *Pirke de Rabbi Eliezer* is from the edition of Gerald Friedlander. Friedlander gives the original MS page and column numbers as 31a, ii; see *Pirkê de Rabbi Eliezer: (The Chapters of Rabbi Eliezer the Great) according to the Text of the Manuscript belonging to Abraham Epstein of Vienna* (tr. Gerald Friedlander; 4th ed.; New York: Sepher-Hermon, 1981) 187.

And I will uproot your *ăšērîm* from your midst
And I will destroy your cities.

In an example of the Targumic interpretative technique, which Michael L. Klein has identified as "converse translation,"[18] Targum Jonathan to Mic 5:13 changes the meaning of the verse. It reads:

ואעקר שתלי עממיא מבינך ואשיצי בעלי דבבך:

And I will uproot the planting of the nations from among you
And I will destroy your enemies.

Aside from the fact that the Targum has turned a judgment against the people into a declaration of God's intent to cleanse them from the corruption of enemies in their midst, this variant reading provides an additional depiction of *ăšērîm* which is complementary to the understanding of *ăšērîm* as trees found in the Targumim to Deut 16:21. According to this free rendering in Mic 5:13, *ăšērîm* either literally are, or represent, corrupting "foreign" influences "planted" within Israel. This image of corruption which is "planted" goes very nicely with the verb עקר, "to uproot."

The translations of Deut 16:21, and the free rendering of Mic 5:13, then, indicate that there was, at some level, an understanding among the Targum translators that *ăšērîm* were trees. Aside from the Targumim of Deut 16:21 and Mic 5:13, however, all the remaining references to *ăšērîm* in the Hebrew Bible are simply transliterated in the Targumim. This is the case even in passages in which images are made of or for the *ăšērāh* (1 Kgs 15:13; 2 Kgs 21:7), passages in which the meaning "tree" could be considered awkward. While this leaves open the possibility that the Targumim had more than one understanding of *ăšērîm*, or at least acknowledged that the Hebrew did, they offer no additional information about what that understanding might have been.

A.2. Midrashic and Mishnaic interpretations

The second aspect of *ăšērîm* noted by Jastrow, that *ăšērîm* were dedicated to idolatry, is specifically stated in the Midrashim *Sifre Deuteronomy* and *Sifra* (on Leviticus) and in the Mishnah tractate *ʿĂbôdāh*

---

[18]"Converse Translation: A Targumic Technique," *Biblica* 57 (1976) 515-37. See also idem, *Geniza Manuscripts of Palestinian Targum to the Pentateuch* (Cincinnati: Hebrew Union College Press, 1986) xxxi. The current author is indebted to Martin McNamara for his references to Klein's work (see McNamara's, *Neofiti*, 31).

Zārāh. While *Sifra* has relatively little to say on the subject of *ăšērîm* (owing, no doubt, to the fact that the term does not occur in Leviticus), *ʿĂbôdāh Zārāh* devotes five paragraphs to *ăšērîm* and the ritual considerations regarding contact with them or benefits derived from their use, and *Sifre Deuteronomy* contains many of the same opinions, but with some additional commentary. In addition to *ʿĂbôdāh Zārāh*, three other tractates make passing mention of *ăšērîm* (*ʿOrlāh*, *Sūkkāh*, and *Məʿîlāh*).

The passage which introduces the *Sifra* section entitled *Qədōšîm* begins its discussion with Lev 19:1-4, which, among other issues, touches upon the prohibition against idols.[19] In commenting on this biblical passage, *Sifra* lists ten objects as belonging to the practice of idolatry along with short axioms which use word play to explain how one can tell that they should be considered idolatrous. For instance, *ĕlîlîm* are said to be *ḥalul*, "empty," and *pəsîlîm*, *nipsal*, "invalid." *massēkôt* are suspect because one serves them with *nəsākîm*, "libations," and so on. In addition to these objects commonly thought of as idols, *maṣṣēbôt* are included as idolatrous because they must be made to stand (*ûmdîm*), as are *ḥammānîm* because they stand in the sun (*ḥammāh*), and *ăšērîm* because they make themselves rich or establish themselves (*mitʾašrîm*) through others.[20] This last interpretation about *ăšērîm*, while not making an explicit comment concerning what they were, does make clear the fact that, for this commentator, *ăšērîm* were included in the overall definition of what constituted idolatrous worship. It does not state that they actually were idols themselves, but it definitely does see the use of them as idolatrous.[21]

More detail concerning *ăšērîm* and their relation to idolatrous worship is set forth in *Sifre Deuteronomy* and the Mishnah tractate *ʿĂbôdāh Zārāh*, which, as noted, cover much of the same ground. Unlike the cursory mention of *ăšērîm* in *Sifra Qədōšîm*, both of these sources discuss *ăšērîm* at length, making it clear that they understand *ăšērîm* to be trees as well as features of idolatrous worship.

---

[19] *Sifra Qədōšîm* section ten, chapter 195; see the translation of Neusner, *Sifra*, 3.87-89.

[20] Neusner favors the translation "because they get rich through others," (*Sifra*, 89), while Jastrow prefers "because they are put up by others" (*Dictionary*, 130).

[21] A later midrash which draws some connection between *ăšērîm* and idolatry is *Pirke de Rabbi Eliezer*. In his translation, Gerald Friedlander notes that one passage in *PRE* (his chapter 26, original MS p. 31a, col. ii) states that Abraham despised idols and graven images. He also notes, however, that earlier editions read *ăšērîm* in place of idols in this passage (see Friedlander, *PRE*, 188 n. 2).

Ăbôdāh Zārāh 3:5 states that *ăšērîm*, in the sense of contact with them, use of their wood, or other benefits from them, are prohibited. The passage reads as follows:

העובדי גלולים העובדים את-ההרים ואת-הגבעות הן מותרין

If those who worship idols worship the mountains and the hills, they (the mountains and hills) are permitted (for use).

ומה-שעליהם אסורים, שנאמר לא תחמוד כסף וזהב עליהם ולקחת לך

But that which is upon them is prohibited (for use), as it is said, "You shall not covet the silver or gold which is upon them and take it for yourself." (Deut 7:25).

רבי יוסי הגלילי אומר אלהיהם על ההרים ולא ההרים אלהיהם

Rabbi Jose said, "Their gods are on the mountains," not "the mountains are their gods."

אלהיהם על הגבעות ולא הגבעות אלהיהם

"Their gods are on the hills" and not "the hills are their gods."

ומפני מה אשרה אסורא

And so, why is an *ăšērāh* prohibited (for use)?

מפני שיש-בה תפיסת ידי אדם, וכל-שיש-בה תפיסת ידי אדם אסור

Because human hands have had contact with it and everything which has had human hands in contact with it is prohibited (for use).[22]

אמר רבי עקיבא אני אובין ואדון לפניך, כל-מקום שאתה מוצא הר גבוה, וגבעה נשאה, ועץ רענן, דע שיש שם עבודת גלולים.

Rabbi Akiba said, "I will explain and expound this for you. In every place in which you find a high mountain, or a raised hill, or a leafy tree, know that there will be worship of idols there."[23]

---

[22]Presumably this refers not to any and all human hands, but specifically to the hands of those who worship idols.

[23]Blackman, *Mishnayoth*, 4. 463.

This passage reveals that for its compiler, *ăšērîm* and the *ʿēṣ raʿănān* were essentially equivalent. After posing the question, "Why is an *ăšērāh* prohibited," a comment of Rabbi Akiba's concerning the *ʿēṣ raʿănān* is cited. The compiler of this ruling, then, does not feel it necessary to distinguish between *ăšērîm* and the biblical *ʿēṣ raʿănān*. Biblical passages related to *ăšērîm* are not cited, nor is any attempt made to explain what the term *ăšērāh* meant. *ăšērîm* are depicted as the equivalent of the *ʿēṣ raʿănān* without any explanation of biblical passages which would not fit this interpretation. Moreover, the ruling assumes that wherever one finds the *ʿēṣ raʿănān*, or presumably, *ăšērîm* as well, one will find idols or idol worship.

Sifre Deuteronomy 60, which comments on Deut 12:2, quotes the same opinion of Rabbi Akiba, and also includes a continuation of the above quote of Rabbi Jose as well. Rabbi Jose's main teaching here is that it was not the trees themselves which were deities to the Canaanites. Hammer's translation renders Rabbi Jose's opinion as follows:

> R. Jose the Galilean says: One might think that if they worship mountains and hills you are commanded to destroy them, too. Hence the verse goes on to say, *Upon the high mountains, and upon the hills, and under every leafy tree* (12:2). Their gods are under the leafy trees, but the leafy trees themselves are not their gods; their gods are on high mountains, but the high mountains themselves are not their gods. Why then is the asherah forbidden? Because it is man's handiwork, and anything that is man's handiwork is forbidden.[24]

From Hammer's translation, "man's handiwork," one might infer that Rabbi Jose considered the *ăšērîm* to be constructed objects. It is more likely that by this phrase Rabbi Jose means that *ăšērîm* were subject to the continuous contact with those who put in the effort of planting and maintaining them.[25] Various types of contact with pagans are discussed in *ʿĂbôdāh Zārāh* as a whole. In addition to the laws concerning use of trees dedicated to idols, there are laws covering when one can resume dealings with pagans after their holy days (1:1-4), what one can sell pagans without contributing to their idolatry and its practices (1:5-9), what sort of food and lodging and contact through labor is appropriate between Jews and pagans (4:8-12; 5:1-

---

[24]Hammer, *Sifre*, 115. An abbreviated form of this opinion of Rabbi Jose is also quoted in *ʿĂbôdāh Zārāh* 3:5: "Rabbi Jose the Galilean says, *their gods upon the mountains* and not *the mountains are their gods, their gods on the hills* and not *the hills are their gods*" (Blackman, *Mishnayoth*, 4.463).

[25]This is the assumption of Blackman who elaborates in a paranthetical addition: "Because the hands of man had been concerned with it [in its planting and tending]," Blackman, *Mishnayoth*, 4.463.

12), how to dispose of idols one finds (3:1-3; 4:4-6), and when and how one can make use of a structure that used to house an idol (3:6-7). These passages make it clear that contact with pagan people and their belongings, of both an intimate and casual nature, was an issue with which the Rabbis were actively concerned.

There can be no doubt, given one additional point made in *Sifre Deuteronomy* 60, that this source clearly views *ʾăšērîm* as live trees. The first comment made in *Sifre Deuteronomy* 60 takes note of the intensive construction אַבֵּד תְּאַבְּדוּן found in Deut 12:2, asking: "Whence do we learn that if one cuts down an asherah and it grows back even ten times, one must cut it down each time? From the emphatic verb."[26] This opinion reveals a clear understanding of *ʾăšērîm* as actual live trees.

What both *ʿĂbôdāh Zārāh* and *Sifre Deuteronomy* are attempting to communicate is that the trees which served as *ʾăšērîm* for idolaters were not gods in and of themselves (such that one should destroy them, as Rabbi Jose states one might assume regarding mountains or hills if one thought they were being worshipped). Nevertheless, their benefits were not to be indulged in because they were known to be in constant contact with those who served idols in their immediate vicinity.

Another type of opinion regarding *ʾăšērîm* is shared by *Sifre Deuteronomy* 61 and *ʿĂbôdāh Zārāh* 3:7. This is the idea that there are three types of *ʾăšērîm*. For *ʿĂbôdāh Zārāh*, the three types of *ʾăšērîm* are: a tree which is planted specifically for idolatrous practices, a tree from which limbs are lopped off for idolatrous practices, a tree under which an idolater set up an idol.[27] *Sifre Deuteronomy* 61 repeats these same types of *ʾăšērîm*, attributing the classification to "the sages." This section of the Midrash goes on to state the opinion of Rabbi Eliezer that one must also uproot the *ʾăšērîm* in order to be in accordance with Deut 12:2 which states "you shall destroy their names," (which in the biblical passage could refer, either to the names of the gods of the nations, or the names of the nations themselves). It is possible, then, that Rabbi Eliezer saw uprooting *ʾăšērîm*, either as a way of totally destroying them, or as a way of eradicating the gods which were buried beneath them.[28]

In addition to the opinions it shares with *Sifre Deuteronomy* 61, *ʿĂbôdāh Zārāh* 3:7 goes on to quote an opinion concerning *ʾăšērîm* which appears to contradict the opinion of Rabbi Jose quoted in *Sifre*

---

[26]Hammer, *Sifre*, 115.
[27]Blackman, *Mishnayoth*, 4.465-6.
[28]Hammer, *Sifre*, 116.

Deuteronomy 60. When asked "What is an *ăšērāh*?," *'Ăbôdāh Zārāh* answers "Any [tree, understood] beneath which there is an idol," but goes on to
mention that Rabbi Simon (whose opinion is ultimately rejected) said "any
[tree, understood] which they worship." *'Ăbôdāh Zārāh* then relates this
story:

> It once happened in Sidon that they used to worship a tree and they found
> underneath it a heap. Rabbi Simon said to them 'Examine this heap,' and when
> they examined it they found an image. He said to them, 'Since it is the *image* that
> the idolaters used to worship we permit them [namely the local Jews to make use
> of] the tree.[29]

Apparently the fact that the idol was present proved that it was not the tree
which was being worshipped and so, in this case, the tree was allowed for
use. This corresponds to *Sifre Deuteronomy* 61, that the idol must be
removed before the tree could be used.[30]

'Ăbôdāh Zārāh has additional instructions concerning under what circumstances use might be made of a tree which was considered to be an
ăšērāh. Chapter 3:8 states that neither humans nor the vegetables they plant
are to take benefit from the shade given by an *ăšērāh*. Humans are not to sit
in or pass through its shade unless the shade is cast some distance from the
tree or over a public thoroughfare. Plants are allowed by some authorities to
be planted beneath an *ăšērāh* in the rainy season in that the shade is not a
benefit at this time. Rabbi Jose, however, points out that even then the
leaves which fall benefit the plants below by fertilizing them and therefore
no planting should ever take place beneath an *ăšērāh*.[31]

'Ăbôdāh Zārāh 3:9 states that no benefit may be obtained even from
the wood of an *ăšērāh*. It may not be used for cooking because any food
made in this way is contaminated. If a new oven is heated for the first time
with *ăšērāh* wood, it must be dismantled, while a previously used oven in
which *ăšērāh* wood has been burned can be purified again simply by cool-
ing it. Additionally, if *ăšērāh* wood is used to make a shuttle for a loom, no
garment made on it can be used. Finally, *'Ăbôdāh Zārāh* 3:10 states that an
ăšērāh can be "desanctified" with regard to pagan practices if an idolater
trims it, prunes it, or breaks branches off, unless, of course, he or she should
be doing this to better the health of the tree or to improve its appearance.[32]

---

[29]Blackman, *Mishnayoth*, 4.465-6.
[30]Hammer, *Sifre*, 116.
[31]Blackman, *Mishnayoth*, 4.466.
[32]Blackman, *Mishnayoth*, 4.467-68.

The three tractates that mention *ăšērîm* only in passing reinforce *ʿĂbôdāh Zārāh*'s rulings concerning the use of *ʿăšērîm* and their by-products. *ʿOrlāh* 1:7-8 (which discusses the three years of fallow time allowed new trees before their produce can be used) excludes *ăšērîm* from such trees.[33] *Sūkkāh* 3:1-3 pointedly excludes *ăšērîm* from the trees whose branches can be collected to make the *lūlāb* for the Festival of Sukkoth.[34] *Məʿîlāh* 3:8, however, allows birdnests to be collected from *ăšērîm* by ruling that removing them does not violate any rules of sanctity which might apply to a tree which was otherwise dedicated for some ritual purpose.[35] Apparently the nest was not considered to be a direct by-product of the tree itself.

In addition to the opinions concerning *ăšērîm* which it shares with *ʿĂbôdāh Zārāh*, *Sifre Deuteronomy*, in chapter 145, gives some additional information in its commentary on Deut 16:21. From this passage, the midrash explains that not only is planting an *ăšērāh* a transgression of a negative commandment, but the planting of any tree on the Temple Mount is also a violation of this commandment because the verse says you should not plant any tree near the altar of the Lord your God.[36] This section also continues the understanding that *ăšērîm* were trees, as it reasons that when Deut 12:3 says one should burn existing *ăšērîm* with fire one could logically reason that one should never plant one, and that when verses such as Deut 16:21 state that one should not plant an *ăšērāh* they also mean that one should not allow an existing *ăšērāh* to remain planted, meaning one should uproot existing *ăšērîm*.[37]

A.3. Synopsis of early Jewish interpretation concerning *ăšērîm*

The predominant opinion among the early Jewish commentators was that *ăšērîm* were trees, and more specifically, trees devoted to idolatry. This is clearest in the relevant portions of the Mishnah and midrashim, but it may also be inferred from the Targumim, although this evidence is at points ambiguous. There is a difference of opinion among the Rabbis whether the

---

[33]Blackman, *Mishnayoth*, 1.446-47.

[34]Blackman, *Mishnayoth*, 2.327-29.

[35]Blackman, *Mishnayoth*, 5.447.

[36]The view that Deut 16:21 constitutes a prohibition against planting a tree in the Temple compound is said by Blackman to be the view of Deut 16:21 as it is listed among the rabbinic *Taryag Mitzvot*, the 613 commandments derived from the Torah. The *Taryag* list, however, simply repeats the Hebrew of the verse. Blackman, *Mishnayoth*, 7.71, 78, 87.

[37]Hammer, *Sifre*, 184.

trees themselves were objects of worship, or simply provided the locus for idolatrous worship. There does not seem to be any overt suggestion among the Jewish commentators that *ăšērîm* were anything other than actual live trees, such as shrines, or statues, or even poles. Nor is there any rabbinic discussion which entertains the notion of legitimate *ăšērîm*, whether in biblical times or during the time of the Rabbis. The understanding of *ăšērîm* as trees used for idolatrous worship has apparently been completely leveled through the early Jewish sources.

In light of the fact that the LXX leveled through a similar understanding of *ăšērîm* by the time of its formulation circa 200 BCE, one might posit that the Rabbis were following the interpretative lead of the LXX translators in their understanding of *ăšērîm*. As noted in the previous chapter on the LXX, however, the concept of a "grove" is not identical to the concept of a singular tree beneath which one might find an idol buried. While the LXX and the early Jewish interpreters cited in this chapter certainly had a common concern about idolatry and its contaminating influence, the Rabbis appear to focus less on the institution of the "sacred grove" as it appeared in the Hellenistic and Roman eras, and more on individual trees maintained by pagans and featuring somehow in their religion.

The similarity between the interpretations of *ăšērîm* in the LXX and in the early Jewish sources rests mainly in the identification of *ăšērîm* as trees devoted to a foreign deity. It is most likely that both these traditions shared a common early Jewish interpretation of *ăšērîm* (perhaps based on Deut 16:21) and each tradition simply chose to depict this concept in a manner which communicated best to their own particular audiences. In both the Hellenistic and rabbinic eras, idolatry appears to be a major concern for Jewish communitites.[38] The fact that rabbinic opinion discusses *ăšērîm* as a feature of idolatrous worship gives a clear indication of what the most important issue related to *ăšērîm* was for the Rabbis. Their concern was not for any identification of biblical *ăšērîm*, but rather the inclusion within the full definition of idolatry of a certain pagan religious practice involving trees with which they were apparently familiar.

The rabbinic concern about idolatry is a function of the continuous challenge of Jewish life under Roman and other foreign domination in the Diaspora. How one was to avoid contact with idols and idol worship appears to have been a major problem for Diaspora Jews as witnessed by sources such as *ʿĂbôdāh Zārāh*. The challenge of living alongside pagan

---

[38]See chapter ten for discussions of Jerome's possible concern regarding idol use in his era (pp. 298-306, 314-16).

people and within pagan society required guidance for everyday life on a wide variety of subjects generally related to whether certain types of contact with pagans constituted undue contact with their gods. Contact with the trees under which pagans bury their idols is only one of many such issues.

The Rabbis do not appear to question whether labeling such trees as *ăšērîm* is true to the biblical depictions of *ăšērîm*. The name *ăšērîm* and biblical injunctions against *ăšērîm* are simply applied to the trees devoted to idols with which the Rabbis are concerned. In this way, the Rabbis evidence both continuity and discontinuity with the biblical depiction of *ăšērîm*. They retain the view of *ăšērîm* as live trees suggested by Deut 16:21, yet they appear to merge the biblical *ăšērîm* with the biblical *ēṣ ra'ănān* and other trees such as the landmark tree in Gen 35:4. *ʿĂbôdāh Zārāh* 3:7 describes an example of an *ăšērāh* from Sidon which sounds very similar to the tree in Gen 35:4. The tree of Gen 35:4, however, is not referred to as an *ăšērāh* in the biblical text, but the early Jewish interpreters equate *ăšērîm* with this type of tree. The rabbinic treatment of *ăšērîm*, then, essentially subsumes discussion of them under the rubric of idolatrous worship.

B. EARLY JEWISH INTERPRETATION CONCERNING *maṣṣēbôt*

B.1. Targumic renderings

qāmāʾ/qāmtāʾ: 34 out of 35 occurrences

One verse contains a contextually specific reading: Isa 6:13[39]

The standard Targumic rendering of the biblical Hebrew term *maṣṣēbôt* is קָמְתָא/קָמָא, which is used to translate not only *maṣṣēbôt*, but also *nəṣîb* which means "pillar" (*Targum Onqelos* of Gen 19:26) and *qāmāh*, which means "standing grain."[40] The term for *maṣṣēbôt* used by *Neofiti* and

---

[39]In this unusual verse which likens a *maṣṣēbāh* to a tree stump, the Targum of Isaiah uses נצבתהון for מצבתה, and expands the verse to make clear that it refers to the future return of Israel from exile. For a discussion of this expansion, see Chilton, *Isaiah Targum*, 15.

[40]*Targum Onqelos* of Exod 22:5; *Targum Jonathan* of Judg 15:5f; *Targum Jonathan* of Hos 8:7. *qāmāʾ* also occurs in the later text of *Targum Pseudo-Jonathan* of Num 22:24 where the Hebrew has גְּדֵר, which means "wall." It is possible that the presence of *qāmāʾ* in this verse is the result of an acoustic confusion with חוֹמָה, meaning "wall." *Targum Jonathan* of Judg 9:6 also uses *qāmāh* in the passage about the "standing oak" of Shechem, perpetuating the obliqueness of any possible reference to a *maṣṣēbāh* in

The Fragment Targums is the related term קיימא.[41] Regardless of which term is employed by the various Targumim, each appears to be consistent in their use of their respective translations, employing them in all cases where the biblical text reads *maṣṣēbôt*.

One interesting expansion, however, can be found in the Targum Jonathan of Hos 3:4. Below the verse is presented with the material added to or altered from the MT in bold print:

ארי יומין סגיאין יתבון בני ישראל לית מלכא **מדבית דויד ולית דעביר שולטן על ישראל** ולית דדבח **לרעוא בירושלם** ולית קמתא **בשומרון** ולית אפוד **ומחוי:**

For the people of Israel shall dwell many days with no King **from the house of David and with no one to exercise authority over Israel and no one to offer an acceptable** sacrifice in Jerusalem and no *maṣṣēbāh* in Samaria, no ephod and **no interpreters.**[42]

By spliting the parallelism in this passage into two descriptions, one of worship in Jerusalem and the other of worship in Samaria, the Targum locates the use of *maṣṣēbôt* within the questionable worship practices of the northern kingdom. Unlike the MT, in which this verse leaves the prophet's evaluation of *maṣṣēbôt* open to question, the Targum makes a negative evaluation of *maṣṣēbôt* clear by contrasting their use to acceptable sacrificial practice and linking them with Samaria. What might have been understood as a contrast between acceptable and unacceptable social institutions *within* Israel has become a contrast between the southern and northern kingdoms with the latter evaluated negatively.

B.2. Midrashic and Mishnaic interpretations

As noted above, the introduction to *Sifra Qədōšîm* on Lev 19:1-4 mentions *maṣṣēbôt* in its discussion of idolatrous practices, stating that

---

the passage. See Jastrow, *Dictionary*, 1383b.

[41]For references from *Neofiti*, see Kaufman and Sokoloff, *Concordance*, 1193-97. In *Neofiti*, two other related terms also occur, the adjective קיים meaning "enduring," and the noun קיים meaning "covenant" (p. 1205). Perhaps the frequent use of patriarchal *maṣṣēbôt* to mark occasions of covenant with an enduring monument influenced the consistency with which *Neofiti* chose קיימה to translate *maṣṣēbāh*. The term קיימתהון for "their *maṣṣēbôt*" is only preserved in *The Fragment Targums* of Exod 23:24. No other verses mentioning *maṣṣēbôt* are preserved in this source.

[42]The MT here reads *tərāpîm*. For the text of this passage see Sperber, *Bible in Aramaic*, 3.390. For a discussion, see Cathcart and Gordon, *Minor Prophets*, 35.

maṣṣēbôt are of a type with idols because they must be made to stand.[43] This midrash is repeated in *Sifra Behar* in the section which comments on Lev 26:1. The only additional comment on the subject of *maṣṣēbôt* in this passage is the statement that *maṣṣēbôt*, like idols, are unacceptable because they are manufactured.[44] It is unclear if *Sifra* actually means us to understand that *maṣṣēbôt* were themselves idols, or simply that they, like idols, were inert manufactured objects whose veneration constituted idolatrous worship.

Jerome, however, appears to have arrived at the understanding that *maṣṣēbôt* were idols, and it is possible that he derived this understanding from rabbinic opinions such as those in *Sifra*.[45] The LXX does not evidence this opinion, which makes it impossible to argue that Jerome's interpretation is dependent upon the LXX. As has been argued in the previous chapter on the Vulgate, it is most likely that the existence of rabbinic opinion linking *maṣṣēbôt* with idolatry reinforced Jerome's own hermeneutical goals. Jerome's primary goal was to create a translation specifically for Latin Christianity. The historic struggle between the early Church and the religion of the Roman Empire may have inspired Jerome to read with rabbinic opinion with regard to *maṣṣēbôt* and against the LXX.

One source which appears to find *maṣṣēbôt* and idols analogous, though perhaps not identical objects, is *Sifre Deuteronomy* 146 on Deut 16:22. In this section, the midrash notes that the prohibition against *maṣṣēbôt* in Deut 16:22 applies only to *maṣṣēbôt*, but then asks how one might reason that this prohibition also applies to idols. Hammer translates the paragraph as follows:

> *Neither shalt thou set thee up a pillar* (16:22): This refers only to a pillar [*maṣṣēbāh*]. Whence do we learn that this applies also to an idol? It is a matter of logic: if pillars, which were favored by the Patriarchs, are to be an abomination to the children, idols, which were an abomination to the Patriarchs, should certainly be an abomination to the children.[46]

Aside from the result of declaring *maṣṣēbôt* to be illicit, this section appears more interested in the use of logic to apply a law regarding one object to another even though it does reveal certain views held by the commentator. The commentator apparently saw *maṣṣēbôt* and idols as similar objects in

---

[43]Neusner, *Sifra*, 3.89.

[44]*Sifra Behar*, chapter 259.2, section 9. See Neusner, *Sifra*, 3.343-44.

[45]See chapter ten (pp. 294, 314f.), on Jerome's use of rabbinic materials.

[46]Hammer, *Sifre*, 185.

that they were both prohibited, but at the same time the commentator reveals the view that *maṣṣēbôt* are less objectionable than idols because they were once favored by the patriarchs. If these objects, then, which were once good are now bad, how much worse are idols which were always considered bad. There is no attempt, however, to explain why *maṣṣēbôt* became an "abomination to the children." The fact that they did is simply noted.

The fact that *maṣṣēbôt* are not specifically discussed in the Mishnah, even in tractates such as *'Ăbôdāh Zārāh* which deal extensively with idolatry may indicate that *maṣṣēbôt* were not objects of pressing concern for the Rabbis. Various types of stones which were prohibited are touched upon, but in all cases, these are stone bases upon which idols stood (*'Ăbôdāh Zārāh* 3:7) or which formed the base of pagan monuments (*'Ăbôdāh Zārāh* 4:1). No connection is drawn between them and biblical *maṣṣēbôt*. However, Lev 26:1 and Deut 16:22, which instruct Israel not to erect *maṣṣēbôt*, are listed as two of the *Taryag Mitzvot*. When translating the verses and listing their import, Blackman reiterates the view that *maṣṣēbôt* were prohibited because they were viewed as idolatrous.[47] The original list, however, does not elaborate on the Hebrew of the verses.

B.3. Synopsis of Early Jewish interpretation concerning *maṣṣēbôt*

According to the Targumim, *maṣṣēbôt* were simply standing stones described with a term derived from the verb *qwm* which accurately translates the biblical term derived from the verb *nṣb*. There is no further interpretation concerning the nature of *maṣṣēbôt* in the Targumim. Other early Jewish sources, however, associate *maṣṣēbôt* with idols, drawing conclusions that the laws regarding one also apply to the other. This indicates either that the sources saw *maṣṣēbôt* as a type of idol or that they viewed *maṣṣēbôt* as part of a complex of worship features which involved idolatry as its predominant practice. *Sifre Deuteronomy* notes that *maṣṣēbôt* were once approved by the patriarchs, and so were not as completely negatively charged as idols; however, like *'ăšērîm*, *maṣṣēbôt* were viewed by the Jewish commentators as objects whose only purpose was the practice of idolatry and as such they were disapproved. As in the case of *'ăšērîm*, the Rabbis seem less concerned with standing stones *per se* (even though the use of standing stones in neighboring cultures continued through the rabbinic era[48]) than with idolatry in the broadest sense.

---

[47]Blackman, *Mishnayoth*, 7.84, 87.

[48]For example, see Graesser ("Studies in *maṣṣēbôt*," 114-24), for a discussion of Phoenician *betyls*.

One point of continuity between early Jewish interpretation of *maṣṣēbôt* and biblical interpretation is that, in Lev 26:1, the Holiness Code lists *maṣṣēbôt* among types of idols as if they were a type of idol themselves.[49] In keeping with this view of Leviticus, the midrashic commentary *Sifra* twice recounts the opinion that the use of *maṣṣēbôt* constitutes idolatry. Lacking any other extensive comment on *maṣṣēbôt* in the rabbinic material, *Sifra*'s view of *maṣṣēbôt* as idolatrous has secured a singular position among Jewish commentary, representing the strand of biblical interpretation on *maṣṣēbôt* likely originating in the Holiness Code.

C. EARLY JEWISH INTERPRETATION CONCERNING *bāmôt*

C.1. Targumic renderings

bāmāh: 50 out of 84 occurrences

bāmāsāʾ: 15 out of 84 occurrences

bêt ʾasḥārûtāʾ: 7 out of 84 occurrences

rāmāh: 6 out of 84 occurrences

bêt kəništāʾ: 1 out of 84 occurrences

miqdaš: 1 out of 84 occurrences

Four verses have variant readings, Mic 1:5; 3:12; Jer 17:3; 26:18

Despite the fact that the Targumim have much more variation in their translations of *bāmôt* than they have in their translations of *ʾăšērîm*, *maṣṣēbôt*, or *mizbəḥôt* (see below), בָּמָה remains the most common translation of the biblical term *bāmôt*, either as the cultic installation or as part of a place name, in the early Jewish sources. Jastrow defines בָּמָה as the "name of the legitimate altars prior to, and of the illegitimate after the establishment of a central sanctuary (at Shiloh) and of the Temple at Jerusalem; temporary or improvised altar."[50]

---

[49]For further discussion, see chapter seven under the heading of *maṣṣēbôt* and cultic statuary, pp. 219-21.

[50]Jastrow cites *Zəbāḥîm* 14.4-8; *Tosefta Zəbāḥîm* 13:17; and *Məgillāh* 1.10 (*Dictionary,* 176). Apparently unrelated to בָּמָה is the term בִּימָה which is used for

bmh is the term chosen in the Targumim in 50 of the 84 biblical occurrences of *bāmôt*. It is found throughout the Targumim of Leviticus and Numbers (with the exception of *Neofiti* and *The Fragment Targums* which choose *bms*),[51] 1-2 Kgs, Amos, Hosea, Isaiah, and Ezekiel. It is also used in the Targum of Jeremiah in four out of six instances, and as part of a place name in Josh 13:17.[52] In the case of the other place names, all of which are in Numbers, *Onqelos* regularly substitutes the term *rāmāh*, meaning "height," while *Neofiti* and *The Fragment Targums* contain variant translations.[53] The second most frequent term used to translate *bāmôt* in the

---

"elevated stands used for public meetings," Jastrow, *Dictionary*, 162.

[51]The only references to cultic *bāmôt* in the Pentateuch are Lev 26:30 and Num 33:52. In both of these verses *Neofiti* reads the variation *bms/byms* which is apparently derived from the Greek βωμός (*Neofiti* Lev 26:30 = *bmsykwn* "your altars;" *Neofiti* Num 33:52 = *bymsyhwn* "their altars"). None of the manuscript traditions of *The Fragment Targums* have extant renderings of Lev 26:30, but Num 33:52 reads *bmsyhwn* in all the manuscript traditions of these Targumim. *Neofiti* uses *bmsyh* also in Deut 32:13 as a translation for Hebrew *bāmôtê*. *Neofiti* and *The Fragment Targums* are not the only Targumim which translate *bāmôt* with *bms/byms*. This is also the predominant translation in the *Targum to Chronicles* (see discussion below, p. 335). The only time that *Neofiti* uses the term *bmt* is in its translation of place names in Num 21:28 and 22:41. *The Fragment Targums* use this lexeme only as part of the term *bāmôtê* in Deut 32:13 and 29, and in the place name Bamoth in Num 21:20. See note 53 below for a discussion of these place names in *Neofiti* and *The Fragment Targums*.

[52]The exceptions to the use of *bmh* for *bāmah* in the Targumim of Jeremiah and Micah are as follows. *Targum Jonathan* of Jer 17:3 mirrors the previous Targum translation of the parallel verse, Jer 15:13, in which the Hebrew has *bimḥîr* rather than *bāmôtêkā*. Targum of Mic 1:5b changes the Hebrew's rather dissimilar parallelism between *peša᾿ ya῾ăqōb* and *bāmôt yəhûdāh* to the parallelism found in 1:5a, *peša᾿ ya῾ăqōb* and *ḥaṭṭā᾿t yəhûdāh*. Finally, like the LXX, the Targum of Micah 3:12, (which is quoted exactly in the Targum of Jer 26:18) translates the phrase *bāmôt yā῾ar* with חורשת חורשא, which means "thicket of bushes." The LXX has ἄλσος δρυμοῦ, which means "grove of thickets." For the Targum texts of these passages, see Sperber, *Bible in Aramaic*, 3.196, 444.

[53]*Neofiti* the *The Fragment Targums* vary from *Onqelos* as follows: Num 21:19, *Onqelos*: *rāmātā᾿*, *Neofiti*: *ryš ṭwryh*, *The Fragment Targums*: *ryšy ṭwry᾿* "the tops of the mountains;" Num 21:20, *Onqelos*: *rāmātā᾿*, *Neofiti*: *r᾿šy ṭwryyh rm<y>h*, "the tops of the high mountains," *The Fragment Targums*: *bmwt*; Num 21:28; *Onqelos*: *rāmtā᾿*, *Neofiti*: *bmth*, *The Fragment Targums*: *ṭ῾wwt d᾿rnwn᾿*, "abominations/idols of Arnon;" Num 22:41, *Onqelos*: *ramat*, *Neofiti*: *bmth*, *The Fragment Targums* are not extant. What appears in *Neofiti* and *The Fragment Targums* of Num 21:19-20 are a series of puns and expositions on the place names, Mattanah, Nahaliel, and Bamoth. Beginning in v.18 the passage reads: "and from the wilderness *they were given a gift* (*ytyhybt lhwn mtnh*) . . . and after they had been given the gift, it became *torrential streams* for them (*nhlyn štpyn*) . . . and after it became torrential streams for them, it began to ascend with them *to*

Targumim is the Greek loan word *bāmāsā'*, derived from *βωμός*. *bāmāsā'* occurs 15 times in the *Targum to Chronicles* (as well as twice in *Neofiti* and once in *The Fragment Targums* as noted above), in contexts where the other Targumim have *bāmāh*. In the *Targum to Chronicles*, however, a distinction is maintained between those later *bāmôt* which are condemned and the approved *bāmāh* of Gibeon. Only those *bāmôt* which are condemned are referred to by the term *bāmāsā'*. The Gibeon installation is called a *bêt kəništā'*, "meeting house" in the Targum of 1 Chr 16:39. In the Targum of 1 Chr 21:29 it is called a *miqdaš*, and in the Targum of 2 Chr 1:3 and 13 it is called a *rāmâ* "height." These variations reveal the translator's desire to distance the Gibeon traditions even further from the taint of unorthodoxy than the biblical Chronicler had done by never once calling the installation at Gibeon a *bāmāh*. To distinguish this accepted site from others which were condemned, the translator chooses different translations for the Gibeon installation, but for this installation alone among all *bāmôt* mentioned in Chronicles.

Another creation for one particular context is the third most frequent translation for *bāmôt*. *Targum Jonathan* of 1 Samuel uses the term *bêt 'ašārûtā'*, "banqueting hall," to translate *bāmāh* in the passages in which Samuel presides over a sacrifice at a *bāmāh* and where Saul meets a band of prophets coming down from a *bāmāh* (1 Sam 9:12, 13, 14, 19, 25; 10:5, 13). This term, *bêt 'ašārûtā'*, is also used as the translation of *liškâ* in 1 Sam 9:22. This translation, reserved for the *bāmôt* of Samuel's time, appears to be an attempt on the part of the translator to distance this venerated person from association with *bāmôt*, not unlike what the Targumic translator of Chronicles did with the Gibeon installation.

This translation of *Targum Jonathan*, however, does not recur in passages that deal with the Gibeon installation. This *bāmāh* remains a *bāmāh* in *Targum Jonathan*, perhaps because Solomon's reign would eventually be tainted by his later association with the *bāmôt* which he built for the gods of his wives after his connection with the Gibeon *bāmāh*. Samuel, however, could be absolved from this association by the rendering of *bāmôt* related to him with another term, which the translator has apparently done. Martin McNamara has pointed out that euphemistic translations aimed at showing respect for the ancestors occur at various points in the Targumim.[54] It is

---

mountain tops" (*lryšy ṭwry'*). For this passage in *The Fragment Targums*, see Klein, *Fragment Targums*, 1.101, 2.72.

[54]*Neofiti*, 32. See also idem, *Targum and Testament: Aramaic Paraphrases of the Hebrew Bible: A Light on the New Testament* (Shannon: Irish University Press, 1972) 74. In support of this statement, McNamara also cites the work of Michael L. Klein. See

quite possible that the examples of variant translations of *bāmôt* listed above should be added to this category in that all of them appear to function as a buffer between a famous personage (or institution) and a *bāmāh*.

The only remaining term used to translated *bāmôt* is *rāmāh*, which occurs 6 out of 84 times in the Targumim. It is used by the *Targum to Chronicles* twice to describe the *bāmāh* of Gibeon (2 Chr 1:3 and 13), and by the *Targum Onqelos* of Numbers in place names which contain the term *bāmôt* (Num 21:19, 20, 28; 22:41).[55]

In addition to the choices of terminology used to translate *bāmôt*, which reveal some of the views of *bāmôt* held by the Targum translators, other verses contain expansions or modifications which provide additional information. For instance, the MT of Isa 16:12 reads:

וְהָיָה כִי־נִרְאָה כִּי־נִלְאָה מוֹאָב עַל־הַבָּמָה וּבָא אֶל־מִקְדָּשׁוֹ לְהִתְפַּלֵּל וְלֹא יוּכָל׃

And it will come to pass when Moab appears and wearies himself on the *bāmāh*, then he will go to his sanctuary to pray but it will accomplish nothing.

In this passage, *bāmāh* is in parallelism with *miqdāšô*, implying simply that *bāmôt* were places where Moabites worshipped. Targum Jonathan of Isa 16:12 adds a nuance to this verse, however, by replacing *miqdašô* with *bêt ṭaʿûtêh*. The whole verse from the Targum reads:

ויהי ארי יהלי ארי ילאי מואב על במתא וייעול לבית טעותיה למבעי ולא יכול׃

And it will come to pass when Moab is tired and wearies himself upon the *bāmôt* and he comes to the house of his idol to beseech, he will not prevail.[56]

The substitution of "the house of his idol" for "his sanctuary" results in a parallel not simply between *bāmôt* and places of worship, but between *bāmôt* and places of idol worship.

Klein's *Genizah Manuscripts of Palestinian Targum to the Pentateuch* ([Cincinnati: Hebrew Union College Press, 1986] 1.xxxii), as well as his article, "The Translation of Anthropomorphisms and Anthropopathisms in the Targumim," in *Congress Volume: Vienna 1980* (ed. J. A. Emerton; VTSup 32; Leiden: E. J. Brill, 1981) 162-77; and *Anthropomorphisms and Anthropopathisms in the Targumim of the Pentateuch* (Jerusalem: Makor, 1981).

[55]As mentioned above in note 53, *Neofiti* and *The Fragment Targums* vary widely from the other Targumim in their translation of these place names.

[56]Chilton, *Isaiah Targum*, 35. The term used for "idol" in this passage (טעות) comes from the root טעה and literally means "error" (Jastrow, *Dictionary*, 542).

C.2. Midrashic and Mishnaic interpretations

Sifra Behuqotai on Lev 26:30[57] makes no additional comment on this verse's prediction of the destruction of *bāmôt* other than to state that the verse should be taken literally. The Mishnah tractate *Zəbāḥîm*, however, contains five paragraphs which discuss *bāmôt* and which offer an explanation of why *bāmôt* were once approved and then later prohibited. *Zəbāḥîm* 14:4 explains that *bāmôt* were allowed prior to the establishment of the Tabernacle, but prohibited thereafter. 14:5 states that *bāmôt* were allowed again once the tribes arrived in Gilgal with only the most holy sacrifices being restricted to the Tabernacle. 14:6 explains that *bāmôt* were once again prohibited when the shrine at Shiloh was constructed, and 14:7 states that after the destruction of Shiloh and the retreat to Nob, *bāmôt* were once again allowed and that Gibeon is an example of such *bāmôt*. Finally, 14:8 states that once the Temple in Jerusalem was constructed the *bāmôt* were prohibited, never to be permitted again.[58] This interpretation is essentially a merging of the centralization concerns of Dtr and P. It projects Dtr's rejection of *bāmôt* which competed with the Temple back into the time period of P's Tabernacle. In this way it can be seen as a continuation of the strand of interpretation on *bāmôt* begun by Dtr.

Further comment concerning the biblical *bāmôt* and their rituals occurs in *Məgillāh* 1.10. This passage states that the only difference in ritual between a small or local *bāmāh* (*bāmāh qəṭannāh*) and a large or national one (*bāmāh gədôlāh*), like the one at Gibeon, was that the Passover sacrifice could be offered only on a larger one.[59]

One additional type of reference to *bāmôt* occurs in *Mənāḥôt* 13:10. This passage uses the exclusion of *bāmôt* priests from service in the Temple described in 2 Kgs 23:9 as the basis for negative comparisons between offerings made or vows fulfilled at the Egyptian temple to YHWH built by Onias IV. The passage also states, based on 2 Kgs 23:9, that the priests who have served at the temple of Onias may not serve at the Temple of Jerusalem. What is interesting here is that this law is also said to apply even

---

[57]Section 6, chapter 267.2; Neusner, *Sifra*, 3.368.

[58]Blackman, *Mishnayoth*, 5.91-93. Chapters 14.9-10 discuss the relative sanctity of the various offerings made at *bāmôt* as opposed to those made in the Tabernacle or Temple (Blackman, *Mishnayoth*, 5.93-94). Mishnah tractate *Məgillāh* 1:10 discusses a distinction between a large *bāmāh* (בָּמָה גְדוֹלָה) and a small *bāmāh* (בָּמָה קְטַנָּה), indicating which type of Passover sacrifices were appropriate to each (Blackman, *Mishnayoth*, 2.445).

[59]Blackman, *Mishnayoth*, 2.445.

more strongly to idolatrous priests.[60] Apparently the Rabbis recognized that
the Onias temple was dedicated to YHWH, and thus afforded it a kinder
treatment than idolatrous temples even though it was in competition with
the Jerusalem Temple. The use of 2 Kgs 23:9 as the basis for this ruling may
indicate that the Rabbis recognized that the *bāmôt* surrounding Jerusalem at
the time of Josiah may also have been YHWHistic but on a lower level than
Jerusalem, like the Onias temple, regardless of the fact that this did not prevent their being destroyed in the interests of centralization. If this was
indeed the view of the Rabbis it would constitute a continuity with the
views of the Chronicler, specifically 2 Chr 33:17.

C.3. Synopsis of Early Jewish interpretation concerning *bāmôt*

Among the Targum translators there appears to have been an
abundance of possible translations for *bāmôt* even though the corresponding
bmh is used most often. Both *Targum Jonathan* and the *Targum to
Chronicles* substitute other terms for *bāmôt* in key passages, perhaps in an
attempt to distance important personages from association with these
installations which were later condemned. *Targum Jonathan* transforms
Samuel's *bāmôt* into "banqueting halls," while the *Targum to Chronicles*
uses various terms such as "sanctuary," "meeting house," and "height" to
describe the *bāmāh* of Gibeon. The *Targum to Chronicles*, *Neofiti*, and *The
Fragment Targums* use the Greek loan word *bms* for *bāmôt*.

The other early Jewish commentators do not appear to have needed
discussion concerning what *bāmôt* were. For them the biblical *bāmôt* seem
to have been understood as legitimate places of sacrifice, which did, at various times, preclude the existence of a more formal sanctuary. The exclusion
of *bāmôt* priests from service in the Jerusalem Temple (2 Kgs 23:9) is also
directly applied to priests in the Second Temple period who served in
YHWHistic temples outside of Israel, and who therefore should be excluded
from service in Jerusalem. In both of these cases, the assumption regarding
bāmôt is that they were YHWHistic installations which were prohibited
primarily in the interests of centralization and as such, they were similar to
YHWHistic temples built outside of Jerusalem in the Second Temple
period.

This view regarding *bāmôt* is almost completely lacking in negative
connotations. There is no connection made between *bāmôt* and idolatry.
Concern for cultic centralization is the primary emphasis in rabbinic interpretation of *bāmôt*. Although some attempt to distance prominent figures

---

[60]Blackman, *Mishnayoth*, 5.173-74.

from connection with *bāmôt* occurs in the Targumim, the reason for this distancing is not stated. Perhaps it is simply an attempt to distance these persons from the accusation that they violated the demand for cultic centralization. No hint of any other reason for such distancing can be found in the sources.

By maintaining a view that *bāmôt* were YHWHistic installations, prohibited only out of a concern for centralization, the early Jewish sources seem most in agreement with the views of the Chronicler. Although the Chronicler mentions idolatrous *bāmôt* (referring to them with the Greek loan word *bms*), the early Jewish sources do not. There is no attempt in the Jewish sources to deny that some biblical *bāmôt* were used for idolatry. The rabbinic sources may have preferred to focus on centralization as the main issue related to *bāmôt* because they could not do away, either with biblical references which linked *bāmôt* to idols or with biblical references which linked *bāmôt* with the Tabernacle and important figures such as Samuel. Failure to link *bāmôt* with idolatry may indicate that there was no contemporary parallel to this use of *bāmôt* about which the Rabbis wished to comment. The Rabbis apparently preferred to use *bāmôt* as an antique type of the later Diaspora temples which competed with Jerusalem, thus continuing the claim of 2 Chr 33:17 that *bāmôt* were essentially YHWHistic.

D. EARLY JEWISH INTERPRETATION CONCERNING *mizbǝḥôt*

D.1. Targumic renderings

madbǝḥā᾽/madbaḥ: 273 out of 330 occurrences.

᾽ēgôrā᾽/᾽ēgôrā᾽: 57 out of 330 occurrences.

The basic Aramaic term for altar is מַדְבְּחָא/מַדְבַּח, which is the Aramaic cognate of the Hebrew מִזְבֵּחַ.[61] There is also another term for altar used in the Targumim, namely, אֱגוֹרָא/אֱגוֹרָא. Jastrow defines this term as "heathen altar (cmp. b.h. גַּל)." Terms which are related to this word are אֱגוֹר/אֱגוֹר which Jastrow defines as "heap, hill . . . a mound of arable ground . . . heaps of crops on the ground prior to harvest," and the verbal root אֲגַר which Jastrow defines as a "verbal root related to b.h. גרר: 'to gather, collect, store up, to heap up.'"[62]

---

[61]For Jastrow's definition, see *Dictionary*, 731.

[62]Jastrow, *Dictionary*, 12–13. There is also a second root אֲגַר II: "to hire, employ, rent," sometimes used of the hiring of prostitutes which might also shed light on the

Similar to the manner in which the Greek uses both βωμός and
Θυσιαστήριον, and the Vulgate uses both *ara* and *altaria*, to translate
Hebrew *mizbēᵃḥ/mizbəḥôt*, with the former of each pair being negatively
charged in context, some Targumim use *madbaḥ* for acceptable altars and
'ēgôrā' for unacceptable ones. Not all Targumim, however, make this distinction. *Neofiti* does not make any distinction in types of altars, using *madbaḥ* for all the altars it mentions, whether accepted or not.[63] *Onqelos*, on the
other hand, uses *'ēgôrā'* for the disapproved altars of Exod 34:13, Deut 7:5,
and 12:3, but uses *madbaḥ* for all the other Pentateuchal altars. In addition
to *Onqelos*, *Jonathan* and the *Targum to Chronicles* use *madbaḥ* and *'ēgôrā'*
to distinguish between acceptable and unacceptable altars.[64]

Just as the Vulgate and the LXX do not always agree on their use of
their alternate and negatively charged terms for altar, so the Targumim do
not always agree in their use of such a term with either the LXX or the Vulgate. Below is a list of verses in which an alternate and negatively charged
term for altar is used by the LXX, the Vulgate, and the Targumim:

Targum verses using *'ēgôrā'*	LXX verses using βωμός	Vulgate verses using *ara*	context/type of altar
Exod 34:13	Exod 34:13	Exod 34:13	non-Israelite
	Num 23:1, 2,	Num 23:1, 2,	Balaam's altars
	4, 14, 29, 30	4, 14, 29, 30	to YHWH
Deut 7:5, 12:3	Deut 7:5, 12:3	Deut 7:5, 12:3	non-Israelite
	Josh 22:10, 11	*altaria*[65]	Transjordanian
	Josh 22:16		

---

wider connotations noun in question (Jastrow, *Dictionary*, 13-14).

[63]*The Fragment Targums* also use *madbaḥ* only; however, the only verses related
to altars preserved in these targums refer to YHWHistic altars (Exod 17:15; 20:24 [21],
25 [22], 26 [23]; 21:14; 27:5; 32:5; Lev 1:9, 15, 16, 17; 6:3; 7:31; 9:24; Num 4:13; 17:3;
Deut 33:10).

[64]The verses which use *'ēgôrā'* are: *Targum Onqelos* of Exod 34:13; Deut 7:5;
12:3; *Targum Jonathan* of Judg 2:2; 6:25, 28, 30, 31, 32; 1 Kgs 12:32, 33; 13:1, 2, 4, 32;
16:32; 18:26; 2 Kgs 11:18; 21:3, 4, 5; 23:12, 15, 16, 17, 20; Isa 17:8; 27:9; 36:7; Jer
11:13; 17:1, 2; Ezek 6:4, 5, 6, 13; Amos 2:8; 3:14; Hos 4:19; 8:11; 10:1, 2, 8; 12:12;
Targum to Chronicles of 2 Chr 14:2; 23:17; 28:24; 30:14; 31:1; 32:12; 33:3, 4, 5, 15;
34:4, 5, 7.

[65]The Vulgate does not use *āra* in this instance but does use the phrase *altare
sacrilegum*, "sacrilegious altar."

Targum verses using 'êgôra'	LXX verses using βωμός	Vulgate verses using ara	context/type of altar
	Josh 22:19,[66] 23, 26, 34		
Judg 2:2		Judg 2:2	non-Israelite
Judg 6:25, 28 30, 31		Judg 6:25, 28, 30, 31	Ba'alistic
Judg 6:32		altaria[67]	
1 Kgs 12:32, 33			northern
1 Kgs 13:1, 2, 4 32[68]			Bethel
1 Kgs 16:32		1 Kgs 16:32	Bethel
1 Kgs 18:26			Ba'alistic
2 Kgs 11:18		2 Kgs 11:18	Ba'alistic
2 Kgs 21:3, 4		2 Kgs 21:3, 4	Ba'alistic
2 Kgs 21:5			for astral gods
2 Kgs 23:12, 15 16, 17, 20			northern/pagan
Isa 17:8	Isa 17:8		HB condemns
Isa 27:9	Isa 27:9		HB condemns
Isa 36:7	No LXX		destroyed in HB
Jer 11:13	Jer 11:13	Jer 11:13	Ba'alistic
Jer 17:1, 2		Jer 17:1, 2	HB condemns
Ezek 6:4-6, 13		Ezek 6:4-6, 13	HB condemns
Amos 2:8; 3:14			HB condemns
Hos 4:19; 8:11; 10:1, 2, 8; 12:12			HB condemns
2 Chr 14:2			not YHWH's
2 Chr 23:17		2 Chr 23:17	Ba'alistic
2 Chr 28:24			HB condemns

---

[66]This verse contains two references to altars. The accepted one is translated with θυσιαστήριον and the unaccepted one with βωμός. Similarly, in Josh 22:28-29, when the Reubenites swear they are only making a copy of YHWH's altar and that they would never dream of building an altar to rival that of YHWH's tabernacle, the LXX uses the term θυσιαστήριον.

[67]Oddly, though the Vulgate uses the term altaria as expected in 6:26 when the altar being referred to is YHWH's altar, and alternates the use of āra and altaria in verse 28 when both YHWH and Ba'al's altars are mentioned in the same verse, it also uses altaria in 6:32 for an altar of Ba'al, ignoring the alternating distinction it had set up earlier in the previous verses. It is possible that altaria in 6:32 is a mistake for āra but this cannot be proven.

[68]In this passage, the term madbaḥ is used for the altar at Bethel in 13:2-3 and in 13:5. All the other references to it use the term 'êgôrā'. See discussion below, pp. 342-43.

Targum verses using 'êgôra'	LXX verses using βωμός	Vulgate verses using ara	context/type of altar
2 Chr 30:14			HB condemns
2 Chr 31:1	2 Chr 31:1		HB condemns
2 Chr 32:12			destroyed in HB
2 Chr 33:3		2 Chr 33:3	Ba'alistic
2 Chr 33:4, 5			for astral gods
2 Chr 33:15		2 Chr 33:15	HB condemns
2 Chr 34:4		2 Chr 34:4	Ba'alistic
2 Chr 34:5, 7			HB condemns

As the above chart shows, the translated traditions share, essentially, only the feature of *having* an alternate and negatively charged term for altar, without, apparently, sharing the exact same understanding of when that alternate term should be used. The three do not always agree in their use of such a term, nor do any two of the three agree always. Two examples illustrate the divergence among the three translations in this practice. One is Numbers 23. The LXX and the Vulgate use their alternate, negative term. *Targum Onqelos* does not, perhaps because Balaam's altars, though in Moab and built by a non-Israelite, were nonetheless understood to be YHWHistic. A second example is Judges 6. In Judges 6, both Targum Jonathan and the Vulgate use their negatively charged term for Ba'al's altar at Ophrah and their positively charged one for YHWH's altars. The LXX makes no such distinction, referring to all the altars in the chapter with Θυσιαστήριον.

It is noteworthy, however, that while there are LXX verses which use an alternate, negative term for altar when the Targum counterparts of those same verses do not, and there are Vulgate verses which do the same in conjunction with the Targum over against the LXX, which does not, there are no verses in which the Vulgate alone uses the alternate term without either the Targum or the LXX also using theirs. The Vulgate does not follow either the LXX or the Targum exactly in this practice, but it nevertheless does not use the term *āra* in any context in which the Targum or the LXX has not also used their alternate term for altar.

Although the Targumim, then, are by no means alone in their use of an alternate and negatively charged term for altar in contexts in which it was deemed appropriate, the Targumim use their alternate term more frequently than either the LXX or the Vulgate. In addition to this fact, the Targumim's use of their alternate term in one passage, 1 Kings 13, makes it appear that there was another interpretative rule in place that may have governed the use of this term in certain contexts.

In 1 Kings 13, the anonymous man of God comes to Bethel to curse the altar that Jeroboam ben Nebat has built. Throughout this passage, the Targumim have been using the term *ĕgôrā'* to translate references to the altar at Bethel. This practice stops, however, in 13:2-3 and 5 and the translator switches back to *madbaḥ* to refer to the altar. The reason for this switch appears to be that the term *madbaḥ* is being reserved for the quotations of the man of God (13:2-3) and the confirmation statement in which it is announced that his curse concerning the altar has come true (13:5). All the other references to the altar at Bethel in the Targumim use the term *ĕgôrā'*. This passage makes it appear that the Targum translators, aware of the fact that they were introducing a distinction into their translation which did not exist in the Hebrew (using two words for altar where the Hebrew has only one), made a second conscious decision, for reasons of reverence, to leave the prophetic speech of the man of God and its confirmation as close to the original Hebrew as possible.

D.2. Midrashic and Mishnaic interpretations

Although there is a wealth of material which discusses the accepted *mizbəḥôt* of the biblical text in the Mishnah, especially the *mizbəḥôt* built by the patriarchs, and those of the Temple and Tabernacle,[69] there is less dis-

---

[69]All six passages related to *mizbəḥôt* that appear in the *Taryag Mitzvot* are related to the legitimate altars of YHWH. Lev 6:3 (Blackman, *Mishnayoth*, 7.68, 75, 81) instructs that the ashes are to be removed regularly from YHWH's altar; Lev 6:5 (Blackman, *Mishnayoth*, 7.68, 75, 81) instructs that its fire be kept lit; Lev 21:23 (Blackman, *Mishnayoth*, 7.69, 76, 83) prohibits any priest with a blemish from officiating on YHWH's altar; Lev 22:22 (Blackman, *Mishnayoth*, 7.70, 76, 83) prohibits the offering of any animal with a blemish upon YHWH's altar; and Deut 16:21 (Blackman, *Mishnayoth*, 7.71, 78, 87) prohibits the planting of any tree near YHWH's altar.

Below is a list of the biblical references to acceptable altars (or rituals belonging to them) to which reference is made in the Mishnah: Gen 22:9, *Tāmîd* 4.1; Exod 27:5, *Zəbāḥîm* 14.10; Exod 29:36, *Yômā'* 5.5; Exod 29:38, *Yômā'* 1.2; Exod 30:1, *Yômā'* 1.2, 5.5, *Ḥăgîgāh* 3.8; Exod 30:18, *Sûkkāh* 4.10; Exod 30:20, *Zəbāḥîm* 14.10; Exod 39:38, *Kərîtôt* 1.1; Lev 1:5, *Məgillāh* 2.5, *Zəbāḥîm* 4.4, 5.4, 14.10; Lev 1:9, *Zəbāḥîm* 9.5, *Mənāḥôt* 13.11; Lev 1:11, *Zəbāḥîm* 14.10; Lev 1:15, *Qiddûšîn* 1.8; Lev 1:16-17, *Zəbāḥîm* 4.4, *Mənāḥôt* 13.11; Lev 2:2, *Qiddûšîn* 1.8, *Zəbāḥîm* 4.3, 6.1, *Kēlîm* 17:10, *Məgillāh* 2.5; Lev 2:8, *Məgillāh* 2.5, *Zəbāḥîm* 14.3, 10, *Mənāḥôt* 5.5; Lev 2:9, *Mənāḥôt* 13.11; Lev 3:2, *Məgillāh* 2.5; Lev 3:8, *Məgillāh* 2.5; Lev 3:11, *Zəbāḥîm* 2.3; Lev 4:7, *Yômā'* 5.6; Lev 4:10, *'Ēdûyôt* 8.6, *Hôrāyôt* 2.1; Lev 4:18-19, *'Ēdûyôt* 8.6; Lev 4:26, *Pārāh* 8.3; Lev 4:30-35, *Yômā'* 8.2, 8, *Sanhedrîn* 7.8, *Hôrāôôt* 1.4, 5, 3.1, *Kēlîm* 17.12; Lev 5:9, *Šəbûʿôt* 1.2, 3.1, 8.6; Lev 5:12, *Kərîtôt* 6.6; Lev 6:2, *Bərākôt* 1.1, *Šəbûʿôt* 4.8, *Zəbāḥîm* 9.1, *Kərîtôt* 2.2; Lev 6:3, *Tāmîd* 1.2, *Zəbāḥîm* 5.6, *Mənāḥôt* 7.4; Lev 6:6, *'Ēdûyôt* 8.6, *Ḥûlîn* 2.10; Lev 7:2, *Məgillāh* 2.5; Lev 7:31, *Ḥûlîn* 10.1; Lev 14:20, *Məgillāh* 2.5; Lev

cussion of illegitimate altars. For instance, although Exod 34:13; Deut 7:5; and 12:3 mention *mizbəḥôt* along with *ʾăšērîm* and *maṣṣēbôt*, *ʿĂbôdāh Zārāh* 3:5 focusses on the *ʾăšērîm*, the high hills, and the green trees in these contexts and passes over the *maṣṣēbôt* and the *mizbəḥôt* in them without comment.

One source which does discuss illegitimate altars is *Sifre Deuteronomy* 61 on Deut 12:2. This passage discusses the destruction of *mizbəḥôt* belonging to the prior inhabitants of the land which were believed to be specifically "hewn" for idol worship,[70] presumably in contrast to YHWHistic altars which were not to be "hewn" (Exod 20:25). This section concludes with a discussion concerning the injunction "you shall not do so for the Lord your God," which ends Deut 12:2. There Rabbi Eliezar asks:

> Whence do we learn that if one chips out one stone from the Hall of the Temple, from its altar, or from its courtyards, he violates a negative commandment? From the verse, *Break down their altars and dash in pieces their pillars...Ye shall not do so unto the Lord your God.*[71]

Gamaliel apparently felt this was not the best understanding of this verse. The midrash quotes him as saying:

> Could you possibly imagine that Israelites would tear down their own altars? Heaven forbid! Rather, the verse means: do not do as the heathen do, for your evil deeds would then cause the Temple of your fathers to be destroyed.[72]

The principle of interpretation at work in this midrash is not aimed at expounding what type of altar the former nations had, or why it was to be destroyed. Rather, it is aimed at deriving the fullest understanding of how all altars, YHWHistic ones included, should be treated under the law. The assumption is already in force that "heathen" altars should be destroyed and the worship practices connected with them avoided.

16:12, *Yômāʾ* 4.4, *ʿĒdūyôt* 8.1, *Kēlîm* 17:11; Lev 16:18, *Yômāʾ* 5.5; Lev 17:6, *Zəbāḥîm* 14:10; Lev 17:11, *Zəbāḥîm* 3.1, *Məʿîlāh* 3.3; Lev 21:23, *Məgillāh* 4.7; Num 18:7, *Zəbāḥîm* 1.2; Num 18:17, *Ḥallāh* 4.9, *Bəkôrôt* 2.2, *Zəbāḥîm* 5.8, *Bəkôrôt* 2.5; Deut 12:27, *Zəbāḥîm* 9.5; Deut 26:4, *Tərûmôt* 3.7, *Bikkûrîm* 3.4; Deut 27:5, *Middôt* 3.4, *Sôṭāh* 7.5; Josh 8:30-31, *Sôṭāh* 7.5; 1 Kgs 3:4, *Zəbāḥîm* 14.7; 1 Kgs 8:64, *Ḥăgîgāh* 3.8; 2 Kgs 23:9, *Mənāḥôt* 13.10; Ezek 8:16, *Sûkkāh* 5.4; Ezek 41:22, *ʾĀbôt* 3.3; Ezek 47:1, *Middôt* 2.5. For further citations from other Jewish sources, see Myron B. Lerner's article, "Altar," *EncJud* 1.767-71.

[70]Hammer, *Sifre*, 116.
[71]Hammer, *Sifre*, 117.
[72]Hammer, *Sifre*, 117.

On the issue of altars and cultic centralization, *Sifre Deuteronomy* 65 and 66 on Deut 12:8-9 discuss when individual altars were replaced by the central altars of the Tabernacle or the Temple. The rulings on when altars were allowed and when they were not, found in *Sifre Deuteronomy* 65, is identical to the discussion of *bāmôt* and the relative timing of their acceptance or rejection found in the Mishnah tractate *Zəbāḥîm* (14:4-8). *Sifre Deuteronomy* 65 simply presents a more condensed version of the Mishnah portion and directs the argument toward *mizbəḥôt* instead of *bāmôt*. According to *Sifre Deuteronomy* 66, altars were allowed in the countryside within the land from the time of Israel's "resting" there until the time of Israel's "possessing" of the land. It is noted that Rabbi Simeon believed that "possessing" referred to the Shiloh era and "resting" to the time of the acquisition of Jerusalem, while Rabbi Judah believed just the opposite.[73]

What is striking about the similar treatment given multiple altars and *bāmôt* in these sources is that both appear to be treated, not as examples of idolatrous worship, as are *ăšērîm* and *maṣṣēbôt*, but as examples of possible violations of the principle of cultic centralization. It is not stated that these various altars or *bāmôt* were dedicated to any god other than YHWH. In fact, these passages explain, rather, why even YHWHistic altars outside Jerusalem are not allowed once the Temple has been constructed.[74]

One final source of early commentary concerning *mizbəḥôt* can be found in *Mekhilta de-Rabbi Ishmael* (chapter 57.1), *Bahodesh* 11 on Exod 20:24-6.[75] In this passage, several observations are made concerning what the instructions in these verses mean. First it is noted that the instruction to make altars for YHWH implies that they are being made for the first time and are therefore not altars that have ever been devoted to any other god. Next it is stated that the phrase "an altar *of earth*," means that each altar should sit directly on the ground and thus not be held up off the ground by stones or pillars.[76] Following this statement are two rabbinical opinions

---

[73]Hammer, *Sifre*, 120-21.

[74]Two later texts also witness to the desire to reinforce biblical trends toward cultic centralization. Midrashic expansions in *Targum Pseudo-Jonathan* on Gen 8:20 and 22:9 state that Adam built an altar upon which he and Cain and Abel sacrificed and which Noah rebuilt and reused after the flood. It was this same altar upon which Abraham was prepared to sacrifice Isaac. This equation of three different and widely separated incidents has the virtue of reducing three possible altars outside Jerusalem to one altar only. *Genesis Rabbah* 34.7 goes the necessary one step farther by stating that both Noah and Adam had also sacrificed on the one great altar in Jerusalem. For a discussion of these interpretations, see Maher, *Targum Pseudo-Jonathan*, 43-44, 79.

[75]Horovitz and Rabin, *Mechilta*, 242-45. See also Neusner, *Mekhilta*, 2.99-103.

[76]The interpretation that altars should be "grounded in the earth," also appears in

concerning the construction of altars, one which advises that they be hollow, and another which states that the metal altars constructed for the Tabernacle and the Temple were subsequently filled with earth.[77] Following these observations, the passage goes into much detail concerning rituals performed at accepted altars,[78] before returning to the subject of altar construction.

When the text's attention returns to altar construction, the biblical passage which begins, "if you make me an altar of stone," is addressed. The text points out that the biblical passage makes it clear that stone altars are optional. When discussing the requirement that stone altars not be made of hewn stone, the text uses two lines of argument. First it is argued that though one might not use hewn stones in an altar, one might use them to build the Temple. Then it is stated that the commandment to use "whole" stones symbolizes the wholeness and peace God desires for humanity.[79] On the subject of altar steps and the "nakedness" which might be revealed should one construct an altar in this fashion, the text notes that Exod 28:42 instructed the wearing of pants by priests to cover their nakedness, and so, this passage must refer to the length of stride (small being preferable to large), which should constitute the style of walking in the holy precinct. One must walk in such a way as to treat the altar with reverence.[80]

D.3. Synopsis of Early Jewish Interpretation concerning *mizbəḥôt*

As noted above, the Targumim use two distinct terms to translate the Hebrew *mizbēªḥ/mizbəḥôt*, the cognate *madbaḥ* for acceptable altars and the term *ʾĕgôrāʾ* for unacceptable altars. This use of two terms to translate one Hebrew antecedent also appears in the LXX and the Vulgate, but not always in the same contexts in which the Targumim make use of the distinction. The Targumim also appear to avoid using this distinction when a prophet's direct speech is being quoted (1 Kgs 13:2-3, 5).

The Midrashic and Mishnaic commentaries on *mizbəḥôt* deal more with acceptable altars than with unacceptable ones; however, alien altars are acknowledged and their destruction taken as a matter of course. As for

---

The Fragment Targums to Exod 20:24. While the MT of Exod 20:24 states, "you shall make me an *altar made of soil*" (מִזְבַּח אֲדָמָה), the Vatican manuscript tradition of *The Fragment Targum* reads, "you shall make me an *altar fixed in the earth*" (קביע בארעא). For this text, see Klein, *Fragment Targums*, 2.134.

[77]Neusner, *Mekhilta*, 2.99.

[78]Neusner, *Mekhilta*, 2.99-101.

[79]Neusner, *Mekhilta*, 2.101-02.

[80]Neusner, *Mekhilta*, 2.102-03.

acceptable altars, several passages interpret issues related to cultic centralization, carefully laying out the meaning of cultic centralization for Second Temple times, as well as expounding on the rules of sacrifice and the ways in which these rituals were to be understood. Some attention is also given to the manner of constructing of acceptable altars.

What comes through in this material is the concern for understanding ritual, especially as it relates to the practices current in the periods of the authors. What constituted an alien altar is straightforward for the early Jewish commentators. They are altars dedicated to a deity other than YHWH. Of more interest is whether altars outside Jerusalem are allowed, and if so, under what circumstances. What rituals may be performed outside Jerusalem? What category of worshipper may engage in such ritual? All of these questions were particularly pressing for Second Temple times given the vast changes in life situations among Jews in the various regions of the Diaspora as well as for those living in the land. It is about this world, even more than about biblical times, that the early Jewish commentators are speaking regarding *mizbəḥôt* and ritual. This may account for why there is more information about which altars are acceptable than discussion of ancient altars which were condemned.

CONCLUSIONS

With regard to *ăšērîm*, the early Jewish sources have leveled through an understanding of *ăšērîm* as trees (probably based upon Deut 16:21) and tended to equate the *ăšērîm* with the *ʿ̄eṣ raʿ̆ănān* of biblical literature. This interpretation occurs in the Targumim as well as in the Mishnah and midrashim. The image of the tree in Gen 35:4, beneath which idols were buried, most closely resembles the rabbinic *ăšērîm*, even though this tree is not called an *ăšērāh* in the biblical text. The primary rabbinic concern regarding *ăšērîm* is their connection with idolatry. Similarly, *maṣṣēbôt* are not interpreted to any great extent by the early Jewish commentators, but they, like *ăšērîm*, are related to the practice of idolatry and so condemned. The biblical source which most closely resembles the rabbinic material on *maṣṣēbôt* is H (Lev 26:1).

Both *maṣṣēbôt* and *bāmôt* are acknowledged as items once beloved of the patriarchs but later condemned. With regard to *bāmôt* and also *mizbəḥôt*, a careful timeline is given in certain sources concerning when their use outside the Temple or Tabernacle was sanctioned and when it was condemned. Two major issues, then, can be seen in the early Jewish commentaries related to these items. One, related more to *ăšērîm* and *maṣṣēbôt*, is the issue of idolatry. The other, related more to *bāmôt* and *mizbəḥôt*, is the issue of cultic centralization.

While the Targumim have constant and straightforward translations for *ăšērîm* and *maṣṣēbôt*, *bāmôt* and *mizbəḥôt* are variously translated in ways that reveal certain interpretative tendencies in the literature. In what some scholars have seen as an attempt to sanitize certain passages so that they cannot reflect badly on respected ancestors or institutions, *bāmôt* are often translated with completely different terms such as "banquet hall," "meeting place," or "sanctuary." The *Targum to Chronicles* goes one step further in its distancing of *bāmôt* from the ancestors when it uses the Greek loan word *bāmāsā'* (from βωμός) to translate its remaining references to *bāmôt* other than the installation at Gibeon.

Finally, *mizbəḥôt* are translated differently depending upon context, but in this case the distinction is aimed at designating certain *mizbəḥôt* as acceptable and others as unacceptable. This use of two terms to translate one Hebrew antecedent also occurs in the LXX and the Vulgate (although not in the exact same contexts as it occurs in the Targumim). This distinction between acceptable and unacceptable altars constitutes an added layer of interpretation on the part of the translators than is found in the original biblical Hebrew text.

In their treatments of the items under discussion, the early Jewish translators evidence both continuity and discontinuity with biblical interpretation. Parts of the rabbinic view of *ăšērîm* are derived from the biblical text, though only peripherally from biblical statements specifically about *ăšērîm*. By leveling through the image of the tree in Gen 35:4, the Rabbis offer a description of *ăšērîm* which is in keeping with their own situation, but only marginally in keeping with the biblical text (by virtue of Deut 16:21). *ăšērîm* become, for the Rabbis, ancient types of the contemporary tree devoted to idolatry with which they apparently had to deal. *maṣṣēbôt* also become subsumed under the category of idolatrous worship, continuing the view of *maṣṣēbôt* which appears in the Holiness Code. Rabbinic treatment of *bāmôt* continues the view of *bāmôt* expressed in 2 Chr 33:17, namely that *bāmôt* were essentially YHWHistic even if they did violate the command for cultic centralization. In these examples it becomes evident that various trajectories of biblical interpretation make their way into the rabbinic material, primarily, though not exclusively, from the later biblical sources.

Conclusion

In recent years many studies have explored both the boundaries between what might be called "popular" religion and "normative" religion and the possibility of multiple forms of accepted religious practice within ancient Israel.[1] Although not yet the majority view among scholars, the understanding of ancient Israel as a society with as much diversity in religious belief and in practice as our own seems more and more the best way to view the evidence when both text and archaeology are fully taken into account. It is this theological and practical diversity that the current study has sought to demonstrate through analysis of textual views expressed regarding cultic paraphrenalia. The target of this analysis was to test the prevailing opinions regarding these items found in the secondary literature.

At the beginning of this study, an overview of the secondary scholarship pertaining to *ăšērîm*, *bāmôt*, and *maṣṣēbôt* demonstrated that it has generally been assumed that these objects were universally viewed as unacceptable by the biblical writers and that this unacceptability resulted from the putative Canaanite origins of these objects and the fear, on the part of biblical writers, of the influence of Canaanite religion upon YHWHism. This judgment was best seen in works which treated these items only cursorily as part of larger studies on other issues related to Israel or Israelite religion. Studies which analyzed these items in detail, however, were frequently more absorbed in the task of attempting to identify these objects than in understanding what they represented to the various biblical writers. Appeals to archaeology, linguistic evidence, and testimony from the early translated versions were often made, but none of these avenues of inquiry has succeeded in offering any lasting insight into how these items were actually viewed by the biblical writers.

The current study has demonstrated that most biblical writers had their own particular understanding of these objects, how they should be used, when they were appropriate, and what their use signified. Similarly,

---

[1]See, for example, Ackerman, *Under Every Green Tree*; Jacques Berlinerblau, *The Vow and the "Popular Religious Groups" of Ancient Israel: A Philological and Sociological Inquiry* (JSOTSup 210; Sheffield: Sheffield Academic Press, 1996); and Diana V. Edelman, ed. *The Triumph of Elohim: From Yahwisms to Judaisms* (Grand Rapids: Eerdmans, 1996).

the early interpreters each carried over or adapted the biblical trajectories of opinion regarding these objects into their own time, but with each transforming their treatment of these items to fit their own concerns. Contrary to what is often hoped by biblical researchers, these early interpretations, regardless of their vantage point in history so much closer to the biblical period than are we, were not interested in providing modern readers with an historically rooted depiction of these items as they existed in ancient Israel.

What the current study has shown is that these items of cultic paraphernalia presented the biblical writers as well as the early interpreters with an abundant source of material related to Israel's religion, from which to draw lessons of import for their own specific communities. The breadth and detail of information regarding these items from among the sources and translated traditions consulted is fascinating. Below are just a few of the nuances that have been discussed.

Regardless of the persistent belief that these items were the exclusive province of the Canaanites and their religion, there is very little evidence in the biblical text which supports this view for any of the objects, with the possible exception of *ăšērîm*. This view is only applicable to *ăšērîm*, however, if one accepts the statement that the Canaanite goddess ᵓAsherah and *ăšērîm* were directly related and that ᵓAsherah was by definition a Canaanite deity. This identification of *ăšērîm* with the Canaanites, however, does not hold up if one rejects a connection between *ăšērîm* and ᵓAsherah, or accepts the idea that ᵓAsherah may have been as thoroughly an Israelite goddess as she was a Canaanite goddess. It remains the case, however, that the insistence upon Canaanite origins for the objects under discussion has little support in the actual biblical sources themselves.

For many biblical writers, however, *bāmôt* apparently did call to mind a foreign culture, namely the culture of Moab, its religion, and its topography (J, E, P, First Isaiah, Jeremiah, and Dtr). For Jeremiah, this connection was expanded until *bāmôt* became irrevocably connected with the Judean monarchy's practice of child sacrifice, a practice in which the kings of Moab were also said to have been engaged. For Dtr, however, Moab was regarded as the site of Moses' retelling of the law, and *bāmôt* represented ancient sites of legitimate worship of YHWH. For the early Jewish interpreters, *bāmôt* served as analogies to Diaspora temples which existed in Second Temple times, devoted to YHWH but still in violation of a purist's view of centralized worship. This illustrates how a single item (in this case *bāmôt*) might be positively associated with a foreign culture, or negatively associated with one, or interpreted completely independently by yet another source in relation to another issue altogether.

Another view of *ăšērîm*, *bāmôt*, and *maṣṣēbôt* found in the secondary literature is that these objects were all universally condemned in the sources. Far from being universally condemned, however, *bāmôt*, as noted above, are championed by Dtr as early shrines of central importance to YHWHism. *ăšērîm*, though condemned by D and Dtr, are portrayed in these same sources as objects whose use was often associated with YHWH's cult and was extremely resistant to attempts at eradicating it. *maṣṣēbôt* functioned within ancient Israel in a variety of acceptable ways. For E they were the quintessential emblems of patriarchal piety. They served as thoroughly acceptable boundary stones, witnesses to covenant, memorial monuments, or grave markers in E as well as in other sources.

maṣṣēbôt are also an example, however, of how the same object could be viewed completely positively by one source, and negatively by another. With one exception, Dtr speaks of *maṣṣēbôt* as if they generally symbolized the worship of gods other than YHWH. H mentions *maṣṣēbôt* in lists among types of cultic statuary in such a way that it appears that H equated their use with the use of cultic statuary.

Even on the subject of altars, the central cultic fixtures in Israelite religion, the Bible contains more nuances than are usually assumed, not all of which result in a positive evaluation of *mizbǝḥôt*, even YHWHistic *mizbǝḥôt*. Some sources mandate the use of natural field stones and earth for the building of YHWHistic *mizbǝḥôt*. Others depict elaborate craftsmanship and careful regulation regarding their manufacture. Some sources affirm only altars built by Israelites, and some only those altars carefully constructed by the priesthood. Others accept any altar builder as long as YHWH is the god to whom the altar is dedicated; and Dtr even ignores its stated concern for cultic centralization when the person erecting altars to YHWH outside of Jerusalem is the preeminent figure of Elijah the prophet.

With regard to the early translated traditions, the in-depth analysis undertaken in this study has revealed that modern scholarly use of these sources primarily as historical witnesses to biblical phenomena mistakes the intention of the early traditions by ignoring their primary interest in the religion of their own time. The early Jewish sources, for instance, in continuity with the Holiness Code, passed on an understanding of *maṣṣēbôt* as linked to cultic statuary to Jerome, who included injunctions against *maṣṣēbôt* in his larger message against idol worship in pagan religion.

Jerome, however, nuanced his treatment of *maṣṣēbôt* by using two negatively charged terms to translate unacceptable *maṣṣēbôt* and two positively charged ones to translate acceptable *maṣṣēbôt*, so that the theological nuances in the biblical text might be linguistically demonstrated in the Latin.

The LXX made special hermeneutical use of *ăšērîm*, relating them to the groves of Greek religion rather than simply translating into Greek what the ancient biblical *ăšērîm* were thought to be. The analogy which the LXX provides between *ăšērîm* and the ἄλσος, or sacred grove, provided a useful contemporary parallel to the challenges facing Jews within pagan Hellenistic culture. Through this analogy, the ubiquitous ἄλσος of Hellenistic culture, and the worship of foreign deities which it represented, were placed under the censure of biblical law by virtue of the LXX's equation of them with the *ăšērîm* of ancient Israel. Similarly, the Rabbis transformed *ăšērîm* into single trees under which pagan idols were buried, thus communicating the prohibition of such idolatrous practices by virtue of their identification with *ăšērîm*.

Finally, rather than merely reproducing or elaborating on biblical treatments of these items, the early interpreters felt free to introduce ideological content into their translations. As in Jerome's treatment of *maṣṣēbôt*, the Jewish, Greek, and Latin sources indicated by vocabulary choice exactly when they viewed biblical *mizbəhôt* as legitimate and when they viewed them as illegitimate. Despite the fact that they all engage in this practice, they did not march in lockstep concerning when and under what circumstances an altar should be translated as illegitimate. They each nuanced their translations, but according to separate criteria.

Another type of hermeneutical device found in the LXX, which is the opposite of an analogy, such as the one drawn between ἄλσος the *ăšērāh*, is the LXX's coining of a completely new Greek word (θυσιαστήριον), with which it referred to the altars in the biblical text of which it approved. By so doing, the LXX translators made a complete separation between the altars of Greek religion and the altars of the Bible and later Judaism. In this way the LXX evidences two complementary techniques of interpretative translation, each was driven, not by a desire to be slavishly literal to the biblical text, but rather by a desire to produce sacred scripture that would be of use to its community, a community placed, for good or ill, in continuous contact with Hellenistic religion.

Throughout the current study the complexity of testimony from the Hebrew Bible and the early interpretative traditions has been demonstrated on the issue of how *ăšērîm, bāmôt, maṣṣēbôt,* and *mizbəhôt* were viewed by the various ancient communities which either contributed to or commented on the Hebrew Bible. The few examples of the nuances in this material mentioned above are merely samples of the myriad details afforded by study of the sources and interpretative traditions, and their views of cultic life in Israel. Far from presenting a world in which one accepted notion of what the proper worship of YHWH entailed was forced upon all and leveled through all the textual traditions, the text and the later translated traditions evidence a remarkable variety of opinions existing alongside one another. This evidence demands that we begin anew an evaluation of Israelite religion that is free of the presupposition of "one normative YHWHism" and gives credence to the many understandings of the biblical writers and later interpreters concerning what constituted the proper religion of ancient Israel.

Bibliography

Achtemeier, Paul J. ed. *Harper's Bible Dictionary* (San Francisco: Harper & Row, 1985).

Ackerman, Susan. "Asherah," *OCB* 62.

_____. *Under Every Green Tree: Popular Religion in Sixth-Century Judah* (HSM 46; Atlanta: Scholars Press, 1992).

Ackroyd, Peter. "Hosea" in *Peake's Commentary on the Bible* (London: Thomas Nelson and Sons, 1962) 603-13.

Aharoni, Yohanan. *The Archaeology of the Land of Israel: From the Prehistoric Beginnings to the End of the First Temple Period* (tr. Anson Rainey; ed. Miriam Aharoni; Philadelphia: Westminster, 1982).

_____. "The Horned Altar of Beer-sheba," *BA* 37 (1974) 2-6.

_____. "The Israelite Sanctuary at Arad," in *New Directions in Biblical Archaeology* (ed. David Noel Freedman and Jonas Greenfield; Garden City, N.Y.: Doubleday, 1971) 28-44.

Ahlström, G. W. *Aspects of Syncretism in Israelite Religion* (Horae Soderblomianae V; Lund: Gleerup, 1963).

Albright, William F. *Archaeology and the Religion of Israel* (Baltimore: Johns Hopkins University Press, 1956).

_____. *From the Stone Age to Christianity* (2d ed.; Garden City, N.Y.: Doubleday Anchor Books, 1957).

_____. *Yahweh and the Gods of Canaan: A Historical Analysis of Two Contrasting Faiths* (Winona Lake, Ind.: Eisenbrauns, 1968).

_____. "The High Place in Ancient Palestine," in *Volume du Congrès: Strasbourg 1956* (VTSup 4; Leiden: E. J. Brill, 1957) 242-58.

Alexander, Philip S. "Targum, Targumim," *ABD* 6.320-31.

Andersen, Francis and David Noel Freedman. *Amos: A New Translation with Introduction and Comentary* (AB 24A; New York: Doubleday, 1989).

_____. *Hosea: A New Translation with Introduction and Commentary* (AB 24; Garden City, N.Y.: Doubleday, 1980).

Anderson, Gary. *Sacrifices and Offerings in Ancient Israel: Studies in Their Social and Political Importance* (HSM 41; Atlanta: Scholars Press, 1987).

Arav, Rami and Richard Freund. "The Bull from the Sea: Geshur's Chief Deity?," *BAR* 24/1 (1998) 42.

Attridge, Harold W. and Robert A. Oden. *Philo of Byblos: The Phoenician History—Introduction, Critical Text, Translation, Notes* (CBQMS 9; CBA: Washington D.C., 1981).

Badé, W. F. *The Old Testament in the Light of Today* (New York: Houghton Mifflin, 1915).

Barr, James. "Man and Nature: The Ecological Controversy and the Old Testament," *BJRL* 55 (1972) 9-32.

_____. "Philo of Byblos and His 'Phoenician History,'" *BJRL* 57 (1974) 17-68.

_____. "Seeing the Wood for the Trees? An Enigmatic Ancient Translation," *JSS* 13 (1968) 11-20.

_____. *The Semantics of Biblical Language* (London: Oxford University Press, 1961).

Barrick, W. Boyd. "The Funerary Character of 'High-Places' in Ancient Palestine: A Reassessment," *VT* 25 (75) 565-95.

_____. "High Place," *ABD* 3.196-200.

_____. "The Word BMH in the Old Testament," (Ph.D. diss., University of Chicago Divinity School, 1977).

Barrois, G. A. "Pillar," *IDB* 3.815-817.

Barthélemy, Dominique. *Les Devanciers d'Aquila: Première publication intégrale du texte des fragments du Dodécaprophéton* (VTSup 10; Leiden: E. J. Brill, 1963).

Baumgarten, Albert I. *The Phoenician History of Philo of Byblus: A Commentary* (Leiden: E. J. Brill, 1981).

Beck, Pirhiya. "The Drawings from Horvat Teiman (Kuntillet ʿAjrud)," *Tel Aviv* 9 (1982) 3-68.

Beebe, H. Keith. *The Old Testament* (Belmont, Calif.: Dickenson, 1970).

Beer, Georg. *Steinverehrung bei den Israeliten* (Berlin: de Gruyter, 1921).

Benzinger, Immanuel. *Hebräische Archäologie* (Tübingen: J. C. B. Mohr, 1907).

Berlinerblau, Jacques. *The Vow and the "Popular Religious Groups" of Ancient Israel: A Philological and Sociological Inquiry* (JSOTSup 210; Sheffield: Sheffield Academic Press, 1996).

Bernett, Monika and Othmar Keel. *Mond, Stier und Kult am Stadttor: Die Stele von Betsaida (et-Tell)* (OBO 161; Göttingen: Vandenhoeck & Ruprecht, 1998).

Bietenhard, Hans. *Sifre Deuteronomium* (Judaica et Christiana 8; Frankfurt am Main: Peter Lang, 1984).

Binger, Tilde. *Asherah: Goddesses in Ugarit, Israel and the Old Testament* (JSOTSup 232; Sheffield: Sheffield Academic Press, 1997).

Biran, Avraham. "Dan (place)," *ABD* 2.14-15.

_____, ed. *Temples and High Places in Biblical Times: Proceedings of the Colloquium in Honor of the Centennial of Hebrew Union College-Jewish Institute of Religion* (Jerusalem: Keter, 1981).

_____. "Sacred Spaces: Of Standing Stones, High Places, and Cult Objects at Dan," *BAR* 24/5 (1998) 38-45, 70.

Bird, Phyllis A. "'Male and Female He Created Them': Gen 1:27b in the Contest of the Priestly Account of Creation," *HTR* 74 (1981) 129-59.

_____. *Missing Persons and Mistaken Identities: Women and Gender in Ancient Israel* (Minneapolis: Fortress, 1997).

_____. "'To Play the Harlot': An Inquiry into an Old Testament Metaphor," in *Gender and Difference in Ancient Israel* (ed. Peggy L. Day; Minneapolis: Augsburg Fortress, 1989) 75-94.

_____. "Women (OT)," *ABD* 6.951-57.

Birge, Darice Elizabeth. "Sacred Groves in the Ancient Greek World," (Ph.D. diss., University of California at Berkeley, 1982).

Blackman, Philip. *Mishnayoth* (7 vols.; Gateshead: Judaica, 1983).

Blackwood, Andrew W. *Ezekiel: Prophecy of Hope* (Grand Rapids: Baker, 1965).

Blenkinsopp, Joseph A. *A History of Prophecy in Israel: From the Settlement in the Land to the Hellenistic Period* (Philadelphia: Westminster, 1983).

Bloch-Smith, Elizabeth. *Judahite Burial Practices and Beliefs About the Dead* (JSOTSupp 123; Sheffield: JSOT Press, 1992).

Bogaert, Pierre-Maurice. "Versions, Ancient [Latin]," *ABD* 6.799-803.

Boling, Robert G. and G. Ernest Wright. *Joshua: A New Translation with Introduction and Commentary* (AB 6; Garden City, N.Y.: Doubleday, 1982).

Boraas, Roger S. "Pillars," *HBD* 799.

Börner-Klein, Dagmar. *Midrasch Sifre Numeri: Voruntersucheungen zur Redaktions-geschichte* (Judentum und Umwelt 39; Frankfurt am Main: Peter Lang, 1993).

Botterweck, G. Johannes and Helmer Ringgren, ed. *Theological Dictionary of the Old Testament* (6 vols.; tr. John T. Willis and David E. Green; Grand Rapids: Eerdmans, 1974-1986).

Bright, John. *A History of Israel* (3d ed.; Philadelphia: Westminster, 1981).

Brinker, R. *The Influence of Sanctuaries in Early Israel* (Manchester: Manchester University Press, 1946).

Brinkman, John A., Miguel Civil, Ignace J. Gelb, A. Leo Oppenheim, and Erica Reiner, ed. *The Assyrian Dictionary of the Oriental Institute of the University of Chicago* (Chicago: Oriental Institute, 1956-).

Brock, Sebastian P., Charles T. Fritsch, and Samuel Jellico, ed. *A Classified Bibliography of the Septuagint* (Arbeiten Zur Literature un Geschichte des Hellenistischen Judentums VI; Leiden: E. J. Brill, 1973).

Brown, Dennis. *VIR TRILINGUIS: A Study in the Biblical Exegesis of Saint Jerome* (Kampen: Kok Pharos, 1992).

Brown, Francis, S. R. Driver, and Charles A. Briggs. *A Hebrew and English Lexicon of the Old Testament* (Oxford: Clarendon, 1907).

Brown, Raymond E., Joseph A. Fitzmyer, and Roland E. Murphy, ed. *The New Jerome Biblical Commentary* (Englewood Cliffs, N.J.: Prentice-Hall, 1990).

Bucher, Christina. "The Origin and Meaning of 'znh' Terminology in the Book of Hosea" (Ph.D. diss., Claremont Graduate School, 1988).

Buck, Harry M. *People of the Lord: The History, Scriptures, and Faith of Ancient Israel* (New York: Macmillan, 1966).

Budde, Karl. "Zur Bedeutung des Mazzeben," *OLZ* 15 (1912) 248-50, 469-71.

Burkert, Walter. *Greek Religion: Archaic and Classical* (tr. John Raffan; Oxford: Basil Blackwell, 1985).

Buttrick, George Arthur, ed. *The Interpreter's Dictionary of the Bible* (4 vols.; Nashville: Abingdon, 1962).

Carmichael, Calum M. *The Origins of Biblical Law: The Decalogues and the Book of the Covenant* (Ithaca: Cornell University Press, 1992).

Carpenter, J. Estlin and George Harford-Battersby. *The Hexateuch According to the Revised Version* (2 vols.; London: Longmans, Green, 1900).

Cassuto, M. D. *From Adam to Noah* (2d ed.; Jerusalem: Magnes, 1959).

Cathcart, Kevin and R. P. Gordon. *The Targum of the Minor Prophets* (The Aramaic Bible 14; Wilmington, Del.: Michael Glazier, 1989).

Childs, Brevard S. *The Book of Exodus: A Critical, Theological Commentary* (OTL; Philadelphia: Westminster, 1974).

Chilton, Bruce. *The Isaiah Targum: Introduction, Translation, Apparatus and Notes* (The Aramaic Bible 11; Wilmington, Del.: Michael Glazier, 1987).

Conrad, Diethelm. "Studien zum Altargesetz: Ex 20:24-26" (Ph.D. diss., Marburg; 1968).

Coogan, Michael D. "Canaanite Origins and Lineage: Reflections on the Religion of Ancient Israel," in *Ancient Israelite Religion: Essays in Honor of Frank Moore Cross* (ed. Patrick D. Miller, Jr., Paul D. Hanson, S. Dean McBride; Philadelphia: Fortress, 1987) 115-24.

_____. "Joshua," *NJBC* 110-31.

Cook, Stanley A. *The Religion of Ancient Palestine* (Schweich Lecture, 1925; London: Oxford University Press, 1930).

Coote, Robert B. and David Robert Ord. *The Bible's First History* (Philadelphia: Fortress, 1989).

_____. *In Defense of Revolution: The Elohist History* (Minneapolis: Fortress, 1991).

_____. *In the Beginning: Creation and the Priestly History* (Minneapolis: Fortress, 1991).

Corpus inscriptionum semiticarum (Paris: Republic, 1881 -).

Cross, Frank Moore. *Canaanite Myth and Hebrew Epic:Essays in the History of the Religion of Israel* (Cambridge: Harvard University Press, 1973).

_____. *From Epic to Canon: History and Literature in Ancient Israel* (Baltimore: Johns Hopkins University Press, 1998).

_____. "Reuben, First Born of Jacob," *ZAW* 100 Supplement issue (1988) 46-64.

Dahood, Mitchell. *Psalms I, 1-50: Introduction, Translation, and Notes* (AB 16; Garden City, N.Y.: Doubleday, 1965).

_____. *Psalms II, 51-100: Introduction, Translation, and Notes* (AB 17; Garden City, N.Y.: Doubleday, 1968).

_____. *Psalms III, 101-150: Introduction, Translation, and Notes* (AB 18; Garden City, N.Y.: Doubleday, 1970).

Davies, G. Henton. "High Place, Sanctuary," *IDB* 2.602-4.

Davila, James R. "The Name of God at Moriah: An Unpublished Fragment from 4QGenExod[a]," *JBL* 110 (1991) 577-82.

Daniélou, Jean and Henri Marrou, ed. *The Christian Centuries: A New History of the Catholic Church, Volume One: The First Six Hundred Years* (5 vols.; New York: Paulist, 1964).

Day, John. "Asherah," *ABD* 1.483-87.

_____. "A Case of Inner Scriptural Interpretation: The Dependence of Isaiah XXVI.13-XXVII.11 on Hosea XIII.4-XIV.10 (Eng. 9) and its Relevance to Some Theories of the Redaction of the Isaiah Apocalypse," *JTS* 31(1980) 309-19.

Dever, William G. "Asherah, Consort of Yahweh? New Evidence from Kuntillet 'Ajrud," *BASOR* 255 (1984) 21-37.

_____. "Gezer," *ABD* 2.1000.

_____. "Nahariyeh," *ABD* 4.995-96.

_____. "Recent Archaeological Confirmation of the Cult of Asherah in Ancient Israel," *Hebrew Studies* 23 (1982) 37-43.

_____. "Tell el-Qedah," *ABD* 5.579-80.

Díez Macho, Alejandro. *Neophyti I: Targum Palestinense. MS de la Biblioteca Vaticana* (5 vols.; Madrid-Barcelona: Consejo Superior de Investigaciones Científicas, 1968-78).

Dietrich, Manfried, Oswald Loretz, and Joaquín Sanmartín. *Keilalphabetischen Texte aus Ugarit* (Neukirchen-Vluyn: Neukirchener, 1976).

_____. *The Cuneiform Alphabetic Texts from Ugarit, Ras Ibn Hani and Other Places* (Abhandlungen zur Literatur Alt-Syrien-Palestinas und Mesopotamiens 8; Munster: Ugarit-Verlag, 1995).

Dogniez, Cecile. *Bibliography of the LXX 1970-1993* (Leiden: E. J. Brill, 1995).

Donner, Herbert and Wolfgang Röllig, ed. *Kanaanäische und aramäische Inschriften* (Wiesbaden: Otto Harrassowitz, 1962).

Dothan, Moshe. "Sanctuaries along the Coast of Canaan in the MB Period: Nahariyah," in *Temples and High Places in Biblical Times: Proceedings of the Colloquium in Honor of the Centennial of Hebrew Union College-Jewish Institute of Religion* (ed. Avraham Biran; Jerusalem: Keter, 1981).

Douglas, J. D. and Merrill C. Tenney, ed. *The New International Dictionary of the Bible* (Grand Rapids: Zondervan, 1987).

Driver, S. R. *Introduction to the Literature of the Old Testament* (7th ed.; New York: Charles Scribner's Sons, 1898).

Ebach, Jürgen. *Weltentstehung und Kulturentwicklung bei Philo von Byblos: Ein Beitrag zur Überlieferung der biblischen Urgeschichte im Rahmen des altorientalischen und antiken Schöpfungsglaubens* (Beiträge zur Wissenschaft vom Alten und Neuen Testament Sechste Folge 8; Stuttgart: Kohlhammer, 1979).

Edelman, Diana V., ed. *The Triumph of Elohim: From Yahwisms to Judaisms* (Grand Rapids: Eerdmans, 1996).

Eerdmans, B. D. "The Sepulchral Monument 'Maṣṣēbāh,'" *JBL* 30 (1911) 109-13.

Eichrodt, Walther. *Theology of the Old Testament* (tr. J. A. Baker; 2 vols.; Philadelphia: Westminster, 1961).

Eissfeldt, Otto. "Der Gott Bethel," *ARW* 28 (1930) 1-30.

Ellis, Peter F. *The Yahwist: The Bible's First Theologian* (Notre Dame, Ind.: Fides, 1968).

Emerton, John A. "New Light on Israelite Religion: The Implications of the Inscriptions from Kuntillet 'Ajrud," *ZAW* 94 (1982) 2-20.

Engle, James Robert. "Pillar Figurines of Iron Age Israel and Asherah/Asherim" (Ph.D. diss., University of Pittsburgh, 1979).

Epstein, J. N. and E. Z. Melamed, eds. *Mekhilta d'Rabbi Šim'on b. Jochai: Fragmenta in Geniza Cairensi reperta digessit apparatu critico, notis, praefatione instruxit* (Jerusalem: American Academy for Jewish Research, 1955).

Erlandsson, S. "זָנָה zānāh," *TDOT* 4.99-104.

Fensham, F. Charles. "Thunder-Stones in Ugaritic," *JNES* 18 (1959) 273-74.

Finkelstein, Louis, ed. *Sifre on Deuteronomy* (New York: Jewish Publication Society, 1969).

Fischer, B., et al. *Vetus Latina: Die Reste der altlateinischen Bible* (Freiburg: Herder, 1949-).

Fitzmyer, J. A. "The Phoenician Inscription from Pyrgi," *JAOS* 86 (1966) 285-97.

Fohrer, Georg. *History of Israelite Religion* (tr. David E. Green; Nashville: Abingdon, 1972).

Fowler, Arthur B. "High Places," *NIDB* 439-40.

Fraser, James George. *The Golden Bough* (1st ed.; 2 vols.; London: MacMillan, 1890).

Freedman, David Noel, ed. *The Anchor Bible Dictionary* (6 vols.; New York: Doubleday, 1992).

Frevel, Christian. *Ashera und der Ausschliesslichkeitsanspruch YHWHs: Beiträge zu literarischen, religionsgeschichtlichen und ikonographischen Aspekten der Asheradiskussion* (Bonner Biblische Beiträge 94/1-2; Weinheim: Beltz Athenäum, 1995).

Friedman, Richard Elliott. *Who Wrote the Bible?* (New York: Summit, 1987).

Frymer-Kensky, Tikva. *In the Wake of the Goddesses: Women, Culture, and The Biblical Transformation of Pagan Myth* (New York: Macmillan Free Press, 1992).

Galling, Kurt. *Der Altar in den Kulturen des alten Orients: eine archaologische Studie von Kurt Galling mit zwei Abschnitten von Hugo Gressman* (Berlin: K. Curius, 1925).

Geffcken, Johannes. *The Last Days of Greco-Roman Paganism* (tr. Sabine MacCormack; Europe in the Middle Ages 8; Amsterdam: North-Holland Publishing, 1978).

Glare, Peter G. W., ed. *Oxford Latin Dictionary* (Oxford: Clarendon, 1968-82).

Gleis, Matthias. *Die Bamah* (BZAW 251; Berlin: de Gruyter, 1997).

Good, Robert M. "Asherah," *HBD* 74-75.

Gordon, Cyrus H. *Ugaritic Textbook* (4th ed.; Rome: Pontifical Biblical Institute, 1967).

Gottwald, Norman. *A Light to the Nations: An Introduction to the Old Testament* (New York: Harper, 1959).

Graesser, Carl Frank, Jr. "Studies in *maṣṣēbôt*" (Ph.D. diss., Harvard University, 1969).

_____. "Standing Stones in Ancient Palestine," *BA* 35 (1974) 34-63.

Gray, George Buchanan. *Numbers* (International Critical Commentary; Edinburgh: T. & T. Clark, 1903).

_____. *Sacrifice in the Old Testament: Its Theory and Practice* (Oxford: Clarendon, 1925).

Grayson, A. K. *Assyrian Rulers of the Early First Millennium BC: I (114-859 BC)* (RIMA 2; Toronto: University of Toronto Press, 1991).

Gressmann, Hugo. "Dolmen, Masseben, und Napflöcher," *ZAW* 29 (1909) 113-28.

Grønbaek, J. H. "Juda und Amalek. Überlieferungs-geschichtliche Erwägungen zu Exodus 17, 8-16," *Studia Theologica* 18 (1964) 26-45.

Grossfeld, Bernard. "Bible: Translations, Ancient Versions," *EncJud* 4.841-51.

Gruber, Mayer I. "Hebrew Qĕdēšāh and her Canaanite and Akkadian Cognates," *UF* 18 (1986) 133-48.

Hackett, Jo Ann. "Religious Traditions in Israelite Transjordan," in *Ancient Israelite Religion: Essays in Honor of Frank Moore Cross* (ed. Patrick D. Miller, Jr., Paul D. Hanson, S. Dean McBride; Philadelphia: Fortress, 1987) 125-36.

Hadley, Judith M. "Some Drawings and Inscriptions on Two Pithoi From Kuntillet ʿAjrud," *VT* 37 (1987) 180-213.

Hallo, William W. "The Origins of the Sacrificial Cult: New Evidence from Mesopotamia and Israel," in *Ancient Israelite Religion: Essays in Honor of Frank Moore Cross* (ed. Patrick D. Miller, Jr., Paul D. Hanson, S. Dean McBride; Philadelphia: Fortress, 1987) 3-13.

Hammer, Reuven. *Sifre: A Tannaitic Commentary on the Book of Deuteronomy* (Yale Judaica Series 24; New Haven: Yale University Press, 1986).

Haran, Menahem. *Temples and Temple Service in Ancient Israel: An Inquiry into Biblical Cult Phenomena and the Historical Setting of the Priestly School* (Winona Lake, Ind.: Eisenbrauns, 1985).

Harl, M., G. Dorival and E. L. Munnich, eds. *La Bible Grecque des Septante: du Judaisme Hellenistique au Christianisme Ancien* (Paris: Cerf, 1988).

Harrelson, Walter. *Interpreting the Old Testament* (New York: Holt, Rinehart, and Winston, 1964).

Houtman, Cornelius. *Exodus* (3 vols.; Leuven: Peeters, 2000).

Heider, George C. "Molech," *ABD* 4.895-898.

_____. "Molech," in *Dictionary of Deities and Demons in the Bible* (ed. Karel van der Toorn, Bob Becking, and Pieter W. van der Horst; Leiden: E. J. Brill, 1999) 581-85.

Hendel, Ronald S. "The Social Origins of the Aniconic Tradition in Early Israel," *CBQ* 50 (1988) 365-382.

Herdner, Andree, ed. *Corpus des tablettes en cunéiformes alphabétiques* (2 vols.; Mission de Ras Shamra 10; Paris: Impremerie Nationale, 1963).

Hestrin, Ruth. "The Cult Stand from Ta'anach and its Religious Background," *Studia Phoenicia V: Phoenicia and the East Mediterranean in the First Millennium B.C.* (ed. E. Lipinski; Orientalia Lovaniensia Analecta 22; Leuven: Uitgeverij Peeters, 1987) 61-77.

_____. "The Lachish Ewer and the Asherah," *IEJ* 37 (1987) 212-23.

_____. "Understanding Asherah: Exploring Semitic Iconography," *BAR* 17/5 (Sept/Oct 1991) 50-59.

Hillers, Delbert. "Analyzing the Abominable: Our Understanding of Canaanite Religion," *JQR* 75 (1985) 253-69.

_____. *Micah: A Commentary on the Book of the Prophet Micah* (Hermeneia; Philadelphia: Fortress, 1984).

Holladay, W. L. *Jeremiah I: A Commentary on the Book of the Prophet Jeremiah, Chapters 1-25* (Hermeneia; Philadelphia: Fortress, 1986).

_____. "'On Every High Hill and Under Every Green Tree'," *VT* 11 (1961) 170-76.

Horovitz, H. S. and I. A. Rabin, ed. *Mechilta d'Rabbi Ismael* (Jerusalem: Wahrmann: 1970).

Horovitz, H. S., ed. *Siphre d'Be Rab. Fasciculus primus: Siphre ad Numeros adjecto Siphre zutta cum variis lectionibus et adnotationibus* (Leipzig: 1917, repr. Jerusalem: Wahrmann, 1966).

Hurowitz, Victor Avigdor. "אבן משכית—A New Interpretation," *JBL* 118 (1999) 201-8.

Hurvitz, Avi. *A Linguistic Study of the Relationship between the Priestly Source and the Book of Ezekiel: A New Approach to an Old Problem* (Cahiers de la Revue Biblique 20; Paris: Gabalda, 1982).

Iakovidis, Spyridon. "A Peak Sanctuary in Bronze Age Thera," in *Temples and High Places in Biblical Times: Proceedings of the Colloquium in Honor of the Centennial of Hebrew Union College-Jewish Institute of Religion* (ed. Avraham Biran; Jerusalem: Keter, 1981) 54-60.

Ishida, Tomoo. "The Structure and Historical Implications of the Lists of Pre-Israelite Nations," *Biblica* 60 (1979) 461-90.

Jacobsen, Thorkild. "Mesopotamia," in Henri Frankfort, *The Intellectual Adventure of Ancient Man* (Chicago: University of Chicago Press, 1946).

Japhet, Sara. *The Ideology of the Book of Chronicles and Its Place in Biblical Thought* (Beiträge zur Erforschung des Alten Testaments und des Antiken Judentums 9; Frankfurt am Main: Peter Lang, 1989).

Jaroš, Karl. *Die Stellung des Elohisten zur Kanaanäischen Religion* (Göttingen: Vandenhoeck & Ruprecht, 1974).

Jastrow, Marcus. *A Dictionary of the Targumim, the Talmud Babli and Yerushalmi, and the Midrashic Literature* (2 vols.; London: Luzac, 1903; repr. 2 vols. in one; Brooklyn: Traditional Press, 1975).

Jenks, Alan. "Elohist," *ABD* 2.478-82.

_____. *The Elohist and North Israelite Traditions* (SBLMS 22; Missoula: Scholars Press, 1977).

Kamesar, Adam. *Jerome, Greek Scholarship, and the Hebrew Bible: A Study of the Quaestiones Hebraicae in Genesim* (Oxford: Clarendon, 1993).

Kaufman, Stephen A., and Michael Sokoloff. *A Key-word In-context Concordance to Targum Neofiti: A Guide to the Complete Palestinian Aramaic Text of the Torah* (Baltimore: Johns Hopkins University Press, 1993).

Kaufmann, Yehezkel. *The Religion of Israel: From Its Beginnings to the Babylonian Exile* (tr. and abridged by Moshe Greenberg; Chicago: University of Chicago Press, 1960).

Kautzsch, Emil, ed. *Gesenius' Hebrew Grammar* (tr. Arthur. E. Cowley; Oxford: Oxford University Press, 1910).

Kempinski, Aharon. "Joshua's Altar: An Iron Age I Watchtower," *BAR* 12/1 (Jan/Feb 1986) 42-49.

King, Philip J. "Micah," *Jerome Biblical Commentary* (ed. Raymond E. Brown, Joseph A. Fitzmyer, and Roland E. Murphy; Englewood Cliffs, N.J.: Prentice-Hall, 1968).

Klein, Michael L. *Anthropomorphisms and Anthropopathisms in the Targumim of the Pentateuch* (Jerusalem: Makor, 1981).

_____. "Converse Translation: A Targumic Technique," *Biblica* 57 (1976) 515-37.

_____. *The Fragment Targums of the Pentateuch According to their extant sources* (2 vols.; Analecta Biblica 76; Rome: Biblical Institute, 1980).

_____. *Geniza Manuscripts of Palestinian Targum to the Pentateuch* (Cincinnati: Hebrew Union College Press, 1986).

_____. "The Translation of Anthropomorphisms and Anthropopathisms in the Targumim," in *Congress Volume: Vienna 1980* (ed. J. A. Emerton; VTSup 32; Leiden: E. J. Brill, 1981) 162-77.

Kloppenborg, John S. "Joshua 22: The Priestly Editing of an Ancient Tradition," *Biblica* 62 (1981) 345-71.

Knohl, Israel. "The Conception of God and Cult in the Priestly Torah and in the Holiness School" (Ph.D. diss., Hebrew University, 1988).

_____. "The Priestly Torah Versus the Holiness School: Sabbath and the Festivals," *Shnaton* 7-8 (1983-84) 109-46 [Heb]; Eng. tr. *HUCA* 58 (1987) 65-117.

_____. *The Sanctuary of Silence: The Priestly Torah and the Holiness School* (Minneapolis: Fortress, 1995).

Kutscher, Raphael. "The Cult of Dumuzi/Tammuz," *Bar Ilan Studies in Assyriology* (ed. J. Klein and A. Skaist; Tel Aviv: Bar Ilan University Press, 1990) 29-44.

Lang, B. "זָבַח zābhach; זֶבַח zebhach," *TDOT* 4.8-29.

Langlamet, F. *Gilgal et les récits de la traversée du Jourdain (Jos., III-IV)* (Cahiers de la Revue Biblique 11; Paris: Gabalda, 1969).

LaRocca-Pitts, Elizabeth C. "Daughter (or Son or Child) Passed Through Fire, Burned, or Sacrificed," in *Women in Scripture: A Dictionary of Named and Unnamed Women in the Hebrew Bible, The Apocryphal/Deuterocanonical books, and the New Testament* (ed. Carol Meyers, Toni Craven, and Ross S. Kraemer; Boston: Houghton Mifflin, 2000) 224-25.

Lemaire, André. "Les Inscriptions de Khirbet El-Qôm et l'ashérah de YHWH," *RB* 84 (1977) 595-608, pl. 31.

_____. "Who or What was Yahweh's Asherah? Startling New Inscriptions from Two Different Sites Reopen the Debate about the Meaning of Asherah," *BAR* 10/6 (Nov/Dec 1984) 42-51.

Lerner, Myron B. "Altar," *EncJud* 1.767-71.

Levenson, Jon D. "Who Inserted the Book of Torah?," *HTR* 68 (1975) 203-33.

Levi, Doro. "Features and Continuity of Cretan Peak Cults," in *Temples and High Places in Biblical Times: Proceedings of the Colloquium in Honor of the Centennial of Hebrew Union College-Jewish Institute of Religion* (ed. Avraham Biran; Jerusalem: Keter, 1981) 38-46.

Levine, Baruch A. "Research in the Priestly Source: The Linguistic Factor," *Eretz-Israel* 16 (1982) 124-31 [Heb].

Lewis, Theodore J. *Cults of the Dead in Ancient Israel and Ugarit* (HSM 39; Atlanta: Scholars Press, 1989).

_____. "Divine Images and Aniconism in Ancient Israel," *JAOS* 118 (1998) 36-53.

Liddell, Henry George and Robert Scott, ed. *A Greek-English Lexicon* (revising ed., Henry S. Jones and Roderick McKenzie; Oxford: Clarendon, 1968).

Lipiński, Edward. "The Goddess Atirat in Ancient Arabia, in Babylon, and in Ugarit: Her Relation to the Moon-god and the Sun-goddess," *OLP* 3 (1972) 101-19.

Louie, Wallace. "The Meaning, Characteristics and Role of Asherah in Old Testament Idolatry in Light of Extra-Biblical Evidence" (Th.D. diss., Grace Theological Seminary, 1989).

Lund, Shirley and Julia Foster. *Variant Versions of Targumic Traditions Within Codex Neofiti 1* (SBLAS 2: Missoula: Scholars Press, 1977).

Lust, Johan, E. Eynikel, K. Hauspie and G. Chamberlain. *A Greek-English Lexicon of the Septuagint* (Stuttgart: Deutsche Bibelgesellschaft: 1992).

Macalister, R. A. S. *Bible Side-Lights from the Mound of Gezer* (London: Hodder and Stoughton, 1906).

Maher, Michael. *Targum Pseudo-Jonathan: Genesis Translated, with Introduction and Notes* (The Aramaic Bible 1b; Collegeville, Minn.: Michael Glazier/Liturgical, 1992).

Maier, Walter A., III. *ʾAšerah: Extrabiblical Evidence* (HSM 37; Atlanta: Scholars Press, 1986).

Manor, Dale. "Massebah," *ABD* 4.602.

May, Herbert G. "Ezekiel," *The Interpreter's Bible* (New York: Abingdon, 1956) 6.39-338.

Mazar, Amihai. *Archaeology of the Land of the Bible: 10,000-586 B.C.E* (Anchor Bible Reference Library; New York: Doubleday, 1990).

_____. "Bronze Bull Found in Israelite 'High Place' From the Time of the Judges," *BAR* 9/5 (Sept/Oct 1983) 34-40.

_____. "On Cult Places and Early Israelites: A Response to Michael Coogan," *BAR* 14/4 (July/August 1988) 45.

McCarter, P. Kyle. "Aspects of the Religion of the Israelite Monarchy: Biblical and Epigraphic Data," in *Ancient Israelite Religion: Essays in Honor of Frank Moore Cross* (ed. Patrick D. Miller, Jr., Paul D. Hanson, S. Dean McBride; Philadelphia: Fortress, 1987) 137-155.

_____. "High Place," *OCB* 284-85.

_____. *II Samuel: A New Translation with Introduction and Commentary* (AB 9; Garden City N.Y.: Doubleday, 1984).

_____. *Textual Criticism: Recovering the Text of the Hebrew Bible* (Philadelphia: Fortress, 1986).

McCarthy, D. J. *Treaty and Covenant* (Rome: Pontifical Biblical Institute, 1963).

McKenzie, Steven L. *The Chronicler's Use of the Deuteronomistic History* (HSM 33; Atlanta: Scholars, 1984).

McNamara, Martin. *Targum and Testament: Aramaic Paraphrases of the Hebrew Bible: A Light on the New Testament* (Shannon: Irish University Press, 1972).

_____. *Targum Neofiti 1: Genesis Translated, with Apparatus and Notes* (The Aramaic Bible 1a; Collegeville, Minn: Michael Glazier/Liturgical, 1992).

Meshel, Ze'ev. *Kuntillet 'Ajrud: A Religious Centre From the Time of the Judaean Monarchy on the Border of Sinai* (Jerusalem: Israel Museum, 1978).

Mettinger, Tryggve N. D. *No Graven Image? Israelite Aniconism in Its Ancient Near Eastern Context* (Coniectanea Biblica Old Testament Series 42; Stockholm: Almqvist & Wiksell, 1995).

Metzger, Bruce M. and Michael D. Coogan, ed. *The Oxford Companion to the Bible* (Oxford: Oxford University Press, 1993).

_____ and Roland E. Murphy, ed. *The New Oxford Annotated Bible with the Apocryphal/Deuterocanonical Books* (New York: Oxford University Press, 1991).

Meyers, Carol L. "David as Temple Builder," in *Ancient Israelite Religion: Essays in Honor of Frank Moore Cross* (ed. Patrick D. Miller, Paul D. Hanson, S. Dean McBride; Philadelphia: Fortress, 1987) 357-76.

_____. *The Tabernacle Menorah: A Synthetic Study of a Symbol From the Biblical Cult* (ASORDS 2; Missoula: Scholars Press, 1976).

Milgrom, Jacob. *Leviticus 1-16: A New Translation with Introduction and Commentary* (AB 3; New York: Doubleday, 1991).

_____. *Leviticus 17-22: A New Translation with Introduction and Commentary* (AB 3A; New York: Doubleday, 2000).

_____. *Leviticus 23-27: A New Translation with Introduction and Commentary* (AB 3B; New York: Doubleday, 2001).

_____. *Numbers* (JPS Torah Commentary; Philadelphia: Jewish Publication Society, 1989).

_____. *Studies in Cultic Theology and Terminology* (Studies in Judaism in Late Antiquity 36; Leiden: E. J. Brill, 1983).

Miller, Patrick D. "Aspects of Religion at Ugarit," in *Ancient Israelite Religion: Essays in Honor of Frank Moore Cross* (ed. Patrick D. Miller, Jr., Paul D. Hanson, S. Dean McBride; Philadelphia: Fortress, 1987) 53-66.

_____. "Israelite Religion," in *The Hebrew Bible and Its Modern Interpreters*, (ed. Douglas A. Knight and Gene M. Tucker; Philadelphia: Fortress, 1985) 201-37.

_____ and J. J. M. Roberts *The Hand of the Lord: A Reassessment of the Ark Narrative of 1 Samuel* (Baltimore: Johns Hopkins University Press, 1977).

Migne, Jacques-Paul. *Patrologiae cursus completus . . . : Series Latina* (Paris: Migne, 1844-1865).

de Moor, Johannes C. "אֲשֵׁרָה ᵃshērāh," *TDOT* 1.438-44.

Moore, George F. "Massebah," *Encyclopaedia Biblica* (New York: Macmillan, 1902) 3.2982.

Muraoka, T. *A Greek-English Lexicon of the Septuagint (12 prophets)* (Louvain: Peeters, 1993).

Nakhai, Beth Alpert. "What's a Bamah? How Sacred Space Functioned in Ancient Israel," *BAR* 20/3 (May/June 1994) 18-29, 77-78.

Neusner, Jacob. *Mekhilta According to Rabbi Ishmael: An Analytical Translation* (2 vols.; Brown Judaic Studies 154; Atlanta: Scholars Press, 1988).

_____. *Sifra: An Analytical Translation* (3 vols.; Brown Judaic Studies 140; Atlanta: Scholar's Press, 1988).

Nielsen, Kjeld. *Incense in Ancient Israel* (VTSup 38; Leiden: E. J. Brill, 1986).

Nieman, David. "PGR: A Canaanite Cult-object in the Old Testament," *JBL* 67 (1948) 55-60.

Noth, Martin. *The Chronicler's History* (tr. H. G. M. Williamson; JSOTSup 50; Sheffield: JSOT Press, 1987).

_____. *The Deuteronomistic History* (tr. Jane Doull and John Barton; JSOTSup 15; Sheffield: JSOT Press, 1981).

_____. *Exodus: A Commentary* (tr. J. S. Bowden; OTL; Philadelphia: Westminster, 1962).

_____. *History of the Pentateuchal Traditions* (tr. Bernard Anderson; Chico: Scholars Press, 1981).

Obermann, Julian. "Votive Inscriptions from Ras Shamra," *JAOS* 61 (1941) 31-45.

O'Connell, Kevin G. "The List of Seven Peoples in Canaan," in *The Answers Lie Below: Essays in Honor of Lawrence Edmund Toombs* (ed. Henry O. Thompson; Lanham, Md.: University Press of America, 1984) 221-41.

Oden, Robert. *The Bible Without Theology: The Theological Tradition and Alternatives to It* (New York: Harper & Row, 1987).

_____. "The Persistence of Canaanite Religion," *BA* 39 (1976) 31-36.

Olyan, Saul. *Asherah and the Cult of Yahweh in Israel* (SBLMS; Atlanta: Scholars Press, 1988).

_____. "The Cultic Confessions of Jer 2,27a," *ZAW* 99 (1987) 254-59.

Patai, Raphael. *The Hebrew Goddess* (3d ed.; Detroit: Wayne State University Press, 1990).

Paul, Shalom. *Amos: A Commentary on the Book of Amos* (ed. Frank Moore Cross; Hermeneia; Minneapolis: Augsburg Fortress, 1991).

Perlman, Alice Lenore. "Asherah and Astarte in the Old Testament and Ugaritic Literature" (Ph.D. diss., Graduate Theological Union, 1978).

Peters, Melvin K. H. "Septuagint," *ABD* 5.1093-104.

Petrie, W. M. Flinders. *Palestine and Israel* (London: SPCK, 1934).

Pettey, Richard J. "Asherah: Goddess of Israel?" (Ph.D. diss., Marquette University, 1985).

Philips, Elaine A. "On Mekhilta d'Rabbi Ishmael: A Study in Composition and Context," (Ph.D. diss., Annenberg Research Institute, 1991).

Pirḳê de Rabbi Eliezer: (The Chapters of Rabbi Eliezer the Great) according to the Text of the Manuscript belonging to Abraham Epstein of Vienna (tr. Gerald Friedlander; 4th ed.; New York: Sepher-Hermon, 1981).

Polzin, Robert. *Late Biblical Hebrew: Toward an Historical Typology of Biblical Hebrew Prose* (Missoula: Scholars Press, 1976).

Pope, Marvin. *El in the Ugaritic Texts* (VTSup 2; Leiden: E. J. Brill, 1955).

Porter, Joshua R. "High Place," *HBD* 391-93.

Porten, B. *Archives from Elephantine: The Life of an Ancient Jewish Military Colony* (Berkeley and Los Angeles: University of California Press, 1986).

_____. "The Religion of the Jews of Elephantine in Light of the Hermopolis Papyri," *JNES* 28 (1969) 118-21.

Preuss, Horst Dietrich. "גִּלּוּלִים gillûlîm; גִּלֻּלִים gillulîm," *TDOT* 3.1-5.

Pritchard, James B. *Palestinian Figurines in Relation to Certain Goddesses Known through Literature* (AOS 24; New Haven: AOS, 1943).

Provan, Iain. *Hezekiah and the Books of Kings: A Contribution to the Debate about the Compostion of the Deuteronomistic History* (BZAW 172; Berlin: de Gruyter, 1988).

de Pury, Albert. "Yahwist ('J') Source," *ABD* 6.1012-20.

von Rad, Gerhard. *Deuteronomy: A Commentary* (OTL; London: SCM, 1966).

_____. *Genesis: A Commentary* (Philadelphia: Westminster, 1973).

_____. *Old Testament Theology* (tr. D. M. G. Stalker; 2 vols.; New York: Harper, 1962).

Rahlfs, Alfred. *Septuaginta: Id est Vetus Testamentum graece iuxta LXX interpretes* (2 vols. in 1; Stuttgart: Deutsche Bibelgesellschaft, 1979).

Rainey, Anson. "The Order of Sacrifices in Old Testament Ritual Texts," *Biblica* 51 (1970) 485-98.

Reed, William L. "Asherah," *IDB* 1.250-52.

_____. *The Asherah in the Old Testament* (Fort Worth: Texas Christian University Press, 1949).

Rehkopf, Friedrich. *Septuaginta-Vokabular* (Göttingen: Vandenhoeck & Ruprecht, 1989).

Rendsburg, Gary. "Late Biblical Hebrew and the Date of 'P,'" *JANESCU* 12 (1980) 65-80.

Rendtorff, Rolf. *Studien zur Geschichte des Opfers im Alten Israel* (Neukirchen-Vluyn: Neukirchener Verlag, 1967).

Ringgren, Helmer. *Israelite Religion* (tr. David E. Green; Philadelphia: Fortress, 1966).

_____. "The Religion of Ancient Syria," in *Religions of the Past* (eds. C. J. Bleeker and Geo Widengren; Historia Religionum: Handbook for the History of Religions; Leiden: E. J. Brill, 1969).

Roth, Cecil and Geoffrey Wigoder, et al. *Encyclopaedia Judaica* (16 vols.; New York: Macmillan, 1971-72).

Rudolph, Wilhelm. *Der 'Elohist' von Exodus bis Josua* (BZAW 68; Berlin: Töpelmann, 1938).

Russell, Emmett. "Pillars," *NIDB* 790b-91a.

Sabatier P. *Bibiorum sacrorum latinae versiones antiquae seu Vetus Itala* (Rheims, 1745-49).

Sandmel, Samuel. *The Hebrew Scriptures: An Introduction to Their Literature and Religious Ideas* (New York: Knopf, 1963).

Sarna, Nahum. *Genesis* (JPS Torah Commentary; Philadelphia: Jewish Publication Society, 1989).

Schmid, Hans Heinrich. *Der sogenannte Jahwist: Beobachtungen und Fragen zur Pentateuchforschung* (Zürich: Theologischer Verlag, 1976).

Schmidt, Brian B. *Israel's Beneficent Dead: Ancestor Cult and Necromancy in Ancient Israelite Religion and Tradition* (Winona Lake, Ind.: Eisenbrauns, 1996).

Schunck, K. D. "בָּמָה bāmāh," *TDOT* 2.139-45.

Sellin, Ernst. "Zu der ursprünglichen Bedeutung der Mazzeben," *OLZ* 15 (1912) 119-26.

Setel, T. Drorah. "Prophets and Pornography: Female Sexual Imagery in Hosea," in *Feminist Interpretation of the Bible* (ed. Letty M. Russell; Philadelphia: Westminster, 1985) 86-95.

van Seters, John. *In Search of History: Historiography in the Ancient World and The Origins of Biblical History* (New Haven: Yale University Press, 1983).

Shanks, Hershel. "Two Early Israelite Cult Sites Now Questioned," *BAR* 14/1 (Jan/Feb 1988) 48-52.

Shiloh, Yigal. "Iron Age Sanctuaries and Cult Elements in Palestine," *Symposia Celebrating the Seventy-Fifth Anniversary of the Founding of the American Schools of Oriental Research (1900-1975)* (ed. Frank Moore Cross; Missoula: ASOR, 1975) 147-57.

Sifra: Halachischer Midrasch zu Leviticus (tr. Jacob Winter; Schriften der Gesellschaft zur Forderung der Wissenschaft des Judentums 42; Breslau: Stefan Munz, 1938).

Smith, Jonathan Z. "When the Bough Breaks," *History of Religions* 12 (1972) 324-71.

Smith, Sidney. *Early History of Assyria* (New York: E. P. Dutton, 1928).

Smith, W. Robertson. *Lectures on the Religion of the Semites*, (Edinburgh: Adam and Charles Black, 1894).

Snaith, Norman Henry. "Sacrifices in the Old Testament," *VT* 7 (1957) 308-17.

Speiser, E. A. *Genesis: Introduction, Translation, and Notes* (AB 1; Garden City, N.Y.: Doubleday, 1962).

Sperber, Alexander. *The Bible in Aramaic* (5 vols.; Leiden: E. J. Brill, 1973).

Spencer, John R. "Golden Calf," *ABD* 2.1065-69.

Spoer, H. H. "Versuch einer Erklärung des Zusammenhanges zwischen Dolmen, Mal- und Schalensteinen in Palälstina," *ZAW* 28 (1908) 271-90.

Stager, Lawrence E. and Philip J. King. *Life in Biblical Israel* (Louisville: Westminster/John Knox, 2001).

Sun, Henry T. C. "Holiness Code," *ABD* 3.256.

Swete, Henry B. *An Introduction to the Old Testament in Greek* (2d ed.; Cambridge: Cambridge University Press, 1914; repr. Peabody, Mass.: Hendrickson, 1989).

Terrien, Samuel. "The Omphalos Myth and Hebrew Religion," *VT* 20 (1970) 315-38.

The Theodosian Code and Novels and the Sirmondian Constitutions (tr. Clyde Pharr; Princeton: Princeton University Press, 1952).

Thomas, D. Winton. "Some Observations on the Hebrew word רענן," in *Hebraishe Wortforschung: Festschrift zum 80 Geburtstag von Walter Baumgartner* (VTSup 16; Leiden: E. J. Brill, 1967) 387-97.

Toombs, Lawrence E. "Shechem," *ABD* 5.1179.

van der Toorn, Karel. "The Nature of the Biblical Teraphim in Light of the Cuneiform Evidence," *CBQ* 52 (1990) 203-22.

Tov, Emanuel. *Textual Criticism of the Hebrew Bible* (Minneapolis: Fortress, 1992).

_____. *The Text-Critical Use of the Septuagint in Biblical Research* (Jerusalem: Simor, 1981).

Ussishkin, David. "The 'Ghassulian' Temple in Ein Gedi and the Origin of the Hoard from Nahal Mishmar," *BA* 34 (1971) 23-39.

_____. "Megiddo," *ABD* 4.668-69.

Vaughan, Patrick H. *The Meaning of 'Bāmâ' in the Old Testament: A Study of Etymological, Textual and Archaeological Evidence* (SOTSMS 3; Cambridge: Cambridge University Press, 1974).

de Vaux, Roland. *Ancient Israel: Its Life and Institutions* (tr. John McHugh; New York: McGraw-Hill, 1961).

_____. *Studies in Old Testament Sacrifice* (Cardiff: University of Wales Press, 1964).

Weber, Max. *Ancient Judaism* (tr. Hans H. Gerth and Don Martindale; London: George Allen & Unwin, 1952).

Weinfeld, Moshe. *Deuteronomy and the Deuteronomic School* (Oxford: Clarendon, 1972).

_____. "Deuteronomy, Book of," *ABD* 2.168-83.

_____. "Kuntillet 'Ajrud Inscriptions and Their Significance," *Studi Epigrafici e Linguistici* 1 (1984) 121-30.

Weiss, A. H., ed. *Sifra de-Ve Rav* (Vienna: 1862).

Wellhausen, Julius. *Die Composition des Hexateuchs und der Historischen Bücher des Alten Testaments* (2d ed.; Berlin: Reimer, 1889).

_____. *Prolegomena to the History of Ancient Israel* (tr. Black and Menzies; New York: Meridian, 1957; translated from the German edition, Berlin: Reimer, 1883).

Westenholz, Joan Goodnick. "Tamar, *Qĕdēšā, Qadištu*, and Sacred Prostitution in Mesopotamia," *HTR* 82 (1989) 245-65.

Westermann, Claus. *Genesis 1-11: A Commentary* (tr. John J. Scullion; Minneapolis: Augsburg, 1984).

_____. *Genesis 12-36: A Commentary* (tr. John J. Scullion; Minneapolis: Augsburg, 1985).

Wevers, John W. *Ezekiel* (Century Bible; London: Nelson, 1969).

_____. *Notes on the Greek Text of Exodus* (Septuagint and Cognate Studies 30; Atlanta: Scholars Press, 1990).

Widengren, Geo. "Israelite-Jewish Religion," in *Religions of the Past* (ed. Claas J. Bleeker and Geo Widengren; Historia Religionum: Handbook for the History of Religions; Leiden: E. J. Brill, 1969).

Wiener, Harold Marcus. *Altars of the Old Testament* (Leipzig: Hinrich, 1927).

Wiggins, Steve. *A Reassessment of 'Asherah': A Study According to the Textual Sources of the First Two Millennia B.C.E.* (Neukirchen-Vluyn: Neukirchener Verlag, 1993).

Winter, Jacob and August Wünsche, ed. *Mechiltha: Ein tannaitischer Midrasch zu Exodus* (Zürich: Georg Olms Verlag, 1990).

Wolff, Hans Walter. *Hosea: A Commentary on the Book of the Prophet Hosea*, (tr. Gary Stansell; ed. Paul D. Hanson; Hermeneia; Philadelphia: Fortress, 1974).

_____. *Joel and Amos: A Commentary on the Books of Joel and Amos* (trs. Waldemar Janzen, S. Dean McBride, and Charles A. Muenchow; ed. S. Dean McBride; Hermeneia; Philadelphia: Fortress, 1977).

_____. *Micah* (BKAT 14/12; Neukirchen-Vluyn: Neukirchener Verlag, 1980).

Yamashita, Tadanori. "The Goddess Asherah" (Ph.D. diss., Yale University, 1964).

Yeivin, S. "On the Use and Misuse of Archaeology in Interpreting the Bible," *PAAJR* 34 (1966) 141-54.

Zertal, Adam. "Has Joshua's Altar Been Found on Mt. Ebal?," *BAR* 11/1 (Jan/Feb 1985) 26-43.

_____. "How Can Kempinski Be So Wrong!," *BAR* 12/1 (Jan/Feb 1986) 43-53.

_____. "Shechem, Tower of," *ABD* 5.1186-87.

Zevit, Ziony. "Converging Lines of Evidence Bearing on the Date of P," *ZAW* 94 (1982) 481-511.

_____. "The Khirbet el-Qom Inscription mentioning a Goddess," *BASOR* 255 (1984) 39-48.

Zimmerli, Walther. *Ezekiel 2: A Commentary on the Book of the Prophet Ezekiel, chapters 25-48* (tr. James D. Martin; ed. Paul D. Hanson and Jay Greenspoon; Hermeneia; Philadelpha: Fortress, 1983).

Index of Ancient Sources

Biblical verses:

Due to the prohibitively large number of biblical references discussed in this study, individual verses are not listed in a traditional verse index format. Rather, the reader will find biblical references listed in the Subject Index within entries on the topics which they address. The entries will then take the reader to pages within the book which list all of the verses on that topic. Cross-referencing within the text will then lead the reader to other sections of the work where those verses are discussed.

Mishnah:

'Ăbôdāh Zārāh: 322; 328-29; **3:5,** 320 n17, 323-25; **3:7,** 320 n17, 325, 329, 332; **3:8,** 326; **3:9,** 326; **3:10,** 326; **4:1,** 332

Məgillāh: **1:10,** 333 n50, 337 n58

Məʿîlāh: 322; **3:8,** 327

'Orlāh: 322; **1:7-8,** 327

Sūkkāh: 322; **3:1-3,** 327

Zəbāḥîm: **14:4-8,** 333 n50, 337, 345

Midrashic Texts:

Mekhilta de-Rabbi Ishmael: 318; *Bahodesh 11,* 345

Mekhilta de-Rabbi Shimon bar Yohai: 318

Pirke de Rabbi Eliezer: 26, 320 n17; 322 n21

Sifra: 300, 305, 318-319; *Behar,* 331; *Behuqotai,* 337; *Qədōšîm,* 300 n27, 305 n51, 322, 330

Sifre: 318, 322, 332; *60,* 324-26; *61,* 325-26, 344; *65-66,* 345; *145,* 327; *146,* 331

Elephantine: 89; 186

Qumran: 1QIsa[a], 149

Inscriptions:

Dagan Stelae (*KTU* 6:13-14): 149 n58

Kuntillet 'Ajrud: 69 n40; 88; 161-62 n6; 165-68, 165-68 nn21-33; 185-87, 185 n56; 263 n22

Khirbet el-Qom: 161-62 n6; 166, 166 n25; 185; 187; 263 n22

Lachish Ewer: 167, 167 n30

Maʿṣub (*KAI* 19): 185 n58

Mesha (*KAI* 181): 142 n42; 145 n51; 149; 275

Panammû II (*KAI* 215): 35 n39

Palmyra (*CIS* 2.3917): 185 n62

Pyrgi (*KAI* 277): 185 n59; 187 n73; 263 n22

Punic Inscription (*CIS* 1.3): 186 n67

Punic Inscription (*CIS* 1.3779): 185 n58

Sardis (*KAI* 260): 185 n61

Sefirê (*KAI* 222): 96 n26; 185 n60

Ugaritic Texts:

Aqhat: 63, 63 n24

altars: see *mizbəhôt*

'Asherah: Israelite as well as Canaanite deity, 350; as related to *ăšērîm*, 187-92

'Astarte: as translation for *ăšērāh,* in the Hebrew, in the LXX: 260-61

'ăṣabbîm: see cultic statuary

ăšērîm: 161-204; **scholarship on**: 161-68; literary approaches, 162-64; archaeological approaches, 164-68; **biblical data**: summary 168-71; *'ăšērîm* **or related topics in**: Exod 34, 22-26; **E**, 27-28; **P**, 35; **H**, 39; **D**, 48; **Josh**, 54; **Judg**, 59-60; **Kgs**, 68-9; **Chr**, 81-82; **Amos**, 88-89; **Hos**, 92-93; **Mic**, 99-100; **1Isa**, 102-3; **Jer**, 105-6; **Ezek**, 111; **3Isa**, 116; **Zech 1-8**, 119; **Pss**, 122; *ăšērîm as live trees*: 171-85; famous biblical trees, 175-80; the *ēṣ raʿănān* formula, 180-83; trees in the early translated traditions, 183; *ăšērîm as shrines*: 185-87; *ăšērîm as depictions or symbols of 'Asherah*:187-92; **associations with**: *bāmôt*, 192; *maṣṣēbôt*, 193-94; *mizbəhôt*, 195-97; cultic statuary, 197-200; other gods or cultures, 200-01; **conclusions from biblical data**: 201-04; **LXX translations of**: ἄλσος, 255-59; δένδρον, 259-60; Ἀστάρτη, 260-61; other LXX uses of ἄλσος, 261; **Latin translations**: 295-98; *lucus* and *nemus*, 295-96; other Vulgate uses for *lucus*, 296; other Vulgate uses for *nemus*, 296; **Targumic renderings**: 319-21; **Midrashic and Mishnaic interpretations**: as trees with idols buried beneath 321-29; **grouped with other items in Kings**: 73-74

bāmôt: 127-59; **scholarship on**: etymological studies, 127-29; archaeological

studies, 130-35; **biblical data**: summary, 135; *bāmôt* **or related topics in**: **J**, 19-20; **E**, 27; **P**, 35; **H**, 39; **D**, 47; **Josh**, 53; **Sam**, 62; **Kgs**, 64-68; **Chr**, 79-81; **Amos**, 87-88; **Hos**, 91-92; **Mic**, 98-99; **1Isa**, 101-2; in **Jer**, 104-5; **Ezek**, 109-11; **Pss**, 122; **acceptability**, 136-39; 351; **associations with**: Moab, 140-43, 350; child sacrifice, 143-45, 350; temples, 145-48; *ăšērîm*, 148-49; *maṣṣēbôt*, 149-50; *mizbəhôt*, 150-53; cultic statuary, 153-56; the *ēṣ raʿănān* formula, 156-57; **conclusions on biblical data**: 158-59; **LXX renderings**: 270-85; transliteration, 271-73; ὑψηλός, 273-74; βουνος, 274; translations based on cultic associations: 274-80; ἄλσος, 274-75; βωμός, 278-80; Θυσιαστήριον, 280; στήλη, 275-78; other LXX uses for ὑψηλός, 280-82; βωμός, 282-83; **Latin translations**: 306-12; *excelsum*, 306-7; *ara*, 307-8; *fanum*, 308; *altitudo*, 308; *sublimis*, 308; *collis*, 308; other Vulgate uses for: *excelsus*, 308-9; *ara*, 310; *fanum*, 308; *sublimis*, 310; *altitudo*, 311; **Targumic renderings**: 333-37; Targum of Chronicles dual translation, 335; **Midrashic and Mishnaic interpretations**: 337-39, as temples, 337, 350; **grouped with other items in Kings**: 73-74

bāmôtê: as related to *bāmôt*, 127-29; **in**: **Hab**, 108; **3Isa**, 116; **Pss**, 122; **Job**, 123; **LXX translations**: 270; **Latin translations**: *excelsum*

child sacrifice: 1, 9-10, 18, 102 n37, 104-5, 107, 110, 112-114, 123-24, 137, 140, 142-45, 152, 154, 158, 350; **connection with** *bāmôt*: 143-45, 350

cultic statuary: *'eben maśkît*: in H, 39-41; as a sign of Late Biblical Hebrew 41-43; *'ĕlîlîm*: in: H, 40-41; Chr, 83-84; 1Isa, 103-4; Jer, 106-7; Hab, 108; Ezek, 112-14; Pss, 122; Job, 124; *'ĕlō hê kesep/zāhāb*: in: Covenant Code, 34; *'ĕlōhê hannēkār*: in: E, 30; Josh, 57; *gillûlîm*: in: H, 40-41; Dtr, 52-53; Kgs, 71-72; Jer, 106-7; Ezek, 112-14; as a sign of Late Biblical Hebrew, 41-43; *gods of wood and stone*: in: Dtr, 52-53; Kgs, 71-72; Hab, 108; Ezek, 112-14; *massēkôt*: in: Exod 34, 27; E, 30; H, 40-41; D, 50-51; Judg, 60-61; Kgs, 71-72; Chr, 83-84; Neh, 84; Hos, 96-98; 1Isa, 103-04; Nah, 108; Hab, 108; 2Isa, 115-16; Pss, 122; *maśkîyōt*: in: P, 35-36, 38; as a sign of Late Biblical Hebrew, 41-43; *nesek*: in: Jer, 106-7; 2Isa 115-16; *semel*: in Chr, 81-84; *'ăṣabbîm*: in: Sam, 64; Chr, 83-84; Hos, 96-98; Mic, 100-101; 1Isa, 103-4; Jer, 106-7; 2Isa, 115-16; Zech, 9-14; Pss, 122; *pəsîlîm:* in: Exod 20:1-17, 31-32; H, 40-41; D, 50-51; Dtr, 52-53; Judg 60-61; Kgs, 71-72; Chr, 83-84; Hos, 96-98; Mic, 100-101; 1Isa, 103-04; Jer, 106-7; Nah, 108; Hab, 108; 2Isa 115-16; Pss, 122; *ṣalmê massēkōtām*: in P, 38; *ṣelem*: in: Sam, 64; Kgs, 71-72; Chr, 83-84; Amos, 90-91; Ezek, 112-14; Dan, 121; Pss, 122; *ṣîrîm*: in 2Isa, 115-16; *qibbûṣayik*: in 3Isa, 117; *šiqqûṣ*: in: Ezek, 112-14; 3Isa, 117; *tərāpîm*: in: E, 30; Judg, 60-61; Sam, 64; Kgs, 72; Hos, 96-98; Ezek, 112-14; Zech 9-14, 120; *tô'ēbāh*: in Ezek, 112-14

'eben maśkît: see cultic statuary

'ĕlîlîm: see cultic statuary

'ĕlōhê kesep/zāhāb: "gods of silver/gold," see cultic statuary

'ĕlōhê hannēkār: "foreign gods," see cultic statuary

'ēṣ ra'ănān formula: 5, 17 n1, 48, 73-74, 85, 92, 97 n28, 105-11, 116, 122; in Vulgate: 295 n15; in Jewish sources: 324, 329, 347: connections with *'ăšērîm*: 180-83; *bāmôt*: 156-57; *maṣṣēbôt*: 221; and *mizbəḥôt* 247-48; verse list: 65 n33

"foreign gods:" see cultic statuary, *'ĕlōhê hannēkār*

gillûlîm: see cultic statuary

"gods of wood and stone:" see cultic statuary

"gods of silver/gold:" see cultic statuary, *'ĕlōhê kesep/zāhāb*

'ĕlōhê hannēkār: "foreign gods," see cultic statuary

Greek witnesses: see LXX

hammānîm: "incense altars:" in: H, 39, 40-41; Chr, 66 n34, 67 n38, 80-81, 83-85; 1Isa, 102-104; Ezek, 109-11; 3Isa, 93 n17, 116; connections with *bāmôt*: 152 n69, 153 n73; *'ăšērîm*: 194-96, 199; *mizbəḥôt*: 239-41, 243; as a sign of Late Biblical Hebrew, 41-43; in LXX: 276, 280, 282; Vulgate: 305, 313; Jewish sources: 322

high places: see *bāmôt*

incense altars: see *hammānîm*

Jewish Interpretation: see Midrashic and Mishnaic materials, and Targumim. See also the Index of Ancient Sources for Jewish sources cited

Latin witnesses: see Vulgate

"leafy tree and high hill:" see *'ēṣ ra'ănān* formula

LXX: introduction, 253-52; **translations of** *ăšērîm/āh/ôt*: 254-65; ἄλσος, 255-59; δένδρον, 259-60; Ἀστάρτη, 260-61; other uses for ἄλσος, 261; **translations of** *maṣṣēbāh/ôt*: 265-69; στήλη, 265-67; λίθος, 267; variant readings suggesting *maṣṣēbôt*, 268; other uses for στήλη, 268-69; **translations of** *bāmôtê*: 270; **renderings of** *bāmāh, bāmāt, bāmôt*: 270-85; transliteration, 271-73; ὑψηλός, 273-74; βουνος, 274; translations based on cultic associations: 274-80; ἄλσος, 274-75; βωμός, 278-80; Θυσιαστήριον, 280; στήλη, 275-78; other LXX uses for ὑψηλός, 280-82; βωμός, 282-83; **translations of** *mizbē*ᵃ*ḥ/mizbəḥôt*: 285-89; βωμός, 285-86; invention of term Θυσιαστήριον for YHWHistic altars, 286-87, 289, 352; other uses for Θυσιαστήριον, 288; **summary of LXX data**: 289-92

massēkôt: see cultic statuary

maśkîyōt: see cultic statuary

maṣṣēbôt: 205-28; **scholarship on**: 205-8; **biblical data**: summary 208-9; *maṣṣēbôt* **and related topics in**: **J**, 20; **Exod 34**, 22-26; **E**, 28-29; **Covenant Code**, 33-34; **P**, 35-36; **H**, 39-40; **D**, 49; **Josh** 54-56; **Judg**, 58; **Sam**, 62-63; **Kgs**, 69; **Chr**, 82; **Amos**, 89; **Hos**, 93-95; **Mic**, 99-100; **1Isa**, 103; **Jer**, 106; **Ezek**, 111; **3Isa**, 116-17; **Lam**, 124 n85; **acceptability related to function**: 209-11, 351; as markers of covenant, 211-12; as grave markers or memorial stela, 212; as boundary stones, 212-13; other cultic functions, 213-14; **associations with**: specific foreign gods, 214; foreign cultures, 214-15; *bāmôt*, 215; *ăšērîm*, 216; *mizbəḥôt*, 216-19; cultic statuary, 219-21; 351; the *ʿēṣ raʿănān* formula, 221; other stones: 221-26; *ʾeben maśkît*, 221-22; *peger*, 222; *ăbānîm* with similar functions, 222-24; Ezekiel's

"stones of fire," 224-26; **conclusions on biblical data**: 226-28; **LXX translations**: 265-69; στήλη, 265-67; λίθος, 267; variant readings suggesting *maṣṣēbôt*, 268; other LXX uses for στήλη, 268-69; **Latin translations**: 298-306; use of different terms for approved and disapproved stelae: 298-99; negative translations linked to cultic statuary (*statua* and *simulacrum*), 299-300, 351; positive translations *titutus* and *lapis*, 300-302; other Vulgate uses for: *statua*, 302-3; *titulus*, 303; *lapis*, 303-4; *similacrum*, 304-5; **Targumic renderings**: 329-30; **Midrashic and Mishnaic interpretations**: linked with cultic statuary, 330-33; **grouped with other items in Kings**: 73-74

Midrashic and Mishnaic materials: on *ăšērîm*, 321-29; on *maṣṣēbôt*, 330-33; on *bāmôt*, 337-39; on *mizbəḥôt*, 343-46; summary of early Jewish interpretation, 347-48

mizbəḥôt: 229-49; **scholarship on**: 229-30; **biblical data**: summary, 230-31; *mizbəḥôt* **and related topics in**: **J**, 21; **Exod 34**, 23-6; **E**, 29; **Covenant Code**, 33-34; **P**, 37; **H**, 40; **D**, 49-50; **Josh**, 56; **Judg**, 59-60; **Sam**, 63; **Kgs**, 69-71; **Chr**, 82-83; **Ezra/Neh**, 84; **Amos**, 89-90; **Hos**, 95-96; **Mic**, 100; **1Isa**, 103; **Jer**, 106; **Ezek**, 111-12; **3Isa**, 117; **Joel**, 118; **Mal**, 119; **Zech 9-14**, 119; **Pss**, 122; **Lam**, 124; witnesses only to YHWHistic *mizbəḥôt*, 231-33; witnesses on to disapproved *mizbəḥôt*, 233-34; witnesses with both approved and disapproved *mizbəḥôt*, 234-38; biblical criteria for evaluation, 238-39; 351; **associations with**: *hammānîm*, 239-41; *bāmôt*, 241-42; *ăšērîm*, 242-43; *maṣṣēbôt*, 244-45; cultic statuary, 245-46; other gods, 246-47; the *ʿēṣ raʿănān* formula, 247-48; **conclusions on biblical data**: 248-49; **LXX translations**: 285-89;

βωμός, 285-86; *Θυσιαστήριον*, 286-87; other LXX uses for *Θυσιαστήριον*, 288; **Latin translations:** 312-14; *altaria* and *ara*, 312-13; other Vulgate uses for: *ara*, 313; *altaria*, 313; **Targumic translations:** different terms for altars approved and those disapproved, 339-43; **Midrashic and Mishnaic interpretations:** 343-46; **grouped with other items in Kings:** 73-74

Molech: see child sacrifice

nesek: see cultic statuary

pɘsîlîm: see cultic statuary

qibbûŝayik: see cultic statuary

sacred poles, sacred trees: see *ʾăšērîm*

ṣalmê massēkōtām: see cultic statuary

ṣelem: see cultic statuary

semel: see cultic statuary

ṣîrîm: see cultic statuary

šiqqûṣ: see cultic statuary

standing stones: see *maṣṣēbôt*

Targumim: 317-48; introduction, 317-319; on *ʾăšērîm*, 319-21; on *maṣṣēbôt*, 329-30; on *bāmôt*, 333-36; on *mizbəhôt*, 339-43; **summary of early Jewish interpretation,** 347-48

tɘrāpîm: see cultic statuary

tôʿēbāh: see cultic statuary

twelve stones for the twelve tribes: 28-29, 36, 46, 54-55, 70, 210-12, 217, 223-23, 231, 244 n31, 267; **verse list:** 29

Vulgate: 293-316; introduction, 293-94; **translations of** *ʾăšērāh/îm/ôt*: 295-98; *lucus* and *nemus*, 295-96; other uses for: *lucus*, 296; *nemus*, 296; **translations of** *maṣṣēbāh/ôt*: 298-306; use of different terms for approved and disapproved stelae, 298-99; negative translations *statua* and *simulacrum*, 299-300; positive translations *titutus* and *lapis*, 300-302; other uses for: *statua*, 302-3; *titulus*, 303; *lapis*, 303-4; *similacrum*, 304-5; **translations of** *bāmôtê*, **and** *bāmāh/āt/ôt*: 306-12; *excelsum*, 306-7; *ara*, 307-8; *fanum*, 308; *altitudo*, 308; *sublimis*, 308; *collis*, 308; other uses for *excelsus*, 308-9; *ara*, 310; *fanum*, 310; *sublimis*, 310; *altitudo*, 311; **translations of** *mizbē*ᵃ*h/mizbəhôt*: 312-14; *altaria* and *ara*, 312-13; other uses for *ara* and *altaria*, 313; **summary of Vulgate data:** 314-16

Index of Scholars

Ackerman, S., 11 n42; 35 n39; 112 n63; 220 n24; 349 n1

Ackroyd, P., 93 n19; 266 n25

Aharoni, Y., 131, 131 n20; 229 n3

Albright, W. F., 1 n2; 6 n21; 20, 20 n8; 111, 11 n58; 128, 128 nn4-6; 130 n10; 131; 133-34, 133-34 nn26-27, 29; 145 n51; 149, 149 nn57, 59-60; 152 n69; 172 n43; 186, 186 n64; 215 n21; 222, 222 n29; 273; 277 n47

Alexander, P. S., 318 nn5, 7

Andersen, F., 88 n5; 89 n7; 92, 92 n16; 93 nn18-19; 96, 96 nn25, 27; 217, 266 n25

Anderson, G., 7 n22; 229 n2

Arav, R., 130 n11; 131 n18

Attridge, H. W., 226 n37

Badé, W. F., 163 n10

Barr, J., 38 n44; 121 n84; 130 n8; 175 n47; 226 n37

Barrick, W. B., 2 n2; 3-4, 3 n11; 11 n42; 111 n58; 129 nn6, 8; 130-31, 130 nn8, 10; 131 n19; 133, 133 nn28-30; 149 n60; 273 n39; 278 n47

Barrois, G. A., 11, 11 n40

Barthélemy, D., 260 n14

Baumgarten, A. I., 225 n37

Beck, P., 161 n6; 165 n21; 167 n31

Beebe, H. K., 7, 7 n26; 192 n76

Beer, G., 205 n3

Benzinger, I., 205 n3; 206 n4

Berlinerblau, J., 349 n1

Bernett, M., 130 n11

Bietenhard, H., 318 n11

Binger, T., 161 n4

Biran, A., 131-32, 132 nn22-24; 229 n3

Bird, P. A., 38 n44; 121 n84; 247 n37

Birge, D. E., 173 n45; 262, 262 nn18-20; 263, 263 n21; 297 n21; 264, 264 n23

Blackman, P., 318 n8, 324 nn24,25; 327 n36; 332, 332 n47

Blackwood, A. W., 224 n30

Blenkinsopp, J. A., 24 n14

Bloch-Smith, E., 133 n26

Bogaert, P-M., 293 n2

Boling, R. G., 54 n10

Boraas, R. S., 10, 10 n37

Börner-Klein, D., 319 n12

Bright, J., 7, 7 nn23-24

Brinker, R., 93 n19; 266 n25

Brown, D., 293, 293 nn3-4; 294, 294 nn5, 9-11; 296, 296 nn16-17; 305, 305 n53; 315 n91

Bucher, C., 7 n22; 247 n37

Buck, H. M., 8 n28

Budde, K., 206 n4

Burkert, W., 269, 269 n31; 284 n59

Carmichael, C. M., 22 n11

Carpenter, J. E., 13 nn43-45; 19 nn5-7; 21 nn9-10; 23 n13; 28 n21; 29 n22; 32 n30; 54 n10

Cathcart, K., 318 n4; 330 n42

Childs, B. S., 21 n9; 23 n13; 24 n16; 28 n21; 31 n26; 32, 32 n30; 34 nn34-35

Chilton, B., 318 n4

Conrad, D., 34 n35

Coogan, M. D., 56 n12

Cook, S. A., 163 n10

Coote, R. B., 2 n7; 13 nn43-45

Cross, F. M., 6 n21; 23, 23 n12; 37 n42; 69 n40; 96 n26; 143, 143 n44

Dahood, M., 288 n65

Daniélou, J., 298 nn22-23

Davies, G. H., 9, 9 n34; 221 n25

Davila, J. R., 30 n23

Day, J., 9, 9 n33; 97 n28; 102 n38; 181 n52

Dever, W. G., 131 nn13, 15, 17; 161 n6; 165 n21; 166 n26; 167 n32

Dietrich, M., 149 n58; 222 n28

Díez Macho, A., 317 n2

Dogniez, C., 253 n1

Dothan, M., 131 n13

Driver, S. R., 13 n46

Edelman, D. V., 349 n1

Eerdmans, B. D., 206 n4

Eichrodt, W., 5, 5 n17; 6, 6 nn18-20; 140 n39

Eissfeldt, O., 186, 186 n65

Ellis, P. F., 13 n43; 24 n15

Emerton, J. A., 162 n6; 165 n21; 166 n27

Engle, J. R., 2 n2; 3 n10; 162 n6; 164-65, 164-5 nn16, 18-20; 187 n67

Epstein, J. N., 318 n10

Fensham, F. C., 225, 225 nn32-34

Finkelstein, L., 318 n11

Fischer, B., 293 n2

Fitzmyer, J. A., 185 n59

Foster, J., 317 n2

Fowler, A. B., 1 n1; 8, 8 n29

383

Fraser, J. G., 297, 297 n20
Freedman, D. N., 88 n5; 89 n7; 92, 92 n16; 93 nn 18-19; 96, 96 nn 25, 27; 218; 266 n25
Freund, R., 130 n11; 131 n18
Frevel, C., 161 n4
Friedlander, G., 320 n17; 322 n21
Friedman, R. E., 21 n9; 23 n13; 32 n30; 41 n49
Frymer-Kensky, T., 161 n5
Galling, K., 229 n1
Geffcken, J., 315 n90
Gleis, M., 127 n1
Good, R. M., 11 n42
Gordon, R. P., 318 n4; 324 n42
Gottwald, N., 8, 8 n27; 192 n76
Graesser, C. F., 2 n2; 93, 93 n19; 205-8, 205 nn1-3; 206 nn4-5;207 nn7-10; 208 nn11-13; 217, 218 n22; 266 n25; 271 n33; 276 n46; 332 n48
Gray, G. B., 19 n7; 229 n2
Grayson, A. K., 128 n4
Gressmann , H., 206 n4
Grossfeld, B., 318 n7
Grønbaek, J. H., 21 n9
Hackett, J., 18 n4; 143 n45
Hadley, J. M., 162 n6; 165 n21; 166 nn23-24
Hammer, R., 318 n11, 319 n14, 324, 324 n24, 331, 331 n46
Haran, M., 41 n49; 135, 135 n31; 138 n37; 146 n53; 150-51, 150-51 nn63-64, 66; 152 n72; 229 n2; 241 n23
Harford-Battersby, G., 13 nn43-45; 19 nn5-7; 21 nn9-10; 23 n13; 28 n21; 29 n22; 54 n10
Harrelson, W., 8 n28
Heider, G. C., 145 n50
Hendel, R. S., 32 n28
Hestrin, R., 162 n6; 240 n21; 166 n27; 167-68, 167-68 nn30-31, 33-34
Hiebert, T., 19 n5; 33 n32; 235 n10
Hillers, D., 6 n21; 23 n14
Holladay, W. L., 93 n17; 148 n55; 156 n78; 180 n50; 279 n54
Horovitz, H. S., 235 n11; 318 n2, 319 n12
Houtman, C., 33 n31
Hurowitz, V. A., 36 n39; 112 n63; 150 n61; 220 n24
Hurvitz, A., 13 n45; 42, 42 n51; 109 n53; 157 n81
Iakovidis, S., 284 n59
Ishida, T., 23 n18; 140 n40

Jacobsen, T., 264 n23
Japhet, S., 2, 2 n4
Jastrow, M., 320, 320 n16, 321, 333, 333 n50; 339, 339 nn61,62
Jenks, A., 2, 2 n5; 13 n44; 19 n7; 21 nn9-10; 24 n17
Kamesar, A., 294, 294 nn7-9, 11; 305 n54
Keel, O., 130 n11
Kempinski, A., 132 n25; 230 n5
King, P. J., 99 n33; 173 n45
Klein, M. L., 235 n11; 318 n3; 321, 321 n18; 335 n54
Kloppenborg, J. S., 37 n41; 57 n15
Knohl, I., 13 n46; 41 n49; 42-43, 42-43 nn53, 56-57; 85 n4;
Kutscher, R., 114 n76
Langlamet, F., 54 n10
LaRocca-Pitts, E. C., 145 n50
Lemaire, A., 162 n6; 165 n21; 166 nn25, 27; 167 n29; 172 n43; 186 n67; 189
Levenson, J. D., 13 n47; 55, 55 n11; 57 n14; 72 n47; 176, 176 n48
Levi, D., 284 n59
Levine, B. A., 13 n45
Lewis, T. J., 63 n24; 133 n26; 206 n6
Lipiński, E., 173 n44; 185, 185 n56; 186 n67; 187
Loretz, O., 149 n58; 222 n28
Lund, S., 317 n2
Macalister, R. A. S., 131; 163 n10
Maher, M., 318 n5
Maier, W. A.,161, 161 n2
Manor, D., 11 n42
Marrou, H., 297, 298 nn22-23
May, H. G., 225, 225 n35
Mazar, A., 229 n3; 230 nn4, 6; 132, 132 nn21, 25; 133 n25
McCarter, P. K., 11 n42; 63, 63 n24; 165 n21; 166-67; 167 n29; 186, 186 n66; 261 n17
McCarthy, D. J., 23 n12
McKenzie, S. L., 51 n9
McNamara, M., 317 n2, 318 n7, 321 n18, 335, 335 n54
Melamed, E. Z. 318 n10
Meshel, Z., 162 n6; 165 n21; 166, 166 nn22, 27; 185 n56; 263 n22
Mettinger, T. N. D., 206 n6
Meyers, C. L., 35 n38; 82 n2; 172 n42
Milgrom, J., 13 nn45-46; 42-43, 42-43 nn49-50, 54-55, 58; 229 n2; 286 n61

Miller, P. D., 11 n42; 64 n29
de Moor, J. C., 10, 10 n38
Moore, G. F., 205 n3
Nakhai, B. A., 133 n25
Neusner, J., 235 n11; 318 n9, 322 nn19,20
Nielsen, K., 240 n21
Nieman, D., 149 n58; 222, 222 nn27-28; 271 n33; 276 n46
Noth, M., 2, 2 nn6-7; 19 n5, 7; 21 n9; 23 n13; 24 n16; 28 n21; 31 n26; 32 n29; 34 n36
O'Connell, K. G., 26 n18; 140 n40
Obermann, J., 149 n58
Oden, R. A., 7 n22; 226 n37
Olyan, S., 5 n16; 10 n36; 48 n4; 106, 106 n49; 161, 161 n3; 162 n7; 168, 168 n36; 186 n63; 201 n85; 209 n15
Ord, D. R., 2 n7;13 nn43-45
Patai, R., 161 n5; 164, 164 n17
Paul, S., 39 n46; 87-89; 87 n3; 88 n4; 89 nn7-9; 90 nn11-13
Perlman, A. L., 4, 4 n13; 161 n4
Peters, M. K. H., 253 n1
Petrie, W. M. F., 163 n10
Pettey, R. J., 161 n4
Philips, E. A., 318 n9
Polzin, R., 42 n49
Pope, M., 225, 225 n31
Porten, B., 89 n8
Porter, J. R., 9-10; 10 n35
Preuss, H. D., 41 n48
Pritchard, J. B., 3 n10; 162 n6; 164, 164 n17
Provan, I., 65 n32
de Pury, A., 13 n43
Rabin, I. A., 235 n11; 318 n9
von Rad, G., 2 n8; 20 n8; 172 n42
Rainey, A., 229 n2
Reed, W. L., 2 n2; 4, 4 n13; 11, 11 n41; 161-64; 161 n1; 162-64 nn7-15; 172; 320
Rendsburg, G., 42 n49
Rendtorff, R., 229 n2
Ringgren, H., 140 n39; 264 n23
Roberts, J. J. M., 64 n29
Rudolph, W., 13 n44; 21 n10
Russell, E., 11 n42
Sandmel, S., 7, 7 n25
Sanmartín, J., 149 n58; 222 n28
Sarna, N., 20n8; 172 n42
Schmid, H. H., 13 n43
Schmidt, B. B., 133 n26

Schunck, K. D., 9, 9 nn31-32, 34; 10-11, 11 n39; 130 n10; 140 n39; 192 n76
Sellin, E., 206 n4
Setel, T. D., 247 n37
van Seters, J., 13 n43
Shanks, H., 133 n25
Smith, J. Z., 297 n20
Smith, S., 163 n10
Smith, W. R., 205 n3; 206 n4; 264 n23
Snaith, N. H., 229 n2
Speiser, E. A., 20 n8; 172 n42
Spencer, J. R., 71 n45
Sperber, A., 62 n23; 94 n20; 271 n33; 317 n1
Spoer, H. H., 206 n4
Stager, L. E., 173, 173 n45
Sun, H. T. C., 42 n50; 157 n81
Swete, H.B., 253 n2; 254nn3-4; 260 n14; 293n2
Terrien, S., 248 n37
Toombs, L. E., 131 n14
van der Toorn, K., 30 n24
Tov, E., 253 n1; 293 n1
Ussishkin, D., 131 nn12, 15
Vaughan, P. H., 2 n2; 3, 3 n11; 4, 4 nn12, 14; 47 n2; 110, 110 n57; 127-31; 127-30 nn2-7, 9-10; 273, 273 n40
de Vaux, R., 229 n2; 273
Weber, M., 6 n21
Weinfeld, M., 2, 2 n3; 13 n47; 17 n2; 23 n14; 47 n1; 49, 49 n6; 92; 72 n47; 93 n17; 107 n51; 162 n6; 166, 166 n28
Weiss, A. H., 319 n13
Wellhausen, J., 2-3; 3 n9; 19 n5, 7; 23 n13; 31 n26; 32; 232, 232 n9
Westenholz, J. G., 7 n22
Westerma nn , C., 20 n8; 38 n44; 172 n42
Wevers, J. W., 225 n30; 267 nn28-29
Widengren, G., 264 n23
Wiener, H. M., 229 n1
Wiggins, S., 161 n4
Winter, J., 318 n9
Wolff, H. W., 23 n14; 88 n4; 90 n11; 95 n23; 156 n79; 248 n37
Wright, G. E., 54 n10
Wünsche, A., 318 n9
Yamashita, T., 161 n4
Yeivin, S., 3 n10
Zertal, A., 131 n14; 132 n25; 230 n5
Zevit, Z., 42 n49; 166 n25
Zimmerli, W., 224-25, 225 nn31, 36